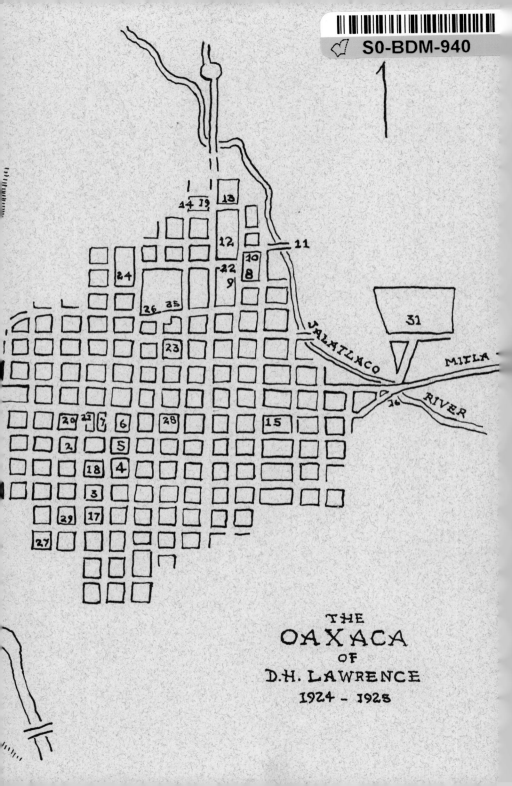

S0-BDM-940

THE
OAXACA
OF
D.H. LAWRENCE
1924 – 1925

32.50

20.00

LAWRENCE
IN
OAXACA

By the Same Author

The Plant in My Window (1949)
Week in Yanhuitlán (1964)
Explorer, Linguist and Ethnologist (1966)
The Awakened Eye (1968)
School of the Soldier (1980)
Four Lienzos of the Coixtlahuaca Valley (1982)
Stages in a Journey (1983)

LAWRENCE IN OAXACA

◆

A QUEST FOR THE NOVELIST IN MEXICO

◆

ROSS PARMENTER

◆

GIBBS M. SMITH, INC.
PEREGRINE SMITH BOOKS
SALT LAKE CITY
1984

➔P

Copyright © 1984 by Ross Parmenter.

No part of this book may be used or reproduced in
any manner without prior written consent from the
publishers.

This is a Peregrine Smith Book.

Published by Gibbs M. Smith, Inc.
Peregrine Smith Books
P.O. Box 667, Layton, UT 84041

First Edition

Library of Congress Cataloging in Publication Data
Parmenter, Ross
    Lawrence in Oaxaca.
    Includes excerpts from D. H. Lawrence's letters
and works.
    Bibliography: p. 363
    Includes index.
    1. Lawrence, D. H. (David Herbert),
1885-1930—Homes and haunts—Mexico—Oaxaca de
Juárez. 2. Oaxaca de Juárez (Mexico)—Biography. 3.
Novelists, English—20th century— Biography. I. Title.
PR6023.A93Z763 1984 823'.912 84-13943
ISBN 0-87905-097-7

Book Design by J. Scott Knudsen

Cover painting, "The Road to Mitla," by Dorothy
Brett and D. H. Lawrence, courtesy of John Harvey,
Santa Fe, New Mexico. Photograph © Len Bouche
1984.

Manufactured in the United States of America

To the memory of

Luisa Linder de Martínez
(1894-1984)
creator and animator of
the Pension Suiza in Oaxaca
within whose sheltering tranquility
this book was written

CONTENTS

Benefits Remembered ix
Prologue
    The Tragedy of García Vigil xv
  1. Lawrence and the Governor 1
  2. Lawrence's Landlord 25
  3. The Market 45
  4. The Kulls and Their _Mozo_ 65
  5. Rosalino 83
  6. Another Walk to Huayapan 109
  7. Favors for Two Writers 135
    Luis Quintanilla 135
    Mollie Skinner 150
  8. Brett with Addenda 159
  9. Correspondence and Other Writings 213
    The Break with Seltzer 214
    "The Hopi Snake Dance" 218
    "None of That" 223
    Tolstoy's "Resurrection" 228
    "Man Is Essentially a Soul" 235
    An Adventure in Recognition 238
10. "Noah's Flood" and More Letters 243
    "Noah's Flood" 243
    "Climbing Down Pisgah" 249
    A Lecture on "Halfness" 255
    The Explosion Against Murry 259
    Letters to the Hawks 269
11. How _The Plumed Serpent_ was Changed
    in Oaxaca 273
    Changes Because of Oaxaca 285
    The Religion Lawrence Invented 290
    Was Lawrence a Fascist? 301
    The Novel and Mexican History 305
    What To Do with Kate? 308
12. The Return to the Francia 317
Afterword
    The Luck of the Draw 345
Appendix
    An Echo of Oaxaca in "The Lovely Lady" 347
Notes 349
Works Consulted 363
Index of Lawrence Works Cited 369
General Index 372

BENEFITS REMEMBERED

My greatest debt is to Lawrence himself, and, wherever possible, I have tried to use his own words to tell the story of his Oaxaca sojourn. Lawrence left autobiographical traces in everything he wrote: in articles, poems, plays, short stories and novels, as well as—most copiously—in letters. How widely I have ranged in locating his first-person evidence can be seen in the separate index of his cited works.

Most of his words relating to Oaxaca and Mexico having been published, I am beholden to many owners of copyright material. Because Viking Penguin Inc. controls more copyrighted Lawrence material than any publisher in the United States, including two heavy tomes I have mined extensively, *Phoenix* and *Phoenix II,* also *Kangaroo, Studies in Classic American Literature,* and *The Boy in the Bush,* my indebtedness to the generosity of this house in granting reprint permissions is particularly deep.

But while Lawrence was in Oaxaca, as the book reveals, he shifted his American allegiance to Alfred A. Knopf Inc. Starting with *St. Mawr* in 1925, Knopf began publishing works by Lawrence particularly pertinent to Oaxaca, including *Mornings in Mexico, The Plumed Serpent, The Woman Who Rode Away,* and *The Man Who Died.* I have drawn on these with great fullness, so my debt to Alfred A. Knopf for permission to quote from its Lawrence holdings is perhaps equally deep, if not, in terms of numbers of words, even deeper. The officials at the two houses who interceded for me to whom I am thankful are Alan D. Williams, editorial director of Viking Penguin, and William Koshland, president of Knopf. The reason I have not cited page numbers for my quotations—and the editions drawn from—has been to avoid confusion. Many of the works have appeared in many editions. But with letters—and Viking controls the two major collections so far, those of Aldous Huxley and Harry T. Moore—I have indicated their dates.

My concern to let Lawrence tell his own story has extended to the women who were with him in Oaxaca, Frieda Lawrence, his wife, and Dorothy Brett. Both published accounts of the sojourn, so with them, too, I am obliged to publishers for permission to quote their words: to Knopf for drawing on *Frieda Lawrence: The Memoirs and Correspondence,* as edited by E. W. Tedlock, Jr., (1964), and to Viking for quotations from Frieda's *"Not I, But the Wind . . ."* (1934). These permissions have been seconded by Gerald Pollinger, who succeeded his father Laurence Pollinger as Lawrence's literary executor and as head of Laurence Pollinger Limited, Authors' Agent in London; and who, since the death of Frieda's son, C. Montague Weekley, has been responsible for the Frieda Lawrence Ravagli Estate. Mr. Pollinger also gave me permission to quote from two letters that Frieda wrote her mother in German.

For Dorothy Brett's published words I thank John Manchester, her artistic and literary executor, who holds the copyright of her *Lawrence and Brett,* which has been such a rich source of direct quotes, as well as her "Autobiography, My Long and Beautiful Journey," published in the *South Dakota Review* in the summer of 1967. I am grateful to Miss Brett, too, for more than thirty letters, as well as personal interviews in Taos, New Mexico.

The others who were in Oaxaca with Lawrence, whom I got to know, are named in the text and thanked by appearing as sympathetic characters in the story, including Hermann and Carola Kull, Ethel R. Doctor, Rosalind Hughes, Jean Akin, Norman Taylor, and Isaac M. Ibarra. Among those I got to know who had met Lawrence elsewhere in Mexico were Luis and Ruth Quintanilla, Willard Johnson, Frederick Leighton, Harloe Hamilton, and Idella Purnell Stone. They are in the story, too. Norman Taylor is the only one of those I interviewed still alive. Surviving relatives helpful in telling me about others in Oaxaca with Lawrence were George E. and Mabel Rickards, nephew and niece of Padre Edward Rickards; Henry W. Winsor, nephew of Jean and Colonel A.D. Akin, and B.C. Girdley, Jr., son of B.C. Girdley.

Many authors have earned my gratitude for what they have written about Lawrence, and in my "Works Consulted" and index I have credited those on whom I have drawn. But here, too, I have acknowledgments to make to individuals and to publishers. An example is John Patrick Carswell, the son of Catherine Carswell, who holds the copyright on his mother's *The Savage Pilgrimage.* Another is Mrs. Dorothy M. Bailey, a daughter of H. M. Tomlinson, who gave me permission to quote her father's description of Lawrence in his *Norman Douglas.* A third is Mrs. Harwood Brewster Picard, the daughter of Earl and Achsah Brewster, who gave permission to quote from her parents' *D. H. Lawrence: Reminiscences and Correspondence.*

To the publishers below giving permission to include copyright material I am glad to extend the requested acknowledgments:

To the International Museum of Photography at George Eastman House for material quoted from *The Daybooks of Edward Weston, Vol. I, Mexico,* 1961.

Selected excerpts from *Letters of Aldous Huxley,* edited by Grover Smith, copyright 1969 by Laura Huxley, reprinted by permission of Harper & Row, Publishers, Inc.

To John Martin and Black Sparrow Press for material quoted in *Letters to Thomas & Adele Seltzer,* edited by Gerald Morris Lacy, 1973.

To Routledge & Kegan Paul PLC for permission to reproduce extracts from letters written by Kai Gótzsche to Knud Merrild published in *A Poet and Two Painters,* 1938.

To Indiana University Press for permission to quote from *A Mexican Ulysses,* José Vasconcelos's autobiography, translated and abridged by W. Rex Crawford, 1963.

Several publishers reminded me that the Frieda Lawrence Ravagli Estate had copyright control of all Lawrence letters, as well as material still unpublished. Gerald Pollinger earned my gratitude for allowing me to reprint many published items still under his control. And I am particularly grateful to him for permission to print one unpublished Lawrence essay, to quote from the typescript of the Chapala draft of *The Plumed Serpent,* and to paraphrase some letters not hitherto published. Holders of the original copies of this material also advised me that I would have to obtain Mr. Pollinger's permission to publish it. Those custodians, who granted their own permission, were the Humanities Research Center of the University of Texas at Austin, the Houghton Library of Harvard University, the Library Board of Western Australia, and William Forster, a London collector who owns the two summarized letters by Lawrence to Constantine Rickards.

Because the Humanities Research Center at Austin also allowed me to work in its comfortable library, where every courtesy was extended, I am especially beholden to it, and its officials, Warren F. Roberts, David Robb Farmer, and Cathy Henderson. There, besides being shown the photographs Brett took in Oaxaca, I was allowed to examine the first and second manuscripts of *The Plumed Serpent,* and the manuscripts in Lawrence's black copybook, "Record," which, besides including the holographs of *Mornings in Mexico,* contained those of several other pieces written in Oaxaca. Most of those others have been published in *Phoenix* or *Phoenix II,* but the philosophical fragment, starting, "Man is essentially a soul," also in "Record," has not been published complete before. I am grateful to the Center and Mr. Pollinger for permission to print it. I thank them too, as well as Professor James Boulton and the Cambridge University Press, for permission to paraphrase the seven unpublished communications to Richard Cobden-Sanderson, William Hawk, A. D. Hawk, Lady Cynthia Asquith, Dorothy Brett, and Thomas Seltzer, detailed in footnote 1 in the chapter "Correspondence and Other Writings."

A typescript of the first draft of *The Plumed Serpent,* catalogued as "fma Eng 967," is the item the Houghton Library, Harvard University, allowed me to read in four happy days in 1970. I am grateful to Carolyn E. Jakeman, who was so helpful to me then, and to Rodney G. Dennis, its curator of manuscripts, who granted the rights of the Houghton Library, insofar as they extended, to draw on material from the typescript.

Communication with the Library Board of Western Australia was by mail. The board owns Lawrence's 17 November 1924 letter to Mollie Skinner from which I have summarized excerpts, and his postscript to Frieda's letter to Mollie of 3 January 1925, which I have paraphrased. The acknowledgment requested by the board is: "Copied from the originals held in the J. S. Battys Library, Perth, Western Australia, from the Mollie Skinner Papers Acc 1396A/31."

William Forster, an ex-policeman, proved one of the jolliest and friendliest persons I met on the Lawrence trail. It is a pleasure to thank him for permission to draw on his Lawrence letters to Rickards.

For illustrative material, my greatest obligation is to the Humanities Research Center at Austin for permission to use thirteen of the photographs Dorothy Brett took in Oaxaca. Cole Weston and the Center for Creative Photography have given permission to reproduce Edward Weston's photograph of Lawrence which is copyright 1981 Arizona, Board of Trustees, Center for Creative Photography. I thank John Harvey of Santa Fe, New Mexico, for permission to use the Brett-Lawrence painting, *The Road to Mitla*. Hermann Kull and Rosalind Hughes generously sent photographs they took in Oaxaca. And I appreciate the work of many Oaxaca postcard makers. I could not trace the identity of them all, but fortunately Alfonso Rivas, with justifiable pride, affixed his name to his.

The men and women of Oaxaca who gave me the most information are named in the text, but not all who helped appear as characters. Among the unnamed who deserve credit are Domingo Aguilar, Anita Bellon de Costes, Eulogio Losado, Colonel R. A. Atkins, María Luisa de Bustamente de Audiffred, Felipe Velasco, and Gloria Larumbe. For specific matters of fact, I thank Frank Waters of Taos for identifying Luis Mirabal; the historian William B. Taylor, who set me straight on the Mercederians and the Bethlehemites as male orders; Thomas J. Carey, astronomer of the Hayden Planetarium of the American Museum of Natural History, for information on the planet Venus; and the late Howard Phillips, editor of *Mexican Life,* for details on the defeat of the de la Huerta forces trapped at Esperanza.

Through their editorial assistance in showing me how to tighten the manuscript and make it less bulky, I received instruction, as well as appreciated practical assistance from the late Marshall A. Best, for forty-four years an official of increasing importance at the Viking Press, and its chief Lawrence expert; and Lavina Fielding Anderson, a skillful copy-editor of Salt Lake City, Utah. Friends who helped with comments, morale-sustaining interest and editorial matters are those veteran aides of other works, Leonard Elliott, Charlotte Isler, and Nona Balakian. I thank Marge Veleta for translating Frieda's two letters in German I have used. And I am grateful for practical help from members of the staff of Peregrine Smith

Books, especially Roberta Vellvé and Leslie Cutler Stitt.

Following the Lawrence trail in Mexico for more than twenty years brought so much joy and interest that it is a pleasure to recall, as well as to thank, all those who helped. And this includes the many charming people of Oaxaca whose names I never learned, among them the obliging and patient men who fetched me the dusty back copies of *El Mercurio* from the files in the Spanish colonial palace now housing Oaxaca's State Library.

PROLOGUE

THE TRAGEDY OF
GARCÍA VIGIL

D.H. Lawrence came into my ken before Mexico did. I began reading him in 1933, the year I left college, and from *The Rainbow* on he was one of my literary heroes. But by December 1961 when I started reading *The Plumed Serpent* for the second time, I was more interested in Mexico then I was in Lawrence. Paradoxically, the reversal of interests turned on Oaxaca, the Mexican city where Lawrence spent the 1924-25 winter.

Capital of the state of the same name, Oaxaca is 350 miles southeast of Mexico City. It is a provincial center that saw one heyday in the eighteenth century when wealth amassed from cochineal, mining, and agriculture brought it to a height of Spanish colonial elegance. The second golden age came in the 1890s. Oaxaca was the birthplace of Porfirio Díaz, and the longtime president of Mexico favored his hometown.

Before the coming of the Spaniards, the Valley of Oaxaca had been a center of several high cultures. The Olmecoid people who first built Monte Alban, the most commanding archaeological site in Oaxaca, were succeeded by the Zapotecs who expanded the site and were themselves succeeded by the Mixtecs who were dominant in the area in the fifteenth century A.D. The artistic skills of these forebears persisted into modern times. Thus, Oaxaca has much to interest the tourist. But with its outdoor cafes, its band concerts, the life of its *zócalo* , or central plaza, its unexpected candlelit processions announcing religious fiestas, and its teeming market, it also has enduring charms for the permanent resident.

Oaxaca's natural setting among the mountains, its responsive and humorous Indians, and its unfailingly lovely climate, in presenting the best that Mexico has to offer, fixed the country permanently in my affection after a first acquaintance in 1947 when I vacationed there. I began vacationing there each year. I traveled elsewhere in Mexico, but the stay in Oaxaca was always the core of the holiday. As the pace of newspaper work in New York stepped up, the more relaxed life of Oaxaca became increasingly important to me. Its colonial architecture furthered my interest in the Spanish period, and its archaeological wealth made me a partisan of its ancient cultures. As my interest in things pre-Columbian grew, it centered on the Mixtec pictorial manuscripts painted on deerhide and this fascination had extended to the manuscripts of the early colonial period when Indians were still employing their ancient artistic traditions.

During my initial visit to Mexico in 1946, I made a swing around the tourist circuit, the only stopover of any length being at Chapala. There I learned that its lake, not far from Guadalajara, was the setting for *The Plumed Serpent,* a Lawrence novel I had not yet read. I made a beeline for it after I returned to New York. Oaxaca was the second place that led me again to Lawrence. When I learned in 1950 that Lawrence had set the first four sketches of *Mornings in Mexico* there, I opened *Mornings* with equal eagerness. Eleven years later I was intrigued to learn that Zelia Nuttall, the American archaeologist who had rediscovered the gorgeous pre-Columbian painted history that bears her name, was the model for Mrs. Norris in *The Plumed Serpent.* How much had her knowledge of pre-Conquest Mexico influenced Lawrence? Reading her *The Fundamental Principles of Old and New World Civilizations* (1901) was the way to find out; and I turned back to *Serpent* to get it fresh in my mind so I could spot how many of its details had been lifted from her book.

By April 1967 I had retired and was living in Oaxaca. Because I had already laid the groundwork for a book on Lawrence's sojourn there, the name of MANUEL GARCÍA VIGIL on a poster halted me one morning as I was strolling to the plaza. Normally I disregarded the announcements of wrestling matches, soccer games, movies, and religious pilgrimages commonly pasted to house walls at principal intersections, but García Vigil had been the Oaxaca governor whose history had shaped Lawrence's revisions of *The Plumed Serpent* and whose career, as I knew from *Mornings in Mexico,* had colored all Lawrence's later Mexican thinking.

The poster also featured the first photograph I had seen of García Vigil. (Plate 1.) His civilian clothes surprised me, for I had always heard him referred to as a general. Obviously he was something of a dandy, younger than I expected, with the face of a poet. Oaxaca had unveiled his bust on a stone plinth in 1950, but the sculptor's efforts, I'd always thought, had made García Vigil look like George Gershwin.

Under the photo were the words *En Justo Homenaje* ("just homage") and the years 1924 and 1967. Before the monument to the "renowned and unforgettable" governor of Oaxaca a civic group was holding a *Solemne Acto* to mark the forty-third anniversary of his *infausta muerte* —"unlucky, unhappy or accursed death." The program promised speeches and renditions by the state band of the "Tannhaüser Overture," "Ase's Death," and Chopin's "Funeral March." Naturally I wanted to attend, and I anticipated a large turnout. After all, the city's principal north and south street was named after the general. According to a marble plaque on the wall of the old Oaxaca Museum, that street, formerly called Libertad, had been changed to García Vigil in 1947,[1] as part of the city's celebration of the twenty-fifth anniversary of the state's constitution, promulgated by García Vigil on 15 April 1922. Two blocks from the *zócalo*

I had noticed another marble plaque affixed to the handsome two-story house where the governor had lived the last four years of his life. This one honored him for "the reconstruction of the material and institutional life" of his native state, "this federative entity."

Calle García Vigil parallels the old aqueduct, cuts the city down the center, and runs past the cathedral to the *zócalo*. The bust of García Vigil faces the street named after him, its back to Calle Allende, a palm-boulevarded cross street leading to the Church of Santo Domingo. When I arrived I saw the bust had been regilded for the *Solemne Acto*. But it was almost starting time and only a handful had assembled. Half of those present—the well-scrubbed children in white dresses, blazers, and slicked-down hair—had been marched to the ceremony by their teachers. There were only two flag parties, both from schools.

One disappointment followed another. In place of the state band, a village dance band from San Juan Chilateca played sad waltzes. The *poema heroico* lauded Bolivar. (Apparently the epic poem about García Vigil is still to be written.) The orator, who mounted the oval rostrum with a balustered railing bearing the Mexican eagle with its serpent in its beak, was a university student. Although most branches of the government had sent bulky white wreaths, no leading political figures were present. As the undergraduate eloquently told how García Vigil had, from his days in the seminary, been a rebel against injustice and oppression, I studied the dignitaries seated at the green baize-covered table shaded from the fierce April heat by a huge tarpaulin. All fourteen were brown-skinned, heavy-set, somewhat shrunken elderly men in suits that had grown baggy. I judged— rightly as it turned out—they were friends who remembered García Vigil and who annually arranged a ceremony on the anniversary of the day he was shot.

The dignitaries surrounded by the floral tributes posed for a group photograph in front of the monument. It was over in less than an hour, and the released children swarmed around the sherbet carts to get their *paletas*.

With mixed feelings, I strolled toward the cathedral. Considering the number of men mowed down by firing squads during the Mexican Revolution, it was reassuring that this civic group was trying to preserve the memory of their leader. But I realized that unless the federal government also encouraged the cult of García Vigil, he would never become a national hero, or even a local folk hero.

Still, if Lawrence had lived to attend the ceremony, he would have been astonished. García Vigil had been executed less than seven months before Lawrence arrived in Oaxaca. At that time the governor was considered an abject failure, his cause so totally lost that a commemorative service before his monument was inconceivable. This eclipse of the dead man's memory only underlined the ruthlessness of those whom the Revolution had brought to power in Lawrence's day. Lawrence, who hated brutality and often saw himself as an isolated and misunderstood leader, had felt the murder of García Vigil, an honorable man only three years the novelist's senior and an impulsive idealist with whom the writer could readily identify, as one more cause for despair about an unregenerated Mexico.

Political events in Mexico influenced Lawrence deeply, especially those in Oaxaca, the city where he stayed the longest. Oaxaca was not an untroubled retreat, unlike the other beautiful places where Lawrence generally lived after he left England in 1919. As shown by *Aaron's Rod* and *Kangaroo,* his novels preceding the Oaxaca period, he came to Oaxaca at the point of his keenest interest in the intersection of politics, history, and human welfare. Because he tried to grasp and convey the temper of the times, his Oaxaca writings are unusually timely, almost as if he were a foreign correspondent chronicling current events.

To understand his Oaxaca writings, one must understand Oaxaca's history. It is not well known. Furthermore, it has been written by the victors; and García Vigil's story, being one of defeat, has been buried. Obviously Lawrence did not know everything that had taken place in Oaxaca between the outbreak of the Mexican Revolution in 1910 and his arrival in Mexico in the first day of spring in 1923. But he learned a great deal, and his Oaxaca writings gain force when they are seen in the light of his knowledge.

García Vigil's tragedy intertwines the ups and downs of the Mexican Revolution as a whole with various uprisings in the state of Oaxaca which resisted that revolution and became a reactionary stronghold. The Mexican Revolution is the story of a series of overthrowers, who, in turn, were overthrown. Francisco I. Madero, who came to power in 1911 by toppling Díaz, was the first of the overthrowers. In 1912 Victoriano Huerta overthrew Madero. A year later Huerta was driven out by Venustiano Carranza, an elderly former senator from the north who, aided by friends, had become the *Primer Jefe* of Mexico. By 1920, Carranza fell to Alvaro Obregón, a former Carranza lieutenant, who had his former chief ambushed and killed when he tried to escape. Obregón had no effective opposition for a time because Pancho Villa's power was destroyed at Celaya in 1915 when his horses charged against Carranza's machine guns. In 1919 Carranza also assisted in the treachery that eliminated Emiliano Zapata. Two men from Sonora, Plutarco Calles, former schoolteacher, and Adolfo de la Huerta (not to be confused with Victoriano Huerta) who had been governor of his native state, were Obregón's chief allies against Carranza. Their names should be remembered. When Lawrence rewrote *The Plumed Serpent* he inserted Calles into the novel as a new character.

De la Huerta was to be a fifth challenger, leading a rebellion against Obregón that almost trapped Lawrence in Mexico as it began in 1923 and which
he learned about in detail after his return in 1924.

With the powers of the central government further weakened each
time a leader was overthrown, Oaxaca went its own way for six years,
developing its own pattern of leaders rising to power and then coming
to grief. In 1914 when Carranza became Mexico's *Primer Jefe,* Oaxaca
acquired a "first chief" too: Guillermo Meixueiro, the son of a Porfirian
governor. Using his wealth and family influence, Meixueiro had risen to
power because he could control the *Serranos.* These unruly men were
so named because they lived in the Sierra de Juárez, the mountainous
birthplace of Benito Juárez, nineteenth-century Mexico's greatest hero.

After three years of struggle, the larger and smaller governments
were more or less stabilized. In Mexico as a whole the Liberals had tri-
umphed. In Oaxaca they had been defeated by those who wanted to restore the conditions which, during the rule of Porfirio Díaz, had benefited
the influential minority. In October 1914, Carranza called a convention
at Aguascalientes to unify the country. But the convention, instead of
ratifying Carranza as the *Primer Jefe,* dismissed him. He had to withdraw
from Mexico City, leaving the capital open to Villa and Zapata.

Unchecked, Oaxaca's rulers continued their reactionary ways. One
of their outrages was the murder of Jesús Carranza. The brother of the
deposed leader had been sent to Oaxaca to find means of cooperation
between Oaxaca and Carranza's Constitutionalists. But in April Obregón's
victory over Villa at Celaya assured Carranza's return to power. Even then
Oaxaca's old-line leaders did not join the main stream of the Revolution.
On the contrary, a move to secede from the union began. On June 3 Meixueiro's puppet governor, José Inés Davila, proclaimed the sovereign state
of Oaxaca a free and independent entity.

Carranza was not able to reenter the capital until mid-October. The
leaders of the Revolution were determined to preserve the Mexican union,
but invading Oaxaca was no easy matter. Because mountains intervened,
the invading army had to proceed from Salina Cruz on the Pacific Coast.
The Constitutionalists were not ready to move into Oaxaca until February 1916. On March 2 they won a crucial victory at Ocotlán. The *Soberanistas,* those claiming Oaxaca was a sovereign state, unable to defend
the open city of Oaxaca, decided to evacuate. Meixueiro and his followers
went back to the Sierra de Juárez. Davila took the government to the Mixteca Alta and established a new capital at Tlaxiaco.

The Constitutionalists surprised the frightened citizens of Oaxaca
by governing in an orderly fashion. They never lost control of the vitally
important Valley of Oaxaca, but it was four years before they succeeded
in crushing the Tlaxiaco government. Finally on 31 May 1919 the

Soberanista capital was taken, Davila was decapitated, and his head was sent back to Oaxaca.

In December Meixueiro recognized Carranza's authority. But this meant less than it would have earlier because a council of *Serrano* leaders had already deposed Meixueiro and chosen as their new leader a man Lawrence was to meet, Issac M. Ibarra.

Ibarra was a *Serrano,* a wiry ex-mine mechanic who had educated himself while working for American mine owners. Gold and silver had lured many foreigners to Oaxaca during Porfirian days. Ibarra had entered the service of Meixueiro and risen to the rank of brigade commander by July 1914 when Meixueiro consolidated his power by capturing Oaxaca and driving out the incumbent governor, Miguel Bolaños Cacho. One other brigade commander in this victory was slated to enter the Lawrence story, Onofre Jiménez, a heavy-set, coarse *Serrano* of little education. Six months later Ibarra and Jiménez helped Meixueiro drive out Jiménez Figueroa, a federal interloper, who for four days had captured the Oaxaca government.

By 1920 Ibarra, a consistent foe of Carranza, was willing to join in the uprising against him even though it meant supporting the northern triumvirate of Obregón, Calles, and de la Huerta. Ibarra's entry into Oaxaca came six days before Obregón's entry into Mexico City. In Oaxaca Jesús Acevedo was declared the new governor. In Mexico City de la Huerta was named the provisional president of Mexico. Six months later Obregón would win a legal election.

García Vigil was away from his native state through most of these developments. He had been born on 24 July 1882 into a distinguished Oaxacan family. His godfather was Emilio Pimentel, a lawyer, who for the last nine years of the old regime was the governor of Oaxaca. According to Lawrence's revised version of *The Plumed Serpent* (which incorporated García Vigil as a character), the boy's mother wanted him to be a priest. After he finished primary school she found an influential sponsor in Oaxaca's first archbishop, Eulogio Gillow. The son of an Englishman who had amassed a fortune in Mexico, Gillow had the wealth to improve the position of the church in his diocese. One institution he rescued was the Seminario Pontifico y Conciliar de la Santa Cruz. Founded in 1673, the seminary had been expelled from its original building as a result of the anti-clerical laws of Juárez. The archbishop had remodeled the abandoned monastery of the Bethlehemite monks as a new home for the seminary. Because he wanted members of good families to study for the priesthood, Gillow arranged a slot for Manuel at Santa Cruz. But there was already something rebellious in the boy's nature, especially when he felt individual rights were threatened. He and the seminary were soon at odds, and his family opted for a military career.

Because Pimentel, his godfather, was able to sponsor him, the seventeen-year-old youth easily managed to get into Mexico's equivalent of West Point, the Colegio Militar de Chapultepec. Three years later, his commission as an artillery lieutenant in Mexico's standing army was signed by General Bernardo Reyes, one of Díaz's most efficient governors, who had entered the federal cabinet as Secretary of War. But García Vigil rebelled against absolutism in the army too; and in 1905, he was discharged for "bad conduct."

By this time he was an ardent champion of democratic freedom and hated dictatorship. Feeling that the truth about the oppression of the poor and landless had to be told, he returned to Oaxaca and, in 1909, began publishing a radical weekly, *El Oaxaqueño.* It espoused the cause of his old idol, General Reyes, who had been dismissed from the Díaz cabinet and had subsequently announced his candidacy for the vice presidency against the running mate chosen by Díaz. Later Reyes prudently withdrew from the political arena by accepting an assignment to study European armies. García Vigil, like many other *Reyistas,* then gave his allegiance to Madero, who was willing to face the personal risk of running against Díaz.

After Madero's overthrow by Huerta, García Vigil reentered military life to fight Huerta. He became an artillery chief for Pablo Gonzalez, a northern regional commander who, by placing his troops at the service of Carranza, helped Carranza come to power. Campaigning for Carranza brought García Vigil into contact with Obregón, Calles, and de la Huerta. García Vigil was one of the victorious soldiers of the north who accompanied Carranza when he made his triumphant entry into the capital in 1914. This gave the fiery, thirty-two-year-old artillery officer a place in the convention in Aguascalientes.

Almost all the delegates were dressed in the new revolutionary style: tieless shirts buttoned at the collar, leather jackets, and Texas sombreros. But the men representing Meixueiro wore top hats and morning coats, thus committing, as one historian observed, "the crass error of presenting themselves in accordance with European etiquette."[2] These delegates were ridiculed and denounced as reactionaries. García Vigil led the denunciation. He claimed the Oaxaca leaders were followers of Félix Díaz, a nephew of the dictator who advocated his uncle's views. The ex-journalist, with his gift for words, raised a storm against the men in morning coats. Others took up the charges; and when the convention could not be quieted, the Oaxaca delegates were forced to leave.

García Vigil was also one of the delegates to the convention called by Carranza in Querétaro which forged the 1917 constitution still in use in Mexico. Subsequently García Vigil became the general of a brigade, a deputy in the federal government and a leading member of the *Partido*

Liberal Constitutionalista. This party was most influential after the over-throw of Carranza. When Obregón came to Oaxaca on his campaign tour, García Vigil came to electioneer with him. In his native city, García Vigil won support for Obregón and also prepared the way for his own election as governor of the state. The *Serranos* soon found that Obregón's acceptance of their support did not enhance their power as much as they thought. Acevedo, whom they had put in as governor, was ousted by the federal government. In the election for a replacement, García Vigil was the victor. Obregón became president of Mexico on 1 December 1920, and García Vigil governor of Oaxaca on December 15. Ibarra was a senator in the new Obregón government.

Since 1911 the governors of Oaxaca had been too concerned with maintaining their own positions and managing immediate crises to restructure the state. But during this time, under Carranza and Obregón, the central government had become increasingly strong. The government of the nation and the government of Oaxaca were in general accord, and García Vigil had won a legal election. He was eager to make basic changes.

One of the changes was personal. He was attractive to women, and one married woman, who loved him, committed suicide. But he did not marry until after he had become governor. Then, near forty, he married a girl not yet out of her teens.

He wanted to make Oaxaca a modern democratic state, informed by the ideals of the Revolution and integrated into the nation. He instituted an agrarian policy which guaranteed the allotment and restitution of lands. He introduced a new taxation system which gave the state fiscal consistency. When businessmen and industrialists opposed his reforms, he used the power of his office to bring them into line. He paved streets, improved drainage systems, worked for better sanitation, tried to combat alcoholism, and in April 1922, created the state constitution. Hence the memorial on his former home praising him for reconstructing the "federative entity." Instead of struggling to hold Oaxaca apart from the nation, as had the *Soberanistas,* he interlocked it more securely into the federal system; his constitution echoed the national one created in Querétaro.

Oaxaca was in need of such aggressive reconstruction when García Vigil came to power. In 1909, before the Revolution began, Oaxaca had been a small but prosperous city of 36,147. By 1921 enough order had been restored for Mexico to hold another census. Oaxaca's population was only 27,792—a quarter of the population lost in the twelve years of upheaval. In one month during the typhus epidemic which coincided with Oaxaca's ill-fated secession, for example, 476 persons had died.

The energy with which García Vigil carried out his reforms brought him enemies. Soon his friendship with Obregón began to fray. But the first half of 1922 was peaceful, and only two events, because of their bearing on Lawrence, need be noted. In the spring Hermann Kull, a Swiss dentist, came to Oaxaca with his wife, Carola. He had practiced for three years in Puebla. Second, on May 18, Eulogio Gillow, the wealthy archbishop who had renovated the Seminario Pontifico and helped García Vigil take the first step toward a priestly career, died. The archbishop had endured almost five years of exile in the United States after the *Constitutionalistas* had closed down his seminary and driven out the seminarians in 1916. But in February 1921 the archbishop had returned to Oaxaca. Although García Vigil and the archbishop were on opposite sides politically, the governor saw that his old benefactor was buried with proper honors.

In the second half of 1922 storms began to brew. Félix Díaz, whom García Vigil had denounced at the Aguascalientes convention, was a rallying figure for the most conservative forces in Oaxaca. Early in May, from the safety of New Orleans, he proclaimed himself Supreme Chief of the Army of National Reconstruction. This gave new hope to the remaining *Felicistas* in the state. They rallied under the leadership of Mario Ferrer. General Fortunato Maycotte, a revolutionary general who had become the *jefe de armas* of the federal government in Oaxaca, did not succeed in crushing them. Obregón began interfering in Oaxaca affairs in arbitrary ways that irritated García Vigil. When troubles between García Vigil and Obregón began to look serious, Senator Ibarra and other *Serrano* leaders made a point of calling on President Obregón to reaffirm their loyalty.

One of García Vigil's enemies was José F. Gómez, a representative from Juchitan in the federal government. He attacked García Vigil verbally in the Chamber of Deputies; and on the night of 15 February 1923, Gómez and four others waited behind trees outside the house where Governor García Vigil was staying in Mexico City. When the governor and a friend appeared, they opened fire. García Vigil and his friend shot back, killing one of the assailants. Although the governor escaped with his life, he received a wound in the left knee that was to trouble him continuously. García Vigil suspected that Obregón had instigated the attack. This deepened into conviction when his attackers were not prosecuted. After he returned to Oaxaca his knee was treated by Lydia Kull, a physiotherapist who had followed her brother, the dentist, to Oaxaca.

This was the year Lawrence began his personal observation of Mexican politics on the first of three trips. He and Frieda began sightseeing their way through Mexico in March 1923 with two friends, poet Witter Bynner and Willard (Spud) Johnson. Lawrence spent June and July at Lake Chapala, developing his ideas about the Mexican Revolution as he wrote the first version of *The Plumed Serpent*. Pancho Villa, the colorful revolutionary leader, especially captured his imagination, largely because his exploits were already subjects for popular ballads. A few days after the Lawrences left Mexico in July 1923, Villa was assassinated. Lawrence worked "the pug-faced notorious Pancho Villa" into the second version of his novel written in Oaxaca in 1924-25, including Villa's killing as a portent of what might happen to his own hero. There Carlota, the hero's antagonistic wife, refers to Villa as a "bandit" who went insane because his pride got the better of him. Pointedly she added that all Mexicans suffer the same madness "as soon as they rise above themselves." Thus, Lawrence learned that assassination, superseded as a political technique in England, was still common in Mexico.

In August 1923 Lawrence, after planning to sail from New York, balked at returning to England and went to California, while Frieda went without him to England. Not only was she eager to get back to Europe, but, as she confided to Adele Seltzer, she was unwilling to submit any longer to Lawrence's bad temper and "eternal hounding." Mrs. Seltzer was the wife of Thomas Seltzer, Lawrence's American publisher. The two couples had become friends when the Seltzers had spent the previous Christmas with the Lawrences at the Hawk Ranch seventeen miles north of Taos, New Mexico.

In September 1923, after four weeks in California, Lawrence arranged to return to Mexico with Kai Götzsche, a Danish painter who had also been at the ranch the winter before. Their plan was to travel down the west coast. On September 24, the day before they set out, the newspapers carried another Mexican bombshell. Adolfo de la Huerta, the Secretary of the Treasury, had broken with President Obregón. De la Huerta had campaigned with Obregón and Calles to overthrow Carranza and had completed Carranza's term of office. So a former president had broken with the present one. Lawrence and Götzsche did not postpone their trip, but they saw increasing signs of the seriousness of the breach as they traveled. As Lawrence was to tell Frederick Carter six weeks later, the political uncertainty was a factor in his decision not to remain long in Mexico. On 19 November 1923, three days before he and Götzsche sailed from Mexico, Lawrence wrote to Spud Johnson, who had been in Mexico with him earlier in the year: "Everything a bit heavier. They expect more revolution—Calles and de la Huerta—probably a bad one. No business doing—and the common people a bit brutal. O heavenly bolshevism."

When Lawrence and the Danish artist reached Veracruz, they learned that Guadalupe Sánchez, the *jefe de armas,* was about to desert Obregón as he had earlier deserted Carranza. His preparations for war made Lawrence and Götzsche feel "threatened by hostile forces"—as Lawrence later told Carter. Lawrence and Götzsche got out none too soon. Two weeks later on December 6, de la Huerta entered Veracruz and took charge of Sánchez's forces. His rupture with Obregón turned into an open rebellion against the government of Mexico. Lawrence had reached England by then, and his December 7 letter to Bynner shows he already knew of the outbreak. "I wish I was in Santa Fe at this moment," he wrote, "as it is, for my sins, and Frieda's, I am in London. I only hope Mexico will stop revolting."

Two days later he was still following de la Huerta's rebellion in the newspapers, for on December 17 he wrote Mabel Luhan that, although he was detesting London, "perhaps it's as well I went away from that revolution in Mexico." The letter also suggests he knew that one side was proving weaker than expected, for he added, "I want, when Mexico is quiet, to go down to Oaxaca. I don't suppose this 'revolution' will last long." His continuing concern about the rebellion showed three days later in a letter to Knud Merrild, the other Danish painter with whom he had wintered on the Hawk ranch: "By March I hope to be coming West again. If Mexico is still revolting we may stay a time in New Mexico."

About this time Ethel R. Doctor, a thirty-one-year-old missionary from Lonsdale, Rhode Island, whom Lawrence would later meet, arrived in Oaxaca. Her assignment was to supervise a home for students from nearby villages operated by the Board of Foreign Missions of the Presbyterian Church of the United States of America.[3] The missionaries in charge of the home were leaving to work among the Zapotec Indians of the Villa Alta district. When she arrived eleven boys and one girl were at the home; but later in the month, Norman W. Taylor and his wife, the former Geraldine Ely, joined her. The Taylors took over the boys, and Miss Doctor looked after the one girl and then the others who joined her. Until Miss Doctor moved to a separate girls' hostel, the three missionaries lived together in the rented home of their predecessors, which faced the southern end of the long park known as El Llano ("The Plain"). The Lawrences later lived near the same park.

Shortly after the missionaries were settled, two more Americans arrived in Oaxaca. Lawrence would later meet Colonel A. D. Akin, a mining engineer, and his second wife, twenty-six-year-old Jean Harmon, who had married the fifty-four-year-old colonel the year before. They had made two trips to Oaxaca earlier in the year. On the first Jean "fell so much in love with it" and on the second the colonel made mining connections. Thus they came to be, in the colonel's language, "interned" by the de la Huerta rebellion.

Many of the revolutionary generals, now military commanders of such states as Jalisco, Puebla, Yucatan, Campeche, Tabasco, and Chiapas, were disgruntled, restless, ambitious, and ready to take up arms again. The navy joined the rebellion. On December 13, García Vigil, who had long been a friend of de la Huerta, brought Oaxaca in on the side of his fellow campaigner.

Maycotte, Oaxaca's military commander, supported García Vigil. One reason for the rebellion was Obregón's plan to impose Calles as Mexico's next president. Obregón's opponents also pointed to summary executions and the assassination of political enemies, including that of Villa and the abortive one of García Vigil. García Vigil, motivated by his hatred of what he considered absolutism, ignored his belief in the need to work through constitutional means and took his state out of the federal union he had helped strengthen. For the second time in eight years Oaxaca had broken from Mexico's central government. Now, however, the situation was reversed. In 1915 a conservative state had seceded from a federal government it considered too liberal. In 1923 the same state, now on the liberal side, had broken with a central power it did not consider liberal enough.

The forty-three-year-old de la Huerta showed little energy. Obregón, an old campaigner, acted quickly. On December 22 his General Juan Andrew Almazán inflicted a crucial defeat on the rebels in Puebla.

Oaxaca had been cut off from the capital from the start. Its peril was strikingly demonstrated on January 12 when three brigades of *Serranos* made good their promise to assist Obregón. Coming down from the hills in the early morning, they raided the city. One of the leaders was that old marcher on Oaxaca, Onofre Jiménez. The invasion was only a one-day affair. García Vigil held El Fortín, the hill that had always been the key to the city, and ably directed his defense from there. The *Serranos,* feeling insecure, withdrew when they saw a train approaching with reinforcements for the governor. As it turned out, only one hundred men from Etla were on the train.

On January 28 Obregón forces led by Almazán inflicted a defeat on rebel forces even more crushing than the one at Puebla. Maycotte, who had been unable to suppress the *Felicistas* in Oaxaca, proved inept again. He let his troop train ride blindly into government entrapment at Esperanza, the junction between the first railroad to Veracruz and the branch line connecting with the railway to Oaxaca. The rebels began to retreat. On February 14, Enrique Estrada, the Jalisco leader, was defeated at Palo Verde near Lake Chapala. His fellow general, Manuel M. Diéguez, and four hundred of his *charros,* as his big-hatted, horse-riding followers were called, took refuge in Oaxaca.

Oaxaca was the next target for the federal troops under Almazán. Diéguez convinced García Vigil of the might of the approaching division and persuaded him to withdraw from Oaxaca rather than to try to defend it. On March 30 the two generals took their forces overland toward the Isthmus of Tehuantepec. The potential power of the rebel forces was further diluted when Maycotte took his forces in a different direction toward Pochutla.

Two days later, General Almazán and his victorious troops entered Oaxaca. With them was General Ibarra, who had ridden into Oaxaca three times previously to throw out governors. As senator he was first in line to become the state's chief executive. As a young man Colonel Akin had been a newspaperman in Georgia, and his instinct for a good news story set him on the spot with his camera when the federal troops "liberated" the city. They entered via Avenida Independencia. (Plate 2.) Three weeks later Ibarra was confirmed as head of the state until a new governor could be elected by the people.

García Vigil took 600 men when he withdrew from Oaxaca. They hoped to get to Chiapas, but the governor's old enemy and would-be assassin, José F. Gómez, was also in revolt against Obregón (but for different reasons). Because Gómez was leading his rebellion from his native Juchitán, that city was unsafe for García Vigil. Generals loyal to Obregón controlled much of the rest of the Isthmus. By the time García Vigil neared the eastern frontier of the state, he was trapped in an impregnable ring. Further fighting, he calculated, would only lead to the useless sacrifice of lives. He decided to surrender, but Diéguez and his *charros* voted against yielding and rode away. The split-off of the Jalisco forces meant another serious reduction in numbers. Félix Gómez, the chief of the Diéguez staff, stayed with García Vigil.

The nearest garrison to which García Vigil and Gómez could surrender was at Tapanatepec at the Chiapas border. By the time García Vigil reached the garrison he had only seventy men left and was in physical misery. His knee wound, from which he had never fully recovered, was now gangrenous. However, the other generals who converged in Tapanatepec treated him like a comrade-at-arms. The men who surrendered were escorted to the nearby railroad town of Chahuities and sent to Ixtepec, the railroad junction where nine years earlier Jesús Carranza, his son, and his nephew had been sentenced to death. At Ixtepec the prisoners were put on the trans-Isthmus railroad which, to García Vigil's surprise, headed north. They might then be taken to Mexico City and be treated as prisoners of war rather than executed as rebels. But the train stopped at Santa Lucretia, another railroad junction four hours away. At this town, now called Jesús Carranza, García Vigil and Gómez were taken from the train at 7:00 A.M. April 19. On an adjacent track was a train headed south. Though García Vigil and Gómez did not know it, it bore two coffins.

García Vigil and Gómez feared the worst when they were told their men would continue to Mexico, but they would be shifted to the southbound train. Dr. Macario Bribiesca, married to one of García's sisters, pleaded to accompany his brother-in-law and give him needed medical attention. The request was brusquely turned down. However, the forty-one-year-old governor was allowed to write a message for the doctor to take home: "To my correligionists and friends. You know well how much I have fought for truth and justice. At the end I die for having defended them, victim of those incapable of appreciating my revolutionary sincerity."

He added a final sentence, particularly touching in view of the memorial service of 1967: "I hope my memory will endure among all those who accompanied me in different epochs struggling for those causes."

García Vigil and Gómez were then forced aboard the other train. Following the pattern of the Jesús Carranza murder, the train was stopped about three hours later. The two generals were marched to the foot of a mango tree near the track and shot. Their bodies were carried to the train, placed in the waiting coffins, and, at Ixtepec, buried.

De la Huerta had managed to escape to the United States. In Los Angeles he pursued an unexpected career for a revolutionary general who had been president of Mexico. He had a fine tenor voice and he taught singing until 1935, when Cardenas exiled Calles, against whose presidency de la Huerta had taken arms. De la Huerta then returned to Mexico and was exonerated. But the tenor's supporting generals were not so fortunate. One by one they were hunted down and killed. Sánchez, the Veracruz leader, was caught in Chiapas. So was Diéquez, the Jalisco leader, who had decided against surrendering with García Vigil. Maycotte, who had fled Oaxaca in a different direction, eluded capture until May 10, but he was tracked down on the Oaxaca coast and executed in Pochutla. José F. Gómez, the would-be assassin of García Vigil, who had rebelled against Obregón for his own reasons, was also captured and shot.

In Oaxaca, all these killings had an embittering aftermath. On the personal side, Lawrence's perceptions were influenced by his misadventure with one of Obregón's chief ministers. The cabinet member was the philosopher and educator José Vasconcelos, Obregón's dynamic Secretary of Public Education. Vasconcelos's name had often come up in the course of the Lawrences' sightseeing. Many of the murals by Diego Rivera and José Clemente Orozco, which they saw with Bynner and Johnson, had been commissioned for the walls of the federal buildings by Vasconcelos.

Vasconcelos was often known as "The Counselor," and his educational program included more teaching of English. To supervise the English-language materials being prepared for the schools he had Frederick W. Leighton, a young U.S. newspaperman (later to operate a famous Mexican gift shop in Greenwich Village) in the Ministry of Education. Leighton met Lawrence on his first visit to Mexico through his old friend Bynner in June 1923. Novels such as *Sons and Lovers, The Rainbow,* and

Women in Love had already won Lawrence considerable fame. Vasconcelos, interested in literature and a man of wide culture, arranged a luncheon that would include the Lawrences, Bynner, Johnson, Leighton, and Carleton Beals, another U.S. newspaperman in Mexico. When the guests arrived at Vasconcelos's office on the third floor of the Ministry of Education, they had to wait. Lawrence, who hated being treated like a visiting dignitary, and had tried to refuse the invitation, became increasingly angry. Finally a subordinate explained that Vasconcelos had been called unexpectedly for an audience with President Obregón. Would the guests excuse him and have lunch with him tomorrow instead? All agreed but Lawrence, who, both Beals and Leighton testify, flew into a rage. When the lunch took place the next day, he did not attend.

Nine months later Vasconcelos had broken with Obregón. He had not joined de la Huerta's rebellion, but Obregón's responsibility for the assassination of a de la Huerta spokesman during the rebellion led Vasconcelos to resign as Secretary of Education. He was persuaded to withdraw his resignation but later resigned again. Outraged by the brutality with which the rebellion was crushed, he denounced the government for abandoning revolutionary principles in favor of militarism. Oaxaca was his native state; and when a number of Oaxaqueños approached him to be a candidate for governor, he agreed to run. The major opponent was the uncultured *Serrano,* Onofre Jiménez, who had been at Ibarra's side whenever the two had descended on Oaxaca to impose a new governor. Besides being Ibarra's choice, Jiménez was backed by Obregón and by Calles, who had relinquished his post as secretary of state to accept the candidacy to succeed Obregón.

The students of Oaxaca and García Vigil's remaining partisans campaigned for Vasconcelos. Saturday 2 August 1924 was election day, and many contend that Vasconcelos won the majority of votes statewide.[4] In the city of Oaxaca, the vote given out by *El Mercurio* on August 4 was 1,515 for Jiménez and 1,031 for Vasconcelos. Less than ten percent of the capital's population either had gone to the polls or had their votes counted. Because Vasconcelos was convinced of his statewide majority, he installed his legislature in a building near the Government Palace. The Ibarra-led legislature had gathered in the palace. The election was in dispute until September 26 when Ibarra's legislature declared Jiménez the winner, claiming he had 106,411 votes against Vasconcelos's 35,131.

Vasconcelos gave up the struggle, wanting neither to beg Obregón to validate his election nor to risk the penalties he had seen inflicted on Obregón dissidents earlier in the year. Later in his autobiography, *Ulise Criolla,* which after his death was published in an abridged English version as *A Mexican Ulysses,* he explained:

We failed to take Obregón into account. His will moved in secret. And Governor Ibarra was his tool. Each one of those who helped me, the elite of Oaxaca at the time, fell into the shade, into oblivion and impotence, with the exception of those who became traitors. My rival, who had been completely apathetic, began to go about the city and speak in private. He never made a speech to the people, but to his friends he made a re-mark that was enough to defeat me: "The Counselor is too big a candi-date for Oaxaca; the Counselor drinks champagne; I drink mezcal; I ought to be Governor." Really, the poor fellow did nothing, did not have to do anything. The incumbent Governor, whose protégé he was, and the Commanding Officer did everything.

I returned to Oaxaca to watch helplessly the trickery, violence, and cynicism. The government did not even bother to hold elections; boxes were missing, ballots were missing, votes were missing, for voters were threatened and frightened. Even so, with the few who turned out, there would have been enough votes to assure us a legitimate victory. But they never complete the count under regimes of barefaced force; the official party carts off the voting urns and never even bothers to open them.

Jiménez was installed as governor of Oaxaca on 1 December 1924, the day that Calles became president of Mexico. Lawrence, who had just missed being in Mexico when Pancho Villa was assassinated in July 1923, who had nearly been caught by the de la Huerta rebellion in Veracruz, who had been invited to lunch by Vasconcelos and who knew the man's calibre because of his transformation of the country's educational sys-tem, had been in Oaxaca twenty-one days. It was long enough to learn what the city had undergone trying to run counter to the will of two strong central governments; long enough, too, to learn about the suffering and fate of an idealistic man like García Vigil. Lawrence had written back to William Hawk, his host and friend at Del Monte Ranch in New Mexico: "Everywhere the government is very Labour—and somehow one doesn't feel very solid. There are so many wild Indians who don't know any-thing about anything, except that they are told that every 'rich' man is an enemy. There may be a bad bust-up in Mexico City: and again, every-thing may go off quietly. But I don't like the feeling."

This is the sort of writing for which people, familiar only with the peaceful Mexico of recent decades, often criticize Lawrence. But he was not talking idly. He knew the name of the general scheduled to lead the "bust-up" and he knew the projected date of the uprising. He had grounds for his general unease. Instead of merely projecting his own fears on an idyllic landscape—as is often charged—he was sensitively attuned to the reality of Mexico after fourteen years of almost constant internecine war.

CHAPTER 1

LAWRENCE AND THE GOVERNOR

In the halcyon days of Porfirio Díaz when foreigners were welcome and mining was booming, Oaxaca had as many as 300 American and British families. The Oaxaca *Herald,* an English newspaper, appeared every Sunday morning. Holy Trinity Church was Anglican with services in English. Perhaps the most famous was the archaeologist Alfred P. Maudslay, who had mines at nearby Zavaleta. Another Britisher was Constantine Rickards, a Scottish merchant and mining man, whose son Constantine G., author of *The Ruins of Mexico,* had a passionate interest in archaeology. Among the Americans were two mine-owners who had employed Ibarra as a mechanic: Claude B. Finney of San Antonio, Texas, who came in 1902, and Charles A. Hamilton of San Francisco, who followed the next year and made a fortune at Taviche. And in this epoch a five-tiered opera house—now the Teatro Alcala—let the cultured and wealthy gather in European elegance. (Plate 3.) But mining began dwindling in 1907, there was a crisis in 1909, the Revolution ruined the industry, and most of the foreigners left.

By 1924 when Lawrence came to Oaxaca, the foreign colony was small. "It was not the old foreign colony destroyed by the Revolution," according to Ethel Doctor, the Presbyterian missionary, "but a new one just beginning." Although a few old-timers were left, she told me that "most of the men in Oaxaca were men staying on, hoping something might come back to them from their lost treasures. Most of them had lands as well as mines. One by one they went away when they saw there was nothing doing: their wealth was not going to be restored. They were idle, living on what they had left. They were sitting around waiting. They would sit under the arcades of the west side of the plaza or across the Zócalo on the opposite side. None of them liked the other."

My search for information about Lawrence's stay in Oaxaca led to a number of these people. Seven or eight I met in person and several more by letter. Whenever anyone named a new member of the colony, I would try to track him or her down. Many had died, but some had living relatives, and I had far more luck in reaching others than I anticipated. I had met Miss Doctor in 1950, and it was her list of names in 1962 that suggested there might be enough information for a book about Lawrence's

Oaxaca sojourn. A decisive factor was Harloe Hamilton, the son of Charles Hamilton, who gave me more names, corrected some of Miss Doctor's, and assured me that certain key figures were still alive. The recollections I gathered lent impact to many references in Lawrence's writings. Particularly this was true for remarks in his letters. Overlapping paragraphs from five letters, for example, provided the genesis for this chapter. All were written from the hotel in which Lawrence and Frieda unpacked their bags on 9 November 1924, the night they arrived in Oaxaca.[1]

The hotel was the Francia, named after its original French owners. It was built in the 1890s and for many years was *the* hotel in Oaxaca. It still exists under the same name, though now the one-story section has an upper story and its once-open patio has been roofed. (Plate 4.)

Now foreigners prefer the Hotel Marqués de Valle or the luxurious Hotel Victoria on a hillside overlooking the town, but the Francia was the choice of foreigners during the first decade of the century, and it was still the home of a number of foreigners during the 1920s. The four best rooms were the front ones of the upper floor of the annex. When the Lawrences arrived, the center two were occupied by the Akins, who had turned one into a sitting room. The red-haired Jean, the colonel's young wife, was visiting her native Kansas, but the photo-taking colonel was on hand, looking after his mining interests and voluminous correspondence. To the left of the Akin suite lived an affable Texan, known as John Duke, whose real name, disguised because of a financial scandal, was Beaumont Clifford Girdley. The room on the right was occupied by Rosalind Hughes, a single California woman of forty-three, who had saved up money as a secretary to fulfill the dream of her girlhood—visiting Mexico. Miss Hughes, who was already eighty-one when I began corresponding with her, had an extraordinary memory, which was aided by her carefully captioned photographs. She lived to be ninety-five, willingly answered questions, and put me in touch with Jean Akin, an equally important source of information.

When the Lawrences arrived, the Francia was run by Doña María Jarquin de Monros, a Catalonian, who nine months before had taken over following the death of her husband Juan Monros, a former pastry-cook. According to Mrs. Akin, the widowed Doña María was a "tall, majestic, rather heavy-set woman" and, Miss Hughes added, one "with considerable personality and character." When Spanish merchants ate at the hotel, Doña María would often sit and converse with the storekeepers. Americans who lived elsewhere would also come in for meals. On the day of her arrival, 14 October 1924, Miss Hughes remembers her encounter with four Americans when she came into the dining room for the big midday dinner: Colonel Akin, Mr. "Duke," and "the Wilson boys." (Robert W. Wilson, aged thirty, and Clyde, aged twenty-one, were the sons of Robert

Wilson, a miner who had come to Oaxaca in 1910 and had been Mr. Hamilton's mine manager at Taviche.) The two young men, who had rowdy reputations, occasionally stayed at the hotel when they came in from the mine. Their father and mother lived next door to the house into which the Lawrences were going to move.

The Francia was not on the main square, but it was only a block away on a street that had long been named 2 de Abril, after the day Porfirio Díaz routed Maximilian's troops at Puebla in 1867. Eight years before Lawrence's arrival, however, the *Constitutionalistas,* in recapturing Oaxaca for the Revolution, had renamed it 20 de Noviembre in honor of the day set by Madero in 1910 for an armed rising against Díaz. It was the north-south thoroughfare that bounded the big covered market on the west; that sprawling market began just a block from the hotel. In front of the hotel ran a tramline with cars pulled by paired mules.

Describing the general insecurity of the time, Miss Hughes wrote, "I heard of various incidents. I do know that many went armed, and that several new revolts were brewing; and it is true, as Dorothy Brett reported, that it was considered unsafe to walk outside the town, and the *bandidos* did rob people of their clothing, etc. I recall walking out somewhere with Colonel Akin. He was armed and very aware of possibilities about bandits, although I could never feel much concern about it. It seemed so peaceful around the town."

Because of the extent to which outside investors, encouraged by Díaz, had exploited Mexico's natural resources, foreigners were a target of revolutionary hatred. Dr. Kull, the dentist, told me that García Vigil had shared these hostile feelings and had red marks placed on their homes to encourage natives to discriminate against them. The marks were fairly inconspicuous, so most foreigners did not know they were there, but an old Indian woman warned the Kulls and advised them to wipe their mark off, which they did. Ibarra, on the other hand, had met enough foreigners and had been treated so well when he was working for Finney and Hamilton that he liked foreigners. After he became governor, he made a point of being friendly to them. The Kulls had a tennis court up near the Llano, and Ibarra often went there for a game. He was the best tennis player of the crowd, wrote Dr. Kull. "I appreciated his good sportsmanship by playing with us, as most of us were just beginners."

Miss Doctor was not disarmed: "He would as soon put a bullet in a man as a ball over a net."

The ruins of Monte Alban, on the crest of a hill which rises steeply from the city, were then little known. This was nearly eight years before the discovery of jewels in Tomb 7 by Alfonso Caso brought them to world attention. Ibarra, however, approached Colonel Akin to raise money for their exploration. The Akins often rode to the ruins with the governor, and Miss Hughes and Dr. Kull once attended a picnic breakfast on Monte Alban at which they were Ibarra's guests.

The governor was accompanied by five or six aides. At six in the morning, after fording the Atoyac River, they climbed to the leveled mountain top and ate their breakfast at the south end of the site's great central plaza near a mound which, when it was later excavated, proved to be the Observatory. Besides Miss Hughes and the Kulls, the guests included Mr. Finney, Duke, and Donald Miller, a young New York mining engineer whose house was across the street from the Lawrences' future home. The Kulls were accompanied by their *mozo,* later a figure in Lawrence's writings. Ibarra, as on his triumphal entry into Oaxaca, wore a Boy-Scout-leader type of hat, which shaded his steel-rimmed glasses, his full moustache, and the lean, rather leathery cheeks of his shrewdly humorous face. (Plate 5.) Because of his native courtesy, he had impressed Mrs. Akin as "one of the old-time gentlemen," but on the picnic he looked very much the outdoorsman.

Wherever Lawrence traveled, he continued to write, and he planned to do so during his first trip to Mexico. But once he had done the rounds of the central highlands as a sightseer, he wanted a quieter place than the capital. A letter of introduction had brought him an invitation to take tea with Mrs. Zelia Nuttall, an American archaeologist whose work on pre-Columbian Mexico would greatly influence Lawrence's *Plumed Serpent.* She had offered to rent him an apartment, which had its own entrance though it was part of Casa Alvarado (her famous home in Coyoacán). Coyoacán was a quiet suburb south of the city. However, Lawrence decided it was still too close. Perhaps, too, he was a little apprehensive about being dominated by his hostess, for when he described the character based on her in The Plumed Serpent he characterized her as a woman who "always put her visitors uncomfortably at their ease, as if they were captives and she the chieftainness who had captured them."

Oaxaca was second choice, but Bynner, in *Journey with Genius,* says that Lawrence rejected it for being too hot. It then took three trains to reach Oaxaca; the first on the British-built Mexican Railway from Mexico City to Esperanza, where Maycotte's forces were fated to be wiped out the next year; the second on the branch line from Esperanza to Tehuacán, a two-hour ride; and, after an overnight stay in Tehuacán, an all-day ride on the narrow-gauge Ferrocarril Mexicano del Sur. Lawrence chose the third alternative, Lake Chapala, and he set off to find a house there the day after the Vasconcelos luncheon that he refused to attend.

The rejected Oaxaca, however, tugged at his imagination. After his second trip to Mexico with Kai Götzsche in the fall of 1923 and while he was enduring his miserable winter in Europe, he wrote Bynner in March 1924, "I want to go back to Mexico—particularly I want to go to Oaxaca."

At Mazatlán he and Gótzsche were warned to take the steamer to Manzanillo because after Tepic there was a hundred-mile gap in the railway. They decided against the comfortable steamer and continued by train to Tepic where they planned to hire horses. None were available. The first day's ride was in a battered Ford over a road so bad that fewer than sixty miles took six hours. At Ixtlán del Río, they hired mules and rode nine hours to La Quemada, over the mountains and down into the *barranca*. The railway was washed out at La Quemada, and they spent six more hours on muleback the next day before picking up the train at Etztatlán. Lawrence wrote a delighted letter the day he and Gótzsche reached the comfort of Guadalajara to the Lawrences' friend, a Scottish newspaperwoman Catherine Carswell:[2]

> We rode two days down the mountains, and got to Eztatlan [his spelling]. Mexico has a certain mystery of beauty for me, as if the gods were here. Now, in this October, the days are so pure and lovely, like an enchantment, as if some dark-faced gods were still young. . . . It is queer, all the way down the Pacific coast, I kept thinking: Best go back to England. And then, once across the *barranca* from Ixtlan, it was here again, where the gods may sometimes be awful, but they are young, here in Mexico, in Jalisco, that I wanted to be.

He wrote a similar letter to his New York publisher, Thomas Seltzer, addressing him affectionately as "Tomasito," partly because Seltzer was hardly more than five feet tall and partly because the diminutive was characteristically Mexican. Ten days later Lawrence's enthusiasm was still running high when he wrote to Adele Seltzer: "There *is* something good about Mexico, something that opens again, at least in part, the floodgates of one's soul. The USA & the world shut the floodgates of my soul tight."

Twelve days later, after he had reluctantly decided not to spend the winter in Mexico and to come to England after all, he wrote to Frieda, "Mexico is still very attractive and a very good place to live in; it is not 'tame.' " The same day he wrote Frieda's mother, the Baroness Anna von Richthofen, "I like it here. I don't know how, but it gives me strength, this black country. It is full of man's strength." And on November 20 he wrote from Mexico City, "I feel I belong here. . . . This is the Indian *source.* " His correspondent was Mabel Dodger Luhan, a Taos patron of the arts whose invitation to the Lawrences had brought them to the United States in 1922.

But October 22 he wrote his friend S. S. Koteliansky: "I was at Chapala for a day yesterday. The lake lovelier than before—very lovely: but somehow gone alien to me. And a sense of suspense, of waiting for something to happen—which something I want to avoid." Thus Oaxaca was chosen as the place in which to settle for rewriting *The Plumed Serpent*.

Lawrence wrote continuously on his second trip to Mexico and completed *The Boy in the Bush,* based on *The House of Ellis* by Mollie Skinner, a nurse-journalist he had met in Western Australia in May 1922. Miss Skinner's novel, about the adventures of her brother as a young pioneer in Australia during the 1880s, had been written at Lawrence's suggestion after he had been stirred to initial enthusiasm by *Black Swans,* an earlier novel of hers he read during his two-week stay at her guest-house in Darlington. *The House of Ellis* had reached Lawrence in New York after his first Mexican trip. He must have begun working on the manuscript almost immediately. Just before he was ready to set out for Mexico the second time he mailed the rewritten first half of the novel to Seltzer from Los Angeles.

Once the third Mexican visit was agreed upon, events determined that the Honorable Dorothy Brett, daughter of Viscount Esher, would come along. She would also accompany the Lawrences to the United States in March 1924 and stay with them in New Mexico. Within a few weeks, Mrs. Luhan would present Frieda with a ranch a mile and a half north of the Hawk ranch where the Lawrences, in company with the Danish artists, had spent the winter of 1922-23. Because this higher ranch, to borrow Joseph Foster's word, was "chipped" out of Mount Lobo, Lawrence was first to call the new acquisition "Lobo," but "Kiowa" became the name that stuck.

When they reached Oaxaca, Lawrence and Frieda struck Miss Doctor as "poor." Indeed they were by present standards, but they were almost as flush as they had ever been. Although Seltzer had been delinquent with payment of royalties, Lawrence noted in his scrappy diary that the day before they left Kiowa ranch—which was now indisputably theirs, because Frieda had given Mrs. Luhan the manuscript of *Sons and Lovers* to seal the bargain—his balance in the Chase National Bank in New York was $2,285.21.

They boarded a Mexican Pullman at El Paso on 20 October 1924 and, after riding two days, arrived in Mexico City just after midnight the evening of October 22. Three nights later he wrote Spud Johnson, on the aftermath of the de la Huerta disaster, which both now knew had not proved to be a true revolution: "They expect more messes here— not revolutions, because nobody has any money to make one. But the place feels depressed." He also reported that Mrs. Nuttall had been to lunch and was "full of news about the murdered Mrs. Evans."

The reference is lighthearted, but Lawrence had described a similar attack on a hacienda in the first draft of *The Plumed Serpent*. Rosalie Evans's story must have reassured him that his imagined attack, with his heroine taking part as one of the defenders, was plausible. The story too must have increased his cynicism about the Mexican Revolution, for Mrs. Evans had died in defense of her hacienda, which she had refused to surrender when Obregón tried to confiscate her land. Because the United States had broken off relations with Mexico following the murder of Carranza and had recognized Obregón in September 1923, it did not want to defend Mrs. Evans and endanger the reestablished diplomatic relations. Since her husband had been English, Mrs. Evans appealed for British help. Great Britain had not had a minister in Mexico since Carranza drove out Sir Lionel Carden in 1914 because of support of Huerta. But it did have as its ranking officer a *chargé des archives,* H. A. C. Cummins, who took up Mrs. Evans's cause with righteous fervor. He defied Obregón and was forced to leave the country. British-Mexican relations were suspended. But Cummins had not managed to save Mrs. Evans. On August 2, two months before Lawrence arrived, Mrs. Evans drove her buggy into an ambush of Agrarians who opened fire. Fatally wounded, she toppled from her buggy. Her long hair caught in one of the wheels, and she was scalped before the horse could be stopped. The leader of the Agrarians responsible for killing Mrs. Evans was Manuel Montes. Lawrence chose Montes as a pseudonym for Calles when he began working him into the revision of *The Plumed Serpent.*

The Evans incident might also have contributed to Lawrence's feeling of personal insecurity in Mexico, for British subjects had no ambassador or minister to turn to. The British consul, Norman King, was "very attentive." But on this visit Lawrence dealt chiefly with the vice-consul, the Oaxaca-born Constantine G. Rickards, who had lost his fortune through the Revolution and had been obliged to abandon archaeology.

Lawrence also had personal contacts with Mexican government officials. Vasconcelos, having opposed Obregón, was no longer Secretary of Education; but the thirty-four-year-old Genaro Estrada, a writer who four years before had published *Poetas Nuevas de Mexico,* was undersecretary in *Relaciones Exteriores.* This Foreign Affairs official was president of the Mexican branch of P.E.N., the international writers organization founded in London in 1921. Lawrence was a member of the English branch, and Estrada called on him promptly after receiving the novelist's note. Thereafter, he showed the Lawrences around and appeared in the Oaxaca revision as the plump poet, García. According to Bynner, Miguel Covarrubias, a nineteen-year-old art student when Lawrence had met him the year before, provided other elements for the young guide. Estrada also arranged a P.E.N. club dinner in honor of Lawrence at the Café Oriental, a modest downtown restaurant that specialized in chop suey.

"I'm not keen a bit on being a swell," Lawrence had written his fiancée, Louie Burrows, thirteen years earlier. Dorothy Brett's memory of this dinner in *Lawrence and Brett* showed Lawrence trying in every way to wriggle out of going to the dinner, but she and Frieda insisted. After all, the club members had been sent a printed folder that was both invitation and program. Lawrence was to be the first member of a foreign P.E.N. club to be fêted by the Mexican membership, and readings of critical studies of his works were promised. Lawrence had taken his dinner jacket on his trip with Gótzsche, and he had it with him now, "green with over-ripeness." Finally he went, "dressed up miserably in a boiled shirt," as Brett describes it. Although Lawrence was dead when she began, her book was an extended letter to him, reviewing the joys and vicissitudes they experienced together. To the Lawrence still living in her memory she recalled the following consequence of the dinner: "That was the beginning of your friendship with Luis Quintana. He sat next to you and was fascinated by you."

Brett, the name she preferred, was deaf. Though she had an electric hearing aid the size of a briefcase as well as an ear trumpet affectionately known as "Toby," she did not always catch foreign words correctly. The name of this twenty-four-year-old Mexican was actually Quintanilla. A member of a group of poets and artists who called themselves *Los Estridentistas* ("The Strident Ones"), he had already published two books of poems and had written and staged *The Theatre of the Bat,* a musical review in which he used Mexican folklore elements as he had seen Russian ones exploited in *Chauve-Souris* in New York. One of his players was Tina Modotti, a beautiful Italian in her middle twenties, who had come to San Francisco at the age of seventeen, and there met the photographer Edward Weston. She and Weston became lovers in 1921, and two years later the thirty-seven-year-old photographer had left his family to go with her to Mexico. Among the brilliant photographs he took in Mexico were some nudes of Tina.

The P.E.N. dinner was held on Friday, October 31, and Lawrence's boiled shirt turned out to be unnecessary. The Mexican writers all wore business suits, and the gathering was relatively intimate since the sixteen writers all sat at a single table. The fair-haired Quintanilla, who had read *The Rainbow* and was already a Lawrence fan, sat happily on Lawrence's right. On his left was Eduardo Villaseñor, who was allocated to such proximity because of his excellent English. Estrada, the president of the club, sat across from Lawrence and read the opening *Saludo,* in which he quoted Martyn Johnson calling Lawrence the most significant figure in English letters of the time. He admitted, however, that because Lawrence's visit was a surprise, he had not yet had time to read his works himself.[3]

The main speaker, Genaro Fernández MacGregor, had read one Lawrence novel, *Aaron's Rod.* It illustrated he said, how Lawrence was an "original, strong, and masculine artist." Lawrence had written Spud

Johnson that he felt Mexican writers were "all a bit of a fraud, with their self-seeking bolshevism. I *really* feel cynical about these 'patriots' and 'socialists' down here." At the dinner, Lawrence, one gathers, outspokenly criticized the Mexican Revolution. Both Brett and Frieda remember the evening as a fiasco. Written nine years later, Frieda's account in *"Not I, But the Wind . . ."* is the more circumstantial and intelligible:

> It was a men's affair and he put on his black clothes and set off in the evening, and I, knowing how unused he was to public functions and how he really shrank from being a public figure, wondered in the hotel room how the evening would go off. Soon after ten o'clock he appeared.
> "How was it?"
> "Well, they read to me bits of 'The Plumed Serpent' [her mistake] in Spanish, and I had to sit and listen, and then they made a speech and I had to answer."
> "What did you say?"
> "I said: here we are together, some of us English, some Mexicans and Americans, writers and painters and business men and so on, but before all and above all we are *men* together tonight! That was about what I said. But a young Mexican jumped up: 'It's all very well for an Englishman to say I am a man first and foremost, but a Mexican cannot say so, he must be a Mexican above everything.' "

Quintanilla was working in the protocol division of Foreign Affairs. At the dinner Estrada assigned him to look after Lawrence for his remaining week in the capital. The young writer, who had been brought up in France and taught by an English nurse, was delighted with the job. Although Lawrence ridiculed American breakfasts, he enjoyed eating them. Quintanilla would accompany him to breakfast at Sanborn's, the drugstore-restaurant in the House of Tiles which is still a leading American meeting place. Lawrence also met the twenty-one-year-old Ruth Stallsmith, a brown-haired American girl with laughing green eyes, who had married Quintanilla a year and a half before. Five years previously the couple had fallen in love when Ruth was a high school student of sixteen at Gettysburg Academy where Luis was gaining proficiency in English. Lawrence was also enchanted by Jane, the Quintanillas' tow-headed baby, then not quite eight months old. Lawrence and Quintanilla often sat in the Alameda, the big rectangular park in the center of Mexico City. Lawrence, according to Quintanilla, would never talk about politics. "His field of interest was always man, especially in his love relationships."

The Sunday after the P.E.N. dinner, Quintanilla took Lawrence to visit Weston, whose first successful exhibition of photographs at Aztec Land Gallery had closed the night before. The novelist made "a most agreeable impression" on Weston, who asked Lawrence to sit for him. Two days later Lawrence did. In his *Daybooks,* Weston recorded that he was in a hurry because he had to get to a lunch honoring James Rockwell Sheffield, the new United States Ambassador to Mexico. Lawrence, he noted, was "a tall, slender rather reserved individual." Weston also recalled a walk that he and Tina Modotti had taken with Lawrence in Chapultepec Park. The novelist seemed so upset and distressed by the capital that Weston felt he was in "a highly neurotic state . . . he wished to leave the city for Oaxaca where he might quietly write."

One of Lawrence's recurring hopes was to establish a community of like-minded friends who could live together in the country away from the rush of modern industrialism. Aldous Huxley described Lawrence's 1915 version of that dream when he wrote his brother Julian, then in the United States, advising him to visit the colony that Lawrence was planning.

> This good man [wrote the twenty-one-year-old Huxley], who impressed me as a good man more than most, proposes, how unwisely soever it may appear, to go to the deserts of Florida there with one Armenian [the writer, Michael Arlen], one German wife and, problematically, one young woman called Dorothy Warren, to found a sort of unanimist colony. The purposes of which are to await a sort of Pentecostal inspiration of new life, which, whether it will come is another question. But Lawrence is a great man, and as he finds the world too destructive for his taste, he must, I suppose, be allowed to get out of it to some place where he can construct freely and where, by a unanimous process, the rest of his young colony might do the same.

The Florida colony fell through. So did Lawrence's 1917 project to have a group of friends go to Colombia, where relatives of David Eder had large estates. But the idea of a colony remained with Lawrence and he continued to use the name he coined for it when he thought it might be established in Garsington. The name was Rananim, inspired by Hebrew words he heard Koteliansky use in quoting a psalm about the righteous. Lawrence's first visit to Mexico reanimated the colony idea, for the country impressed him as offering the right setting at last. "If we were a few people we could make a life in Mexico," he wrote Merrild. On that first visit he inspected a number of haciendas around Chapala to see if they might make suitable sites. A leading purpose of his second visit was to find a ranch where the colony might be established. He and Gótzsche, working their way down the Pacific coast, inspected several sites, including one that was offered in Guaymas. In the same letter to Mrs. Carswell in which he described the gods being in Mexico, Lawrence wrote: "I wish it could be that I could start a little center—a ranch—where we could have our little adobe houses and make a life, and you could come with Don [her husband] and John Patrick [her five-year-old son]. It is always what I work for. . . . And there is room—room for all of us if it could but be.''

But even had Lawrence found an ideal site in western Mexico, the colony would not have materialized. Towards the end of his first return to England he invited seven friends to dinner at the Café Royal and specifically asked them to come with Frieda and himself to create the colony in Mexico. Brett was the only one ready to sail with them on the *Aquitania* eight days later, which is why the Lawrences were honor-bound to take her first to New Mexico, then to Mexico.

In Mexico City Lawrence either read or heard about an incident which he included in *The Plumed Serpent* when he revised it in Oaxaca. A month after winning the election, President-elect Calles had sailed to Europe. Ostensibly the purpose of the visit was to improve his health, but some believed it was to keep him away from the danger of assassination during the interim. While the Lawrences were in Mexico City, Calles returned; and on October 27, the day after his ship, the *George Washington,* docked in New York, the *New York Times* ran a story with the headline ''Calles Welcomed by Nation & City.'' The story noted that the ship was three hours late and that the U.S. Army Band played in Calles's honor at the Battery. Lawrence inserted the reception in his revision. Because Lawrence wanted to get Calles into the story quickly, he worked him into one of the earliest sequences, the already written account of Mrs. Nuttall's tea party. He expanded the conversation of the guests and included the New York arrival as part of the discussion about the president-elect. Besides changing his name to Montes, the novelist transformed Calles's two given names, Plutarco and Elías, into the somewhat similar Socrates Tomás. Kate, the heroine of the novel, says of Calles-Montes: ''I thought it was so nice that they received him in New York with loud music by the Street Sweepers' Band.''

The expanded conversation, besides illuminating character, reflects a remarkable grasp of the political atmosphere of the time. There was a strong likelihood that the army, en bloc, would refuse to serve Calles. Even if the army stayed loyal, an armed uprising was expected led by Angel Flores, a northern general whom Lawrence included in the novel as ''Angulo.'' Flores was a former governor of Sinaloa. He had not taken part in the de la Huerta rebellion but was strongly opposed to Obregón and Calles and ran against Calles in the presidential election. November 23 was the day expected for the Flores revolt, the ''bad bust-up in Mexico City'' that Lawrence mentioned in the November 14 letter to Hawk.

Oaxaca also crept into the conversation Lawrence added to his novel. At the hotel in Orizaba, one of the new characters, a young American named Mr. Henry saw a courageous hotel manager harangue a group of revolutionaries who came to shoot his American and Spanish guests. This was the Hotel Francia.[4]

Brett described how the Lawrences picked the Francia in her book. On the way to Oaxaca their narrow-gauge train made a number of inexplicable stops, and around 7 P.M. when they were finally nearing their destination it made another. Representatives of various hotels came aboard, the names of their establishments on their visored caps. Being a foreign tourist and a desirable catch, Lawrence was soon surrounded. He gave his party's luggage to "the most respectable looking boy," who happened to be the representative of the Francia. There were no reservations in those days and no cabs either. The young porter escorted them through the crowded station to the trolley pulled by two mules, and they rattled slowly along the tracks through the darkened town until they came to the more brightly lighted area where the Francia was situated. (See plan of Oaxaca on the endpapers.)

They found the hotel "homely," and its Catalonian proprietress "very friendly and kind." The Lawrences were shown to a large inner room in the two-story annex, but Brett was given a huge, cool room, looking onto the street in the single-story section. The Lawrences liked it better than theirs, which had no outside window. When they learned Doña María had a double one next to Brett's room "with two large beds swathed in mosquito curtains," they took it. These rooms opened onto a large patio with a fountain in the center. Around the fountain grew coffee and banana trees, roses, jasmine, and other flowering shrubs.

When the three entered the dining room in the two-story wing, Miss Hughes saw them for the first time. (Plate 6.) Of all the people Lawrence was to meet in Oaxaca, Miss Hughes was the only one who had heard of him before. She had read about him in the book section of the *New York Herald Tribune,* which a friend had sent her regularly. The reviews had never aroused her interest, but his appearance did. Lawrence, who had turned thirty-nine two months before, "looked pale and thin," she recalled. "With his red hair, beard, and general facial appearance, he reminded me very much of Bernard Shaw." All three were tired, and Brett was distressed when she found that Toby, her "precious ear-trumpet," was missing. She left the dining room to search their luggage. When Doña María explained that thieves poked nail-tipped poles through the grills of the long windows facing the street, Brett concluded the trumpet must have been fished out of the room by just such an angler.

The Lawrences were in the dining room when the Wilson brothers returned. According to Miss Hughes, one of the brothers exclaimed "Jesus

Christ!'' upon seeing the new guests, partly because profanity came naturally and partly because Lawrence's appearance prompted the irreverent comparison. Miss Hughes recalled that her dinner companions, Colonel Akin and Mr. Duke, agreed that the phrase *Jesu Cristo* never seemed offensive when natives used it, but did when spoken in English. Later in the market Miss Hughes heard Indians from the villages quietly exclaim "Jesu Cristo" when they saw Lawrence, because only in pictures of Jesus had they ever seen a red-bearded man.

Brett had her forty-first birthday the next day, and they celebrated by strolling in the town. The streets, she recalled, were full of Indians, and everybody stared at them: the Indians as they padded softly by, the storekeepers behind the counters in their shops. Miss Doctor reported, "All three were exotic. They attracted your attention, they were so original: Mrs. Lawrence, a stout German Frau with stringy blonde hair; Miss Brett, definitely an English type; and Lawrence, tall, thin, very bearded, and a little stooped." The sun was already hot, and they wandered round and round what Brett mispronounced as "the lovely, shady Zócola."

Oaxaca's *zócalo* has changed little since that time. They would have seen the green-stone Government Palace bounding the plaza to the south. On the east and west they would have seen the arcades under which Miss Doctor said waiting Americans spent much time sitting. (Plate 7.) The five-story hotel had not yet been built to the north but the Cathedral of the same pistachio-colored stone as the Government palace was there. (Plate 8.)

In front of the cathedral's wide façade was the rectangular Alameda, covered with Indian laurels, and the larger square park with its bandstand looking like something from the *Arabian Nights*. Through the trees of the Alameda they would have seen a palatial residence of the same green stone built in about 1760 by the López Ortigoza family. By Lawrence's day it had become the Alameda Hotel, now the Monte Alban, after the archaeological site.

The Lawrences stayed at the Francia eight days. While they were there, Doña María's seventeen-year-old daughter Maruca took Brett to a native tinsmith who produced a serviceable replacement for Toby. Lawrence described it to Clarence Thompson, the good-looking young protégé of Mabel Luhan they had all met in Taos, as "a gramophone horn," adding that it was "the delighted astonishment of these little Indian natives." The device was a boon to Brett, for her battery-operated Marconi hearing machine had begun faltering at the ranch.

Rosalind Hughes and Dr. Kull remembered another minor adventure at the hotel. In an old building near the dentist's office near the Hotel Francia was a shoemaker who worked in an entrance hall. The phonograph in the cantina across the street often played selections from

Rigoletto. The cobbler's parrot, according to Miss Hughes, had learned to imitate the music "amazingly well." While engaged to Louie Burrows, Lawrence had once written her in the flush of his enthusiasm for *Cavalleria Rusticana* and *Pagliacci,* "I love Italian opera—it's so reckless." Strains of raucous Verdi coming from the entranceway had therefore attracted his attention. He was so delighted with the parrot that on another occasion when he and Frieda were strolling with Miss Hughes, he insisted on a detour so she could hear the parrot.

Stories told by John Duke, the Texan who had the room to the left of the Akin suite, were to influence Lawrence considerably. The Lawrences must have met him within a day or two of their arrival. One evening the Texan told a story about the chief of the Labor Bureau in Oaxaca. Indians were encouraged to come in and report complaints in their villages. Then the chief would say he had to report the complaint to the governor, pick up the phone, ask for the governor, and repeat what the Indians had been telling him. He would forward the governor's assurance that the matter would be made right to the awed Indians. The telephone, Duke said, was a dummy. The story confirmed Lawrence's prejudices about Mexican labor leaders, and he worked it into the conversation at Mrs. Nuttall's tea party.

Everyone liked forty-one-year-old Duke. He had been a teller in a bank in Midland, Texas, of which his father-in-law had been president. He was hiding in Mexico under an assumed name because he had been "forced to take the rap for a couple of the bank officers regarding some irregular cattle deals."[5] Because only two friends in Oaxaca knew that Duke was an alias, Girdley would not have told Lawrence about his troubles in Texas or Oaxaca, but others surely did. Brett knew the story.[6] Dr. Kull and Miss Hughes both told it to me.

One player in Duke's story was eighty-three-year-old J. Emerson Gee from Ohio. Gee came to Mexico in 1907 and in 1912 became manager of mines and construction for the Indiana Oaxaca Mining Company of Indianapolis. Gee was another of Ibarra's former employers. When the Department of the Interior had asked Gee what service he could perform in World War I, he had lopped seven years off his age and replied "as scout in Western Mexico; as rifleman anywhere." He and Mrs. Gee lived upstairs at the Hotel Alameda in the big corner room with a wrought-iron balcony.

Harloe Hamilton, who gave me many names of his contemporaries in Oaxaca, was one of Duke's best friends and the only one, besides Jean Akin, who knew of the alias. Harloe, who had followed his father to Mexico when he was twenty, was then in his late thirties. Thinking his friend would be safer if armed, he bought Duke a pistol. Early one morning while it was still dark, Duke was passing the Hotel Alameda and saw a burglar escaping down a pipe under the Gees' balcony. Duke shot at the man, intending to wound him. The man managed to get to the park in front of the hotel and shoot back before he collapsed. He died in the general hospital the next day. Duke was jailed; but because the intruder was a known burglar, Harloe was able to secure the Texan's release on condition that he would not leave Oaxaca for four years.

The Gees had left Oaxaca before Lawrence arrived, and Harloe was away from the city.[7] Brett and Kull's version of the events was somewhat different. This is no doubt the story Lawrence heard. Duke supposedly caught the man in the Gees' bedroom after he had gained entrance by forcing the window bars apart. Kull wrote me about his attempts to console Duke: "When I tried to make him see that he most likely saved the Gees' lives, he answered, 'But I killed a man.' "

Lawrence could well understand this sense of horror. Duke's story may have led the novelist to add the man's arm, "like a black cat crouching on the bottom of the panel-space," to the scene in *The Plumed Serpent* where his heroine lies afraid in the dark. In the original draft, Kate only imagines a prowler, but in the Oaxaca version she screams as she sees the arm coming over the top of the half door.

At the Francia, Lawrence also met Colonel Akin, the mining man who never went out without donning his pith helmet and took strolls armed with a .45. He would certainly have warned Lawrence of the dangers lurking on the outskirts of the city. So the Chapala-Mexico City experience was repeated here: resident Americans plied him with reports of violence and the hardships of being cut off from the rest of the country for four months. Having come within two weeks of being caught in the de la Huerta rebellion himself, Lawrence must have been especially interested in hearing how it affected Oaxaca.

Colonel Akin, according to his young wife, was "absolutely all man" and considered Lawrence "effeminate and a weakling." Jean Akin, who was to meet Lawrence when she returned to Oaxaca, came to disagree with her husband. The Lawrences had also met Hermann and Carola Kull by this time. They soon became acquainted with the Thompsons, who lived in a big house with elegant wrought-iron gates facing a large field in the north section of town where baseball was played and where circuses pitched their tents. Since 1950 this field has been called the Jardín Gonzatti. G. William Thompson had bought a mine at Taviche. Even though the property was almost ten miles square, Thompson was hard up and appealed to Colonel Akin for financial assistance. The two became partners. Mrs. Thompson was the former Emma von Violand, the daughter of an aristocratic Austrian political refugee who had brought his family to America when Emma was a girl. The family had lived near Chicago and subsisted in part by selling jewels and other possessions they had smuggled out of Austria. Jean Akin remembered that Emma still occasionally sold an heirloom in Oaxaca. Mrs. Thompson was an excellent cook and liked to entertain on a grand scale. She inaccurately gave Miss Doctor the impression of being wealthy.

The Oaxaca visit began happily for the Lawrences. Brett recalled: "The train is crowded, but we don't care. The excitement of movement, of adventure, of new rhythm, is on you. Your eyes gleam, and you bite your beard; you are alert and happy." Three days later, as Lawrence wrote his first letter from Oaxaca, he was in the same mood: "We got here all right Sunday night—a very amusing journey, by the Ferrocarril Mexicano to Esperanza, then a wild little railway (2 hrs) to Tehuacan: slept the night there in a very nice Hotel Mexico; came on Sunday, a wild queer lovely journey in a steep gorge."

That journey through the Tomellín Canyon was to haunt his memory. Because of stories he later heard in Oaxaca, his imagination eventually transformed the "steep gorge" into something more sinister. Brett described the journey in some detail.

> We drop down to the tropical belt. The heat is stifling. We buy sugar cane and suck it. We have a very excellent lunch at a village of four houses; the restaurant kept by a Chinaman. All the stations are pock-marked with bullets and there are ruined villages and houses everywhere. At every station, rows of silent men in clean white clothes sit along bits of broken walls, their faces pools of dark shadow from their big hats. But the glinting eyes watch us unceasingly.
>
> We are going into the Canyon, says the Indian guard to you. It is very long and narrow, and the line has only just been repaired since the revolution [the ill-fated de la Huerta uprising against Obregón]. The canyon is indeed lovely: it is so narrow that we keep crossing and recrossing it, sometimes running along near the river, and at other times climbing up to a narrow ledge. Whistling through tunnels, crawling over bridges, the train writhes like a snake. We see some little deer drinking in the river: they do not even look up as we rattle by.

Lawrence also described their destination in his first letter: "Oaxaca is a very quiet little town, with small but proud Indians—Zapotecas. The climate is perfect—cotton dresses, yet not too hot. It is very peaceful and has a remote beauty of its own. The Hotel Francia very pleasant— such good amusing food—4 pesos a day for everything."

At that time the peso was worth about fifty cents, so they were living for two dollars a day. Lawrence had a reason for including this price and the rail fares, because he was writing to Luis Quintanilla, trying to persuade the Quintanillas to visit Oaxaca, as they had promised to do.

"We want to go out to Mitla and Tula and Ejutla," he wrote, "but will wait a bit, and if you come we'll all go together."

Mitla, a village twenty-six miles down the southeast arm of the valley, was famous for its tombs and ruined palaces. "Tula" was Santa Maria del Tule, remembered for its enormous tree. These were the chief sightseeing spots of the area. Ejutla some fifty miles south was a jumping-off place for mines.

"There are two rivers," the letter continued, "but I've only seen one, with naked Indians soaping their heads in mid-stream." The river Lawrence had seen was the larger of the two, the Atoyac. The rainy season had only been over two months in November and there was still water in the river. The Jalatlaco River flowed just a block and a half behind the house Lawrence was soon to rent.

"The Indians go about in white cotton," the letter continued, "they don't make them wear proper trousers as in most towns."

In Chapala, he and Bynner had met an American, John Dibrell. Dibrell would walk about the town dressed in the Indians' traditional *calzones,* which Lawrence called pantaloons. This was Dibrell's statement against the move to modernize the Indians by forcing them to wear store clothing.

> The advantages of Chapala are, of course, the Lake, bathing and the short journey [continues the Lawrence letter]. But this isn't touristy at all—quite, quite real, and lovely country around, where we can ride. A man has already promised to lend me a good Texas saddle. And we can go down to Ejutla and look at silver mines, with this same man.

The man was Donald Miller, who had been on the picnic-breakfast with Governor Ibarra and who proved consistently friendly to the Lawrences.

Lawrence told Quintanilla of inducements. "Very nice people on the train, and wonderful scenery, really." He signed off, "Many greetings to you both and to JANE, from us all."

A postscript[8] illustrates Lawrence's practicality and underlines his eagerness to have the Quintanillas come. "Take a bit of lunch, perhaps, from Tehuacan as you don't get food until 2.15 at Tomellin. The little train is very dusty—wear old clothes as possible. But it is not too hot."

Quintanilla's boss, Genaro Estrada, the under-secretary for Foreign Affairs who had arranged the P.E.N. dinner, had also written the Governor of Oaxaca asking him to do something for the visiting novelist. Estrada's letter must have gone out before the Lawrences left Mexico City, for the governor's request that Lawrence come to the palace arrived only a day or two after the Lawrences did.

The visit occurred within the first three days. Brett wrote this account: "You are taken to visit the Governor, as word has been sent from Mexico that you are to be taken care of. Frieda and I sit in the Zó-cola opposite the Governor's imposing residence, while you sit, bored, in gilded rooms."

I began corresponding with Brett in 1962 and was lucky enough to visit her in Taos in 1964. She was already eighty, but our meeting enabled me to understand why Lawrence said, "She has a way of lighting things up." She still did. Lawrence's interview with the governor was one of the many events I had already questioned her about:

> The whole incident was so colored by Lawrence's fuming and raging at having to go and see him. Lawrence objected, as far as I can remember, at being "summoned," but at the same time his enormous curiosity and interest in people overcame his resistance to what he felt might be a slight. I can remember our walking to the Governor's Palace and his reactions. I don't remember who escorted him into the Palace. I know he was kept waiting, even when inside, which maddened him.

The palace was not the governor's home, as Brett remembered, but the state capital building that Ibarra and his legislature had occupied three months before to frustrate the rival legislature of Vasconcelos. Though Lawrence in "The Flying Fish" was to classify the building as Spanish baroque, it was actually a neo-Renaissance structure built in 1877 during Porfirio Díaz's first term as president of Mexico.

Lawrence's "interest in people" was hardly evidenced in this case, however; communication was compromised by the fact that Lawrence's Spanish was still mostly Italian. Nevertheless, we can assume that Lawrence was secretly flattered by the attention, something that Brett guessed stemmed from his early days as a coal miner's son. He referred to the visit in at least five letters, using much the same wording in each account.

Two letters—one to Curtis Brown, his English agent, and the other to William Hawk, the young rancher, were dated November 14.

> I called on the Governor of the State, in the Palace. [A second letter two days later repeated the theme.] He is an Indian from the hills, but like a little Mexican lawyer: quite nice. Only it's all just crazy. Tomorrow he asked me to go out to the opening of a road into the hills. The road isn't begun yet. That's why *we* open it. And during the picnic, of course he may get shot. It's a fool's world, anyhow, and people bore me stiffer and stiffer. Fancy, even a Zapotec Indian, when he becomes governor, is only a fellow in a Sunday suit grinning and scheming.

The governor was the slim, bespectacled, moustached Isaac M. Ibarra, for the chunky Onofre Jiménez had not yet been inaugurated. Clearly, Ibarra did not appeal to Lawrence's imagination. Lawrence can be forgiven for not seeing behind the façade of the governor: the young mine mechanic working for Americans and educating himself by candlelight; the mechanic who left the mines when Mexicans on every hand were taking sides; the *Serrano* who joined most of his fellow hillmen in espousing the cause of the reactionary Meixueiro; the soldier who showed such tactical skill and gifts for leadership that he rose to be a general; the political leader chosen to replace the deposed Meixueiro; the anti-revolutionary who came out for the revolutionary Obregón; and finally the federal senator who rode with a fourth victorious army into Oaxaca to himself become governor. Lawrence had not been in Oaxaca long enough to hear this remarkable story. But he had amassed enough information about Mexico in general to wonder how an Indian from the hills got to be governor, how an Indian received enough education to resemble a lawyer in a Sunday suit, and what role the Indian had played in the Revolution. The case of Rosalie Evans, murdered for trying to defend her hacienda, had no doubt taught the novelist enough about the Obregón administration to cause him to wonder about Ibarra's relationship to Obregón. Lawrence did sense a man who schemed as he grinned. He expressed what he did see with two obvious stereotypes—the little Indian and the Mexican lawyer. He left the presence of one of the most interesting personalities he met in Oaxaca feeling superior to him and muttering that it was a fool's world.

Such muttering probably reflected more the mood Lawrence brought to the interview than the insights he gained. Even in so peaceful-seeming a spot as Oaxaca with a marvelous climate and abundant natural beauty, he had learned of atrocities and political ineptitude. The interview with the governor reveals Lawrence as a man living very much in the world of his own preoccupations.

Lawrence's observation to Murry that there was a chance Governor Ibarra might get shot at the road-opening suggests that during the four days between this letter and the "Oaxaca is a very quiet little town" letter to Quintanilla, Lawrence had learned what was beneath the city's tranquil exterior. On November 15 he wrote Murry:

> Everything is so shaky and really so confused. The Indians are queer little savages, and awful agitators pump bits of socialism over them and make everything just a mess. It's really a sort of chaos. And I suppose American intervention will become inevitable. You know, socialism is a dud. It makes just a much 9 of people: and especially of savages. And seventy percent of these people are real savages, quite as much as they were 300 years

ago. The Spanish-Mexican population just rots on top of the black savage mass. And socialism here is a farce of farces: except very dangerous.

Note that the "wild Indians" of the letter written the day before to Hawk have become "savages." The native people of Oaxaca have not been savages for at least 2,000 years; but Lawrence's shift of vision also made him something he seldom was: wrong about color. He was right about the high density of Indian population in Oaxaca, and the Indians being small, but "a black savage mass" betrays an emotional attitude triumphing over realistic observation. Yet in this same letter, Lawrence also describes Oaxaca with tenderness: "This country is so lovely, the sky is perfect, blue and hot every day, and flowers rapidly following flowers. They are cutting the sugar-cane, and hauling it in in the old ox-wagons, slowly. But the grass-slopes are already dry and fawn-coloured, the unventured hills are already like an illusion, standing round inhuman."

In Oaxaca one does see hills in every direction. Except for El Fortín and Monte Alban, which are not overbearing, they are far enough away to seem dreamlike. When the rains cease, as they had done before the Lawrences came, the sparsely treed hills lose their greenness and turn subtle shades of beige and brown.

Whenever Lawrence got to a new place where he intended to stay a while, he generally sent out a flurry of letters announcing his new address. His letters which included the descriptions of Governor Ibarra were in this initial group. He also wrote to his sisters, Pamela or "Emily" King, who was three years his senior, and Ada Clarke, two years his junior. His November 15 letter to Ada (which she published in *Young Lorenzo*) gives a further insight into his state of mind at the time:

We got down here all right. There is always a certain risk in Mexico, especially on a little narrow railway that winds for hours & hours in a gorge. This is a little town, lonely, way in the south, with little rather fierce Zapotec Indians. The climate is lovely: just like midsummer, cloudless sun all day, & roses & tropical flowers in full bloom. My chest had got very raw up at the ranch: that very high altitude. That's why we had to come south so soon. Already it's nearly healed up. The altitude here is just above 5,000 ft. They are always expecting more revolutions: it's the most unsettled country, and the most foolish politically, on the face of the earth. But I don't suppose anything will happen to affect us seriously. . . . I hope the country will stay quiet. Otherwise we shan't be able easily to get out. . . . One feels far away here—I want to get my Mexican novel finished if I can.

Of special interest here are his comments about his health. He conceals the fact that he had spat blood while at the ranch, a recurrence of troubles appearing as early as 1913, but he admits he felt chest pain in the rarefied 8,600-foot altitude. Three times before Lawrence had been critically ill. The first was in October 1901 when pneumonia put an end to his first job as a clerk in Nottingham. He was then sixteen and might have died had it not been for his mother's nursing. This illness, he wrote in "Autobiographical Sketch" (one of the *Assorted Articles*), "damaged my health for life." A second terrible illness occurred in 1911 after three years of teaching at the elementary school for boys on Davidson Road in Croydon, a suburb of London. As he reported to Edward Garnett on December 17, "The doctor says I mustn't go to school again or I shall be consumptive." He convalesced at the seaside in Bournemouth. In April 1922 Lawrence was visiting the American painters Earl and Achsah Brewster in Ceylon. Here, on the first stage of his wanderings away from Europe, he got malaria. His investigation of the Orient had lasted only six weeks. And when the novelist wrote to Brewster from Australia, the second stage, he reported he had never "felt so sick" in his life.

Lawrence didn't accept Governor Ibarra's invitation to go to the road opening, but other Anglos including Dr. and Carola Kull and Rosalind Hughes did. The official party rode in a procession of Model-T touring cars. The road ended at Teotitlán del Valle, a village where the finest of Oaxaca's famous blankets are still woven.

"Villages along the way were decorated with flower arches and many little triangular flags," wrote Miss Hughes. "Each village brought its little band, and without rehearsal they all tried to play the National Anthem. Then there was a banquet under the portales for officials and special visitors, while the hungry campesinos looked on. After the speeches, Gov. Ibarra took us to see the Cabrera in the church, and a big crowd followed. Then he took a few of us to the home of Eligio Bazán, the most skillful weaver of blankets with the calendar stone and idols."[10]

And no one took a shot at the governor.

So Lawrence missed a happy outing, which did not deserve the mockery in advance that he passed on to Murry. At Chapala the year before, he had gone down the lake to the weaving village of Jocotepec, where his interest caused him to have blankets woven to his own designs. Because of Lawrence's plans to drape blankets echoing pre-Columbian styles over the shoulders of the men of Quetzalcoatl and Huitzilopochtli in *The Plumed Serpent,* the work on Bazán's looms may have already stimulated the novelist through examples of it seen in Oaxaca. Bazán's chief innovation was incorporating into blankets the *grecas* from the palaces of Mitla. These abstract motifs, named for suggesting Greek frets, have proved a fecund source of beautiful design ever since. (Plate 9.)

I was so convinced that the governor who offered Lawrence hospitality must have been a man in his late fifties that, when I took up the Lawrence trail thirty-seven years after the novelist left Oaxaca, I assumed Ibarra was dead and did not try to find him. I did however, seek out other Mexicans. Guillermo Brena's large establishment facing El Llano at which he sold textiles and honey made him easy to locate. Miss Doctor had named him as one of the young Mexicans who played tennis at the Kulls. But he said she was mistaken. He had no recollection of Lawrence either. But he was a nephew of General Enrique Brena, an opponent of García Vigil and an old companion of the *Serrano* generals, including Ibarra. He knew the Ibarra family and told me that Ibarra was still alive. Brena did not have his address, but Marcelino Muciño would. This was another astonishing name leaping from the past, for Muciño was one of the Kull tennis crowd.

In those days I was still working for the *New York Times,* and it was another year before I was back for my vacation. Then I sought out Sr. Muciño, who proved to be a ruddy-faced, squarish, handsome man with white hair, living with his daughter in the Colonia Viaducto Piedad in Mexico City. His vigor belied his eighty-two years. An athlete, he had gone to Oaxaca in 1906 to form a baseball team for the American colony. Paul Wooton issued the invitation; and when that enterprising entrepreneur launched the *Herald,* the English-language newspaper for the colony, Muciño became a journalist. Later, when he was on his own, he published *El Mercurio,* a newspaper I had heard about from Jean Akin, from 1920 to 1936. He had been in Oaxaca at the same time as Lawrence but had no recollection of the novelist. However, he gave me Ibarra's address in Tacubaya, a formerly independent town now part of Greater Mexico.

The moment I left Muciño I ran for a public telephone. The general was in the phone book. Seconds later, I was ringing his number. Yes, General Ibarra lived there. No, he wasn't in. But I could see him if I came to the house at six that afternoon. I was there on the dot, and when the slim, erect man with wide cheek bones and small genial eyes came towards me, I recognized him immediately from the photograph of the picnic breakfast. He was wearing a beautifully tailored suit of dark brown tweed. His hair was no more than iron gray, and he hardly looked a day older than in the photograph taken forty years earlier. I had heard that the governor never smoked, drank, or accepted invitations to lavish banquets. This had obviously paid dividends. He was one of the softest-spoken, most courteous men I ever met. I could understand why Lawrence had been unable to imagine him as a revolutionary campaigner. Neither could I. Nor in the house with book-lined walls which reminded me of a professor's home could I envisage an unschooled youth from the hills trying to educate himself by candlelight. In fact, despite the brownness of his skin, I hardly saw the Indian in the well-groomed gentleman. He was certainly not someone I would dismiss as a little Mexican lawyer in a Sunday suit.

I appreciated his kindness, especially his tolerance for my mistake-filled Spanish. I had a number of blanks to fill. In which year, for example, was the general born? 1888. Far from being in his fifties when he saw Lawrence, he was three years younger than the novelist. He was born in Lachatao, and before going to work for Hamilton at Taviche he had worked in La Natividad, a mine nearer his native village, which is still in operation. At Hamilton's mine he tried to learn English. He soon could understand much of what he heard, but he spoke in the broken English of a laborer—something that came as a shock to me when this cultivated man tried to speak English.

I asked about the death of García Vigil, recalling Harloe Hamilton's words that if Ibarra had been in the party hunting García Vigil "he would have shot him." Ibarra replied quietly that he had admired García Vigil and that the ending was sad.

Then I broached the subject of the election he had supervised. "Vasconcelos lost it, and Onofre Jiménez won it," he said with a polite firmness.

What had Ibarra done after Jiménez took over? I asked. He had stood for federal senator, he replied, but was not reelected. He then left politics and resumed his military career. He remained in Mexico City and had retired from the army only two years before—in February 1962 at the age of seventy-six. (He would live ten years beyond our interview.)

I asked him if he remembered the road going into Teotitlán which he opened on 10 November 1924. The corners of his dark eyes crinkled behind his steel-rimmed glasses. He did. It was only a *tramo,* or section of a road, he explained. Knowing the road into Teotitlán was still not paved, I asked how his road was surfaced. *Terrazeria,* he answered, packed-down earth and gravel. And he added, with justified pride since he was only in office eight months, that the road had required the construction of two bridges. Then he provided a clue to explain why Lawrence had thought none of the road had been built. The section to Teotitlán, he said, was to be part of the *Carretera Sierra Juárez.* I knew this proposed highway to his native region was not built until almost forty years later, and then via a different route. Instead of going through Teotitlán, it branched off nearer Oaxaca and was called *Carretera de la Patria.*

What could he tell me about his interview with D. H. Lawrence, I asked. He looked puzzled. D. H. Lawrence, the English novelist, I repeated, the author of *La Serpiente Enplumada,* thinking the novel's title in Spanish might be more familiar. But he shook his head. He had no recollection of such a name. I told him the circumstances of the interview, but still nothing came back to him. Even when I produced a photograph of Lawrence, he could not recall the face.

So without knowing Lawrence had ever jeered at him, the "little Indian in the Sunday suit" had his revenge. We can guess that Lawrence, ordinarily so vivid to others, would rather have been recalled in negative terms than be confronted with the humiliating evidence that he had faded completely from the governor's mind.

![CHAPTER 2]

LAWRENCE'S
LANDLORD

One of the Mexican treasures at the Royal Ontario Museum in Toronto is an enormous sixteenth-century painted sheet once known as "Codex Rickards." It is a *lienzo,* the accepted name for Mexican pictorials painted on linen. Because it belonged to a group of Mixtec *lienzos* in which I was particularly interested, I hunted down an article about it published in 1913 by the *Journal de la Société des Américanistes.* Written by the owner who had named the sheet in his own honor, the article provided me his full name, Constantine G. Rickards, author of *The Ruins of Mexico.* He was identified as British vice consul in Oaxaca.

Ethel Doctor knew nothing about the codex, but she knew two men named Rickards. One was "Father Rickards," whose house had been near hers. "With Mrs. Thompson, I called on him once. We had tea. But later, when he knew I was a Protestant, he reluctantly greeted me." The priest's brother, she said, worked in the British Embassy in Mexico City.

This steered me to the *Foreign Office List,* Great Britain's yearbook of diplomats. Constantine was not listed, but I discovered a George E. Rickards who was the current British vice consul. In response to a letter, George E. Rickards promptly replied that he was Constantine's son. On my vacation, when I telephoned him, he was generous enough to invite an inquisitive stranger to his home in Tacubaya for tea. There he told me his father was dead. His uncle, the priest, was Edward Arden Rickards.

Three months later I was already dreaming of my next Mexican vacation. My interest in Lawrence had been revived. If I could find where he had lived in Oaxaca, I would visit the house in September. I remembered that most of Lawrence's letters in Aldous Huxley's edition included the addresses from which they were written. A letter Lawrence wrote Bynner from Mexico City in October 1924 read: "I think we shall go in a fortnight to Oaxaca. The English Vice-Consul has a brother, a priest in the Cathedral Chapter there, and he would sponsor us! Ye gods! But the man says it's very nice down there." Lawrence's "sponsor" could only be a man of the cloth named Edward Arden Rickards.

This made me even more determined to discover the address of the Lawrence house, described in his *Mornings in Mexico* as "a rather crumbly adobe house built around two sides of a garden patio," which suggested something too small to have a street number. But I leafed through more letters. In the first letter to Murry about Governor Ibarra, Lawrence added, "We shall move into a house next week. It's the house of an Englishman who was born here, and who is a priest in the Cathedral Chapter." The priest, then, was also Lawrence's landlord.

On the next page in another letter to Bynner was what I wanted. "We are here in a house," it said, and the letter was headed Av. Pino Suárez #43.

I called George Rickards as soon as I got to Mexico City on my 1962 vacation. He and his wife Mabel cordially invited me to Tacubaya for supper. It was a triple feast. Besides Mabel's chicken pot pie, there were more anecdotes about Constantine and new information about his priest-brother.

"Tio Eduardo," as George called him, was brought up as an Anglican, and Jane Arden, his mother, was the daughter of a Protestant minister. But Jane died when Edward was only nine years old, which left the boy much in the company of women servants who were all Roman Catholics. They used to take him to church and tell him stories of their faith, which he found appealing. His mine-owning Scottish father, who was fifty-one years his senior, was a stern Anglican with an impressive shovel beard and a terrible temper. His sons were afraid of him. When Edward talked about entering a seminary, the father said flatly, "I forbid you to become a priest." But after the death of the seventy-seven-year-old mine owner, Edward, then twenty-six, came into his inheritance and turned for counsel to the half-English Archbishop Gillow, who eight or nine years earlier had helped García Vigil enter the re-housed Seminario Pontifico. Rickards wanted to study in England rather than in Oaxaca. Gillow was probably the one who proposed Oscott College, five miles from Birmingham, which had played an important role in the education of English Catholics excluded from the universities and which since 1897 had been the central seminary for the Midlands and Southern dioceses of England. Rickards was sponsored by Gillow but listed as "unattached" because no diocese financed him. Rickards paid his own way, following the college's normal curriculum of dogmatic and moral theology, sacred scriptures, and minor courses. The Reverend Canon Harold Drinkwater, a fellow-seminarian, remembered him as "an exemplary student, hard working and devout" but not an outstanding personality or a leader because he was "diffident and shy." It seems, however, that he willingly talked about Mexico. In 1908 he wrote two articles for the college magazine about Our Lady of Guadalupe, the manifestation of the Virgin particularly dear to Mexicans. On 29 June 1909, the Day of Saint Peter and Saint Paul, he was ordained by the bishop of Birmingham in Saint Mary's

Chapel at Oscott. Then he returned to his native Oaxaca where, besides taking up pastoral duties, he served as secretary to Archbishop Gillow.

Originally, my wish to inspect Lawrence's house had been only a tourist's desire. But after the evening with George and Mabel I became more serious. When I reached Oaxaca I visited the house, camera in hand, with notes on the features described by Lawrence.

Back in New York, I assembled most of the Lawrence literature already published. My visits to the nephew's and to the Rickards' house had put me in a prime position to watch the chronological emergence of the priest in the books of others.[1]

The visits also helped me to catch some misconceptions. The house, divided into living quarters for three families, was much larger than Lawrence's description had led me to expect. The property was also larger, for a modern house had been built in the huge yard behind the patio. It was by no means "a hacienda," as described by Harry T. Moore in his "Who's Who in the Letters." And if L. D. Clark had discovered the dates of the priest's life—1879 to 1941—he would have realized that Padre Rickards was the wrong generation to be the model for Bishop Severn, a totally new character included in the second version of *The Plumed Serpent.* The model was, in fact, Archbishop Gillow, though Lawrence must have learned about Gillow from Rickards since the archbishop died before Lawrence reached Oaxaca. But if Rickards's birth in 1879 made him too young to be Severn, it made him the same age as Frieda and six years older than Lawrence—the right age to be a congenial companion to the tenants who lived in the southern half of his house.

George Rickards told me how the house came into his uncle's hands. Following the death of the Scottish father, Edward had continued to live with his brother Constantine in their father's beautiful two-story house at Armenta y Lopez No. 8. Constantine had promptly married Adela Durán, the daughter of a Mexican general in Porfirio Díaz's bodyguard. When nephews began appearing, Edward was already studying for the priesthood in England. About a year after his return, a disastrous fire destroyed most of the block, gutting the nonstone part of the Armenta y Lopez house. The brothers bought the single-story building near the outskirts of the city, a block from El Llano, the city's largest park. The house was large enough for them both, but when Constantine's three sons were joined by two daughters, the priest moved to Las Nieves, a church dedicated to Our Lady of the Snows. The Revolution destroyed the brothers' mining interests. Even though Constantine had followed his father's wishes and become a lawyer, he discovered he could not earn a living in Oaxaca. His marriage to the daughter of a Porfirian general and his service as a judge in the Pimentel administration counted against him. His plight, in fact, was almost desperate because *The Ruins of Mexico,* lavishly illustrated with several hundred tipped-in photographs, had been too expensive to sell well. Yet he had contracted with an English publisher to bring out 10,000 copies. Leaving his family in the care of Maximiliano Salinas, his guide, mentor, and friend on several archaeological expeditions, the heavily indebted Constantine went to Mexico City, hoping to improve his lot. He had been born in Oaxaca, but his father had seen that his sons held British citizenship, so Constantine managed to obtain a post in the British consulate, even though the diplomatic staff had been sadly reduced since Carden's expulsion. By 1917, having sold his "Codex" and most of his Zapotec antiquities to Toronto, Constantine was able to send for his family. Edward borrowed money and bought his brother's share of the house.

Today the house is No. 600. But when Padre Rickards took it over from his brother the house was 43, the number cited in Lawrence's letters. Avenida Pino Suárez, bounding the east side of the Llano is one of the city's principal north-south streets. A mule trolley took passengers to and from the market.

Oaxaca has septupled in size since Lawrence's day, with much of its new growth extending towards Mitla. During the winter of 1972-75 the stretch of the Jalatlaco River between the old seminary and the Mitla Road Bridge was directed through a cement channel encased with arched vaulting and the Calzada de la Republica, with its succession of bronze heroes, was built above. The plan (end papers) shows the city as it was during Lawrence's stay, confined between the uncovered Jalatlaco and the larger Atoyac River, where Lawrence saw the Indians soaping their heads in midstream.

Brett gave the impression that the negotiations with Padre Rickards and getting his rooms habitable occurred the same day, but Lawrence's letters show they were separated by at least four. The November 14 letter to the younger Hawk suggests that the house had been seen but not decided on, for Lawrence wrote, "We shall probably take a house here for a month or two." The next day, in the Curtis Brown letter, one learns that the die was cast.

Only one detail is preserved of what Lawrence noticed the day they went up to look at the Padre's house: the young male servant "lurking in the patio, and glancing furtively under his brows." Brett's account is more detailed:

> We are rattling along in the mule-tram on our way to the Padre's house. He has some rooms to let. The street is long and hot until we reach the end: there we find large, shady trees hanging over walls.
>
> A faded number on some big doors shows us the Padre's house. We knock and an old Indian woman peers out. She is expecting us, so

she lets us in. The Padre is out, but she will show us the rooms. Five other Indian women stand looking at us as we walk into the lovely, shady patio.

How quiet and peaceful it is. How sheltered after the streets and the hotel. The little square garden is full of trees. Orange trees, banana trees, and some immense, dark-leaved, silver-trunked trees. The quiet is broken by the shrill, noisy talk of two green parrots, perched in a tree. A small white poodle kind of dog sniffs around our legs.

The patio is red-tiled; so are the huge, high rooms that the Indian woman takes us into. Huge, barren, unfurnished rooms, opening into each other with no doors. The outside doors open onto the patio. There is a nice kitchen with charcoal ovens.

"How like Italy!" you say. It is cool and spacious, the garden lovely; yet you seem dissatisfied. Then Frieda blurts out that she does not think there is room enough for all of us. I realise the difficulty, also the unexpressed wish.

"I can remain at the hotel, easily," I say. "And that will give you more privacy." The air lightens; Frieda becomes immediately possessive— almost in possession.

The Padre appears round a bush: a small, stoutish man. You introduce yourself and us, then begin talking to him about rents and so on. He is a friendly little man, who afterwards becomes one of your best friends in the town.

The rooms are unfurnished, but he knows where furniture can be borrowed; he will ring up.

Brett's description shortchanges the exterior of the house in only mentioning the large doors. In 1962 one of the doors still had a smaller one within it at which a servant could appear without disturbing the larger doors. Those doors still opened onto an important part of the house— the *zaguan,* a roofed entranceway with the same front-to-back dimensions as the rooms. A basic feature Brett did not mention was the house's remarkable width—enough to accommodate one large window on the Padre's side of the *zaguan* and the five windows of the rooms into which the Lawrences were shown on the right. (Plate 10.) Each wing had a right-angled extension at its corner. The main section, paralleling the street, was only a single room deep, though its living area was increased by a veranda-portal running the width of the house.

It was this *corredor* that Brett called the "patio." Her "outside doors" were those opening onto the *corredor.* The immense "silver-trunked" trees in the garden would be Indian laurels. Though none survive now in the Padre's old grounds, the patio of the smaller house next door still retains its dwarfing trees. This was the house of Robert Wilson, the father of the two rough-tongued miners who had commented irreverently on Lawrence's appearance the first night at the Francia.

At the northern corner of the block rose the towers and domes of the green stone Templo del Patrocinio. The street flanking the church led to the bridge crossing the Jalatlaco River which meant it was the chief method of ingress into the city for the Indians from Jalatlaco, as well as from villages closer to the hills in the northeast.

The Indian woman who let the would-be tenants in was Padre Rickards's cook Natividad. She had three daughters; the names of two were Maria de Jesús and Maria del Carmen. Another maid, Pascualita, was a relative of Natividad's, perhaps a sister.

The little white dog, more pug than poodle, was Corasmín, the name Lawrence used in *Mornings in Mexico*. "Uncle was very much in love with the dog," nephew George was to tell me. "He had him for fifteen years." Several of Brett's photographs preserve a record of both master and dog. The Padre was stocky. Although Brett recalled him as "little," Oaxaqueños tend to remember him as tall. I judge he was about five foot eight inches, for those who recalled him tended to say he was my height. His hair, although there was little left except at the sides, was reddish. In his well-rounded chin was a dimple.

One of Brett's photographs shows that even in his own backyard, the Padre dressed as a priest. (Plate 11.) Such attire may have awakened unpleasant associations for Lawrence. In one passage in the novel, Lawrence wrote that henceforth monks and priests were to be allowed to wear no habits in the street "beyond the hideous black vest and white collar of the Protestant clergy."

Even when the decision to move was fixed, Lawrence was not altogether happy. "If only it wasn't winter," he wrote Hawk, "we'd come back to the ranch tomorrow. . . . Thank goodness my chest and throat are better, since we are here in this soft warm air. I want to get them sound this winter."

In his November 17 letter to Murry, he said, "I suppose we shall stay a few months here, since we're moving into a house tomorrow. But if I still feel put out by the vibrations of this rather malevolent continent, I'll sail from Vera Cruz."

Miss Doctor remembered that Emma Thompson, with whom she went to Padre Rickards's for tea, was a particular friend of the priest's and loaned him some of the furniture borrowed for the Lawrences. The Thompsons lived only a few blocks north on the other side of the Llano. Probably the Lawrences knew the Kulls well enough to approach them directly with the same request, for he spoke of "collecting bits of furniture from various people" to Curtis Brown. The Kulls had been in Oaxaca almost three years. Even before the de la Huerta rebellion the dentist's business had slackened, and the rebellion had made most

Oaxaqueños so poor that they could not afford a *dentista Americano*. Kull had already announced he would end his practice on January 15. Since the Kulls did not plan to return, they welcomed the opportunity to help friends and to dispose of furniture they did not want to take to Mexico City. They gave furniture to the Lawrences.

In the first of his *Mornings in Mexico,* Lawrence identified five of the borrowed pieces without saying how he came by them. One was "an onyx table," which Miss Hughes remembered as a round table with an onyx top. The others were three rocking chairs and "a little wooden chair." Brett's account mentions tables, beds, and cupboards, probably chest-of-drawers/wardrobe combinations with mirrors in the doors. Such *roperos* are a common furnishing in Mexican houses which, in the old days, were never equipped with built-in closets. Perhaps eating utensils, sheets, towels, and tablecloths were also loaned. Lawrence told Murry how he and Frieda bought "pots and blankets" at the market. With such limited means one can understand why, two days after moving in, Lawrence should write to a new pen-pal, "The house has a patio with big trees, and great empty rooms. We camp on the verandah."

The new correspondent was Edward D. McDonald, a Philadelphia professor who was compiling a bibliography of Lawrence's writings. The novelist commented, "I am ashamed to think of 28 books. For heaven's sake don't try to make it any more." No one in Oaxaca had read any of them. Although later Frieda confided in Jean Akin, no one knew either about the couple's stormy romance: how Frieda, a cousin of the German war ace, Baron Manfred von Richthofen, had left her English husband, Ernest Weekley, and her three children to go off with her husband's sometime-student and how they had lived and traveled together in Italy before Frieda could get a divorce to marry Lawrence. To the foreigners in Oaxaca, then, Padre Rickards's new tenants seemed both more respectable and less distinguished than they actually were. No one seemed to know Brett was a viscount's daughter with far more claim to put on airs than Lawrence. Because of her desire to be of service to the man she cherished, she was typing Lawrence's manuscripts and was thus accepted as what Miss Doctor called her, "a secretary."

There are also clues as to what the Lawrences thought of the colony. Later Frieda would feel overwhelmed by the kindness of its members, but at the start Lawrence was not so charitable. Perhaps it was their ignorance of the literary world that prompted the remark, but in his letter to Clarence Thompson, Lawrence sized up the situation: "Marvelous sunshine every day, but rather stupid people."

Friends must have told the Lawrences they should have a *mozo,* a young male servant who keeps watch, sweeps the *corredores,* and helps with the marketing. They found one in the youth Lawrence had noticed lurking on the patio the first day. He was about eighteen or nineteen, and his name was Rosalino.

The day the Lawrences moved their trunks and borrowed furniture, Rosalino came to the Francia to help. So did the Kulls' *mozo,* though the young Indians proved less useful than Lawrence expected. The commotion of getting the furniture into the house prompted a gesture of friendliness from the man living across the street, Donald Miller, the slim mining engineer of the Monte Alban picnic. Lawrence's reference to a man willing to show them mines near Ejutla suggests that they had already met Miller. Brett says the miner also "sent in cakes and jam."

Because the writing paper that Lawrence brought was to prove important to his life in the priest's house, it is worth detailing. During the 1913-14 winter in Italy when he still had some of his black and red Nottingham University College notebooks, he had begun writing his poems on loose sheets rather than in exercise books. Because he enjoyed working outdoors, he had extended the practice to novels and short stories as well. By the time he was living in Cornwall during World War I he wrote nearly everything in copybooks that could be easily slipped in and out of the pockets of a jacket and would not blow away or get out of order. Thanks to the Lawrence manuscripts collected at the University of Texas at Austin, we know that Lawrence arrived in Oaxaca with five such notebooks in his luggage, each lined page about nine inches high by seven wide.[2] The two with green spines and mottled dark blue boards contained the draft of the novel that he had come to Oaxaca to rewrite—*Quetzalcoatl* as he called it then. Because this draft occupied only 469 pages, the last half of the second book was empty. The third copybook, which he had bought in New Mexico, was a black pebbled one with "Record" stamped on the front in curving ornamented white letters. It contained "Hopi Snake Dance," "Introduction to Bibliography," which he had written for McDonald, and a short story, "The Princess," three of the final works completed before leaving the ranch. Because they needed only seventy-three pages, this book, too, was only partially filled.

In revising, Lawrence did not chop up an old draft and change it about. Instead, he made a new start and rewrote completely. Planning to do this with *Quetzalcoatl,* he knew the new version would need more space than remained in the incompleted notebooks. Besides, it was going to be a major effort. The year before, he had found copybooks he liked in Mexico City for his Chapala version of the Mexican novel. When he was about to leave for Oaxaca, he went to "El Bufete," a stationery store at Isabela la Catolica No. 39, around the corner from his hotel, and bought two more blue-lined copybooks with numbered pages. They were identical in size and each had unstamped red spines and corners, but the covers of one were purple, while those of the other were a mottled yellow-brown.

The day after moving into the priest's house he wrote at the top of the purple book's first page, "Ave Pino Suarez #43, Oaxaca, 19 Nov. 1924." That day he began the rewriting that was to overflow both the "Bufete" books.

The way the writing went was proof that Lawrence could do in Oaxaca what he came to test: "If I can get any work done." That he could must have been a relief, for although Lawrence wrote freely most of his life, in his first sojourn on the North American continent he had been unable to work in the old way. He had managed to revise his *Studies in Classic American Literature,* write the wonderful essay on the Apaches, "Indians and an Englishman," and compose eight New Mexican poems for *Birds, Beasts and Flowers,* but "in the U.S. I could do nothing," he wrote the Baroness von Richthofen. Only at Lake Chapala, after leaving the United States, had his fiction begun to flow again; and a writer who has been once blocked knows the fear of its happening again.

In his first letters, Lawrence referred to Padre Rickards as a priest "in the Cathedral Chapter." In later ones he spoke of him as being "in the Cathedral Mitra." He wasn't being contradictory. Rickards was a canon of the cathedral, meaning a clergyman on its staff. His nephew George interpreted his duties as those of secretary-treasurer. The Mitra is still the way Oaxaqueños designate the semi-detached building on the northeast corner where cathedral business is conducted, including christenings every weekday evening between 5 and 7. According to George, the Padre put in long hours at the Mitra for thirty pesos a month, but he never complained, for he had entered the priesthood to be of service, and not for the sake of its perquisites. When Muciño, the ex-baseball-player-turned-journalist, wanted some articles from his pen for *El Mercurio,* the priest explained that he had something suitable on sanitation, but it was in English, and he had no time to translate it into Spanish. Padre Rickards was friendly with the Americans in town, and when he explained the predicament to Jean Akin, she translated his thesis. She had been a teacher and welcomed every opportunity to improve her Spanish.

When I called her long-distance in Arkansas, she was cordiality itself. The Padre was "of medium height and slightly bald. One night he came into the hotel for dinner. He saw that we were Americans and came over and joined us. We struck up quite a friendship. He was very interested in improving the life of his people."

That Padre Rickards was away from the house much of the time or perhaps too tactful to intrude into the lives of his tenants is attested by the way he drops from Lawrence's letters. Brett cites his agreement with Lawrence that the *zaguan* was a cold place for the *mozo* to sleep and he joined the Lawrences' Christmas party. But the only extended visit she reports is a walk with the Padre to El Fortín, the leveled space near the top of the mountainous spur which narrows the entrance to the city by jutting towards Monte Alban. This space, named for a small fort that once existed there, has been dominated since 1906, the centenary of Juárez's birth, by a heroic bronze statue of the statesman, imperiously pointing west.

> The Padre takes us up to the old fort [wrote Brett]. It is on a hill and from it we see the town lying below us. How lovely it looks in the evening light, all shades of a delicate apricot color. The cupolas sparkle, and away over the mountains, huge pillars of clouds rise perpendicularly into the sky.
> "If I were a painter, I would paint those clouds," you say to me.

Now the Pan-American Highway climbs over this hill. At the point where the Lawrences stood is a turn-out to provide a view point. A few taller buildings have gone up since 1924, but the churches are still the outstanding feature of the cityscape. Besides large domes rising from their crossings, most of the churches have little cupolas capping twin bell towers, and the sparkling effect that Brett noticed as the sun set is because many of the cup-like shapes are sheathed with glossy tiles.

Perhaps while they were enjoying the view, Padre Rickards told the Lawrences some of the history of the hill. Aztec warriors were stationed there to protect the trade route to Tehuantepec. The fate of Oaxaca had often depended on who held the hill. Hadn't García Vigil, just eleven months before, postponed his downfall by riding to the hill and holding it successfully when the *Serranos* tried their one-day invasion? Brett's later references to what she called "the old Greek house of the President" suggests that the Padre told them about a conspicuously unfinished building with a Greek-style portico visible from the hill. Having been abandoned only ten years before, it was not old, and it was never the residence of a president. But it had been the start of an ambitious project by a governor: a school of agriculture that the wealthy Bolaños Cacho had imported an Italian architect to design. And its lack of completion was connected with the hill, for Bolaños Cacho was the first of the governors whose downfall Ibarra helped bring about. He surrendered to the *Serranos* because his situation became helpless once his forces, which had been holding the hill, defected to the invaders.

Brett wrote at the time of the walk to the hill: "There is something sympathetic between you and the Padre. You like him. He is a sincere, simple man, hard-working and poor. And you feel an even stronger sympathy for him when the old Indian woman, the mother of the four daughters, comes to you and asks if you have any shirts to spare; and if you could give them to her for the Padre, who is so poor and so generous to the poor. This depletes you considerably of shirts!"

Not far from the Padre's house the old colonial aqueduct was still bringing water from the village of San Felipe "del Agua," named for its plentiful water which could be led down a stone canal to the city. Two of Brett's photographs preserved at the University of Texas prove that she went with the Lawrences on an unaccompanied excursion to inspect the stretch near the "Greek" house. Other photographs of hers show that some time later they walked all the way to San Felipe. This was another excursion conducted by the Padre with Maximiliano Salinas, the Rickards' family friend, as bodyguard. Eight years earlier he had looked after Constantine's family in Oaxaca as the older brother sought work in Mexico City. Frieda wore the same derby-style hat as on the walk to the aqueduct, but this time she brought a white parasol against the strong Oaxaca sun. The Padre wore a black fedora and took the cane that his nephew recalls as his constant walking companion. The "bird's nest of a dog"—one of Lawrence's terms for Corasmín—came along. Lawrence wore the same Panama hat as on the earlier walk. (Plates 12 and 13.)

Brett does not say whether Lawrence discussed the book he was writing with the Padre. Since the novelist was claiming that Christianity was an outworn religion, the harmony hints that Lawrence was chary with his views. After all, the priest was a man who daily demonstrated his fidelity to his vocation. Lawrence probably felt no need to affront him. But in his Chapala draft he envisioned some priests "filled with joy at the bigness and splendour of the new conceptions,"—the new religion bringing back the old Mexican gods. In Oaxaca he struck the passage out. Perhaps knowing a Roman Catholic priest personally showed him the unlikelihood of any such rejoicing. Perhaps, too, it was experience with Padre Rickards that caused him to have his Don Ramón write the new open letter to the clergy. "Who am I, that I should be enemy of the One Church? I am catholic of catholics. I would have one Church of all the world, with Rome for the Central City, if Rome wishes . . . . Priests who will come to me do not forsake either faith or God. They change their manner of speech and vestments, as the peon calls with one cry to the oxen, and with another cry to the mules. Each responds to its own call in its own way."

There is certainly evidence that Lawrence gave Padre Rickards absorbed attention when he was talking about Eulogio Gillow, his former boss, for Lawrence, as events proved, was interested in developing a different patron for Cipriano, the Indian boy in his novel. Gillow was ideally tailored for his needs. (Plate 14.) As bishop, he could play a more vital role in the plot. He was rich enough to arrange an Oxford education for the Indian boy, and his birth in 1841 made him the right age. But in order to make his Bishop Severn around seventy-five in 1913, the year Lawrence wanted to eliminate him, the novelist set his bishop's birth back to 1838.

Actually Gillow lived to be eighty-one, dying in 1922, but Lawrence otherwise transcribed Gillow with remarkable fidelity; he would have made him seem more credible, though, had he followed the truth and made him half-English. As it is, Lawrence's Severn is wholly English, whereas Eulogio Gregorio Gillow y Zavalza, was half-Spanish, as his complete name reveals, and his mother, Maria J. Zavalza de Gillow, was the Marquise de Selva Nevada.

The extensive property of the English father, Thomas Gillow, was around Puebla, where the future bishop was born; and after his primary schooling, his father had him educated at the colleges of Dorchester and Stonyhurst in England and then at institutions in Belgium and Rome. He was ordained in Puebla in 1865, but instead of becoming a parish priest he returned to Rome to study diplomacy and political economics. At the first Vatican Council he gained knowledge of his future episcopate, for Vicente Fermin Márquez, the bishop of Oaxaca, was among the 600 clergy who came to Rome to debate and ultimately enunciate the doctrine of the infallibility of the Pope. Gillow was assigned to the recently appointed bishop as assistant and theological counsel. After King Victor Emmanuel's entrance into Rome brought the council to an unscheduled halt, Gillow returned to Mexico where he had economic responsibilities as well as ecclesiastical duties, for his properties included a hacienda at Chiautla, Puebla. In 1887 his old council colleague, Dr. Márquez, died, and Gillow succeeded him as Bishop of Oaxaca. One of his practical acts was collaborating in the building of the railway between Puebla and Oaxaca, the Ferrocarril Mexicano del Sur. And four years after he had been named Oaxaca's first archbishop he built himself a sumptuous palace on Avenida Independencia, around the corner from the Alameda. Thereafter he spent huge sums renovating different Oaxaca churches, bestowing his greatest munificence on his cathedral. Because the Bethlehemite monastery that he had rehabilitated as a seminary was being used as a military hospital when Lawrence moved near it, one suspects that Padre Rickards pointed out the huge building at the head of the park to Lawrence as the place that had housed one of Gillow's dreams. Probably, too, he told the novelist that it was where García Vigil had studied for the priesthood, both pieces of information providing details he was to work into his novel.

In the first version of *The Plumed Serpent,* Lawrence's sub-hero, Cipriano, obtained his Oxford education through an English family with a coffee plantation. But in Oaxaca, the real half-English bishop presented a more appealing option for giving an Indian an English education. The novel shows, too, that in listening to Padre Rickards, Lawrence, not content with learning the incidents of the old archbishop's biography, also tried to get an idea of his character: of his familiarity with hacienda life, of his presence of mind in a crisis, of his understanding of children, and

of his high-minded idealism that might have prevented him from conceiving all that was seething below the surface of his country. Thus, the
novel speaks of "the old bishop's strong, rather grandiose personality."

Birmingham, where Rickards studied, and Eastwood, the coal-
mining village where Lawrence was born and raised, are both in the English Midlands; and Lawrence entered Nottingham University College in
September 1906, which was the year after Rickards entered Oscott. So
the two men were studying simultaneously at colleges within a few miles
of each other, one to be a teacher, the other to be a priest. They must
have worked out the coincidence and speculated on how eighteen or
nineteen years earlier their paths might have crossed in the Midlands.
That the Padre knew the Midlands must have contributed to Lawrence's
feeling at home with him. One wonders if, with the Padre, the "Bert"
in Lawrence—as he was known to the Chambers family at the Haggs, the
farm near Eastwood where he spent his happiest Midland days—came
through. That the boy in Lawrence never wholly disappeared is shown
by his 28 November 1928 response to an unexpected letter from David,
the youngest Chambers son: "Whatever else I am," he wrote, "I am somewhere still the same Bert who rushed with such joy to the Haggs."

The Lawrences left the Padre's house in mid-February 1925, and
the two corresponded for at least two years after that. None of the letters
survived. The priest's reaction to the novel redone under his roof would
have been interesting. Was it a shock that Lawrence felt another religion
should replace Catholicism? Were his feelings hurt that the novelist had
attacked his beloved faith and advocated burning the images of the saints?
A reference to the correspondence preserved in a Lawrence letter written a year after the publication of *Serpent* suggests that the relationship
between them was amicable when they parted. After all, the priest's
brother was a Protestant who had been passionately absorbed in Mexico's pre-Columbian past far longer than Lawrence.

A vivid glimpse into the priest's life in the year following the
Lawrence stay is given in the Mexico volume of Edward Weston's *Daybooks*. Weston, who took Lawrence's photograph in Mexico City, knew
Lawrence's address in Oaxaca because the novelist had written him from
the priest's house. In June 1926, almost two years after the Lawrence sitting, the photographer visited Oaxaca, stayed at the Francia, and "decided
to call on Padre Ricardo,—an English Padre with whom Lawrence spent
some time. We found him gone,—arrested and deported to Mexico the
night before by the military. The neighbors spoke in hushed voices but
with flashing eyes,—the criada we found in tears. He had been well loved.
This was a hint of that which followed in the religious war."

The events leading up to Rickards's arrest were not hard to reconstruct. José Mora y Del Rio, the Archbishop of Mexico, had proclaimed

early in 1926 that the Roman Catholic Church in Mexico did not and could not accept the religious conditions imposed by the Constitution of 1917. Calles, not one to tolerate such defiance, retaliated by being even firmer in enforcing Articles 3 and 130 to which the archbishop was objecting. One measure was to round up and deport foreign-born priests because of the Constitution's stipulation that only native-born Mexicans could be ministers of religion in Mexico. Padre Rickards, like his brother Constantine, was a British citizen.

George Rickards reported that his uncle, though taken into custody on June 19, was not immediately transported to the capital; and his brother, the British vice consul, received word of the arrest by wire and hastened to Oaxaca. Calles, having gained the long-withheld recognition of Great Britain, was not disposed to endanger relations with England again, so Padre Rickards was released in his brother's care. Constantine took him to Mexico City. The Padre remained there about six months, returning to Oaxaca once he was assured that it was safe.

In Mexico City the Padre lived at his brother's house. George was nineteen at the time and his younger sister, Grace, was fifteen. They both remembered how Uncle Edward put aside his reversed collar and black suit, both forbidden by Calles's new legislation. After the priests defied this new legislation and closed all the churches on 1 August 1926, George and Grace also remembered how their uncle continued his priestly duties. Every morning he got up early and took a tram, generally to the Basilica of Guadalupe, though often it was to celebrate mass in some home or another. Grace remembers how, when he came home in the afternoon, he would read his breviary, walking up and down the patio. All the children had great respect for their uncle, Grace said. But Mabel, who was not yet married to George, remembers the Padre joining the young people in the evenings playing "Snap." He would laugh as hard as they did when, in the excitement of the card game, his stuttering would sometimes prevent him from getting out his cry of "Snap" with sufficient celerity.

Though it leaps forward by ten years, another of Grace's memories is worth preserving. Because her father Constantine had remained a Protestant, she had been raised as one but fell in love with Manuel Solano, a young traveling salesman, who was a Roman Catholic. Far from shunning his Protestant niece, Padre Rickards came from Oaxaca to perform the marriage ceremony. The wedding was in a home and Grace remembers with gratitude how Uncle Edward wore his purple robe to add to the impressiveness of the occasion. After she was a young matron, the Padre would send her things from Oaxaca, generally *serapes,* and she would sell the tickets he sent with them so she could help raise money for his parish by conducting raffles among her friends and neighbors.

Once, she remembers, they raffled a twenty-dollar gold piece.

If he sought money for his parish, though, he never sought it for himself. He and his brother were always close and never discussed their religious differences, but George remembers his father remonstrating with his uncle when the old brother discovered the priest did not have a decent pair of shoes. "You should have more money," said Constantine. "I don't need it," the Padre replied. When the consular brother tried to help Edward with material things, Tio Eduardo would reply, "I've got enough. A priest is not supposed to have anything."

"He had no personal ambition," said George, "and in addition to being a devoted priest, he did penances. He slaved all his life and was sick all the time. He suffered from spleen. Yet he was always cheerful. He was happy in what he was doing."

His church, La Merced, was an earthquake casualty. In his house near the end of their stay, with Lawrence ill, Frieda, in *"Not I, But the Wind . . .,"* described how "to my horror I saw the beams of my roof move in and out of their sheaves." This 1925 tremor was too minor to be preserved in the annals of the city, but starting on 9 February 1928 came a series of terrible and repeated shocks, the first three spaced about a month apart, the next two months apart with the last on October 18. As soon as the quakes ceased the Padre would go into the streets and attend the injured and dying in the shattered houses. His own house survived the shocks, but La Merced, the church of which he was the pastor, was so badly damaged that it had to be closed. (Plates 15 and 16.) The cracks that developed in the dome made the cupola especially dangerous. La Merced was founded by the Mercedarian Order in 1570, making it a church with one of the longest traditions in the city. In 1930, he sold his house and used the proceeds to repair the church dome.

Since February 1973, when the old regional market adjoining the church was torn down, that dome, checkered with blue and brick red tiles, has stood clear and free, but in Padre Rickards's day it was partly obscured by the tin roof of the market that overflowed into the church's park-like approach. Then the dome appeared at its best from the cloister, for La Merced was once a monastery. Though it has only a single story, that cloister is especially beautiful and spacious, with seven arches on each side. And after he sold his house Rickards went to live in a room opening onto one of its ambulatories.

In 1931 he would have been obliged to move anyway. In even more terrible earthquakes, a large part of the city was destroyed including the Government Palace and Pino Suárez 43. The beams jerked free of their sheaves, and the roof crashed down. The house was not reconstructed until after the property was purchased by the brothers José and Manuel Alvarez Collando who had the *corredor* rebuilt with iron pillars to replace the plaster-covered piers of the Lawrences' time. (Plate 17.)

When I began seeking people in Oaxaca for memories of Padre Rickards, I met Bethsabe Salinas, the daughter of the grizzled family friend who accompanied the Lawrences on their walk to San Felipe. Bethsabe, who was already an old woman, said Natividad and Maria de Jesús were both dead, and she did not know what had become of the other daughters, or of Pascualita. Even a photograph of Lawrence did not stir any recollection of the novelist, but she certainly remembered the Padre. *"Un Santo,"* she said with feeling. *"Una bellisima persona."*

Between 1928 and 1932 Rickards taught English at García Vigil's old institution, the Seminario Pontifico in San José, another wrecked nunnery that Archbishop Gillow had rehabilitated. Manuel Bejerano, a seminarian of those years, recalled that the Padre got very nervous if his students did not work hard. George Rickards amplified this by saying Tio Eduardo "stuttered if he got nervous." Josefina González Meza de Ruiz Bravo, who studied English under Padre Rickards, said it was only in Spanish that he stuttered. She also remembered him blushing. His eyes, she said, were clear, but not a pure blue. He was *humilde* ("humble"), modest, cultivated, and always lived according to his convictions. He was very much in demand she told me, and one of his innumerable extra duties was as chaplain of the Hospital Vasconcelos de Caridad where he helped the nuns.

The Padre, she said, was especially loved in the barrio of La Merced, where every August 31, the day of San Ramón, the people of the barrio bring their animals to be blessed. On one such day when the atrium was full of adorned animals, an American girl brought a big dog, dressed in a straw hat and white stockings. The Padre gave the girl a smile of such surpassing sweetness that it still haunts the señora's memory. Having attended a latter-day blessing of the animals at La Merced, I could fill in the rest of the picture: the Padre at the ruined second-floor window looking down on the alley between the side of the convent and the long wall of the covered market, beaming on the people holding up their animals, if they were small enough, like parrots and canaries in cages, cats, and dogs; or leading in burros or tugging in huge bulls, some brown, some black and white. I could see the clown's hats on some dogs, the capes on the kittens, the spectacles painted round the eyes of the goats, and a few white-flanked animals painted pink. I could visualize, too, the acolyte beside the Padre, swinging a censer of smoking incense, and every now and then handing the priest a refilled hyssop, so holy water could be continually sprinkled on those pressing to get their turn under the window in the narrow passageway.

On 23 September 1966, an unexpected religious procession called a *calenda* had caused me to hasten my steps to overtake it. It was from

La Merced, Padre Rickards's church, marching in honor of our Lady of Mercy's feast day on the morrow to which everyone was invited. The *calenda* had three floats. In the chief one, a girl dressed as the Virgin of Merced sat on top of a large sphere representing the earth. *Reina del Universo* proclaimed the bulbs in the lighted arch at her back. The second float had a figure on a white horse that might have been Zapata, and the third had another Virgin. There were two bands, and many women carried round baskets on their heads containing lyres, stars, and crescent moons, all upholstered with flowers. The *gigantes* who marched and danced along with them were not very tall, but two of these outsized personages, created by dressed frameworks that men carried on their shoulders, represented the American comic strip characters Maggie and Jiggs. Because the Queen was on so high a sphere, and her height was increased by her ray-like halo, men with bamboo poles with Y's on their tips accompanied the almost hidden truck, lifting the telephone wires high enough so the queen could pass under them safely. I followed the *calenda* for a long time, impressed by its beauty as it circled the *zócalo,* where its spotlit floats and bearers of lanterns with candles burning in inverted cones of colored paper, were seen through the dark tracery of the trunks and overhanging leaves of the trees.

Sunday, September 25, was the climactic day of the fiesta, said one of the men throwing up lighted rockets in the van of the procession. I got to the church at 8:30 P.M. and had the luck to see the Virgin being brought down through the center of the church for the last of her various processions during the festival period. She was followed by women with candles and the church was hazy with pungent incense. The statue was then taken through the side door and carried counterclockwise around the cloister. Many people carrying candles preceded and followed her, and their lights seemed brighter in the ambulatories, causing a golden glow that set the pillars and arches in black silhouette. The candles, too, shone up beautifully on the bronze skin of those bearing them.

In the corner near where the Padre had lived, a woman played a portable harmonium. A man singer, two violinists, and a cellist joined her in providing the main melody, while at close intervals the candle-bearers sang the repeated response, *"Ora pro nobis."* The cloister had a single large tree. Beyond its heavy dark crown, my eye caught the moving gondolas of the neon-lighted ferris wheel from the fair in the street beyond the cloister walls.

Men carried the heavy statue of the Virgin, who was dressed in white with gold embroidery, her long train sustained by those walking behind her. Her crown was like a golden iris. In her right hand she held a gold sceptre and from her wrist hung a scapular with the escutcheon of the Mercedarians. On her left arm she carried her child, dressed very much like herself. Young men preceded her, swinging censers. It was a mild, lovely night, and the black sky glittered with stars. Rising from the dome that Padre Rickards had saved was a neon cross, its green light reflected on the cupola's tiles. I imagined the Padre among his beloved people, glad he had merged with them instead of becoming a member of the British colony in Mexico City.

Music was coming from within the church too, and as the Virgin was taken back through the side portal, I began to hear *"adiós, adiós"* among the words being sung. The people were saying goodbye to their *madrecita,* and they continued their farewells during the process of getting her reinstalled in her arched tabernacle over the high altar, terminating with fireworks. From inside, I could not see the façade's whole display of fireworks, but three silver cascades rained for several minutes over the Roman arch of the main door.

After the Virgin was safely in her tabernacle, most of the electric lights were turned out. The church, which had been full, emptied as the worshippers left to join the crowd at the carnival. Perhaps Padre Rickards too, wandered through the press of people patronizing the shooting galleries, the games of ring toss, and the *loteria* tents, where a form of "Bingo" is played with corn kernels to cover the lucky pictures. Surely he must have loved watching the children riding the merry-go-round.

Around ten o'clock came the entertainment everyone had awaited—the fireworks. First, men donned carapaces shaped like bulls and went dancing about as fireworks shot from them in all directions. After the *toritos* came the *angelitos,* with angel-shaped carapaces that sprouted wings of golden fire. And all the time the band played, as boys alternately dared and fled from the men whose molded shelters protected them from the flashes and explosions they were carrying. The barrio had maintained the character of a closely knit village, even though it is no longer at the outskirts of the city. The village-like aspect was increased by pennants of pink plastic fluttering on cords stretched from roof to roof across all the streets of the neighborhood. I regretted that Lawrence, absent from Oaxaca in August or September, had not seen the blessing of the animals or attended Merced's fiesta. Although he described the priest's house in *Mornings in Mexico,* including his dog and his two parrots, he never mentioned the master. No matter how congenial he may have been to Lawrence personally, Padre Rickards, like Governor Ibarra, was not a man who appealed to the novelist's literary imagination.

After catching a chill on a visit to Mexico City, Padre Rickards died in Oaxaca of a combination of pneumonia and heart failure on 5 March 1941 at age sixty-two. When the news of Tio Eduardo's death reached Mexico City, according to George, Constantine was incapacitated by a stroke, so George and his brother-in-law, Ernest Grether, went to claim the body. They took the night train and arrived in Oaxaca about ten o'clock the next morning. They were pleased to find that Padre Rickards was already laid out in state in the church he had served but could not understand why his parishioners were reserved and hostile.

Mexico, where there is little embalming, requires burial within twenty-four hours of death and forbids burying priests in churches. The nephew found that, in compliance with both laws, the parishioners had arranged for a funeral the following day at the large public cemetery. The route the cortege would follow and the hour of the burial were announced in the newspapers. The next day crowds lined the streets from La Merced to the *Panteón*. But they waited in vain. The night before, in the utmost secrecy, a group had buried the Padre in the crypt under the church altar and immediately plastered over the opening. Faced with a *fait accompli,* the outwitted authorities did not press for an exhumation. Eight years later, the church commissioned an artist to copy a photograph to create a life-size portrait of the Padre in impressive red robes. It now hangs in the church office.

CHAPTER 3

THE MARKET

The Oaxaca market and the Indians who bring their wares to it each Saturday stirred Lawrence's imagination. Symbolic of all markets, he saw Oaxaca's as a benign vortex drawing everything to its center in a series of curving lines. He also saw men and women coming to the market, many from considerable distances, so their lonely lives in the hills and isolated villages could be warmed by something infinitely precious—the spark of human contact. His essay, "Market Day," in *Mornings in Mexico* likens this spark to "the flashing intermediary, the evening star that is seen only at the dividing of the day and night" when it is more beautiful than either the sun or the moon.

Because the first concept has cosmic overtones and the second dramatizes essential human experience, Lawrence may have selected aspects of the market more significant than mere objective description. The objective features he cites are evoked with magical vividness. But there was much about the market that he apparently never noticed, much of historical interest that he did not realize, and much that was veiled from his understanding by the romanticism of the concepts on which he built his essay.

"Market Day" was written after he moved into Padre Rickards's house; and, for the sake of artistic unity, he wrote it as if it were an account of a single visit on the last Saturday before Christmas, which in 1924 was December 20. But internal evidence shows he drew on impressions from a number of visits.

That the market was the first big excitement the Lawrences experienced in Oaxaca is indicated by Brett's early cliff-hanging words: "Then we find the Market Place, a huge corrugated iron building. . . ." The discovery was made after they had repeatedly circled the *zócalo* on their first morning. But the position of their hotel must have given them many signs of the market before they actually entered it. The night of their arrival, they might have seen the yellow flames of candles or unshaded gasoline lamps down the street from vendors hoping for a last late sale. Because it was Sunday, several street merchants would have been camping in the streets surrounding the permanent sheds; many Indians bringing their goods in on Saturday remain till Sunday evening. The clip-clop of burro hoofs must have drawn the unpacking Lawrences to their windows to watch the departure of those who had already taken down their awnings and loaded their mules, burros, and their own backs with their unsold goods. The sound of shoppers likely woke them Monday morning, for the street outside the hotel was a main thoroughfare to the market; and in Oaxaca the market is active daily even though its scale is diminished on weekdays.

From this market came the blankets and pots with which they furnished their quarters at the priest's. On his second Mexican visit, because he was grateful to the Hawks for renting him and the Danes cabins on their Del Monte ranch through the previous winter, he had sent them some pottery from San Pedro Tlaquepaque. This gift is mentioned in a 28 October 1923 letter by the Dane who was Lawrence's traveling companion. "Today," wrote Gótzsche, "we went to St. Pedro on the tram car, a few miles from Guadalajara, where they make pottery. We bought some small things and shipped them." Another purchase was a Mexican blanket with an eagle pattern either owned by the Hawks or seen by Bill at the Lawrences' when they settled on nearby Kiowa. In a letter, Lawrence describes the "big market humming like a bee-hive where you can buy anything from roses to horseshoes. I wish we could send you some of the pottery, such beautiful colours, and costs nothing. But the last lot I sent got smashed. This is where they make the *serapes* like the one with the eagle that hung on the wall: and the little men stalk about in them looking very showy."

Lawrence's vivid beehive simile suggests the market's sheds as well as its sounds. But Lawrence made a mistake he would have been able to correct two days later had he gone to the governor's road opening. The eagle blankets are not made in Oaxaca but in Teotitlán del Valle. The men who "stalk" about in them—they wear them folded in piles over each shoulder—are weavers from the village bringing their blankets to sell in the more exciting city. And "showy" is certainly the word for their outsize epaulettes, especially since the grays, browns, whites, and blacks of natural wools have been augumented by the scarlets, oranges, greens, and blues made possible by aniline dyes.

Saturday, November 15, gave the Lawrences their first opportunity to see the market on its principal day. They took it, and in Lawrence's letter to Murry on his return, he gives another glimpse: "It's the chief market today—such a babel and a hubbub of unwashed wild people— heaps of roses and hibiscus flowers, blankets, very nice wild pottery, calves, birds, vegetables, and awful things to eat—including squashed fried locust-beetles."

Again the description is alive and vivid, but Lawrence had mistaken beetles for grasshoppers; and they are not fried. First they are dropped live into boiling water to be simultaneously killed and cleaned. Then, after being dried, they are boiled again in water flavored with salt, lime juice, oregano, and garlic. By this time the pretty green creatures are the color of mahogany. Dried once again they are taken to the market by the basketful. Generally they are eaten as an appetizer or relish. They are not eaten in other states but they are such a favorite with Oaxaqueños that a man from Oaxaca in a far place will often be nicknamed *El Chapulin,* "The Grasshopper."

Although Lawrence referred to Oaxaca's pottery in his letters, he omits it from his essay, only mentioning the red-brown *ollas* ("great nets of bubble-shaped jars") among the items on the donkey backs in the cavalcade coming to the market. (Plate 18.) Brett, however, includes pottery in her account of the first day:

> The Indians are watchful as we pass down the avenue of stalls. You stop at a stall of pottery: I can feel the interest run from the Indian woman behind the stall along the whole line of men and women. She smiles a questioning smile, and wishes you a polite good-day. The same smiling good-day is returned, the same gentle good manner. Her passing look of bewilderment gives place to an instantaneous friendliness, a recognition of something more nearly akin to herself. The news flashes down the line and like a wave ripples round the whole market. Furtive looks, little smiles of friendliness are given you. Your gentleness, your red beard, thick hair, quiet blue eyes—all add to the mystery of the strange otherness of this soft-spoken man. A message has been subtly broadcast throughout the whole building: A new kind of white man is among us.
>
> A man mutters, "Cristo," and a look of fleeting annoyance passes over your face. A woman sees it, smiles at you, a row of shining white teeth. You smile back at her and give a little, shy laugh. . . . The babies, perched on the stalls, stare at you with huge, solemn eyes, like round globes of dark light.
>
> Señora Monros has now joined us. Frieda listens to the prices, to the bargaining. The basket on the back of the Señora's *mozo,* slung from his forehead, is speedily filled up. And you buy two jugs, after a great deal of bargaining.
>
> "It is," you tell me, "their moment of gossip. If you do not bargain, they are disappointed: they have missed their only bit of excitement in the day."

Lawrence was to develop this idea in his essay. Meanwhile, any one who has enjoyed the friendliness and quick understanding of the vendors and the appeal of their big-eyed children will recognize how precisely Brett caught elements that make marketing such a pleasure in Oaxaca. Lawrence says nothing about the children.

Brett was wrong about the roof. The market is not roofed with corrugated iron but with tin. But her description of the interior is a superb impression.

> We plunge into the Market Place. It is dark, with great splashes of light in large pools here and there. There are flowers, masses and masses of flowers; clean, glistening vegetables and fruit; gorgeous *serapes;* materials; baskets. . . . Color, color everywhere! The whole place blazes and glows, the colors flash in the pools of sunlight, deepening in the rich shadows. The clean white clothes of the men, the big dark hats, the golden straw hats, and the patterned flowing skirts of the women and their speckled *rebozos* —all merge with the flowers and fruits and vegetables. And, above all, how quiet it is. The scent of the flowers, the dry smell of the earth, the soft, low ripple of talk among the Indians, broken now and then by a loud squawk from the turkeys or chickens or ducks lying with their feet tied together in bunches on the floor.

Brett also tried to capture her market impressions with her camera. She did not have much success with the richness of the shadows, but she dramatized the brilliance of "the pools of sunlight" by catching in one photo the shadow of two awning poles lying across Lawrence's back like the ribbon of a foreign decoration. (Plate 19.)

Frieda, on this visit, wore a suit much like a riding habit. Her preference for this style is noted in Lawrence's 10 January 1926 letter to Brett: "F. is still charmed by her clothes. You should see her in the black step-downstairs coat and the bowler riding hat!"

Frieda was also thrilled by the market. In *"Not I, But the Wind . . ."* she wrote, "I loved the market and it was only distressing to see the boy Rosalino with the basket so utterly miserable at my paying without bargaining; it was real pain to him. But the lovely flowers and everything seemed so cheap."

While at the Francia, Lawrence was living near the center of the magnet, seeing the convergence of many of the filings drawn towards it. But at Pino Suárez 43 he observed a line of gravity beyond to the northeast reaching up into the hills. The priest's house provided a grandstand seat as the bridge over the Jalatlaco River was located at the back of the house and determined the traffic's flow towards the market. The people who came over it were from the villages of San Andres Huayapan, Tlalixtac, Ixcotel and Garita de Tepeaca. (See map, page 109.) Watching them approach would have given Lawrence a clear idea of the traffic coming to market from different directions, for by now he must have known that Oaxaca was located where three valley arms met, with traffic coming from Ocotlán in the south, from Etla and other towns to the northwest, and from Tlacolula and Mitla to the southeast. The bridge for the important road from Mitla was only four blocks down from the house and four blocks east. In his day, Lawrence might have found a point from which he could see two lines of market-bound traffic simultaneously (impossible now because of intervening buildings). The streams of traffic were a catalyst for his essay; for, once he knew the lines, he decided not to open with the market itself, but with the people coming to it. Both streams entering his quadrant of the town are described. He alternates between them so that in the narrative they seem to be braided. This mingling makes them hard to disentangle, but it enhances the description. It enables him to achieve his desired effect of many streams from many directions all whirling smoothly forward as if to the center of a vortex.

When the Pan-American Highway was extended to Oaxaca and beyond, towards the Isthmus of Tehuantepec, about twenty years after Lawrence's visit, smooth pavement brought buses, automobiles, and trucks. The hard surface hurt the hoofs of the animals. Since the highway was constructed through the northwest and southeast arms, it also superseded many of the less direct dirt roads that grew dusty in the dry season. But one still sees old modes of travel in the villages; in 1947, when I began visiting Oaxaca, the sights Lawrence described were common. My own experience enabled me to distinguish one stream of traffic from another.

Aldous Huxley comments on Lawrence's descriptions in general. In his 7 October 1940 letter to Frieda, criticizing Melchior Langyel's dramatization of *Lady Chatterley's Lover,* Huxley wrote, "What he failed to do is to give the play those elements which Lawrence gave to the book by means of his astonishing descriptions." He depicted the "unventured hills" with the grass slopes "already dry and fawn-coloured" in a letter dashed off to Murry. To comprehend the effect of similar impressions developed later, we need to see the enormous stage he set for both streams of traffic. "Everything seems slowly to circle and hover towards a central point, the clouds, the mountains round the valley, the dust that rises, the big, beautiful white-barred hawks, and even the snow-white flakes of flowers upon the dim palo-blanco tree. Even the organ cactus, rising in stock-straight clumps, and the candelabrum cactus, seem to be slowly wheeling and pivoting upon a centre, close upon it."

It does not matter that he misspells the sparrow hawks as *gabilanes* for, in the next paragraph, he uses the birds to dramatize the vast space of the sky by describing one bird's banking "as the tips of the broad wings of the hawk turn upwards, leaning upon the air like the invisible half of the ellipse."

Lawrence then describes the smaller stream of traffic from the nearer hills:

Away on the footslope lie the white specks of Huayapa, among its lake of trees. It is Saturday, and the white dots of men are threading down the trail over the bare humps of the plain, following the dark twinkle-movement of asses, the dark nodding of the woman's head as she rides between the baskets. Saturday and market-day, and morning, so the white specks of men, like sea-gulls on plough-land, come ebbing like sparks from the palo-blanco, over the fawn undulating of the valley slope.

They are dressed in snow white cotton, and they lift their knees in the Indian trot, following the ass, where the woman sits perched between the huge baskets, her child tight in the *rebozo,* at the brown breast. And girls in long, full, soiled cotton skirts running, trotting, ebbing along after the twinkle-movement of the ass. Down they come in families, in clusters, in solitary ones, threading with ebbing, running, barefoot movement noiseless towards the town, that blows the bubbles of its church-domes above the stagnant green of trees, away under the opposite fawn-skin hills.

As a schoolteacher reading papers to a literary group in Croydon, Lawrence had already formulated a mode of communicating emotion. "Art and the Individual," one of those papers, defines "picture words." David Cavitch in *D. H. Lawrence & The New World* puts his finger on another mode when he praises Lawrence's "richness of objective material." Anaïs Nin also provides a synthesis in her *D. H. Lawrence: An Unprofessional Study,* by using her own craftsman's knowledge of writing to analyze Lawrence's descriptions. Stressing that a wealth of objective material is not enough in itself, she mocks those authors "who think taking an inventory of the universe is really literature" and concedes that in *Kangaroo* some of the descriptions are "rather enumerative." But overwhelmingly she argues that in Lawrence's descriptions his "rich objective vision" is "transfused by a fine poetic imagination."

Examples of this vision abound in the description just quoted. Yet no one could say they are listed as an inventory. One of Lawrence's secrets, Nin points out, is that he incorporates his poetic sensations into his factual descriptions. Another secret is rhythm, established here by repetition of words. Rhythm, Nin points out, is so important to Lawrence that he is sometimes careless of both syntax and sense. Perhaps his speaking of the invisible half of the ellipse for the hawks' wings in flight is an example. Finally, Nin points out how his descriptions appeal to all five senses. The Nin analytical touchstones—details richly observed, fusing and suffusing poetic imagination, personal sensations, verbal rhythm, and a wide range of sensuousness—can be applied to his description of the larger stream of traffic as well. One must also consider other touchstones—telling similes, an extensive vocabulary, a gift for *le mot juste,* a nature so responsive to impressions that they affected him deeply, and what one can only describe as soul-force, because in Lawrence's descriptions there is such intensity in his desire to communicate his impressions— witness the repetitions—that one feels the pressure of his spirit behind his words.

The account of the traffic on the old Mitla road is contrapuntally interwoven with the description of the people coming from the hills.

> The dust advances like a ghost along the road, down the valley plain. The dry turf of the valley-bed gleams like soft skin, sunlit and pinkish ochre, spreading wide between the mountains that seem to emit their own darkness, a dark-blue vapour translucent, sombering them from the humped crests downwards. The many-pleated, noiseless mountains of Mexico.
>
> Down the valley middle comes the big road, almost straight. You will know it by the tall walking of the dust, that hastens also towards the town, overtaking everybody. Overpassing all the dark little figures and the white-specks that thread tinily, a sort of underworld, to the town.
>
> From the valley villages and from the mountains the peasants and the Indians are coming in with supplies, the road is like a pilgrimage, with the dust in greatest haste, dashing for town. Dark-eared asses and running men, running women, running girls, running lads, twinkling donkeys ambling on fine little feet, twin great nets of bubble-shaped jars, twin bundles of neat-cut faggots of wood, neat as bunches of cigarettes, and twin net-sacks of charcoal. Donkeys, mules, on they come, great pannier baskets making a rhythm under the perched woman, great bundles bouncing against the sides of the slim-footed animals. A baby donkey trotting naked after its piled up dam, a white, sandal-footed man following with the silent Indian haste, and a girl running again on light feet.
>
> Onwards, on the strange current of haste. And slowly rowing among the foot-travel, the ox-wagons rolling solid wheels below the high net of the body. Slow oxen, with heads pressed down nosing to the earth, shovel-shaped collar of wood pressing down on the necks like a scoop. On, on, between the burnt-up turf and the solid, monumental green of the organ cactus. Past the rocks and the floating palo-blanco flowers, past the towsled dust of the mesquite bushes. While the dust once more, in a greater haste than anyone, comes tall and rapid down the road, overpowering and obscuring all the little people, as in a cataclysm. (Plate 20.)

There are two more paragraphs, equally fine, which describe the appearance of the "specks" of people from closeup.

The advance to the market occupies almost five pages, followed by another five-page description of the market itself—the building occupying the block bounded on the north by Las Casas, on the south by

Aldama, on the west by 20 de Noviembre, the street of the Francia, and on the east by the continuation of García Vigil, which below the *zócalo* is called Miguel Cabrera in honor of the painter. In reality, this building is less than half the market, but it is the only part Lawrence describes.

Unlike Brett, he makes no mention of corrugated iron. "The market," he says, "is a huge roofed-in place." But when I returned to the market in 1962, camera in hand and eyes alert to see the market, his ghostly presence made me look at the market in a way I had never done before. My first stop in retracing Lawrence's route was on the north side. After I had taken a photograph of its central section, I then made a point-by-point inspection of its architectural features. (Plate 21.) I noticed for the first time the name of Mercado Benito Juárez Maza in faded black under the triangular pediment that gave the façade a Neo-classic touch. So it was named for the son of the great Don Benito, Oaxaca's governor for seven months during the early days of the Revolution. He maintained stabililty but died suddenly of a heart attack in April 1912, and his death unleashed the real troubles of the Revolution in the state.

Circling the block, I found the building's north and south façades identical, but the east and west entrances lacked the three handsome arches. Nevertheless, these side entries were imposing. In its outer aisles, the Mercado Juárez Maza resembles an enormous cloister. Lawrence's impression focused on sounds:

> Most extraordinary is the noise that comes out, as you pass along the adjacent street. It is a huge noise, yet you may never notice it. It sounds as if all the ghosts in the world were talking to one another, in ghost-voices, within the darkness of the market structure. It is a noise something like rain, or banana leaves in a wind. The market, full of Indians, dark-faced, silent-footed, hush-spoken, but pressing in in countless numbers. The queer hissing murmurs of the Zapotec *idioma,* among the sounds of Spanish, the quiet, aside-voices of the Mixtecas.

His description has life and pulsing individuality, and was something he felt inwardly and later brought up from inside. The basic differences are illustrated in a conversation that Brett recorded later in New Mexico. First she and Lawrence had agreed that, "because the imagination works better that way," most pictures should be painted from memory. Then Lawrence had asked: "Why do all painters have to sit in front of what they paint? It's because they feel nothing inside them, so they must have it before their eyes. It's all wrong and stupid: it should all be brought up from inside oneself."

When I entered the building, I found a cloister within a cloister, for the four interior tin roofs, supported only by steel trusses upheld by girders, joined at right angles to form an inner frame, leaving the center of the market open to the sky. A plaque that did not survive the 1965 reconstruction gave the market's date, 1893, and two English names: Read y Campbell, Ingenieros-Contratistas.

The first was H. Hudston Read, the second Albert J. Campbell. Read and Campbell were English engineers who in May 1888 built the railway, the narrow-gauge line from Puebla to Oaxaca that Lawrence picked up at Tehuacán. Although they contracted to build the railway in ten years, they completed it in four. President Díaz inaugurated it on 12 November 1892.

A new, enlarged market was a logical outcome of a railway that brought Oaxaca into easy contact with the commerce of the nation's capital. Undoubtedly Díaz had a hand in seeing that his birthplace got a structure resembling those built for the great expositions in Europe. The Indians I saw in the market might have been what Lawrence saw—survivors of a culture going back several centuries. But the place in which they were gathered was part of a new era of Porfirian modernism. "Round the center of the covered market where there is a basin of water, are the flowers." In the unroofed center was a large circular fountain with water spouting from a life-sized iron crane. It was another victim of reconstruction. Gladioli were mostly being sold when I was there, though Lawrence described "red, white, pink roses in heaps, many-coloured little carnations, poppies, bits of larkspur, lemon and orange marigolds, buds of madonna lilies, pansies, a few forget-me-nots, . . . lilies wild from the hills, and . . . . mauve-red orchids." (Plate 22.) In the Oaxaca market all goods of one class are grouped in the same location. I had long wanted to map the goods and was amazed at the varieties of peppers. I recognized the big green stuffers readily enough, as well as the jade green ones the size of gherkins. But what were the dark vegetables that looked like small deflated balls? *Chiles,* the attendant said. And the wide black pointed ones as wrinkled and sticky-looking as prunes? *Chiles,* too. The same for the paprika-red ones shaped like shrimps, and those wrinkled as raisins and raisin in color, too. Many were the color of tomatoes, others the color of pumpkins. Some were mahogany, some a leathery nutmeg brown, some the color of port wine, some as lustrous as scarlet pottery, some as dark green as the pottery of Azompa. Some were long and pointed, some blunt and fat, some straight, some crescent-shaped.

The beans were a revelation, too, I recognized those like licorice jelly beans as *frijoles,* but what were the little white pebbles? *Frijoles,* said the attendant. And the things that looked like unpeeled Spanish peanuts? *Frijoles.* And those like slightly roasted cashew nuts? *Frijoles.* *Frijoles* were also the objects like tiny red-speckled larks' eggs and those that resemble cranberries. Noticing small white eyes in some of the black beans made me see also the pale brown beans with white eyes. There were beans the color of port, and some the color of heather in the distance; shiny beans and dull beans.

Lawrence had not noted either the chiles or the beans. Even more surprising was his neglect of the fruit. Below is his only paragraph that is at all comprehensive, and because it comes just after the account of purchasing a bunch of mixed carnations, it suggests a view from the now destroyed fountain: "The stalls go off in straight lines, to the right, the brilliant vegetables, to the left, bread and sweet buns. Away at one end, cheese, butter, eggs, chickens, turkeys, meat. At the other, the native-woven blankets and *rebozos*, skirts, shirts, handkerchiefs. Down the far-side sandals and leather things."

Lawrence did not take notes. Friends, who later read his detailed descriptions of shared sights, have expressed their incredulity that merely from memory he could reconstruct so fully what they had seen together. That he was relying on memory became apparent to me when I studied his summary in the light of my map. True enough, there is a point where the vegetables are on the right and the bread on the left; but there the cheese is adjacent, not "away at one end," and the booths lining the aisles of the outer cloister are not visible from the inner complex. Lawrence's description, which suggests a single vantage point, is actually a composite of many viewpoints. The ready-made wares on my map—such as dresses, pants, children's clothing and pharmaceuticals—when contrasted with their absence in Lawrence, made me realize how many more manufactured items there were in the market in the 1960s than in the 1920s. Even so, I was surprised at how many things Lawrence must have seen that he did not include: the shrimp, the coconuts, the knives, the toys, the tablecloths, the ribbons, the fruit drinks, the ironware, the tinware. And in recalling eggs, his English memory must have tricked him into conjuring up butter, for butter is almost nonexistent in Oaxaca's diet. He did not include some of the items mentioned in his letters, like horseshoes and "awful things to eat," such as grasshoppers. Nor did he mention the round white cheeses wrapped in banana leaves, nor the crisp, ruffled sheets of cooked pig's skin, nor the women seated by cylindrical baskets filled with tortillas that they extracted from protective napkins when people heeded their calls of *"Blandas, blanditas"* and paused to buy.

Lawrence conveys most of his sense of the market in three scenes. He is the central figure in them, although by referring to himself as "you" rather than "I" he elicits the participation of the reader and reduces the impact of his own personality. He tells of not purchasing a blanket: "The *serape* men spy you, and whistle to you like ferocious birds, and call Señor! Señor! Look! Then with violence one flings open a dazzling blanket, while another whistles more ear-piercingly still, to make you look at his blanket. It is a veritable den of lions and tigers, that spot where the *serape* men have their blankets piled on the ground. You shake your head and flee.''

The men of Teotitlán del Valle, who are the chief vendors of their own creations, can be charmingly and ingeniously persistent, but they make a *"hist"* sound rather than a whistle, and never have I, in more than twenty years, seen them act like "ferocious birds."

One of the thrills of mapping was finding that the hat stalls still come after passing the *huaraches* as in the Lawrence essay.

"Señor! Señor! Look! *Huaraches!* Very fine, very finely made. Look, Señor!"

The fat leather man jumps up and holds a pair of sandals at one's breast. They are of narrow woven strips of leather, in the newest Paris style, but a style ancient to these natives. You take them in your hand, and look at them quizzically, while the fat wife of the *huarache* man reiterates, "Very fine work. Very fine. Much work!"

"How much?"

"Twenty *reales.*" [1]

"Twenty!"—in a voice of surprise and pained indignation.

"How much do you give?"

You refuse to answer. Instead you put the *huaraches* to your nose. The *huarache* man looks at his wife, and they laugh aloud.

"They smell," you say.

"No, Señor, they don't smell,"—and the two go off into fits of laughter.

"Yes, they smell. It is not American leather."

"How much do you give?"

"Nothing, because they smell."

And you give another sniff, though it is painfully unnecessary. And in spite of your refusal to bid, the man and wife go into fits of laughter to see you painfully sniffing.

You lay down the sandals and shake your head.

"How much do you offer?" reiterates the man gaily.

You shake your head mournfully, and move away. The leather man and his wife look at one another and go off into another fit of laughter, because you smelt the *huaraches,* and said they stank.

They did. The natives use human excrement for tanning leather. When Bernal Díaz came with Cortés to the great market-place of Mexico City, in Montezuma's day, he saw the little pots of human excrement in rows for sale, and the leather-makers going around sniffing to see which was best, before they paid for it. It staggered even a fifteenth-century

Spaniard. Yet my leather man and his wife think it screamingly funny that I smell the *huaraches* before buying them. Everything has its own smell, and the natural smell of *huaraches* is what it is. You might as well quarrel with an onion for smelling like an onion.

This scene reveals Lawrence as an observer. It not only tells about the market and its people, it also represents him at his best. Yet Lawrence displayed a lack of curiosity and humility arising from a conviction of knowing it all. He was over-confident of his intuition and relied too much on a vivid, but tricky memory. He was reluctant to admit that a vendor of wares might know more about his offerings than he did and was careless about checking facts and references. The scene also illustrates that Lawrence was by no means indifferent to objects, but he tended to be more interested in his responses to them. If he had been seriously interested in one of Oaxaca's best handicrafts, he would have asked where the pair of *huaraches* held out to him had been made. The man would have replied Oaxaca itself, for one can recognize the city-made style in his description. But if he had asked the place of origin of the simpler sandals with the wider straps of red-brown leather, the man would have answered Tlacolula, the main village on the way to Mitla. Those with two sets of double thongs of soft cream-colored leather were from Juchitan in the Isthmus of Tehuantepec. Those with three bands in front that cross diagonally over finer strips behind, were from Ocotlán, one of the chief *huarache*-making towns in the state. Such questions would have emphasized how Oaxaca towns and villages specialized in certain goods, each producing work of a distinctive style, and how the Oaxaca market served as a clearing house for village handicrafts from a wide area.

L. D. Clark, in *Dark Night of the Body,* has ingeniously worked out that Lawrence read Bernal Díaz's *The Discovery and Conquest of Mexico* as early as 1920, four years prior to his visit to Oaxaca. In Díaz's account of his visit to the Aztec market at Tlalteloco he tells of seeing little jars and of hearing of boatloads of human dung kept in inlets near the plaza. The dung, he was told, was sold to tan hides. The old soldier was not appalled; but Lawrence, when he read the account, obviously was. His imagination manipulated the chronicler's facts in the intervening years. It shifted the heaped-up dung from the boats, had it divided into categories and distributed by class into little jars; brought the pots right into the market; invented Aztec tanners acting like connoisseurs testing wine bouquets, and then envisaged a Lawrence-like Bernal Díaz staggered by such sniffing. This transmutation was a prime example of what Lawrence tended to do with books. As he blithely confessed in his *Fantasia of the Unconscious,* "I only remember hints—and I proceed by intuition."

Thus in "Market Day," one finds Lawrence giving a highly fanciful version of Bernal Díaz; and, worse, assuming that because the Aztecs used human excrement for tanning in the 1520s Oaxaca sandal-makers still used it in the 1920s. Had he asked the vendor he would have known that the delicate bark of *timbre,* a small holm oak grown in the Mixteca Alta, was the chief tanning agent. Other tree barks were also used as well as juice of a fruit like tamarind called *cascalote.* I asked *huarache* makers in Ocotlán and various *huarache* salesmen in Oaxaca whether human excrement was used as a tanning agent. They all said it wasn't.

Lawrence's scene not only spreads misinformation, but the joke was actually on him. He depicts the vendor and his wife as coarse people joking at a white man's distaste in smelling dung. In reality they were probably enjoying the funny faces he made while smelling the leather. Thinking he was smelling feces when he wasn't and feeling more refined than the vendors, the joke was on him. The element of poignance comes from the lack of true communication between the stranger and the natives, and the stranger not realizing his misjudgment. Certainly, the natives had no idea what he was thinking.

Brett relates this incident in their first visit to the market.

> The big burly Indian in the stall, grins at you as you pick up the sandals and sniff them over.
>
> "My sandals do not smell," the man says proudly—which is strange, as the smell among his sandals is simply appalling. I pick out a much-patterned pair and sniff at them gingerly. I hand them to you, and you smell them all over, carefully.
>
> "They are all right," you say. "If they fit, buy them at half the price he asks." They do fit, and after a bit of shy haggling, they are wrapped up in paper. We each get an unsmelly pair. Outside you explain:
>
> "They tan the leather with human excrement, that's what makes them smell." The expression on my face is too much for you, and you shake with laughter. "It was even a bit too much for Cortez and his Spaniards, and they were none too squeamish in those days," you add.

Lawrence did not shake "his head mournfully and move away;" he bought the sandals he said he rejected, boyishly enjoying Brett's shock when he gave her the erroneous Díaz information. The Lawrence of Brett's account is much more likable than the Lawrence in his own. That Lawrence in person was often more likable than Lawrence in his self-portraiture is attested by Murry who in his *Reminiscences of D. H. Lawrence* recalled watching Lawrence at a dinner party "talking with all his quick gaiety and sensitive response." The man's charm stirred the question, *"Why* is there a gulf between this Lawrence and the writer?"

As Murry continued to watch Lawrence he became "bewildered and depressed by the strange discrepancy." Later when Lawrence asked Murry the cause of his depression, Murry answered, "You always deny what you actually are. You refuse to acknowledge the Lawrence who really exists."

Ernest Collings, an English artist and poet, who had opened communications by a fan letter, elicited especially fine letters from Lawrence. In his fourth letter to Collings, written on 17 January 1913, while still in Italy with Frieda, Lawrence said: "We can go wrong in our minds. But what our blood feels and believes and says, is always true. The intellect is only a bit and bridle. What do I care about knowledge. All I want is to answer to my blood, direct, without fribbling intervention of mind, or moral, or what not."

The *huarache* incident portrays a clear case of "fribbling intervention" of mind in the distorted recollection of Bernal Díaz, but one can easily imagine him defending this scene against the charge of misrepresentation. The leading charge that Mexicanists bring against him is that he didn't care enough for knowledge; he reported only what his "blood," a combination of intuition and animal response, told him about Mexico. This approach, illustrated in the *huarache* scene, was his strength as well as his weakness as a reporter of Mexico. Because his response was always passionate, it always had vitality. His intuitions often uncovered the truth. But because he was not seeking knowledge and because he did not care enough for factual information, he tends to be incomplete and sometimes totally wrong.

In defense of his own approach, he sometimes went overboard, as here in this letter to Collings where he attacks knowledge and the intellectual approach.

> I conceive a man's body as a kind of flame, like a candle flame, forever upright and yet flowing; and the intellect is just the light that is shed on to the things around. And I am not so much concerned with the things around—which is really mind—but with the mystery of the flame, forever flowing, coming God knows how from out of practically nowhere, and being itself, whatever there is around it, that it lights up. We have got so ridiculously mindful, that we never know that we ourselves are anything—we think we are only the objects we shine on. And there the poor flame goes on burning ignored, to produce this light. And instead of chasing the mystery in the fugitive, half-lighted things outside us, we ought to look at ourselves. . . .

What Lawrence says here is applicable to those who see Mexico differently than he does. The world that each of us sees is always partly imaginary, overlapping reality but not always corresponding with it. Mex-icophiles who criticize Lawrence because his vision of Mexico does not square with theirs should rejoice that he provides so luminous a candle for sights and people they love.

Lawrence wrote the four Oaxaca essays of *Mornings in Mexico* around Christmas time when he was also deeply occupied with *The Plumed Serpent*. Perhaps he broke off the market essay shortly after the *huarache* scene because of his general plan to keep the sketches "nice and short," but one also senses he was tired, may have delivered as many market details as the reader could absorb, or felt he had given as many as were needed to make his two chief poetic points. Thus, he withdraws as a character following the ensuing scene.

> The great press of the quiet natives, some of them bright and clean, many in old rags, the brown flesh showing through the rents in the dirty cot-ton. Many wild hillmen, in their little hats of conical black felt, with their wild, staring eyes. And as they cluster round the hat-stall, in a long, long suspense of indecision before they can commit themselves, trying on a new hat, their black hair gleams blue-black, and falls thick and rich over their foreheads like gleaming bluey-black feathers.

Lawrence employs a characteristic but derogatory device for break-ing off. "But already the fleas," he writes, "are travelling under one's clothing." Certainly there are fleas in the market, but it is not flea-infested and I've never found one in my clothing after a visit. Lawrence always hated being among a "great press" of people and, unless the fleas were a lot worse in 1924 than they have been since 1947, I suspect Lawrence's discomfort grew from the crowded market which led him to imagine the fleas crawling on his skin. If he were going to describe the market's in-sects, it is surprising he did not mention the more obvious ones: the flies swarming over the purple-red strips of unrefrigerated meat, or the wasps, with their long narrow wings and tiger-striped abdomens, hovering over the macaroons, turnovers, meringues, cubes of cake and other sweet breads, piled neatly on boards supported by X-shaped folding stands.

Because he ended so abruptly, Lawrence omitted one of the mar-ket's most fascinating areas, now gone and replaced by the ugly Mercado 20 de Noviembre, with its sawtoothed roof like an assembly area in a factory. Across Aldama and through the narrow lane behind the little church of San Juan de Diós was the great uncovered market—the high-walled, wide, sunny place where they sold the brilliantly colored pot-tery, the baskets nested in each other to form straw towers of Pisa, the mats woven of pale gold palm strips, the hanks of rope and lengths of cream-colored cordage, and best of all, the great piles of vari-colored corn kernels displayed on palm leaf mats. (Plates 23 and 24.) The sheds roofed with shingles and reeds, and the numerous sheets strung up at odd angles or supported on Robinson Crusoe-like frames to provide shade make the scene all the more picturesque. In the large courtyard, pottery could be seen in abundance: some black, some bright red, some dark green, hundreds of lustrous nested bowls with daisy-like interiors. Brett photographed him looking down on just such bowls. (Plate 25.)

This market adjoining a church was at one time the Mercado San Juan de Diós, and, in more secular times, the Mercado de Industria, as it was devoted to handicrafts. Lawrence could have used both it and the church to illustrate one of the points he makes in the essay. "To buy and sell, but above all, to commingle. In the old world, men make themselves two great excuses for coming together to a centre, and commingling freely in a mixed, unsuspicious host. Market and religion."

The little church of San Juan de Diós, built on the site of Oaxaca's first cathedral, is the oldest church in the city, proving that the Indians of Oaxaca have been combining the two excuses since 1526, the year the church was founded. In fact, the market might have been encouraged to grow up around the church, for Oaxaca was only an Aztec garrison at the time of the coming of the Spaniards and had never been the site of a pre-Columbian market. The important city of the region was Zaachila, the Zapotec capital. San Juan, whose belfry barely clears the market roofs, has been much remodeled, Bishop Gillow giving it a thorough overhauling in 1889. Notwithstanding, it still remains one of the city's outstanding churches. A series of circular portraits around its upper walls depicts Oaxaca's bishops and church leaders of four centuries. Had Lawrence taken note of them he would have realized that before Shakespeare was born Oaxaca was already a Spanish-style city with cultivated inhabitants and spiritual leaders. He would have seen also a portrait of Gillow, his Bishop Severn, as a relatively young man, and Urbano Olivera's lively, semi-primitive murals of historical events which line the lower walls: a Spanish-Victorian reconstruction of the first mass said in Oaxaca, when Padre Juan Díaz elevated the Host under a *guaje* tree beside the Atoyac River in 1521; the baptism of Cosiojeza, the last Zapotec king, at Zaachila, for whom the cross street of Lawrence's rented house was named; and the events of 14-16 September 1700, in San Francisco Caxones, in the Villa Alta district where principal citizens had reverted to paganism. In these last paintings, two district attorneys lead Dominican friars to arrest a secret celebration of pagan rites; then enraged villagers break into the Dominican monastery to haul out the attorneys and behead them with machetes. These paintings would have excited Lawrence. In the draft of his novel he had already imagined and described men loyal to Quetzalcoatl executing priest-inspired marauders.

San Juan de Diós is proof of Lawrence's markets and religion theory. A large altar to the Virgin of Soledad almost blocks the entrance,
and the patroness of Oaxaca attracts so many kneeling worshippers that
to get into the church one generally has to squeeze between them. A chapel
dedicated to Christ carrying his cross also inspires intense devotion. In
a sense, the little church is almost a compendium of all the churches of
Oaxaca, for here are gathered San Juan Bosco, San Judas Tadeo, San Francisco de Paula, San José, San Felipe de Jesús, San Antonio de Padua, Santa
Rita, Jesus seated as the mocked king of the Jews, with a rope around
his neck; Jesus as a corpse laid out in a glass coffin, the Virgin of Carmen,
the Virgin of the Rosary, the Virgin of the Light, and the Virgin of Guadalupe, the Trinity, and, since Lawrence's day, the black San Martín de
Porres. Silver arms, legs, eyes, breasts, and hearts pinned to the holy personages' velvet backdrops indicate the organs the saints have cured or
been asked to cure. Each little shrine is adorned with fresh flowers, showing that marketers often drop in to pray to intercessors not found in their
own villages and whose larger altars elsewhere in the city they lack the
time to visit. Essentially it is the church of the peasant vendors and not
the storekeepers.

> Market lasts all day, [Lawrence went on.] The native inns are great dreary
> yards with little sheds, and little rooms around. Some men and families
> who have come from far, will sleep in one or other of the little stall-like
> rooms. Many will sleep on the stones, on the earth, round the market,
> anywhere. But the asses are there by the hundred, crowded in the inn-
> yards, dropping their ears with the eternal patience of the beast that knows
> better than any other beast that every road curves round to the same centre
> of rest, and hither and thither means nothing.

Lawrence might have also added that the Oaxaca market illustrated
the historic tendency of trade and religion to support each other. The
greatest of the inn-yards, the largest of the seven patios contained in the
Casa Fuerte, was part of a church establishment. This enormous two-story
building was constructed by the Jesuits on the north side of the market
shortly after their arrival in 1578 and covers all of the block except the
northeast corner, which they reserved for La Compañia, one of the hand-
somest churches in the city with the purest of baroque façades. One patio
was so large that it could be roofed over later to make a movie house,
the Cine Reforma.

But the largest one has been left uncovered. This great, arcaded,
secular cloister became the central parking place for the donkeys who
brought vendors and their goods into the market. The Jesuits were expelled from the New World in 1767. Lawrence should not have lumped

it as one of the "dreary yards with little sheds." Here, as elsewhere, his imagination failed in envisaging Oaxaca's elegance in the seventeenth and eighteenth centuries. To him it remained a wild and primitive little capital.

Lawrence's two previous trips to Mexico had taught him to haggle in the marketplace; the natives, he told Brett, were disappointed if you did not bargain. His statement that they liked their "moment of gossip" indicates that the seed of his market essay may have already been forming in his mind. In the essay itself, he says that of all the things exchanged in the market, the most cherished is human contact.

"That is why they like you to bargain, even if it's only the difference of a *centavo,*" he wrote. Then he describes refusing to buy a bunch of cherry-pie heliotrope because a woman would not let him have it for ten *centavos,* when she asked fifteen. "You put back the cherry-pie, and depart," he said, adding complacently what he could only speculate: "But the woman is quite content. The contact, so short even, brisked her up."

They pass on to another flower seller, and here he presents Brett as the bargainer. The vendor offers red pinks for thirty *centavos.*

"No, I don't want red ones. The mixed."

"Ah," The woman seizes a handful of little carnations of all colors, carefully put together. "Look Señorita! No more?"

"No, no more. How much?"

"The same. Thirty *centavos.*"

"It is much."

"No, Señorita, it is not much. Look at this little bunch. It is eight *centavos.*" Displays a scrappy little bunch. "Come then, twenty-five."

"No! Twenty-two."

"Look!" She gathers up three or four more flowers, and claps them to the bunch. "Two *reales,* Señorita."

It is a bargain. Off you go with your multi-colored pinks, and the woman has had one more moment of contact, with a stranger, a perfect stranger. An intermingling of voices, a threading together of different wills. It is life. The *centavos* are an excuse.

Although he never wallowed in self-pity, Lawrence seems to have been a lonely man. His motive behind the colony idea might have been his own need for human contact. And though he did not admit directly to loneliness, he sometimes revealed it through his characters. "All his life he had secretly grieved over his friendlessness," he poignantly states about Somers, his self-portrait in *Kangaroo.* And in December 1918 he summarized his case squarely to Katherine Mansfield, whose husband was Middleton Murry. "I do believe in friendship. I believe tremendously in friendship between man and man, a pledging of men to each other inviolably. But I have never met or formed such a friendship. Also I believe the same way in friendship between men and women, and between women and women, sworn, pledged, eternal, as eternal as the marriage bond, and as deep. But I have not met or formed such friendship."

Lawrence had always been frustrated in finding "the heart's brother, the answerer," terms he used in *Studies in Classic American Literature.* Concluding the Mansfield letter, he wrote, "I begin to despair altogether about human relationships—feel one may just as well turn into a sort of lone wolf, and have done with it." Four years later in his 29 September 1922 letter to Mrs. Carswell written after he had visited Ceylon, Australia, and the United States he stated, "Perhaps it is necessary for me to try these places. Perhaps it is my destiny to know the world. It only excites the outside of me. The inside it leaves more isolated and stoic than ever." Although Lawrence had the companionship of Frieda, she did not fill all his needs for friendship, love, and company. He was never able to be the lone wolf that he told Katherine Mansfield he felt he should be nor as stoical as he told Mrs. Carswell he was. As early as 1916, when he and Frieda were moving to Cornwall, he had persuaded Murry and Katherine to come and live with them in an adjoining cottage. From 1923 onward he repeatedly asked others to join him on his travels. In Mexico, even with Brett along, he had asked the Quintanillas to come to Oaxaca. Two years later in a July 1926 letter to Rolf Gardiner he said: "I should love to be connected with something, with some few people, in something. As far as anything *matters,* I have always been very much alone, and regretted it." However, he continually reached out to new friends. One sees a man fiercely insistent that he be left alone but always dreading actually being alone. This market essay betrays his inner loneliness more poignantly than any of his other writings. His heart went out to the Indians of Oaxaca because he saw them as lonely, too. He saw in them a symbol of humanity, traveling for miles and sleeping on rocks at night, just to achieve that thing as beautiful as the evening star, "the spark of contact."

Lawrence's view of the Oaxaca market was romantic even though he mentions fleas and pungent leather. Yet *centavos* do matter. People bring their little bunches of heliotrope to market to buy bread or a little cloth to dress a child. And the woman who he said was quite content when he rejected her flowers probably hid real disappointment.

The vortex vision of the market is also romantic, setting aside the economic force of the vortex. The Oaxaca market is only part of a larger market system. The Sunday market at Tlacolula, the Monday market at Miahuatlán, the Wednesday markets at Etla and Zimatlán, the Thursday market at Zaachila and the Friday market at Ocotlán all lead up to it and serve as relay stations for professional vendors who go from one to another. Thus villagers can bring wares to nearer markets. By the same token, not all villagers have to come as far as Oaxaca to buy things unavailable in their own villages, which is particularly important for the single-craft villages like Teotitlán del Valle (weaving) and Coyotopec and Azompa (pottery). The Oaxaca market helps sustain a great part of the state, as well as a way of life, "a peasant-like economy," as Ralph Beals, the anthropologist, calls it in "The Structure of the Oaxaca Market." In that article, a predecessor to his full-length study, he spells out how the Oaxaca market is a crucial part "in a system of exchange which links village with village in an extensive interdependent network." Because such a network functions well, the villages within it, despite their economic dependence on each other and on Oaxaca, can retain a good deal of social and political autonomy.

Lawrence's highly praised essay catches much of the spirit and the appearance of this important Mexican market; nothing else on the Oaxaca market can match it as literature. But gifted as Lawrence was, he did not capture the reality that teemed before his senses. He reduced Oaxaca's variety and scope, failed to include the market's past as well as its continuity, and by minimizing its economic basis, reduces a major phenomenon to an almost fairy-tale vision. However, no one before him had seen the market with his particular insight, and his vision is marvelously poetic. After describing the joy of being "part of a great stream of men flowing to a centre" and having "felt life concentrate upon them," he describes their departure: "And towards nightfall the dusty road will be thronged with shadowy people and unladed asses and new-laden mules, urging silently into the country again, their backs to the town, glad to get away from the town, to see the cactus and the pleated hills, and the trees that mean a village. In some village they will lie under a tree, or under a wall and sleep. Then the next day, home."[2]

CHAPTER 4

THE KULLS
AND
THEIR *MOZO*

"**T**hey kept more company with us than with anyone," was how the Swiss dentist sized up their relationship with the Lawrences in Oaxaca. "D. H. and Frieda took to us, and we to them, and we enjoyed their company very much. Perhaps because we also were Europeans, and perhaps because he felt that we comprehended him best."

Hermann Kull is "the foreign resident" whose kindness to his servant is detailed in "The Mozo," the third of the Oaxaca essays in *Mornings in Mexico.* He was the only non-Mexican Lawrence wrote about.

Ethel Doctor told of an Austrian or German dentist in Oaxaca who was often entertained by the Lawrences. The wife was an artist. She did not remember his first name nor did Harloe Hamilton but predicted I would find it in the Mexico City telephone book. Kull, he said, was the Swiss consul. A friend who was renting the house answered my phone call and laughed at the idea of Kull being the Swiss consul. They had moved to a house in Cuernavaca which had no phone. I began writing to them in 1962 and met them 7 October 1963.

The Kulls had been away from Oaxaca for thirty-seven years, had lost touch with the Lawrences, and had no idea that either *Mornings in Mexico* or *Lawrence and Brett* had been published, much less that they had appeared in both books. Hermann wrote back promptly and cordially in fluent English. He had left Switzerland at twenty-one and had lived nine years in the United States, where he received nearly all his dental training. Born in Olten in 1889, he was four years younger than Lawrence and his wife, Carola, was a Lithuanian of German parents, born near Riga. She was not a professional artist, as Miss Doctor thought, but a self-taught amateur. (Plate 26.) The fifth letter included a snapshot of them smiling on a tennis court "in their younger days." Their new home, Villa Carola, was in the Lomas de San Antón, a new *colonia,* located in the hills above the San Antón Falls.

They invited me to call on them and greeted me cordially, even though I had arrived in advance of my confirming telegram. Carola rustled up a lunch of sausages, spaghetti, cucumber salad, brownies, and coffee.

The sausages prompted me to exclaim, "But I thought you were vegetarians!" They did not let it interfere with their hospitality, they said. Then I remembered what Hermann had written: "We never discuss either religion or vegetarianism with our friends, but serve them their flesh-pots. So I don't remember whether or not Lawrence was interested in our way of life in this respect."

Carola was plumper than in her snapshot, but her somewhat scraggly hair was the same red gold I had anticipated and I loved the humor in her bright blue eyes. Hermann, too, was a good deal heavier than in his tennis-playing days, but his big frame carried the extra weight easily. He was a ruddy, hearty man, whose blue eyes protruded slightly behind his glasses. How compatible they were was emphasized at the end of the visit. "Good-bye, old girl," he said, as he was about to drive me to the limousine station. And they gave each other a good kiss, even though the parting was to be so short.

Hermann explained how they happened to live in Oaxaca. His wanderlust had propelled him beyond the United States to Mexico, where he had become a junior partner of Dr. Cornish, an Englishman with a practice in Puebla. The older dentist announced he was returning to England. He told Hermann how much Oaxaca needed a modern dentist.

Rosalind Hughes, a friend of the Kulls, had described their tennis court and garden as "the center of much of the social life. He was a tall, slender, handsome blonde, and she a little, lively, bright young woman who brought many people together on their court or garden for refreshments. They did much to enliven the social life of Oaxaca and had many friends."

Curious about where the court was located I brought a little map of Oaxaca and asked the Kulls to show me where it had been. They could only say it was "up near the river." They could not recall a single Lawrence visit, even as spectators, but had vivid memories of Brett on the court. "Oh bother," she used to exclaim whenever she missed the ball.

Inocente Cruz was the Kulls' *mozo* who had ridden on his pony to the picnic-breakfast on Monte Alban and had helped the Lawrences move from the Francia. He was about twenty at the time, from a village in the Sierra de Juárez about two days journey away. Besides keeping the court and garden in order, he used to collect the balls for the players. With impressive endurance, he would pick up tennis balls on both ends of the court, running like lightning. Inocente was also unusually handy, and Hermann trained him to help with his laboratory work, polishing the bridges and plates.

Kull's office was at the front of the second floor above the Farmacia Hidalgo next to the Alameda Hotel. For the first part of their stay the

Kulls lived behind the office, with their living quarters divided from the working ones by only a curtain.

During this period Carola contracted typhoid fever and nearly died. "The doctors in those days, and in Oaxaca, knew little or nothing about the disease. They did not have the defenses of the antibiotics. There was a moment when Carola was floating off into the higher spheres, as she put it, where all was peace and harmony. But I wouldn't let her stay there long, but brought her back by other 'spiritual means'—a good shot of brandy."

They moved later, a block up 20 de Noviembre and then around the corner to the second house on Independencia. From Hermann's description of two French windows with fancy ironwork facing the street, I identified it later in Oaxaca as Independencia 506. Since 1955 the front *sala* has been rented to Emy, a beauty parlor, and one of the French windows now serves as an entrance. It is up the street from "the Bishop's Palace," Carola's description of the archducal mansion that wealthy Gillow built for himself in 1895, a building that now houses Oaxaca's post office and telegraph office.

The Kulls intended to move to Mexico City but in December 1924 some German coffee planters near the coast offered to pay well if he would bring his dental equipment to a central point in the region of the coffee *fincas* so they could get caught up on necessary dental work. Thus commenced their biggest Mexican adventure. With the help of Inocente, they packed the dismounted foot lathe in a specially made flat box, folded the portable chair into its neat case, sealed the plaster needed for eight months work in ten-gallon alcohol cans, and packed the rest of the necessary material in grocery cartons. On 5 February 1925, with their luggage, boxes, and Inocente, they boarded the train to Ejutla, which was as far as the railroad went. There on nine mules sent by the planters, they began a four-day ride over rocky trails that took them over some of the highest passes in that part of the Sierra Madre. The lead boy and the three additional *mozos* provided by the planters made the trip barefoot.

Hermann gave dental service for two months to people from four coffee plantations in Alemania. Then he moved nearer the coast of Pochutla. Here Carola saved Hermann's life by grabbing the knife-wielding arm of a man about to stab him in the back, who was furious at Hermann for not putting as many false teeth into his wife's mouth as the number extracted. He thought he was being cheated.[1]

Glad to get out of Pochutla alive, the Kulls moved to Puerto Angel, took a little steamer up the coast, and finally, in November, after working in a number of cattle and cotton towns ravaged by the Revolution, headed for Mexico City riding saddle-horses. In the capital Hermann bought a practice and worked sixteen years in his own office. But in 1941, when he was fifty-two the combination of waiting for patients and the tension of the work, aggravated by the strain on the eyes, led him to give up active dentistry. First he taught it, then in 1945 he became a professional representative in Mexico and Central America for the Dentist's Supply Company of New York. He lived in a small house with a beautiful garden in the Lomas of Chapultepec, but he still traveled to show dentists how to use the new materials.

The Kulls had never heard of D. H. Lawrence when he arrived in Oaxaca and could not recall their first meeting. Hermann wrote in an early letter, "Foreign residents in a town the size of Oaxaca are few and far between and therefore get to meet each other readily. Most likely they had heard of the Swiss dentist and were first in calling on us. They were rather on the poor side, and neither made a big impression when they arrived. It was only later, through his conversation, that Lawrence impressed me as a genius. He always called me Dr. Coll. We got together quite often, sometimes for dinner at our flat, and sometimes for a chat at their home. While we did most of the entertaining, we went to dinner several times to the Lawrences'." Brett also refers to the hospitality of the Kulls and of others who had been through the de la Huerta rebellion:

> We are lunched and dined. Our social life is looked after by the few Americans who have weathered the storm of the Revolution and are thankful beyond measure to have someone to talk to. But you make one firm stipulation:
>
> "I will come," you say, "if the meal is at the time you mention—if I have not to wait from seven until nine. If the dinner is at seven, I will come at seven; if at nine, I will come at nine—but I don't like waiting."

Suspecting it might have been at the Kulls' that Lawrence was not fed until the customary hour for *cena* in Oaxaca, I asked Brett. She recalled "It was very ornate, marvelous food, but so late Lawrence was starved and tired before it appeared," and she could not recall the hosts. It sounded more like a party at Emma Thompson's. Hermann recalled that "only once did we have a rather large crowd at dinner. After that it was Lawrence's express wish that our get-togethers be of a more intimate nature and that we keep to ourselves."

Three years earlier, when Mabel Luhan had invited Lawrence to come to New Mexico, he had given her the warning that she included in *Lorenzo in Taos:* "We are very practical, do all our own work, even the washing, cooking, floor-cleaning and everything here in Taormina: because I loathe servants creeping around. They poison the atmosphere. So I prefer to wash my own shirts, etc. And I like doing things."

Hermann gave evidence that Lawrence kept house in Oaxaca as he had in Sicily. "When we went to dinner," Hermann said, "it was he who did the cooking and the setting of the table. It was very nice food." Rosalind Hughes corraborates: "I had tea with them several times on the *corredor,* at a small onyx table, and Lawrence himself made the tea and brought it out in a clay pot."

That Lawrence liked housework is shown by the paean to dishwashing in "Education of the People," begun as an unsuccessful foray into journalism when he was desperate for money at the end of World War I: "If I wash the dishes, I learn a quick, light touch of china and earthenware, the feel of it, the weight and roll and poise of it, the peculiar hotness, the quickness or slowness of its surface. I am at the middle of an infinite complexity of motions and adjustments and quick, apprehensive contacts." In the same essay he elevated into an ideal for education what he himself had learned as a boy. To become independent and self-reliant he said, every child should "clean its own boots, brush and fold its own clothes, fetch and carry for itself, mend its own stockings, boy or girl alike, patch its own garments, and as soon as possible make as well as mend for itself." In a November 1927 letter to Frieda's mother he told the Baroness, "Thank the Lord, I am still small enough to mend my socks and wash my cup."

The Lawrences did not talk about their pasts with the Kulls, who refrained from prying. Hermann knew little about Frieda's life in England. He gathered after knowing her for three months that she had first been married to an English lord for twenty-five years and had two grown sons. That her husband had been a Nottingham professor fifteen years her senior; that the marriage lasted thirteen years; that Frieda abandoned a boy and two girls in running off with Lawrence; and that she had lived with him unwed until her divorce in 1914, were surprises. They already knew that Frieda was related to von Richthofen, the German war ace, whose inherited title and prowess as a fighter pilot in World War I earned him the nickname "The Red Baron." Hermann, not knowing how much Frieda liked to scrub floors, attributed Lawrence's housekeeping to her aristocracy.

"She was born into a family, which would have never thought of training her to be a *hausfrau*. Children and young ladies of her time lived a sheltered life, under the guidance of a governess almost up to the time of marriage. But Frieda was an outspoken, frank and down-to-earth soul and we liked her very much indeed. Never did she make you feel she was of 'noble birth.' " Later he said he thought Frieda might have been over-sexed and that she was "kind of husky, heavy-set, more on the fat side, blonde, a good skin, a cultured woman."

"A good scout," was Carola's verdict.

"Brett," Hermann said, "treated Frieda as if she, 'Lady' Brett, was in first place. Brett," he continued, "could not hide a certain British snobbishness. She could be rather pleasing company, but she did keep you at a distance. Perhaps this attitude, though, had to do with her defective hearing. All in all, we think Brett to be not only just naive or dumb, but downright cruel by wedging herself constantly between Frieda and Lawrence, who were fond of each other, but who for years had seldom had a moment to themselves."

With a roughness, quickened perhaps by her criticism of Carola's painting, Hermann described Brett as "the third wheel on the wagon." He remembered both Frieda and Lawrence complaining about her. Frieda said, "She simply won't be put out. If only I could get rid of her." Lawrence's opinion was a shade kindlier: "She's a lonely old thing. She insists that I need a secretary and I can't get rid of her."

Two stories in *Lawrence and Brett* depict the Kulls as bystanders in her triangular relationship. The first is set in one of Oaxaca's pleasantest features—the outdoor cafés. They are located in the *portales,* the arcades in front of the shops and bar-restaurants bounding the square. The activity of the square, the lovely weather, and the lack of pressure to order and move on make the cafés always popular, especially in the evenings when people have time to sit and talk. In the first story Frieda was at home and Brett and Lawrence were in the *portales* together:

What can be the matter? A giggling crowd is staring into a shop window. You and I have been having some drinks in the Zócola. We are so intrigued by the giggling crowd that, finishing our drinks, we go and look. The crowd parts to let us through; the waiters are now grinning. There, in the middle of the window, is a caricature of you: a good one, too, after a fashion. The crowd is delighted and watches you with amusement. You are amused, too, in an impersonal way.

We go off, laughing, and join the Kulls. This means more drinks— but they are light and easy, these drinks. Then the Kulls invite us to their flat to have some brandy. You talk about the cruelty of races, especially of the dark races—when suddenly you realize it is nine o'clock. You get up and run home.

Next day, when I come up, you tell me Frieda was in a towering rage. Then Frieda joins in the tale:

"He kept me waiting," she cries, "Kept me waiting!" The emphasis on the "me" astonishes me.

"Why not?" I ask, rather tactlessly and fruitlessly.

In Brett's second story,

Frieda is in a rage this afternoon, when I come up. She is attacking me. You are not here—you are hurt and angry and have gone out. Frieda says

I spoil all her fun, that I laugh at her and so on. And now she has run into the garden. I am perplexed and vexed.

"Come on, Frieda," I call to her. "Let us have a talk." I talk and talk to her, but her eyes are still mistrustful, they dart about, looking at nothing; her mouth is a tight line.

Then the Kulls come and the moment is broken. I go out with them, down to the town; and in the Zócola on a bench I see you sitting. You are pale, remote, abstract, your eyes unseeing, your whole figure withdrawn, untouchable. Therefore we must needs go up and break into your isolation. I cannot prevent it. I feel your strong resistance; I am appalled at the feeling of hate that pours out of you as you are disturbed. It makes me shiver, nervous as I am already from the earlier scene. What is happening? What is it all about?

Hermann and Carola knew the triangle caused tension, but they "did not remember any 'scenes' between D. H. and Frieda and I never saw Lawrence angry," said Hermann. "The resistance Brett sensed was probably what poor Lawrence must have really felt towards her. What a brazen intrusion into the life of a married couple! No wonder Lawrence and Frieda were sick so often." Lawrence's illness on one occasion frustrated the Kulls when they were all planning to ride to Monte Alban. Lawrence was not feeling well enough to undertake the excursion. Frieda stayed home too, but Brett went. She wrote me about the outing in November 1962, but a better account of her visit to the ruins appears in the portion of her autobiography, "My Long and Beautiful Journey" which was published in the 1967 summer issue of *South Dakota Review.* "Only one Indian, with a machete that was as long as he was tall, was there guarding the first attempt to dig. I went with the dentist, Dr. Kull, and his wife: it was a long ride on uncomfortable wooden saddles. I had no idea how near the place I was, as I was riding somewhat behind the others, but all of a sudden I could feel the strong vibrations of the last spirit of the place. Just as at Mitla, I could almost smell the blood of sacrifices."

That climb was probably on 6 January 1925 for there is a Lawrence letter of that date at the University of Texas which tells the younger Hawk that this morning "Brett went riding horseback with the dentist and his wife—Swiss—and she came home almost in tears, for the ranch. I never saw her so depressed."

Kull was amused at anyone smelling blood at ruins that had been abandoned more than four centuries. But he remembered the climb and agreed that the ancient ceremonial center, even in its unexcavated state, made a strong impression.

Because the Kulls arrived in Oaxaca shortly before the death of Archbishop Gillow, they were able to meet him. "Gillow," wrote

Hermann, "was a fine old gentleman who had the good grace to invite us to one of his receptions, even knowing that we were not members of his Church. There was something of the Irish wit about him. When it came to shaking hands with him and kissing his ring by the faithful there was just an imperceptible little smile on his features when, just ahead of Carola, a fat old lady got down on her knees and could hardly get up again, after doing what was her religious duty. He was pleased, evidently, that we just shook hands, with a little reverent bow in recognition of his high station."

Since Hermann relished his own stories and remembered this one so well forty-two years later, he told me that he probably told it to Lawrence, who was also collecting Gillow stories from Padre Rickards. Since the Kull house was in the next block from Gillow's palace, another safe assumption is that Kull explained the conspicuous residence to Lawrence. Humorous, anticlerical—his niece in Oregon "had already made it known that there is no salvation for poor old Uncle Hermann"—he undoubtedly pointed out to Lawrence a joke built into the façade of the palace. The Gillow coat of arms appears in the arched pediment over the neo-Classic main entrance, and sheltering the armorial bearings is a wide-brimmed pontifical hat with a full complement of cardinal's tassels. When Gillow built the palace he was convinced he would become a cardinal. Porfirio Díaz, who proposed him as Mexico's first cardinal, and Gillow would have had their wish had there not been a law forbidding a Mexican cardinal.

Because the *Hospital Militar,* which had preempted Gillow's seminary, was across from the Kulls' tennis court, it is likely that the dentist also told Lawrence that he was now living near where García Vigil had rebelled against theology. Lawrence, hearing the same story from Padre Rickards, was more influenced by the career of García Vigil than by that of Benito Juárez in remodeling his character Cipriano. L. D. Clark first suggested Juárez as Lawrence's leading model for his political figure who started his career in a seminary. It was probably from Juárez that Lawrence got the idea of making Cipriano a Zapotec Indian, for García Vigil was a mestizo with relatively little Indian blood. But Lawrence was well acquainted with the Juárez story earlier and could have used him in the first draft. Oaxaca undoubtedly made Lawrence more conscious of Juárez, but it was finding a second instance of a revolutionary patriot beginning as a seminarian that gave the novelist his new idea, and fit well with his idea of giving Cipriano a bishop for a patron. Futhermore García Vigil took up the soldier's profession (Juárez never did), became a general in the Revolution (Juárez, a lawyer, died thirty-eight years before it began), lived in the epoch of Lawrence's novel, and though by no means entirely like the recast Cipriano, in his campaigning against drunkenness, his military quickness, his impulsiveness, and his sexual vitality, resembled Lawrence's hero far more than the austere and unbending Don Benito. Kull appears to be one who told Lawrence most about García Vigil and who gave him the clearest idea of the energetic personality of the young governor. Vicariously acquainted with the governor through his sister, Kull saw him as "a young and rather brave man," a view from which he never wavered despite the red mark the governor ordered painted on the homes of all foreigners.

"Somehow," wrote Kull, "García Vigil had heard of my sister [Lydia] and sent for her to see if she could ease his condition. She could alright, for it wasn't long before he could get around with a cane only as a support." Meanwhile in December 1923 came the outbreak of the de la Huerta rebellion, into which García Vigil drew the state.

Oaxaca was immediately cut off from the rest of the nation. When the isolation became protracted, as Kull was to write, it "caused a complete collapse of the city's economy." Miss Doctor explained, "While Oaxaca was incommunicado with the rest of the world, we received no mail, no lights, no trains. Fortunately, we were able to borrow money to live on. In fact, a certain merchant who knew he would get it back later, was glad to give us the money because Governor Vigil demanded money from all who had it."

Using these accounts and combining them with memories of his trip from Mexico City, Lawrence described the situation in his own terms in "The Flying Fish," his last work written in Oaxaca.

> Little revolutions had again broken the thread of railway at the end of which the southern town hung revolving like a spider. It was a narrow-gauge railway, one single narrow little track which ran over the plateau, then slipped down, down the long *barranca,* descending five thousand feet down to the valley which was a cleft in the plateau, then up again seven thousand feet, to the higher plateau to the north. How easy to break the thread! One of the innumerable little wooden bridges destroyed, and it was done. The three hundred miles to the north were impassable wilderness, like the hundred and fifty miles through the low-lying jungle to the south.

In this passage, he reconstructs his own journey in reverse to picture leaving the Valley of Oaxaca as the start of the trip, then the descent into the Tomellín canyon as the second stage. He even imagined the wild, mountainous, railroadless area between Oaxaca and the Pacific Coast that he never traversed, but which he heard about. The image of Oaxaca as a spider revolving at the end of one of its own strands is powerful and no doubt original.

A month after the spider's thread snapped, there was suddenly sharp excitement. "About 5 o'clock one morning we were awakened by shooting going on in the streets," recalled Kull. "The shooting spree lasted all day until about 5 P.M. Result: one dead Serrano and several wounded. Among the pictures I am sending you'll notice the one marked 'sad remnants of a revolutionary army.' They must have been the ones who defeated the Serranos, under García Vigil's leadership. Somewhere I have a small bullet, I believe a 22 caliber, or a 38, which I found later on my tennis court." (Plate 27.)

The horsemen outside the cathedral had been among those who saved the city by keeping control of El Fortín. The "shooting spree" was the one-day attack of 12 January 1924 that García Vigil repulsed.

Miss Doctor also dramatized the one-day invasion. Living with Mr. and Mrs. Norman Taylor, looking after a dozen children from the hills, she wrote: "One night, I was awakened by a soldier climbing a ladder (over a bedroom window to the roof.) I called Norman and we went to see what was up. The soldier was taking over our house as a strategic firing point. They expected a rebel group to attack the city."

Because the governor's troops wanted to use their house as a watch-tower each night, Miss Doctor, the Taylors, and the native girl arranged to sleep thereafter at the McEwens' house. Charles McEwen, one of the mining engineers, was a one-armed Canadian. His home is significant to the Lawrence story because it was across the street from Padre Rickards's. Miss Doctor must have pointed to it as the one in which they took refuge each night after their roof was commandeered:

> The boys stayed in their quarters, which was a separate house in the second patio of our house. They slept on *petates* on the floor. We figured they could climb over the back walls and come out through the yards of houses on other streets—if they must. Each morning we went back to our house when the soldiers left, to live and make our meals. Business went on everywhere as usual during the day. Trenches were built where the Pan-American highway is now. What is now Oaxaca Courts was out of bounds. No one went out of the city—that far.[2]

Perhaps Lawrence thought it strange that fate had brought him to live in a battle zone of the rebellion that had almost caught him in Veracruz; his house was near García Vigil's defense point. Undoubtedly Kull told the novelist what he told me: that the day García Vigil had to ride to El Fortín to fend off the *Serranos,* the effort of mounting his horse tore open the knee that Lydia Kull had helped by massages. Perhaps, too, Kull relayed two of his vignettes of the "holing in": how he saw one of the mercenaries ready to defend the city with the German Iron Cross pinned on his khaki uniform; and how at another time he met a defender who was a "drunken down-at-heels, who had been a colonel in Pancho Villa's army."

Jean and Colonel Akin were other members of the foreign colony who also lived through the isolation. They had been at Taviche near their mine when the rebellion broke out and, like other mining personnel, had to leave the mines unguarded to come to safer precincts in the city. Not liking Lawrence, Colonel Akin was probably not very communicative to the novelist about the experience, but after it was over he wrote about it at some length—and with some exaggeration for dramatic effect—to his friend, Hugh A. Smith, the cashier of the Farmers Nations Bank in Topeka.

> We were absolutely cut off from all communications for over four months—not a letter, in or out, not a newspaper, not a telegram, nor anything, and for three months we were confined to the City of Oaxaca, where we refugeed in December. . . . We did not have a particularly joyful, nor did we have an especially sad time during our internment, but it is gone now and we are safe. We went through one battle [this would be the invasion of the *Serranos*] in which several hundred were killed, and there were a number of skirmishes of little import. A four-inch ventilator back of our room had eleven bullet holes in it and the balcony of our sitting room some bullet marks, so you can judge how near we were to the center of things. The governor's palace, which was the objective, is exactly one block from the hotel in which we stayed in Oaxaca during our internment. All's well that ends well.

Jean's relatives, having heard nothing, had sought the aid of the Red Cross in getting word of her. She told them the story in person on her visit home at the time of Lawrence's arrival in Oaxaca. Lawrence had already moved to Padre Rickards's before she got back.

A result of the *Serrano* attack was a wholesale imprisonment of *Serranos* who García Vigil feared might betray him. Inocente Cruz, the Kulls' *mozo,* was picked up outside his hut on the Kulls' tennis court.

The city jail was then in the remodeled convent of Santa Catalina at the corner of Cinco de Mayo and Abasolo (Plate 28), and even after its renovation to a luxury hotel in 1976, the words JUZGADO, almost erased by time, could still be read in the high wall around the corner from the façade. The jail was en route to the priest's house and Lawrence must have passed it often on the way home. In "The Mozo" he describes prisoners being taken to it by armed soldiers. Lawrence retells Inocente's story, disguising his identity as Aurelio.

Yet that little Aurelio, the friend's *mozo,* who is not above four feet six in height, a tiny fellow, fared even worse. He, too, is from the hills. In his village, a cousin of his gave some information to the *losing* side of the revolution. [At this juncture, the cousin's fellow-*Serranos* were the losers.] The cousin wisely disappeared.

But in the city, the winning side [that of García Vigil] seized Aurelio, since he was the *cousin* of the delinquent. In spite of the fact that he was the faithful *mozo* of a foreign resident, he was flung into prison. Prisoners in prison are not fed. Either friends or relatives bring them food, or they go very, very thin. Aurelio had a married sister in town, but *she* was afraid to go to the prison, least she and her husband should be seized. The master, then, sent his new *mozo* twice a day to the prison with a basket; the huge prison, for this little town of a few thousands.

Meanwhile the master struggled and struggled with the "authorities"—friends of the people—for Aurelio's release. Nothing to be done.

One day the new *mozo* arrived at the prison with the basket, to find no Aurelio. A friendly soldier gave the message Aurelio had left. *"Adiós a mi patron. Me llevan."* Oh, fatal words: *"Me llevan"* —They are taking me off. The master rushed to the train: it had gone, with the dwarf, plucky little *mozo,* into the void.

Months later, Aurelio reappeared. He was in rags, haggard, and his dark throat was swollen up to the ears. He had been taken off, two hundred miles into Vera Cruz State. He had been hung up by the neck, with a fixed knot, and left hanging for hours. Why? To make the cousin come and save his relative: put his own neck into a running noose. To make the absolutely innocent fellow confess: What? Everybody knew he was innocent. At any rate, to teach everybody better next time. Oh, brotherly teaching!

Aurelio escaped, and took to the mountains. Sturdy little dwarf of a fellow, he made his way back, begging tortillas at the villages, and arrived, haggard, with a great swollen neck, to find his master waiting, and another "party" in power [Ibarra's, supported by Federal troops]. More friends of the people.

Tomorrow is another day. The master nursed Aurelio well, and Aurelio is a strong, if tiny fellow, with big brilliant black eyes that for the moment will trust a foreigner, but none of his own people.

"Of course it was the García Vigil gang who put Inocente in jail," Kull wrote me after I had sent him the Lawrence account.

These poor devils had to pay for something in which they had not taken a direct action. I know nothing about a cousin of Inocente being mixed up with or being guilty of his arrest. Inocente, to my knowledge, was not the political type. But, as I recollect it, every *Serrano* being caught was just put into prison on "general principles." Otherwise Lawrence's story is correct and complete in every respect. I was foolhardy enough to think that I could get Inocente out of jail, but of course didn't get even near the Governor's office. He then had other worries of greater import than to think of getting a mere *mozo* out of jail. I think the reason of Lawrence not mentioning my name was precaution. He probably thought that getting me mixed up with those troublesome times might still incriminate me as a foreigner.

The worries of greater importance on García Vigil's mind were the advancing federal troops under the leadership of General Almazán. General Diéquez, the defeated Jalisco leader who sought refuge in Oaxaca with his 400 charros convinced García Vigil that a garrison on the hill and trenches on the outskirts of the city would not hold off the government's approaching division. Accordingly, García Vigil evacuated the city six weeks after he had beaten off the *Serranos*. Almazán and Ibarra entered Oaxaca two days later.

This ended the city's isolation. Soon trains began arriving regularly from Mexico City and payment of federal employees was resumed. The *Mercurio* of those days conveys a sense of relief. Meanwhile, to the south, the fleeing García Vigil was suffering from gangrene in his knee until he was shot.

The governor's gangrenous leg appears in the Mexican chapters of Aldous Huxley's *Eyeless in Gaza,* a novel, written after Lawrence had returned to Europe and renewed his friendship with Huxley, written— in fact after Lawrence's death. Huxley wanted to include a Mexican insurrection. All was quiet on his 1933 visit. He drew on Lawrence's stories of the de la Huerta rebellion with four parallels too striking to be coincidental. First, Huxley's hero and the soldier of fortune he accompanied to Mexico missed the abortive insurrection they planned to assist. (Although not wanting to participate, Lawrence also missed a rebellion that failed.) Next, Huxley set his uprising against the state government in Oaxaca (the area where Lawrence learned most about the rising against Obregón.) Third, Huxley's hero was shocked by the way the defeated rebels were shot in the cemetery where their graves were already dug (just as Lawrence was shocked by the way Obregón hunted down the de la Huerta rebels.) Fourth, Huxley's characters were unable to reach the rebels because the soldier of fortune smashed open his left knee, insisted on pressing on, and developed gangrene.

Kull's stories deepened Lawrence's sense of tragic cynicism about Mexico.

Inocente had returned by the time the Lawrences shifted from the hotel to the priest's house, for he helped them move. "Van" is the word Lawrence used for the horse-drawn transport, but Kull, remembering no closed vans in Oaxaca then, describes it as an open wagon. Piled on it were the pieces of furniture the Lawrences had borrowed. Miss Hughes remembers that one of the beds was a double one, and that there were also a chest and a brazier. Included were also two trunks, a suitcase, and a hat box; Lawrence's brown satchel that is preserved in the Museum of New Mexico at Santa Fe included the American Railway Express Company receipt for the baggage made out on 30 March 1925 in Santa Fe when the Lawrences reclaimed their luggage on their return from Mexico.[3] Since Lawrence carefully detailed for his mother-in-law the luggage with which he and Frieda had left Taormina more than two years before, it can be judged that one of the trunks was his and the other Frieda's, and that they took most of their belongings to Mexico except the "household trunk" and the "book trunk" they had in Sicily. Probably those held many of the "better things," like "silverware, rugs, . . . pictures" that they had left in the care of the Hawks at Del Monte.

Also in the satchel preserved in Santa Fe was Lawrence's sewing kit, inherited from his mother, with thimbles, needles, wool, and thread. Brett records that on the first leg of their train trip to Oaxaca, the ride to Esperanza, "you have disappeared. Frieda is trying to sleep, so I go off to look for you. I find you further down the carriage, sitting quietly, mending your socks. Your bag is open beside you, with your little case of threads and needles and scissors laid out on the seat. . . . You smile and your eyes twinkle as you see me eyeing the socks and your bare foot on the opposite seat. "Might as well," you say. "Nothing else to do."

Lawrence kept his money and checkbooks in the satchel; while he was in Australia, he had a nightmare about it, recorded in *Kangaroo*. "They are going to steal my little brown handbag from the bedroom, which contains all the money we have." At the time of the move, Brett recorded:

> "One tiny little Indian, the *mozo* of the dentist, Dr. Kull, is reluctant to carry anything very heavy; and as for the *mozo* that has been found for you, he seems to dread anything of any weight on his back also. You are astonished and annoyed."
>
> "Are they lazy?" you enquire.

Brett wrote her recollections after Lawrence's death and without checking her memories against *Mornings in Mexico*. Her versions often differ from his. In retelling Inocente's story, she ignores his *Serrano* background, includes the "cousin," says both were suspected of robbing the cathedral collection box, and speaks of the hanging first "to try and wring a confession out of him" and the transportation to Veracruz second. She agrees that Inocente "escaped and returned, starving and ill, neck still swollen, to Dr. Kull" and for this reason he shrank from lifting and carrying.

The grateful *mozo* remained loyal to the Kulls. After they left the Costa Chica, he returned to Oaxaca, married, and raised a large family. In the 1950s he made a special trip to Mexico City to show off his wife and children to his old *patrón,* bringing gifts of eggs and plants from the country.

The Kulls could not date their encounters with the Lawrences, but I was able to learn approximate dates of four of them. The *Mercurio* of 7 December 1924 announced the opening of the tournament of the Oaxaca Lawn Tennis Club with the first round of the mixed doubles: Mrs. Kull and Muciño, the editor of the paper, vs. Mrs. Akin and Robert Wilson.

Carola and Muciño, both nearing forty, were considerably older than their opponents, but they beat the younger players handily. Jean, whom Hermann remembered as being a "southpaw" and whom Carola recalled as having "beautiful eyelashes," protested the verdict and asked that the set be replayed. Again the older pair won, and this time, according to the Kulls, Jean got mad. The Kulls thought she was a poor sport, especially when she took revenge through a tea party on 7 January for a group of diplomats visiting Oaxaca. Ernest Lagarde, the secretary of the French legation, was the senior member with Dr. Francisco Sedlacek, secretary of the Czechoslovakian legation, Stuart Grummon, secretary of the United States embassy, and Lieutenant-Colonel George M. Russell, military attaché of the United States embassy. Oaxaca's mayor designated them guests of the city. They were taken to the ruins of Mitla, and on 10 January all Oaxaca society turned out for a grand ball in their honor at the opera house and an elaborate tea given by Jean Akin. Colonel Russell was "a particular friend of my husband," Jean recalled. "Frieda was quite popular" at the event which the Kulls recall as a tea in her honor. "It was quite a nice tea," remembered the hostess, but Carola Kull was not invited. When Frieda asked why, Jean explained that she hadn't invited the Lithuanian-German Mrs. Kull because she was "a foreigner."

"Well, so am I," retorted Frieda, adding, "And so are you."

The Kulls, who must have heard the story from Frieda, thought this squelch richly deserved and narrated it with relish. Lawrence did not attend the tea by his own choice.

As Christmas was approaching, Frieda wanted to give the Kulls some present to thank them for their kindness. Brett took a photograph of the Lawrences in the Hall of Columns at Mitla, and Frieda sent it, "with a note scribbled by Frieda on the reverse, asking us to accept the little Christmas gifts they were sending us, or rather my wife, consisting of a lovely bead purse and a light-as-a-feather cashmere shawl, still treasured possessions." (Plate 29.)

The purse was an evening bag for opera glasses in dark blue worked with red roses. It had a bead tassel hanging from its rounded base and could be hung from the wrist by drawstrings. Wanting to see that Carola had something she could not get in Oaxaca, Frieda had parted with one of her keepsakes.

During this period Lawrence was eager to acquire copies of some of his books. In his card of 7 December to William Hawk he requested, "If a parcel of books comes— *The Boy in the Bush* or *The Memoirs of the Foreign Legion,* send me a copy of each here, please, so that I can give them to people." About eleven days later he wrote Edward Weston: "There is supposed to be a parcel of my books on its way to me, but it must have fallen into somebody's pocket." The books still had not arrived by 23 December for on that day he had to turn down Lady Cynthia Asquith's request for an autographed volume to be sold for charity. He could not oblige his loyal friend of World War I days, he explained, because he did not have any of his books on hand. When the requested two arrived, he promised to autograph one and send it, even though it would be too late for her bazaar. On 6 January 1925 he wrote young Hawk again, "The post is such a weariness & struggle here, & they keep on *losing* the things sent me from New York; so that one gets disheartened." But on January 14, a parcel arrived containing a book he had asked Hawk to send, Maurice Magnus's *Memoirs of the Foreign Legion,* for which he had written a long introduction. Lawrence characterized this edition of Martin Secker as looking "like a Church hymnal."

"His conversation was always fascinating," Kull had written me. "I remember one particular dinner when he gave us a very interesting account of how he got hold of the manuscript of 'The Foreign Legion.' He had received a copy of the first edition of that book that very day, which he generously gave as a present to Mrs. K. with his signature." Lawrence had written the date under his signature. Carola recalled that they had sat around the table in the dining room behind the patio in their home as Lawrence had told them his memories of Magnus.

Magnus was a forty-six-year-old journalist, whose mother was thought to be the illegitimate daughter of a Hohenzollern kaiser. He had been born in New York City but spent most of his adult life in Europe where his varied career had included acting as manager for Isadora Duncan. Lawrence's first portrait of Magnus was as the good-humored Mr. May in *The Lost Girl.* Magnus borrowed money from everyone, including Lawrence, until he finally killed himself by swallowing prussic acid as his creditors' police closed in on him. Lawrence blamed himself for that suicide because he had refused to lend more.

They had met when their mutual friend Norman Douglas had introduced Magnus to him in Florence in November 1919. Three months later, he visited Magnus at Montecassino.

During his three-day stay in the ancient monastery, Lawrence, then thirty-four, made a crucial decision not to retreat into the past as he saw the monks doing but to move forward, fighting, into the main stream of modern life. Magnus had showed him a number of manuscripts, including "Dregs," his memoir of his Foreign Legion experience. Lawrence felt it was publishable but needed revisions. He made specific editorial suggestions and Magnus rewrote the manuscript.

After Magnus's death, this revision came to Lawrence from a fellow-creditor. Magnus's will left his literary remains to Douglas, but when Lawrence asked him what to do about the memoir, Douglas replied "Damn the Foreign Legion. . . . By all means do what you like with the Ms." In 1921 Lawrence wrote his introduction and began trying to get the work published. Seltzer, his American publisher, wanted to bring out only the introduction and, when Lawrence refused, hung onto the manuscript for almost two years. Murry showed the manuscript to Secker who, though he had turned it down earlier, now accepted it.

Feeling his friend had been wronged, Douglas, then living in Sicily, dashed off a pamphlet, *D. H. Lawrence and Maurice Magnus: A Plea for Better Manners,* which he dated 24 December 1924, the Christmas Eve that Lawrence was in Oaxaca. Lawrence would not reply to Douglas's charges until 1926.[4]

Many memoirs of Lawrence illustrate his storytelling ability in congenial company including a genuine gift for mimicry. However, he found few people sympathetic in Oaxaca and thus there is little comment. Miss Doctor even reported that "he kind of mumbled. He was reserved and you could hardly hear him. He talked with his head down." But he felt expansive with the Kulls and entranced Carola with the people and places he conjured up in the story of Magnus, the plump, bird-like man, "almost smart . . . all in gray." She recalled telling Lawrence: "If you write as well as you talk, it must be a marvelous book."

"Lawrence," added Hermann, "was very proper in his talk. It never even bordered remotely on sensuality. His speech was that of a very cultured gentleman. In fact, he was a gentleman in every way. I never expected such a man would produce a *Lady Chatterley's Lover.*"

Carola understood and sympathized with the character supposed to be the uncouth brute, Lawrence's father, in *Sons and Lovers.* "Hermann doesn't realize when his harsh words hurt," she said, "and I felt Mrs. Lawrence and her son in the book didn't either."

The last encounter with the Lawrences that the Kulls remembered can be dated shortly after 30 January when Frieda reported to Brett, "I have got to go to Kull for my teeth, beastly and expensive," she said. Lawrence became too ill to be left alone. Carola volunteered to tend Lawrence while Frieda kept her appointment at the dentist's office.[5]

The Kulls were not surprised by Lawrence's illness. When Carola, after describing how his red beard covered a lot of his face, had added that he was "slender, tall and very thin," Hermann had corrected, "emaciated." Lawrence, he said, had looked "sickly" from the start.

"Several times, Lawrence had expressed a wish to come with us on our trip," Carola recalled. "The day I took over the nursing from Frieda, he pleaded with me to wait a few days before we started south. He said he was sure he would be well enough to come. When I told Hermann about his request, Hermann said "Oh, no, he'll be on our hands! We always lived in a primitive way on our journeys and we knew such a trip would be the death of him." The Kulls left on schedule.

On a second visit to the Kulls in 1964, I learned the golden wedding anniversary trip to Switzerland had been a disappointment. They had found few old friends left and Hermann had had a heart attack. Both seemed in vigorous health until Carola, then eighty, died suddenly in 1966. When I visited Hermann in 1967, his memory was worse. His heart prevented him from going down to the garden because of the difficulty of mounting the stairs to get back. His feet kept swelling and cataracts had formed over his eyes. Saddest of all, he had lost "a good companion."

"I'm not over the shock yet," he said. He died before the year was over.

CHAPTER 5

ROSALINO

The people who stir writers' imaginations are often not the expected ones. Governor Ibarra and Padre Rickards are interesting people Lawrence met in Oaxaca, but they made no literary impact on him. Although he wrote about Kull, he made no attempt to individualize him. García Vigil influenced the revised *Plumed Serpent, Mornings in Mexico,* and "The Flying Fish," but never emerges as a character. Archbishop Gillow holds a supporting role only. Because Lawrence's usual imaginative response to people is quick, he must have been too preoccupied with finishing *The Plumed Serpent.* However, Rosalino, the Indian *mozo* he inherited from Padre Rickards, captured his imagination.

Rosalino is the chief character in three of the four Oaxaca sketches in *Mornings in Mexico.* Part of Lawrence's interest in the handsome young Indian arose out of his fascination with Indians as a whole. Although the *mozo* caught his eye on his first visit to the priest's house, their first real encounter was the day the furniture was moved in. Inocente could not lift anything heavy. Rosalino had equally good reason for not carrying anything on his back. When García Vigil was desperate for resources, during the de la Huerta rebellion, he sent press gangs to round up men to fight for him. Rosalino was among the chosen.

> But Rosalino refused, said again *No quiero!* He is one of those, like myself, who have a horror of serving in a mass of men, or even being mixed up with a mass of men. He obstinately refused, whereupon the recruiting soldiers beat him with the butts of their rifles till he lay unconscious, apparently dead.
>
> Then, because they wanted him at once, and he would now be no good for some time, with his injured back, they left him, to get the revolution over without him.

Clearly Lawrence identified personally with the *mozo:* "He is one of those, *like myself,* who have a horror of serving in a mass of men." Lawrence assumes the horror for one of Rosalino's characteristics, as Lawrence repeatedly illustrates, was his silence about his inner feelings. Koteliansky in October 1927, had asked for advice about publishing an "intimate series" and Lawrence had brought up the difficulty of writing an intimate manuscript. The poems in *Look! We Have Come Through!* published in 1917, provide an extraordinarily close and unreserved account of his early life with Frieda, but a decade later he protested: ''I find it terribly difficult to write intimately—one feels colder and colder about unbosoming oneself.''

Lawrence was speaking about writing for publication, for his letters reveal he never found it difficult to unbosom himself to friends. However, the sketches in *Mornings in Mexico,* written for publication, contain what amounts to a confession. His feelings about fighting were vaguely positive—he saw it as a manly duty—but felt repulsion at the military machine. During World War I, he was summoned three times for medical examination but was rejected as physically unfit. He fiercely disapproved of this war and resented being examined. The first two humiliations—as he saw them—did not trouble him as much as the third, less than seven weeks before the armistice, in which he was examined naked before other men in his native Midlands, after he had already been spied upon, visited by the police, and driven out of Cornwall. Under the guise of fiction he described its indignities in the ''Nightmare'' chapter of *Kangaroo.* Knowing how he recoiled from being ''pawed'' then, one can judge his response to the atrocity of soldiers beating a recruit into insensibility with their rifle butts. One can understand how he admired Rosalino for refusing service and how he sympathized with the youth for what he saw as an affront to his essential nature, as well as to his body.

Lawrence did not disguise Rosalino's name, although he never gives the surname, nor could I discover it. Rosalino's mother had a bit of land and some orange trees. The boy was born around 1904 and, like the other children of the village, was brought up speaking only Zapotec. Rosalino had a sister, who was married by the time he came to Oaxaca, and a younger brother. Moving backwards from Lawrence's ''now''— 1924—Rosalino came to Oaxaca for the first time in 1922. He began working as a *mozo* by day and going to night school in the evenings. During the two previous years he had picked up a little Spanish.

Rosalino probably came from Santa María Zoogochí, a village in the region of the Sierra de Juárez known as La Rinconada. Zoogochí, which is beyond Ixtlán on the other side of the mountain, is a two-day walk from Oaxaca which is as Lawrence describes it. Further, it is an orange-growing town. The people of La Rinconada are very timid and pacific, as opposed to those around Ixtlán, a third indication, and speak a special form of Zapotec, something that Lawrence noted in Rosalino. Even more conclusive is Rosalino's costume in the Brett photograph of Lawrence in the uncovered San Juan de Diós Market. Brett took this picture (Plate 25) in late November because Lawrence sent her prints as postcards on December 4 to his sister Emily, on 5 December to his sister Ada, and on

9 December to Secker, explaining to the publisher, "The boy in the picture is our *mozo* Rosalino—marketing with us."

Ubaldo Garces, a *Serrano* who has traveled throughout his region, identified Rosalino's sandals, blouse, pants, and Japanesy straw hat as the distinctive garb of the men of Zoogochí.

Lawrence also notes: "Rosalino seemed to like doing things for us. He liked learning his monkey-tricks from the white monkeys. And since we started feeding him from our own meals, and for the first time in his life he had real soups, meat-stews, or a fried egg, he loved to do things in the kitchen. He would come with sparkling black eyes: *'Hé comido el caldo, Grazias!'* ("I have eaten the soup. Thank you.")—, And he would give a strange, excited little yelp of a laugh."

In one place the novelist said the youth had never returned to his village; but in the story of the boy's being beaten by the soldiers, seven paragraphs later Lawrence said he had been back the year before. One statement or the other is incorrect. Francisco Martínez,[1] a *Serrano* of the same age who was an acolyte for Padre Rickards's friend, the priest of the Patrocinio, suggests that he could only have been beaten in the city for the Vigilista recruiters did not dare go into the Sierra.

The Rosalino sketches contain a greater inconsistency. Lawrence wanted to present Rosalino as a prototype of the Mexican Indian, while on the other hand, he wanted to characterize him with all individuality and exactness. However, Rosalino as an individual did not square with Lawrence's view of the average Indian. "Our Rosalino is an exception," he says. Nevertheless, he persists in using him as a literary peg for his ideas about Indians in general, simultaneously at his best as a novelist and his worst as an anthropologist.

Lawrence also used Rosalino as a device for conjuring up the priest's house and the novelist's own life in it. Lawrence's mood when he moved into the priest's house is revealed in his letter to McDonald, his Philadelphia bibliographer: "I don't feel up to anything—as if the world had sort of come to an end. As you feel about politics. Perhaps it has. Anyhow, I'll lie low a bit, and get my pecker up." His use of English slang for courage brought him the amused thought that perhaps to an American he might have seemed to have referred to his penis. "Myself," he added, "I don't know American slang, and I'm sure pecker isn't improper in English. If it is, *tant mieux.*"

Despite his lassitude, he was in a good humor, and there can be little question that his life at Pino Suárez 43 began happily. Contradicting his resolve to lie low, he immediately began work on the new *Plumed Serpent.* Thereafter his energies rallied quickly. Four weeks later, the opening of "Market Day" reveals his contentment:

This is the last Saturday before Christmas. The next year will be momentous, one feels. This year is nearly gone. Dawn was windy, shaking the leaves, and the rising sun shone under a gap of yellow cloud. But at once it touched the yellow flowers that rise above the patio wall, and the swaying, glowing magenta of the bougainvillea, and the fierce red outbursts of the poinsettia. The poinsettia is very splendid, the flowers very big, and of a sure stainless red. They call them Noche Buenas, flowers of Christmas Eve. These tufts throw out their scarlet sharply, like red birds ruffling in the wind of dawn as if going to bathe, all their feathers alert. This for Christmas, instead of holly-berries. Christmas seems to need a red herald.

Knowing, as Bynner attests, that Lawrence was always an "early bird," and that the room where he slept gave onto the red-tiled *corredor* whose open side was to the east, one can visualize the novelist standing there, perhaps still in his old-fashioned, almost ankle-length nightshirt[2] watching the sun make each garden color more brilliant as it rose high enough to hit the flowers directly. I have watched the same effect in Oaxaca, and in December it comes around a quarter to seven, so perhaps on that particular morning the novelist got up at 6:30 A.M.

The Yucca is tall, [the description continues] higher than the house. It is, too, in flower, hanging an arm's length of soft creamy bells, like a yard-long grape cluster of foam. And the waxy bells break on their stems in the wind, fall noiselessly from the long creamy bunch that hardly sways.

The coffee-berries are turning red. The hibiscus flowers, rose-coloured, sway at the tips of the thin branches, in rosettes of soft red.

In the second patio, there is a tall tree of the flimsy acacia sort. Above itself it puts up whitish fingers of flowers, naked on the blue sky. And in the wind these fingers of flowers in the bare blue sky, sway, sway with the reeling, roundward motion of tree-tips in a wind.

Though Lawrence apparently did not seek the identification of the "flimsy" tree, his description is so precise that it can be identified readily as the *guaje,* a member of the acacia branch of the pea family, which has its flowering peak in November and December, and in July produces fruits in pods resembling jumbo beans. It is pronounced WAH-hay and may be related to Oaxaca's name. An earlier passage about the patio of the *guaje* tree shows it was the fenced-off rear part of the property. "Ours is a double square, the trees and flowers in the first square, with the two wings of the house. And in the second patio, the chickens, pigeons, guinea-pigs, and the big heavy earthenware dish or tub, called an *apaxtle,* in which all the servants can bathe themselves, like chickens in a saucer."

Note the word *apaxtle*. In *The Plumed Serpent* he preempted it for the name of the town of the justice-seeking villagers who were fooled by the dummy telephone in the story told by Duke.

The presence of Lawrence was only implicit in the description of the sunrise, but in "Corasmín and the Parrots" Lawrence paints himself in the picture. Curiously enough, he includes himself in this first sketch as a single individual with a particular vantage point. Ironically in everything else he wrote about Mexico for publication, he assumes an omniscient perspective, not as an outsider who visited Mexico during a particular period. Perhaps it was because he was aware of what he was doing in *The Plumed Serpent* that he felt the need to add this cautionary note:

> One says Mexico: one means, after all, one little town away South in the Republic: and in this little town, one rather crumbly adobe house built around two sides of a garden patio; and of this house, one spot on the deep, shady veranda facing inward to the trees, where there is an onyx table and three rocking chairs and one little wooden chair, a pot with carnations, and a person with a pen. We talk so grandly, in capital letters, about Morning in Mexico. All it amounts to is one little individual looking at a bit of sky and trees, then looking down at the page of his exercise book.

Brett portrays Lawrence vividly: "Your large rooms are beautifully cool, the long patio a delight, with its big, shady trees and flowers and quietness. The scarlet poinsettias are out, the parrots incessantly chatter in their tree, and the little dog snoozes comfortably at your feet." Though Lawrence never let a photographer catch him wearing glasses, he was "a bit short-sighted," as he admitted in his essay "On Coming Home," and he had required spectacles for his work since he was in his twenties, a fact revealed in his anguished P.S. to Edward Garnett on 30 October 1912. "I'm in great misery having broken my spectacles, and have no eyes to write with, so must feel in the dark."

He was writing with a fountain pen sent to him by Thomas Seltzer as the publisher's thank-you gift. In September 1927, after Frieda's sister, Else Jaffe, had the pen repaired for him, he wrote her: "Many thanks for the pen, which I am so glad to have in my fingers again—it's an old friend: it wrote *Boy in the Bush* and "St. Mawr" and "Princess" and "Woman Who Rode Away" and *Plumed Serpent* and all the stories in between: not bad, even if it is a nasty orange brown colour. But I've got even to like this colour. They seem to have mended it all right, it goes well."

The book in which the bespectacled Lawrence was writing with the orange-brown pen is preserved at the University of Texas and thus we know which of the five exercise books that he brought to Oaxaca he was using on this particular morning. It was the black one with

"Record" stamped on the cover in white curved letters. As it already contained three pieces completed in New Mexico, he was starting the new reflections on page seventy-four.

Another detail can be gained from Helen Corke's "Portrait of D. H. Lawrence: 1909-10." "David Lawrence has always a cough." This affliction, noted by his friend of teaching days at Croydon, had persisted, for Joseph Foster in *D. H. Lawrence in Taos* recalls how the novelist coughed "incessantly" before going to Oaxaca. The cough continued and in 1928 he wrote stoically to his sister Ada calling "that asthmatic cough, my old friend" but another time, feeling less resigned, he described it to Mabel Luhan as "this accursed cough."

Lawrence had become a connoisseur of mornings as early as the autumn of 1913, when he walked from Germany across Switzerland to Italy, as recounted in *Twilight in Italy:* "Everything was very clean, full of the German morning energy and brightness, which is so different from the Latin morning. The Italians are dead and torpid first thing, the Germans are energetic and cheerful." It is not surprising then, the essay he was starting was headed "Friday Morning." "Saturday Morning" was the original title of the market essay. "Friday" became "Corasmín and the Parrots" later when it seemed prudent to title each essay separately for the magazine market.[3]

Continuing his argument about the need to have the reader envision a specific author, Lawrence wrote:

> When books come out with grand titles like *The Future of America* or *The European Situation,* it's a pity we don't immediately visualize a thin or a fat person, in a chair or in bed, dictating to a bob-haired stenographer or making little marks on paper with a fountain pen.
>
> Still, it is morning, and it is Mexico. The sun shines. But then, during the winter, it always shines. It is pleasant to sit out of doors and write, just fresh enough, and just warm enough. But then it is Christmas next week, so it ought to be just right.
>
> There is a little smell of carnations, because they are the nearest thing. And there is a resinous smell of ocote wood, and a smell of coffee, and a faint smell of leaves, and of Morning, and even of Mexico. Because when all is said and done, Mexico has a faint, physical scent of her own, as each human being has. And this is a curious, inexplicable scent, in which there are resin and perspiration and sunburned earth and urine among other things.
>
> And cocks are still crowing. The little mill where the natives have their corn ground is puffing rather languidly. And because some women are talking in the entrance-way, two tame parrots in the trees have started to whistle.

Lawrence's finest collection of poems, *Birds, Beasts, and Flowers,*
is noted for his ability to describe living things. Colette is the only other
writer I know who can match him. After the double poinsettias, the yucca
blossoms, the hibiscus, and the *guajes,* he spends the next three pages
on the parrots. In the course of detailing how they can imitate sounds
made by others, Lawrence describes how they mimic Rosalino whistling,
calling the Padre's dog, and the dog himself.

> Now they are yapping like a dog: exactly like Corasmín. Corasmín is a
> little fat, curly white dog who was lying in the sun a minute ago, and has
> now come into the veranda shade, walking with slow resignation, to lie
> against the wall nearby my chair. "Yap-yap-yap-! Wouf! Wouf! Yapyap-
> yapyap!!" go the parrots, exactly like Corasmín when some stranger comes
> into the *zaguan,* Corasmín and a little more so.
>
> With a grin on my face I look down at Corasmín. And with a silent,
> abashed resignation in his yellow eyes, Corasmín looks up at me, with
> a touch of reproach. His little nose is sharp, and under his eyes there are
> dark marks, as under the eyes of one who has known much trouble. All
> day he does nothing but walk resignedly out of the sun, when the sun
> gets too hot, and out of the shade, when the shade gets too cool. And
> bite ineffectually in the region of his fleas.
>
> Poor old Corasmín: he is only about six, but resigned, unspeakably
> resigned.

Corasmín is one of Lawrence's best dog portraits, ranking almost
with the dogs in "Rex" and "Bibbles." The dog's exact responses are
observed for several additional paragraphs, increasing both his vividness
and Lawrence's own likability.

Rosalino's day begins as follows:

> His duty is to rise in the morning and sweep the street in front of the house,
> and water it. Then he sweeps and waters the broad, brick-tiled verandas,
> and flicks the chairs with a sort of duster made of fluffy reeds. After which
> he walks behind the cook—she is very superior, had a Spanish grandfather,
> and Rosalino must address her as *Señora* —carrying the basket to market.
> Returned from the market, he sweeps the whole of the patio, gathers up
> the leaves and refuse, fills the pannier-basket, hitches it up on his shoul-
> ders, and holds it by a band across his forehead, and thus, a beast of bur-
> den, goes out to deposit the garbage at the side of one of the little roads
> leading out of the city.

It is while Rosalino is on his third round of duties, sweeping the
patio, that Lawrence glimpses the parrots mocking him. Perhaps it was

because Lawrence was such a good mimic himself that he enjoyed the parrots so much:

> The parrots, even when I don't listen to them, have an extraordinary effect on me. They make my diaphragm convulse with little laughs, almost mechanically. They are a quite commonplace pair of green birds, with bits of bluey red, and round, disillusioned eyes, and heavy, overhanging noses. But they listen intently. And they reproduce. The pair whistle now like Rosalino, who is sweeping the patio with a twig broom; and yet it is so unlike him, to be whistling full vent, when any of us is around, that one looks at him to see. And the moment one sees him, with his black head bent rather drooping and hidden as he sweeps, one laughs.
>
> The parrots whistle exactly like Rosalino, only a little more so. And this little-more-so is extremely, sardonically funny. With their sad old long-jowled faces and their flat disillusioned eyes, they reproduce Rosalino and a little-more-so without moving a muscle. And Rosalino, sweeping the patio with his twig broom, scraping the littering leaves into little heaps, covers himself more and more with the cloud of his own obscurity. He doesn't rebel. He is powerless. Up goes the wild, sliding Indian whistle into the morning, very powerful, with an immense energy seeming to drive behind it. And always, always a little more than life-like.

Birds, Beasts and Flowers was completed not long before Lawrence's first visit to Mexico; the poems include successive contemplations of a fish he caught, a turkey-cock, a humming bird, a blue jay, and Bibbles, the little black dog that so often exasperated him during his winter on the Hawk ranch. The reflections these creatures stirred are continued in this Oaxaca essay, for the parrots, the white dog, and Rosalino increased his sense of how each creature belonged to a different order. When he realized, too, how different Rosalino's world was from his own, he initiated what might be called a fantasia on an Aztec theme. Behind it was one of his major conflicts with modern science, which he enunciated as early as October 1921 in the foreword to his *Fantasia of the Unconscious:* "I do not believe in evolution but in the strangeness and rainbow-change of ever-renewed creative civilizations."

> Myself, I don't believe in evolution, like a long string hooked on to a First Cause, and being slowly twisted in unbroken continuity through the ages. I prefer to believe in what the Aztecs called Suns: that is Worlds successively created and destroyed. The sun itself convulses, and the worlds go out like so many candles when somebody coughs in the middle of them. Then subtly, mysteriously, the sun convulses again, and a new set of worlds begin to flicker alight.

> This pleases my fancy better than the long and weary twisting of the rope of Time and Evolution, hitched on to the revolving hook of a First Cause. I like to think of the whole show going bust, *bang!* —and nothing but bits of chaos flying about. Then out of the dark, new little twinklings reviving from nowhere, nohow.

Both his belief and disbelief meant that when Lawrence learned the Aztec theory of the origin of species it overlapped his own notions while appealing to his imagination. Instead of postulating evolution from a single creation with men descending from apes, the Aztec theory postulated five creations, each of a different order with each destroyed by a different cataclysm. Perhaps Lawrence heard the Aztec theory from Mrs. Nuttall in Mexico City. But the "Corasmín" essay shows that he had deliberately refreshed his memory of it in Oaxaca from Lewis Spence's new book, *The Gods of Mexico.* Thanks to Brett, we know he read it there. It was also part of Lawrence's priming himself for one of the major imaginative efforts he had to make for his revisions of the *The Plumed Serpent.* His Chapala version had told of the upsurge of a new religion reviving old gods but without detail. To make its appeal more convincing, Lawrence knew it had to have a more vivid mythological base. So one of his tasks was to learn more about the pre-Columbian religions to work their details into the mythology he had to construct.

He calls the Aztec view his "fancy" and he had defended Frederick Carter's early manuscript, "The Dragon of the Apocalypse," by exclaiming, "Thank God for fantasy, if it enhances our life." So he changes and reshapes that myth. He correctly summarizes Spence's description of the four preceding suns and the jaguar that destroyed the first sun, but he states incorrectly that its inhabitants were "mercifully forgotten insects." According to the Aztecs, they were giants. The second Sun was destroyed by "a great wind." But recollections of the very Darwinism that he deplored led him to be wrong about the inhabitants of this sun too. They weren't "big lizards," but people. Those who survived turned into monkeys. The third sun, the one destroyed by fire, Lawrence omits from his summary altogether and along with it the belief that its inhabitants were children, with those that were not burned turning into birds. The fourth sun he confuses with the third. It was destroyed by water as he says; but he is wrong in saying it was inhabited by "the first attempts at animal men," for the Aztecs believed premonkey men existed in the second Sun.

Ironically, the anti-evolutionist has this to say of the fifth and present Sun: "Out of the floods rose our own Sun, and little naked man." He mixed Darwinism and Aztecism, and no creation went "bust, *bang!*" even though he liked to picture them all doing it.

The scene, however, warns us that the pre-Columbian material in

Lawrence is not as close to the aboriginal mythology as it appears to be. Part of Lawrence's magic as an artist is to make his own legends, borrowing but changing Aztec elements. Also, Lawrence sometimes sent his recollections of books into the world as his misinterpretation without recognizing—or perhaps caring—how his imagination had jumbled what he had read.

When Aldous Huxley challenged Lawrence on evolution and asked him to look at the evidence, Lawrence's retort, according to Huxley, was, "But I don't care about evidence. Evidence doesn't mean anything to me. I don't feel it *here.*" Huxley, telling the story in his introduction to his edition of Lawrence's letters, pokes fun at his friend by the way he indicated that "here" was "his solar plexus." Lawrence may have been baiting this overly intellectual challenger nine years his junior. In "Introduction to These Paintings," which Lawrence wrote for the Mandrake Press's reproductions of his paintings in 1929, he explains his position more rationally: "I find I can't, with the best will in the world, believe that the species have 'evolved' from one common life-form. . . . I have to violate my intuitive and instinctive awareness of something else, to make myself believe it." Lawrence does not define that "something else" but the evidence he considered contradictory to evolution—the reality he felt he could not deny—is stated in "Corasmín and the Parrots":

> If you come to think of it, when you look at the monkey you are looking straight into the other dimension. He's got length and breadth and height all right, and he's in the same universe of Space and Time as you are. But there's another dimension. He's different. There's no rope of evolution linking him to you, like a navel string. No! Between you and him there's a cataclysm and another dimension. It's no good. You can't link him up. Never will. It's the other dimension.
>
> He stands in one Sun, you in another. He whisks his tail in one Day, you scratch your head in another. He jeers at you, and is afraid of you. You laugh at him and are frightened of him.

It was easy for Lawrence to imagine this monkey-human confrontation because he had already envisaged other animal-human confrontations, notably, the horse-woman conflict envisaged that summer at the ranch in writing *St. Mawr.* Describing the horse confronting its mistress, he wrote, "the wild brilliant alert head of St. Mawr seemed to look at her out of another world. It was as if she had had a vision, as if the walls of her own world had suddenly melted away, leaving her in a great darkness in which the large, brilliant eyes of the horse looked at her with demonish question."

His intense awareness of real differences between species prevented Lawrence from accepting the premise of "one common life-form." Watching the dog and the parrots in the priest's garden brought their differences—and the differences between other creatures—home to him. Those who have lived in Oaxaca will know why he thought of the earwig as still another creature, with its lengthwise black and yellow stripes and two-pronged tail. The natives call them *tijerillas,* "little scissors," a name derived from the characteristic noted by Lawrence: the way "they turn up their tails and nip with them."

In "Corasmín," besides giving us a sense of the priest's garden in a given moment of time, Lawrence writes significantly of birds, animals, and men of different cultures coexisting in the same world, and yet because of differences in heritage, nature, and mental endowment, existing in different worlds. Rosalino points out for Lawrence the differences among men.

> Rosalino, the Indian *mozo,* looks up at me with his eyes veiled by their own blackness. We won't have it ["the other dimension"] either; he is hiding and repudiating. Between us also is the gulf of the other dimension, and he wants to bridge it with the foot-rule of the three-dimensional space. He knows it can't be done. So do I. Each of us knows the other knows.
>
> But he can imitate me, even more than life-like. As the parrot can him. And I have to laugh at his *me,* a bit on the wrong side of my face, as he has to grin on the wrong side of his face when I catch his eye as the parrot is whistling *him.* With a grin, with a laugh we pay tribute to the other dimension.

Lawrence used the capital D in saying the monkey "whisks his tail in one Day, you scratch your head in another," showing that he was thinking increasingly of a theme that had been developing in his mind since *The Trespasser* of 1912, where the hero muses, "For me the day is shrivelling. I can see the darkness through its petals." *Aaron's Rod* illustrates that by 1922 Lawrence had already begun using contrasting "days" to distinguish between types of consciousness, even types of existence. Aaron reflects in Sir William Frank's garden after reaching Florence: "He felt like a man who knows it is time to wake up, and who doesn't want to wake up, to face the responsibility of another sort of day."

The year before, in his "Moby Dick" essay, Lawrence wrote: "Doom of our white day. We are doomed, doomed. And the doom is in America. The doom of our white day. Ah, well, if my day is doomed, and I am doomed with my day, it is something greater than I which dooms me, so I accept my doom as a sign of the greatness which is more than I am."

Though Lawrence does not mention it, he sometimes used Rosalino as a messenger, generally to Brett. When the University of Cincinnati purchased the bulk of Lawrence's letters to her in 1953, the collection included even undated notes in pencil, which Rosalino had brought to the Francia. Three notes involved books. With the first, Rosalino delivered a book to Brett, along with two baskets belonging to Mrs. Kull. In the second Lawrence explained, "Here is Rosalino for the book—I have to send a note, or he's too shy to ask." The third is described by Brett: "This morning I have a crashing headache. Rosalino had banged and banged on my door and finally I struggled out of bed. It is a note from you about a terrible train hold-up. I cannot send a note back, my head is too bad."

The hold-up was not a robbery but a breakdown in service. Lawrence's note stated that "Father Rickards said rebels had broken our railway bridge, but no word in the *Mercurio.*" Lawrence tended to over-dramatize the incident, for the *Mercurio* of December 6 said that the train of the day before for Puebla had been able to get only as far as Cuicatlan because two bridges beyond had been burned.

On December 7 the *Mercurio* reported that service was back to normal. The bridges, less than a third of a mile apart, had been repaired in time for the Puebla train to leave on schedule. The newspaper reported that it was not known who burned the bridges, but Lawrence, in a note dated "Sunday" to William Hawk, repeated "Rebels" and spoke of the bridge being burned rather than broken, adding, "but it's mended, so the train comes again." He and Padre Rickards may have settled on rebels as the culprits because earlier stories in the *Mercurio* had blamed *rebeldes* for a series of derailments on the Veracruz-Isthmus of Tehuantepec line.

Four years after Lawrence had left Indians of both New and Old Mexico behind, he confided his ambiguous feelings to Mabel Luhan: "Somewhere underneath in myself I feel a deep sympathy with the Indians—superficially I don't really like them." His earlier thoughts are revealed in a letter to the Baroness von Richthofen written from Lake Chapala:

> Mexico is very interesting: a foreign people. They are mostly pure Indians, dark like the people in Ceylon but much stronger. The men have the strongest backbones in the world, I believe. They are half civilized, half wild. If they only had a new faith they might be a new, young, beautiful people. But as Christians they don't get any further, are melancholy inside, live without hope, are suddenly wicked, and don't like to work. But they are also good, can be gentle and honest, are very quiet, and are not at all greedy for money.

A year and a half later in Oaxaca he garbled Aztec mythology and ignored the fact that the energetic, militaristic, self-regimenting Aztecs were by no means a characteristic Indian people to open another fantasia on an Aztec theme:

> The Aztec gods and goddesses are, as far as we have known anything about them, an unlovely and unlovable lot. In their myths there is no grace or charm, no poetry. Only this perpetual grudge, grudge, grudging, one god grudging another, the gods grudging men their existence, and men grudging the animals. The goddess of love is goddess of dirt and prostitution, a dirt eater, a horror, without a touch of tenderness. If the god wants to make love to her, she has to sprawl down in front of him, blatant and accessible.

Lawrence worked an echo of this into *The Plumed Serpent* when he had the infuriated Don Ramón say scathingly to Kate, "There have been pretty goddesses, I assure you, in the Aztec pantheon."

This generalization of Aztec deities is another product of Spence's *The Gods of Mexico* and the Christmas season. One of the Aztec birth myths summarized by Spence gave Lawrence the idea of retelling the myth in the style of Christmas carols and Handel's *Messiah*. He begins with a confusion between two goddesses. Having introduced the excrement-eating goddess, he then starts talking about the female half of the primal couple (variously known as Citlalicuie, Omecihuatl and Tonacaciuatl) as if he were still talking about Tlazolteotl, the dirt eater.

> And then, after all, when she conceives and brings forth, what is it she produces? What is the infant-god she tenderly bears? Guess, all ye people, joyful and triumphant!
>
> You never could.
>
> It is a stone knife.
>
> It is a razor-edged knife of blackish-green flint, the knife of all knives, the veritable Paraclete of knives. It is the sacrificial knife with which the priest makes a gash in his victim's breast, before he tears out the heart, to hold it smoking to the sun. And the Sun, the Sun behind the sun, is supposed to suck the smoking heart greedily with insatiable appetite.
>
> This, then, is a pretty Christmas Eve. Lo, the goddess is gone to bed, to bring forth her child. Lo! ye people, await the birth of the saviour, the wife of a god is about to become a mother.
>
> *Tarumm-tarah! Tarumm-tarah!* Blow the trumpets. The child is born. Unto us a son is given. Bring him forth, lay him on a tender cushion. Show him, then, to all the people. See! See! See him upon the cushion tenderly new-born and reposing! Ah, *qué bonito!* Oh, what a nice, blackish,

smooth, keen stone knife!

And to this day, most of the Mexican Indian women seem to bring forth stone knives. Look at them, these sons of incomprehensible mothers, with their black eyes like flints, and their stiff little bodies as taut and keen as knives of obsidian. Take care they don't rip you up.

Lawrence seems to believe that the first Mexican was a flint knife from which all Mexicans are descended. But the legend does not say this. As Spence, Lawrence's source, tells it, the primal mother had already given birth to a number of sons before she produced the knife which so horrified them they threw it out of heaven. When it struck the earth it turned into 1,600 gods, who were miserable because they had to work for a living. Feeling that this drudgery was unfair to beings of divine origin, they petitioned heaven for the right to create men. Their unsympathetic mother referred them to the Lord of the Realm of the Dead, saying he might have some relics of past generations, "which, if subjected to the magical influence of sacrifice, might provide the beginnings of a new earth race." One of the complaining gods—Xolotl in one version, Quetzalcoatl in another—was delegated to make the hazardous journey. In the underworld he managed to obtain an enormous bone, which he got to earth, but not until after it had been shattered as he fell, chased as an escaping thief. The cherished splinters were then placed in a vessel and the 1,600 brothers drew blood from their bodies to mix with the bone fragments. On the fourth day a human boy emerged from "the gory mass," so the gods again drew their own blood to moisten the bone, and on the fourth day a girl emerged. This boy and girl became the progenitors of the human race.

In the Mexican legends, then, the first people, far from being descendants of a flint knife, were the children of a couple created from a bone of their predecessors fertilized by the blood of gods. Instead of an inhuman concept, as postulated by Lawrence, it is a human one, not without tenderness. Although Lawrence believed in the wisdom of blood, he did not see its beauty. He preferred the concept gleaned from a careless reading because the flint knife story supported his fixed idea of the Mexican Indian.

Lawrence's notion of a woman giving birth to a knife surfaced in "Cocksure Women and Hensure Men," a magazine piece republished in *Assorted Articles* which explained how modern women had surrendered their "hensureness" in order to be cocksure: "They find often, that instead of having laid an egg, they have laid a vote, or an empty ink-bottle, or some other absolutely *unhatchable* object which means nothing to them."

In 1928, he was being satirical in a light-hearted way, but in Oaxaca he was in earnest, and the view of the Mexican Indian given in the unfortunate passage—and implicit in much of *The Plumed Serpent*—is another reason many Mexicophiles boil at the mere mention of Lawrence's name. They believe that he implies too much danger, malevolence, and slumbering violence below the Mexican surface and maligns its Indians. Finding the Indians good, gentle, and honest—as Lawrence himself earlier said they were—they are angered by his presentation of these charming people as personified flint knives.

I am sure that by the end of 1924 many Indians, after all they had suffered during the Revolution, were moody, suspicious, and hostile. Lawrence correctly observed an ugly mood but he asserted that this mood was inherent. Those who claim he was wrong about the Indians are ignorant of Mexican conditions at the time Lawrence was there. Most of them have known only the more relaxed, more trusting Indians of the long period of stability since 1937. In the peaceful decades many tourists have been so enchanted by the Indians, particularly those of Oaxaca, that they have idealized them. The truth lies in between. Lawrence's views must be judged in terms of his time. There is much realism in his observation of individual Indians; if he erred about the Indians as a whole, at least he did not err on the side of naive sentimentalism. A personal factor must also be considered. Lawrence felt unduly threatened by anything that he interpreted as hostility; he found hostility in the eyes of swarthy-skinned strangers. In her beautiful "Elegy," Rebecca West reveals Lawrence's distrust of Sicilian peasants; it is apparent in his Mexican writings as well.

Take, for example, his simile for the black eyes of the Indians. "Like flints," he said. Indians to this day stare at fair-skinned people. It is partly because they do not share our cultural prohibition against staring. Besides, a white person's size, pale eyes, and light skins are intensely interesting. Eyes so dark that iris is difficult to distinguish from pupil can disconcert people used to irises of blue, green, and amber. If one feels uncomfortable or insecure, it is easy to mistake innocent curiosity for a whole spectrum of negative feelings.

Lawrence was a rare specimen in Oaxaca in 1924. With his red beard, he must have astonished black-haired Indians who have difficulty growing beards of any kind. Brett has shown how the market Indians immediately responded to his gentleness. "Wherever you go," wrote Brett, "there is surprise and wonder among the Indians. The sensitive approach, the understanding, the quiet friendliness, the perfect manners, matching their perfect manners, warms them to you quickly. What we are told is so different to what we experience in our contacts with the Indians."

Lawrence disagreed: "Usually, these people have no correspondence with one at all," he wrote. "To them a white man or white woman is a sort of phenomenon, just as a monkey is a sort of phenomenon; something to watch, and wonder at, and laugh at, but not to be taken on one's own plane." His assessment might have been more objective than Brett's, and it applies almost equally to white people's observation of Indians. Generally, however, Lawrence is more subjective, and again and again he saw in the Indian eyes flint-knives ready to rip him up, profoundly influencing his reading of the aboriginal character. But his portrait of Rosalino shows he could see other things in Indians, too—when he got to know them and suspended his theorizing.

> He is not one of the erect, bantam little Indians that stare with a black, incomprehensible, but somewhat defiant stare. It may be Rosalino has a distant strain of other Indian blood, not Zapotec. Or it may be he is only a bit different. The difference lies in a certain sensitiveness and aloneness, as if he were a mother's boy. The way he drops his head and looks sideways under his black lashes, apprehensive, apprehending, feeling his way, as it were. Not the bold male glare of most of the Indians, who seem as if they had never, never had mothers at all.
>
> He drops his shoulders just a little. He is a bit bigger, also, than the average Indian down here. He must be about five feet four inches. And he hasn't got the big, obsidian, glaring eyes. His eyes are smaller, blacker, like the quick black eyes of the lizard. They don't look at one with the obsidian stare. They are just a bit aware that there is another being, unknown, at the other end of the glance. Hence he drops his head with a little apprehension, screening himself as if he were vulnerable.

Moreover, Rosalino's reticence informed his manner of speech, talking in "half-audible crushed tones." Often, when he had to admit ignorance when asked a question, his voice had "the inevitable flat resonance of aloofness touched with resignation, as if to say: It is not becoming to a man to know these things." Yet sometimes, he would break into "a great grin," and occasionally he would give "a sudden yelp of laughter" that made Lawrence feel Indians laughed "as if it were against their will, as if it hurt them, giving themselves away."

Taking out the garbage, watering the garden, and sprinkling the swept patio occupied most of the morning for Rosalino. "In the afternoon he sits without much to do. If the wind has blown or the day was hot, he starts again at about three o'clock, sweeping up leaves and sprinkling everything with an old watering-can." Rosalino studied in the afternoons and went to night-school in the evenings.

Then he retreats to the entrance-way, the *zaguan,* which with its big doors and its cobbled track, is big enough to admit an ox-wagon. The *zaguan* is his home: just the doorway. In one corner is a low wooden bench about four feet long and eighteen inches wide. Whoever gets into the house or patio must get through these big doors. There is no other entrance, not even a needle's eye. The windows to the street are heavily barred. Each house is its own small fortress.

He works for four *pesos* a month, and his food: a few tortillas. Four *pesos* are two American dollars: about nine shillings. He owns two cotton shirts, two pairs of calico pantaloons, two blouses, one of pink cotton, one of darkish flannelette, and a pair of sandals. Also, his straw hat that he has curled up to look very jaunty, and a rather old factory-made, rather cheap shawl, or plaid rug with fringe.

By half-past nine at night Rosalino is lying on his little bench, screwed up, wrapped in his shawl, his sandals, called *huaraches,* on the floor. Usually he takes off his *huaraches* when he goes to bed. That is all his preparation.

Lawrence completes the picture by describing the other youth from Rosalino's village who served as a fellow guard. "In another corner wrapped up, head and all, like a mummy in his thin old blanket, the *paisano,* another lad of about twenty, lies asleep on the cold stones. And at an altitude of five thousand feet, the nights can be cold."

One night a cold north wind rattling the worm-chewed window frames made Lawrence aware of how Rosalino might be suffering, which led him to give the youth a blanket. Self-effacingly, he tells the story to illustrate how Rosalino expressed agreement by repeating *"Como no, Señor?"* meaning "Why not, sir?"

"Rosalino, I am afraid you will be cold in the night."
    "Como no, Señor?"
    "Would you like a blanket?"
    "Como no, Señor?"
    "With this you will be warm?"
    "Como no, Señor?"

Lawrence details Rosalino's bargaining prowess:

He loved to go to the market with the *patrones.* We would give him money and send him forth to bargain for oranges, *pitahuayas* [garnet-fleshed cactus fruit], potatoes, eggs, a chicken and so forth. This he simply loved to do. It put him in a temper to see us buying without bargaining, and paying ghastly prices.

He bargained away, silent almost, muttering darkly. It took him a long time, but he had far greater success than even Natividad, the cook. And he came back in triumph, with much stuff and little money spent.

Brett retells the same story:

You have changed into your beloved black and white befrogged check suit and *huaraches.* You have sewn the mattress; I have painted the chairs white, while Frieda has sewn the blinds. You light the charcoal fire. It is the same you tell me, as the charcoal fires in Italy. The kettle boils and the priest comes to tea. The Indian women peep furtively from their doorways at you. Our *mozo,* Rosalino, beams. He shows you where he sleeps and you look doubtful, perplexed. It is a wooden bench near the big double doors onto the street. That, and the threadbare *serape,* is all he has for a bed.

"But the nights are chilly," you say to the priest.

"They are used to it," he answers. But somehow you are not satisfied; and when we go to the market, with Rosalino following with the basket for the stuff we buy, you take him to the *serape* heap and tell him to choose one, a nice warm one for himself.

For a moment he stares at you incredulously; then, with a broad smile and a gleam of white teeth, he begins to bargain. He sees the one he wants, and in true Indian fashion he goes about getting it as cheaply as he can. We move off, knowing that the job will be a long one. Finally he catches up with us and touches you on the arm. He tells you he can get the blanket he wants for so much—incredibly cheap. You give him the money and he hurries back, returning with the treasure folded over his shoulder. From that moment, he is your slave.

Brett adds another detail: "He is observant and discovers that you take a bath regularly every Saturday evening, and that Sunday morning means a clean shirt. Rosalino religiously goes to the public baths on Saturday evenings from the moment he makes this discovery; and every Sunday he appears in a gorgeous flowered shirt, spotlessly clean. He has but two, until you give him two more; but his appearance on Sundays is always dazzling."

What Brett remembered as the "gorgeous flowered shirt" was probably Rosalino's pink one, for men of the Sierra do not wear embroidered shirts. The reference to the public baths was to a *baño,* which for a small fee, provides shower baths. It is doubtful that the novelist's weekly bath gave Rosalino the idea of donning clean linen on Sunday—a clean shirt on Sunday is a Mexican village tradition.

Another Rosalino story that only Brett tells occurred just after moving in:

All through the market, all the way home, an Indian woman follows you with four ducks squeezed in a basket. Nothing you say deters her; she is determined to sell you the ducks. She follows you into the patio, and there the poor cramped ducks are pulled out of the basket and shown to you. By this time you are so bored, so defeated by her persistence, that you buy the ducks and she goes off happy; while the four Indian servants gather round and tell you that a little pond must be made for them.

Our *mozo* is grinning. He has decided that he likes you and that he will stay; so he leads us to a small, high-walled yard and there digs a round hole, pours water into it—and then unties the ducks' legs. They give a few stiff scuffles and then, with a clack, slip into the water and wag appreciative tails.

The ducks are fattened and heartlessly eaten one by one—all except the last one, which when you go one day into the yard to catch, suddenly rises on unsuspected wings and flies over the wall. How angry you are, after all the feed and care it has had, to lose the good meal! Enquiries are made to all the neighbors, but not one has seen a duck lately—although it has been clearly seen in the neighboring garden.

A Rosalino story Brett and Lawrence both tell is about his studies:

One evening you find him on his bench, poring over a copy-book [wrote Brett]. "What is it?" you ask him. Shyly he hands up the book. He attends a night school for reading and writing. His copy-book is full of long poems that he has to learn and copy over and over again.

"I will help you in the morning," you tell him. "Then you'll get on quicker." And every morning you teach him an hour. Sometimes, coming up in the morning, I find you and Rosalino with a face of agonized concentration on the simple things you are trying to teach him.

Lawrence tells about the studies as follows:

In the obscurity of the *zaguan* he sits and pores, pores, pores over a school-book learning to read and write. He can read a bit, and write a bit. He filled a large sheet of foolscap with writing: quite nice. But I found out that what he had written was a Spanish poem, a love-poem, with *no puedo olvidar* and *voy a cortar* —the rose of course. He had written the thing straight ahead, without verse—lines or capitals or punctuation at all, just a vast string of words, a whole foolscap sheet full. When I read a few lines aloud, he writhed and laughed in an agony of confused feelings. And of what he had written he understood a small, small amount, parrot-wise, from the top of his head. Actually, it meant just words, sound, noise, to him: noise called Castellano, Castilian. Exactly like a parrot.

From seven to eight he goes to the night-school, to cover a bit more of the foolscap. If he goes two years more he will perhaps really be able to read and write six intelligible sentences: but only Spanish, which is as foreign to him as Hindustani would be to an English farm-boy. Then if he can speak his quantum of Spanish, and read it and write it to a very uncertain extent, he will return to his village two day's journey on foot into the hills, and then, in time, he may even rise to be an *alcalde,* or headman of the village, responsible to the Government. If he were *alcalde* he would get a little salary. But far more important to him is the glory: being able to be boss.

Modestly, Lawrence does not report helping Rosalino with his studies. The Lawrence he presented for print was not as likable as the real Lawrence. Again he felt the public figure had to be less human, more superior, more the man of wide knowledge informing the world about the nature of the Mexican Indian. The conclusion about Rosalino's aspirations may simply be Lawrence's own assumption, like his misconception that all Indians wanted to be literate. He was flatly wrong about village officials receiving salaries: to this day, they serve without pay.

Brett had several prints made of her market photograph including Rosalino; Lawrence gave Rosalino an envelope and a stamp so the *mozo* could send a copy of the photograph home to his mother. The gift would later play a role in a crisis that began the evening of Sunday 21 December. The precipitating event was an excursion into the hills that Rosalino made during the day with the Lawrences. During the excursion he had been unusually cheerful.

But in the evening he lay mute on his bench—not that he was really tired. The Indian gloom, which settles on them like a black marsh-fog, had settled on him. He did not bring in the water—let me carry it by myself.

Monday morning, the same black reptilian gloom, and a sense of hatred. He hated us. This was a bit flabbergasting, because he had been so thrilled and happy the day before.

And now, the reaction. The flint knife. He had been happy, *therefore* we were scheming to take another advantage of him. We had some devilish white monkey-trick up our sleeve; we wanted to get at his *soul,* no doubt, and do it the white monkey's damage. We wanted to get his heart, did we? But his heart was an obsidian knife.

He hated us and gave off a black steam of hate, that filled the patio and made one feel sick. He did not come to the kitchen, he did not carry the water. Leave him alone.

At lunch-time on Monday he said he wanted to leave. Why? He said he wanted to go back to his village.

Very well. He was to wait just a few days, till another *mozo* was found.

At this a glance of pure, reptilian hate from his black eyes.

He sat motionless on his bench all the afternoon, in the Indian stupor of gloom and profound hate. In the evening, he cheered up a little and said he would stay on, at least till Easter.

Tuesday morning. More stupor and gloom and hate. He wanted to go back to his village at once. All right! No one wanted to keep him against his will. Another *mozo* would be found at once.

Tuesday afternoon, and he thought he would stay.

Wednesday morning, and he wanted to go.

Very good. Enquiries made; another *mozo* was coming on Friday morning. It was settled.

The characterization of hatred and anger seems highly fanciful. Furthermore Lawrence does not mention that Thursday was Christmas Day. Rosalino, it seems, could not resist the promised excitement of Christmas morning marketing. "So again that afternoon he was staying on. The spell was wearing off."

By this time, Lawrence had a new theory about the youth's moodiness. According to Brett, Padre Rickards had explained that "the mountains had given Rosalino a nostalgia for his own mountain home—an irresistible urge." Lawrence reported "that the Indians of the hills have a heavy, intense sort of attachment to their villages." Of the town they had visited, he said that its "black Indian gloom of nostalgia must have made a crack in his spirits." Very unsympathetically, Lawrence, without ever having seen Rosalino's mother, exclaimed: "Seeing the photograph, the mother, who had completely forgotten her son, as far as any keen remembering goes, suddenly, like a cracker going off inside her, wanted him: at that very moment. So she sent an urgent message."

By referring to Christmas only as "fiesta" Lawrence gives no inkling of what his flint-hearted Indians were probably feeling. After not seeing Rosalino in several years, the widowed mother must have longed to have her son home for Christmas, and very likely the photograph intensified her feelings. Similarly one can guess the youth's feeling. A visit to a village resembling his own must have made him homesick. It is likely that the flint was in Lawrence's heart.

On the afternoon of Christmas Eve "arrived a little fellow in white clothes, smiling hard." It was his brother from the hills, someone to walk back with. On Friday, after the fiesta, he would go.

Thursday, he escorted us with the baskets to the fiesta. He bargained for flowers, and for a *serape* which he didn't get, for a carved *jicara* [gourd shell] which he did get, and for a number of toys. He and the Niña [Frieda, employing the affectionate term for the mistress] and the Señorita [Brett] ate a great wafer of a pancake with sweet stuff on it. The basket grew heavy. The brother appeared, to carry the hen and the extra things. Bliss.

He was perfectly happy again. He didn't want to go on Friday; he didn't want to go at all. He wanted to stay with us and come with us to England when we went home.

So, another trip to the friend, the Mexican, who had found us the other *mozo*. Now to put off the other boy again: but then, they are all like that.

Just after the excursion that caused so much other trouble Lawrence caught Frieda's cold and by Tuesday was so sick he had to go to bed. Rosalino's refusal to carry the water caused him hardship since his response to sickness was nearly always to get irritable. He had written his editor-mentor, Edward Garnett, as early as 7 January 1912, "But there, one is always churlish after an illness." Rosalino's shilly-shallying and the extra trouble of first engaging another *mozo* and then having to put the new boy off would be further irritants. Lawrence himself was suffering from the Christmas blues in Oaxaca as indicated by a section he added to *The Plumed Serpent*. "How awful, Christmas with hibiscus and poinsettia!" he has his Kate exclaim when she feels the tug of England as Christmas-time nears. "It makes me long to see mistletoe among the oranges, in a fruiterer's shop in Hampstead [a section of London where the Lawrences had lived]. To see the buses rolling on the mud in Piccadilly, on Christmas Eve, and the wet pavements crowded with people under the brilliant shops." There is a good deal of poignance in the friction between the man and the equally temperamental youth, each so isolated in his own self-centered feelings, and neither understanding the other.

Brett relates a story revealing Rosalino's kindness, even during his Christmas moodiness. Brett volunteered to do the marketing when Frieda was still not feeling well and Lawrence was in bed. Rosalino went along. When they returned, she was "flustered and obviously full of news."

"Well, what is it?" you ask, impatiently.

"An Indian hit me!" I blurt out, excitedly. You look askance at once.

"What on earth do you mean? That's bad," you say, seriously.

"I was in the market, pushing through the crowd, when a very ugly Indian came up. Rosalino reached out from the other side of me and touched him, whereupon the Indian hit back at me with his fist and caught me a hard blow on the side. But Rosalino got between me and him immediately and spoke to him. Then he went off. Rosalino says he was drunk." My eyes are still round with my adventure. Frieda, from her room, is calling out to know what it is all about.

"Rosalino!" you call to him; and then in Spanish: "What is all this about the Señorita?" Rosalino deposits the basket in the kitchen; then comes up to you with a beaming smile and repeats the tale to you in Spanish with delicate gestures of his dark hands.

Lawrence gives one of his most sympathetic glimpses of Rosalino in his account of how he reacted when wakened unexpectedly in the night:

Usually everybody is in by half-past-nine in our very quiet house. If not, you may thunder at the big doors. It is hard to wake Rosalino. You have to go close to him, and call. That will wake him. But don't touch him. That would startle him terribly. No one is touched unawares, except to be robbed or murdered.

"Rosalino! *estan tocando!*" —"Rosalino! they are knocking!"

At last there starts up a strange, glaring utterly lost Rosalino. Perhaps he just has enough wit to pull the door-catch. One wonders where he was, and what he was, in his sleep, he starts up so strange and wild and lost.

Rosalino's fears appear in two stories about soldiers, arising from his beating and Inocente's unjust jailing. Brett likewise relates an experience of hostility when she and the Lawrences were on their way home. It might have been at the barracks on García Vigil, just beyond Carmen Alto or at the cavalry barracks behind Santo Domingo at the corner of Reforma and Constitución. "A huge Indian soldier (with his head hunched in his shoulders, one hand in a pocket, the other holding a rifle) confronts us. He points to the road. His motion is silent and savage. Frieda and I hurry past on the edge of the curb. You, who are anyhow walking in the street, turn white with fury. The soldiers, the terrible, dreaded soldiers!"

The threatening soldier brought to her mind what she had previously seen: "prisoners, sometimes guarded by these soldiers and being marched to prison. The prisoners are a sickly green, green with the fear and horror of the prisons." She described the nearby jail as "a huge, desolate stone building, dreadful even from the street."

Lawrence's soldier story, which he uses to close "The Mozo," recalls passing the jail in the company of the two *mozos* he knew.

Is it any wonder that Aurelio and Rosalino, when they see the soldiers with guns on their shoulders marching towards the prison with some blanched prisoner between them—and one sees it every few days—stand

and gaze in a blank kind of horror, and look at the *patrón,* to see if there is any refuge?

Not to be *caught!* Not to be *caught!* It must have been the prevailing motive of Indian-Mexico life since long before Montezuma marched his prisoners to sacrifice.

This poignant ending ironically represents a complete reversal on Lawrence's part. The essay, which begins by presenting all Mexican Indians as flint knives, ends by depicting them as human beings who through the ages have lived in dread of the flint knife, whether wielded by pre-Columbian priests, the Spanish conquerors, or revolutionary leaders. The cry Lawrence imagined as being so constant showed how deeply his tender nature had absorbed the pain of the Revolution's victims. Perhaps in his very contradiction, Lawrence has conveyed something important about Mexico. People who live in dread of flint knives and have often seen them wielded, can come to harbor them in their own hearts; sometimes, when drink or a blind drive for retaliation drives them crazy, they slash about wildly with flint knives themselves.

Because Christmas is the last day covered by the Oaxaca sketches in *Mornings in Mexico,* we know little about Rosalino's final weeks with the Lawrences. Lawrence made a point of working a further sympathetic portrait of the *mozo* under the name of Lupe, into the final pages of *The Plumed Serpent,* suddenly and without advance preparation. Kate, married to General Viedma and living at the Villa Aragon, would naturally have a new set of servants, since Juana, her daughters, and her sons were attached to the house Kate had left. Just before Kate sets off to visit Ramón's *hacienda* for the last time, she calls "a man servant" to row her down the lake. He looks up at her "with dark, pregnant eyes" when they both hear singing as the boat approaches the jetty of the *hacienda.*

In the garden near the shore Kate sits on a bench to listen to the new song Ramón is teaching the singer.

> Her *mozo,* a man-servant, had followed her into the garden, and sat at a distance on his heels, under a tree, with his back to the trunk, like a crouching shadow clothed in white. His toes spread dark and hard, in his open *huaraches,* and the black braid of his hat-string hung against his dark cheek. For the rest he was pure white, the white cotton tight on his thighs.
>
> When the singing had finished above and the drum was silent, and even the voices speaking in low tones, were silent, her *mozo* looked up at Kate, with his black hat-string dangling at his chin, his black eyes shining, and a timid sort of smile on his face.
>
> *"Esta muy bien, Patrona?"* he said shyly. "It is good, isn't it, Mistress?"

He looked so young, when he smiled that gay, shy, excited little smile. Something of the eternal child in him. But a child that could harden in an instant into a savage man, revengeful and brutal. And a man always fully sex-alive, for the moment innocent in the fullness of sex, not in the absence. And Kate thought to herself, as she had thought before, that there were more ways than one of "becoming again as a little child."

But the man had a sharp, watchful look in the corner of his eye: to see if she were feeling some covert hostility. He wanted her to acquiesce in the hymn, in the drum, in the whole mood. Like a child he wanted her to acquiesce. But if she were going to be hostile, he would be quick to be first in the hostility. Her hostile judgment would make a pure enemy of him.

Brett left Oaxaca on January 19, extending the story beyond the cut-off date of *Mornings in Mexico.* She tells how the urge that rose in Rosalino so powerfully before the holiday, finally overcame him, although she is probably wrong in placing the event before Christmas:

One day he disappears. You are hurt, but it shows in bitterness. "It is always the same: give friendship and they deceive you and go. They don't really care—they really hate us. It makes me hate them," you say.

"He will come back," says the priest. Two days later Rosalino is back on his bench.

"Where have you been?" He waves a vague arm to the mountains.

"I go home to my village, to see my people."

But he has returned, with his faithful devotion, and now he begs and begs you to take him with you always wherever you go. This you know would be fatal; he would die of homesickness and cold. Meanwhile you teach him, and he guards you faithfully.

In August 1970, while going through Moore's two-volume edition of Lawrence's letters I came upon an unsuspected letter about the *mozo* that Lawrence wrote on 11 November 1927. The letter was in response to one written by Maria Cristina Chambers, a Mexican who had come to the United States at the age of fourteen and who, twenty years later, was the wife of Henry Kellett Chambers, a senior editor of *The Literary Digest.* She had never met Lawrence but introduced herself when her story with a Mexican setting, "John of God, the Water Carrier," followed Part I of Lawrence's "Flowery Tuscany" in the October 1927 issue of the *New Criterion* published in London.

A few months earlier Alfred Knopf had published *Mornings in Mexico* in New York, and the essay, "The Mozo," had excited her so much that she had persuaded her husband to publish a boiled-down version in his magazine, which appeared in the *Digest's* 24 September 1927 issue as "A Look Inside a Mexican Indian's Head." Her interest was personal. Lawrence wrote to Mrs. Chambers: "Is it possible you really are the godmother of Rosalino—the actual Rosalino of Oaxaca? [he asked incredulously.] Or do you mean, in the spirit merely? (pardon the merely.) But if in the flesh, do you know how he is, poor lad? The last I heard from Father Rickards he was in hospital, and not likely to live. Poor Rosalino, such a shy gentle soul—it's an awful shame."

Inocente's story, with his eggs, plants, beaming wife, and large family, had a happy ending, but Rosalino's did not. Mrs. Chambers had been dead five years by the time I discovered her story, and when her stepson, Colin K. Chambers, searched through her papers, he could find no trace of Rosalino.

CHAPTER 6

ANOTHER WALK
TO HUAYAPAN

San Felipe del Agua is at the base of
the mountain wall that rising sharply gives Oaxaca a lofty and dramatic
northern background. The town is quite well known; yet on a line heading almost due east are three other villages hardly known at all: Donaji
and San Luis Beltrán, which, like San Felipe, are still on the valley floor,
and San Andrés Huayapan, a little higher up the slope. All four villages
can be seen in their relationship to Oaxaca in the map, abstracted from
Cecil R. Welte's large-scale map of the valley. The Pan-American Highway, not yet built in Lawrence's day, is omitted, but it mounts the hill
of El Fortín, crosses the Jalatlaco River, and then proceeds through Ixcotel in the direction of the old road to Mitla shown on the map. The
contours of the hills are indicated by fence-post lines.

Lawrence's walk to Huayapan was on Sunday, 21 December 1924.
Mine was on Tuesday, 11 September 1962. His, as he confesses in his
"Walk to Huayapan," was an accident, probably before Padre Rickards

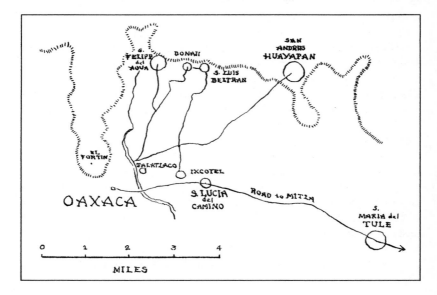

and Maximiliano Salinas showed him the shortest way to reach San Felipe. Their excursion was a spur of the moment affair, for when Frieda, infected by Sunday morning restlessness, said, "Let's go somewhere," Lawrence was likewise discontented. They decided to take a picnic lunch to San Felipe. My walk was an effort to follow Lawrence's footsteps, complete with a pocket edition of *Mornings in Mexico*. I planned to repeat my experiment at the market: to take pictures whenever I came upon sights described by Lawrence. I had never been to Huayapan, but felt sure I would recognize features he described so precisely.

My walk began paying dividends even before I started, for at breakfast I read over his introduction. My hotel was the Monte Alban, which had been the Alameda in his day. As it was in the center of town, the evening before I had only needed to step outside to enjoy the gala sight of the people of Oaxaca strolling round the plaza. Yet what did I find in his very first paragraph? "Humanity enjoying itself is on the whole a dreary spectacle." It seemed an incredible statement to make in a place like Oaxaca. Never had I been in a town where I had taken such pleasure in watching families relax together as they enjoyed the mildness of the evening air in an atmosphere of sociability. And when I read "I will avoid the sight of people enjoying themselves—or try to," I realized how much Lawrence felt alienated from humanity at that point. Having visited the house on Pino Suárez, I could visualize this indrawn man, who found holidays, "more disheartening than drudgery" making the determined resolution quoted in the essay: "On Sundays and on *fiestas* I will stay at home, in the hermitage of the patio, with the parrots and Corasmín and the reddening coffee-berries."

Lawrence's essay did not indicate the length of the walk to Huayapan and I resolved to time my own walk to find out. The walk between his house and the center of town took twenty minutes. But I walked slowly because there was so much that was pleasant and interesting to see, including the church of Santo Domingo. I had discovered that, except for the prison, Lawrence's walks home had held many enjoyable sights; I enviously recalled how Miss Doctor had sometimes accompanied him because she was going the same way.

It was just before ten o'clock when I reached the old house; finally I was in a position to make a point-by-point comparison between my Huayapan walk and Lawrence's. They would have emerged from the small door inset in the right wing of the large doors. Frieda had worn "a plain hat of bluey-green woven grass, and a dress of white cotton with black squares on it," and from her photograph in the priest's garden I knew that dress was ankle-length. Rosalino would have carried the picnic basket.

Lawrence described "the peculiar looseness" of the sunshine on the morning of their walk. My sky was overcast.

I had once seen Huayapan from a distance, so I knew its general direction. I had to continue north to the Pan-American Highway, and then head east until I found the right dirt road branching towards the hills. But I did not know the start of Lawrence's route because the highway did not exist then. At the end of his block, however, the towers of the Church of El Patrocinio rose above its high stone wall, the first landmark in their stroll. "So we walk around the wall of the church."

At the end of the park, adjoining the Santuario of Guadalupe, was Lawrence's "huge old monastery enclosure that is now barracks for the scrap-heap soldiery." An automobile blocked the view into the cloister. Lawrence had made a joyful point of saying, "Thank God, in Mexico at least one can't set off in the 'machine.' It is a question of a meagre horse with a wooden saddle: or a donkey; or what we called as children, 'Shanks' pony'—the shanks referring discourteously to one's own legs."

"At once there are hills," wrote Lawrence to dramatize the effect of suddenly clearing the walls of the monastery-hospital. My view was obscured by many intervening structures, including a gasoline station. Here, instead of continuing straight ahead going north, the threesome took a road branching off to the right. "In a stride, the town passes away," said Lawrence. But I had to walk almost ten minutes along the tree-planted boulevard before, through the opening of a vacant lot, I could glimpse the view that had greeted Lawrence immediately.

"Before us lies the gleaming, pinkish ochre of the valley flat, wild and exalted with sunshine." It captured atmosphere as well as topography, yet I saw green. Why did he call it pinkish ochre? I looked more closely at the earth visible where the vegetation was sparse. It was pinkish and a little yellow. His walk had been in December in the dry season and I had known the valley only in the rainy season. There was corn in the fields, but his must have seemed "wild." The rainy season, too, meant a heavy roof of clouds while his was "exalted with sunshine."

"I will lift up my eyes unto the hills, whence cometh my strength." This line of a psalm had come into Lawrence's head as he cleared the Bethlehemite monastery and he added the somewhat grudging compliment, "At least one can always do *that,* in Mexico. . . . On the left, quite near, bank the stiffly pleated mountains, all the foot-hills that press savannah-coloured into the savannah of the valley. The mountains are clothed smokily with pine, *ocote,* and, like a woman in a gauze *rebozo,* they rear in a rich blue fume that is almost corn-flower blue in the clefts. It is their characteristic that they are darkest-blue at the top."

When I lifted my eyes to the same mountains I saw gray, wet clouds rolling quite far down their flanks. The slopes were uniformly serge. Where ridges could be discerned through the clouds, the crests were indeed darkest at the top. "Clothed smokily with pine," too, was a very precise description, but the phrase I envied most was "stiffly pleated" for those down-running side ridges.

Not there in Lawrence's day were the Vasconcelos baseball park, the big trucks lumbering along the road, the whizzing automobiles, the jeeps, the already superseded airstrip of the old airport, the new Colonia Reforma served by a wide avenue of orange lamp posts along its dividing boulevard, and the new white-walled penitentiary with its turreted gray corners. A snatch of marimba music coming from a radio in a thatched hut made me think that the radio had hardly been developed in Lawrence's day. As the spacious valley arm towards Ocotlán began opening on my right, I concluded that if Lawrence ever looked south, he did not reveal it in his essay. His eye was only on the villages at the foot of the pleated mountains.

It was eleven o'clock before I was in open country and then, for the first time, I was able to see Lawrence's logic in comparing the hills to "some splendid lizard with a wavering, royal-blue crest down the ridge of his back, and pale belly, and soft, pinky-fawn claws." I tried to catch the effect with my camera but could not. However, I later captured it in a sketch.

Lawrence's lizard simile is useful for colors as well as forms. The foothills and lower slopes are different in hue and lighter in tone than the tree-covered upper slopes. The description continues, written like a stage direction: "Between the pallor of the claws, a dark spot of trees, and white dots of a church with twin towers. Further away, along the foot-hills, a few scattered trees, white dot and stroke of a hacienda, and a green, green square of sugar-cane. Further off still, at the mouth of a cleft of a canyon, a dense little green patch of trees, and two spots of proud church."

As I searched for the features described, I was amazed at his accuracy.

Clearly, he looked from left to right. At the left I saw the "dark spot of trees" obscuring San Felipe del Agua. I understood why he skipped over Donaji; it was hardly visible. At San Luis Beltrán the trees were indeed more scattered and I saw the "stroke" of the hacienda's long flat roof. On the right I saw how "dense" was the green patch of trees representing Huayapan. Although the overcast did not allow me to discern the "two spots of proud church," I saw "the cleft of the canyon" at whose mouth the village seemed to lie.

"Rosalino, which is San Felipe?" Lawrence asked when they had reached this point.

"Quien sabe, Señor?" Rosalino replied.

Lawrence had proposed a picnic in San Felipe relying on Rosalino to act as guide. After walking an hour in the wrong direction, he had made the discovery that the youth knew as little about the region as he did.

"Have you never been to any of these villages?" Lawrence asked incredulously.

"No, *Señor,* I never went."

"Didn't you want to?"

"Como no, Señor?"

Since they weren't seriously lost and it really did not matter where they had their picnic, "we decided for the farthest speck of a village in a dark spot of trees. It lies so magical, alone, tilted on the fawn-pink slope, again as if the dark-green napkin with a few white tiny buildings had been lowered from heaven and left there at the foot of the mountains, with the deep groove of a canyon slanting in behind. So alone and, as it were, detached from the world in which it lies."

The description was so accurate that anyone aware of the topography would know they had decided on Huayapan, even if, at the time, they did not. Later I left the highway, crossed some fields, and reached a point on a dirt road leading to the hills where the distant Huayapan looked exactly as he described it. But the poignance of Huayapan's isolation which Lawrence felt so keenly seemed even sharper under a lowering sky.

The poignance Lawrence sensed, resembling the feeling that had often swept over him in Mexico, led him to generalize:

Nowhere more than in Mexico does human life become isolated, external to its surroundings, and cut off tinily from the environment. Even as you come across the plains to a big city like Guadalajara, and see the twin towers of the Cathedral peering around the loneliness like two lost birds side by side on a moor, lifting their white heads to look around in the wilderness, your heart gives a clutch, feeling the pathos, the isolated tininess of human effort. As for building a church with one tower only, it is unthinkable. Here must be two towers, to keep each other company in this wilderness world.

This passage capturing so uniquely the tragic poetry of so much of the Mexican landscape, makes one count as minor the instances where Lawrence made mistakes.

Remembering how unfriendly Lawrence had found the people of Huayapan, I was charmed when the country people I began greeting invariably smiled and replied, *"Buenos días. Pase Usted."*

"A donde va?" asked a bricklayer in a friendly tone, building a small wall. He assured me I had found the right road to Huayapan and told me I should follow it straight ahead. Later, after clearing the unroofed old barracks begun during World War II and passing a grove of feathery green jacaranda trees, I came to a fork in the road. *"A la izquierda. Que le vaya bien,"* said a man with a heavy cylindrical basket on his back who came along at my moment of doubt. I felt especially touched as I watched his figure diminish towards Oaxaca. I was a privileged foreigner with no heavy load but he had wished me well.

The Lawrences had crossed a little river; as I came to a dry stream bed, arched over by a brick bridge, I wondered if I had reached the point where Frieda had rested under the shade of a bush. Lawrence had mentioned no bridge, but the one I saw might be new. I asked a pleasant man in a black felt sombrero the name of the waterless stream. *"Rio Tecolote* (River of the Owl)," he replied. Then he volunteered that further on I would cross two more rivers, the Rio Cazaguate, which was also dry, and the Rio Zoogochí, which had water.

As I stood at the bridge, I had a pleasant surprise, a Lawrence touch I was sure of, for two women I had not noticed reached the bridge, prototypes of Lawrence's "occasional women taking a few vegetables to market," or as described in more detail: "Down the trail that had worn grooves in the turf—the rock is near the surface—occasional donkeys with a blue-hooded woman perched on top come tripping in silence, twinkling, a shadow. . . ."

It was with just such a woman that this dialogue occurred.

Rosalino, prancing behind with the basket, plucks up courage to speak to one of the women passing on a donkey. "Is that San Felipe where we are going?"—"No, that is not San Felipe."—"What, then, is it called?"—"It is called Huayapa."—"Which, then, is San Felipe?"—"That one"—and she points to her right.

Lawrence's report that she called her village Huayapa shows a good ear, for villagers generally omit the final consonant and there is disagreement about what it should be. "M" is often given, but I follow the census records in using an "n."

Taking advantage of the bridge's shade, I read on to see what was coming next; I wanted to vary the procedure of reading Lawrence solely as commentator on what I had found for myself. Since leaving the highway I had entered a world·apparently unchanged since 1924, and Lawrence's visual accuracy up to that point had given confidence that I would find little change in thirty-eight years.

"Ten o'clock, and the sun getting hotter," began the first of the paragraphs. "Not a spot of shade, apparently, from here to Huayapa. The blue getting thinner on the mountains, and an indiscernible vagueness, of too much light, descending on the plain."

Since it had taken me until 11:40 A.M. to reach the point he had reached by ten, I calculated he and Frieda must have left home about 8:15 A.M. It was also getting hotter for me with little promise of shade. Although the clouds were still too numerous for the "indiscernible vagueness of too much light," soon the day would be totally sunny. Although it was not "thin" yet, the blue on my mountains was decidedly paler, and all colors, especially the greens of the corn stalks, had grown more vivid.

The second river, the Cazaguate, was dry as predicted by the man in the black hat. I discovered that Lawrence, although giving the impression of describing every inch of the way, was artist enough to simplify by leaving features out. This stream bed, which had given so little advance warning of its presence and which was in a very narrow, steep-walled gorge, was not mentioned. In another paragraph he implied that the first stream bed contained water. I had reached a second dry stream bed, and it was the season more likely to have water than in Lawrence's December. But the unmentioned stream beds were included nevertheless; this realization taught me more about his artistry. Although he wanted to relate a specific walk, he also wanted a prototype conveying the character of most walks to Mexican villages. He generalized in introducing the first stream, another example of his gift for pinning down the essence of the Mexican landscape. The two undescribed streams must have stirred his imagination to write:

The road suddenly dips into a little crack, where runs a creek. This again is characteristic of these parts of America. Water keeps out of sight. Even the biggest rivers, even the tiny brooks! You look across a plain on which the light sinks down, and you think: Dry! Dry! Absolutely dry! You travel along, and suddenly come to a crack in the earth, and a little stream is running in a little walled-in valley bed, where is a half-yard of green turf, and bushes, the *palo-blanco* with leaves, and with big white flowers like pure white, crumpled cambric. Or you may come to a river a thousand feet below, sheer below you. But not in this valley. Only the stream.

The Rio Zoogochí conformed exactly to this description. I knew I had been wrong in thinking the dry Rio Tecolote might have been his stream. The flowers he saw here, like "crumpled cambric," settled a botanical question. When he spoke of the distant "palo-blanco" blossoms in the market essay as "snow-white flakes of flowers," I had wondered what species he was referring to. Books on Mexican flora had not supplied the answer, but they were clearly *cazaguates*. I felt double envy for his choice of words. I had seen big floppy *cazaguate* flowers often enough. So many grow on the slopes of Monte Alban that some believe the sacred hill was called "White Mountain" because of them. Why couldn't I have thought of crumpled white linen? Or of snowflakes for the distant effect?

Sitting down at the very ford where the Lawrences had stopped, I was in a special position to visualize the incidents of their rest:

"Shade!" says the Señora, subsiding under a steep bank.

"Mucho calor!" says Rosalino, taking off his extra-jaunty straw hat, and subsiding with the basket.

Down the slope are coming two women on donkeys. Seeing the terrible array of three people sitting under a bank, they pull up.

"Adiós!" I say, with firm resonance.

"Adiós!" says the Señora, with diffidence.

"Adiós!" says the reticent Rosalino, his voice the shadow of ours.

"Adiós! Adiós! Adiós!" say the women, in suppressed voices, swerving, neutral past us on their self-contained, sway-eared asses.

When they have passed, Rosalino looks at me to see if I shall laugh. I give a little grin, and he gives me back a big explosive grin, throwing back his head in silence, opening his wide mouth and showing his soft pink tongue, looking along his cheeks with his saurian black eyes, in an excess of *farouche* derision.

I could almost hear the splashing of the donkey's feet as the women passed through the ford, and I saw how they would have had to swerve to get past three people sitting where I was, for the shady spot was practically athwart the narrow path leading up the bank on my side of the stream.

Lawrence called "good-bye" to the approaching women as a reassuring greeting, from its broad meaning, "to God." He had the women say it three times as they passed, for they were following the custom of wishing each person they passed the same divine protection. I doubt that Rosalino's grin was derisive. It was more likely sheer pleasure that he and the *patrón* had shared a secret understanding, both appreciating the women's timidity.

The women who dropped the consonant had swerved away from the Lawrences. Others did too. "They all swerve away from us, as if we were potential bold brigands," he wrote. Then forgetting his doubts about his British slang when he wrote McDonald, he added: "It really gets one's pecker up."

"The presence of the Señora only half reassures them," he continued. "For the Señora . . . is almost a monster of unusualness. *Prophet art thou bird, or devil?* the women seem to say, as they look at her with keen black eyes. I think they decide she is more of the last." Lawrence felt that the men looked also at him with the same questions. He felt they likewise sized him up as mostly devil. Rereading the passage as I sat in the shadow of the bridge, having received so many kindly greetings, I wondered if Lawrence had misinterpreted the looks he received. In 1962 natives were still not accustomed to seeing tourists on this particular road. In 1924, a man with a red beard and a blonde woman, who by native standards was mountainous, must have seemed strange indeed. This was also a period when members of Oaxaca's foreign colony were remaining strictly within the city limits, convinced that unlawful elements made it unsafe to venture into the countryside. The Lawrences were doing something daring and unusual, something their friends would probably have counseled them against. Perhaps in those days the people coming from the hills were as fearful and suspicious as Lawrence believed. On the other hand, they might have swerved away because they misinterpreted the Lawrences' own looks. They might have felt they were being glared at, and Mexicans are quick to sense dislike. If the Lawrences had known more about the Indians, they would have anticipated intense and mistrustful scrutiny, especially now that they were out of the city, for among the country folk, unaccustomed to outsiders, the Revolution's bitter campaign against foreigners had undoubtedly raised uncertainties.

While they were still resting, "a great hawk, like an eagle, with white bars at the end of its wings," swept low over them. Lawrence interpreted it as "looking for snakes" and added, "One can hear the hiss of its pinions." When Rosalino identified the bird as a *gavilan*, Lawrence asked him what it was called in the *idioma*, meaning Rosalino's native Zapotec.

>*"Psia!"* —He makes the consonants explode and hiss.
>"Ah!" says the Señora. "One hears it in the wings. *Psia!"*

From their vantage point, they saw this scene:

Down the creek, two native boys, little herdsmen, are bathing, stooping with knees together and throwing water over themselves, rising, gleaming dark coffee-red in the sun, wetly. They are very dark, and their wet heads are so black, they seem to give off a bluish light, like dark electricity.

The great cattle they are tending slowly plunge through the bushes, coming up-stream. At the place where the path fords the stream, a great ox stoops to drink. Comes a cow after him, and a calf, and a young bull. They all drink a little at the stream, their noses delicately touching the water. And then the young bull, horns abranch, stares fixedly, with some of the same Indian wonder-and-suspicion stare, at us sitting under the bank.

Up jumps the Señora, proceeds uphill, trying to save her dignity. The bull, slowly leaning into motion, moves across-stream like a ship unmoored.

The bathing lad on the bank is hastily fastening his calico pantaloons round his ruddy-dark waist. The Indians have a certain rich physique, even this lad. He comes running short-step down the bank, uttering a bird-like whoop, his dark hair gleaming bluish. Stooping for a moment to select a stone, he runs athwart the bull, and aims the stone sideways at him. There is a thud, the ponderous, adventurous young animal swerves docilely round towards the stream. *"Bacerro!"* cries the boy, in his bird-like piping tone, selecting a stone to throw at the calf.

Glancing down the creek, I saw there were reeds in it still. When I looked upstream I could hardly believe my eyes. (Plate 30.) One of Lawrence's little "herdsmen" had actually materialized—barefoot, dressed in a red baseball cap, worn with the visor reversed, a red T-shirt and ragged blue pants. Though a long pole sloped over his shoulder, I saw no sign of his cattle. Slung over his shoulder, the boy had a white sack bulging with what might be stones.

"*Buenas tardes,* " I called, since it was now past noon. The boy returned the greeting and assured me the water was pure enough to drink. I took him at his word and knelt to scoop up handfuls. The boy's name was Bernabé and he was twelve years old.

As he accompanied me towards the village, we met a man with two burros loaded with kindling. The man said I would find a famous retable in the church. After he was gone the boy explained that besides raising corn, the men of the village gathered wood, often going high into the hills to cut it, which they would sell in Oaxaca.

"We proceed in the blazing sun up the slope," Lawrence continued. "There is a white line at the foot of the trees. It looks like water running white over a weir. The supply of the town water comes this way.

Perhaps this is a reservoir. A sheet of water! How lovely it would be, in this country, if there was a sheet of water with a stream running out of it! And those dense trees of Huayapa behind."

At this point, Frieda asked Rosalino if it were water they saw. *"El blanco? Sí, agua, Señora,* " the *mozo* replied. Lawrence comments that if Frieda had asked if it were milk, Rosalino would have agreed. "That dumb-bell," repeated Lawrence, apparently not stopping to think that the boy was in no better position than they were to explain the white line.

On the last stretch to the town Lawrence implied there was nothing to see until the white line resolved "into a broken, whitewashed wall." Perhaps he was fatigued for he spoke of walking "amidst a weight of light, out of which one hardly sees." On a cooler, less trying day, I found the approach to the village interesting: the first near glimpse of the two white towers of the church, two more woodsellers and, in a wide field, a man plowing the brown-red earth with a team of yoked oxen. After another dip in the landscape, the unrutted, dirt road began paralleling the Zoogochí, and the going became decidedly pleasant, for trees lined the river banks, including willows, bananas, and *guayabas,* which I recognized from their round green-yellow fruit. Bernabé paused to hurl his long stick into a particularly well-loaded tree, gathering the *guayabas,* putting them in his sack. He then shinnied up the tree to pull free others that had not yielded to his whirling stick. When he rejoined me, he gave me a handful.

After a while the road crossed the river on a pretty brick bridge shaded by trees. Beyond the mountains, the sky was gray with rain. A young mother, her baby slung in a *rebozo* on her back passed, taking her husband's lunch to the fields. Everyone who passed was friendly, helpful, and apparently pleased that a stranger should be coming to visit. Finally, we reached the larger trees on the outskirts, not a moment too soon, for the rainstorm from behind the mountains was suddenly on top of us. But a *busache,* a big white-flowered tree, provided shelter dense enough for both of us. I could even read. Two men approached protected by plastic sheets, with a train of seven burros loaded with wood.

When the rain let up, Bernabé and I started off again, only to be overtaken by another rainstorm. We waited this one out under a huge fig tree. After it had passed, the sky was a pristine blue. Resuming our way, we came to Lawrence's wall. The wall surrounded a cemetery, or *pantéon* as Rosalino called it. The baroque entrance gate still had whitewash, but none was left on the rustic stone walls, explaining why I had not seen them from afar as the Lawrences had. Besides, screening eucalyptus trees now make the cemetery much less exposed.

"Hello, mister," called a cheery wood-seller in English as we reached *la Calle de Pocito,* the Street of the Little Well. We followed it into the town plaza. It was 1:30 P.M.; the walk had taken three and a half hours.

When I turned to thank Bernabé, he had vanished.

Lawrence's account of Huayapan is longer than his story of the approach to the village. I was confused. When I had reached the *plaza* so quickly after the cemetery, why did he describe all those intervening streets? It was not until later in the afternoon, when I had walked through a number of streets myself, that I reconstructed the party's route.

Though Huayapan is built on a slope, the slope is broad enough to accommodate the classic Spanish town plan: a grid of straight streets, crossing at right angles. In Huayapan's case the grid is tilted, the short streets running down, the long ones traversing the slope from west to east. The Lawrences, instead of proceeding straight along *Calle de la Pocito,* took a left turn up the *Calle de la Mina,* which Lawrence remembered as *Calle de las Minas;* an understandable confusion since the village has both a Street of the Mine and a Street of the Mines.

They went up the Street of the Mine, rightly described as "a rocky stream gutter, disappearing to nowhere from nowhere between cactus and bushes." Then they turned right at Magnolia, a long transverse street conforming to his "just a track between the stiff living fence of organ cactus, with *poinsettia* trees holding up scarlet mops of flowers, and mango trees, tall and black, stonily drooping the strings of unripe fruit." Their stems were now red, though the fruits were definitely stone-shaped, which enabled me to admire his "stonily drooping." I also noticed that fences of reeds bound tightly together far outnumbered those of organ cactus. Lawrence was probably combining memories of Mitla with those of Huayapan. Very few houses were plastered, so one saw their brown adobes, the color of maple sugar.

The Lawrences walked along Magnolia until they saw Reforma "and at the end of Reforma the great church." Scarcely a town in Mexico lacks a Calle de la Reforma named for the 1856-59 Reform Laws of Juárez. "A stony stream-bed, emerging out of tall, wildly swaying reeds," well described Reforma's upper part, where the Lawrences turned right to reach the plaza.

Up to now Lawrence's choice of color words had been subtle, original, and enviably right, but here he called the village's adobes black. Was it his mood? A projection of his internal state on the external landscape? One recalls his dislike and perhaps fear of Oaxaca's Indians; he called them "a black savage mass." He describes the village negatively:

> Not a soul anywhere. Through the fences, half-deserted gardens of trees and banana plants, each enclosure with a half-hidden hut of black adobe bricks crowned with a few old tiles for a roof, and perhaps a new wing made of twigs. Everything hidden, secret, silent. A sense of darkness among the silent mango trees, a sense of lurking, of unwillingness. Then actually

some half-bold cur barking at us across the stile of one garden, a forked bough over which one must step to enter the chicken-bitten enclosure. And actually a man crossing the proudly labelled: First Street of the Independence.

If there were no churches to mark a point in these villages, there would be nowhere at all to make for. The sense of nowhere is intense, between the dumb and repellent living fence of cactus. But the Spaniards, in the midst of these black, mud-brick huts, have inevitably reared the white twin-towered magnificence of a big and lonely, hopeless church: and where there is a church there will be a *plaza.* And a *plaza* is a *zócalo,* a hub. Even though the wheel does not go round, a hub is still a hub. Like the old Forum.

This otherwise excellent passage—though extremely subjective—is marred by a mistake. In Mexico a *plaza* is a *zócalo,* but that does not mean a hub. It is the Spanish equivalent of our architectural term *socle,* a projecting member, usually molded, at the foot of a wall, pier, or pedestal.

"In front of the church," he wrote, "is a rocky *plaza* leaking with grass, with water rushing into the two big, oblong stone basins." (Plate 31.) Even the stone basins were still there, used by the village women for washing. It seemed incredible that the *plaza* had remained so little changed in thirty-eight years. But in 1962 it was considerably enhanced by handsome Indian laurels that might not have been there in Lawrence's day.

While drinking an orange soda I discovered that Lawrence had described the very establishment I was in and its neighbors as well: "On the bottom of the *plaza* is a shop. . . . Next door is another little hole of a shop." Perhaps in his day the middle third of the portal's tile roof had not yet fallen in, but his description conveyed such decrepitude that I felt it probably had.

Because it was Sunday, they found the church open. The church was closed on Tuesday, the day of my visit. Arriving during the midday meal, I had found the town as quiet and deserted as the Lawrences did, but asked a neatly dressed young man who came into the *plaza* if he knew how I could get into the church. He would help me find the verger. His slightly citified air indicated that he was one of the local schoolteachers. Some of his pupils would be along soon and they could guide me to the verger's house. Meanwhile his wife, also a schoolteacher, joined us. They were Leonardo Santiago López and Soledad Ramírez de López. They had been teaching in the village for four years and liked Huayapan. *"Gente muy pacífica, muy tratable,"* said Sr. López. I had consulted the census of 1921—the nearest census to Lawrence's visit—and found Huayapan then had 233 men and 251 women in it. I asked the teacher how many it now had. He told me the census two years earlier showed 565. In forty years the town had grown by only 81 people. They all spoke Zapotec.

"Was there ever a man here named Valentino Ruiz?" I asked. That was the name Lawrence gave the villager who he felt had overcharged him for three oranges. Valentino was dead now, said the teacher, but his son, Valente, still lived in his father's old house with the brown and red tiles on Calle de 12 Magnolia. So Lawrence had even named the street correctly.

I asked the teacher if he knew that the English novelist D. H. Lawrence had written a famous essay about Huayapan. He didn't, so I slipped my book from my pocket and showed the essay to Sr. López and his wife. If he would deliver the book to the Presidente Municipal, I would send two copies, one for the teacher, the other for the village archives. The teacher willingly agreed, promising he would explain the gift to the mayor when it arrived.

As two little girls came by, the teacher asked them to take me to the verger's. Even in this new part of town the adobes were brown, not black. Marciano García Cortez, the caretaker of the church willingly agreed to open it for me. On the way, he told me he had been the sacristan since 1950. The village had no resident priest, relying on priests from Oaxaca who came out for special occasions.

The church tower on the left had obviously been reconstructed in 1951-52, noted by a little sign under the belfry. So it revealed the village care shown since the novelist's visit, but if one looked at the right tower through the trees one could appreciate the exactness of Lawrence's words: "The great church stands rather ragged, in a dense forlornness, for all the world like some big white human being . . . held captive in a world of ants." For the church as a whole still conformed to this description. (Plate 32.) With the church, as with the *plaza,* he chose unusual words to bring out the spirit of what he saw; relying on subjective impressionism rather than technical terms like pilasters, cornices, tiled cupolas, an octagonal choir window, and a baroque cresting. The phrase "a dense forlornness" is characteristic of the sort of thing Frieda argued about with Lawrence in Italy in 1912. "He is so stupid, I think, in *seeing* things that cannot be seen with eyes, or touched, or smelt or heard," she wrote their friend Edward Garnett. "The peculiar looseness" of the sunshine, a "weight of light," and a *plaza* "leaking with grass" are other examples of sensuous impossibilities. What Lawrence conveyed were the emanations that came to him from things; he was right to persist, in spite of Frieda's criticism, for the captured emanations are what make his descriptions so amazingly alive and, in some mysterious way, so easy to visualize. Perhaps objects can be more easily conjured up in the imagination by the vibrations than by catalogues of their parts.

The church had a side chapel on the left so large that it had its own entrance. My first impression, once Don Marciano had let me in, was of a simple cruciform with a dome rising over the crossing. The cream-colored walls were divided by pilasters rendered conspicuous by terra-cotta paint, and the nave seemed unusually spacious because only two side altars intruded on its width. The shallow domes of the ceiling were separated from the walls by a blue-gray cornice. Crystals dripped from a scrawny central chandelier. The floor was clean and well-swept. The Lawrences had come three days after the feast of the Virgin of Soledad, the patron saint of Oaxaca, and "sprays of wild yellow flowers" were still trailing on the floor.

I quickly discovered why Lawrence first described "the great Gulliver's Travels fresco picture of an angel having a joy ride on the back of Goliath," for the moment we cleared the underside of the choir gallery we saw on the left a huge fresco of Saint Christopher carrying the Christ Child over the legendary river. Recently renovated, the fresco was probably even more conspicuous than when Lawrence saw it, and I had to smile at his exuberant description. But why did he mistake the Child for an angel when it had no wings? Was it possible that his Congregational upbringing was so void of images that he did not recognize Saint Christopher? Or was he joking?

Indifferent to Roman Catholic images and unaware of their significance, he was silent about the gilded two-story reredos that rose behind the main altar. Above, in a semi-circle was a grim painting of a *Pietá*. Below, set off by pillars suggesting gold filigree, were two paintings of Christ at the Column flanking a niche with a small saint clad in red and gold. If Lawrence did not recognize the little saint as Saint Andrew, surely, as a good Briton, he should have recognized the patron saint of Scotland in the adjacent version, for this larger statue was backed by an identifying X-shaped cross. But apparently he didn't, thus explaining why his essay omits *San Andrés,* the patron saint, from the name of the village.

The reredos also offered an interesting clue to the early history of Huayapan and the founding of the church. Saint Dominic, the founder of the Dominican Order, was represented by two statues, which showed that the village, like the majority in the state of Oaxaca, had been under Dominican control. The Indian name indicated that the community probably antedated the coming of the Spaniards. Being beside a river having plentiful water all year round, its name (deriving from the Nahuatl *huey,* meaning "great," and *apam,* meaning "river") suggests, too, that its location was pre-Conquest. If the sixteenth-century Dominicans did not establish the village, they certainly had a hand in making its plan conform to the Spanish grid. But the man who did not recognize Saint Andrew was even less likely to recognize Saint Dominic, despite the striking black and white habit of his order. Besides, five years earlier, Lawrence had written to Nancy Henry, an editor at Oxford University Press, "I do loathe the broken pots of historical facts."

The side chapel, extending from the left transept, was as large as the church itself. The sacristan explained why by the proud tone in which he gave its name—the Sanctuary of *El Señor,* pointing with a reverent gesture to a little crucified figure over the altar that was dwarfed by the life-sized angels holding crystal chandeliers before it. *El Señor,* he said, perspired with human sweat. When this was discovered in the seventeenth century, the bishop of Oaxaca tried to claim the miraculous image, but the villagers refused to give it up. Ever since, it had attracted many pilgrims. But I was more excited by a statue in a high-arched niche in the left wall still wearing real clothing, and unmistakably, the one statue in the church that Lawrence had described: "a life-sized Christ— undersized; seated upon a little table, wearing a pair of woman's frilled knickers, a little mantle of purple silk dangling from His back, and His face bent forward gazing fatuously at his naked knee, which emerges from the needlework frill of the drawers." When Lawrence saw the image it was near the altar steps, but this niche was clearly its permanent home. Obviously it had been set near the altar for the fiesta of Soledad, because Soledad, a version of Mary at the foot of the cross, is intimately associated with Christ's Passion.

Lawrence was right about this Christ being a little undersized, and he still had a purple cape, but his frilled knickers had been replaced by *calzones,* the white ankle-length trousers worn by field workers. I found the expressive figure especially touching, not fatuous, and Lawrence's unsympathetic, uncomprehending, and superior attitude towards the villagers' feeling for the anguish of Jesus seemed particularly unfeeling. The sacristan told me the figure was named *El Señor de la Humildad Paciente,* the Lord of Patient Humility, venerated on Holy Thursday, the day before his crucifixion. Had Lawrence understood this, despised and rejected himself—witness the 1915 suppression of *The Rainbow,* his most beautiful book—surely the knickers would not have filled him with such prejudicial scorn.

I took notes as Don Marciano spoke, as I had during my whole walk to Huayapan. How did Lawrence, who did not write from notes, manage such accuracy in remembered impressions? Was his memory photographic and his recall total? If so, one can understand how he found the words he did to evoke his impressions so vividly. He could rerun his memories in his mind's eye when there was leisure to seek for perfect expressions. Also, he seems to have grasped specific appearances and general identities simultaneously. Evocative words rose effortlessly in his mind the moment he saw anything. Joseph Foster recalled "the instant way he verbalized beauty." "Words welled out of him," wrote Lady Cynthia Asquith in describing what it was like walking with him. Frieda testified similarly in a statement E. W. Tedlock, Jr., found among her papers: "All those that ever went for a walk with him remember what an experience it was. It seemed all he saw out of doors he saw for the first time, and he noticed everything, every first flower in the spring, every color, every smell." And in *"Not I, But the Wind . . ."* she wrote, "travelling with him was living new experiences vividly every minute."

Lawrence's view of the Huayapan church provides an example of his richness of detail:

> We sit silent, motionless, in the whitewashed church, ornamented with royal blue and bits of gilt. A barefoot Indian with a high-domed head comes in and kneels with his legs close together, his back stiff, at once very humble and resistant. His cotton jacket and trousers are long-unwashed rag, the colour of dry earth, and torn, so that one sees smooth pieces of brown thigh, and brown back. He kneels in a sort of intense fervour for a minute, then gets up and childishly, almost idiotically, begins to take the pieces of candle from the candlesticks. He is the Verger.

And this was only one of hundreds of scenes that kept flashing on him during that walk. In contrast, I have no recollection at all of what my verger was wearing, except that he was not ragged. If Lawrence had not led me to look for the characteristic, my notes would never have preserved the fact that Don Marciano, too, had a high-domed head.

Mrs. Carswell had observed: "It might be said of him that he was the most incurious of men," denying that Lawrence always had to be "fed with new travel by way of excitement." Pictures, not curiosity, stirred his seeing; at this stage of his life he must have been aware of his penetrating vision which never needed questioning, making him over-confident in the completeness of his impressions. If he had been less intuitive and less naturally gifted at articulating his views, scenic and otherwise, he would have been more exhaustive in his investigations and slower in coming to judgment. But he would not have been the man he was.

Depressed during World War I, Lawrence wrote to Lady Cynthia Asquith, "I hate humanity so much, I can only think with friendliness of the dead." "Damn humanity!" became an increasingly common expression in his letters. His misanthropy had been building up in Oaxaca and, although getting out into the country had lightened it at first, being in Huayapan revived it. He grew increasingly unfair to the village. When first reading the Huayapan essay I was a fairly sentimental tourist, having only visited Mexico four times and having imbibed most of my ideas about the Revolution from left-wing American writers of the 1930s who praised what the Revolution had done to make Mexico truly democratic. I had fallen under the sway of Diego Rivera and Orozco's art and I had thrilled at what men like Vasconcelos had done to foster public education. I was almost ready to give up Lawrence forever as an observer of Mexican life when I came to his treatment of the village meeting. Never had I read anything so exasperatingly unjust to semi-literate people who were making admirable strides in establishing a new and better form of government.

On the uphill side of the *plaza,* a long low white building with a shed in front, and under the shed crowding, all the short-statured men of the *pueblo,* in their white cotton clothes and big hats. They are listening to something: But the silence is heavy, furtive, secretive. They stir like white-clad insects.

Rosalino looks sideways at them, and sheers away. Even we lower our voices to ask what is going on. Rosalino replies, *sotto voce,* that they are making *asuntos.* But what business? we insist. The dark faces of the little men under the big hats look round at us suspiciously, like dark gaps in the atmosphere. Our alien presence in this vacuous village, is like the sound of a drum in a churchyard.

The intelligent thing for the Lawrences to have done would have been to explain that they were lost picnickers. Instead they went into the church without a by-your-leave. "Outside, the gang of men is still pressing under the shed. We insist on knowing what is going on. Rosalino, looking sideways at them, plucks up courage to say plainly that the two men at the table are canvassing for votes: for the Government, for the State, for a new governor, whatever it may be."

But the elections had taken place several months ago, for it was now December 21, and Jiménez had been installed on December 1. Rosalino, obviously guessing, did not guess right. But Lawrence, again forgetting that Rosalino had never been in Huayapan before, swallowed the *mozo's* explanation and composed the following address.

Votes! Votes! Votes! The farce of it! Already on the wall of the low building, on which one sees, in blue letters, the word *Justizia,* there are pasted the late political posters, with the loud announcement: Vote for this Mark **+**. Or another: vote for this Mark **–** .

My dear fellow, this is when democracy becomes real fun. You vote for one red ring inside another red ring and you get a Julio Echegeray. You vote for a blue dot inside a blue ring and you get a Socrate Ezequiel Tos. Heaven knows what you get for the two little red circles on top of one another. Suppose we vote, and try. There's all sorts in the lucky bag. There might come a name like Peregrino Zenon Cocotilla.

Independence! Government by the People, of the People, for the People! We all live in the Calle de la Reforma, in Mexico.

Those paragraphs angered me when I read them, even though the details were accurate. The differing parties still use circle-surrounded initials in their campaigns, and I could see the cleverness of identifying one party as Plus and the other as Minus. Now that I know how many candidates were originally in the 1924 political campaigns, I appreciate his accuracy still more. In the final showdown for the presidency were Plutarco Elías Calles and Angel Flores, the general who was expected to revolt rather than abide by the official decision. But Nicolás Flores Magon had been an earlier opponent of Calles. Heliodoro Díaz Quintas and Francisco Alonso were among the Oaxaqueños who were anti-Calles. In the contest for governor, besides the leading candidates, Jiménez and Vasconcelos, there had been Rubén Morales, whose *Gran Partido Liberal Independente* only managed to muster 760 votes. So Lawrence had cause for making such a play of funny-sounding names. Since *tos* means "cough," he even devised an amusing pseudonym for Calles, whom he was working into *The Plumed Serpent,* less satirically, as Socrates Tomás Montés. But the basic attitude underlying the novelist's mockery seemed grossly unfair.

Ignorantly Lawrence dismissed the brick portal as a "shed"; it actually fronted the village's city hall. *Justicia,* the word painted in blue, over the doorway to the *Sala Municipal,* or council chamber, was not, as Lawrence implies, a slogan expressing an ideal. Furthermore, he misspelled it as *Justizia.* Yet Lawrence's contempt and disgust came from a more accurate picture of Oaxacan politics than mine.

Five weeks had passed since he had called on Ibarra, and in that time the boorish Jiménez had been installed as the new governor. Longtime residents of Oaxaca, like the Kulls, Miss Doctor, and Duke, had revealed the ugly facts behind the new regime. Lawrence had learned how García Vigil, who had given the state its democratic constitution, had been hunted down and killed. He had learned Ibarra's early record in using force to put in and overthrow governors and of the rigged election that imposed an ignorant lout over Vasconcelos, the educational reformer. He had reason for terming the 1924 Oaxaca election a "farce," reason for knowing that what hopefully self-asserting villagers like those of Huayapan could do in the face of the Calles-Obregón political machine was hardly worth considering. His long series of disillusions also included disillusion with democracy. The conduct of the British common people during the first World War had convinced him that people were not capable of governing themselves anywhere. "No man who has consciously lived through this," he said of the war in *Kangaroo,* "can believe again absolutely in democracy." *Kangaroo* was his last novel written before coming to Mexico, and what he had learned in Mexico had deepened his distrust of people's political capacities. Skepticism about the whole democratic process, as well as inside knowledge, made him think Huayapan's democracy a mockery.

During the war Lawrence had often compared human beings to beetles. "White-clad insects" was his Mexican image to convey comparable disgust. Intensity of reaction was one of his traits, and the sight of the villagers, especially their seeming hostility, led him to vent feelings churning in him from the earlier disheartening events in Oaxaca. Vasconcelos, who was cheated of Oaxaca's governorship, and who, after his bid for the presidency of Mexico in 1929, was forced into seven years of exile from the country he loved so passionately, remained bitter about Lawrence's refusal to come back to have lunch with him. "Lawrence," he wrote in *A Mexican Ulysses,* "was nothing but a sexually inadequate man devoted to sublimating the potency that he did not have, and making a divinity out of it." Yet in a later part of his autobiography Vasconcelos recorded a more favorable verdict with Francis de Miomandre, a French author who had translated *Don Quixote* and gained fame from his book, *Written on Water.* Miomandre admired *The Plumed Serpent:* "He asked me how right the mystico-gloomy interpretation of the famous English novelist was. One cannot deny, I told him, that this is a case where there are insights of real genius; to such a point that certain predictions which made me angry when the book appeared were later confirmed, convincing me that I was the mistaken one, having been misled by excessive patriotic optimism."

The Lawrences' lunch included sandwiches and some lemonade poured into an empty wine-bottle. But they had counted on getting fruit in San Felipe. Even though they had reached a different village, they did not abandon their idea and hunted fruit for five pages. It became a narrative thread on which to string many aspects of village life, but the bad temper of the account reveals that he did not realize how vividly he was also revealing himself.

The first place the Lawrences sought their fruit was the shop at the bottom of the plaza where I had bought my orange drink. He reports the conversation with the owners: "*'Hay frutas?* Oranges or bananas?'—'No, Señor.'—'No fruits?'— *'No hay!'* —'Can I buy a cup?'— *'No hay.'* —'Can I buy a *jicara,* a gourd-shell that we might drink from?'— *'No hay.'* "

Lawrence did not preface his request with *por favor.* Perhaps he did not want to have to explain to the non-Spanish reader it meant "please" as his narrative forced him to explain that *No hay* means "there isn't any." *No hay,* he added, was "the most regular sound made by the prevailing

Plate 1. Manuel García Vigil, the Governor of Oaxaca, who was shot about seven months before Lawrence arrived.

Plate 2. A segment of federal cavalry entering Oaxaca on 1 April 1925. Photograph by A. D. Akin.

Plate 3. Oaxaca's opera house, which was opened with a performance of *Aïda* in 1909. Photograph by Alfonso Rivas.

Plate 4. The Hotel Francia as it was at the time of Lawrence's visit to Oaxaca. Dorothy Brett lived at the hotel during her whole stay in Oaxaca, and she commented on this photograph (letter of 4 February 1963) "My room . . . was one of those front ones to the left hand side, either the first or second window, the long ones."

Plate 5. Isaac M. Ibarra, Governor of Oaxaca, the day of the picnic-breakfast on Monte Alban. Photograph by Hermann Kull.

Plate 6. Rosalind Hughes, the year before Lawrence met her.

Plate 7. This photograph, taken at the time of the Lawrences' visit, shows the *Portal de Mercaderes,* devoted mostly to shops. The cafés had not spread to this side of the *zócalo.*

Plate 8. The façade of the Oaxaca Cathedral which Lawrence described in "The Flying Fish." Postcard by Mexico Fotografico.

Plate 9. A Oaxaca *serape* vendor with examples of *greca* motifs borrowed from the ruins of Mitla. Photograph by Alfonso Rivas.

Plate 10. The house on Pino Suárez where the Lawrences lived during most of their stay in Oaxaca. They occupied the five rooms represented by the five openings onto Pino Suárez to the right of the taller principal entrance. This photograph was taken in August 1962 when two of the five Lawrence windows had been turned into doorways for separate apartments. The smaller house of Robert Wilson is beyond the Rickards' house, and, at the corner, the church called La Patrocinia. Photograph by Ross Parmenter.

Plate 11. Frieda Lawrence, behind the wooden pillar, D. H. Lawrence in his black and white checked suit crouching to hold Corasmín still, and Padre Edward Rickards, the dog's owner and Lawrence's landlord. The sun is catching one of the priest's parrots in the tree rising behind Lawrence's head. Lawrence wrote about both the dog and the parrots in *Mornings in Mexico.* Photograph by Dorothy Brett. All Brett photos in this volume are in the Humanities Research Center Library, University of Texas, Austin, and are reproduced here by permission.

Plate 12. Lawrence standing on the channeled wall carrying water from San Felipe del Agua to Oaxaca. Frieda strides on ahead. The colonial aqueduct still exists but no longer carries water. Photograph by Brett.

Plate 13. On the excursion into the hills beyond San Felipe del Agua, Padre Rickards (in black on left) led, with Maximiliano Salinas, a Rickards family friend, as a companion. Frieda is seen with her parasol and Lawrence is resting on the side of the road. Photograph by Brett.

Plate 14. Eulogio Gregorio Gillow y Zavalza, Oaxaca's first archbishop and the model for Bishop Severn in *The Plumed Serpent*. Photograph by Armando Vasquez.

Plate 15. The dome of La Merced, Padre Rickards's church, above the cloister of the former monastery. Photograph by Ross Parmenter.

Plate 16. Padre Edward Arden Rickards in the cloister of his church, La Merced.

Plate 17. D. H. Lawrence and Frieda sitting in the red-tiled *corredor* of the house they rented from Padre Rickards. The priest's part of the house is seen at the rear. The *corredor* faced a garden. The Lawrences are using furniture borrowed from foreign residents of Oaxaca. Photograph by Brett.

Plate 18. A vendor on the road coming into Oaxaca bringing in what Lawrence described as great "bubble-shaped jars." Postcard by Osuna.

Plate 19. The Lawrences in the Mercado Benito Juárez Maza, Oaxaca's old covered market. Frieda, dressed in riding clothes, wears a bowler-like hat. The two dark stripes across Lawrence's back are shadows from the bamboo framework, which under ordinary circumstances would support a canvas awning. Photograph by Brett.

Plate 20. Ox carts piled high with corn leaving Oaxaca on market day. Postcard by Mexico Fotografico.

Plate 21. The north entrance to Oaxaca's covered market, only a block from the Lawrences' hotel. Photograph by Ross Parmenter.

Plate 22. This 1962 photograph shows the central fountain in Oaxaca's covered market around which the flowers were sold, as described in *Mornings in Mexico*. Since then the fountain has been removed and the area above it roofed over. Photograph by Ross Parmenter.

Plate 23. A stand of baskets in the subsequently roofed open market adjoining the Church of San Juan de Diós. Photograph by Alfonso Rivas.

Plate 24. An area of the old uncovered market specializing in *petates,* the Indian sleeping mats made of woven strips of palm leaves. Photograph by Alfonso Rivas.

Plate 25. The Lawrences in the old open market examining pottery bowls. The native holding the basket is Rosalino, the Lawrences' *mozo*. Photograph by Brett.

Plate 26. Hermann Kull, the Swiss dentist, with his wife, Carola, on their tennis court, a gathering place for the Oaxaca foreign colony.

Plate 27. This faded photograph was taken 12 January 1924, the day Governor García Vigil and his followers successfully frustrated the *Serranos'* attempt to capture the city. It shows some of the victorious cavalry drawn up in front of the cathedral, with others coming from the direction of El Fortín to join them. Photograph by Hermann Kull.

dumb-bells of the land," hardly a kindly comment on a country suffering from poverty, poor communications, political upheaval, and remoteness from industrial centers. " 'What is there, then?' A sickly grin. There are, as a matter of fact, candles, soap, dead and withered chiles, a few dried grasshoppers, dust and stark, bare wooden pigeon-holes. Nothing, nothing, nothing."

Lawrence fumed when the next "little hole of a shop" was equally empty. When he found that it did have *tepache,* however, a mildly alcoholic drink, he added, "There is probably *mescal* too, to get brutally drunk on." *Mezcal* is the chief hard drink of the region, but he might have seen its consumption as a calamity arising from, and compounding poverty, rather than a further sign of the awfulness of Huayapan. "The village is exhausted in resources. But we insist on fruit. Where, *where* can I buy oranges and bananas? I see oranges on the trees, I see banana plants."

A woman, who waved her hand "as if she were cutting the air upwards," directed them to a house outside the *plaza.* The woman there said, *"No hay."* Next they tried at "a yard with heaps of maize in a shed, and tethered bullocks; and a bare-bosomed, black-browed girl." When the girl said she had no fruit, Lawrence protested, "'But yes! There are oranges—there!' " "She turns and looks at the oranges on the trees at the back and imbecilely answers: *'No hay.'* " She probably meant they were not for sale—an understandable attitude in a village where oranges were scarce. But this did not seem to occur to Lawrence, who saw only "a choice between killing her and hurrying away."

The description of the house of their third attempt makes another scene, as in a play:

> A yard with shade around. Women kneading the maize dough, *masa,* for tortillas. A man lounging. And a little boy beating a kettledrum sideways, and a big man playing a little reedy wooden whistle, rapidly, endlessly, disguising the tune of *La Cucaracha.* They won't play a tune unless they can render it almost unrecognisable.
> *"Hay frutas?"*
> *"No hay."*
> "Then what is happening here?"
> A sheepish look, and no answer.
> "Why are you playing music?"
> "It is a *fiesta."*
> My God, a feast. That weary *masa,* a millstone in the belly. And for the rest, the blank, heavy, dark-gray barrenness, like an adobe brick. The drum boy rolls his big Indian eyes at us, and beats on, though filled with consternation. The flute man glances, is half appalled and half resentful, so he blows harder. The lounging man comes and mutters to Rosalino, and Rosalino mutters back, four words.

Four words in the *idioma*, the Zapotec language. We retire, pushed silently away.

In demanding to know why they were drumming and piping, Lawrence must have struck the people in the enclosure as rude and intrusive. Again there is recognition that his own conduct might have caused his troubles.

"What language do they speak here, Rosalino?"
"The *idioma.*"
"You understand them? It is Zapoteca, same as your language?"
"Yes, Señor."
"Then why do you always speak in Spanish to them?"
"Because they don't speak the *idioma* of my village."

Lawrence might have learned a good deal from this. In those days only the best-educated villagers were bilingual. Undoubtedly his questions had not always been understood, and those addressed had been unable to reply in a language he could understand. What alternative had they but to be uncomfortably silent? But all Lawrence deduced was, "He means, presumably, that there are different dialects"; something he could have learned far sooner. After all, he had been in Oaxaca six weeks.

By this time Lawrence was undoubtedly very tired, and we know from subsequent events that he was coming down with Frieda's cold. Perhaps there was rueful irony in his comparison of their hunt for fruit to the trek of Mary and Joseph looking for rooms in Bethlehem. But they persisted.

We went down every straight ant-run of that blessed village. But at last we pinned a good-natured woman. "Now tell us, *where* can we buy oranges? We see them on the trees. We want to eat them."
"Go," she said, "to Valentino Ruiz. He has oranges. Yes, he has oranges, and he sells them."
From black hut to black hut went we, till at last we got to the house of Valentino Ruiz. And lo! It was the yard with the *fiesta*. The lounging man was peeping out of the gateless gateway, as we came, at us.
"It is the same place!" cried Rosalino, with a laugh of bashful agony.

Even Rosalino was embarrassed for them. But Lawrence, commenting wryly on how his compatriots often behaved abroad, added, "We don't belong to the ruling race for nothing. Into the yard we marched."

"Is this the house of Valentino Ruiz? *Hay naranjas?* Are there oranges?"

We had marched so long, and asked so often, that the *masa* was made into tortillas, the tortillas were baked, and a group of people were sitting in a ring on the ground, eating them. It was the *fiesta.*

At my question up jumped a youngish man, and a woman, as if they had been sitting on a scorpion each.

"Oh, Señor," said the woman, "there are few oranges, and they are not ripe, as the Señor would want them. But pass this way."

We pass up to the garden, past the pink roses, to a little orange-tree, with a few yellowish-green oranges.

Even then, I can only get three of the big, thick-skinned, greenish oranges. But I spy sweet limes, and insist on having five or six of these.

He charges me three cents apiece for the oranges: the market price is two for five cents: and one cent each for the *limas.*

"In my village," mutters Rosalino when we get away, "oranges are five for one cent."

A patently loaded quotation with which to end the sequence. Of course, the oranges would be cheaper where Rosalino lived. It was a village devoted to raising oranges in an environment where oranges flourished; not a woodcutters' village among semi-arid mountains at an altitude precluding exuberant tropical vegetation.

Once the fruit was in Rosalino's basket, Lawrence's humor improved. When they met men coming from the town meeting, he wrote, "They watch us as if we were a coyote, a *zopilote,* and a white she-bear walking together in the street." A *zopilote* is a familiar Mexican sight, a large black scavenger bird resembling a vulture, the simile he conceived for Rosalino, a strange Indian from a different village. The animal parallels arose from his experience with the Taos Indians. His leanness and his red beard had led them to call him the Red Wolf, as he acknowledges in his poem of that name; Brett says the Taos Indians nicknamed Frieda "Angry Winter." It was only a brief leap for Lawrence to think he might seem like a coyote to these southern Indians. Frieda, wearing an ankle-length white dress in combination with the earlier nickname, suggested the polar bear.

This time the Lawrences spoke: "*Adiós,*" they said politely, and the men returned the courtesy: " '*Adiós*' comes the low roll of reply, like a roll of cannon shot." Remembering that the Lawrences had come upon an aqueduct after climbing above the village to find a spot for their picnic, I asked the verger if the village still had an aqueduct. It did, and he found a boy, Genaro Cortés López, who served as my guide.

"The water rushes downhill in a stone gutter beside the road," Lawrence wrote of the route they took. Genaro must have taken me along the same street, for as we climbed the hill, we, too, came to a point where the rushing river water crossed the road "unchanneled." The Lawrences waded through it, and he reported, "It is the village drinking supply," a mistake he never corrected, even though later he told of meeting a woman who showed his supposition was wrong.

Genaro said the spring from which the drinking water originated was far in the hills. As we climbed, I again had the sensation of being in Lawrence's exact steps. "Up, up wearily. . . . At last, the last house, the naked hills. We follow the water across a dry maize-field, then up along a bank. Below is a quite deep gully. . . . Shall we go down into the gully into the shade? No; someone is bathing among the reeds below, and the aqueduct water rushes along in the gutter here above." Above the town, were *guayaba* trees.

> On, on, [the text had said] till we spy a wild guava tree over the channel of water. At last we can sit down and eat and drink on a bank of dry grass, under the wild guava tree. We put the bottle of lemonade in the aqueduct to cool. I scoop out a big half-orange, the thick rind of which makes a cup.
> "Look, Rosalino! The cup!"
> *"La taza!"* he cried, soft-tongued, with a bark of laughter and delight. . . . And one drinks the soft, rather lifeless, warmish Mexican water. But it is pure.

A "chock, chock" attracted Lawrence's attention so he got up to seek its source and found it came from the gully and from above he looked down on: "a woman, naked to the hips, standing washing her other garments upon a stone. She has a beautiful full back, of a deep orange colour, and her wet hair is divided and piled. In the water a few yards up-stream, two men are sitting naked, their brown-orange giving off a glow in the shadow, also washing their clothes."

Lawrence had described an architectural feature that I was certain would be more permanent than a guava tree: "A sort of bridge where the water divides, the channel water taken from the little river, and led along the top of the bank." I asked Genaro to show me where the water divided. He understood, taking me down into the gully. It was too deeply shaded to allow an adequate photo, but I recognized Lawrence's "sort of a bridge," though it was more like a low dam, with the spillway taking the water into a channel on the other slope of the gully, while a shallow U-cut in the middle of the dam wall caused a cascade as part of the river pursued its natural course. Genaro pointed below the little artificial falls to where people bathed; but this day no one was there.

As the Lawrences were eating they had a visitor, whom he described as "an old woman . . . with naked breast and coffee-brown naked arms, her under-garment fastened on one shoulder, round her waist an old striped *serape* for a skirt, and on her head a blue *rebozo* piled against the sun. "She was holding three or four *chirimoyas,* or custard apples, to her bosom.

> She lectures us, in slow, heavy Spanish:
> "This water, here, is for drinking. The other, below, is for washing. This, you drink, and don't wash in.". . . And she looked inquisitively at the bottle of lemonade. . . . Then she gave us the *chirimoyas,* I asked her to change the *peso,* I had no change.
> "No, Señor," she said. "No, Señor. You don't pay me. I bring you these, and may you eat well. But the *chirimoyas* are not ripe; in two or three days they will be. . . . But I make a gift of them to you, and may you eat well. Farewell. Remain with God."

The old woman's loving look at the bottle cooling in the channel had not escaped Lawrence. As a result, "When we had drunk the lemonade, we sent Rosalino to give her the empty wine-bottle, and she made him another sententious little speech. But to her the bottle was a treasure."

Lawrence does not let the taste of the single pleasant meeting linger. Three days later they found that the *chirimoyas* were wormy, implying that the woman had outwitted them to get the bottle. His parting shot at the villagers was fired in the following comment: "And I, going round the little hummock behind the wild guava tree to throw away the papers of the picnic, came upon a golden-brown young man with his shirt just coming down over his head, but over no more of him. Hastily retreating, I thought again, what beautiful, suave, rich skins these people have: a sort of richness of the flesh. It goes, perhaps, with the complete absence of what we call 'spirit.' " Certainly a broad generalization for a brief visit, but immediately Lawrence wins one back with his final description: "We lay still for a long time, looking at the tiny guavas and the perfect, soft high blue sky overhead, where the hawks and the ragged-winged *zopilotes* sway and diminish."

Lawrence broke off at this point, leaving the "long, hot way home" to the reader's imagination. But my walk home was as pleasant as the walk to the village. A lovely view of distant Oaxaca bathed in soft golden light met my eyes. In the foreground, more cattle than I anticipated were grazing in the peaceful fields. I felt calm and tranquil, and only then realized I had missed lunch. At the ford where Bernabé had attached himself to me I met the two woodsellers with the seven burros. They were on their way home and their burros were unburdened. I asked whether they had received a good price for their wood. Yes, they said smilingly. I got broad smiles from other returning woodsellers, too. I did not hesitate to tell them that I had liked Huayapan. Once in sight of the highway, I looked back to see the mountain resembling "a splendid lizard." Its blue crest was partially concealed in a cloud and Huayapan was lost in gray rain, but in the ten minutes I needed to reach the highway, winds swept all overhead clouds towards the hills, leaving the westering sun to shine unobstructedly into the retreating rain. Over the valley arched a perfect rainbow, the seven bands of its left foot resting on Huayapan.

Oaxaca's plaza that evening was especially cheerful and lively. The band was playing and, because Independence Day was near, the red, green, and white bulbs strung between the tall trees added a garden party note. As I sat on a bench enjoying the promenade, I thought over the walk to Huayapan. The walk was one I would have enjoyed under any circumstances; but with the peppery ghost of Lawrence for a companion, it had sharpened my vision and stirred my imagination as no such walk had ever done before. I was grateful for the continuity of the peasant way of life; if Huayapan had changed more, I could not have followed Lawrence so well.

CHAPTER 7

FAVORS FOR
TWO WRITERS

LUIS QUINTANILLA

When Lawrence returned to North America in the spring of 1924, he came by way of New York. He wanted to retrieve the two blue copybooks containing the manuscript of *Quetzalcoatl,* which he had left the previous summer with Seltzer, his American publisher. Also, as he wrote Bynner just before sailing, Seltzer had been "behaving queerly." Checking why the publisher had been defaulting on royalties, however, was not Lawrence's only literary business during his five-day stay in New York. Since 1920, publishing stories, sketches, and poems in American periodicals had helped keep him alive. Magazine payments, in fact, had reached the point where he needed to pay American income tax. Lawrence was also interested in developing the magazine market further. As Joseph Wood Krutch recalls entertainingly in *More Lives Than One,* Oswald Garrison Villard, owner of the *Nation,* was one publishing potentate with whom Lawrence lunched. Another grew from a contact Seltzer had established in 1922 with a less earnest publication of broader circulation, *Vanity Fair.* In January 1924 the glossy Condé Nast publication had printed its first Lawrence article, "The Proper Study of Mankind." A month earlier it had appeared in London in the *Adelphi,* a magazine that Middleton Murry had founded the previous June, partly to provide an outlet for Lawrence's nonfiction. Making no mention of the prior publication, *Vanity Fair* introduced the article with considerable fanfare and dressed it up with a seated portrait of Lawrence that Frank Crowninshield had arranged for Nicholas Muray to take the previous summer.[1] Crowninshield, who brought many a brilliant writer to *Vanity Fair,* was the editor who also welcomed Lawrence into the fold.

One of Lawrence's other New York missions was to become acquainted with A. W. Barmby, the new manager of the New York office of Curtis Brown, Lawrence's English agent. Due to his break with Robert Mountsier, Lawrence had been without an American agent for a year. Barmby, a north-of-England man, struck the novelist as "a very decent sort" and inspired his confidence. Though Seltzer had been the one who initially urged Lawrence to write for *Vanity Fair,* it was probably Barmby who arranged that his new client and Crowninshield should lunch together. The genial editor did not remain clear in Lawrence's mind. But perhaps the writer did not impress "Crownie" very much either, for neither his grand-nephew, Frederic Bradlee, who was later to coedit *Vanity Fair: A Cavalcade of the 1920's and 1930's,* nor Geoffrey Hellman, Mr. Crowninshield's biographer for the *New Yorker,* had any idea the editor had ever met Lawrence. However a Lawrence letter from Oaxaca, which preserves a record of the luncheon, reveals they talked business. Perhaps one topic was Lawrence's "On Human Destiny," another *Adelphi* pick-up that *Vanity Fair* was publishing in the May issue. In any event, the lunch cemented a relationship between Lawrence and the magazine that was to result in his appearance in many subsequent issues.[2] Crowninshield must have been cordial, and Lawrence came away from the lunch feeling the connection was strong. The meeting, also stimulated him to write the "Mornings in Mexico" sketches, for the editor was interested in more short pieces from Lawrence. "Mornings" never did appear in *Vanity Fair,* nevertheless, the Crowninshield lunch leads on to Luis Quintanilla.

In 1936 Edward D. McDonald published *Phoenix,* his massive edition of lesser-known Lawrence writings including many never published in the novelist's lifetime. One item brought to light was "See Mexico After, by Luis Q," a rather puzzling monologue of an excitable young Mexican working in Mexico City for the Bureau of Information. Because McDonald had only undated typescripts to work from, neither his introduction nor his notes tell of the piece's place of origin; nor do they say whether "Luis Q" was a real person, or a character invented by Lawrence. It was Nehls, who hunted out the Rickards family connection, who also flushed out the identity of the problematic "Luis Q." His run-down on Quintanilla's career in volume two of the *Composite Biography* reveals that Quintanilla rose to be one of Mexico's most important diplomats. On several occasions he was Mexico's chargé d'affaires in Washington, D.C. During the first four years of World War II, he was Mexico's ambassador to the Soviet Union. When the United Nations General Assembly met for the first time in San Francisco in 1945, Quintanilla was Mexico's delegate; thereafter he played a major role in his country's behalf in the Organization of American States.

He lived until 15 March 1980, but in 1969 he was another Lawrence associate I had thought must surely be dead. In May of that year by chance I opened *Novedades* at its editorial page and discovered that he was still an active columnist for the large Mexico City paper. This enabled me to track him down and to draw from him the details that filled out the story. While rewriting *The Plumed Serpent* in Oaxaca, Lawrence expanded the number of guests and the amount of conversation in both his tea party scene and the dinner party. I was eager to find the models for the new guests at this second social gathering. García, who also showed the heroine the revolutionary murals of Orozco and Rivera in government buildings was, I had discovered, in part Genaro Estrada, the P.E.N. president, but who was Mirabal, the other "pale young man?" " 'What do you think, Mrs. Leslie,' cried the pale-faced young Mirabal, in curiously resonant English, with a French accent. 'Don't you think it would be wonderful if the gods came back to Mexico? Our own gods.' He sat in intense expectation, his blue eyes fixed on Kate's face, his soup-spoon suspended." Mirabal is obviously Quintanilla as Lawrence saw him in 1924. (Plate 33.)

What other Mexican intellectual of the time had blue eyes and spoke English with a French accent? Or conformed to the description of another added guest who, in stressing the diversity of Mexicans, called him "mixed French and Spanish." Quintanilla admitted that in those days he loved the names of the pre-Columbian gods and very much liked the idea of their being revived. Quintanilla, nearing seventy, with a trim figure, light complexion and straight, brushed-back hair, still with traces of brown, easily resembled the man conjured by Lawrence. His words still came in a "torrent." Everything he told me about himself confirmed that in his early days he must have been "burning with an intense, crazy energy." Lawrence captured even the voice, still "curiously resonant" though, in 1969, somewhat husky and no longer marked by a French accent.

"If you were taught English by an English nurse," I asked him, "how is it that you don't have a British accent?"

"I did," he replied. During his year at the Gettysburg Academy the American students mocked it; so he suppressed it.

Quintanilla's father was Luis Fortuño Quintanilla and his mother, Ana María del Valle y Lerdo de Tejada, a granddaughter of Miguel Lerdo de Tejada, who helped draft Mexico's constitution of 1857. Though born in Mexico, she was of French descent. She was the one who transmitted to the young Luis the blue eyes of her Basque mother. In the latter days of Don Porfirio, upper-class Mexicans looked towards France as the fount of gentility and culture. Quintanilla, Sr., a man of comfortable means whose love of things European included an intense admiration of Wagner, decided to make his residence in the country of his wife's people—a fashionable decision. Luis Siegfried was born in Paris in 1900.

The Quintanillas were friends of the Maderos, and though, like the Maderos, they were members of the elite, they were also liberal. Don Luis Fortuño supported Francisco Madero's uprising against Díaz; and after Madero became president, he asked Quintanilla to become revolutionary-Mexico's Minister to France. Quintanilla had never been a diplomat but willingly assumed the post.

The Quintanillas made periodic visits back to Mexico, but it was not until 1917 that young Luis returned to live permanently in Mexico when the Revolution was in full swing. "The train I was riding in from Veracruz," he said, "was shot at. Nevertheless I fell madly in love with my own country." He also caught the Revolutionary enthusiasm. And he became a poet, though, because of his French schooling it was easier for him to first write the poems of *Avión* and *Radio* in French. The titles of those first two books show how up-to-date his subjects were. He also wrote in *vers libre,* a later link with Lawrence.

Lawrence made the long trip to visit the Quintanillas' small apartment where he met Ruth Quintanilla and Jane, the baby. "He was kind to everybody," Quintanilla said, "and he relaxed with children." Material Lawrence wrote for Quintanilla shows that the novelist also visited *Relaciones Exteriores* where Quintanilla worked. How else could he have been so accurate about the office "poked in the corner of a would-be important building," on the top floor of a four-story structure without elevators? When Lawrence came with Frieda to pick Quintanilla up, perhaps he even puffed a bit going up those stairs, as one does climbing stairs at 7,000 feet. The office, as Lawrence wrote, looked "over the flat roofs and bubbly church domes and streaks of wire" of the city. It commanded a view of the volcano Popocatépetl "lounging his heavy shoulders under the sky, smoking a cigarette end à la Mexicaine."

"He was very simple in all his habits," Quintanilla said. "I was assigned to accompany him as an official to see he had everything he needed. But he never asked for anything. I never met a more modest man. He avoided publicity and would blush when an interview was mentioned. There was something of Saint John the Baptist about him, with his red hair and blue eyes. He had a refinement of manners that was almost Oriental, and he loved the delicacy of feeling of the Indians. But he did not see delicacy and beauty in the ruins. He wanted delicacy and smiles. His feelings for Mexico were mixed. He had tremendous interest and unbearable fright.

"He came at one of the most traumatic and tragic times. Life didn't count here, and for him life was everything.

"He loved to walk slowly without being noticed. He loved Chapultepec Park, and we often sat in the Alameda with my brother José. He never monopolized the conversation. He kept silent and spoke softly. He never raised his voice and he loved to listen. He loved the coolness of the morning, and he hated rain. He hated bullfights and he was suspicious of the *mestizos.* "

Forgetting, or perhaps not knowing that Lawrence had visited Ceylon, he exclaimed, "What a pity he was never in the Orient. Indian Mexico was the nearest to the Orient he experienced. And he immediately understood that the greatness of Mexico was the Indian.''

Buddhist statues lined the walls of the Quintanilla living room in his luxurious home in San Angel, souvènirs of the Orient. The heavy-lidded man recalling his youth paused to relight his pipe.

"He was very much in love with Frieda and she was always very sweet and kind to him. She was the very image of health: wholesome, good-natured and unusually plain and straightforward. Very much of a German country girl. Brett was like the mother. She would tell him when to stop writing, when he was getting a cold, and so on. She had red hair and was slim.''

Quintanilla showed Lawrence his poems and the novelist was clearly impressed.

"He wanted me to get out of *Relaciones Exteriores,* and to give up the career of diplomacy on which I had started. 'Be exclusively a writer,' he said to me. 'Come to Oaxaca. I will help you to start. You are a born writer.' He insisted that I write a novel. A first novel, he said, should be a man's own life, because if a writer can't understand himself, how can he pretend to understand others? 'Never write in the afternoon, and never at night,' Lawrence told. 'Always rise early. In the morning the mind is more at ease and more efficient. Always write with a pen. Don't dictate. You go too fast, but with the pen you can feel as you write.' "

"He wanted me to continue to write in English," said Quintanilla, " 'Spanish is too damn musical,' he said. He felt its words were too long and the vocabulary not rich enough. Those writing in Spanish, he said, were always in danger of succumbing to the rhythm and the music, forgetting content and sense. An advantage of English was that it had many more monosyllables to dispose of. And I remember him reading me his description of men milking cows at the start of *The Rainbow.* He pointed out that it was written mostly in monosyllables, and he wanted to show how easy it was for English to convey feeling. Long words, said Lawrence, delayed the transition of thought. English, he said, was more concise, and not so much like a melody. Lawrence cared for music, but he thought it was important to combine music and content.''

Just before our first interview ended, Quintanilla took me upstairs to point out one of his prized possessions, a large framed portrait of Lawrence. It was the sensitive and beautiful profile study that Edward Weston had made. (Plate 34.) Lawrence had autographed it on the right with a large, finely written signature in pencil. And had added on the left "Edward Weston, Mexico, 1924.''

Lawrence's hope for ideal friendships was never extinguished, despite repeated disillusions. His first act in relation to Quintanilla in Oaxaca was writing a cheery letter singing the city's praises and giving him travel tips. The tone suggests that Lawrence felt in the young Mexican the potentiality of a heart's brother. His second act was to add Quintanilla to the growing cast of new characters being introduced into *The Plumed Serpent*. Quintanilla was added for the same reason as "Bell," "Montes," "García" and "Mr. Henry," which also dictated the expansion of the conversations at the tea and dinner parties. In the sixteen and a half months since completing the Chapala version of his novel, Lawrence had realized that one of his tasks was to present more fully the intellectual background of Mexico. Particularly he needed to make what he had postulated more convincing: the emergence of Ramón's religion because there were many Mexicans emotionally ready to revive the pre-Conquest gods. Nearly all the new material contributes to that goal. On his first two visits, Lawrence had met Mrs. Nuttall and other Anglos in Mexico, but it was not until his third visit that he mingled with Mexican intellectuals. The articulate young Quintanilla was made to order for his literary requirements. "If you like the *word* Quetzalcoatl, don't you think it would be wonderful if he came back again? [Lawrence has Mirabal ask Kate.] Ah, the *names* of the gods! Don't you think the *names* are like seeds, so full of magic, of the unexplored magic? Huitzilopochtli!—how wonderful! And Tlaloc! Ah! I love them!"

Lawrence had other reasons, too, for making Mirabal one of Ramón's dinner guests. Kate had just seen a newspaper story about the Quetzalcoatl movement. Mirabal could reveal the possibilities of the new religion to her, and he later appears as one of the two white-skinned men among the circle of initiates at Ramón's hacienda. When Mirabal reappears in peon costume as one of the "Lords of the Day and Night" in chapter eleven, we understand why he had spoken with such enthusiasm about the old gods to Kate.[3]

Shortly after the Lawrences' visit to Mitla, Quintanilla wrote that because of a job offer from *Relaciones Exteriores* too lucrative to turn down, he could not keep his promise to visit Oaxaca. Frieda, who was less gregarious than her husband and tended to be happiest when they were living quietly together, was probably relieved. Lawrence, however, probably felt dashed. As early as 1909 when he was having no luck placing his short stories, he wrote Louie Burrows, "I am beastly disappointed about one thing & another, but it's no use letting on." This remained the pattern of his response to disappointment, and, his reply was warm:

> Dear Quintanilla, I was sorry you couldn't come down, but glad to hear of Pesos 20 per diem. Sounds almost as good as an engine-driver. I think in many ways you are a born diplomat—who knows, you may save Mexico yet. She needs a bit of saving: even along with Calles's nice words. Personally, I believe he means them. But it's a far cry to Lochaber.
> We are settled in half the Rickards' house. . . . Of course we know

all the Americans: there are no English. I am working at my novel, which is just beginning to digest its own gall & wormwood.

Saluti cordiali to Señor Estrada. I am almost afraid to write his name, in view of the "strained relations" & Mexican national sensitiveness. But risk it.

The picture is Mitla: top of my head. Miss Brett has taken to photography. The other man is José García, whom I think you know. All good wishes to M. le diplomate - & to Madame - & Jeanne, not of Arc.

The letter was one of six written by Lawrence to Quintanilla that Nehls published for the first time, explaining that the Scottish saying about Lochaber meant "There is still much to be done about it." When Quintanilla produced the original, I was surprised to find that it was written on the reverse of a photograph familiar to me from *Lawrence and Brett.* (Plate 35.)

This explained "The picture is Mitla" and Lawrence's reference to the top of his head, for his bearded chin was obscured by the large sombrero of the guide showing them the zigzagging *grecas* in the Hall of Mosaics. "Jeanne, not of Arc," was a playful reference to Quintanilla's daughter. Estrada was Quintanilla's boss at *Relaciones Exteriores* and the president of the P.E.N. Club. Quintanilla said he thought the "strained relations" referred to the hot words that flew between Lawrence and his hosts at the club dinner, but the novelist was wrong in thinking he knew the José García looking at the camera. Neither his face nor his name stirred any memory.[4]

About a week after learning Quintanilla was not coming to Oaxaca, Lawrence heard from Weston. "The D. H. Lawrence negatives were not up to standard," Edward Weston had written in his *Daybooks,* adding, "Damn the ambassador's banquet for my hurry!" Nevertheless he made two prints and sent them to Lawrence—one showing the author looking downward in profile that I had seen in Quintanilla's study, and the three-quarter shot of the novelist with his head tilted back that Mabel Luhan and Richard Aldington used as frontispieces for their Lawrence books.

In another letter Lawrence revealed that during the sitting he had discussed the possibility, if the photographs turned out well, of submitting them to *Vanity Fair.*

Dear Mr. Weston,

Thank you very much for the photographs. I like them very much: think I like the one with the chin up better than the other looking down but like them both.

I would write to *Vanity Fair* myself, but have clean forgotten the editor's name: and I had lunch with him in the spring. But I am doing one or two little articles [he was referring to "Mornings in Mexico"] which will probably suit *Vanity Fair*. Next week I shall send them to my agent, A. W. Barmby of Curtis Brown Ltd. 116 West 39th St. New York, and tell him about the portrait too. He would look after it if you like. And I'll tell my English agent, Curtis Brown, 6 Henrietta St. Covent Garden, London W.C. 2, to approach one of the big London illustrated periodicals, if you like. You write to Barmby and to Curtis Brown if you feel so inclined. It seems to me you have reached the point where you should go in for a bit of publicity. *Vanity Fair* might like some of your less startling nude studies, if you could stand seeing them reproduced & ruined.

Let me know if I can help you in any way. Tackle the world, it's a rather stupid bull, to be taken by the horns, not dodged.

Greet the Signora [Tina Modotti]. Let me know when you leave. Those two addresses of my agent are always good. Wish I had a copy of *Aaron's Rod* to send you.

On December 19 Lawrence wrote Quintanilla:

I had the portraits from Edward Weston: they are very good, I think. I want them to get published, in New York *Vanity Fair* and in London, perhaps the *Sphere*. They like to have a bit of text too. Why don't you do a little article on Mexico, D.F.—& me thrown in—& Weston thrown in—for *Vanity Fair*. Sounds as if I want to get publicity for myself, but it's not that. *Vanity Fair* knows me already very well. But it would be quite nice for me, & good for Weston, because they ought to know a wee bit about him when the photograph is published. It's time he tackled the world. And then you, with your Paris-Post-bellum amusing style, you could very successfully do little articles—two or three thousand words—for a paper like *Vanity Fair*, which everybody reads. Little amusing articles, even on Calles etc. to hurt nobody. Why don't you do that? I think I can get them accepted all right. Do the P.E.N. Club a bit funnily. And the mother of Janey can help you, she'll know what to put in. [This was because Ruth Quintanilla, being from Pennsylvania, would know American interest.] Don't say you're used up by the FOREIGN OFFICE, that's too farcical.

Lawrence's suggestion appealed to Quintanilla and he dashed off an article which he called "Mexico, Why Not" after an advertising slogan the railroads used to follow up the success of "See America First." But he did not take Lawrence's advice to write about Mexico City. Instead he wrote about the American tourists he was being obliged to show around because of his government job. He had been meeting them singly and in groups, for many American organizations were sending commissions to Mexico. Most of the visitors rubbed him the wrong way, especially when they complained about Mexico not having the blessings they had back home, like corn flakes and pie à la mode. Type after type he ticked off the oil men, the average young married couple (the gum-chewing husband and the wife expecting all Mexicans to look like Ramon Navarro or Rudolf Valentino), the "wealthy" old maids, the labor politicians, the husbands fleeing their wives and acting very rugged in Mexico, the nouveau riche "Little town heroes" from "Santa Burro, Texas," or "Little Bull, Arizona," etc. Quintanilla's style was amusing though sometimes heavy-handed and unflattering. Some of the caricatures, especially of those seeking oil rights, have a savage intensity. But he made one exception. Acting on the need to include something about the photographer who was to illustrate the piece, he wrote:

> At last, comes the American artist.[5] At last comes Edward Weston, the photographer who has peacefully conquered the Mexican intellect, and probably the last of the American bohemians. Tired of Los Angeles' standard atmosphere, the day he sold a dozen pictures at $30.00 a piece he went south in search of color and line. Once in Mexico, he spent his time photographing Indian beggars, colonial churches, poets, volcanoes and blue-lacquered birds. After a few months of such unfruitful work, hunger drives him back north. But you have caught the very heart of Mexico, Edward Weston. The Indian pyramids pierce the sky more majestically since you have seen them. And that insolent little Mexican straw-general that your magic lens imprisoned behind the picture-glass will remain forever swearing at you, within his crystal prison.

One sees Quintanilla's literary gifts, too, though somewhat disordered, in what he wrote about the P.E.N. dinner. This, he tells us, is what he planned to say in his prepared speech:

> Poor old Mexico, your old age is your greatest sin. In spite of the revolutionary contest that you have been resisting for the last 200 years, in spite of the nation-wide shooting contest which will win you "some sunny day" the Olympic honors in a Stadium, you can not get rid of your millennial civilization, you can not shake off your mountainous spine the hundreds and thousands of ruins and idols which grow wherever true Mexicans have lived. And Fate has ironically placed you, the oldest and probably the first civilization, near the newest and probably the last of earthly civilizations.
>
> Civilization, that old clown, has almost completed her trip around the earth. She started in Yucatan and when the ATLANTIDA sank, like

an old ship, she went through the Orient and then Europe. Now she is coming back to America. . . .

But Quintanilla's speech, as his article tells, did not come off as planned:

> I stood up, stiff and determined to say this and still deeper trifles, but the presence of D. H. Lawrence's red beard among the guests (I even think he was the GUEST OF HONOR only because of his red beard) impressed me so much, that I started stammering and felt quite unable to expose myself before such a distinguished Englishman.
>
> Now the genial author of *Women in Love* writes me from the Mitla ruins, in Oaxaca, that he is working at his Mexican novel, which is just beginning to digest its own gall and worm-wood.
>
> Maybe, in spite of the "strained" Anglo-Mexican relations, the subtle and deep talent of the great English writer will catch the strange beauty of this Mexican atmosphere; with her crimes and her poetry, with her ruins and her social utopias, with her bandits and her dreamers.
>
> The blossoming of gun-shots in the clear sky. A total scorn for human life. A romantic charro aiming his pistol at the moon: this is Mexico— WHY NOT?

The eight-page, double-spaced article occupied only four sheets, because Quintanilla typed on both sides of paper. He dated it "Mexico City, December 30th, 1924," and sent it off promptly.

The article caused Lawrence a good deal of moral struggle. He felt responsible for encouraging Quintanilla to write it, yet he did not like it. He had guessed wrong on Quintanilla's ability to write congenially for *Vanity Fair,* but still wanted to help the younger author. At first Lawrence did not know how to salvage the article; but thinking over the problem, he decided on a stopgap measure that would do something to allay Quintanilla's anxiety. He made arrangements to have him receive one of Weston's photographs.

Then he got to work, first editing the article in pencil between the lines. After going through the first five pages, he realized it was not working out. From Tedlock's *The Frieda Lawrence Collection of D. H. Lawrence Manuscripts: A Descriptive Bibliography* we know that Frieda had a yellow scribbler with a trademark drawing of a pheasant on its outer cover which she was using for her Spanish lessons. Lawrence borrowed it and began his first stab at an independent rewrite of the Quintanilla article, abandoning it after twenty lines.

Quintanilla's article presented its author's views as the objective truth, giving no clue as to who he was, what work he did, or why he was in a privileged position to observe visitors to Mexico. After two tries at revising the piece, Lawrence decided it needed to establish the author as a personality, with his setting, his credentials, and enough changes so that the reader, particularly the reader who had visited Mexico would know he was getting the views of a single, perhaps biased individual. This brought Lawrence to a workable solution: to incorporate many of Quintanilla's ideas, phrases, thumbnail sketches, thoughts, and feelings—as well as his own impressions of Quintanilla and remembered snatches from Quintanilla's conversation—into an interior monologue that would evoke a vivid picture of the man and his work. Once Lawrence had this idea, he turned to "Record," the black copybook containing the just completed *Mornings in Mexico* and wrote in unhesitating longhand the eight pages of "See Mexico After." Then he took an eraser and scrubbed hard over the first five pages of Quintanilla's typescript to eliminate what he had written in pencil between the lines. He was conscientious about his erasing, and although he succeeded in making almost all he had written illegible, there was no concealing the fact that the typescript was no longer pristine. He apologized for this in a letter of 10 January 1925.

"Did you get the photograph?" he began, by way of softening the blow. And the next sentence—"I signed them and sent them back"—suggests he had returned both pictures to Weston and asked Weston to give one to Quintanilla. Then followed the words he had delayed saying:

> And the little article came. I was a bit sad, because it was sad and rather bitter: in fact very: with undigested spleen. Is that how you really feel about them: I doubt if they'd print it, because the touch isn't light enough. I'm afraid I had to go scribbling on your MS.—By the way, type on one side only, for literary MSS.
>
> I couldn't help writing out your little article again. I'll get it typed, & send it to you. You could, you know, easily write these little sketches. Only it means conquering your own sadness and heaviness inside first, and being able to laugh at it all, if only on the wrong side of your face.
>
> My wife wants to go to Germany to her mother. Probably at the end of the month we shall come up to Mexico to arrange a ship, & sail in February. But then, should see you & Jane [&] Jane's mother.
>
> Till then, adios!

The signing off showed more affection than Lawrence usually did before his signature. But Quintanilla still did not know what the novelist had done to his article as it was not included. Lawrence mailed it, retyped by Brett, on January 12. Quintanilla was confronted with a piece in the flippant anti-American vein of Lawrence's *Studies in Classic American Literature*. He also found he had been made the subject of a Lawrencean character sketch in which the protagonist reveals himself by musing in the first person. It began

> *My home's in Mexico*
> *That's where you want to go.*
> *Life's one long cine show. . . .*
>
> As a matter of fact, I am a hard-worked, lean individual poked in a corner of a would-be important building in Mexico, D.F.
>
> That's that.
>
> I am—married, so this is not a matrimonial ad. But I am, as I said, lean, pale, hard-worked, with indiscriminate fair hair and, I hope, nice blue eyes. Anyhow they aren't black. And I am young. And I am Mexican: oh, don't doubt it for a second. *Mejicano soy.* La-la-la-la! I'll jabber your head off in Spanish. But where is my gun and red sash.

The young man, excitable and energetic, is portrayed dashing up and down the four flights of his building twice after being asked by a tourist, "Not American, are you?" While in New York, the young man had observed "See America First" posters everywhere and the assumption that the United States was the only America had riled his pride. Mexico was also part of the North American continent.

Then, after some verbal play over the pronunciation of Popocatépetl—obviously Lawrence's idea of adding a "light touch"—the article takes up the Quintanilla sequence of tourist types. They are all rewritten, though the English Lawrence, for all his amiable intentions, was hardly kinder to the United States tourists than the French-reared Mexican. He preserved Quintanilla's "Little Bull, Arizona" as a parody name for the U.S. hometown, but he substitutes "Old Hat, Illinois," for "Santa Burro, Texas." And he adds a type not included by Quintanilla, perhaps recalling Quintanilla's own description: "Then the young lady collecting information! Golly! Quite nice looking too. And the things she does! One would think the invisible unicorn that protects virgins was ramping around her every moment. But it's not that. Not even the toughest bandit, not even Pancho Villa, could carry off all that information, though she as good as typed out her temptation to him."

Despite his own suggestion, Lawrence cut the references to Weston and himself. But he did save something from Quintanilla's proposed P.E.N. speech, something almost unintelligible without knowledge of what the Mexican wanted to say. However, when Quintanilla's words are recalled, Lawrence's ending has a good deal of irony: "Of course Mexico went in for civilization long, long ago. But it got left. The snake crawled on, leaving the tail behind him. The snake crawled, lap by lap all around the globe, till it got back to America. And by that time he was some snake, was civilization. But where was his tail? He'd forgotten it. . . . But before civilization swallows its own tail, that tail will buzz. For civilization's a rattler: anyhow Mexico is."

Lawrence's accompanying letter said:

> I send you your little article, which I'm sorry I went scribbling on and also mine. You mustn't take offense at anything I say: because of course I don't mean any. —I find even my article barely covers its rancor, and it is a bit bewildering. There must be a terrible bitterness somewhere deep down between the U.S.A. and Mexico, covered up. When one touches it, it scares one, & startles one.—But just put my little article in the fire, if you don't like it.—Or if you like it, send it to *Vanity Fair* or some paper, and see if they'll print it over Luis Q. I doubt if they will. It'll make them too uneasy. But fun to try them.
>
> I have done a lot of my novel again—I had the biggest part done last year. It is good, but scares me a bit, also.

Writing that he planned to sail for England from Veracruz on 20 February, Lawrence added, "I don't feel very easy in my skin, in Mexico this time. Perhaps I ought to go home for a bit." Acting out of consideration for Brett, he added some further news, without letting on that it was largely because of Frieda's insistence that Brett was leaving Oaxaca:

> Miss Brett doesn't want to go to England—wants to go straight back to our ranch in New Mexico—and leave any time now. If she arrives in Mexico City, will you & your wife look after her a bit. Ask Mrs. Quintanilla if she will. And if you hear of anybody nice with whom Miss Brett might travel up to El Paso, tell me, will you. I don't like to think of her going alone.
>
> The little article is yours to do as you like with, entirely. Perhaps just make an auto-da-fe.
>
> It's lovely & warm now here. What is it, makes one want to go away? Best wishes to you.

"See Mexico After, by Luis Q," when its bewildering elements are clarified, emerges as a less flimsy piece than on first reading. "What Quetzalcoatl Saw in Mexico," that bitter fourth hymn in chapter seventeen of *The Plumed Serpent* which condemns foreign exploiters of Mexico, owes a good deal of its intensity of feeling, especially in its denunciation of the oilmen, to the anti-U.S. passages of Quintanilla's original article. Quintanilla influenced *The Plumed Serpent,* both by his own views and by serving as the inspiration for the new character Mirabal. Lawrence's writing in Oaxaca included two character sketches of him. Quintanilla recalled his reaction to Lawrence's work: "I *never* resented Lawrence's revisions of my article which finally I decided not to send to *Vanity Fair*. On the contrary, I thought and still think it was a great honor to have a genius like Lawrence read and scribble over something I had written. It showed, among other things, a rare quality in Lawrence: his innate kindness and modesty."

Yet some time later when Quintanilla and I were in his study and we read over Lawrence's letter of transmittal together, he read the sentence about learning to "laugh about it all," (his Revolutionary feelings) and observed: "We couldn't laugh at it at all. It was so damn serious to us. I wrote my article spontaneously and quickly," he added. "Lawrence's version was the polished one of a literary man. The two were written from different points of view. I never tried to place the Lawrence version because I did not agree with everything in it. And it did not seem fair to send out under my own name what was actually written by another."

As a later Lawrence note shows, the Mexican maintained a long silence indicating an emotional distance.

Quintanilla's article has brought us well past the walk to Huayapan; and completion of the Quintanilla story necessitates glimpses of Lawrence's stay in Mexico City after leaving Oaxaca. In his first days in the capital he was too ill to see people; he and Frieda remained by themselves in two sunny rooms on the top floor of the Imperial Hotel, which under the name Hotel Francis, still stands near the statue of Columbus, a Porfirian landmark on the Paseo de la Reforma. But by March 2 Lawrence had the strength to write Curtis Brown, and the next day he made a sortie from the hotel. Quintanilla, who had got wind of the Lawrences' return, paid a call but, finding his friends out, left a note. When he received it Lawrence must have been feeling considerably stronger, for his immediate reply was one of four notes he wrote on March 3.

> They gave me your note this evening. I went & got malaria, plus grippe, so badly in Oaxaca, that I was a month in bed & can still hardly crawl through the days. My wife got it too. We were lying absolutely low here, not having the energy for a thing. But come in & see us: we are almost always stuck here. We are sailing to England on the 17th—two weeks today—& till that time, struggling through the days with some difficulty, feeling done in by this dirty sickness.
>
> I thought you had gone to Guatemala, Washington or Pekin: are you sure you've not?
>
> Kindest regards from both of us to Mrs. Quintanilla. We'll muster up courage in a few days to have our teas in Sanborn's, shall we?

Quintanilla took up the invitation to visit the Lawrences at the hotel, and he tells of one visit in the letter he wrote Nehls for the *Composite Biography:*

I was with my brother José at Lawrence's bedside in the Hotel Imperial, with Frieda, when we called a doctor because D. H. was suffering, at least so we thought, from a bad case of grippe. It was then that the doctor took me apart to announce that is was not a case of grippe but definitely an advanced case of tuberculosis. You can imagine what a shock it was to my brother and me! We broke the news as gently as we could to Frieda, and decided not to say anything to Lawrence, for the time being.

This memory is particularly interesting, for it presents the doctor in a much more kindly light than Frieda does. In *"Not I, But the Wind . . ."* she wrote:

I had Dr. Uhlfelder come and see him. One morning I had gone out and when I came back the analyst doctor was there and said, rather brutally, when I came into Lawrence's room: "Mr. Lawrence has tuberculosis." And Lawrence looked at me with such unforgettable eyes.

"What will she say and feel?" And I said: "Now we know, we can tackle it. That's nothing. Lots of people have that." And he got slowly better and could go to lunch with friends. But they, the doctors, told me:

"Take him to the ranch; it is his only chance. He has T.B. in the third degree. A year or two at the most."[6]

In the period when Lawrence rallied enough to lunch with friends, Quintanilla saw him once more. This time the Mexican brought Manuel Maples Arce, the Veracruz poet, who though only twenty-four, was the acknowledged leader of "The Strident Ones." Arce, like Quintanilla, was enthusiastic about the Mexican Revolution and both were riled by Lawrence's criticism of their country. Perhaps Lawrence was unusually cutting because of his Oaxaca experience. As his letters show, he blamed Mexico for the breakdown of his health; if a relatively small illness always left him "churlish," one can imagine what a serious illness caused. Tension increased, and when Quintanilla's belief in his friend's talents led him to claim that Arce was a genius, Lawrence blurted out scornfully, "What genius has Mexico ever produced?"

"This made me so angry and hurt my feelings so badly," said Quintanilla in recalling the scene years later, "that I got up and left the restaurant. Arce came with me and I was glad that, not knowing English, he had not understood what had been said. I never saw Lawrence after that."[7]

Meanwhile, Lawrence and Frieda, having canceled their plans for a sea voyage to England, left March 25 on the train for the sunny New Mexico ranch. Lawrence's last note to Quintanilla shows that he tried to see the impulsive young Mexican again, suggesting that the still-smouldering Quintanilla used the amoebic dysentery contracted by his infant daughter to form a polite excuse rather than blame the blow-up.

> We were very much distressed to hear Jane was ill, [wrote Lawrence five
> days before he was to leave Mexico.] I hope it's not bad, & that Mrs. Quin-
> tanilla will be able to sail. [She was planning to take the baby to the United
> States.] Really, there is a doom on us all in Mexico: best for us to depart.—
> We are due to leave on Tuesday morning: I am finished with the doctor
> thank God.—Let us know how it is: we don't go out till about 11.00; and
> if we can do anything for you in any way, let us know.

Quintanilla never answered; in fact, he never wrote Lawrence again.
Five years later, when he heard Lawrence was seriously ill, the breach
troubled him more than ever. Brett had liked Ruth Quintanilla, whom
she described as Quintanilla's "gay American wife." Their acquaintance-
ship was improved after Brett returned to the Mexican capital where Ruth
had indeed looked "after her a bit." Concerned about her husband's feelings, Mrs. Quintanilla confided them to Brett, telling her how sorry he
was to hear of Lawrence's failing health and how he felt about "the unfortunate discussion that broke a friendship so precious" to him.

The kindly Brett, then in New York, replied to Ruth, saying:
"Lawrence has been for the last three years abroad—Italy & France—
most sick and fragile—but tell your husband this—that Lawrence never
thought of him as other than a friend. Lawrence fully realized your husband's feelings for his country. Believe me nothing but friendship
survives."

The letter was dated 24 February 1930, only six days before
Lawrence died. As Quintanilla wrote Nehls, the assurance made him feel
"a lot better," but his relief was quickly mingled with sadness. Almost
the day the letter came he read of Lawrence's death in the newspapers.

Forty years later, on my first visit to Quintanilla's home, he still felt
keenly about the breach. He had many photographs autographed by famous persons—Stalin, Franklin Roosevelt, and Ho Chi Minh of Vietnam—
and his movement in the intellectual world is attested by photographs
from such luminaries as Bertrand Russell and Albert Einstein. Yet when
we got to the bottom of the stairs, Quintanilla said with obvious feeling,
"I will regret *all* my life that I did not continue my contact with D. H.
Lawrence. Perhaps I was too young to appreciate him."

MOLLIE SKINNER

Mollie Skinner, whose novel Lawrence had finished rewriting into *The
Boy in the Bush* on his second trip to Mexico, is another writer whose
career he generously tried to promote while in Oaxaca. I found the

manuscript of a preface for her revised version of *Black Swans,* the novel which, when he read it in Darlington, Australia in 1922 led him to urge her to write the one that developed into *The Boy.* The manuscript was in "Record," the black copybook containing *Mornings in Mexico.* The text said it was written on Christmas Eve, and the manuscript was signed, "Oaxaca, 1924, D. H. Lawrence."

Miss Skinner's letter announcing the acceptance of *Black Swans* must have arrived not too long before Lawrence moved to Padre Rickards's house. The day before he moved, he replied, in a letter not yet published,[8] that he was pleased that Jonathan Cape had accepted her novel and that Edward Garnett was to be her editor. Garnett, he said, was his very good friend. Implying that Garnett would roar at her to improve the novel, he asked to be sent a copy as soon as it was published so he could see how it had been revised.

He wrote the preface five weeks later by request. The problem posed in her now missing request is stated in the preface's opening words: "Difficult to write about *Black Swans* when I have barely seen so much as the egg of the book. Yet I suppose the MS I did see in Western Australia may be considered the egg. It was a wild MS, climbing the mountain of impossibilities and improbabilities by leaps and bounds: a real rolling stone of an egg, no doubt."

Because of this difficulty, the rest of the preface discusses *The Boy in the Bush,* but there is this further word about the work being introduced: "I wonder very much how *Black Swans* has wound up. When I saw it, it was about a girl, a convict, and a Peter: Lettie, I think her name was, poised between the entirely praiseworthy Peter and the fascinating convict. But there the tale tumbled away into a sort of pirate-castaway-Swiss-Family-Robinson-Crusoe-Treasure Island in the North West. This "adventure" part was rather pointless. I suggested to Miss Skinner that she work out the Peter-Lettie Convict combine on ordinary terra firma. I believe she has done so in *Black Swans.* "

When Lawrence knew so little about the revised novel, when he had so much writing of his own to do, and when he was confined to bed with a cold, why was he willing to undertake Mollie's assignment? The preface gave him an opportunity to pay tribute to Edward Garnett, but more significantly the forty-five-year-old nurse, who, like the heroine of his novel, *The Lost Girl,* had studied midwifery in London, was on Lawrence's conscience in a particularly troubling way. How much sympathy he felt for her and how troubled he was on her behalf were revealed in 1970 when Martin Secker's letters to and from the novelist were published. While he was in New Mexico six months before going to Oaxaca, Miss Skinner had written him her big news. She had redone *Black Swans* and was on a ship headed for London, planning to arrive there with the new manuscript shortly before the publication of *The Boy in the Bush.* Lawrence replied July 8:

> I was very much surprised to get your shipboard letter, and to know that by now you will be in London. I hope you will have a good time: and that you won't be disappointed at waiting until September 1st for *The Boy.* Secker sent me his advertisment leaflet: too bad that he leaves you out so much: it is not *my* wish, not a bit: just a publisher's attempt to use a known name and suppress an unknown one. I hope Lettie [the heroine of *Black Swans*] meets with a warm reception.

Fifteen days later he wrote Secker: "I hear Miss Skinner is in London. Now be nice to her. I know she's hard up, wish you would advance her £ 25 or £ 30 on *The Boy* —unless she's had her advance on that. I hope her new novel is good. I read a beginning that I liked very much, but it went wrong. So she wrote it again. If necessary, I must help her a bit. Write and tell me what you think of *Black Swans* —her book."

On August 8 when Lawrence got his own first copy of *The Boy,* he wrote Secker again. "Be sure and tell me about Miss Skinner and her new novel." By August 13 Secker had rejected *Black Swans* and told Lawrence it was "quite hopeless . . . as it stands." On August 31 Lawrence wrote the publisher, "I'm sorry about Miss Skinner and her novel, she'd be so disappointed. But I don't think I want to re-write another."

Lawrence's September 13 letter to Secker shows that now something else was troubling him. The British reviewers of *The Boy in the Bush* were not giving Mollie the attention she deserved: "I do wish they mentioned Miss Skinner's share and praised it. I do wish people were nice to her. Are you sure her *Black Swans* wasn't good. Why not? She seemed so depressed, and no wonder."

Miss Skinner's fate in London awakened Lawrence's sympathy. His reference to "literairy" coteries shows his disrespect, and he was scornful of the *Times Literary Supplement* that had mistaken her gender.

> She sailed off penniless, with a steerage ticket from Tremanitlo [an allusion to Fremantle] to England, the MS of *Black Swans* in her bag, and hopes, heaven high! Ay-ay! Anticipations. *The Boy in the Bush* was not yet out.
>
> She arrived in London to be snubbed and treated as if she did not exist, and certainly *ought not* to exist, by the same-as-ever London Literairy people. Those that esteemed me, literairily, decided that *Mr.* Skinner was probably a myth, and didn't matter anyhow. Those that didn't esteem me declared that *Mr.* Skinner, if he existed, couldn't amount to anything, or he would never had made such a connection. Certainly I am

a safe mark for the popular moralists to aim their slosh at. "Mr. Skinner" was buried before he went any further.

Of course Miss Skinner felt badly. But if Stafford put not his trust in Princes—or realized that he shouldn't have done—the first business of anybody who picks up a pen, even so unassuming a pen as Miss Skinner's now, is to put no trust in the literary rabble, nor in the rabble of the critics, nor in the vast rabble of the people. A writer should steer his aristocratic course through all the shoals and sewerage outlets of popular criticism, on to the high and empty seas where he finds his own way into the distance.

The part of "The House of Ellis" that Lawrence changed most in *The Boy in the Bush* was the ending. As he worked on it, he warned Miss Skinner from Guadalajara: "The end will have to be different, a good deal different. . . . Your hero Jack is not quite so absolutely blameless an angel, according to me. You left the character psychologically at a standstill all the way: same boy at the beginning and end. I have tried, taking your inner cue, to make a rather daring development, psychologically. You may disapprove."

On 3 March 1924 when Lawrence still had not heard from Miss Skinner about the revision sent her in typescript almost two months before, he wrote to jog her, defending his ending in the process: "You may quarrel a bit with the last two chapters. But after all, if a man really has cared, and cares, for two women, why should he suddenly shelve either of them? It seems to me more immoral to drop all connection with one of them, than to wish to have the two."

Miss Skinner's ending, as Lawrence reveals in the Oaxaca preface, had Jack, the hero, finding he really loved the virtuous Mary after all, once her cousin Monica, his early love, "went to the bad." Then Jack and Mary live happily ever after. In the last three chapters—not just the last two—Lawrence had Jack marry Monica, loving her still, even though she had lived with two other men and had a child by each. In this respect his Jack was even more of a gentleman than Mollie's; but in the last chapter Lawrence had Jack ask Mary to become his common-law wife, telling her frankly that her cousin Monica did not satisfy all his needs in a wife. Thinking the proposal indecent and being unwilling to undercut her cousin even though she loved Jack, Mary refused. Jack rode back to Monica in chagrin.

But Lawrence did not leave the matter there. Listening in on the dinner table conversation where Jack outlined his ideas of a man being like Abraham in his need for several wives, was an attractive, slightly deaf younger girl called Hilda Blessington (a very charming portrait of Dorothy Brett as Lawrence knew her in 1915). This girl was "one of the odd borderline people who don't and *can't* really belong." She rather liked the idea of being "a man's second or third wife: if the other two were living." Boldly she rode after Jack, letting him know her feelings. The novel ends with the agreement that at Christmas she will come and visit Jack and Monica in the Northwest.

When Miss Skinner read this ending, as she confided in a memoir[9] written twenty-six years later, she wept. Family reasons intensified her feelings. Her war-crippled brother, Jack, was the model for her hero, and Lawrence was presenting him as a polygamist. But her objections were delayed in reaching her collaborator. On April 4 Lawrence wrote her from the ranch: "Your letter about *The Boy* MS has come here. I have written to Secker and Seltzer to make the alterations you wish, if it is not too late. Also I tell them they may leave out both chapters at the end, if they wish. But here, if the book is set up, the publishers will not agree unless they wish to of their own accord."

Secker felt "very strongly" that Lawrence's last two chapters "should not be scrapped,"[10] and the novel was published as Lawrence ended it in both England and the United States. Knowing Miss Skinner was unhappy about this too made Lawrence regret that he had given her additional pain. Yet, as an artist, he believed in his ending and had a strong impulse to defend it.

If Lawrence felt his ending was psychologically plausible when he wrote it a year earlier in Guadalajara, he had reason for being even more convinced about its soundness in Oaxaca. Perhaps unlike Jack he was not as happy as he thought he would be with an extra, devoted woman on hand. But hadn't the very girl he portrayed proved the correctness of his insight by willingly joining Frieda and himself in real life? He had written of her joining the married couple in the novel without any knowledge that a month or two later, after a four-year absence, he would remeet the model for his Hilda in London. Brett's coming to the New World with the Lawrences was an amazing example of life imitating fiction.

Lawrence's defense of his ending is reflected in "The Novel," an essay written in New Mexico a few months after leaving Oaxaca. One of his points favoring the novel as an art form is that it illustrates the relativity of everything in life, how "everything is true in its own relationship, and no further." Giving an example, he wrote: "So, if a character in a novel wants two wives—or three—or thirty: well, that is true of that man, at that time, in that circumstance. It may be true of other men, elsewhere and elsewhen. But to infer that all men at all times want two, three, or thirty wives; or that the novelist himself is advocating furious polygamy; is just imbecility."

Miss Skinner's request for a preface, then, came at a time when Lawrence wanted both to rebut and befriend her. To spare her any blame for his work, to state her side of the case, and to make amends for hurting her personally, he climaxed his account of his efforts on behalf of *The Boy* by saying: "Yet let me here make the confession that the last chapters and anything in the slightest bit shocking are, of course my fault; not Molly Skinner's."[11]

He could not let well enough alone, however. In her ending Miss Skinner, he said, had fallen back on "evasions and sentimentalities." He added, "Forgetting, as Miss Skinner's Jack forgot Monica, is all bunk. Once you care, and the connection is made, you keep the connection, if you are half a man."

McDonald's questions for his bibliography, in forcing Lawrence to review his publications, must have encouraged him to write about Garnett, the editor who had helped his career so much between 1911 and 1914. Two things had come together: Miss Skinner had asked for a preface, and the book she wanted it for, having won an acceptance on its second submission, was being edited by Garnett. The conjunction obviously wakened Lawrence's memories of his struggles with Garnett, as well as of his reasons for gratitude, for in obliging Miss Skinner, he wrote:

> Poor Molly Skinner, she had a bad time. But two sorts of bad time. The first sort, of being informed she ought not to exist, and of having her *Black Swans* turned down. The second sort, when old Edward Garnett tackled her. He saw her *Black Swans* floundering and flopping about, and went for them tooth and nail, like a rough-haired Yorkshire terrier. Poor old Molly Skinner, she saw the feathers of her birds flying like black snow, and the swans squawked as if they were at their last gasp. But old Edward twisted at them till they knew what's what.

Glimpses of the Lawrence-Garnett relationship already given show how Frieda was included in the friendship, too. This was important, for when Lawrence first ran off with the "ripping Mrs. Weekley"—it was thus Lawrence described "the woman of a lifetime" in his first letter about her to the editor—Garnett did not disapprove. Although he was seventeen years older than the novelist, he was a friend to them both. Garnett's acceptance of them when other people had cut them off was something they long remembered. Lawrence summarized his editorial relations with Garnett when he wrote Ernest Collings: "Hueffer sent me to Wm. Heinemann with *The White Peacock,* and left me to paddle my own canoe. I very nearly wrecked it and did for myself. Edward Garnett, like a good angel, fished me out."

Hueffer was Ford Madox Hueffer, "later Ford," who in 1909 launched Lawrence's literary career by publishing some of his poems in the *English Review*. Subsequently, he printed some Lawrence stories and got Heinemann to publish his first novel, *The White Peacock*. But Hueffer had disliked Lawrence's second novel, *The Trespasser,* and his adverse comments had so undermined the author's faith in it that he told Heinemann he would not have it published, even though Heinemann had accepted it. Garnett's first approach to Lawrence had been two years after Hueffer's, when he asked the twenty-five-year-old schoolteacher if he had any stories for the *Century,* an American magazine for which Garnett was scouting. Garnett turned down the stories Lawrence submitted, but they remained friends, for Garnett obliged with genuinely helpful comments after Lawrence wrote, "If, any time, you would give me a word of criticism on my MS, I should go with surer feet." Garnett was particularly helpful with *The Trespasser*. Besides restoring Lawrence's faith in it by enthusiasm for its essential worth, he gave Lawrence many detailed suggestions for its improvement. In his convalescence at Bournemouth, after the breakdown of health that ended his teaching career, Lawrence rewrote the novel under Garnett's guidance. Gerald Duckworth, for whom Garnett was working, brought out the revised version in May 1912.

Meanwhile, having gone to Italy with Frieda, Lawrence was working on "the colliery literary novel," which was to end as *Sons and Lovers*. Garnett furnished literary counsel for it, as well as reading plays, short stories, and articles for Lawrence. "Why do you take so much trouble for me?" asked the incredulous writer in one letter to Garnett. Nevertheless, on 1 July 1912 Heinemann rejected "Paul Morel," as the novel about the coal miner's son was then called. Again Garnett rallied Lawrence's spirits with practical suggestions. "What a Trojan of energy and conscientiousness you are!" Lawrence wrote, in thanking Garnett for a letter full of notes that were "awfully nice and detailed." Garnett, in the meantime, persuaded Duckworth to accept Lawrence's first book of poems, *Love Poems and Others*. Through Garnett's influence Duckworth Ltd. also published *Sons and Lovers*. Appearing in May 1913 it was dedicated to Garnett. In a presentation copy of the novel now owned by the University of Texas, Lawrence wrote on the flyleaf, "To my friend & protector in love & literature—Edward Garnett, from the author."

Lawrence's words written in Oaxaca about Mollie's swans being plucked and twisted until they squawked show his awareness that Garnett as an editor could be overbearing and sometimes, for all his skill, rough on the feelings of his authors. A breach opened between the two men in June 1914 when Garnett told Lawrence that "The Wedding Ring" (the long manuscript that was to develop into *The Rainbow* and *Women in Love*) was shaky and wrong in its psychology. By this time Lawrence, more sure of his direction, was no longer willing to take Garnett's strictures and advice. Though the novelist does not admit the "upset" to which Frieda testifies, in his June 5 reply to Garnett he explained that he had lost interest in "the old-fashioned human element" in characters, and wanted instead to deal with what was "non-human in humanity." People, he said, were animated by inhuman wills, and he wanted to deal with them as phenomena—"inhumanly, physiologically and materially." He rebelled against the old-fashioned human element because it obliged a novelist "to conceive a character in a certain moral scheme and make him consistent." He went on to speak in very difficult terms about a different kind of ego passing through "allotropic states." If Garnett was bewildered, he can't be blamed, for it was not until "Education of the People," started in 1918 and taken to completion in 1920, that Lawrence could state his new ideas clearly and simply. There he wrote, "We have got to get a new conception of man and of ourselves," which involved seeing men as inconsistent beings, not understandable to themselves and driven by inhuman forces.

Perhaps, in receiving that hard-to-understand letter, Garnett felt as hurt in having his advice rejected and in being told he restricted Lawrence in his new attitude to his character as Lawrence was in having his work misunderstood. As a result Lawrence insisted on paddling his own canoe, and Duckworth lost him as an author. *The Rainbow,* the first of the interlinked novels, was published by Methuen.

How was it that in Oaxaca, Lawrence, when given the chance, was glad to write affectionately and even admiringly of Garnett? In the meantime, they had partially made up. Garnett, who shifted to the new firm founded by Jonathan Cape in 1921, broke the ice in October of that year by asking Lawrence, who he knew could read German, to serve as publisher's reader for Emil Lucka's *Grenzen der Seele.* Lawrence gave an opinion of the book and refused to accept the guinea that was offered. But he added a personal note: "I was glad to hear from you again—wonder what you are doing—still looking after books, pruning them and re-potting them, I know." The next month, however, Lawrence showed his independence from his former mentor, now fifty-three. "No, my dear Garnett," he wrote, "you are an old critic and I shall always like you, but you are also a tiresome old pontiff and I shan't listen to a word you say." Three years later in Oaxaca, he ended his preface for Miss Skinner by writing: "I am dying to see *Black Swans* now, since Edward put their mistress through her paces. She is fleeing breathless back to Australia. I am laughing in the Mexican sun. Tonight is Christmas Eve, and who knows what sort of child the Virgin is going to bring forth, this time!"

Christmas Eve was the day Rosalino's younger brother had arrived and lifted the gloom from the Lawrence household, perhaps making

Lawrence laugh as he wrote the finale of his preface. But perhaps he was also laughing at his buried joke about the Aztec goddess bringing forth a flint knife.

Black Swans, appearing after considerable delay toward the end of the next year, was published without Lawrence's preface. Thus a second piece written in Oaxaca to help a writer-friend misfired and was buried; the preface to *Black Swans* had to wait thirty-two years longer than "See Mexico After, by Luis Q." to be published. In 1968 when it finally was printed, Oaxaca as a place of origin suffered the same bad luck as it did with "See Mexico After." Despite the fact that Tedlock's 1948 catalogue of Lawrence manuscripts owned by Frieda called attention to Oaxaca's being included in the signature of the manuscript, Warren Roberts and Harry T. Moore, the editors of *Phoenix II,* in which it first appeared, did not indicate where it was written. The preface, like "See Mexico After," belies its first impression of triviality. It, too, is more significant when its puzzling elements are dispelled, providing a telling example of Moore's dictum that biography is more important for an understanding of Lawrence's works "than for most other authors." Sometimes Lawrence seemed to expect readers to know his whole life story, and, as in these two pieces, he wrote as if he was sure they did.

On 3 January 1925 Lawrence wrote Mollie about the preface; not in a whole letter, but in a postscript added to Frieda's.[12] He had written an introduction to *Swans,* but he felt she would be better off without it. He feared critics would injure her by associating him with the novel, but he would speak to Garnett if he got to London in March.

The postscript suggests that Lawrence had decided not even to show Mollie the preface. Yet a letter from Kiowa Ranch, written a month after leaving Oaxaca suggests that he did send it and that Mollie turned it down. She probably would have felt pain at the preface's criticism of her own ending of her brother's story. Later in the summer, Lawrence told Secker he might try rewriting *Black Swans* after all; at one time Cape announced that the novel would appear with Lawrence's introduction. But if Miss Skinner did reject it, Lawrence's response is amazingly without rancor:

> We are thinking about you, and wondering about *Black Swans.* I'm looking forward to reading it soon. When is it due? I'm sure it's best for it to appear absolutely without any connection with me. That way you'll exist in yourself and by yourself, for the tribe. I'll write an introduction to your third novel, if you like.[13]

CHAPTER 8

BRETT WITH ADDENDA

Lawrence's stay in Oaxaca is indelibly colored by the presence of Dorothy Brett for most of the time. He left a vivid portrait of Brett in his short story "The Last Laugh," depicting her as "the deaf nymph" known by her surname James. She was "slim," "very erect," with a "quick, quiet voice," a "quick chuckling laugh," "fine bobbed hair," "round staring brown eyes," and "a fresh soft face." "Very practical" with a "quick, cool unemotional way," her occasional imperiousness showed she was "not the daughter of a peer for nothing." All her life she had held herself "intensely aloof from physical contact . . . never having let any man touch her." She was a painter and he describes one of her self-portraits, with "its nice brown hair and its slightly opened rabbit mouth and its baffled, uncertain rabbit eyes." (Plate 36.)

Shortly after the story opens, James's escort (a portrait of Middleton Murry) hears strange laughter. "The girl, with her alert pink-and-white face, looked at him sharply, inquisitively. She had an odd, nymph-like inquisitiveness, sometimes like a bird, sometimes a squirrel, sometimes a rabbit: never quite like a woman." When she wants to test if she can hear the mysterious laughing too, she hands the man her "little brown dispatch-case, which was really a Marconi-listening machine. He held it while she opened the lid and attached the wires putting the band over her head and the receivers at her ears, like a wireless operator. She switched on: little yellow lights in glass tubes shone in the machine. She was connected, she was listening."

The listening machine played a negative and troublesome role in Oaxaca; a passage in *Fantasia of the Unconscious* reveals Lawrence's feelings when "the vulcanite ear" of such a machine was pushed near his mouth. "I want to shout down the telephone ear-hole all kinds of improper things, to see what effect they will have on the stupid dear face at the end of the coil of wire. After all, words must be very different after they've trickled round and round a long wire coil." Lawrence, acknowledging "I . . . am a bit deaf myself," wrote about James: "She was used to the sensation of noises taking place which she could not hear."

Frieda is also vividly described in a Lawrence short story, "The

Border Line," where he gives her the name Katherine Farquhar. (Plate 37.) The substitution of Russian for Polish in her lineage is the only attempt to disguise his wife:

> A handsome woman of forty, no longer slim, but attractive in her soft, full feminine way. The French porters ran around her, getting a voluptuous pleasure from merely carrying her bags. And she gave them ridiculously high tips, because, in the first place, she had never really known the value of money, and secondly, she had a morbid fear of underpaying anyone, but particularly a man who was eager to serve her.
>
> It was really a joke to her, how eagerly these Frenchmen—all sorts of Frenchmen—ran round her, and *Madame'd* her. Their voluptuous obsequiousness. Because, after all, she was Boche. Fifteen years of marriage to an Englishman—or rather to two Englishmen—had not altered her racially. Daughter of a German baron she was, and remained in her own mind and body, although England had become her life-home. And surely she looked German, with her fresh complexion and her strong, full figure. But, like most people in the world, she was a mixture, with Russian blood and French blood also in her veins. And she lived in one country and another, till she was somewhat indifferent to her surroundings. So that perhaps the Parisian men might be excused for running round her so eagerly, and getting a voluptuous pleasure from calling a taxi for her, or giving up a place in the omnibus to her, or carrying her bags, or holding the menu card before her. Nevertheless it amused her. . . . Katherine understood so well that Frenchmen were rude to the dry, hard-seeming, competent Englishwoman or American. She sympathized with the Frenchman's point of view; too much obvious capacity to help herself is a disagreeable trait in a woman.

These two women of aristocratic background—brought so much more vibrantly to life by the novelist's own words than by others' descriptions—were Lawrence's companions in Oaxaca. It was inevitable that tension would mount, especially when one considers an aspect of Brett's nature, not suggested in "The Last Laugh," but developed in Frieda's posthumously published memoir "And the Fullness Thereof . . ." pulled from her chaotic papers by Tedlock. In commemorating her associates, Frieda likewise resorted to the guise of fiction, selecting Andrew as her pseudonym for Lawrence, Paula for herself.

After describing R—, a clear portrait of Mabel Luhan, the memoir turns to S—, an equally recognizable portrait of Brett, saying, "The other woman who attached herself to Andrew was a different type, the serving self-effacing." She added "herself to another's being . . . feeling very superior in her self-abnegation." Complicating the situation was that "blindly and humbly she adored Andrew, seemingly seeking in return a delicate spiritual recognition of her service."

What could be expected of Lawrence under the circumstances? His early letters show how he was sure to react in the field of forces running between two such different women.

As early as 29 December 1912 when he had been living with Frieda for only eight months, he wrote Edward Garnett's son David: "Do you think you might persuade one or two quite tender young ladies to lionize me a bit when I get back to England. Frieda pulls all my tail-feathers out, and I feel as if a little gentle adoration would come remarkably soothingly unto me." Humor in his suggestion is shown by his after-thought, "Not that lions have tail-feathers. Put it at a tuft." Nevertheless, he was expressing genuine wishes.

In a letter six months earlier to David's father, Lawrence wrote: "God, how I love her—and the agony of it. She is a woman who also makes a man suffer, by being blind to him when her anger or resentment is roused."

These letters reveal what made Lawrence happy and what made him miserable. He needed recognition and respect, suffering keenly when people were blind to him. In a letter to Sir Thomas Dacre Dunlap, the English consul at Spezia, six days before he married Frieda he said, "To love, you have to learn to understand the other, more than she understands herself, and to submit to her understanding of you." Although Frieda was often blind to him, he was very rarely blind to her. One of his remarkable qualities was that he was hardly ever blind to anyone. He was certainly never blind to Brett. Because he saw her emotional needs so clearly, she appealed to his tenderness. But her sympathy and understanding were not an unmixed blessing. "I can't stand it when she clings too tight," he wrote Earl and Achsah Brewster on 11 April 1926 following his visit to Brett in Capri after the breach between himself and Frieda, generated when his sister Ada and Frieda's two daughters, Barbara and Elsa, were all together at the Villa Bernarda at Spotorno on the Italian Riviera near Genoa. In their later years the Lawrences were by no means a happy couple. The bloom of their first two years together and of the early years of their marriage, so splendidly celebrated in *Look! We Have Come Through!*, has been extended by some commentators to cover their whole life together. Those who see them in the romantic light of the *Look* poems tend to think the "glorious equilibrium" achieved early in their marriage lasted until the end, often treating their repeated quarrels as part of their love—stormy scenes indulged in chiefly for the pleasure of making up afterwards. But Lawrence was more serious than that and more easily wounded. "The hurts and the bitterness sink in, however much one may reject them with one's spirit," he wrote in his reopened correspondence with his early champion, Lady Ottoline Morell. Three months before his death, on 28 December 1929 he wrote to Secker, *"Dio mio!* how awful is a dissatisfied woman." The shafts were not aimed at Frieda directly but indicate how often she made him feel miserable.

The earlier rift between them in August 1923 when they were in New York, has already been revealed. Lawrence had not been back to England since his departure in 1919 and somehow he found it extraordinarily difficult to face his homeland again—so difficult, in fact, that he canceled his passsage, even though Frieda insisted she would sail. Because neither would yield to the other, they agreed to part. "He can go to blazes," Frieda wrote from the boat to Adele Seltzer. Lawrence's letters express resigned sadness, rather than anger, but they also show the separation was left open-ended. No plans for a reunion were made. After Frieda sailed, Lawrence went to California and from there set off with Gótzsche on the important second Mexican journey. He missed Frieda and wanted her to rejoin him. But she was firm that the reunion should be in England; he yielded to her will. The return to England was miserably unhappy for him, and in *"Not I, But the Wind . . . ,"* written after his death, Frieda conceded, "I think he was right; I should have gone to meet him in Mexico, he should not have come to Europe; these are the mistakes we make, sometimes irreparable."

December's awful weather was a minor factor in Lawrence's misery. During this period Frieda had an affair with another man and even though they returned to the New World together in the spring of 1924, they were not on the best terms. Futhermore, even though Brett worked like a laborer helping them rehabilitate the ramshackle cabins on Kiowa Ranch, her constant presence through the summer had not improved matters. Consequently, they were still estranged when they came to Oaxaca. They concealed the situation so that neither Quintanilla nor the Kulls suspected anything wrong, and Miss Doctor attributed Frieda's complaints about her drinks, etc., to a disagreeable disposition rather than to marital trouble. What Miss Hughes observed was polite neutrality. "I never saw any sign of estrangement or difficulty between Lawrence and Frieda. They were always courteous and seemed considerate of each other." But she added, "Neither did I see any display of affection or tenderness."

The situation was difficult, even if Brett had not been along. But Brett was very much in the picture. That Frieda was so often blind to Lawrence at the ranch and again in Mexico—the presence of Brett certainly caused her anger and resentment—undoubtedly increased his suffering. That suffering, in turn, would make Brett's sympathy especially sweet to him, which further maddened Frieda.

The explosiveness of the pre-Oaxaca situation is dramatized in a scene that took place while the three were still traveling between El Paso and Mexico City. Brett places it in a "restaurant":

The passengers stare at you. They watch you furtively as you sit reading a magazine. We seem to be the center of all eyes in the restaurant. Then Frieda picks up your magazine, after lunch, and begins to read it. You ask her for it, but she pays no attention.

"I was just in the middle of a story," you say to me. "Don't you think Frieda ought to let me finish it?"

"Yes," I say, "I don't think it is fair." Whereupon Frieda hurls the magazine at your head angrily.

"Take it," she shouts. "You two make me sick!" The other passengers are all sniggering and giggling. You pick up the magazine and turn to your story, while Frieda settles down as well as she can to sleep. I, as usual, feel wretchedly embarrassed and full of hatred for the giggling passengers.

Lawrence's version of this same El Paso-Mexico City journey contains nothing about the magazine throwing. Instead he observed Mexican generals on the train. One general was "a real peasant Indian, travelling with a frizzy half-white woman who looked as if she had fallen into a flour-sack"; and neither had ever ridden in a Pullman before. Lawrence used their guzzling to build the cynicism and lack of idealism in Mexican leadership. Once in Oaxaca beginning revisions on the second chapter, he wrote in the general and his mistress as they struck his heroine: "It had annoyed Kate to see this general and this woman eating chicken and asparagus and jelly in the Pullman, paying fifteen pesos for a rather poor dinner, when for a peso-and-a-half apiece they could have eaten a better meal, and real Mexican, at the meal-stop station. And all the poor, barefoot people clamouring on the platform, while the 'general,' who was a man of their own sort, nobly swallowed his asparagus on the other side of the window-pane."

Thus passengers could get meals in two ways: in the dining car or at restaurants in stations. Lawrence complained to Bynner that "the food in the Pullman [is] the same swindle," suggesting he submitted to it. But Brett's story shows that he rebelled and descended with his womenfolk to eat economically in the station. Probably, it was as he returned to the train that he saw the general in the dining car, and it would have been back at their seats that he continued reading the disputed magazine as Frieda tried to sleep.

Besides visiting the market, meeting the other English-speaking residents, calling on the governor, and arranging to move into Padre Rickards's house, the Lawrences did some sightseeing during their first eight days in Oaxaca. It is a city of churches and potters, and, thanks to Brett, we know that the Lawrences sampled both aspects of their new community. Brett wrote, "We have seen nearly all of the churches, inside and out, because we scramble up onto the roofs among the cupolas." Unfortunately, however, she gave no names and few precise details. There are only two glimpses of church interiors. "We are haunted by the intense *santos* —the agonized Christs and saints." The other glimpse contains a mistake attributable in part to her deafness and in part to a confusion of Christian and Hindu iconography. In Mexican churches, often at the summit of the tallest altars, the Divine Providence of the Most Holy Trinity is represented by an eye, usually in a triangle supported by clouds and bristling with rays. Such an eye must have caught Brett, and she exclaimed:

> "Look Lawrence, look at the eye in the middle of the forehead."
> "Good gracious, Brett," you answer angrily, "Have you never heard of the third eye?"

Only in Hindu and Buddhist iconography is "the third eye of spiritual perception" set in the forehead of images. The scene continues:

> And you disappear up a small, corkscrew staircase in a turret.
> "Call me if there is a parapet and I can't be giddy," I cry. Then I hear a faint, far-away call:
> "Come on; it's quite safe, and too lovely to miss: So I creep cautiously up the stairs out onto the roof and look over the golden-colored town."

The incident evokes one of the pleasures of Oaxaca and the church in question was probably Santo Domingo, the city's most famous church and the one with the roof most likely to be climbed by tourists. The view of the town from among its cupolas is one that Lawrence might well find too lovely to miss. If Frieda were present in the church, she did not bother to make the climb. Brett, despite her fear of heights, was happy to follow Lawrence to share his enthusiasm. The Lawrence presented is a man in high spirits and good health, impatient of church interiors, indifferent to images and eager to get into the fresh air or a high place commanding a wide view. If the church were Santo Domingo, Lawrence had a special reason for not wanting to linger in its interior. We know this from a letter he wrote George R. G. Conway, the English managing director of the Mexican Light and Power Company and a collector of Spanish colonial documents. On 10 June 1925, the novelist wrote him: "I shudder even when I look at the little MS you gave me and think of that beastly Santo Domingo Church, with its awful priests and the backyard with a well-ful of Baby's bones."

Harry T. Moore was the first to publish this particular letter as one of the new Lawrence letters in *The Intelligent Heart*. A photograph sent by Rosalind Hughes taken on 13 August 1924 by Colonel Akin, was captioned in his hand, "Baby Bones found in Secret Room, Santo Domingo Convent." Part of the monastic complex of Santo Domingo was being used then, as it still is, as a barracks. According to Jean Akin, the bones were discovered by treasure-hunting soldiers, who tapped the walls for hollow-sounding places, broke through one reverberant spot, and found a passage twenty feet long and almost five feet wide covered "four feet deep with baby bones," generally assumed to be those of children illicitly begotten by the Dominican friars. After General Ibarra heard the news, he asked Colonel Akin if he wanted to see the gruesome evidence. Ever alert for good news photographs, the Colonel took his Graflex to the spot, and Ibarra, according to Jean, helped the Colonel pose some of the bones. Mr. Duke also learned of the tiny bones and gathered some in a wooden box. He still had them two months later when Miss Hughes arrived at the Francia and asked her if she would like some. Although he later recalled them as found in a well rather than behind a wall, the bones gave Lawrence a horror of Santo Domingo, even though its friars had been driven out in 1859 when Juárez's Reform Laws abolished the monasteries.

In *Twilight in Italy* Lawrence explained that he never became interested in a church until "a living connection" was established between him and it. In the same book he describes how he felt on entering a church where such a connection had been made. "My senses were roused, they sprang awake in the hot, spiced darkness. My skin was expectant, as if it expected some contact, some embrace, as if it were aware of the contiguity of the physical world, the physical contact with the darkness and the heavy-suggestive substance of the enclosure. It was a thick, fierce darkness of the senses. But my soul shrank."

With such sensibility, and such mastery of words, one regrets exceedingly that Lawrence never established a living connection with Santo Domingo. It is one of the glories of the western hemisphere with its Tree of Jesse, its rosary chapel, and its painted and sculptured barrel-vaulted ceiling.

Nor did he make a connection with either the little market church of San Juan de Diós or with the Jesuit church of La Compañia, whose largest patio provided house-room for burros on market days. Apparently he never responded to La Merced, Padre Rickards's church, nor to La Patrocinio on his own corner, whose wall he rounded to go to Huayapan. Even the conspicuously placed cathedral, with its walls of pale green stone and its façade, wonderfully carved in a harder, light brown stone, is never mentioned in his correspondence, and all he gave it by way of description in his other writings is a vivid sentence in "The Flying Fish": "The yellow cathedral leaned its squat, earthquake-shaken towers, the bells sounded hollow." La Soledad was the only church in the city he mentioned at length.

Brett's incidents are chronological although her implied sequences are sometimes unreliable. For example, the visit to the governor occurred three or four days after Lawrence's arrival but she places it after the move to the Padre's house. She also describes a visit to a pottery as occurring after they were in the house, although it more probably occurred during the sightseeing days when the Lawrences were still at the Hotel Francia. Miss Hughes remembered going with them, and perhaps she showed the way, for the pottery they visited five blocks from the hotel was one she had visited previously with Mr. Duke.

> We go this afternoon to the pottery factory [wrote Brett]—the little yard full of bowls drying in the sun. A half-naked Indian is digging clay out of a pool of water; there is an air of busy quietness and of peace. We go down some steps into a dark shed—and there sits the potter at his wheel: a dark, slender Indian with large, dreamy eyes and small, delicate, sensitive hands. He looks up at us and smiles, and willingly puts a large lump of clay on his wheel. Then with his bare toes, he turns the great stone wheel under the table until the smaller wheel on the top of the table spins. As it spins, with his nimble fingers he models the clay, wetting his hands at intervals. For modelling the inside of the bowl, he uses a piece of shaped clay: for the rim and outside, a piece of leather.

The potter was Armando Ramos. Tracking down his identity required three stages. First, I knew I had to locate the pottery. Taking my copy of *Lawrence and Brett* with a picture of the Lawrences visiting it, I had luck at the first pottery I tried in August 1970. Antonio García Díaz, the owner, recognized the young man with the wide belt standing behind the crouching Lawrence as Juan Toboada who used to work for Alfarería Jiménez. The Jiménez pottery was still in existence. Don Antonio told me I would find it at Zaragoza 13, and to ask for Adela Jiménez. The street number was now changed to 402, and the yard did not look as it did in Brett's day, but Doña Adela assured me I had the right place and took me under the second-story addition at the back to the potter's shed. Apolinar Jiménez had founded the pottery in 1901, but by 1924, the time of the photograph, Apolinar had been dead three years and his son, Ignacio, then eighteen, was in charge. She had married Ignacio in 1927. Now he is dead, but she has carried on with her son, Rafael, as her partner. I did not ask about Armando then, because I did not know Brett had taken his picture. That discovery came two months later when I examined Brett's negatives at the University of Texas and found two photos of individual potters. (Plate 38 is one.) Obtaining prints of them, I took them on my second visit to the pottery in April 1971 along with one of Miss Hughes's pictures.(Plate 39.) Doña Adela immediately identified Armando as one of the potters and the other as her husband. Doña Adela could recognize the three men on the left in the Hughes photograph. The smiling young man with the bowl in his hand was Toboada, who had been identified in the Brett picture. The taller young man in the black felt hat was Armando, and the third was her husband, Ignacio. But she could not identify the other four men.

"Who is the little girl?" I asked.

"That's Catalina," was the quick reply. In a few minutes, Catalina arrived. She was a sturdy and well-preserved matron of fifty-six who was a shy nine at the time the photograph was taken. The old man with the apron and bare legs was her uncle, Manuel Caballero. The men on either side of Uncle Manuel were the Lara brothers, Eliseo the short one and Guillermo, the tall one. Eliseo was the only man in the picture still alive. The last one in the line was Guillermo Contreras. One of Catalina's three sons is a potter, carrying on the family tradition.

Doña Adela told me that the wheels the potters turned with their feet were of wood, not of stone. The axles leading up to the turntables were called *flechas* or arrows, and were also of wood. The turntables from which the vessels were drawn up from the clay were *discos*. The pool of water in which the half-naked Indian was digging clay was the *estanque* or tank. It no longer exists. In those days the tanks were used as trampling areas in which the barefooted potters walked on the clay to get it soft and uniform in consistency. Now the work is done at mills with power-driven machinery.

Although the rear part was now all *reformado*, Doña Adela said the property was the same size as in Lawrence's day. On the ground I could see earthen vessels drying on boards, and slipped vessels drying on the earth, just as in Brett's picture.

Brett had said that it was in the potters' shed that they felt "peace and serenity for the first time,"a reflection of how they were influenced by "the constant rumor of revolution, the uneasiness of the white people," the "tales of unspeakable horrors in the mountain villages; of nameless, incurable diseases that are poured into your ears by the doctors." The reference to the doctors, immediately following her words, "you have had a stomachache most of the night and are feeling low," indicates that Lawrence's condition had required medical attention.

According to Brett, the fear that he might be trapped in Oaxaca by the blowing up of the railway was already depressing Lawrence "terribly" as was the feeling that his freedom was curtailed. "Our walks, our talks, are all restricted. Even our mail is opened," she reported, until Lawrence put a stop to this by complaining to the post office. "A strange feeling is coming over us: a dual feeling [Brett wrote]. One of imprisonment, and then another of a fierce desire to sally forth armed to the teeth, and to shoot—to assert ourselves noisily in this noiseless unease. We can find no freedom, for ourselves or in anyone else. Everybody is virtually a prisoner. The Indians are afraid of the Mexicans, the Mexicans are afraid of the Indians, and the Americans are afraid of both."

Lawrence confirmed these words in a January 6 letter to William Hawk. "It's so queer here, never free, never quite safe, always a feeling of being hemmed in, & shut down. I get sick of it myself: —feel I shall burst."

By the time they visited the pottery, the first joy in Oaxaca had evaporated. Its interest as a place for sightseeing had worn thin. The Lawrences had failed to make the sort of contacts with the natives that they had in Italy, and the atmosphere was surcharged with tension. Frieda was disenchanted: "Frieda of course pines for her ranch, and the freedom," he wrote the younger Hawk on November 14. Three days later, on the eve of moving into the Padre's house, he wrote Clarence Thompson, "Frieda wears her best frocks, but doesn't really enjoy it." He added, "I'm wishing I'd gone to Europe, instead of coming here."

Getting settled in the priest's house and back to a regular writing schedule, however, brought an upswing, and on December 9, when Lawrence sent his new address to Secker, he wrote, "I like it! It gives me something. When one once gets over the peculiar resistance Mexico offers always."

Lawrence and Brett states that Brett's decision to stay at the Francia was her own, made because of Frieda's hostility the day they went to inspect the priest's house. This may well have been when Brett herself first had the idea of not moving in but the idea had been in Lawrence's mind as well as Frieda's even before they left the ranch. On October 8 he wrote Mrs. Carswell, "Brett will go down with us. But if we take a house, she must take a little place of her own. Not to be too close." Perhaps, though, Lawrence did not have the heart to break this decision to Brett, and left it to Frieda to deliver the sledge-hammer hint. Whatever the explanation, the departure of the Lawrences from the Francia made a sharp difference in Brett's life. "I do most of the visiting [she wrote]. Now that you are in the Priest's house, I go about a good deal alone. I usually go up to your house at about four, unless there is a special trip on, or you come and fetch me for a walk."

The restriction of Brett's visiting to the late afternoons was due to Lawrence working in the mornings which were sacrosanct as soon as they moved into the house. Brett kept in touch with him vicariously at the hotel by typing his manuscripts.

She describes: "I once more begin my slow, painful typewriting . . . and our spelling does not match any better in Mexico than it did in America." Though it might be construed the other way round, this was a comment on Brett's own difficulty in spelling. She had begun typing for Lawrence when she was living in the one-room cabin near them. In one of her first letters to me she told an amusing story of the Lawrence machine she used. It had become dirty and Frieda undertook to clean it. "She boiled it," Brett wrote. "It never moved again. Just died in its tracks." The explanation reveals what lay behind Lawrence's 15 September 1924 letter to the older Hawk that Paul Delany published in the *D. H. Lawrence Review.* "I wonder if you would lend me your typewriter for a couple of days?" asked Lawrence. "Mine has just gone wrong, when there is a last bit of work to finish & send away in a hurry: oh tiresomeness of all machinery." Lawrence needed another typewriter to take to Mexico, and Mrs. Luhan lent him a portable. It was this portable that Brett worked on in Oaxaca, doing her transcribing sitting at her window. It was a congenial work place:

> As I sit in my hotel room, near the long, barred window, the Indians go softly, swiftly by in the sunny street. The women, folded in their *rebozos,* in their full white skirts and with their bare feet, scarcely giving me a glance. The men, wrapped up in their *serapes* like colored pillars, topped by their huge felt hats, go by quietly, but slow up and cast stealthy looks at me— more aware of me than the women, more inquisitive; more wondering and curious; and more aware of themselves, too. The strangeness of the place crowds in to me—our utter difference and, beyond all, our complete isolation.

Brett's sense of isolation was intensified by her deafness. She could not hear the sounds outside her window, especially now, for her hearing machine, with the headphones and the yellow lights, was working "very fitfully." When it was turned on and working well, Brett wrote me, "I could hear a pin drop." She could find no one in the city to repair it and had to send it to Veracruz. Its absence greatly increased her communication problems. "It's very difficult," she wrote me thirty-eight years later, "to convey to people the sort of twilight existence that partial deafness gives. Everything so disjointed and uncertain." In another letter she said, "Most of my stupidity about facts and names and so on was my difficulty with hearing."

Brett also painted in her room. This activity attracted even more interest than her typing. Miss Hughes recalled how "often there were from two to three to a crowd of natives, mostly men, standing at her window watching her paint." Brett wrote nothing about her indoor painting nor she did stay indoors every morning. "I sit most often on the Mitla road, painting or watching the hill people come in to market. The men take off their huge hats to me; the women stare. Sometimes the men and women come and sit down for a while beside me and watch me painting. My Spanish is limited and so is theirs. I take many photographs: the Indians are always willing to be taken."

Then, after a passage on the road traffic influenced from her memory of "Market Day," she adds, "I sit by the hour, in the shade of a tree and watch."

But Brett wasn't always alone when she wasn't with the Lawrences. "It was so hard to try to talk to her," said Jean Akin, remembering the tin horn she had to shout into, but Mrs. Akin was friendly nevertheless. Miss Hughes visited several potteries with Brett, while Brett sometimes went to the market with Doña María Monros. On one such visit there were several adventures. Brett bought a baby squirrel and a cage for it. Then she ran into a decidedly cool Frieda, who was shopping with Rosalino. While they were all together, an Indian from the hills came by, "carrying round the market a small box with folding doors." It was a little shrine of the Virgin and Child. "He presents it to everyone he meets and everyone kisses the glass over the image. Even Señora Monros. I don't kiss it, nor does Frieda."

Two of Brett's outings with the Lawrences have been illustrated by her photographs. She does not mention the walk to San Felipe with Padre Rickards and Maximiliano, but the book includes a walk which might have been the one on which Brett photographed the aqueduct.

It is hot, piping hot; and we explore small roads, wander into deserted houses and gardens. Frieda longs for one house in a beautiful shady garden, full of flowering trees and flowers.

"It's no good," you say. "They would never let us live out here. The only way to live in Mexico is to possess nothing." By this time, we are so hot that we can hardly move. We find a field with a stream in it.

"Let us paddle," cries Frieda; and off come our shoes and stockings. "Look at the lovely cows," says Frieda, again, "How big they are!" The cows approach to have a look at this strange sight in the river. They come quite close and surround us. Then one of the cows jumps onto the back of another: it is an enormous bull. Frieda's face is a study: she rushes for her shoes. They are nearly all huge bulls. You are laughing, laughing so much tears are in your eyes; but all the same you are hurrying into your shoes also. I am already in mine.

"Don't run," you say to us. "Let us go quietly." Then the bulls begin to fight. Heads lowered, they rush at each other, bellowing. They are a silvery gray; big, with large horns. We move off quietly, turning to watch them. We have armed ourselves with large sticks, but there is no need; they are too taken up with their own fight to bother about us. We scramble back into the road and sit and rest under a tree. Further on we pass a man ploughing: a couple of oxen hitched to an odd, ancient, wooden plough.

At this time the Lawrences began to see more of Donald Miller, their across-the-street neighbor. His was the house which had protected Miss Doctor and the Taylors each night when the roof of their own was commandeered by García Vigil's soldiers. McEwen, the hospitable one-armed Canadian mining engineer who had given shelter to the missionaries, moved out after his five-year-old daughter died from typhoid fever. Thereupon Miller, who formerly lived near the *zócalo,* moved in.[1]

Miller, who was three years younger than Lawrence, was a fine-boned, slender man with light brown hair, deep-set eyes and sharply cut features. Everyone testified that he had charming manners and was always socially very correct. Dr. Kull remained permanently grateful to him, for Miller was the man who introduced the dentist to Flit. Though Miller was a bachelor, he liked to entertain and Jean Akin recalled that it was at a party at his house where she first met the Lawrences.

Miller was one of the few mining men in Oaxaca who was riding high. He had come to develop a silver mine abandoned at the start of the Revolution. Its location gives the clue that he was the man who promised to lend Lawrence a good Texas saddle, because Lawrence said the loaner had also offered to show him silver mines near Ejutla; and the abandoned mine was at La Garzona, a tiny settlement not far from Ejutla. The mine was called "San José la Garzona" and Miller's employer was Cinco Minas de Jalisco, an American company backed by James Watson Gerard, who had been United States Ambassador to Germany in the neutral years of World War I. The Mimiaga family, which owned the mine, would not sell it but was willing to rent it, and Miller worked out a contract giving his company the right to work the mine from 1923 to 1927. The mine had been flooded, so the first major task was to pump out the water. When it was discovered that the vein was slender, the American company lost interest, ordering Miller to give up the work and close down the mine. But Miller and one of his miners, Jesús Herrera, had faith in the property, and Miller decided to take it over for himself. Shortly after this, Herrera set an explosion where he had a hunch a large vein of silver would be exposed. His hunch was correct, and the vein, which appeared to be about six feet wide when it was discovered, widened into nine feet as it was pursued. The high-grade ore yielded eighteen kilograms of silver a ton as well as some gold. Miller became rich, enabling him to move into the large house and to purchase a car, which had to be brought to Oaxaca on a railroad flat car.

The ruins of Mitla were still the thing for visitors to Oaxaca to see in the 1920s. Lawrence had asked Seltzer, his American publisher, to send him *Terry's Guide to Mexico,* before setting out for Mexico the first time. T. Philip Terry, its compiler, was nothing if not dogmatic, and Lawrence had exploded against his judgments many times the year before. Nevertheless, he was still relying on him, and Terry's description of Mitla filled five pages with small print, almost equaling the coverage for Oaxaca itself, in sharp contrast to the scornful paragraph on Monte Alban. Since the latter's ruins have subsequently so far eclipsed those at Mitla, it is amusing to read that in those days Terry could write of Monte Alban: "The hill shows evidence of having been the centre of a considerable population in ancient times. There are rock-carvings, the remains of fortresses and whatnot. The view is attractive, but an almost equally comprehensive *vista* may be had from the *Cerro del Fortín,* and with less exertion."

Terry also suggested taking the mule trolley to Santa María del Tule and hiring a car there, or taking the train twenty miles to Tlacolula and hiring a car or buggy there. One could stay at Mitla, for it had "a quaint, ranch-like hotel, primitive in character, but hospitable withal." With a car from Oaxaca, however, even though the road was unpaved, the round trip could be managed in a day. The Lawrences had their neighbor to drive them so did not stay in Mitla overnight.

The Mitla ruins, like most of Mexico's important archaeological sites, are under the jurisdiction of the Instituto Nacional de Antropología e Historia. Tickets are sold and no record is kept of the names of the visitors. But in Lawrence's day, Fausto Quero, the son of Felix Quero who owned the hospitable hotel, was in charge of the zone and Don Fausto had all visitors sign a large guest book. I hoped to learn the date of the Lawrences' visit by finding their signatures in the 1924 book, but could not. The market traffic from Oaxaca that Brett tells us slowed down their return suggests they went on a Sunday. If so, it was probably November 30 for by the following Sunday, Lawrence had several of Brett's Mitla photographs to send as postcards.

> We start early in the morning [wrote Brett]. I have to be up at your place at six. Escorted by the hotel *mozo,* I arrive to find the car has disappeared. But it finally turns up and we pile in and off we go.
>
> The Mitla Road is full, even at this early hour. We have to go slowly—the oxen cannot be moved quickly out of the road. Frieda is shouting like a schoolboy; you are quieter than quiet. Disturbed by Frieda's exuberance, you turn suddenly on her and snub her into silence.

Poor Frieda! Her exuberance, which so many have written about, was seldom seen in Oaxaca. Brett did not defend her. "I am squeezed in between the two of you, as usual. On the front seat is Mr. Miller and his young engineer friend." Thanks to Lawrence's identification on the back of the Mitla photo he sent Quintanilla, we know the friend was José García, an Oaxaqueño particularly friendly to Americans engaged in mining. He was not an engineer, as Brett thought, but a caretaker who kept an eye on mines for owners who could not live near them, especially those around San Miguel Peras, where he lived for many years. The day of the Mitla visit, as Brett's photographs show, he wore a gray fedora, a tie, a dark suit coat, and white pants. Brett wore a pleated cotton dress and a striped cardigan jacket. Whether her hat with the small brim was the one Lawrence compelled her to buy in Oaxaca "to make more of a woman" of her, one cannot tell. But it was not the "big Stetson" that she preferred. Frieda's hat was large and quite floppy, but dark —not "the new white felt" one chosen for her by Lawrence at the same time he chose Brett's. Lawrence wore the same white Panama with the narrow black ribbon that we see in photographs at the market, the pottery, and on the walk to examine the aqueduct. Remaining a proper English gentleman by wearing a tie, he was formal enough to wear his waistcoat under his neat single-breasted suit. "A mile or two out of town [according to Brett] the good road ends in a sort of rambling affair. Along this we bump for hours [they only had seven miles to go] until we reach Tuli. [Santa María del Tule.] There we stop to see the great tree. It is huge standing in the yard of a small church."

Baron Alexander von Humboldt never got to Oaxaca, but probably, like most modern tourists, they were shown the 1802 board with the baron's name, which is slowly being swallowed under the approaching lips of the tree's cinnamon-colored bark.

"In spite of mud holes, through which we crawl carefully," Brett continued, "we manage to reach Mitla about twelve—a strange lonely little village. The road is lined by single organ cactus. They have been planted as fences, except for the irregularity of height. Behind these cactus fences, lurk little leave-villages, so crouched in among the undergrowth and foliage of trees, that they are hard to see."

Her photograph of the inn, "with oxen carts drawn up outside" warranted a picture preserving the fact that the inn had the same name then as now, "La Sorpresa." (Plate 40.) The Museo Frissell de Arte Zapoteco is now behind the doors and windows, but then the space was occupied by a store, and Darío Quero, a grandson of Felix Quero, said that the ox-carts would be waiting while their drivers were inside buying feed and other supplies. La Sorpresa was also the village post office. The building had been the center of an eighteenth-century *hacienda* and had belonged to the Quero family for more than 200 years.[2]

This Sorpresa photograph was another of Brett's Mitla pictures that Lawrence used as a postcard. "This," he explained, in sending it to the younger Hawk, "is outside the Hotel at Mitla, where the ruins are. If you look in the picture you'll see a white hat—me—we motored out there—3 1/2 hours to do 33 miles—and supposed to be a good time. Oh roads! I was battered and shattered."

One wonders why the scene Brett took in front of La Sorpresa should have induced "a feeling of isolation . . . that makes us shudder." Perhaps she was influenced by Terry's translation for *Mictlan,* the Aztec word from which the town derives its name: "hell or a place of sadness." Lawrence's description shows they had also heard the more common translation, "Place of the Dead."

Mitla is in a cul-de-sac leading off to the left at the end of the southeast arm of the valley. The land is still level at the village with the ruins about a half mile beyond where the ground begins to rise towards the hills. In those days the major adobe structure, covered by earth and surmounted by a little brick chapel, seemed like a natural hill. Palm-leaf thatching was the common roofing in Mitla and other villages. "We walk up to the ruins along the cactus-lined road," Brett writes. "It is terribly dusty, but when we reach the ruins [undoubtedly the walls of cream-colored stone of the great palace called the Hall of Columns], their beauty and strangeness make up for the dreariness of the village. The carving is magnificent." She was referring to the three-dimensional mosaics known as *grecas,* varied frets composed of hundreds of geometrically cut stones, which, in the exterior walls, are embedded in panels framed by long, flawlessly plain horizontals.

At the entrance, she reported, "a well-nourished, well-dressed Indian becomes our guide." Present guides identified him as one of the owner's sons because he was wearing shoes instead of *huaraches* (something I had never noticed). They guessed he was Ambrosio Quero, the oldest son. Darío confirmed that his rotund Uncle Ambrosio had an impressive white moustache and a predilection for big sombreros, white shirts, and pants resembling jodhpurs. Undoubtedly, like guides who have succeeded him, he pointed out the precise cutting of the individual *grecas,*the way they fitted so closely that no mortar was needed, and the wonder that such work was done without the benefit of steel tools.

The room with the finest interior *grecas* is behind the columned hall that gives its name to the whole palace. The party, therefore, had to pass through the hall twice. The six monolithic columns dividing it down its length gave Brett a photographic idea, and she persuaded her companions to pose before the smooth pillars rising from below the floor to support a now-vanished roof. García stood in front of the nearest column, Lawrence in front of the next, Frieda in front of the third, and Miller in front of the fourth. Frieda used this shot as an enclosure card for her Christmas gifts to Carola Kull. (Plate 29.) After the front-to-back picture was taken, Miller must have borrowed the camera to take his guests disposed before the columns in a conventional row. (Plate 41.)

The Patio of the Tombs is described most fully by Brett; in her account of human sacrifice, one gets a sharp sense of how she was either handicapped by her poor hearing or misled by the combination of her imagination and Don Ambrosio's. There might have been sacrifices at Mitla at one time, but it was Zapotec and Mixtec, not Aztec, and no sacrificial stone has been discovered there. Yet Brett got the idea that Don Ambrosio took them to see one when he led them into the cruciform tomb very close to the surface, whose roof at the crossing is supported by a central column. The imagined stone oppressed her: "We go up into the open air thankfully, away from that sacrificial stone and the smell of blood that somehow pervades the whole ruin. It seems lifeless and yet full of a dark, fierce life."

In the tomb, Don Ambrosio told them the superstition about the column that guides still tell tourists: that it had "the power of foretelling the length of one's life." The guide asks a tourist to embrace the column, then calculates the number of hand-widths by which the finger tips of the embracing arms do not touch. These he translates into years and the result is the number of years left for the embracer. A child with short arms, of course, has many; and an adult, especially if his arms are long, has few. With the Lawrences, " 'Put your arms round,' " says the guide. 'And I can tell you how long you are to live.' Frieda flatly refuses; but you and I, one after the other, clasp the pillar firmly. You have eighteen years to live, and I twenty."

The calculation shows that Lawrence's reach exceeded Brett's, for the space between his finger ends and hers was smaller. By living to be ninety-three Brett had more than twice the number of years promised by the column. Lawrence, on the other hand, had less than a third. If the column had made the true prophecy for him of five years and three months, the trio could not have emerged so lightheartedly from the tomb. Frieda at forty-five still had thirty-two years more.

That it was the dry season is emphasized by Brett's recollection of leaving the ruins. "The wind has become almost a gale and the dust is thick in the air. We are tired and a bit depressed. An excellent lunch in the little hotel cheers us up, but it is hard to shake the feeling of blood and fierceness that the ruins give out." The ride back to Oaxaca, because of the market traffic clogging the road, must have equaled in length the three-hour ride out. "The long, slow drive home tires you terribly," wrote Brett, hinting at what was to become increasingly evident: that the thin, frail man did not have the physical stamina of his two women companions.

Lawrence used the Mitla visit in revising *The Plumed Serpent*. He had reached his heroine's first major debate with herself over whether to flee from Mexico or to let herself be drawn more deeply into it, to leave the country or go on to Lake Chapala where the new Quetzalcoatl religion was stirring. Lawrence's changes show that he felt the need for a more compelling presentation of Mexico's power, both to draw and to repel. One step was to transform the debate from a weak coda in the previous chapter into the nucleus of a new, independent chapter, "To Stay or Not to Stay." Another was to relate the ideas more urgently to Kate's personal problems. A third was to build up the looming sense of Mexico's pre-Columbian past by adding Mitla. So after the evocation of Teotihuacán and Cholula, he writes:

> Mitla under its hills, in the parched valley where a wind blows the dust and the dead souls of the vanished race in terrible gusts. The carved courts of Mitla, with a hard-sharp-angled, intricate fascination, but the fascination of fear and repellance. Hard, four-square, sharp-edge, cutting, zigzagging Mitla, like continual blows of a stone axe. Without gentleness of grace or charm. Oh America, with your unspeakable hard lack of charm, what then is your final meaning! Is it forever the knife of sacrifice, as you put out your tongue at the world.

The powerful description is graphic, but idiosyncratic. The style is so obviously Lawrence's own, however, that it is difficult to imagine a woman formulating her impressions in such terms. Since Kate is part Lawrence anyway, the effect is not too incongruous. In her list of the contradicting aspects—the charming elements of Mexico—he inserted a detail drawn from the town of their overnight stay between trains on the way to Oaxaca: "The voices of the boys, like birds twittering among the trees of the plaza of Tehuacan!"

The two inserts show how his novel—his major preoccupation—was in the back of Lawrence's mind throughout all the external events of this particular visit to Mexico. Everywhere, including Mitla, he was on the alert for material to make "Quetzalcoatl" more fully the novel he wanted it to be.

The Lawrences liked to read, yet they were never settled in one place long, and as Lawrence wrote once to Frederick Carter, "one can't carry books around." When Kyle S. Crichton, one of the few U.S. newspapermen to obtain an interview with Lawrence, asked how they managed for reading materials, the author replied that they read whatever books anybody sent them.

"We never carry any when we travel," Lawrence told Crichton, "and take whatever our kind friends foist off on us. In that way we learn things we'd never in a hundred years pick off a library shelf."

This reliance on unexpected and unanticipated reading often stimulated Lawrence. But sometimes he asked friends to send specific books, like Terry's *Guide,* and he was constantly receiving copies of his own, as either new ones or reprints were issued in England or the United States. When he found books on friends' shelves that interested him, he borrowed them. Miller proved a source of books. Brett gives an instance:

> The three of us are in Mr. Miller's house, drinking cocktails and eating very good sandwiches. You ask him if he can lend you a book. He is most willing and eager, and goes to the bookcase, you following. You kneel down and take a look along the line of books. You pull out one and glance through it. As you kneel there, turning over the pages of the book, Mr. Miller hands you another with a laugh, saying:
> "This is just the book for you." You take it and hold it in your hands. On the cover is the picture of a woman pulling off her chemise, a man in evening suit watching her. You take it in your hands, a look of astonishment on your face. You hold it for a few minutes in silence then hand it quietly back to Miller without even saying a word. He looks baffled, but he puts it back on the shelf and does not offer you any more books. You finally choose a book on Mexico.

When I asked Brett for her memories of Miller in 1962, she said he had visited Taos and she had seen him there. "He was very grieved at my talk about him," she explained, in the incident of the sexy novel. "I can remember Lawrence sputtering over it afterwards. It always made him mad. The man was a very nice man, very kind to us, but a bit obtuse in certain matters. Miller was grieved that I told about the books. I can almost remember the lurid cover of one of them. I think now I should not have mentioned it. Why humiliate the man, as there are many other ways of describing Lawrence's hatred of 'dirty stories' and dirty books."

The Lawrences did not attend the grand ball for the visiting diplomats at Oaxaca's charming little opera house,[3] but Brett's book shows they went there at least twice. She describes the first visit: "In the evening, we go to the magnificent theatre. It is an amateur performance, clever at moments, but long and tedious; only relieved for us by Frieda and myself getting the most hopeless giggles. The tears are running down our faces; we are purple in the face. We cannot stop. You sit between us, rigid, unsmiling, completely disowning us."

The opera house also presented occasional movies; the other visit to the theater described by Brett was on December 7, for I found from *El Mercurio* that this was the Sunday of the showing of *The Thief of Baghdad,* starring Douglas Fairbanks. "He thrills us," Brett reported. "You enjoy it just as much as Frieda and I do."

According to the advertisement, the picture began at five P.M. and nine P.M. Brett specified going "later in the evening" to the second showing. Surely they sat in the *Luneta* or orchestra as tickets were only seventy-five centavos, and one can't see the three of them climbing to the *Paraiso* just to save twenty-five centavos. *Thief* was a silent film. Lawrence had written in *Twilight in Italy* how the movies, "that triumph of the deaf and dumb," had come "to give us the nervous excitement of speed—grimace, agitation, and speed, as the flying atoms." Sooner or later, Lawrence made artistic use of nearly every scrap of his experience. In his story, "Mother and Daughter," the Armenian suitor looks incongruous in a dinner-jacket when "his sort of fatness called for a fez and the full muslin breeches of a bazaar merchant in *The Thief of Baghdad.*"

Thief ended the day that had begun with Rosalino banging on Brett's door to get a book when Brett had a "crashing" headache. She did not send back an answer; and when she visited the Lawrences later in the day she was surprised that Lawrence was angry.

> After lunch and five aspirins (feeling lightheaded, but with the pain gone) I take the mule tram up to your house. You are cold, aloof: what has happened? I suddenly realize that it is because I never answered your note. I hurry after you into the kitchen where you are fanning the charcoal fire, and I explained and apologize for not sending an answer back by Rosalino. You understand immediately, and immediately are warm and friendly again.
>
> We go out into the patio and you sit down next to me in so gentle and charming a way—so anxious to show me you are not cross and don't think me rude. We say nothing. Somehow we don't need to say anything: that is the mystery of our friendship. Frieda comes out of her room and casts a sharp glance at us.

The book Lawrence wanted may have been Spence's *The Gods of Mexico,* the book on Mexico that Lawrence chose for himself from Miller's shelf. When a passage of a book stirred him, he read it aloud. The account of the goddess who bore a flint knife was one Spence passage he read to Brett. When she reminded him of it later, she added jokingly, " 'That's just what might happen to me with my passion for knives.' And you laugh and laugh at this, and heartily agree."

Brett was eager to buy a knife produced in Oaxaca, where knives are a specialty. The helpful Mr. Miller knew the workshop where the finest knives were made and volunteered to take Brett there. "I go off with Mr. Miller to see the knife-maker, an Indian with an Italian great-grandfather, who had inherited the secret of steel-making. This secret the Indian refuses to sell, though offers have been made to him from big American and European firms. He keeps his secret—he and his handsome sons. They make swords and knives that are famous the world over. I just have to have one, and so we go to the man's house."

Brett did not name the knife-maker, but her description was so specific that I felt the memory of such a smithy would still be alive in Oaxaca in 1970. Eloy Gopar was the first master knife-maker I visited for help, but his shop was not hers. He was the first of his family to make knives, but he had learned his art at the Casa Aragón, which had been in one family for years. He said it still existed and that I could find it at Jota P. García 503, the address where it had always been. When I entered the salesroom in the front of the old house, I knew I had the right place. Photos of knife-makers of several generations lined the walls and there were framed gold medals won at three world fairs, including the Saint Louis Exposition in 1904. The family member now carrying on is Guillermo Aragón Guzman, a man of twenty-five or twenty-six, who is a sixth-generation knife-maker. Between us, we figured out that when Brett came, a member of the fourth generation, his grandfather Austreberto Aragón García, was in charge. Austreberto Aragón Maldonado, a member of the fifth generation, one of the handsome sons Brett noticed, was still alive but left most of the work to Guillermo.

When I saw the big oval photo of the third generation knife-smith, the one who set up a branch of the business in Oaxaca in 1900, I realized why Brett spoke of an Italian great-grandfather, for under the portrait was "H. Aragón, Ejutla." Through her ear trumpet, *Ejutla* must have sounded like *Italy* to her. In Ejutla, near Miller's mine, Felipe Aragón had founded the family forge in 1750. Hermenegildo Aragón, who brought the business to Oaxaca, was a refined-looking man with a moustache, a spade beard, and a large black bow tie. Brett did the man who waited on her an injustice to describe him merely as an Indian. Austreberto the First, whose photo was also on display, had an even more refined face than his father. He lived until 1954, thirty years beyond the Brett-Miller visit. Guillermo confirmed that the family had a secret for tempering steel that it refused to sell.

"Swords of all kinds," wrote Brett, "knives of all kinds are shown to me; also the anvil and a half-made sword." Guillermo led me through the family living quarters to the forge in a blackened courtyard behind the house where a man was pulling down on a bellows cord to fan up a flame as he heated a blade, then moved to the anvil and pounded on the red-hot steel.

Christmas was coming, so Brett ordered two knives with deer horn handles, a large one for herself, and a smaller one "as a surprise" for Lawrence. She asked that his name be put on it, and her words, "The patterns of the blades are all drawn and designed by the Indian, and then stamped on," indicated that she did not watch this phase of knife-making. Guillermo told me that the family at one time had patterned blades *a golpe,* that is, by hammering the steel around the designs to be left standing clear. But since 1910 they had used the less laborious method of painting the designs with ink that resisted the acid into which the blades were briefly dipped.

Both knives, Brett told me, had subsequent histories. When she went fishing by herself in New Mexico, she wore hers in the top of her right cowboy boot and it frightened "the Mexicans out of their wits." In 1962, at the age of seventy-nine, when her fishing days were over, she wrote, "I gave it a few years ago to a young friend who used to go fishing with me." Lawrence used his knife as a paper cutter and after he died it figured in an attack (no harm was done) on Frieda. In 1971, Brett added additional details.

After Lawrence had returned to Frieda following the Spotorno rift, her daughters were still with her, and on 10 April 1926 he wrote about them to Koteliansky: "F.'s daughters are really very funny: they sit on their mother with ferocity, simply won't stand her cheek, and fly at her very much in her own style. It leaves her a bit flabbergasted, & is very good for her, as you'll guess." Her daughter Barbara lost her temper while siding with Lawrence in a dispute between him and Frieda and threatened her mother with Brett's gift-knife. Although this story contradicts Brett's earlier story that it was after Lawrence's death, Barbara was often at odds with her mother.

After the visit to the knife-maker, Miller disappears from Brett's story. He stayed in Oaxaca until 1927 when his lease on "San José la Garzona" ran out. Understandably, the Mimiaga family was not willing to renew the lease. Futhermore, Miller, having developed ulcers, was ready to leave Oaxaca. The family, now headed by son-in-law José Sántibañez, began working the mine in its own interest, and in 1933 it yielded another bonanza, which enabled Sántibañez to build the large Hotel Marqués del Valle on the *zócalo* to take advantage of the influx of tourists expected from the completion of the Pan-American Highway. By this time Miller was back in New York, where he lived until 1950, then moved to California, where he died three years later.

Brett began to take Spanish lessons; and as the feast of the Virgin of Soledad neared, her instructor told her some of the legends associated with the patroness of Oaxaca, whose name Brett never got straight, repeatedly calling her the Virgin of San Felipe. The Oaxaca historian, José María Bradomín, sets 1543 as the year of the chief legend; it sounds like a sixteenth-century story, for in spirit it resembles that of the appearance of the Virgin of Guadalupe on the outskirts of Mexico City in 1531, although the Church of Soledad accepts the much later year of 1620.

Whatever the year, there is agreement that as dawn was breaking one December morning the drivers of a pack train, loaded with merchandise and precious stuffs from Veracruz, discovered an unaffiliated mule carrying a large box. No one saw her join the train and because the men were afraid they would be accused of having stolen her, they decided to leave her with the mayor of the city. On the outskirts of Oaxaca at a hermitage dedicated to Saint Sebastian, the strange mule sat down, and all the kicking and pulling of the muleteers could not get her to move. Finally, the drivers decided to remove the heavy box. She got up, took ten or twelve steps, and dropped dead. Now the men felt they would be accused of killing the mule. The mayor was sent for and ordered the box to be opened. To everyone's amazement, the box held a statue of Christ of the Resurrection. Even more mysterious were a beautiful head and a pair of praying hands with an inscription identifying them as those of Our Lady of Solitude. Everyone dropped to his knees. The bishop of Oaxaca was sent for. He didn't come, but the Vicar General did. He, too, felt in the presence of a miracle and gave two orders: that the head and hands should be left at the Hermitage of Saint Sebastian to be venerated there and that the Christ should be taken to the hermitage of la Santa Vera Cruz.

Brett's version, as she got it via her ear trumpet and relayed to Lawrence, was somewhat different, although many of her discrepancies may have been due to the imagination of her instructor. In her story, the pack-train, the hermitage of Saint Sebastian, and the other statue are omitted, the animal is a burro rather than a mule, and, instead of being mysteriously unaffiliated, it is the property of a known master. A governor and an archbishop are introduced, both of whom try personally to heave the reluctant pack-animal to its feet; and the animal dies after its cargo is disclosed, rather than before. But she was right about two essential things: a body, or at least a form, was made to support the head and hands, and a church was built in the Virgin's honor. The present great cruciform church, however, was not begun until 1682, planned so that the original walls of the hermitage would form a chapel behind the right transept. When the ground was leveled for the nave, the rocky outcropping where the mule fell was left untouched at the base of the north wall near the entrance. Seven years later, when her new home was ready, the Virgin was moved from the one-room hermitage to her sumptuous new sanctuary above the altar of the magnificent baroque church.

The head and hands are a shade more than life-size and the form created to support them is concealed by a dress of black velvet. The effect of a triangle is heightened by her cloak, also of black velvet, which falls to the ground in wide spreading angles from under her golden crown. (Plate 42.) The hands hold a lily of golden filigree, except in Lent when they support a crown of thorns and three diamond-headed nails. Except during Lent when it is unrelieved black, the Virgin's clothing is richly embroidered with foliage-surrounded monograms stitched in gold and silver and adorned with pearls.

Since her installation, Soledad has been credited with her quota of miracles, especially in saving sailors caught in storms at sea. Brett's instructor related a legend accounting for Soledad's many pearls, which she passed on to Lawrence:

> Away at sea, pearl-fishers in a sailing-ship are in agonies of fear in a great storm. The ship is tossing wildly in heavy seas. The sailors pray fervently to the Virgin, and suddenly they have a vision. They see the burro kneeling on the mound; they see the crowds, the Governor, and finally the Archbishop as he takes the head and hands of the Virgin out of the box. They see the workmen building the church; they see the church finished. They swear among themselves that if they are saved, they will send their cargo of pearls to the Virgin as a thanks-offering for the saving of their lives.
>
> The storm calms down; the ship sails into harbor. A sailor is sent running from the coast to Oaxaca with the precious pearls. He gives them, with a letter telling of the vision and their desire to have a pearl robe made for the Virgin, to the Archbishop. And ever since, at the Fiesta of San Felipe, the Virgin is brought out in her robe of pearls.

Although invented, this reinforcement of the first miracle by a second is symptomatic of how belief in one miracle begets belief in others. Lawrence, according to Brett, was not scornful of her recital, and she quoted him as saying: "If I could only believe that these tales are true, not just inventions. And yet they must spring from something. It is, though, quite a lovely story."

Lawrence's readiness to believe in some psychic force bringing such stories into human consciousness must have come from sitting quietly before Soledad and feeling her force. The experience could only have been in Oaxaca, for Soledad is not, like many other manifestations of the Virgin, a reappearance of a Virgin first appearing elsewhere. Although it may have been created entirely by the faith projected into her by those who have come to her for help in the last three centuries, her numen exceeds that of any sacred figure I know. Lawrence felt its force and simultaneously came to know how it affected others as attested by the passage he added to *The Plumed Serpent*. Wanting to characterize Cipriano and to convey how the Indian general felt when he saw Kate weeping, he wrote: "He looked at her soft, wet white hands over her face, and at the one big emerald on her finger, in a sort of wonder. The wonder, the mystery, the magic that used to flood over him as a boy and a youth, when he kneeled before the babyish figure of the Santa Maria de Soledad, flooded him again. He was in the presence of the goddess, white-handed, mysterious, gleaming with moon-like power and the intense potency of grief.''

Not the Day of San Felipe, which is May 26, but December 18 was established as the day of Soledad's feast, the day the mule refused to carry its burden further. In Oaxaca the celebration of Soledad's feast is a major event. In the previous description of the feast of the Virgin of La Merced, which occurs across the town three months earlier, I have introduced the main elements of a Oaxaca church fiesta: the *calenda,* or procession through the streets inviting everyone to attend; the carnival in the streets adjoining the church; the outpouring of devotion for the patron saint generally culminating with its image being carried among the faithful; and the fireworks that somehow manage to be both sacred and profane. Soledad's fiesta has them all, but always on a larger scale, for she is not just the patron saint of one neighborhood but the patroness of the whole state, and her sodalities from other towns and villages come in organized groups to give her thanks and honor. The throngs attract more merry-go-rounds, more ferris wheels, more games of ring toss, more food stands, and more tents for the native form of bingo. There are attractions that are not available at other fiestas: fireworks on two nights, instead of one; and the procession through the city of twenty-foot standards with hanging velvet banners of solid colors—burgundy, red, blue, yellow, green—encrusted with silver. The standard-bearers always wait until two-thirty in the morning before starting out so that it will be almost dawn when they and their candle-bearing attendants get back to the church to greet the Virgin on her day with *Las Mañanitas,* the traditional aubade for a loved one's birthday. Soledad's fiesta takes on added happiness from beginning the Christmas season.

The 1924 fiesta must have been particularly festive, in contrast to the year before when the city was cut off from the rest of the country, when money was running out, when Oaxaca's military allies were being routed, and when the de la Huerta Rebellion was facing inevitable defeat. Peace had been restored to the state and city, trains were running again, salaries were being paid, a firm government was supported by federal power, and the nightmare of deprivation and suspense was over. However, the Lawrences did not fully enjoy the three-day spectacle. From Brett's descriptions one gets the impression they hardly knew what was going on.

How queer and strange the constant little Fiestas are! We are sitting in the *Zócola* when a small band comes blowing around the corner. The men are wrapped in *serapes* and from under their huge hats, protrude the queerest and strangest of musical instruments: old, ancient wind instruments. The drums keep up a monotonous rapping and not one

> instrument is in tune or in time with the others. They march around the *Zócola,* guarded by five soldiers on horseback. The pathetic little procession is followed by crowds of men, women and boys. You are touched by the sadness of it, the poverty.

The description is accurate but there is no sign of awareness that the rustic band was announcing a forthcoming event at a church. A few nights later Brett wrote: "Another procession. Men and women, Indians, moving slowly, gently, with Chinese lanterns on sticks. The lanterns are lovely in the half light—but how stealthy it all is. There is no shouting, no singing. Ghost-like."

Brett is seldom at fault when using only her eyes, but there is lack of comprehension that these marchers with their candles in paper lanterns were part of a *calenda* inviting all to join them at the church the next night for the eve of Soledad's fiesta. There was probably a rustic band in this procession too, with a man in advance hurling up rockets from time to time. There is never shouting or singing when a *calenda* passes. Even though they had been primed for Soledad's feast, they did not know what they were seeing, and they were too wrapped up in their own concerns to care. Brett reported their conversation:

> You are tired; the dinner-party last night has tired you. I, who sat just behind you and another man, there being no room for me to sit between you, had caught at intervals your distressed eye turned for a moment my way. I was helpless: what could I do to help, with two backs to talk to?
>
> And now we are in the midst of a heated argument. Frieda is cross and getting furious. You reproved her for taking an impersonal conversation personally, and she is angry at you for reproving her before me—and angry at me, anyhow, because I stick up for you.

They did go to see Soledad's first night of fireworks, but Brett adds them as an afterthought to her main description of the feast. "The fireworks last night at twelve were just as silent, just as mirthless." She was wrong to expect rowdiness and gaiety when the mood is always wonderstruck enchantment. If Lawrence really "explained" things as she said—accepting his words as gospel—he was in this case totally in error. "The people are not allowed to shout and sing, in case of too much excitement rousing more trouble. The rulers want to keep the people quiet," she reports him as saying. He did not know the people of Oaxaca are quiet by nature, even when, as on national holidays, they are unsuccessfully encouraged to shout lusty *vivas.*

The Lawrences did not wait to see the assembling of the great banners and their setting out through the dark streets, accompanied by hundreds carrying candles and chanting responses to the prayers of a leader. But the Lawrences returned the next morning, accompanied by Señora Monros of the Hotel Francia, still wearing widow's weeds, and a compadre of hers, Ramón Allenta, a fellow-Catalan who lived at the hotel and loved poker. (Plate 43.) Before the Lawrences ascended the steps leading to the church's side door, Brett crossed the street to get a photograph of them. (Plate 44.) In her account she wrote:

> We three, with Señora Monros, are trying to get into the Church. It is packed. We struggle through the crowd at the door and find the church a sea of kneeling Indians. They kneel holding up a candle or holding up and out both arms. Thus for hours they kneel with rapt, absorbed faces. There is something beautiful in their endless patience.
>
> The Virgin has not yet been brought out. [She is never brought out until evening] and we do not feel strong enough to stand and wait in the hot, dense crowd; so we go out and walk up and down the street among the booths. We watch the gambling and eat the large flat cakes with golden syrup which drips down our chins.[4] You refuse to eat, but Frieda and I are more enterprising, having stronger stomachs. We watch the little merry-go-round with its silent riders whirling round, pushed by a dozen small, perspiring boys. It is all so silent: no laughter, no singing, no shouting.

They did not wait for the climax of the festival when Soledad, to the sound of solemn music by the state band, is carried under a canopy in slow procession through the atrium. Nor did they see the second and more spectacular round of fireworks after her return to the golden tabernacle above the altar. "A blind beggar, with a brilliant scarlet *serape* over his shoulder, kneels down in the road in front of you, his arms out as they pray in the church. He kneels there immovable. You drop a coin into his box, but he remains kneeling long after we go. At the end of the street, I look back and catch a glimpse of him through the crowd, still kneeling."

This final glimpse of the fiesta probably misinterprets the beggar's kneeling as well. Soledad's feast was on Thursday and the next morning, December 19, Lawrence began "Friday Morning," the first essay in *Mornings in Mexico*. For the next month Brett's, Frieda's, and Lawrence's stories are closely interwoven. Lawrence suddenly emerged from the work in which he had isolated himself and took on a variety of other writing tasks. The number of pages covered by his neat handwriting in the purple copybook shows that once back to work on "Quetzalcoatl," he must have written at furious speed and almost unceasingly during the first four weeks in the quiet of the large house. Although he was recopying much of the first version, he was, nevertheless, involved in an immense imaginative effort, conceiving not only a mythology, but also bringing into sharp focus the essential religious vision that was still indistinct at Lake Chapala. Mounting tension, fatigue, restlessness, and physical confinement probably all contributed to the change. His progress must have given him confidence that, at last, he could relax a bit. His pace would allow him to finish in the time he had allotted—two and a half months. But ten days earlier his situation was still uncertain for in his December 9 letter to Secker he said: "Frieda wants to come to Europe in the spring to see her mother and children, don't quite know if we shall manage it." Frieda was becoming restless under his writing regime. Lawrence's letter to Bynner the next day—"Frieda is sniffing Europe-ward once more: her mother and children"—shows that her restlessness was complicating his problem. At this time Frieda's mother was seventy-three and living in a home for elderly widows in Baden-Baden, Germany. Barbara, the youngest daughter, was already twenty, Elsa was twenty-two, and Frieda's still-unreconciled son, Charles Montague Weekley, was twenty-four. One reason Frieda would be so eager to be with her daughters again was that the year before they had reentered her life as adults, willing to meet Lawrence, and ready to forgive her for deserting them when they were young. If Frieda were feeling estranged from Lawrence, she would be longing more for her own family.

By the time of Soledad's fiesta, Lawrence knew where his work stood and was ready for a break. The arrival of Edward Weston's photographs seems to have been a catalyst. As we have seen, he wrote Weston saying he should try to place his pictures in *Vanity Fair*. He began writing with *Vanity Fair* in mind himself and urged Quintanilla to start a series of articles for the magazine. As Brett shows us, he began to vary his routine still further by doing what he used to do at the ranch, at Chapala and elsewhere, leaving the house to write outside, preferably under a tree. To do this, he switched copybooks, leaving at home the purple one and the blue Chapala ones, which he consulted as he rewrote, and slipping "Record" into his pocket instead.

> You and I have decided to try and go out and sit in the desert, [Brett opens her account of the first day of the new regime]. You want to get out in the mornings to write (you are beginning to write "Mornings in Mexico"), and I have a longing to paint.
>
> "Let us try," you say. "Two of us must be safe. Frieda can join us with lunch: Rosalino can carry the basket and look after her."
>
> I come up in the tram in the early morning for you. You are ready with your copybook and pen; I have my paints. Off we go, out into the lovely morning. It is the radiant fragrance of the air that is the beauty of Oaxaca.

On their way they would have seen, off to the left, the high-walled grounds of Oaxaca's large cemetery, for it is at the outskirts of the city close to the Mitla Road where they were headed. There is evidence that Lawrence, as well as Frieda, visited it. At the head of a short boulevard they would have come to a neo-renaissance arched gateway, reading *Postraos: Aqui le Eternidad Empieza y es Polvo aqui la Mundana Grandeza:* "Kneel humbly: here Eternity begins and here worldly grandeur is dust." Passing through the gateway, the English visitors would have found themselves in a vast cloister of yellowish stone surrounding a courtyard large enough to enclose a ruined, unfinished chapel and a multitude of white and gray tombs. Built into the outer walls of the cloister like five tiers of lockers were compartments for coffins. The newer section to the east had regular streets of tombstones and little mausoleums, too close together to allow grass.

Beyond the cemetery, Brett's words continue:

> We walk away onto the desert, far out, facing the great mountains. We walk slowly, happy to have the great space around us. Not a soul in sight. Occasionally we pass a man with cattle, or in the distance, along some trail, an oxen cart slowly crawls.
>
> We find two bushes—far apart, but within easy calling distance. You settle down under one, I under the other; and you begin to write in your easy, steady way. I fix up my paint box and begin to paint. The sun pours down. I creep back into my bush as far as I can and peer out to see how you are faring. You have taken off your coat and have laid it over the bush as a sort of umbrella. Under it you are sitting in your shirt sleeves, writing steadily. A couple of women ride by in the distance, the burros were specks; and up in the pure blue sky great birds are wheeling, gold in the sun. Suddenly your shadow falls over my painting.
>
> "I have finished," you say. "How are you getting along?" I hold up my painting, proudly.

From that painting[5] we know that Brett had faced north and was painting the wall of mountains that Lawrence likened to "a great splendid lizard," with a pink underbelly and the double cusp of San Felipe as its head. Her aim was to paint a profile view of one of the great streams of traffic coming to market that Lawrence had described in prose. Although she had defined the contours of the hills with extreme accuracy, Lawrence was critical. Her narrative continues:

> "Oh Brett," you say testily, "Do look at the mountain. It has great bare toes, where it joins the desert. Here, let me have a try." Down you sit, and with delicate finger-touches, you proceed to give the mountain its

toes. You roughen the fir trees on the mountain and darken the blue of the sky. "You are dumb, Brett; you don't look at things; you have no eyes."

"Tomorrow," I say darkly, "I will put in the figures," knowing that you can't paint figures. At that you laugh and with a sigh look at your watch.

"Frieda can't be coming, after all; so we must start home." And we collect our things reluctantly, and wander slowly back.

Frieda refused to bring out the picnic while Brett was with Lawrence, but the next day she suggested just such a picnic when Brett could be left behind. Not included, Brett learned of the walk to Huayapan second-hand. Either her faulty hearing or exaggerations (sounding more like Frieda than Lawrence) caused her to write: "The people had fled; you had seen them peeping around trees at you, frightened at your white face and red beard. The people fled in all directions, whenever you appeared, so little were they used to white people."

The seven hours walking to and from Huayapan took its toll on Lawrence. Nevertheless, the following day he went out with Brett again, walking the same long distance as on their first day together, for the lower part of her painting, which would form its foreground, was not finished, and she wanted the same view of the mountains.

This morning, somehow we are not so successful. As we start I have an idea you are not feeling well. The morning is just as lovely, just as radiant, the desert perfect in its solitude and quiet; but you are not the same. You are quiet, moody, uneasy. We find our little bushes, but your writing does not seem to flow so readily today. And my painting goes so stodgily that I put it aside and just watch the desert. Now and then I rouse myself and put in a group of figures. I am transplanting the ceaseless flow of the Mitla Road to my desert picture. At last you shut up your book, put your coat over your arm, and come over to my bush. You look at my figures, and sit down, taking the picture in your hands.

"It needs some animals, but it is nice," you say; and you paint in the right hand corner some women, burros, goats and dogs . . . "Don't you like my animals?" I do; they are lively and amusing. But we have to go home.

"What about tomorrow?" I ask, as we reach the door. You hesitate.

"I don't know," you reply. "You had better come up and see. I don't think Frieda likes it."

But in the evening when I come up, I find you in bed not feeling at all well; and Frieda worried.

Brett makes no mention of *Las Posadas,* ("the inns") indicating how seldom outsiders in Oaxaca were taken into the homes of the Mexicans. Had she been aware of the custom of organizing parties to enact the travels of Mary and Joseph in trying to find quarters in Bethlehem, she would surely have described how for nine successive nights before Christmas children and adults go singing to different houses, being refused admittance the first eight nights and admitted to the ninth house only on Christmas Eve. The songs to be sung outside the closed doors of *Las Posadas* are very charming. However, Brett did participate in *"La Noche de Rabanos"* ("The Night of the Radishes"), always on December 23. Frieda, still suffering from the effects of her bad cold, did not want to go and Lawrence, who had caught Frieda's cold, was still in bed. Brett went with Rosalind Hughes, another single woman at the Hotel Francia.

> I go to the *Fiesta of the Rabanos* with Miss Hughes. It is late, but she and I stroll through the streets lined with booths. I have no idea what to expect: nor has she. I press through the crowd to a largish booth and I am utterly astounded. Hanging like dolls all over the booth, are large radishes: pink and white *male* radishes! Nude male figures, little life-like men, hardly touched by the knife. No portion of their anatomy is missing, and certain unmentionable portions are so exaggerated that I am overwhelmed with embarrassment. There are giggles as I look: the expression on my face is amusing the Indians. I turn and hurry away to the next booth, hoping to free my embarrassment. Not a bit of it: the next booth is worse. All the booths are the same; the radishes are glowing and defiant, naked and unashamed.

Miss Hughes has no recollection of having seen any such figures or, as she put it more discreetly in a letter of 25 October 1962 "I do not recall the 'embarrassing' ones that Miss Brett describes." Miss Hughes remembers seeing the stalls being set up in the late afternoon and being decorated with flowers. Then, at night "the happy crowds around them; the beautifully decorated turnips and carrots, cut in the form of roses, etc., and the many fantastically shaped radishes, some of enormous size, cut to represent human figures, using fine black roots for hair. Some were decorated with a pen knife to form scallops around charro jackets, and stripes down the sides. Very skillful work."

The Night of the Radishes I attended in Oaxaca was in 1965. I saw no nude male figures, but people have told me that in the past occasional radishes have had exposed genitalia. Never, however, have I heard of wholesale displays such as Brett reports, and though I have inquired often, never have I heard Brett's explanation that they are displayed because the fiesta is a mating festival. After her first shock, Brett had an impulse described as follows: "At last, with some diffidence, I buy a fairly modest, unexaggerated radish and hiding it under my coat, I smuggle it into the hotel.'' But she felt her guilty secret was exposed to all, for she added, ''As I go through the hall, everyone notices the bulge in my coat and they all smile.''

She wanted the radish as a Christmas present for Lawrence, but she guarded her secret through the morning of Christmas Eve, when she helped with the special marketing.

> Frieda and I go down to the market and buy a Christmas tree, Rosalino staggers away with it while we buy all kinds of knick-knacks for the Padre's Indian servants—something for the Padre, too. But I go up again to your house at four to help fix the tree. I take up my radish. You are still in bed, but better. I bring the radish in to you and begin by telling about the Fiesta. A look of surprise and incomprehension comes over your face: I am not telling my story well. Then I produce my radish and your eyes twinkle: a gleam of wicked amusement shines in them. I am becoming more and more embarrassed as I tell my tale, and the laughter is dancing in your eyes: they are two gleaming specks of light. You are biting your beard and you are vexed at having missed it all.
>
> ''Damn these people who come and see me and give Frieda their beastly colds, which she gives me! But hang the radish on the tree.'' So I hang it up in a conspicuous place.

Lawrence had many subsequent chuckles over Brett's gift, for it provided a private joke that he played at least twice in public, and that he exchanged, in veiled fashion, in several letters to Brett after he had begun painting himself. But he did not start painting originally (as distinct from copying) until almost two years after leaving Oaxaca. His paintings later brought him trouble with the police largely because of the exposed genitalia of his male nudes.

Brett's gift delighted Lawrence for being a tangible embodiment of a metaphor he had already conceived. In his letter of 9 January 1924 that Johnson published as an article the following May in his magazine, *The Laughing Horse,* he states, ''But talking seriously, Spoodle, man must be a centaur. This two-legged forked radish is going flabby. . . . Let the forked radish do the lamenting. . . . I've got to ride on a laughing horse. The forked radish has ceased to perambulate.'' The Oaxaca radish became for Lawrence a symbol for male virility, one he used as a euphemism in ''The Novel,'' the essay in which he defended his ending of *The Boy in the Bush.* There it emerges in his denunciation of those who present man ''as if he were all books of geometry with axioms, postulates and definitions in front.'' ''Man,'' he exclaims scornfully, ''a geometric bifurcation, not even a radish.'' In ''Introduction to Pictures,'' which first appeared among his posthumously published papers in *Phoenix,* the first sentence says, "Man is anything from a forked radish to an immortal soul."

How the radish joke passed between Brett and Lawrence in correspondence requires awareness of "The Feast of the Radishes," a painting reproduced in color in Mervyn Levy's *Paintings of D. H. Lawrence.* The painting shows in the foreground a young girl and a youth interchanging a radish similar to the one Brett bought. In the background, hanging in booths vaguely festooned with electric light bulbs, are nine other similarly carved radishes. Between the booths and the couple are nine men in big blacks hats and brown and red *serapes,* two women in black *rebozos,* and two boys examining the exhibits. Most have their backs to the viewer, but among them, in profile, is a hatless portrait of Lawrence resembling other portraits of him painted by Brett. Thus he is presented in a scene that Brett saw but he didn't. The book ascribes the painting to Lawrence, but in his epilogue to the 1974 edition of *Lawrence and Brett,* John Manchester, Brett's art executor, neighbor, and biographer, claims it was done by Brett. Manchester said Brett could not remember painting it, but she had no recollection of Lawrence's painting it either. Lawrence did not do it in Oaxaca as he denied all original painting before 1926 in "Making Pictures," one of his *Assorted Articles.* And having come to shrink at the very mention of the city's name, he certainly did not paint it after leaving Oaxaca.

Lawrence's query to Brett in his 20 January 1927 letter indicates that in Taos she called on her memories of Oaxaca to paint this picture. His words further suggest she promised to send it to him as a gift. "My 'Men Bathing' and 'Red Willow Trees'," he wrote, "is nearly done—how are your radishes? I shall only be too glad to have my eyes popping." On March 8 he queried her about it again. "Even my pictures," he said, "which seem to me absolutely innocent, I feel people *can't even look* at them. They glance, and look quickly away. I wish I could paint a picture that would *kill* every cowardly and ill-minded person that looked at it. My word, what a slaughter! How are your radishes? Since my 'Eve Regaining Paradise,' I've not done anything." Lawrence had just finished the second version of *Lady Chatterley's Lover,* finally published forty-five years later as *John Thomas and Lady Jane.* In his letter of March 24 to Brett there is a veiled reference suggesting he had received her painting. Of *John Thomas* he wrote, "I daren't send you my novel to type, though I'd like to. But it's so improper, the American authorities would arrest you. Well, well, a man is a forked radish!" Knowing his continual need for copybooks, Brett had given him several. He added in this letter, "But my novel is done in the two best books you gave me, very neat and handsome." Because the University of Texas[6] has the manuscripts of all three versions of the novel, we know those books are the same size with leather spines and corners, but floral urns decorate the covers of the first, and the red boards of the second are dotted in white, with each dot encircling a star.

That Frieda had a strong feeling for Christmas has been shown in her parting with her cashmere shawl and evening bag to the hospitable Carola Kull. As Frieda shows in "Christmas at Home," the most charming chapter in her posthumous memoir, "And the Fullness Thereof . . . ," Christmas was always a particularly happy day for the Richthofens, one they prepared for long in advance. Besides all the special foods brought in, the wild boar and the partridges, the presents bought and wrapped for their parents, the making of the marzipan candy, etc., the three sisters saved their pocket money, repaired their old toys, and redressed their dolls so they could give the eight children of their washerwoman a happy Christmas as well. Accordingly, a Christmas tree was always set up in the kitchen and the girls gave the children their presents before they received their own. It was around the second tree in the brown-gold living room that the girls and their parents later opened their own presents. This tree was as high as the ceiling, "streaming its light from many candles shimmering over silver and gold." Then came friends bringing more presents, and a special feast: "the hares that came every Christmas," and, for dessert, coffee cream and fruit. The evening ended with saying goodbye to friends as they made their way home through the snow.

Christmas at the Lawrences' was entirely different. They lived in a coal-mining village and, Lawrence was among the miners' children invited to receive oranges and pennies at Lamb Close House, the residence of the mine-owning Barber family. At home the money for presents had to be divided among five children, the house was small, the father and mother had no love left for each other, and, as Ada stated in *Young Lorenzo,* they never had a Christmas tree. But they did gather holly to decorate the house and until 1900 Mrs. Lawrence contributed to the Christmas cheer. But in 1901 brother Ernest died and after that on Christmas Eve, Mrs. Lawrence would stay in the kitchen in her rocking chair. The Christmas of 1910 was especially miserable. Mrs. Lawrence died sixteen days before it, and in the last stages of her illness had been unable to appreciate what it meant when, a week before her death, Lawrence laid an advance copy of his first novel, *The White Peacock,* in her lap. Neither he nor Ada could bear to be at home in Eastwood that Christmas.

How differently Lawrence and Frieda felt about Christmas is reflected in the Lawrence letters. Frieda tried to make each Christmas seem a bit like the holiday she had known in her happy childhood home in Germany. "Drew an almost blank Christmas," Lawrence wrote Brett of the 1925 Christmas at Spotorno, the first after Oaxaca. "Just as well, for I hate these strained rejoicings." The next year at Villa Mirenda, seven miles from Florence, they set up a Christmas tree and had a party for the people on the estate. They were still at the villa in 1927; and as Christmas neared, Lawrence wrote Else Jaffe, Frieda's sister: "We are staying here for Christmas and making a tree for the peasants. This year there'll be at least thirty of them. Dreadful thought. But Frieda wants it." Eleven days later he reported to his friend Koteliansky, "As for Christmas, damn it. We're having in the peasants to the tree." Just prior to Christmas of 1929, which would be his last, he wrote Koteliansky, "There are various friends here at the hotel [at Bandol in the south of France], we shall have a certain amount of Christmas fuss. I hate it, but Frieda seems to think it essential."

Although Lawrence included events just before Christmas in his essay on Rosalino and revealed his pre-Christmas homesickness in the nostalgia for the buses and the gleaming wet pavements of Piccadilly that he worked into *The Plumed Serpent,* I have found nothing beyond the account of Rosalino's happy Christmas morning shopping—which included a "number of toys"—in the novelist's writings about the day itself. With Frieda I have drawn an equal blank, but thanks to Miss Hughes and Brett, I know enough to report that the holiday ran as expected. It was not a Christmas brimming over with happiness, but on the whole it was agreeable, cheered by the arrival of Rosalino's younger brother and the dispersal of the difficulties with the homesick *mozo.* For Lawrence certainly, and perhaps even a little bit for Frieda, Brett's high spirits and thoughtfulness were a help; and although the Lawrences were renters, the Padre's establishment was definitely a home.

"I am going to all the parties which you are not well enough to go to," wrote Brett of Christmas Eve. But Miss Hughes presented documentary evidence that here Brett's memory was at fault. In a letter she wrote a day or two later, Brett did not just flit off and leave a glum Frieda attending a husband too sick to stir from bed. "Christmas Eve, after a supper and Christmas tree for the small American colony—and the British—(D. H. Lawrence, the author, and his wife, and Eng. girl artist spending winter)," wrote Miss Hughes. Lawrence, who had had energy enough during his day in bed to dash off the preface for Mollie Skinner, was strong enough to get up in the evening to attend the chief party, which meant Frieda also went. Miss Hughes remembered that it was given by Emma Thompson, who with her husband, William, the hopeful miner, had loaned the Lawrences some of their furniture. A deciding factor in the Lawrences' attendance was that it did not entail a long walk, since the Thompsons lived only a block or two away. Besides recalling that Mrs. Thompson had a Christmas tree and a good meal for her guests, Miss

Hughes remembered that the lively Jean Akin was there with her husband, the Colonel. At midnight Oaxaca would stage one of its most beautiful and touching sights, the competition of the *calendas*.

Each church organizes a procession to carry its particular Christ Child to the awaiting manger on Christmas Eve. Each church tries to outdo the other in the beauty of its candlelit procession, vying for the approval of the citizens by converging on the *plaza* around eleven o'clock. There they circle the square with light, each group carefully timing its departure from the *zócalo* to arrive at its church just before midnight. Then on the stroke of twelve in each church the Christ Child is laid in the manger.

Emma Thompson's party broke up early, allowing the guests to get to the square to see the processions. The Lawrences, deciding not to make the effort, crossed the park to their home. Brett did not write about the *calendas,* and thirty-eight years later she had no memory of them; so perhaps she went home too. But it seems unlikely, considering how much she liked to see everything, and Miss Hughes recollects Brett being with the Thompsons, the Akins, and herself as they watched the different parishioners reenact the Nativity.

> When we left about ten P.M. [Miss Hughes wrote me in 1962]—we found the *calendas* in full swing. Parades of groups, different churches and organizations, from bootblacks and paper boys up. Men, women and children. Each with its own band or string orchestra. Each group carrying different colored paper torchlights—like heads of lettuce, bells, stars, crescents, globes, etc. Then representations of Mary (dressed in long blue robe and white veil) on a burro, and Josephs with children carrying a doll on a pillow, surrounded by flowers, to be given to the Marys at midnight. Children dressed as angels with white feather wings. The Three Wise Men in the offing in suitable Oriental robes, etc. All going later to midnight mass in different churches.

Miss Hughes had loved her two-month stay in Oaxaca, but she was leaving on the early morning train of December 26. For her, the tenderness and beauty of so many groups, each cherishing its own particular Child, was a culmination of all that was heart-warming, reverent, and good about Oaxaca.

One indication that Brett saw the same spectacle is her description of another Oaxacan Christmas Eve custom. "Every one is buying old bowls," she wrote, "and throwing them into the air. The air is full of the sharp splintering sound of breaking pottery. So I buy some and break them too." What is curiously incomplete about this recollection is that the bowls are not empty. They are the imperfect serving dishes of coarse ware handed to customers who buy *buñuelos,* the great wafers also sold at the fiesta of Soledad. After eating your *buñuelo,* the custom is to drop your bowl or toss it into the air. Some say the custom dates to the Aztec rite of breaking all old household dishes before kindling the New Fire, so they could start over entirely fresh when the rising of the sun had assured them of the world's continuance. But more people see it as a mere releasing of inhibitions. Next morning Brett found the streets "full of bits of bowls—the ground is littered with broken pottery."

> I play tennis in the morning [Brett opened her account of Christmas Day], and go up to your place at four. You are going to get up. I present the lovely knife with your name on it. You look at it and say:
> "I am not such a knify person as you, but I must give you a penny, so as not to cut our friendship." And you hand me a penny from among your things on a table near your bed. Then you get up to finish decorating the tree. Afterwards you paint a little, and then the Padre comes to a supper of cold ham and eggs.
> Then the Indians are called. They come shyly to the door, look at the Christmas Tree, then a broad smile spreads over all their faces. They murmur to each other, but you have caught what they are saying.
> "They have seen the radish," you say to me. Even the Padre is smiling broadly. The Indians come and give me some tiny pottery: little cups and saucers and bowls in a dark green color. [These would come from the pottery village of Azompa.] They give something to you, too, and then we hand out the presents from the tree. They are delighted with everything.
> Finally nothing hangs on the tree but the radish. Then you ask one of them about it and she tells you that it is the day when the young man can declare his love for his girl and his desire for her. The delicate way he does it, is by buying and giving her a radish.

By 1962 Brett wrote me that in the "Betrothal Fiesta" the girl gave the radish to the man. Thus she recalled her gift as a proposition to Lawrence. "Of course the servants knew the meaning, hence the giggles. So did Lawrence but he never turned a hair." But Brett did not want to be too bold, for she added, "The radish I bought for Lawrence was the most modest one of its kind I could find."

The radish joke probably did not amuse Frieda. In fact, many moments in her life with Lawrence were difficult, and in a letter to Bynner four months after Lawrence's death, she wrote, "My pride is that I saw him right through, and you know it was diabolically hard at times." Particularly hard for her to endure was his insistence, as she saw it, that she should submit to his domination. But she never did. She fought him "like blazes."

Lawrence was explicit about his concept of a wife's role in *Fantasia of the Unconscious,* which he wrote during the summer of 1921 at the age of thirty-six. He did not see a wife's role in isolation. He had an equally firm idea of the husband's role. Both men and women, he held, had to make a resolution that was basically the same: "to come to rest within themselves, to possess their own souls in quietness and fullness." But he was aware that for each sex such a resolution required a different kind of courage. On the woman's part it required the courage "to give up her hopeless insistence on love and her endless demand for love, demand for being loved." On the man's, the courage "to withdraw at last into his own soul's stillness and aloneness, and *then,* passionately and faithfully, to strive for the living future." Lawrence himself italicized *then* because he wanted to emphasize a step that came after love and sexual fulfillment. "When a man approaches the beginning of maturity and the fulfillment of his individual self, about the age of thirty-five, then is not his time to come to rest. On the contrary. Deeply fulfilled through marriage, and at one with his own soul, he must now undertake the responsibility for the next step into the future. He must now give himself perfectly to some future purpose, some passionate purposive activity."

That he was speaking for himself—and that he had acted on his own beliefs—are both shown by his visit to the monks of Montecassino when, at the age of thirty-four, he resolved to push forward actively into the life of his time. *Aaron's Rod* and *Kangaroo* reflect his indecisions, but *Fantasia* shows that he had found his own great "purposive activity." "We have got to get back to the great purpose of manhood, a passionate union in actively making a world," revives the colony idea. "The accomplishment of religious purpose, the soul's earnest purpose," is another clue in defining the second and "greater" way of fulfillment. First, he felt he had to join with others—and, if they failed him, alone—to show what men needed to create a life more worth living than the diminishing, destructive life he saw on every hand. As more associates seemed to fail him, he realized that his gifts as a writer had to be his great means of demonstration.

A man, he said, must have "the courage to withdraw into his own stillness and singleness, and put the wife under the spell of his fulfilled decision." The woman, however, must have "the greatness of soul to relinquish her own self-assertion, and believe in the man who believes in himself and in his own soul's effort."

Thus he did not want to dominate Frieda just for the sake of dominance, but wanted her to give up insistence on being "queen, goddess, mistress, the positive, the adored, the first and foremost and the one and only." He wanted her to give him "wife-submission" of her own free will and because of her belief in his talents and the worth of his mission. Even more than when he wrote the poem, "Lady Wife," he wanted her to "serve, as a woman should," which meant, to "add your strength to mine." Because his task was a large one, he felt deeply the need for strength and support.

During his second visit to Mexico, when Frieda was back in Europe, Lawrence's resolve to persist in his purpose grew stronger. On that trip he confided to Frieda's mother that he was tired of his wife's talking so much about love. "Frieda must always think and write and say and ponder how much she loves me." What he wanted more, he said, was supportive strength. He spelled out clearly what he felt was Frieda's blind spot. "Frieda doesn't understand that a man must be a hero these days and not only a husband: a husband also but more." Because of Lawrence's many weaknesses, it was perhaps hard for the practical Frieda to see him as a hero (as it was for many of his contemporaries). Yet we now know that in his fight to extend human awareness and to make men and women live more nobly, especially when we consider the handicap of his poor health, he was behaving heroically. It is little wonder that Frieda found him different when he finally succumbed to her wishes and joined her in Europe. Thirty years later she recalled the difference in a letter to Murry: "I think L. had become strange to me, when he came back and I was scared and your warmth was good to me and I was happy about it and deeply grateful."

Another year had passed and Brett's constant presence with the Lawrences, at the ranch and then in Oaxaca, had certainly not increased Frieda's desire to be "wife-submissive." Because she had been resentful of a hero-recognizing woman who was happy to be "wife-submissive," we can assume that Frieda had not been very supportive during that year. Lawrence, on the other hand, needing more support elsewhere as his wife withheld it, must have found Brett's attentiveness welcome in the same way Frieda found Murry's warmth. Feeling sympathy for Brett and knowing that his intentions toward her were innocent, Lawrence must have considered Frieda hard and lacking in understanding to resent the relationship. Yet he would have understood her, and I am sure part of his suffering of the period was due to his sympathy for all three of them, Frieda, Brett, and himself. One can judge the extent of his awareness of the cross-currents through passages such as one he wrote in *Psychoanalysis and the Unconscious:* "The amazingly difficult and vital business of human relationship has been almost laughably underestimated in our epoch. All this nonsense about love and unselfishness, more crude and repugnant than savage fetish-worship. Love is a thing to be *learned,* through centuries of patient effort. It is a difficult, complex maintenance of individual integrity throughout the incalculable processes of interhuman-polarity."

In his fiction there are extraordinary demonstrations of Lawrence's awareness of all three people in triangular relationships. An example is the scene in the military hospital in "The Ladybird" where the wife listens as her husband and the Bohemian count are "locked in the combustion of words." Every moment the novelist is alive to the inner feelings of each member of the trio and of how their respective presences are determining the responses of one to the other. One sees the same uncanny three-way awareness between two women and a man in *The Fox*. The novella was written three years earlier; thus, Lawrence had already imagined how women, basically friendly, can feel when a man precipitates a struggle between them and how a man reacts to the tensions when he wants to pursue his own aims.

A touching passage in Lawrence's early letters was one written on 17 January 1913 to A. W. McLeod, his best friend among the teachers at the school in Croydon. He was living with Frieda at a beautiful spot on Lake Garda. *The White Peacock* and *The Trespasser* had been published, but writing seemed to hold little prospect of providing enough money to live on, and there were almost insurmountable difficulties in the way of Frieda's divorce. "I got the blues thinking of the future," he wrote McLeod, "so I left off and made some marmalade. It's amazing how it cheers one up to shred oranges or scrub the floors."

The remembered passage gave new poignance to Brett's first post-Christmas scene:

> Frieda is now sick in bed, so you and I cut up the oranges for the marmalade. And while we cut them, we talk of England. You are thinking of England again, of an English spring, that you have not seen for five years. A note of homesickness is in your voice, and a great longing. You feel the need of supporters; you think you might find them in England, maybe; but disappointment seems to dog your footsteps, and your questing generally ends in your getting deeply hurt. You seem to have a sort of fear of the ranch, the fear that being ill in a place always gives you; and the ill ease of Old Mexico hurts you. One more summer at the ranch would surely be healthier for you, but I say nothing. It is better not to say anything, when the restless fit seizes you.

Brett understood Lawrence's fear for his health at the ranch, for she had been there the summer before when he spat blood. It is through her vivid description that we know of the frightening experience. Because his chest got so "raw" they had left the ranch earlier than planned. Her silence on these things and on her medical views indicates how much she understood him at that moment, but she had no inkling that she herself might be a factor in Lawrence's distress. Up to this point Lawrence had been too kind to tell her that he sometimes felt she was a responsibility he did not totally welcome, especially in view of what her presence was doing to Frieda and their relationship. Meanwhile, despite the interruptions of Christmas and the extra work of writing Mollie's preface and the four "Mornings in Mexico," Lawrence pressed on with *The Plumed Serpent*. On 31 December 1924 having filled all 381 pages of the purple scribbler, he turned to the matching yellow-brown one, numbering its first page 382 and dating it. He had written almost 400 pages in six weeks. And he would sustain the pace. In the next six he was to write even more, as well as additional side pieces. A good deal of the rewriting of *The Plumed Serpent* involved writing poetry, which would have been a remarkable achievement for a man in the best of health, completely free of all emotional harassment. Yet Lawrence was neither. His creative flame was burning with an intensity hard to imagine.

His physical appearance at this time is conveyed in one of Brett's finest passages:

> I have been waiting for you in the hotel for so long that I begin to wonder if you are coming after all. I stroll slowly to a corner of the *Zócola* and stand for a few minutes watching the people. Suddenly I see you, walking along the street. Your head is up, your feet move over the ground lightly, so lightly that you might be floating. You drift along dreamily, looking as if you were seeing nothing, hearing nothing; your head is slightly tilted back, your pointed beard sticking out. Slight, narrow-shouldered,[7] in pale grey, your big Stetson shadowing your face, your face pale, luminous in the shadow of the hat—you are almost a dream figure. I watch wonderingly, so little do you seem to belong to this earth.
>
> What is it that flows from you? It is hard to describe. It is that something from the heart, that has nothing to do with upbringing or training. Compassion . . . can it be that? I wonder, watching you. Compassion . . . understanding . . . or both . . . or what? I can find no word. How describe the real aristocracy of the heart and mind? I have tried so often, from the first days I knew you, but I have never been able to find the words. I watch you now and know that it surrounds you, gives you that strange "quality" that others see and feel as well as I, and which clothes you even from that distance as I watch you drifting lightly across the street and around the corner. I know the way you must come, so I hurry to meet you.

Brett's "the first days I knew you," were in the autumn of 1915 when Lawrence was planning to leave England to found a colony in Florida. Brett first met him at tea in his "tiny box of a house" on the Vale of Heath, escorted by fellow-artist Mark Gertler, who felt she and Lawrence should know each other. After that she gave the Lawrences two "farewell" parties for the sailing that never took place. She made an extremely favorable impression on Lawrence, and they talked intimately even then, as shown by his portrait of her in his ending for *The Boy in the Bush:* "There was a frail beauty about that odd young woman: frail, highly-bred, sensitive, with an uncanny intelligence." He describes her "wide, quick, round" eyes, and her "fleecy brown hair." Her brothers jeer at her "slight deafness" but "she kept an odd, bright, amusing spark of revenge twinkling in her all the time." Jack thinks of Hilda what Lawrence must have thought of Brett: "She was a new thing to him. She was one who knew the world, and society, better than he did, and her hatred of it was purer, more twinkling, more relentless in a quiet way. She had gone further along that line than himself." And she said she didn't care for men at all. "All that sort of thing is impossible to me."

> She had such an odd, definite decisiveness and self-confidence. . . . She seemed the queerest, oddest, most isolated bird. . . . Exceedingly well-bred, with all the charm of pure breeding. By nature, timorous like a hare. But now in her queer state of rebellion, like a hare that is perfectly fearless, and will go its own way in determined singleness. . . . And she had a great capacity for remaining silent and remote, like a quaint rabbit unmoving in a corner.

In *"Not I, But the Wind . . ."* Frieda relates how her exasperation with Brett had built up before they left for Oaxaca:

> When the Brett came with us, Lawrence said to me: "You know, it will be good for us to have the Brett with us, she will stand between us and people and the world." I did not really want her with us, and had a suspicion that she might not want to stand between us and the world, but between him and me. But no, I thought, I won't be so narrow-gutted, one of Lawrence's words, I will try.
>   So I looked after Brett and was grateful for her actual help. She did her share of the work. I yelled down her ear-trumpet, her Toby, when people were there, that she should not feel out of it. But as time went on she seemed always to be there, my privacy that I cherished so much was gone. Like the eye of the Lord, she was; when I washed, when I lay under a bush with a book, her eyes seemed to be there, only I hope the eye of the Lord looks on me more kindly. Then I detested her, poor Brett, when she seemed deaf and dumb and blind to everything quick and alive. Her adoration for Lawrence seemed a silly old habit. "Brett," I said, "I detest your adoration for Lawrence, only one thing I would detest more, and that is if you adored me."

Frieda condensed her experience in Oaxaca into the following sentences: "The Brett came every day and I thought she was becoming too much part of our lives and I resented it. So I told Lawrence: 'I want the Brett to go away,' and he raved at me, said I was a jealous fool. But I insisted and so Brett went up to Mexico City."

Her later version in the posthumously published "*And the Fullness Thereof . . .*" was longer, but hardly kinder. The memoir's categorization of Brett (called S—) as the "serving self-effacing" type has already been quoted. After that Paula (as Frieda called herself) characterized S—'s feeling for Andrew (Lawrence) as "her lollipop of imagined spiritual communion"; going on to say that S—wanted to dominate Andrew. S—, the memoir continues, "hated Paula's aggressive nature particularly." But "her negative being roused the aggression." The stage set, Frieda tells her side of the story, starting from pre-Oaxaca days.

S— had got away from her conventional surroundings and had come to stay with Andrew and Paula at the ranch. Paula was impressed with the way S— had thrown over her past, so comfortable and even luxurious, for this simple life. She lived in a tiny cabin with only the absolute necessities, she saddled the horses and helped to build sheds and carry stones, exerting herself like a man. It was admirable and S— was happy. Paula did all she could to make S— happy. Though she knew quite well that S— was not in the least grateful for Paula's efforts. S—'s one-track adolescent mind, that had always, since she was sixteen years old, existed in the adoration, the *Schwarm,* for somebody or other exclusively. . . .

It exasperated Paula, chiefly that her own good will towards this incomplete being was so ignored. She put up with her because she helped Andrew in many things, she was a faithful servant but the kind of servant that bosses you in the end with her service. S— did not hear very well, so whatever Paula said was one thing and what S—'s ears heard was another. Every teasing remark of Andrew's turned into criticism, every argument turned into tragedy. She encroached more and more on the privacy of Andrew and Paula's daily life, till Paula would stand it no more.

"She goes or I," she had declared one morning. The eternal critical hostile eye on herself had got on Paula's nerves, the hostility took her freedom away. S—'s hatred of her was all the stronger because unconscious. So S— went.

The only concern for Lawrence shown in the account is that he should have a faithful servant. And in its self-centeredness there is no recognition that, once he got to Oaxaca, the ailing Lawrence was struggling with what seemed to him the greatest book he had ever written. Neither of Frieda's accounts indicates how many acts there were in the drama. It was not as quick and simple as "I insisted and so Brett went up to Mexico City" suggests. If the acts might be named, they were "The Gathering Storm" in which all three appeared; "The Ultimatum," which was between Frieda and Lawrence; "The Breaking of the News," between Lawrence and Brett; and "The Final Week," in which they all tried to be considerate of each other.

A number of the "Gathering Storm" scenes have been given. In Oaxaca, no magazines seem to have been thrown, but Frieda did look "sharply" at her husband and Brett when they ended their misunderstanding over the unreturned book so affectionately. She refused to join them on the Mitla Road with a picnic lunch. Lawrence, in turn, reproved Frieda for taking an impersonal argument personally as a *calenda* passed almost unnoticed. A further scene occurred after Lawrence and Brett returned, "excited, happy, exhilarated" by a long walk.

> We came into the shady patio. Frieda is sitting smoking in a rocking chair—she looks up at us. Our joyousness radiates out of us, permeates the air of the patio. Frieda's eyes begin to dart about, her mouth tightens, but she says nothing to me. I am still immersed in the talk I have had and I notice nothing: for the moment I am obtuse.
>
> Tea is a silent meal and it is then that I begin to feel the change in the atmosphere. I say something to Frieda, she gets up and goes into the bedroom. At last it dawns on me. I rise and say I think it is time for me to go home. You come and open the great doors for me, saying nothing.

Then there was the scene when Brett arrived in the afternoon, and, Lawrence being absent, the long-silent Frieda attacked her openly, with the arrival of the unsuspecting Kulls averting the explosion that might have ensued when Brett laughed at the onslaught.

There were also build-up scenes in the "Ultimatum" act. When Lawrence discouraged Brett from a third morning working under their respective bushes, he told her that Frieda did not like such excursions. Clearly, Frieda opened up to him before she did to Brett. Because he hated the position he was in, Brett felt his "strong resistance" when she and the Kulls found him sitting on a bench in the *zócalo*.

Since Brett knew nothing of it and Lawrence does not mention it, we will probably never know just when the "she goes or I" ultimatum was delivered. It may have been what drove Lawrence out of the house before the Kulls' visit, or he may have left because of a preliminary round, with the actual showdown coming later. All we know for sure is that in one of the skirmishes, when Frieda either took her stand or threatened to take it, Lawrence "raved" and called her " a jealous fool."

There is considerable evidence of Lawrence's dependence on Frieda. One finds it most movingly expressed in the poems in *Look! We Have Come Through!*:

> How quaveringly I depend on you, to keep me alive,
> Like a flame on a wick! . . .

> Suppose you didn't want me! I should sink down
> Like a light that has no sustenance. . . .

In the same collection he expressed the element of painfulness in the dependence by titling a poem about it "Humiliation." Among its lines are:

> I have been so innerly proud, and so long alone,
> Do not leave me, or I shall break,
> Do not leave me. . . .

> And God, that she is necessary!
> Necessary, and I have no choice!

This dependence still existed at the time of their Mexican travels for in *A Poet and Two Painters,* Gótzsche reveals how Lawrence longed for Frieda after she had insisted on going to Europe. As the two men neared the end of their Mexican trip, Gótzsche wrote Merrild: "It would be too difficult to live with a man like Lawrence in the long run. Frieda is at least an absolute necessity as a quencher. I have sometimes the feeling that he is afraid she will run away from him now, and he cannot bear to be alone."

Aldous Huxley, too, gives evidence of the continuing dependence, and he wrote about it two years after Lawrence's death in a letter to Flora Strousse. Of Frieda he said, "I like her very much; but she's in many ways quite impossible. She was only possible for someone who happened to be in love with her and married to her—and not only in love and married but, as Lawrence was, in some strange way dependent on her presence, physically dependent, as one is dependent on the liver in one's belly, or one's spinal marrow."

Lawrence was not going to sacrifice Frieda for Brett. Frieda would win. She had won when he gave in by returning to England, although it had been a fiasco. He must have bitterly resented the thought of giving in to her again on this new issue, especially when he wanted her "to relinquish her own self-assertion" and believe in his "soul's effort." What right had Frieda to be angry at a relationship that was innocent and justifiable? How could he think of himself as heroic in any way if he bowed to her ultimatum, particularly when he had invited Brett to come with them? Then, if he did give in, how was Brett to be told? He had to be manly enough to break the bad news himself, for he could not just let Frieda order her out while he sat by in mute discomfort. Yet knowing how happy Brett was and how sensitive, he must have shrunk from administering the blow, even if he was also exasperated with her for precipitating the crisis by not being more independent.

Once he decided to ask Brett to leave, Lawrence could not bring himself to make the request face to face. The prospect of having to raise his voice to an ear trumpet made him resort to a letter. Instead of delivering it personally, he sent it via Rosalino, and Brett reported its arrival as follows: "This morning I wake up with a sort of apprehension hanging over me. There is a loud knock on the door: it is Rosalino with a letter from you. I tear it open. It is fierce, cruel, telling me that the three of us are no longer a happy combination and that we must stand apart."

This letter has been published, with few recognizing it as belonging to Oaxaca because it is marked only "Friday evening." Harry T. Moore mistakenly placed it among the letters written at Kiowa Ranch three months later. Peter L. Irvine of the English Department of the University of Cincinnati, which owns the letter, first called it to my attention by showing how its text squared with Brett's description, adding that the original was not headed "Kiowa Ranch."

> Dear Brett, The simplest thing is to write, as one can't shout everything.
>   You, Frieda and I don't make a happy combination now. The best is that we should prepare to separate: that you should go your own way. I am not angry: except that I hate "situations" and feel humiliated by them. We can all remain decent and friendly, and go the simplest, quietest way about the parting, without stirring up a lot of emotions that only do harm. Stirred-up emotions only lead to hate.
>   The thing to do is to think out, quickly and simply, the best steps. But believe me, there will be no more ease between the three of us. Better to take your own way in life, not this closeness, which causes strain.
>   I am grateful for the things you have done for me. But we must stand apart.

Far from being "fierce," the letter tries to soften the blow; and to avoid being "cruel," Lawrence wrote in a way that seemed ambiguous to Brett, for this was her response.

> I am upset and puzzled. I do nothing. Rosalino returns with the word that there is no answer. I have no answer, I want to think. I sense behind it

all, something that has no bearing on me and my doings.

At four, I go up to your house as usual. You give me a quick glance. I am so quiet, so noncombatant, that you become gentle—gentle and considerate in feeling—for, as usual, we say nothing. Frieda is hintingly hostile; her eyes are hard, her mouth a line. The tea-table is balanced on a volcano. You are looking seedy. I think it wise not to stay too long. I begin to recover my equipoise and I return to the hotel in a clearer and more peaceful frame of mind. Suddenly, as I am sitting typing in my window, you appear: excited, stormy, despairing.

"Frieda broke out again the minute you left," you say. "She made such a scene that I can no longer stand it. I am at the end of my tether—in despair. The only thing I could think of was to come down and ask you not to come up again to the house."

Again he held back from directly asking her to leave Oaxaca. But this time Brett was not obtuse.

I tell you to sit down, and down you sit. You rumple your hair, despairingly. "Look here, Lawrence," I say, "Let us be calm and sensible. This is too much of a strain for you; it makes you ill, doesn't it?"

"Yes," you reply, wearily, "It is unbearable. I shall be ill if it goes on."

"Well," I say. "The simple, easy way out is for me to go. I will go back to Del Monte [the Hawks' ranch in New Mexico] for a while. This will relieve you of the strain."

"That will be best," you reply, more hopefully. "If you think you can manage the journey alone. I don't altogether like your taking that long journey by yourself, but I don't see what else can be done."

This scene was in the late afternoon of Saturday, January 13;[8] and when Brett settled her date for leaving she did not mean the coming Monday but the Monday of the week after, or nine days later.

Thus we arrange it. I decide to go the following Monday. I know it is the only thing to do. You sit for awhile and we talk of the ways and means of the journey. You don't like the idea—the danger, the difficulties for me—but gradually you calm down, the tension loosens. Something intolerable has ceased to exist and you become alert, but you give me a long, strange look as you sit there, leaning slightly forward. That side of me that keeps an impersonal hold on my emotions, that at times puzzles and vexes you, and yet is so invaluable to you, is puzzling you now. I see the desire to say something flit across your face; the fleeting, momentary wonder at my attitude; a queer annoyance, too: all pass through the intense deep gaze of your eyes as you sit and look at me. They are dark and big and shine brilliantly. You leap up so suddenly that I jump out of my skin.

"I will go and tell Frieda, and maybe things will be better," you say. And your step is more springy as you go out of the room.

Lawrence's quailing at having to shout was due to Brett's Marconi ear machine being in Veracruz for repairs. One of her anxieties, when she was suddenly faced with leaving, was about the machine, which had not been sent to her in Oaxaca. Fortunately, she had met Constantine Rickards in Mexico City, so she wrote the British vice-consul as follows: "Dear Mr. Rickards: I am in difficulty again. The Vera Cruz people sent me some papers, asking if I would pay the bill. I wrote to them asking them to send me the bill and I would pay it. Since then I have heard nothing. Would you kindly write to them as I haven't their address. If you ask them for the account and to send the machine to you, then, when I arrive in Mexico on Tuesday 20th it may come in time for me to take it with me from Mexico to Santa Fe. . . ."

On January 16, not knowing Brett had already written Rickards, Lawrence showed his concern for her and her hearing aid by writing the vice-consul himself. His letter, now owned by William Forster of London and not yet published, gives insight into Lawrence's relations with the consul and demonstrates how the novelist wrote personally even in business letters. After enclosing a check for stamps and thanking Rickards for sending mail, he told him how Miss Brett would be arriving in Mexico City on Tuesday, January 20, on her way to New Mexico. He and Frieda, he said, expected to arrive the first week in February. Meanwhile, showing his own exasperation at the trouble caused by Brett's listening machine, he asked if Rickards could get it sent from Veracruz so Brett could pick it up in Mexico City. All was quiet in Oaxaca, he reported, except that Padre Rickards, the consul's brother, had not recovered from his cough.

Finishing her typing for Lawrence was the only business Brett had to attend to in the remaining days of her stay; and now there was less to do. She had completed the four "Mornings in Mexico" essays and Lawrence had sent them to Barmby in New York the very day of his we-must-stand-apart letter. By this time, having met no harm on previous walks beyond the town, Lawrence was less credulous about the dangers involved, as was Brett. He and Brett took a number of afternoon walks. Because Brett was leaving soon, Frieda apparently tolerated the walks, but on the two described she did not unbend enough to go along. The first walk was to Santa Lucia del Camino, the first village beyond the railroad bridge crossing the Jalatlaco River on the train route to Tlacolula. Its position about two miles east of the center of the city can be seen on the map, page 109. Brett begins the story with Lawrence's calling for her at the hotel:

"Let us get out into the country, over the railway bridge and out into the open," you say; and I agree. We walk a long way and talk of many things, mostly of friendship. But a weariness has fallen on you again. I ask no questions.

We pass through a lovely little leaf village, with cows and chickens but no Indians: they are hiding to watch us. We find a church and sit on the steps, tired and hot. Your book is tiring you, as well as all the friction. We talk of friction, of how mutual friends of ours had spoiled their life together with too much of it; and we are both agreed that friction is wearing beyond endurance. I tell you what I think about friendship, what it means to me. You shake your head, wearily, and sadly, and say:

"It is easier said than done," with a sardonic smile. I try to urge you to start a little group, however small, to put your authority over it and build some new way of living among a few of us. "I wish I could," you say, sadly. "But what is the use—it's no good."

Suddenly, out of your heavy, gloomy silence, you say: "You know Frieda hates you. Why, knowing that, cannot you understand how hard it is for me?" I stare at you in astonishment.

"Frieda likes me," I reply. "I think she feels I am one of the few friends she has."

"Really, Brett," you say. "Are you so stupid? Can you really be so dense as not to know that Frieda hates you? Or—"

"But," I say, astonished. "Do you mean to say that all this time while I have been thinking Frieda likes me, that she has been hating me?"

"Of course," you reply, impatiently. "Of course she hates you. What do you suppose all our quarrels are about?" At this I turn and stare at you incredulously.

"But," I say, astounded. "But you are famous all over the world for your quarrels! How could I know it was me?" For a moment you are nonplussed. You look at me intently, silently. Then, very quietly, with conviction, you say:

"I believe you. I do believe you do not know. I thought you were doing it on purpose."

So Lawrence had harbored a further exasperation with Brett. Underestimating the innocence of her friendliness, he had thought she was deliberately baiting Frieda. After he realized he had misjudged her, they rose from the church steps.

We walk along in silence, my mind in a turmoil. "I must be an idiot,"
I think to myself. You are sunk once more in silence, but not so heavy,
not anything like so gloomy a silence. Something seems to have lifted off
you. The Greek House looks wretchedly deserted. The far away mountain with its little trails lures me.

"You wouldn't like it, Brett," you say. "They look lovely, but they
are poisonous and dangerous; bitterly cold, too; ice on the trails at the top."

This conversation indicates that they did not resume talking until
they were nearly back in the city, for the "Greek House" was undoubtedly the unfinished agricultural school with the classic portico that Governor Bolaños Cacho began shortly before he was driven from office. The
abandoned school would become visible only when they were nearing
the northern outskirts of Oaxaca. The "far away mountain" yearned for
by Brett must have been San Felipe, which at a certain point does seem
to rise directly above the Greek portico.

Lawrence's memories of European passes had shaped his vision of
hills into which he had never ridden. Mexico has mountains that reach
into the snows, but none around Oaxaca. Even in January, it is like summer on the top of San Felipe. "We turn back along the avenue," wrote
Brett, showing they were approaching the park. The church that caught
their attention might have been the Santuario of Guadalupe at the head
of the park, but probably it was El Patrocinio at the corner of the
Lawrences' block.

At the church, groups of Indian women with candles are going through
the big doors standing black against the white walls.

"That's the kind of picture I wonder you don't paint," you say,
as we stroll past on towards your house. I leave you at your door and
go home to the hotel.

The new version of Luis Quintanilla's article was mailed on January
12, but Brett had committed herself to further projects. "I am still typing. I want to do as much as I can before I go," is the way she introduced
the other walk described, which must have been northward towards San
Felipe. Again the meeting spares Frieda having Brett in the house. "You
come down in the afternoon, looking tired and exhausted. You want to
go to the bank. It is shut. We stroll along as far as the old Greek House
of the President. It looks more of a ruin than ever—I suppose because
we are both tired and spiritless. Your spirits are so low that you can hardly
talk at all; and I feel compunction at even trying to break through your
weary silence."

Among the Brett negatives at the University of Texas were three related to Oaxaca that I could not place. At first I thought they were taken on the visit to Mitla, for they have a background of *organos* planted to form a fence like those characteristic of Mitla. In one of Brett alone she was wearing the round-domed hat, the striped cardigan, and the pleated dress she wore to Mitla. Lawrence, too, was dressed similarly with a tie and a waistcoat under his single-breasted suit. But his hat was not the white Panama with the narrow black ribbon, but a new-looking felt hat, with a wide pale ribbon, which must have been the one Brett called his "big Stetson" when she saw it shadowing his face as he approached the *zócalo.* The fact that he consented to stand still and pose for two pictures, one with his hat on and one with it in his right hand, leads me to guess that he made this special concession to Brett on one of their last walks. (Plate 45.) The absence of Frieda and the late afternoon shadows help support this, as does the fact that the one of Brett is taken from exactly the same location as the two of Lawrence. If this supposition is correct, Lawrence's was the hand that shook too much to produce a clearly focused picture.

When John Manchester relayed my question to Brett shortly after her eighty-seventh birthday, she could not recall the circumstances under which she took the pictures of Lawrence with his felt hat. But she remembered his two hats and replied that "the straw hat was for general everyday wear and the felt one was reserved for more special occasions." She added "Lawrence hated to wear any kind of a hat and he had difficulty buying what he did wear because his head was so large.[9]

By capitulating at the hotel without a scene and by keeping out of Frieda's way, Brett had robbed Frieda of something important to any woman caught in a triangle: the chance to state her side of the case to the rival. Perhaps Brett's generosity in retiring graciously was also making Frieda feel a little mean. Whatever the motivation, Frieda came to feel she must confront Brett. Because she also blanched at the ear-trumpet, she, too, resorted to a letter. In her case, however, as revealed by Brett, she delivered it personally.

> Frieda has come rushing in this morning. She says she cannot bear that I should think it is her fault any longer. She has with her a letter which she had written me, explaining it all. I take it and read it in amazement. In it she accuses us, Lawrence and myself, of being like a curate and a spinster; she resents that fact that we do not make love to each other. She says that friendship between man and woman makes only half the curve. Well, maybe.
>
> "But Frieda," I say, "How can I make love to Lawrence when I am your guest; would that not be rather indecent?" She stares at me suspiciously.

"Lawrence says he could not possibly be in love with a woman like you—an asparagus stick!" she answers. I laugh.

"He is none too fat himself," I reply. "If you goad a man long enough he will say anything." Her eyes are hard like blue ice, she is so unbalanced, so extreme, at this moment: an emotional, unguided vessel. I listen quietly; friendliness seems to ooze out of me and begins suddenly to ooze out of her. In some mysterious fashion, we end amicably; mutual friendliness is restored and we both end in shouts of laughter over some trivial joke. Frieda leaves me in a state of complete bewilderment. Are we friends or are we not? And what is the correct behaviour in a triangle?

Frieda's visit to the hotel with her letter was on Sunday morning, January 18. Later in the day Lawrence also came to the hotel.

In the afternoon you came down and we settle the money question: I borrow some from you. I tell you of Frieda's visit, but I do not tell what she said. I feel we have all had enough for the moment.

I finish packing; then I go up to you for supper. You are tired—a headache all day. You are lying on the sofa. Frieda and I pull the supper table up near you. We try to be a bit gay, but none of us are feeling at all gay.

After supper I sit near you and I try, shyly, to thank you for all you have done, for bringing me to Old Mexico. I fumble along. Your mouth pulls down at the corner, a sardonic smile comes over your face, and you give me an angry glance. I know, you are annoyed at my shy blundering. Why am I shy again all of a sudden? I don't know. I stop, and turn the subject to Del Monte. You are relieved and we talk of the horses, of the ranch, of all I am going back to.

"I wish I were coming, too," you say. "But I must finish my book. Then we'll see."

On that slim hope, I get up and go. A warm handclasp, and a promise to come and see me off at the station. I leave you lying on that sofa. You idly pick up your book, wave your hand, and that is the last time I ever see those great bare rooms and that sunny patio.

Brett did not tell how she got to the station the next morning, but Doña María, the Catalan widow who ran the hotel, who had located a tinsmith to make a new ear-trumpet, who had taken Brett to market, and who had gone with the Lawrences to the fiesta of Soledad, was thoughtful to the end. She accompanied Brett to the station.

I am at the station. Doña María Monros is with me. The train is in; I have my seat. At last, you and Frieda come hurrying along. You are just in time.

"I hope you will be all right," you say, still anxious, still worried over my long journey alone. I have the address book you have written out for me: I am all right.

You shake my hand, warmly. I kiss Frieda. She is astonished; so am I. I get into the train and we wave and wave until the train turns a corner and I am alone.

CHAPTER 9

CORRESPONDENCE AND OTHER WRITINGS

For a long time I did not know how many letters Lawrence wrote in Oaxaca. Huxley published nine in his 1932 edition. Harry T. Moore revealed three more in *The Intelligent Heart* in 1954. Edward Nehls uncovered seven new ones for the second volume of his *Composite Biography* (1958). Four years later Moore, in his two-volume *Collected Letters of D. H. Lawrence,* published sixteen Oaxaca letters, including five not previously published by Huxley, Nehls, or himself. And Secker's edition of his letters from Lawrence in 1970 brought two more not in the earlier collections. That brought the published total to twenty-six.

But there must be more. Through *Lawrence and Brett* I knew of two Rosalino brought to Brett at the Hotel Francia. Miss Hughes told me Lawrence wrote her twice about looking after Brett in Mexico City. I calculated on another to Mollie Skinner, for there must have been at least a note about his preface for her *Black Swans.* Since it was while he was in Oaxaca that Lawrence broke with Seltzer, his American publisher, I counted on at least one letter to Seltzer. And what about letters to his sisters and such faithful correspondents as the Brewsters?

My conjecture was accurate. Lawrence was even more energetic as a letter-writer in Oaxaca than I had thought. On my second visit to the University of Texas in July 1971, I encountered the two-month-old two-volume dissertation of Gerald Morris Lacy, "An Analytical Calendar of the Letters of D. H. Lawrence." This unassuming title described a chronologically ordered list of more than 4,300 letters, a summary of each, whether published or unpublished, if published where, and, where possible, pinpointing the letter's present location. The Oaxaca letters were in the second volume—numbers 2636 to 2691, fifty-six in all! Sure enough, there were four communications to sister Ada, and Lacy gave their page numbers in *Young Lorenzo.* There were four to sister Emily, and a postcard apiece to her daughters, Joan and Margaret. A letter to Miss Skinner and one to Seltzer verified other conjectures; and Lacy pointed to where I would find two communications to the Brewsters in their

D. H. Lawrence: Reminiscences and Correspondence. Of the twenty-five unpublished Oaxaca communications listed in the "Calendar," seven were available right there in the University of Texas Academic Center Library.[1] And Lacy's "Calendar" pinned down the elusive date when Lawrence left Oaxaca.

Because Lawrence's Oaxaca letters illuminate his other writings, emphasis in this chapter and the next will shift between letters, essays, and fiction. After Christmas, substories continued to crystallize but they are shorter and more numerous because the pace of his life stepped up. When all the works he wrote in Oaxaca are revealed, it will be seen that his months there may well rank as the most productive period of comparable length in his creative life.

THE   BREAK   WITH   SELTZER

Lawrence's letter to Curtis Brown of 10 January 1925 summarizes where Lawrence stood with his work at the time of the showdown with Brett and discusses his plans after he finished "Quetzalcoatl." It also has family information which becomes clear when one remembers that Lawrence's father, Arthur John Lawrence, died on 10 September 1924, the day before the novelist's thirty-ninth birthday. Lawrence was at the ranch, far from the bedside of the seventy-eight-year-old coal miner who had caused him so much emotional turmoil. His absence, too, meant that he had not seen his younger sister, Ada, the member of the family to whom he was closest, since their father's death.

> I am getting ahead with the Mexican novel [Lawrence wrote his agent]. If heaven is with me, I should finish it this month. I had a good deal done from last year.—It will probably make you open your eyes—or close them: but I like it very much indeed. If I finish by the end of this month, then about 2nd February we shall go to Mexico City, to see about a ship. My wife feels she must see her mother, and my father died, and my sister keeps worrying to see me. So perhaps we'll be in England by March.

The Curtis Brown letter also reveals that while Lawrence was being torn apart over Brett, he had simultaneously been obliged to make a painful decision involving another important figure in his life: Thomas Seltzer, the New York publisher to whom he had turned after unfortunate experiences with Mitchell Kennerley, his first American publisher, and what he considered "such vagueness and evasiveness" on the part of B. W. Huebsch. Lawrence's association with the new publisher had begun in 1920, the year after the Russian-born Seltzer had started his own firm.

The play *Touch and Go* and the novel *Women in Love* were Seltzer's first Lawrence publications. Seltzer's willingness to take a chance on the novel was particularly important to Lawrence. After four years, no English publisher had been willing to touch it because the police had suppressed its predecessor, *The Rainbow*. But Seltzer agreed to a United States edition of 1,250 numbered copies, distributed only to subscribers. Following this breakthrough, in 1921, Secker brought out a public edition in England and Seltzer brought out the first American trade edition the following year. When John S. Sumner's Society for the Suppression of Vice tried to prosecute Seltzer for the publication, he stood up manfully for the book, which was saved from suppression when Magistrate George W. Simpson dismissed the charges. In addition to his help with *Women in Love*, Seltzer had published *The Lost Girl, Aaron's Rod, Kangaroo, The Boy in the Bush, Fantasia of the Unconscious, Psychoanalyis and the Unconscious, Sea and Sardinia,* collections of short stories, two books of poems and *Studies in Classic American Literature*. He had also brought out the first book written about Lawrence: Herbert J. Seligmann's sensitive and appreciative short monograph, *D. H. Lawrence: An American Interpretation.* Because of Lawrence's tendency to make friends of everyone with whom he dealt, he had done so with Seltzer; and in 1922 he had his first face-to-face meeting with his publisher when the Seltzers spent Christmas with the Lawrences at the ranch. There he had found Seltzer "a nice tiny man," and Seltzer had been surprised by Lawrence's "small but sweet voice" as he sang Christmas carols. Frieda had also liked Adele, who aided her husband in his publishing business and shared his literary enthusiasm for Lawrence. The next summer the Lawrences had been the guests of the Seltzers, in New York and at their cottage in Dover, New Jersey.

Later in the year, trouble started. During Lawrence's 1924 visit to New York when he saw Crowninshield of *Vanity Fair,* he also looked up Seltzer because the publisher had been "behaving queerly." Actually these words to Bynner were a charitable understatement. Mrs. Carswell told the story more fully in *Savage Pilgrimage:* "Lawrence, waiting in vain week after week for some reply to the letters and cables which he had been sending to his New York publisher, had begun to be anxious about money." Quite a lot was involved, too, for *Women in Love* the year before had sold more than 15,000 copies in the United States "I wonder why Seltzer has not written to me," Lawrence wrote Mrs. Luhan two days after Christmas. "For about six weeks I have nothing from him. I wonder if something has gone wrong with him or his business. Hope not, that would dish me in another direction." On 7 February 1924, Lawrence wrote Murry from Baden-Baden, "I still have no word from that miserable Seltzer." Mrs. Carswell reports that, on his way back to

London from Germany, Lawrence "wasted five days in Paris hoping to get a reply to his cables from New York. None came."

When he got to New York in March, Lawrence discovered why he had been receiving no payments. "Seltzer had a bad year," he reported to Mrs. Carswell, adding that the publisher had lost $7,000. "But," continued the letter, "he's going to scrape together a few hundreds, and we're going West on Tuesday morning. . . . Friendly relations preserved." After settling at Kiowa Ranch, Lawrence revealed that he had shrunk from applying the screws to his friend personally. Writing to Frederick Carter, he said, "I got an agent in New York to tackle my publisher, and the thing will be straightened out—but will take about a year. It wasn't nice." This 3 June 1924 report turned out to be overly optimistic. Lawrence, however, still hesitated. But in Oaxaca, urged by Barmby, he finally decided to cease publishing exclusively with Seltzer in the United States. The news of the decision is revealed in the January 10 letter to Brown, Barmby's boss. "I wired Barmby to proceed with Knopf for the next book." But Lawrence did not let the matter rest so brutally. Later in the letter he betrayed what he felt was justifiable anger: "As for Seltzer, if only he'd been open and simple with me, I'd have borne with him through anything. But a furtive little flea who hides his hand from me, as if he were going to fleece me—whether fleas have hands and fleece or not—why—*Basta!*"

"Stirred up emotions only lead to hate," Lawrence had written Brett. In the last weeks of writing *Serpent* Lawrence did not want to further stir up his own emotions or get involved in Seltzer's as evidenced by two letters he wrote on February 15. One to Brown showed that in the five weeks since he decided to change publishers, Lawrence had been unable to tell Seltzer directly. "Had a long cablegram from Seltzer," he reported to his agent. "Is it true that you are going to Knopf? etc." The cablegram ended Lawrence's procrastination, and the other letter of the same day was to Seltzer: "Yes, I agreed at last with Barmby that he should offer the short novel *St. Mawr* to Knopf. It seemed better all round: in the end even better for you.—But that does not mean I shall never offer you anything more. I am not so very sure that one exclusive publisher is wisest. Let us see how things work out: & if Knopf does one book, why should you not do another, if you wish to."

Lawrence was serious about not wanting a total break with Seltzer. Recapitulating his own words to the publisher he wrote Brown: "I didn't see why, in the future, we couldn't offer another novel to Seltzer, if all goes well, and I mean that. I don't quite believe that it is good for me to be monopolized by one publisher in each country. I think two publishers stimulate the sales much better than one. . . . I believe you think it wisest to put all one's works into the hands of one publisher—but seriously, I don't agree. One becomes like a special sort of medicine."

Lawrence gave Mrs. Carswell another report after he left Mexico. Writing on 20 June 1925, he said, "As far as prosperity goes—I have left Seltzer, who hangs, like a creaking gate, long: and gone to Knopf, who is a better business man. But of course I still have to live on what is squeezed out of poor Seltzer."

Three days later he wrote Brown in some indignation: "Knopf advertises that I shall henceforth publish exclusively with him. He's not justified in so doing. Seltzer writes an expostulation. I never made any 'exclusive' promise to Knopf, and I don't think Barmby ever did."

Seltzer had a Lawrence book in the works at the time of the break, a translation of Giovanni Verga's *Novelle Rusticana.* It came out before Lawrence left Mexico as *Little Novels of Sicily* and proved to be their last collaboration. Nevertheless, when Lawrence passed through New York for the last time in September 1925, he went to see the Seltzers. Remembering the image he had conceived in Oaxaca, he wrote the young Hawks about the visit:

> I didn't care for New York—it was steamy hot. I had to run about and see people: the two little Seltzers dangling by a single thread over the verge of bankruptcy, and nobody a bit sorry for them. The new publishers, the Knopfs, are set up in great style, in their offices on Fifth Avenue—deep carpets, and sylphs in a shred of black satin and a shred of brilliant undergarment darting by. But the Knopfs seem really sound and reliable: am afraid the Seltzers had too many "feelings." Adele said dramatically to Frieda: "All I want is to pay OUR debts and DIE." Death is a debt we all pay: the dollars are another matter.

The next year Seltzer sold his business to his nephews, Albert and Charles Boni, with whom he had helped to create the Modern Library. But he still brought out a few books under his own imprint and towards the end of 1926 he wrote Lawrence a letter whose contents can be gauged from Lawrence's reply. In contrast to the "Dear Seltzer" of the Oaxaca letter, it began "Dear Thomas":

> Your letter, with Adele's, came a week ago. I don't know why it took so long.—I had, in all conscience, to ask Curtis Brown his opinion. I can't promise to come back to you, not now at least.—You say you will pay me the arrears if I come back, but not if I don't; which is a sort of threat. And you know why I left you: because you left *me* quite in the dark.— And Adele says I am to come back with a best seller under my arm. When I have written *Sheik II* or *Blondes Prefer Gentlemen,* I'll come. Why does anybody look to me for a best seller? I'm the wrong bird.

> I'm awfully sorry things went to pieces. Blame me, if you like, for leaving you. But blame yourself, now as ever, for not knowing how to be simple, and open with me.
>
> And I do hope you will get rich one day—honestly I do.

Two years later, from the south of France, Lawrence wrote Seligmann, author of the pioneer book about him published by Seltzer in 1924. Now Seligmann had done the novelist a second favor—reviewing *Lady Chatterly's Lover* favorably and losing his job with the *New York Sun* in the process. Lawrence wanted to thank him. Remembering Seltzer's publication of the Seligmann *American Interpretation,* and thinking (wrongly, as it turned out) that the two men might be friends, the novelist asked:

> Do you ever see Thomas Seltzer? I think of him always with affection and a sad heart. I wish to God he had been able to prosper on me. But I'm afraid I am not the stuff prosperity is made of. I always feel so unhappy about him—not because I left him, for his affairs would have gone just the same, if not worse, had I stayed with him—but because of the great disappointment to him. Myself I don't expect money success, so it doesn't matter. But a publisher has to have it.

''THE HOPI SNAKE DANCE''

Lawrence's insight, human sympathy, and basic friendliness tended to put him on intimate terms with people in very short order, for which Frieda often criticized him. When he found himself simultaneously confronted with three tangled relationships, he must have felt she was right. His need to break with Seltzer coincided with his worry over handling Quintanilla's article without hurting the poet's feelings and with Frieda's ultimatum about Brett. He must have been relieved that at least "Mornings in Mexico" had been sent off. Another palliating factor is hinted at in a January 10 letter to Brown. "Did Barmby," it asked, "send you a copy of *The Theatre Arts* with my 'Hopi Snake Dance' article?"

This article, the first piece he wrote into "Record," was close to his heart, and was first seen by him in print in Oaxaca. Lawrence had begun seeing Indian dances in the American Southwest the moment he arrived in Taos in September 1922, when Mabel Dodge insisted that Lawrence let Tony Luhan drive him to the Jicarilla Reservation to see the Apaches' annual Encampment there. Two weeks later he saw the spectacular races of the annual harvest festival at Taos on the day of San Geronimo, described in both "Taos" and "New Mexico." On his second visit to Taos in 1924, he extended his knowledge of Indian dances and religious customs, unquestionably with intensified interest, for he had drafted "Quetzalcoatl," coping with the problem of presenting a new Indian religion arising from the roots of the old. The first new dance he saw on his return was the Dance of the Sprouting Corn at the Keres pueblo of Santo Domingo. This was a spring dance observed on April 23, the Wednesday after Easter. He wrote a short but vividly descriptive account of it which his literary agency, now working for him on both sides of the Atlantic, submitted to Murry's *Adelphi* in London and the *Theatre Arts Magazine* in New York. Both accepted it, the *Theatre Arts* published it in July 1924 and *Adelphi* published Part I in January 1925 and Part II in February 1925. Lawrence's other major dance experience that summer—again arranged by Mabel Dodge, now Mrs. Luhan, again with Tony as the chauffeur—came after the long drive west to the Hopi area of northeast Arizona. He saw the annual Hopi snake dance, which that year was in Hotevilla, a village on the farthest of the "three tall arid mesas" that rise from "greyish, unappetizing desert." Actually, he saw two dances, for he watched the prelude to the main dance on August 17 and the final snake dance the next day. He was back in Taos by August 25 and he must have dashed off his article on the experience rapidly, for on August 30 he wrote Murry: "I'm sending Curtis Brown my article on the Hopi Snake Dance. No doubt it's too long for you, but read it anyhow, as it defines somewhat my position. . . . This animistic religion is the only live one, ours is a corpse of a religion."

Meanwhile, Mrs. Edith J. R. Isaacs, editor of *Theatre Arts,* pleased with "Dance of the Sprouting Corn," had written Lawrence asking for another article. On September 6 Lawrence replied that he had already asked his agent to send her the Hopi article: "I did an article on The Hopi Snake Dance [he said], and feel rather deeply about the said essay. But no doubt it is far too long and far too speculative for your magazine. I don't want to cut it down at all:. not for anybody. But if you wish I will try to write a little purely descriptive essay such as the 'Corn Dance' one."

So Lawrence braced himself for rejection with both magazines. Because he wrote an early draft of the article, without speculation, we are in an excellent position to know why the article meant so much to him and what he thought so speculative in it. Johnson published this early draft in his *Laughing Horse* of September 1924. In the preliminary study the snakes are described merely as emissaries to the rain god. Between writing that somewhat flippant account of the dance and the longer serious one, Lawrence either had a flash of intuition or was told something that transformed the "men with snakes in their mouths, like a circus" into truly religious celebrants. From that point, he saw the snakes as emissaries to something Lawrence believed in deeply: not a mere local corn goddess, but the invisible dark sun at the center of the earth that was the source of life's potencies. The snakes were chosen for the ambassadorial role because snakes lie nearer than other creatures to the earth's dark center.

In her *Lorenzo in Taos* Mrs. Luhan says the flippant account of the dance had "no vision, no insight, no appreciation of any kind," and she let Lawrence know how it "disappointed and incensed" her. Perhaps through her own vision of the dance, she played a shaping role in his new concept. At all events, her dissatisfaction led Lawrence to try again, as he acknowledged in a note thanking her for the trip: "I'll write a sketch for the *Theatre Arts,* and draw one, too, if I can; not for the *Horse* to laugh at."

It was the second article that Murry saw, and, after first saying he liked it, he proved lukewarm and niggling about it, leading Lawrence to write him from Oaxaca on November 17: "The article you wearily mention is the Snake Dance article, I suppose. If you really cared about it, I'd tell Curtis Brown to let you have it at the price you can afford to pay. But if you don't really care, what's the good."

With this disappointment in the background, Lawrence was particularly delighted by two magazines he received as he was struggling with his Seltzer-Brett-Quintanilla-Frieda problems. *Theatre Arts* had published his Hopi article in full and illustrated it handsomely with three photographs and two sketches by Indian artists. He ordered additional copies for his sisters, Emily and Ada; and on January 10 he expressed himself as follows:

> "Dear Miss Isaacs,—The two copies of *Theatre Arts* have come: thank you very much. I must say it's a *very* attractive production, and amazingly without printer's errors. Makes one believe it *can* be done. Yes, I like my 'Hopi Dance' extremely, in appearance. I'd rather see it in *Theatre Arts* than in among the ads of those great and profitable periodicals that have so much space and so little room for anything."

That Lawrence expressed his thanks for the Hopi dance article the same day that he sent out "Mornings in Mexico" might be considered a prophetic coincidence. Two years later the earlier article would meet the four newer ones in a book. The idea for the book, *Mornings in Mexico,* was not Lawrence's, but Secker's, who was eager for a successor to *Sea and Sardinia* published in 1923. "Secker has been worrying me to write a travel book," Lawrence wrote Ada from Villa Mirenda on 3 May 1926. But, as he explained to his sister, he didn't "want to do an ordinary travel book, just of places." He was interested in visiting Etruscan areas to gather material on the mysterious precursors of the Romans but did not get around to making his Etruscan tour until the next year. Meanwhile, Secker had an alternate idea. Though Lawrence was disappointed in how long their placement took, the four "Mornings in Mexico" essays had finally been accepted, two by the American magazine *Travel*, "Market Day" by the English *New Criterion,* the other three of the series by Murry's *Adelphi.* Secker's new idea for getting a travel book out of Lawrence was to use material already published. Lawrence was not at all enthusiastic. Responding to Secker's proposition on 15 November 1926, he wrote:

> Do you really think those essays are good enough? It seems to me they are rather half-baked, some of 'em. The four essays called "Mornings in Mexico"—there must be four, they are a set—are good. But what about the others. I doubt if I want them put in a book—they're not good enough. . . . I hate the thought of half-baked essays in vol. form. Let me know exactly what you think—and send me the material you think genuinely suitable for a book, so I can look through it—if you have it, I feel very doubtful.

Eight days later Lawrence had Secker's proposal for the articles to accompany the Oaxaca sketches: the Sprouting Corn and Hopi pieces from *Theatre Arts* and "Indians and Entertainment," a more generalized piece about Indian dances written at the same time as the other two and published in the *New York Times* on 26 October 1924. Saying "the essay book sounds all right," Lawrence proposed a final eighth piece incongruously dealing with an evening in Italy, "A Little Moonshine with Lemon." This, too, had already been published, the first piece in the April 1926, all-Lawrence issue of Johnson's *Laughing Horse.* In describing Saint Catherine's night in Spotorno, Lawrence dramatized his nostalgia for the far-away New Mexican ranch on 25 November 1925, prompting a connection to the other three sketches. A stronger and much more logical candidate would have been "Indians and an Englishman," describing the Apache Encampment, which had appeared in the February 1923 *Dial.* The publisher accepted Lawrence's suggestion for the coda, however, and the oddly assorted collection was issued by Secker in London in July 1927 and by Knopf in New York the same year. It was dedicated to Mabel Luhan, who had taken Lawrence to the corn and snake dances. Oaxaca, then, inspired only half the volume, and the book does not have the consistency and well-roundedness of its predecessors, *Twilight in Italy* and *Sea and Sardinia,* and the one he would write later, *Etruscan Places.*

"The Hopi Snake Dance" has a further link with Oaxaca. More important than the arrival of the article was the influence of the dance's animistic religion on one of the new sequences worked into *The Plumed*

Serpent there. In the sermon to his peons just before the coming of the first rain, Ramón, too, speaks of a snake as an ambassador between the earth's surface and its invisible dark center. The Hopi idea had grown in Lawrence's imagination. Instead of picturing the released snakes leaving *for* the earth's center, as in the article, Ramón pictures a snake returning *from* that center, bringing some of the power from the central sun— or fire, as it is called here. To awaken his listeners to a sense of that snake, Ramón begins dramatically, "'Serpent of the earth, snake that lies in the fire at the heart of the world, come! Come! Snake of the fire of the heart of the world, coil like gold round my ankles, and rise like life around my knees, and lay your head against my thigh. Come, put your head in my hand, cradle your head in my fingers, snake of the depths. Kiss my feet and my ankles with your mouth of gold, kiss my knees and my inner thigh, snake branded with flame and shadow.' "

Later, inducing audience participation in his rituals, Ramón addresses himself directly to the peons with the instructions, "'Speak then to the snake of the heart of the world, put oil on your fingers and lower your fingers for him to taste the oil of the earth, and let him send life into your feet and ankles and knees, like sap in the young maize pressing against the joints and making the milk of the maize bud among its hair.' "

In sending the magazine with the Hopi piece, Mrs. Isaacs must have asked for a comparable dance piece from Oaxaca. Perhaps she had heard that it was a state particularly rich in folk dances. But Lawrence who had been no further from the state capital than Mitla, replied in the lordly vein he sometimes used in "Mornings in Mexico": "There's never a dance down here. They're terribly un-dancy, these Zapotec and Mixtec Indians. But when I see something that might do for you, I'll have a whack at it and send it along."

Had Lawrence queried some oldtimers in Oaxaca he would not have spoken so hastily. All seven of the state's principal regions have distinct folk dances, and when they are demonstrated at the annual *Lunes del Cerro,* on the third Monday in July on´*El Fortín,* they make a wonderfully varied program, visually enlivened by the whites, blacks, reds, blues, and purples of the richly embroidered regional folk costumes. But in Lawrence's time the traditional program, dating back to pre-Conquest days, was not being held. Still, it is strange that he had not heard of the Plume Dance, one of the most spectacular of the old Indian dances that have survived in Mexico. Teams of feather dancers, with their great disk headdresses measuring a yard across, often dance in Oaxaca and at the fiestas of such nearby villages as Cuilapam and Teotitlán del Valle. I have watched them, for instance, in the cloister of La Merced, Padre Rickards's church. As the men advanced towards each other in ranks, as if intending to clash their headdresses like cymbals (yet never letting the great feathered disks tip or touch), and as I have seen them leap backwards, shaking their rattles while making turns in the air, I have often wished Lawrence had seen and described the ancient ritual dance. Then it would have had a word-master equal to its athleticism, intricacy, beauty, and inner significance.

''NONE OF THAT''

Lawrence's short story "None of That" is linked to Oaxaca by internal evidence. The chief male character, a bullfighter, is the son of a Mixtec Indian woman, and the description of his build—"short, and broad, and rather fat"—shows that, by the time of its writing, Lawrence had come to know enough about the Oaxaca Indians to distinguish the Mixtecs from the leaner, more aquiline Zapotecs. By 1971 the story had grown vague in Brett's memory, but when Manchester read it aloud to her, enough of its history returned to bring her a moderately certain feeling that Lawrence had started it in Oaxaca and a strong feeling that she had typed it at the ranch.

Bynner, in *Journey with Genius,* says "None of That" was not written until after Lawrence had seen his second bullfight on his Mexican journey with Gótzsche. And by correlating a passage in *Lawrence and Brett* with the date that Lawrence met Dora Carrington, a painter friend of Brett's, I was able to establish that the story was still not written before Lawrence left England. The novelist studied the young blonde artist "keenly," according to Brett, who added, "I think you used her later in your story 'None of That.' " Because Carrington wrote about this meeting to Gerald Brenan, we know it occurred at a party on 1 March 1924, four days before Brett, Lawrence, and Frieda sailed for New York.

The story was based on a *grand scandale* in Mexico City, which Lawrence probably did not hear until he got there. The English-educated Eduardo Rendón, who identified the scandal for me, was one of the Mexican intellectuals Lawrence met at this time. (Plate 46.) Although the urbane, elegant, silver-haired Don Eduardo said he did not remember telling Lawrence about the Arbuckle-like case, the novelist could have easily learned about it during his stop-over in the capital. It had been in the papers, and the newspaper *El Universal* was then distributing free to its subscribers *Mis 20 Años de Torero,* a ghost-written "intimate" life of the popular bullfighter involved. Lawrence's story, then, may have been started in Mexico City and finished in Oaxaca, with Brett typing it there. Dealing with it here is chronologically plausible. The story is obviously related to the three stories Lawrence wrote on the ranch before returning to Mexico for the third time.

Opinions differ as to which was written first, *St. Mawr* or "The

Woman Who Rode Away," but we know "The Princess" was third, for it was the last piece written into "Record" before Lawrence took the copybook to Mexico. Because E. W. Tedlock, L. D. Clark, and David Cavitch have all noted the relationship between the three stories, it is remarkable that none of them placed "None of That" as the fourth member of the quartet. "None of That," too, is a story of a wealthy American woman responding to the sexual appeal of a dark-skinned Mexican male. This common theme is enough to give the foursome unusual interest, but they become an even more interesting set when one understands why Lawrence gave the theme so much time, thought, and creative energy. Since creating Cicio in *The Lost Girl* and Count Dionys in "The Ladybird" he had considered the swarthy-skinned male as sexually potent. After getting to know Mexico he had come to see the Mexican male, especially the Indian, as an incarnation of the phallic mystery, a human survival still possessing some of the ancient physical animism that Lawrence felt had been all but sapped from white men by modern civilization. The theme, then, was congenial to his thought because it enabled him to dramatize the phallic mystery by showing how four modern heroines behaved on encountering it in human embodiments. When one knows both versions of *The Plumed Serpent* one realizes Lawrence also had a more pressing and more practical reason for treating the theme so often. He needed a number of trial runs to solve a major problem left on his hands when he finished the first version of the novel: what to do with Kate.

Kate, as we have seen, is the heroine of *The Plumed Serpent* and her dilemma, as revealed in the account of the Mitla visit, was whether to run away from Mexico or to settle there. In the Chapala version, the novel ends with Kate packing up and leaving, and Lawrence's subsequent thought on the matter shows that he knew this was doubly unsatisfactory. Making Kate merely an observant tourist who got close to a new Mexican movement and then withdrew reduced the novel to a thinly disguised travel book. By the same token, the novel was diminished by having a heroine who did not really participate in the action. Lawrence recognized he had to handle Kate's dilemma differently. But how?

An invitation to join the Quetzalcoatl movement made Kate's dilemma acute. Besides committing herself to stay in Mexico, she agreed to see herself as an incarnation of an ancient Mexican goddess and to marry a Zapotec Indian, Cipriano, the military leader of the movement who believed himself an incarnation of another Mexican deity, Huitzilopochtli. Perhaps hardest of all, in becoming part of a particular circle of Mexican life she agreed to surrender her own will.

The heroine of *St. Mawr* is Lou Witt, a twenty-five-year-old rich American girl brought up chiefly in Europe. The Mexican who comes into her life is Geronimo Trujillo, "an odd piece of debris," son of a

Mexican father and a Navajo mother, nicknamed "Phoenix" because he came from Arizona. Mrs. Witt, Lou's mother, adopts him as a sort of stray after nursing him through shell-shock during World War I. Lou's dilemma is never acute. Her affairs and her marriage have so disgusted her with most men's copulating that her resolution, despite the admitted physical appeal of Phoenix, is to renounce sex altogether and merely keep Phoenix as a groom on her New Mexico ranch—a sort of outdoor nunnery where she hopes to find peace of soul by coming to terms with unseen presences. She likes having him near but rejects the idea of surrendering her body to him and never considers surrendering her will.

The heroine of "The Princess" is Dollie Urquhart, a woman of thirty-eight brought up to think of herself as a princess by a widower father, now dead. Her rejection of sex had begun in childhood. Like Lou Witt, her early life was spent mostly in Europe. The story proper begins on a ranch in the same area of New Mexico as the ranch bought by Lou. But unlike Lou's primitive ranch, it is a dude ranch. The Mexican who kindles a sexual spark in the virginal Dollie of "the apple blossom face" is Domingo Romero, with eyes "black and Indian looking." Romero, the son of the Spanish sheep-rancher who formerly owned the ranch, is now reduced to serving as a guide for its guests. The Princess sets up a trip on horseback to a shack high in the mountains, and there she provokes him to rape her. When she finds herself revolted by intercourse, Romero insists he will keep her captive until she likes it. But Dollie does not yield. After Romero is killed in a shootout with two rescuing Forest Service men, Dollie blames him, saying he went out of his mind. Again the female will remains unconquered; here the man suffers death, in contrast to the comfortable servitude agreeable to Phoenix.

In the two other stories the scales tip against the woman. Both can be seen in fresh and more logical light if they are viewed as nightmares Kate might have had while trying to make up her mind about the conflicting forces tugging at her. "The Woman Who Rode Away," closest in plot to *The Plumed Serpent,* gives a particularly lively idea of how the novel's problems remained operative in Lawrence's mind in the fallow period. Perhaps the participants and the locale of the story were suggested to Lawrence in New Mexico when he learned about the raids of the 1880s of the Chiricahuas across northwest Chihuahua, northeast Sonora, and into the United States. For the Chiricahuas remained the last Apache tribe to be brought into reservations because they had mountain retreats to which they could escape when Mexican and United States troops pursued them. In this story the heroine, never named, is the thirty-three-year-old wife of a mine owner in Chihuahua and still "the girl from Berkeley at heart." She is drawn not to one Mexican, but to a whole tribe. Lawrence calls this nonexistent tribe the Chilchuis, and the woman wants to ride away from the mine and join them. She acts on the impulse, and the Indians she meets on the trail take her to their village high in the mountains. There, aided by drugs, they slowly prepare her to willingly submit herself to be a white sacrifice whose death will restore to the Indians the powers taken from them when the whites conquered Mexico. A handsome young Indian attendant, always respectful, helps her will slip away. The story ends with the sacrificial knife about to be plunged into her breast. If taken literally, the story in many respects is crazy and implausible, but when viewed as something a woman in Kate's situation might have dreamed, it is a brilliant evocation. Kate was close to being irrevocably drawn into a group of religiously inclined Mexicans, and the integrity of her will was very much at stake. A woman, feeling that joining meant self-sacrifice, could easily dream of it as being sacrificed to the gods in the manner familiar to her from stories of the Aztecs.

The heroine of "None of That" is Ethel Cane, a wealthy American woman of "between thirty and forty" who comes to revolutionary Mexico about 1914, feeling drawn to men of dramatic power. The Mexican compelling her fascination is Cuesta, a half-Mixtec bullfigher. Ethel's attitude toward men interested in bedding her has always been the "None of That" of the title. She wants to dominate Cuesta, as she has dominated other men, by her will. But in this case she is greatly drawn by his animal magnetism. Aware of this, he uses the lure of his body to conquer her, wanting both her subjugation and her fortune. Ethel is driven emotionally, for she has so much faith in the power of her imagination that she always held that she would kill herself if her imagination lost its control of her body. Finally, however, she agrees to visit Cuesta in his home, knowing she is likely to surrender to him bodily. But instead of taking her himself, he hands her over to "half a dozen of his bull-ring gang." Finding her shaken imagination inadequate to raise her above such violation, Ethel poisons herself three days later.

When Manchester refreshed Brett's memory of the story, she held to her earlier belief that Carrington, her friend of Bloomsbury days, was the physical model for Ethel. But she hastened to add that the inward character of the heroine was closer to Mabel Luhan—an opinion which Frieda shared, as she confided to Harry T. Moore. Support for this belief is found in Mrs. Luhan's own exclamation in *Lorenzo in Taos* —"But I wanted none of that"—when she was angry at Lawrence's decision to quit her hospitality in favor of her son's ranch, seventeen miles away. Even more decisive is the way Lawrence repeatedly characterized Mabel in direct confrontations. In his letter to her of 21 May 1926, he commented on the portrait she had drawn of herself in her *Intimate Memories,* which she had sent him to read in manuscript. "With your men," he wrote, "you only want to resist them, fight them and overthrow them." This was also the pattern of his heroine Ethel Cane, who finally was conquered by impersonal male force in "None of That."

In his 8 October 1927 letter to Secker, Lawrence said the story was "founded on fact." This was only partly true. Even if the heroine was based on two real models, Lawrence invented the foreign woman's involvement with the bullfighter and her subsequent suicide. Rodolfo Gaona, a famous Mexican bullfighter whom Bynner says Lawrence learned about on his first visit to Mexico, had in fact gotten into hot water because, during one of his gang's orgies, a Mexican girl had accidentally been killed. Gaona's name, too, was much in the air when Lawrence got back to Mexico City in October 1924, not only because of the "intimate life" that the newspaper was distributing, but because he was in his last triumphant season as an idol of the Mexican bullring. To disguise his sources, Lawrence set his story ten years earlier, but how closely he modeled Cuesta on Gaona can be gauged from Gaona's career. Gaona, born in Léon in 1888, made his debut in the ring in Mexico in 1905 at the age of seventeen. After triumphs in Spain he returned to Mexico for the 1908-09 season. Soon he was known as the *Indio Grande*. Later, perhaps because his success with women suggested the lord of a harem, he was called the *Califa de León*. In the ring he performed with elegance and style and introduced a new kind of lance known as a *gaonera*. Even though he lived until 1975 and was succeeded by many native-born matadors, he is still acknowledged as one of the greatest bullfighters Mexico has produced. Like the matador in Lawrence's story, he had amassed a fortune by the time he retired at the age of thirty-seven, and his farewell appearance in the ring was a few weeks after the Lawrences left Mexico.

In contrast to the repugnance to bullfighting in *The Plumed Serpent,* "None of That" is totally nonjudgmental. Lawrence must have listened carefully to whomever supplied him with background, for the story is vividly realistic in its details. It also has a plausibility lacking in "The Woman Who Rode Away," for one can believe in Ethel's violation, whereas no tribe resembling the one sacrificing the unnamed woman has survived into the twentieth century. "None of That," therefore, is not a psychological fantasy, like "Woman." Nevertheless, its *raison d'être* becomes clearer when it is also seen as another of Kate's nightmares—in this case, of a different kind of death as the price of surrendering the white female will to the dark Mexican one. It is a death, not at the hands of religiously motivated Mexicans, but by brutal ones. Taking score of the stories, we find that in two, victory goes to the women; in the other two, to the men. The four solutions weighed were: willing submission leading to sacrificial death; submission, partly willing and partly unwilling, leading to gang rape and the woman's subsequent suicide; submission of the same equivocal kind leading to one-to-one rape, with the man being killed; and renunciation of sex altogether. Only the last did not end in disaster, but it was not a solution Lawrence generally favored. Obviously, Kate's dilemma required a solution different from any of the four.

TOLSTOY'S ''RESURRECTION''

Finding "Record," the black copybook Lawrence had with him in Oaxaca, was the greatest thrill of the Lawrence hunt. That I found it by accident added to the excitement. It happened on Saturday morning, 31 October 1970, in the Academic Center Library of the University of Texas. At that time I had little idea of how many Lawrence manuscripts the library had, nor had I read Tedlock's *The Frieda Lawrence Collection of D. H. Lawrence Manuscripts.* I had never heard of "Record's" existence, much less that around 1965 it had found its way to Austin in the second batch of Lawrence manuscripts acquired from the late T. E. Hanley, a collector from Bradford, Pennsylvania. My business in Austin was to go through Brett's negatives hoping that she took more photographs in Oaxaca than the five reproduced in *Lawrence and Brett.* After I had finished this principal task, I had a little time left, and, because I thought it would be foolish not to check for further Oaxaca possibilities, I asked to see the tray of index cards for the library's Lawrence manuscripts. When I got to the M's my eyes popped. The library had something I had not known had survived: the manuscript of "Mornings in Mexico." I asked Dorotha Collins if it would be possible to see it, fully believing that, if it were not far away in a safe, it was at least in a glass case. "Of course," she said casually, and within a matter of moments a page brought me a little black book that might have been a housewife's ledger. Not only did it contain the four Mexican "Mornings," but it had a number of other manuscripts as well. Suddenly I found that Lawrence had written a lot more in Oaxaca than I had realized. "See Mexico After" was the only one I recognized for sure, though I had a suspicion "Resurrection" might have been the piece of that name I had read in the first *Phoenix.* And even if it was, I had learned *where* it was written. The sequence of the manuscripts provided a clue to the order in which they were written. Because "Resurrection" was sandwiched between the last "Morning" and "See Mexico After," I deduced that it was written while Lawrence was beset by all his problems of the first week of the New Year.

Being fortunate enough to have a copy of the then out-of-print *Phoenix,* I was able to reread the essay. As I did, I felt that Lawrence's sensitivity to the pain in his own relationships in early 1925 had kept Jesus' first three words to Mary Magdalene after his resurrection reechoing in his mind, words that had haunted him, too, at other painful junctures: "Touch me not!" With these words Lawrence opens the article. If unconscious motivation for their use is speculation, one knows for sure that at this time Lawrence also had a tangible stimulus for using them. The article itself discloses how the essay was prompted by the most significant of his reading experiences in Oaxaca. The experience also touched off a more important essay, "The Novel," which he wrote three months after leaving Oaxaca. "Resurrection" shows, too, that the seed for the novella of four years later, *The Man Who Died,* began sprouting in Padre Rickards's house in Oaxaca.

"I have just read, for the first time, Tolstoy's *Resurrection,*" Lawrence records. Because he found the novel about the sufferings of those sent to Siberia and Tolstoy's attitude towards them repugnant, he was stirred to many responses. It repelled him as a thinker, as an artist-novelist, and as a prophet of salvation. For an understanding of the range of his response, what he wrote about the Tolstoy novel at Kiowa Ranch must be coupled with the Oaxaca piece.

"Resurrection" began like a book review, but soon it started sounding like another "Hymn of Quetzalcoatl." He wrote "Resurrection" after "Hymn," for "The Novel," the second response to the book, is unquestionably an essay-review of *Resurrection.* Since the essay makes the Oaxaca hymn easier to understand, let us outline it first.

Lawrence's relationship with Tolstoy goes back to when he was a young intellectual in Eastwood. "Turgenev, Tolstoy, Dostoievsky—mattered more than anything, and I thought them the greatest writers of all time," he recalled to Mrs. Carswell in a letter of 2 December 1916. Moore in *The Intelligent Heart* relates how in 1907, Lawrence, then twenty-two, praised *Anna Karenina* as the greatest of novels when he argued with Jessie Chambers and her family over which parts were the finest. By 1909, when he was a schoolteacher at Croydon, he had also read *War and Peace,* and the "raptures" he felt on that first reading are recorded in his posthumously published *Apocalypse.* But after Lawrence had come to grips with the central experience of *Anna Karenina* by running off with another man's wife himself, he found Tolstoy's handling of the situation too moralistic. Thereafter, his admiration for the novelist waned. Somewhat inarticulately he expressed new reservations about Tolstoy in a letter which rejected Garnett's criticism of "The Wedding Ring" and led to the break between the two men. In defending how his characters differed from those in other novels, Lawrence wrote, "The certain moral scheme is what I object to. In Turgenev and in Tolstoy, and in Dostoievsky, the moral scheme into which all the characters fit—and it is nearly always the same scheme—is, whatever the extraordinariness of the characters themselves, dull, old, dead."

Lawrence returned to Tolstoy when, in the first few months of World War I, he wrote his "Study of Thomas Hardy." Here Tolstoy's moral scheme is defined as "a metaphysic of self-justification, or a metaphysic of self-denial." Tolstoy, like Hardy, applied his metaphysic to the world, instead of *vice versa*.

Lawrence continued feeling strongly about Tolstoy, especially about his debasing treatment of Vronsky, the man who won another man's wife, and had an outburst against the Russian novelist in his *Fantasia of the Unconscious*. In *Studies in Classic American Literature*, though Lawrence acknowledged Tolstoy as one of the greatest novelists, he could not refrain from noting he "failed with the soil." With his shifting and ambivalent attitude towards the older novelist, it is not surprising that Lawrence, who found most people in Oaxaca limited, should have gratefully seized upon the one major Tolstoy work he had not read— *Resurrection* — when he discovered it in the possession of a member of the foreign colony. Reading *Resurrection* brought home to Lawrence passionately and with full clarity the basic flaw he found in Tolstoy as a novelist. Since his views had now clarified on the qualities a novel should have, he wrote his essay-review, rejoicing at last in writing directly about Tolstoy instead of just referring to him glancingly in relation to others. On 29 June 1925, when he sent it to the Centaur Press for inclusion in *Reflections on the Death of a Porcupine,* he confided to McDonald, whose bibliography had just been issued by the same publisher, that Frieda thought the essay was "too much." Discussing Tolstoy gave him an excellent opportunity to say things he wanted to say about the novel "as the highest form of human expression so far attained." He also talked about a distinction that was crystallized by *Resurrection:* that novelists, as philosophers with a purpose, can and do lie; but the novel itself "won't let you tell didactic lies, and put them over." In other words, novelists were one thing when they were thinkers, another when they were artists, and it was always as artists that they were more honest.

In the Oaxaca piece, Lawrence says only that *Resurrection* represents "the step into the tomb." When one recalls the horrors Tolstoy evoked in dramatizing the fate of those held in Russian jails and transported to Siberia, one realizes the force and justness of the statement. Tolstoy's hero is the Russian Prince Dimitri, who wishes to atone for the downfall of the girl he seduced on his aunts' estate by entering that tomb. Lawrence, in "The Novel," calls the would-be pious Prince "a muff, with his piety that nobody wants or believes in." The attack which follows becomes more intelligible when we realize Lawrence's Oaxacan preoccupation with the metaphor of a candle flame, a revival of an interest manifest eleven years earlier when he wrote Collings about confusing our own flames with the objects they shine on. In "The Novel," he calls character "the flame of a man, which burns brighter or dimmer, bluer or yellower or redder, rising or sinking or flaring according to the draughts of circumstance and the changing air of life, changing itself continually, yet remaining one single, separate flame, flickering in a strange world; unless it be blown out at last by too much adversity.''

In "the silly duplicity of *Resurrection,*" Tolstoy, as a Christian-Socialist, wanted to show the Prince as a hero, a man redeemed by his beliefs. Lawrence will have none of it: "When that Prince in *Resurrection* so cruelly betrayed and abandoned the girl, at the beginning of her life, he betrayed and wetted on the flame of his own manhood. When, later, he bullied her with his repentant benevolence, he again betrayed and slobbered upon the flame of his waning manhood, till in the end his manhood is extinct, and he's just a lump of half-alive elderly meat.''

As Lawrence points out, the novel does not allow a romantic or heroic view of Dimitri. The prince, who joins the girl in her suffering by accompanying her somewhat more comfortably to Siberia, looks upon her as his "dear cross.''

"But," says Lawrence, "you can't fool the novel. Even with man crucified on a woman: his 'dear cross.' The novel will show you how dear she was: dear at any price. And it will leave you with a bad taste of disgust against these heroes who *turn* their women into a 'dear cross,' and *ask* for their own crucifixion.''

To be quick, to be vitally and organically interrelated in all its parts, and to be honorable—these Lawrence held were the three essential qualities a novel must have. In defining quickness, he wrote, "In every great novel, who is the hero all the time? Not any of the characters, but some unnamed and nameless flame behind them all. In the great novel, the felt but unknown flame stands behind all the characters, and in their words and gestures there is a flicker of the presence." The "God-flame," then, is quickness. Later he wrote that if one tries to find out wherein the quickness of the quick lies, "It is in a certain weird relationship between that which is quick and—I don't know: perhaps all the rest of things. It seems to consist in an odd sort of fluid, changing, grotesque or beautiful relatedness. The Prince in *Resurrection,* following the convict girl, we must count dead. The convict train is quick and alive. But that would-be expiatory Prince is dead as lumber.''

Lawrence did not mind a novel having a didactic "purpose"—how could he, writing the novels he did?—but he insisted that, if there be such a purpose, it must comply with two requirements: it must be large enough, and it must not be "at outs with the passional inspiration." What he held against Tolstoy, in *Anna Karenina* and *War and Peace,* as well as in *Resurrection,* was imposing on them a purpose that was contrary to his passional inspiration. For this reason he found the novels were not honorable. "Of course Tolstoy, being a great creative artist, was true to his characters. But being a man with a philosophy, he wasn't true to his *own character,* "is how he summarized it. Tolstoy's character, said Lawrence, made him a lion, and punning on the novelist's baptismal name, he wrote: "When the lion tries to force himself down the throat of the huge and popular lamb—a nasty old sheep, really—then it's a phenomenon. Old Leo did it; wedged himself bit by bit down the throat of woolly Russia. . . . What a dishonorable thing for that claw-biting little Leo to do! And in his novels you see him at it. So that the papery lips of *Resurrection* whisper: *Alas! I would have been a novel. But Leo spoiled me.*"

The Oaxaca "Resurrection" piece was the response, not of the novelist-critic, but of the prophet of salvation. And in it, laying artistic considerations aside and goaded by Tolstoy's gospelizing, Lawrence preaches as a counter-prophet, setting forth his own gospel. In the novel, the Prince leaves the prisoners and, after a transcendent experience reading the Gospel of Saint Matthew, decides that, instead of trying to aid the convicts, his first responsibility is to "seek the Kingdom of God and His righteousness." This resolve is presented as a personal resurrection for the Prince—the "Resurrection" of the title. The novel ends, implying that each man should take the same road to salvation. To Lawrence this withdrawal into mysticism was not the way out. He was angered that the novel never took "the third step": that it left the reader in the tomb with the stone "rolled upon him." Lawrence held that it was time to roll away the stone and to rally round the Lord who had not only stepped from the tomb but ascended unto the Father. It was time to accept the Ascension as well as the Resurrection, that is, to realize that "Christ is not put twice on the Cross." The article's last direct comment on Tolstoy is that "it seemed to him, Christ would go on being crucified everlastingly."

The rest of the piece is addressed to "the Men of the Risen Lord." Even though there is no further reference to the Russian novelist, the reader with memories of *Resurrection* recognizes in the imagery and the talk of the Lord's being out of prison that Lawrence's imagination was still haunted by Tolstoy's descriptions of the multitudes of the prisoners, tormented by fleas, marching through the wastes after wagons often stalled in the deep Siberian mud. In all the latter part it is as if Lawrence were trying his hand at an exhortatory hymn for Christians, similar to the hymns for the followers of Quetzalcoatl that he was composing for *The Plumed Serpent.* And it is written in a style deserving notice. In *Apocalypse,* in recalling his day school, his Sunday school, his home, the Band of Hope and Christian Endeavour, Lawrence noted somewhat rancorously how the Bible was "poured into the childish consciousness day in, day out, year in, year out, willy-nilly, whether the consciousness could assimilate it or not." But in his article "Hymns in a Man's Life," he acknowledged a good side of this inpouring by saying, "I should have missed bitterly a direct knowledge of the Bible." One can gauge how truly he prized his boyhood exposure to it by the use he made of the Bible in his writing. How deeply its rhythms passed into his subconscious can be seen by the facility with which he could reproduce them. An early instance in which he did so is the foreword for *Sons and Lovers* written only for Edward Garnett's eyes in January 1913. In the second year of World War I came "The Crown;" and this Oaxaca "Resurrection" piece provides a further example of his biblical style which he was to use twice more in Oaxaca. How easily in "Resurrection," touched off by poetically garbled memories of Anaximander's wheels and Ezekiel, he can proclaim in the visionary manner of an Old Testament prophet: "The wheel of fire is starting to spin in the opposite way, to throw off the mud of the world. Deep mud is on the staggering wheel, mud of the multitudes. But Christ has rejoined the father at the axis, the flame of the hub spurts up. The wheel is beginning to turn in the opposite way, and woe to the multitude."

He continues:

> Men of the Risen Lord, the many ways are one. Down the spokes of flame there are many paths which are one way still, to the core of the wheel. Turn round, turn round, away from the mud of the rim to the flame of the core, and walk down the spokes of fire to the Whole, where God is one.
>
> For the multitudes shall be shaken off as a dog shakes off his fleas. And only the risen lords among men shall stand on the wheel and not fall, being fire as the wheel is Fire, facing in to the inordinate Flame.

In its way, it is quite wonderful, but we must restrict ourselves here to the imagery of Good Friday and Easter. These ideas that stirred in Oaxaca grew more important with time, for on Good Friday of 1927 he wrote Mrs. Luhan: "This is the day they put Jesus in the tomb—and really, those three days in the tomb begin to have a terrible significance and reality to me. And the Resurrection is an unsatisfactory business—just *noli me tangere* and no more. *Poveri noi!* But *pazienza, pazienza!* The wheel will go round."

One of the verses using Easter imagery is: "Put away the Cross; it is obsolete. Stare no more after the stigmata. They are more than healed up. The Lord is risen and ascended unto the Father. There is a new body and a new Law."

Of special interest here is how this foreshadows Part Two of *The Man Who Died* with its hero whose wounds are already mere scars. Other verses foreshadow another piece he was to write back in Europe, "The Risen Lord," which was published in *Everyman* in 1929; notably the verse "Since the War, the world has been without a Lord. What is the Lord within us, has been walled up in the tomb." In fact, this Oaxaca article might be considered as a liturgical offering for the Christian church. In the *Everyman* piece, Lawrence was urging the church to preach the Risen Lord so that man might have a new vision of himself, the World War having destroyed his vision of himself as the Christ Child on the Virgin's lap and the subsequent peace having destroyed the war-born vision of himself as Christ Crucified:

> The Lord is risen. Let us rise as well and be lords. The multitudes rolled the stone upon us. Let us roll it back.
> Men in the tomb, rise up, the time is expired. The Lord is risen. Quick! Let us follow him.

One can pinpoint just how far along Lawrence was in rewriting *The Plumed Serpent* when his mind was being churned by Tolstoy's *Resurrection,* for the signs of its influence come as he was expanding the account of Kate's first visit to Ramón's *hacienda.* The first is to be found when Carlota, in complaining about her husband to Kate, says mockingly, "You didn't know my husband had become one of the people—a real peon—a Señor Peon, like Count Tolstoy became a Señor Moujik." The second comes in a later complaint of Carlota. In implying that her husband was treating Jesus cruelly, she asks rhetorically, "Ah, Señora, what woman would have the heart to put Christ back on the cross, to crucify him twice!"

Then in the sermon to the peons later in the evening, Ramón starts introducing the idea that Quetzalcoatl's rising from his place of sleep beyond the sun had points in common with Christ's resurrection. " 'So he had risen,' [says Ramón of Quetzalcoatl] 'and pushed the stone from the mouth of the tomb, and has stretched himself. And now he is striding across the horizons even quicker than the great stone from the tomb is tumbling back to the earth to crush those that rolled it up.' "

Quetzalcoatl's rising is told from an even closer viewpoint in the second of the leaflets that Kate, a short time later, hears Julio reading to her servants. Here Quetzalcoatl himself is the speaker, relating his dialogue with himself as he woke: "Now all was heavy upon me, like a tombstone of darkness. I said: Am I not old? How shall I roll this stone away? How art thou old, when I am a new man? I will roll away the stone. Sit up! I sat up, and the stone went rolling, crashing down the gulfs of space."

In the bitter hymn "Quetzalcoatl looks down on Mexico" the men of the new religion are addressed in terms similar to those Lawrence used in his Christian exhortation. Here Quetzalcoatl gives the instruction to a messenger to the Mexicans,

So tell the men I am coming to,
To make themselves, clean, inside and out
To roll the grave-stone off their souls, from the cave of their bellies,
To prepare to be men.

The verses of both hymns, to the Christians as well as to the followers of Quetzalcoatl, show the image Lawrence wanted men to hold
of themselves. In Tedlock's good phrase, he wanted to make men into
"gods with a revolutionary program." Besides showing how one division of his brain was working in Oaxaca, the Christian verses also illustrate a characteristic of Lawrence's mental life singled out by his friend
Brigit Patmore: "The harsh demands his genius made on his unbelieva-
ble crowd of intuitions and perceptions." When one thinks how his "Art
and Morality," "Morality and the Novel" and almost indubitably "Why
the Novel Matters" were written within a few days of the "The Novel"
as part of the same Tolstoy stimulus, one gains an idea of the incredible
activity of Lawrence's mind as he was reading *Resurrection*. Besides taking in the novel's plot and characters, and arguing with its thought, his
mind, not content with new ideas for *The Plumed Serpent,* was stirred
to ideas for six or seven new pieces—eight, if "The Flying Fish" be included. And this was the man who had just finished "Mornings in Mexico," who was struggling against an end-of-the-month deadline for his
novel, who was caught in a painful bind between two women, who had
recently broken with a publisher-friend, and who was worrying about
Quintanilla's feelings. It is hard to conceive a brain capable of sustaining
such a program. Astonishment grows when one realizes how many of
his literary ideas he acted on. Instead of letting them lie dormant, he actually wrote a high percentage of the pieces he had ideas for—certainly
he did with those stirred by reading *Resurrection*. And this despite a body
that tired easily and emotions that were always intense.

"MAN IS ESSENTIALLY A SOUL"

Aaron's Rod closes with a one-sided dialogue in which the flute-playing
Aaron listens skeptically to Rawson Lilly, a fictional Lawrence, who insists that lesser souls always have a need to submit "to the heroic soul
in a greater man." When Aaron is told he is one of the submitters, he
asks, "And whom shall I submit to?" "Your soul will tell you," Lilly
answers.

Lawrence finished *Aaron's Rod* in Taormina in 1921, and "Record" shows that these views persisted in Oaxaca. Indeed, they had grown
firmer, as demonstrated by the sixteen-paragraph discussion of them in
the black copybook, a discussion arising from his renewed preoccupation

with the metaphor of the candle. Because those paragraphs are not separated from the prior "Suggestions for Stories" by even a blank space, because they are untitled, and because, like the "Suggestions," they are in pencil, I missed them the first time through. But when I read Tedlock's book on Frieda's collection of Lawrence manuscripts, I learned he called the paragraphs "a philosophical fragment." Naturally I sought them out on my second visit to Austin. I would have known they were related to "Resurrection," even if they had not begun on page 130, only nine pages after "Resurrection's" close, for they are related to the same new section of *The Plumed Serpent:* the expanded account of Kate's first visit to Ramón's *hacienda*. These paragraphs, however, deal with the prayer meeting of the initiates, preceeding the service for the peons. Obviously, thinking about that prayer meeting, in which disciples were to meet with a leader, had made Lawrence want to redefine the leader-disciple relationship. He felt both sides were free, even though the followers had to be submissive. The brief essay—it is really too well-rounded and complete in itself to be called a fragment—can be placed in the second week of the New Year. Only the "Suggestions for Stories" stand between it and the rewritten piece for Quintanilla, which was mailed on January 12. The January 6 letter to William Hawk shows how some of the essay's ideas were moving in Lawrence's mind at that time. "Freedom is a gift inside one's own soul, you can't have it if it isn't in you."

Because the essay has not been published previously and because both the University of Texas and Gerald Pollinger, agent for the Frieda Lawrence Ravagli Estate, have given me permission to include it, I would like to present it in its entirety, for it is a noble statement, summarizing many of Lawrence's chief ideas about man's nature in simpler, more comprehensive terms than in most previous tries. It is interesting to compare Lawrence's flame metaphor with his explanation to Collings eleven years earlier in 1915: "I conceive a man's body as a kind of flame . . . and the intellect is just the light that is shed on the things around." Now it is the soul—an entity not mentioned to Collings—that is viewed as the flame. Another new entity—the spirit, is introduced, too, closer to the French *esprit,* meaning intelligence, than to anything churchly. The soul burns between the body and the spirit. The intellect is no longer a light, but an instrument bringing awareness of the flame.

The prayer meeting for the initiates is in Chapter XI, "Lords of the Day and Night." But the essay is related to later parts of *The Plumed Serpent* too. Witness Kate's response as she watches the wounded Ramón after the attack on his life: "Kate saw, vividly, how the body is the flame of the soul, leaping and sinking upon the invisible wick of the soul." And the essay's dictum—"The finest soul in the world is the first man of the world"—is clearly associated with Ramón's answer to Cipriano's question about what would happen if Mexico became a Quetzalcoatl country. "I shall be the First Man of Quetzalcoatl—I know no more." Because Ramón then goes on to discuss the natural aristocrats of the world (related to the "new order of aristocracy" in the essay), the essay is related even more intimately to Chapter XVII, "Fourth Hymn and the Bishop." But whether Lawrence wrote the essay to prime himself for the "Fourth Hymn" chapter or whether the discussion in the chapter fired him to make a more general statement, I do not know. The chapter may well have come first, for in the foreword to *Fantasia of the Unconscious* Lawrence said his thinking always arose out of his "unwatched" novel and poems, not *vice versa*. Only later, when the poems and the works of the imagination had been completed, did an "absolute need . . . . for some sort of satisfactory mental attitude towards oneself and things in general 'make him' try to abstract some definite conclusions: from his 'experiences as a writer and a man.' "

The essay, then, is evidence that in Oaxaca Lawrence had one of his periodic compulsions to see what his life and his works had taught him by that time. His conclusions can be read below:

Man is essentially a soul. The soul is neither the body nor the spirit, but the central flame that burns between the two, as the flame of a lamp burns between the oil of the lamp & the oxygen of the air.

The soul is to be obeyed, by the body, by the spirit, by the mind.

The mind is the instrument of registering the soul in consciousness.

The soul is instinctive. Real education is the learning to recognize & obey the instincts of the soul.

The most subtle & sensitive thing in life, is the recognizing and responding directly to the instinctive soul. All men do it in their own degree. But to catch the finest and ultimate flickers of intimation that can come from within needs a rare, pure, burning soul, a pure body, a sensitive strong spirit, and a quick, imaginative mind—And this is rare.

So men are really arranged in hierarchies of the soul, from the finest down to the dullest in hierarchies of the soul.

This is the new order of aristocracy, and it is a world-order. The finest soul in the world is the first man in the world, and the rest form themselves naturally into hierarchies.

By the movement of his soul within himself, a man knows the soul within another man, & whether it be a pure, stronger flame, whether the man belongs to a higher hierarchy or not. Man knows at first hand, *if he will*.

Body & spirit both must learn to obey the soul, since both are consummated in the soul. The soul is a flame that forever quivers between oil and air, between body and spirit, between substance and non-substance, between the senses and the mind. It is born of both and partakes of both and surpasses both. But it is always midmost between the two.

If the flame of the soul dies out, or is blown out by perverse living, the body begins to go corrupt in life, and the spirit takes on its murderous aspect.

So that there must be *authority* and discipline—The soul itself is the source of all authority, and the man of the purest, strongest soul-flame is the highest authority in the world. But even he must discipline his senses, his spirit, his mind and body, all the time, to the fulfillment of the soul. And every man's life, in so far as it is truly lived, is a long self-discipline.

If the body is disciplined to the soul, then the senses are consummated in the soul, and pleasure is transmuted into joy. And when the spirit is disciplined to the soul, then delight and ecstasy likewise fall into the deeper harmony of joy, without shrillness.

There is no such thing as absolute freedom. True, soul is the only authority, and each man primarily obeys his own soul. But obeying his own soul means, in every man, realising that he cannot know his own soul or come at its intimations without help from a purer, stronger being, to whose authority he must submit himself. Yet he only submits because his own soul tells him to. And this is freedom. Freedom in the sense of escape from all authority is illusion and disintegration. There is *always* authority imposed from the soul within, and obedience & discipline exacted. This we cannot escape, without falling into corruption & running into disintegration.

There is no absolute Word or Logos, even no *absolute* Law. All depends on the soul.

Neither is there any One Way. The soul takes many & different ways, all of them right.

Neither is there one supreme passion, like love & sacrifice. No sacrifice is final, not even Christ's. And every sacrifice man can make will in its turn be sacrificed, when the time comes. And every supreme passion will yield in its turn to another passion, which will then be supreme for its own time. So pride yielded before love, & love will yield before the passion of integrity.

AN ADVENTURE IN RECOGNITION

Lawrence received his first copy of Edward McDonald's bibliography three months after leaving Oaxaca and acknowledged it in a letter of 29 June 1925, to David Jester, the junior partner of its publisher, the Centaur Book Shop. "I feel I have lived in such a state of ignorance of my own fate. I really am pleased with the bibliography. Almost it makes me feel important."

His modesty also comes through one of the letters he wrote in Oaxaca. His correspondent was Carlo Linati, a Milan literary critic who had written an appreciative article about him in a newspaper that Lawrence considered "about the best paper in Europe," the *Corriere della Sera.* The article arrived in Oaxaca three days after Brett's departure, and Lawrence thanked Linati immediately. Though the praise did not turn his head, his morale obviously improved by having his work surveyed so prominently by such an important newspaper. The letter is in the second volume of Moore's collection. Two of its disclosures are pertinent to study Lawrence's self-assessment at this stage of his career. Lawrence had come to a clearer notion of the type of writer he felt he was and wanted to be. "Whoever reads me will be in the thick of the scrimmage, and if he doesn't like it—if he wants a safe seat in the audience—let him read somebody else." Lawrence liked his new style, apparent in *Studies of Classic American Literature,* which shocked many by its slangy, self-assertive, almost obstreperous tone. Also the Linati letter, like the one to Jester, shows that Lawrence had not paused long enough to see his writing in historical perspective—or even how the sum of it might strike a single reader. For Lawrence, however, Linati's article was clearly not so great an adventure in recognition as McDonald's bibliography.

When he first encountered Lawrence's work in 1915, McDonald was a thirty-two-year-old assistant professor of English at Trinity College in Hartford, Conneticut. At that time the sandy-haired young don from Coldwater, Ohio, was already interested in such "moderns" as Wells, Conrad, Bennett, James, Ibsen, Shaw, and Strindberg. But when *Sons and Lovers* came his way, almost by accident, he heard a new voice. He found that Lawrence had three previous books to his credit. When he had read them too, he felt Lawrence met his "ideal of what a writer should be—versatile, germinal, prolific—and a poet." The United States's entry into World War I took McDonald away from literature, and for a year he was a member of the War Department's seven-man Committee on Education and Special Training, organized to inform male college and university students of war issues. After the war he returned to teaching as head of the English Department of the Drexel Institute in Philadelphia. Here, in his own words, he became "a serious Lawrence buff." Besides reading Lawrence, he began collecting his books, letters, and manuscripts. By 1924 his personal collection was so complete that he knew he could use it as the basis of a Lawrence bibliography. He broached the idea to the novelist that summer. Lawrence replied from the ranch on July 3 that he didn't give "a snap for first editions," but "I'll help as much as I can." By September 10 he had sent McDonald the "little introduction" he had promised to contribute.

When he was eighty-two, McDonald told his side of the story in his preface to *The Centaur Letters,* published by the University of Texas in 1970: "After recovering from his bewilderment at the thought of a bibliography [wrote McDonald], Lawrence was of immense help to me. Answering promptly all questions, he gave me many leads to his early fugitive publications. This seems to show, in spite of his disclaimers to the contrary, that Lawrence's remembrance of his early work was far from shaky."

McDonald also played a central role in the creation of the first *Phoenix* (1936), a posthumous memorial edition of Lawrence's work, which ultimately had more significance for Oaxaca. In editing and compiling that monumental volume, McDonald published five of Lawrence's Oaxaca pieces not printed in the novelist's lifetime. Originally *Phoenix* was the brainchild of the London publishing company bearing the name of its founder William Heinemann. In 1930, ten years after Heinemann's death, the company gained control over all of Lawrence's titles in England. *Phoenix* was to be a further memorial tribute, following the publication of the Huxley edition of Lawrence's letters. McDonald, who had published his second Lawrence bibliography bringing the record up to the novelist's death, and Edward Garnett, who had served so well as an editor early in Lawrence's career, were asked to collaborate in editing the proposed volume. Both agreed. Garnett was then in his late sixties and, as it turned out, within three or four years of his death. When the typescripts began coming to him from Curtis Brown's London and New York offices, ailing Garnett saw the magnitude of the editorial labors involved, decided it was too much for him, and withdrew. But McDonald continued alone, and to the 80 percent of the material amassed by Garnett and Heinemann Ltd. he was able to add another 20 percent from his own collection, including items unknown to Garnett.

The five Oaxaca pieces uncovered from the Curtis Brown files were undated typescripts with no indication of where they were written. McDonald was eager to pin them down. Naturally he thought of turning for help to Mrs. Lawrence, whom he had met under happy circumstances in New York in 1925. But the publishers ordered, "Don't go to Frieda, we're having trouble with her," McDonald recalled in Salisbury, Connecticut, in February 1972, five years before his death. Because McDonald believed a man should abide by the wishes of his employer, he didn't contact her. When I asked why the publishers were against his consulting the novelist's widow, he said, "Probably Frieda wanted more money."

Consequently McDonald never learned of the existence of "Record," which proved that four of Lawrence's five unpublished pieces were Oaxaca products. Nor did he see Frieda's evidence that the fifth was also written in Oaxaca. He never identified them with the city, and ironically did not know what he was doing in Oaxaca's behalf when he published them. But because of the Lawrence letter already quoted—the one about "camping" on the Padre's veranda—McDonald was fully conscious that his first Lawrence bibliography was part of the Oaxaca winter.

As Lawrence's preface for Mollie Skinner shows, by the time he came to Oaxaca he was well aware of journalistic reviews of his individual works and had nothing but scorn for the "sewerage outlets of popular criticism." Seligmann's brief *American Interpretation* was the only book that had been written about him, which explains why he was bewildered when McDonald first approached him. Lawrence's Oaxaca letter to his bibliographer also gives instances of the sort of help the novelist provided, such as the color of the binding of the first edition of *Movements in European History* (Lawrence's history written under the pseudonym, Lawrence H. Davidson, that McDonald had overlooked) and the source of the Hiroshige print that appeared on the cover of *Tortoises*.

The letter refers to the introduction that Lawrence had written for McDonald two months earlier, and which was the second piece in "Record." That introduction explains why in the letter Lawrence speaks so bitterly of two of his early English publishers. William Heinemann, who published *The White Peacock,* had treated its two successors badly—accepting *The Trespasser* but denigrating it, and rejecting *Sons and Lovers* outright: "William Heinemann [according to Lawrence's introduction] said he thought *Sons and Lovers* one of the dirtiest books he had ever read. He refused to publish it. I should not have thought the deceased gentleman's reading had been so circumspectly narrow."

Sir Algernon Methuen, who was made a baronet in 1916, was Lawrence's other target in the letter. The gossip he passed on to McDonald about Sir Algernon was private retaliation added to the public retaliation in the introduction. What Lawrence held against Methuen were his actions when *The Rainbow,* which Methuen had published, was suppressed in 1915. Said the introduction: "Then came the first edition of *The Rainbow.* I'm afraid I set my rainbow in the sky too soon, before, instead of after the deluge. Methuen published that book, and he almost wept before the magistrate, when he was summoned for bringing out a piece of indecent literature. He said he did not know the dirty thing he had been handling, he had not read the work, his reader had misadvised him—and *Peccavi! Peccavi!* wept the now be-knighted gentleman."

Seltzer, who, in contrast, had defended the Lawrence novel he had published, was therefore not the only publisher on Lawrence's mind in Oaxaca. The McDonald letter shows he was still smarting from treatment by Heinemann and Methuen; and the preface for Miss Skinner shows he also thought of Gerald Duckworth, to whom he shifted because of Garnett and whom he left when he no longer saw eye-to-eye with Garnett.

The malicious glee in the letter to McDonald from Oaxaca illustrates the extent to which the bibliography's compiling was an adventure Lawrence enjoyed from start to finish.

"It is nice to have a bit of grateful recognition, whatever one may say," Lawrence wrote to Else Jaffe two years later. Just how seriously grateful Lawrence was for McDonald's bibliography was tangibly demonstrated in August 1926 when McDonald visited England. Lawrence was staying with his sister Ada in Lincolnshire while McDonald was in London, so they did not see each other. But McDonald did see Frieda in a studio-flat in Rossetti Mansions in Chelsea. He recalls that Aldous Huxley had left just before his arrival; that Frieda described the studio, which looked over roofs, as "a pretty poor show"; and that she was jubilant over the fact that, not long before, Lawrence and her finally reconciled son, Montague Weekley, had met and liked each other. "They were like two kittens together," McDonald remembered Frieda saying. Shortly after McDonald's visit, Frieda did something that she and Lawrence must have planned together. She came to McDonald's hotel with a package, and when she found he was not in, left it with the desk attendant, accompanied by a note saying it would be "safer with you than with us." When McDonald opened the package, he found about half the manuscript of *Women in Love,* including a sequence of chapters written in pencil in nine exercise books of the size Lawrence had in Mexico.

CHAPTER 10

"NOAH'S FLOOD"
AND
MORE LETTERS

"NOAH'S FLOOD"

"**N**oah's Flood" was the third Oaxaca piece that McDonald published in *Phoenix* without realizing its place of origin. Discovering that this start of an ambitious play also belonged to my territory was another of the strikes of the bonanza day when I first saw "Record" at Austin. But I did not read through the manuscript then. Time was short and I counted on having McDonald's text to study. When I turned to it, however, it baffled me. The scene's position in the copybook—immediately following the essay on the soul—showed it must have been written towards the end of the Oaxaca stay. The great white bird sustaining the sun echoed the sun-behind-the-sun cosmology of *The Plumed Serpent,* but nothing else indicated what prompted the writing. McDonald said only that the unfinished play was "comparatively negligible" and that it had never been published before. This meant that I had to start using my own resources to make the Oaxaca connection.

The scene that McDonald published was apparently all of the play that Lawrence wrote, for no more is given in the 1966 Viking edition of *The Complete Plays of D. H. Lawrence.* There is no explicit reference to the flood, only a hint of some imminent meteorological change as the days get colder and the sun seems to be sick, merely limping across the gray dust of the sky each day. McDonald notwithstanding, it opens with great promise when three sons of men conspire to steal the Red Flutterer, the marvelous scarlet chicken owned by the demi-gods, Noah and his sons. One of the conspirators has heard it called Fire. Fire, "which hatches the pale dough into bread," is the one Noah-secret the sons of men do not possess. With the sun apparently failing, its possession seems all the more desirable. With it, the conspirators feel they will be able to kill the demi-gods and become free. Frustratingly, the scene ends with Noah's entrance.

Besides the conspirators, Noah and his three sons, Shem, Ham, and Japhet, the *dramatis personae,* show that Lawrence planned to introduce three other characters, all promising interest: Kanah (the Echoer; it was, it shall be), Shelah (Flux) and Cosby (female-male: Kulturtrager ["upholder of civilization"]). Did Lawrence create them or draw them from some obscure mythology? What part were they to take in the action? And why should Lawrence want to write it in Oaxaca? It seemed unrelated to anything that happened to him there or to anything else he wrote in the city. Being in the biblical vein might have linked it to "Resurrection," but the connection seemed tenuous. They were unlike in thought, and "Resurrection" grew out of the New Testament.

Months later as I was shaving, I remembered a passage in *The Plumed Serpent* describing men in the days before the flood. Perhaps it held a clue? Eagerly I sought it out. It was in the penultimate chapter and gave hope that I was on the right track. But only after I had checked a number of intervening facts did it prove conclusive.

The passage is in still another of Kate's debates with herself about whether to stay in Mexico, an odd passage that suddenly introduces a note not previously sounded in the novel: not the world of pre-Columbian gods, but of "the old prehistoric humanity, the dark-eyed humanity of the days perhaps, before the glacial period." The description was much more intelligible than it had been in any previous readings, since I had, in the meantime, come upon Lawrence's introduction to his *Fantasia of the Unconscious.*

In that introduction, written a year before he had visited North America, he boldly names Atlantis, along with Asia and Europe, as one of the geographical areas of the world, saying that the Azores are the only part of it now showing above the sea. With equal assurance he named another huge drowned land area, "the Polynesian continent," of which only the Easter Isles and the Marquesas remain. Instead of accepting the commonly held view that men developed slowly from crude beginnings during the last great glacial period, he makes other assumptions common to believers in Atlantis and cites them as historical facts: that highly civilized men existed before the Pleistocene Epoch. World travelers could pass easily from one continent to another because the sea basins were comparatively dry. The waters of the earth were held in glaciers.

"Then came the melting of the glaciers," continues the introduction, "and the world flood. The refugees from the drowned continents fled to the high places of America, Europe, Asia and the Pacific Isles." Most forgot the universal culture of the pre-flood world. But some, "like Druids or Etruscans, or Chaldeans or AmerIndians or Chinese, refused to forget, but taught the old wisdom, only in half-forgotten, symbolic forms."

The parallels between these ideas and those Lawrence set stirring in Kate's mind reveal that Kate believed in Atlantis, too, reinforcing the other factors tugging her to stay in Mexico. Irish, she feels an affinity for the Mexicans, other survivors of the "mysterious, hot-blooded, soft-footed humanity" of the pre-flood culture.

> Sometimes in America [says the novel] the shadow of that old pre-flood world was so strong, that the day of historic humanity would melt out of Kate's consciousness, and she would begin to approximate to the old mode of consciousness, the old dark will, the unconcern for death, the subtle, dark consciousness, non-cerebral, but vertebrate. When the mind and the power of man was in his blood and his backbone and there was the strange, dark intercommunication between man and man and man and beast, from the powerful spine.
>
> The Mexicans were still this. That which is aboriginal in America still belongs to the way of the world before the Flood, before the mental-spiritual world came into being. . . . Kate was more Irish than anything, and the almost deathly mysticism of the aboriginal Celtic or Iberian people lay at the bottom of her soul. It was a residue of memory, something that lives on from the pre-flood world, and cannot be killed. Something older, and more everlastingly potent, than our would-be fair-and-square world.

This section of the novel, then, revealed that Lawrence was thinking about a world flood while he was in Oaxaca, but it was the flood that destroyed Atlantis. Did he believe that Noah's flood was a legend of the flood that destroyed Atlantis preserved in Jewish mythology while Plato's story preserved it in Greek? Possibly. The first similarity between the play and Kate's musing was the coldness. In the play it had been growing steadily worse. "Even in the daytime shivers seize us, since the sun has moulted his rays," says the most militant of the conspirators. "When the world was colder, and the seas emptier, and all the land-formation was different" are leading conditions envisaged by Kate. And then she added, "When the waters of the world were piled in stupendous glaciers on the high places, and high, high upon the poles. . . ." In the play, the militant conspirator envisions using fire to "unleash the waters from the ice."

I found the clinching connection in *Birds, Beasts and Flowers.* "Grapes," a poem written in September 1920 in San Gervasio, Italy, muses about "the world before the floods" where men were "soft-footed and pristine." And although Atlantis is not named, that world existed:

> Before the glaciers were gathered up in a bunch out of the
> unsettled seas and winds,
> Or else before they had been let down again, in Noah's flood.

Clearly, the flood of Lawrence's play had little connection with God intending to destroy the wicked men by prolonged rain. Even though Lawrence planned to borrow characters from the Bible, he was imagining not the world of Genesis, but the world of Atlantis.

A textual question pertinent to Oaxaca was this: Were Kate's musings on Atlantis composed at Chapala and recopied verbatim in Oaxaca? My four days at Harvard's Houghton making notes about its typescript of the first version of *The Plumed Serpent* showed definitely that the Atlantis section was new. Thus, it was in Oaxaca that a great flood was on Lawrence's mind. And here the discoveries made through studying the different pieces provoked by Tolstoy's *Resurrection* came to my aid. Knowing how a single stimulus often gave Lawrence parallel inspirations, I found it entirely possible that imagining Atlantis before the flood that destroyed it could give him the idea for a play about Noah. Having learned, too, how he generally acted promptly on his literary ideas, I could envision how, despite his pressing deadline on the novel, he immediately began the play. Was there any evidence that Kate's Atlantean musings and the start of the play were written at the same time?

The combination of Lawrence's letters to friends and the position of "Noah's Flood" in "Record" provided that evidence. On January 29 Lawrence wrote Secker, "I have finished *Quetzalcoatl,* or at least am in the last chapter." So by January 29 he had gone beyond the penultimate chapter, "Kate Is a Wife." The "Noah's Flood" scene was written sometime after "See Mexico After" was posted to Quintanilla (January 12). Both "Flood" and the musings, then, fall assuredly between January 12 and 29, with a strong probability that the time between them was considerably less than seventeen days. It is regrettable that Lawrence never had the will to finish a play that must have been clearly outlined in his mind.

Even though I had solved most of my puzzle, I was haunted by the unfinished play. What would have come of the sons of men's attempt to steal fire from Noah? The Bible provided a clue for the ending. The Noah story ends with the rainbow. But would Lawrence have the rainbow play the same optimistic role in the drama as it did in his novel, *The Rainbow?* Was Noah, like Ursula at the end of the novel, going to see "in the rainbow the earth's new architecture, the old brittle corruption of houses and factories swept away, the world built up in a living fabric of Truth, fitting to the over-arching heaven"? It is an intriguing question. Intriguing, too, are the roles of those nonbiblical characters.

After I had abandoned all hope of learning anything more about "Noah's Flood," I was in San Antonio's beautiful new public library on the banks of the river, once again looking into Tedlock's book on the manuscripts formerly owned by Frieda. I hoped to find some nuggets I might have missed earlier in the New York Public Library and was mortified to discover a section which I had totally overlooked. It included a discussion of *two* manuscripts of "Noah's Flood." One, in a copybook Lawrence bought in Florence in the spring of 1928, showed that he had not completely abandoned the play, for in Italy he made a fair copy in ink of the scene that three years before he had written in pencil in Oaxaca. It was the ink version, according to Tedlock, that McDonald published. The penciled manuscript was the one I had glimpsed in "Record." It contained a second scene. Tedlock, too, furnished another clue I could follow in Austin about why Lawrence had the urge to write a play in Oaxaca.

Lois Garcia, the librarian in Austin, brought me "Record" and immediately I turned to page 133. In this version Lawrence provided more information about the characters he envisaged. The copybook had the names thought of first for the three mysterious characters. Rhea, one of the names crossed out, was clearly a woman's name, showing that Shelah (which I had not recognized as a variant of Sheila) was to be a woman, and therefore linked to Ham, not just because he represented Heat and she Flux, but because she was his wife. Kenah's discarded names were Phoebe and Achsah, the latter the given name of Lawrence's friend, Mrs. Brewster. So Kanah was also to be a woman, and besides being the Echoer of Shem, she was to be married to him. The first name contemplated for Cosby was Lilith, making her a woman too, one mythologically linked to sexual temptation. The further description of Japhet as the "male-female," in contrast to Cosby, the "female-male," indicated that Cosby, who in the additional scene is dragged in as an outsider, was to become Japhet's wife.

The androgynous Japhet, in the fuller description, is also the "father of fire, the injurer," in addition to "encompassing, spreading, Father of all: also Destroyer." And Shem's descriptive tag, "The Utterer," because of Lawrence's amplified use of the term in "Education of People," shows Shem was meant to be the great man in the hierarchy of souls, "the perfect utterer" at the summit of the populace. With such men married to such women, Lawrence's ark gave promise of being lively indeed. Surely he envisioned a collision of magnificent speech from the Destroyer and the Utterer. Noah was not to be a strong controlling factor. Lawrence had written, then stroked through "rather faint-hearted" in his description of Noah, but it was in the back of his mind for his figure of "Cronos, father." The drama was thus ambitious, perhaps too ambitious, in fact, to complete.

When Noah, wearing a black and white robe, comes upon the conspirators in the second scene, he asked, "The women are sweeping the fern-seed for bread, what are the men about?" The third man replies "The Men are cold, my lord." They tell Noah they were talking about the bird,

Fire. All are summoned to a counsel by the blowing of a conch shell, and Noah takes his place under a tree. The sons enter. Shem, the Utterer, is in yellow, Japhet, the Destroyer, is in blue and white, and dark Ham, the personification of Heat, is in red. Noah is distressed by adultery among the sons of men. A strange woman is brought in, Cosby. The sons of men are angry with her because she will not take up with them. "I am weary of the world of men," she tells Noah. She seeks the Sons of God, of whom Noah is the last. Noah's people want the gods to go but leave them the red bird. "I cannot open my hand, Son of man," says Noah, "till the Great One breathes on it. And even if I give you the gift of fire, think you can live by it forever?" The unfinished scene ends with Noah's prophecy that once men obtain fire "you will drown it in blood, and quench it in tears."

Tedlock's lead about why Lawrence began a play in Oaxaca took me back to Mrs. Luhan's *Lorenzo in Taos*. There I found she had liked "Altitude," the unfinished comedy about her guests straggling into her kitchen for breakfast that Lawrence started before leaving for Oaxaca, and had urged him to return to playwriting seriously. The Lawrence letter Tedlock referred to showed him favorable to the project. If he got an idea, he intended to write a play in Oaxaca. The letter, written 29 October 1924, a week after his arrival in Mexico City, said: "Don't talk to me about plays, the very word makes me swear. At the minute there's not a play-word in me, & I'd rather be in New Mexico. If we don't like Oaxaca, we shall probably toddle back. . . . If I can sit still in Oaxaca, I shall probably pull off a play. But *Quien Sabe!*"

When this was written, a scorching letter from Mrs. Luhan was on its way. She wrote it on the train headed for New York, telling Lawrence she was cutting him from her life. Thus, his playwriting came because the impulse was strong, not because he wanted to please Mabel. The force of the impulse is measured by the fact that when he recovered his strength in the summer after leaving Oaxaca he wrote a whole play, *David,* telling of Saul's hatred for the Lord's Anointed after the slaying of Goliath, of Jonathan's friendship, and of David's exile to await the coming of his day. Clearly he continued to be haunted by the appeal and challenge of a pageant-like drama based on the Old Testament.

Because it was in Oaxaca that Lawrence turned back to the theater, it is worth noting that the theater was always more important to him than is commonly recognized. Indeed, his novels and short stories are so much better known than his plays that many never think of Lawrence as a playwright at all. But his first work for the stage, "A Collier's Friday Night," was written while he was still a schoolmaster at Croydon. Before he gave up teaching, he had finished *The Widowing of Mrs. Holroyd* and "The Merry-go-Round." In the 1912-14 period, besides revising *The Widowing,* he wrote three more, *The Married Man, The Daughter-in-law,* and

The Fight for Barbara. He returned to playwriting in 1920 with *Touch and Go,* which, like its predecessors, had a modern setting. Between this and "Noah's Flood" there is only "Altitude," the skit about Mrs. Luhan's friends in Taos. So "Noah's Flood" awakened an old impulse that continued with *David* and the revising of *The Married Man.* In all, then, Lawrence wrote eight full-length plays. The fact that its realistic forerunners had not been more successful must have weighed on him as he began "Noah's Flood." Perhaps, too, it was lack of success in the commercial theater that turned his hopes to poetic drama in the classical tradition.[1]

''CLIMBING DOWN PISGAH''

The piece crowded into the last pages of "Record," "Climbing Down Pisgah," brought still another article written in Oaxaca to my attention. Published in McDonald's *Phoenix,* it was even more baffling than "Noah's Flood." The use of *tampoco* ("not that either"), and the vision of "the demon of the beginning," first a great taloned bird, then a serpent coiled to strike, were the only elements that connected it with Mexico. The essay was clearly not a travel piece and its many non sequiturs made it almost unintelligible. Only when I came to understand three keys did its mysteries start yielding.

Why did Lawrence write it in Oaxaca? The key that helped with this was learning how Lawrence often composed. His own account is to be found in "Trees and Babies and Papas and Mamas," in *Fantasia of the Unconscious.* Picturing what happened to him on a particular morning when he planned to write about babies, he recalled: "I come out solemnly with a pencil and an exercise book, and take my seat in all gravity at the foot of a large fir-tree, and wait for thoughts to come, gnawing like a squirrel on a nut. But the nut's hollow. I think there are too many trees. . . . And they won't let me get on about the baby this morning."

So instead he writes about the trees. In other words, he sometimes succumbed to writing about unanticipated things. Dorothy Brett in her *South Dakota Review* autobiographical fragment helps complete the picture: "Once I asked him whether he planned his stories, knew what he was going to write." He said, "Up to a certain point, I have an outline, but then I don't know: it seems to come down to me from the air."

When this occasional unexpectedness of his writing is coordinated with the facts of his life in Oaxaca towards the end of January, the opening of "Climbing Down Pisgah" ceases to be puzzling. It is straight autobiography arising out of the frenzied activity of starting an ambitious play before having finished a major novel, and then going on to write still another essay. This is how it begins: "Sometimes one pulls oneself up short, and asks: 'What am I doing this for?' One writes novels, stories, essays: and then suddenly: 'What on earth am I doing it for?' "

Later he isolates his own chief imperative for writing: "Probably it is the sense of adventure, to start with. Life is no fun for a man, without an adventure." He weighs and discards other reasons for writing. The first was "for the sake of humanity," and though he never really dismissed it in practice, he disclaims it contemptuously in the essay: "Pfui!" he says, echoing his misanthropy of the period. "The very words *human, humanity, humanism* make me sick. For the sake of humanity as such, I wouldn't lift a little finger, much less write a story."

"For the sake of the Spirit" is the second imperative he considers. "*Tampoco!*" he replies in good Mexican fashion. "But what do we mean by the Spirit? Let us be careful. Do we mean that One Universal Intelligence of which every man has his modicum? Or further, that one Cosmic Soul, or Spirit, of which every individual is a broken fragment, and towards which every individual strives back, to escape the raw edges of his own fragmentariness, and to experience once more the sense of wholeness?"

The distinctions between Intelligence, Spirit, and Soul parallel the preoccupations of "Man Is Essentially a Soul." And in the phrase, "the raw edges of his own fragmentariness," one can hear overtones of his feelings after the struggle between Frieda and Brett had left him feeling painfully detached from both. It is another echo of Birkin's anguished cry in *Women in Love:* "And why? Why should we consider ourselves, men and women, as broken fragments of one whole?"

The issue of wholeness led Lawrence to the third reason, which he weighed more carefully.

> Does one write books in order to give one's fellow-men a sense of wholeness: first, a oneness with all men, then a oneness with all things; then a oneness with our cosmos, and finally a oneness with the vast invisible universe? Is that it? Is that our achievement and our peace?
>
> Anyhow, it would be a great achievement. And this has been the aim of the great ones. It was the aim of Whitman, for example.

A lengthy denunciation of "oneness" follows, for a long time almost incomprehensible. The problem was another instance of a difficulty that Lawrence's nonfiction often poses: presupposing that the reader has more information than he or she in fact possesses. He assumes the reader's knowledge of his life, of his other writings, and of his allusions. Nowhere, for example, does he explain what happened on Pisgah to make it a mountain of symbolic significance: that from its summit Moses viewed the Promised Land he could not enter.

The essay made me alert to Lawrence's views on oneness. He had begun exploring the theme as early as "The Crown," the six-part essay he wrote for *The Signature,* the ill-fated publication that he and Murry began in 1915 to take action against World War I. There he characterizes preachers of two types of oneness: those "adhering to one eternity of darkness" who advocate oneness with the Source, and those who advocate oneness with "the opposite eternity," the Goal. He denounced them both, claiming they deny the dualism of existence.

The next year, when *Twilight in Italy* was published, Lawrence's visit to his landlord's lemon gardens forms the setting for a discussion of two eternities which have become the two Infinites:

> It is past the time to cease seeking one Infinite, ignoring, striving to eliminate the other. The Infinite is two fold, the Father and the Son, the Dark and the Light, the Senses and the Mind, the Soul and the Spirit, the self and the not-self, the Eagle and the Dove, the Tiger and the Lamb. The consummation of man is two fold, in the Self and in Selflessness. By great retrogression back to the source of darkness in me, the Self, deep in the senses, I arrive at the Original, Creative Infinite. By projection forth from myself, by the elimination of my absolute sensual self, I arrive at the Ultimate Infinite, Oneness in the Spirit. They are two Infinites, two fold approaches to God. And man must know both.

To this second infinite, "Oneness of the Spirit," Lawrence was most antagonistic. In speaking of the Spirit and the Soul as opposites, Lawrence reveals that he saw the spirit as related essentially to the intelligence. Man, he felt, besides knowing both Infinites, must know the relation between them. In *The Signature* essay he chose the crown between the lion and the unicorn on the British coat of arms as the symbol for the relationship. In "The Lemon Gardens" essay he chooses the Holy Ghost; adding, "And it is this, the relation which is established between the two Infinites, the two natures of God, which we have transgressed." Wholeness thus included the two Infinites and the relationship between them. If one infinite was excluded, so was wholeness.

In "Education of the People," Lawrence criticizes the "One—and-Allness" claimed for the mental consciousness; and *Studies of Classic American Literature* attacks Edgar Allen Poe and Walt Whitman as examples of deplorable insistence on different kinds of oneness. A fifth denunciation of oneness came three months before Lawrence left for Oaxaca. On 4 July 1924, in his first letter to Rolf Gardiner, he must have staggered the then-unknown fan who wrote him from the blue, by starting his third paragraph so vehemently: "Myself, I am sick of the farce of cosmic unity, or world unity," he wrote. "It may exist in the abstract—but not elsewhere." Then he went on:

To tell the truth, I am sick to death of the Jewish monotheistic string. It has become monomaniac. I prefer the pagan many gods and the animistic vision. . . . I have known many things that may never be unified. . . . To me, chaos doesn't matter so much as abstract, which is mechanical, order. To me it is life to feel the white ideas and the "oneness" crumbling into a thousand pieces, and all sorts of wonder coming through. . . . I hate "oneness," it's a mania.

Lawrence's attitudes toward oneness provided the second key to "Climbing Down Pisgah." Because Lawrence hated preachers of single panaceas and was deeply aware of the diversity of the universe, a factor in making him reject evolution, dislike of oneness was increasingly smoldering in his thought. In "Man Is Essentially a Soul," he states: "There is no absolute Word or Logos. Neither is there any One Way." Thus, the matter was on his mind in Oaxaca too. Not surprisingly when he began to write in an undirected manner, his unconscious brought this subject down "from the air."

Pisgah, I found, was another theme that had haunted him for years, probably from his childhood attending the Congregational chapel in Eastwood, where he heard of Pisgah, the level summit of Mount Nebo, the mountain before Jericho on which Moses died, in sight of Canaan, the Promised Land. The article itself confirms this hypothesis by quoting the children's hymn, "Fair waved the golden corn in Canaan's pleasant land" that was one of the nonconformist hymns that he loved most as a boy according to his confession in "Hymns in a Man's Life." "Climbing Down Pisgah," then, though not written in the biblical style of "Resurrection" and "Noah's Flood," was further evidence that Lawrence's religious background came surging to the surface in Oaxaca.

Pisgah appears as the title of a chapter in his first novel, *The White Peacock*. The allusion is unexplained, and neither Moses nor Canaan is mentioned. But the way George parts from Lettie reveals that Lawrence was using the mountain as a term for a lookout point where one comes to a parting of the ways. The Pisgah metaphor is also implicit in the title of the ensuing chapter, "The Scarp Slope," for Lawrence's interest in Nebo led him to grasp its geographical reality, its cliff-like western slope immediately overlooking the desolation of the Jordan basin and the Dead Sea. In his Oaxaca essay, he exploits the fact that the slope down from Pisgah is much more precipitous than the slope to the ascent. The essay quotes another of the nonconformist hymns of Lawrence's youth:

They climbed the steep ascent of heaven
Through peril toil and pain:
O God to us may grace be given
To scramble down again.

The fourth line is a boyish parody of the hymn's hortatory fourth line: "To follow in their [the martyrs'] train."

In "Craving for Spring," a poem written either in 1916 or 1917 in Cornwall, Lawrence, recognizing the full promise embodied in the opening of violets, cried out, "Pray not to die on this Pisgah blossoming with violets." But, perhaps significantly for his Oaxaca thinking, he made fullest use of Pisgah as a metaphor in *Fantasia of the Unconscious* where he outlined his Atlantis ideas. There he dramatizes the plight of those caught on Pisgah. Speaking for himself, he says:

> We refuse any *Cause,* whether it be Sex or Libido or Elan Vital or ether or unit of force or *perpetuum mobile* or anything else. But also we feel that we cannot, like Moses, perish on the top of our present ideal Pisgah, or take the next step into thin air. . . . The promised land, if it be anywhere, lies away beneath our feet. Idealism and materialism amount to the same thing on top of Pisgah, and the space is very crowded. We're all cornered on our mountain top. . . .
>
> The Moses of Science and the Aaron of Idealism have got the whole bunch of us here on top of Pisgah. It's a tight squeeze, and we'll be falling very, very foul of one another in five minutes, unless some of us climb down.

Then he lampoons many types of reformers by singling out the various promised lands they say they can see that he can't, including "the home of successful Analysis, surnamed Psycho." Instead of searching for them further, he said, "I'm going to sit down on my posterior and slither full speed down this Pisgah, even if it cost me my trouser seat. So ho! Away we go."

His verbal play with the metaphor goes on for several high-spirited pages, and when he exhorts—"To your tents, O Israel! Brethren, let us go down. We will descend. The way to our Canaan lies obviously downhill. An end of uplift."—one realizes he sees the descent as a leaving of false notions to descend into truth.

There is another reference to Pisgah in the Whitman study where Lawrence comes close to doing what he was finally going to do in Oaxaca: to bring his oneness and Pisgah themes together. But three pages separate his mocking picture of Whitman driving an automobile "along the track of a fixed idea" and his different vision of the Whitman who faced death. In the latter, he says, "Whitman's camp is at the end of the road, and on the edge of a great precipice. Over the precipice, blue distance, and the blue hollow of the future. But there is no way down. It is a dead end. Pisgah. Pisgah sights. And Death. Whitman like a strange, modern American Moses. Fearfully mistaken. And yet the great leader."

Since there are several references to Whitman in "Climbing Down Pisgah," a rereading of the poet in Oaxaca may have been a factor stimulating the essay. However, if this essay was not planned in advance, it is easy to see why his unconscious should have brought him Pisgah from the air, as well as oneness. And there is a strong indication that "Climbing Down Pisgah," like "Noah's Flood," was stirred by Kate's new musings about staying in Mexico. Shortly after she sees the need for a new connection between the blood of white Europeans with the blood of the survivors of the pre-flood world, she comes to a new vision of Don Ramón's movement. "Now she understood Ramón's assertion: Man is a column of blood: Woman is a valley of blood. It was the primeval oneness of mankind, the opposite of the oneness of the spirit." So again we see a single stimulus stirring Lawrence's mind to work in two directions at the same time, for as Kate gets a better idea of oneness of the spirit by gaining a vision of its opposite, Lawrence writes a new essay on this particular oneness that he deplored for excluding sensual oneness with the dark source.

In this essay, as in the *Fantasia* introduction, Lawrence also speaks of the view from Pisgah. Instead of ridiculing invented "Pisgah-sights," he writes more soberly: "The Pisgah-top of spiritual oneness looks down upon a hopeless squalor of industrialism, the huge cemetery of human hopes. This is our Promised Land." But quickly the mood changes: "Hie, boys, over we go! Pisgah's a fraud, and the Promised Land is Pittsburgh, the Chosen Few, there are billions of 'em, and Canaan smells of kerosene. Let's break our necks if we must, but let's get down, and look over the brink of some other horizon. It's an adventure. And there's only one left, the venture of consciousness."

The rest of the essay recommends the adventure of crawling down the dark side of Pisgah or slipping down on a sore posterior. Old men won't try it, he says, "but young men with hearts still for the life adventure will rise up with their trouser-seats scraped away, after the long slither from the heights down the well-nigh bottomless pit, having changed their minds."

After Lawrence's death, the ribbon copy of this piece was located in the New York office of Curtis Brown and the carbon copy in the agent's London office; neither office had found a magazine to print it. One is not surprised. But once the connection of the essay with Lawrence's earlier sounding of its themes is demonstrated, it emerges as a significant record of the movement of his thought. As such it may be the most important of the essays not previously indentified with Oaxaca. Certainly it illustrates an aspect of Lawrence that is commonly overlooked. Many have seen that Lawrence was a prophet as well as an artist; but, because a good deal of scorn has been poured on his logic, few older critics have acknowledged that once he hit his stride with *Sons and Lovers,* Lawrence was a thinker and a creator simultaneously. Until Lawrence the thinker is recognized more clearly, the man, I feel, will never be seen in his true fullness. And "Climbing Down Pisgah," his final theoretical piece written in Oaxaca, besides giving new evidence of how active was the thinking Lawrence, shows with what eagerness and courage he was ready to push into unexplored areas.

A LECTURE ON "HALFNESS"

In Mexico City, Brett stayed at the Hotel Isabel, around the corner from the noble Augustinian church that is now the National Library. Miss Hughes recalled she had a room overlooking the street on the fourth or fifth floor. "Her favorite spot," Miss Hughes wrote, "was on the wide window ledge, her back against the side of the window, where she looked out on the city's tiled domes, and had quite a view, and could watch pedestrians below. Now and then someone spied her up there, and became concerned she would fall." Despite her elevated viewpoint, Brett must have painted a dismal picture of the capital in her first letter back to Lawrence, which arrived in Oaxaca on Monday, January 26, exactly a week after she left. "If Mexico City is so unpleasant," replied Lawrence, "we shall probably stay here an extra week or fortnight, and go straight to Vera Cruz. I don't like the sound of it."

Besides enclosing a letter Murry had written her, Brett's letter must have contained a statement of her feelings for Lawrence, for he quotes what she said about "delicate friendship." And one can guess at her words from those she wrote in the *South Dakota Review:* "There was no crush in that sense of the word—it was a far deeper, more delicate, remote attachment. Lawrence knew this. But Frieda's colossal femaleness bitterly hated my lack of femaleness."

Somewhere in her now-lost letter, Brett must have included a reference to Christ. She touched off a landslide of a letter in Lawrence's immediate response. The man referred to as "Toronto" was Frank Prewett, a Canadian poet and protégé of Ottoline Morell, who in August 1919 was a fellow-guest with Brett at Garsington, the Morell estate near Oxford. He was known by his nickname to Koteliansky and W. J. Turner as the letters of Dora Carrington and Mark Gertler show. Maruca, whose marriage without love apparently shocked Brett, was the daughter of Doña María Monros, the proprietress of the Hotel Francia. Brett was a close friend of Katherine Mansfield, and the mentioned friendship with Murry must refer chiefly to the interval between Katherine's death in January 1923, and Murry's second marriage in April 1924, for during this period he continued living next door to Brett, taking his meals with her and enjoying her sympathetic understanding. Captain Seeley sounds like a fellow-guest at the Hotel Isabel, whom the Lawrences and Brett had met in Mexico City before their departure for Oaxaca. William was the thirty-three-year-old son of A. D. Hawk, the owner of the Del Monte Ranch, where the Lawrences had rented cabins during the 1922-23 winter. He and his wife, Rachel, had remained neighbors when the Lawrences returned to New Mexico with Brett the next spring, for Kiowa, the ranch Mrs. Luhan gave Frieda, was less than two miles up the slope from Del Monte. The "good William and Rachel," as Lawrence described them, lived in a log house and ran a small dairy farm on their parents' ranch. Every evening Lawrence and Brett had ridden down to get milk and their mail. Lawrence's counsel to Brett about her attitude to the young Hawkses was pertinent because she would soon be accepting further help and hospitality from them when she got back to New Mexico.

Lawrence's letter is cruel in many ways, and there may be an element of retaliation in it for the emotional distress Brett had caused him. But he was also convinced that he was telling her needed home truths. Easy to discern, too, is that Lawrence told her things in the letter that he held back in Oaxaca.

The letter announces to Brett: "Friendship between a man and a woman, as a thing of first importance to either, is impossible: and I know it. We are creatures of two halves, spiritual and sensual—and each half is as important as the other. Any relation based on the one half—say the delicate spiritual half alone— *inevitably* brings revulsion and betrayal. It is halfness, or partness, which causes Judas."

To bring this home to her, he made it personal:

Your friendship for Murry was spiritual—you dragged sex in and he hated you. He'd have hated you anyhow. The halfness of your friendship I also hate, and between you and me there is no sensual correspondence.

You make a horrid mistake of trying to put your sex into a spiritual relation. Old nuns and saints used to do it, but it soon caused rottenness. Now it is half rotten to start with.

Then he turned to less spiritual cases:

When Maruca *likes* a man and marries him, she is not so wrong. Love is chiefly bunk: an over-exaggeration of the spiritual and individualistic and analytic side. If she likes the man, and he is a man, then better than if she loved him. Each will leave aside some of that hateful *personal* insistence on imaginary perfect satisfaction, which is part of the inevitable bunk of love, and if they meet as mere male and female, *kindly,* in their marriage, they will make roots, not weedy flowers of a love match.

Plate 28. The abandoned city jail in 1971, built by remodeling the former convent of Santa Catalina. In 1976 the turrets and the rest of the Porfirian façade were stripped away and the building was converted into a hotel. Photograph by Ross Parmenter.

Plate 29. The Hall of Columns in the most beautiful of the Palaces of Mitla. José García is beside the first pillar. Donald Miller, the host, is in front of the fourth. Photograph by Brett.

Plate 30. The ford that Lawrence described as follows: "Down the creek, two native boys, little herdsmen, are bathing. . . . The great cattle they are tending slowly plunge through the bushes, coming up-stream. At the place where the path fords the stream, a great ox stoops to drink." Photograph by Ross Parmenter.

Plate 31. "In front of the church is a rocky *plaza* leaking with grass, with water rushing into two big, oblong stone basins." Photograph by Ross Parmenter.

Plate 32. "The great church stands rather ragged, in a dense forlornness, for all the world like some big white human being, in rags, held captive in a world of ants." Photograph by Ross Parmenter.

Plate 33. Luis Quintanilla at the time of the Lawrence visit.

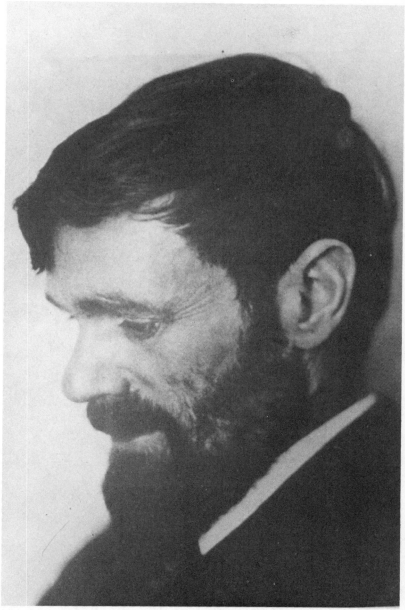

Plate 34. Edward Weston took this photograph of Lawrence in Mexico City on 2 November 1924. Lawrence received two poses in Oaxaca and returned this autographed copy to Quintanilla. © 1981 Arizona Board of Regents, Center for Creative Photography, Tucson, Arizona.

Plate 35. A photograph of the Mitla excursion that Lawrence sent to Quintanilla. Ambrosio Quero is the guide showing Lawrence and Frieda a room of mosaics. José García, a fellow guest, looks at the camera. Photograph by Brett.

Plate 36. Self-portrait of Dorothy Brett
painted in 1922 at Garsington, Lady Ottoline
Morrell's home near Oxford. Lawrence
described the portrait in "The Last Laugh,"
a short story whose heroine is modeled on
Brett.

Plate 37. Frieda Lawrence as sketched in New Mexico by George Schreiber. The original drawing is in the possession of the Humanities Research Center Library of the University of Texas at Austin and is reproduced with its permission.

Plate 38. Frieda looks over Lawrence's shoulder as he crouches to examine un-fired vessels drying in the sun in the patio of the Alfarería Jiménez. The potter with the wide belt in the rear is Juan Toboada. The pottery, about six blocks away from the Lawrences' hotel, is now operated by the third generation of the founding family. Photograph by Brett.

Plate 39. The personnel of the Jiménez pottery visited by D. H. and Frieda Lawrence. Left: Juan Toboada, Armando Ramos, Catalina Jiménez, Ignacio Jiménez, Eliseo Lara, Manuel Caballero, Guillermo Lara, and Geronimo Contreras. Catalina was the nine-year-old sister of Ignacio Jiménez, who had inherited the pottery three years earlier following the death of his father, Apolinar Jiménez, its founder. Photograph by Rosalind Hughes.

Plate 40. Taken in front of "La Sorpresa," the store and inn at Mitla where the Lawrences had lunch. The inn still exists with the same name, but the space occupied by the store is now occupied by a museum of Zapotec and Mixtec art. Lawrence is in the Panama hat behind the second ox-cart. The man in the fedora is José García. Photograph by Brett.

Plate 41. Though taken with Brett's camera, this photograph must have been snapped by Donald Miller, the host for the excursion to Mitla. His guests, standing in front of one of the monolithic pillars in the Hall of Columns, are, left, José García, Lawrence, Brett, and Frieda Lawrence. The boy in the background is carrying what looks like the case for Brett's camera.

Plate 42. The image of the Virgin of Solitude, Oaxaca's patron saint.

Plate 43. Lawrence at the festival of Soledad, 18 December 1924. The woman in mourning beside him is Doña María Jarquin de Monros, the proprietess of the Hotel Francia. Ramón Allenta, like her a Catalan, often visited the hotel. Photograph by Brett.

Plate 44. Lawrence and Frieda (on the other side of the ice cream freezers) visiting the church of Soledad during the fiesta of its patron virgin. The steps behind them lead up to the atrium and the side door. Photograph by Brett.

Plate 45. Lawrence holds his Stetson in front of a fence of organ cacti. Photograph by Brett.

Plate 46. Eduardo Rendón, an English-educated Mexican, photographed with Lawrence in the Borda Gardens in Cuernavaca by their mutual friend George R. G. Conway.

Plate 47. Dorothy Brett's pencil portrait of John Middleton Murry, a friend of both Brett and Lawrence.

Plate 48. Manuel Gamio, Mexican archaeologist, who discovered the Quetzalcoatl heads Lawrence saw at Teotihuacán and inspired *The Plumed Serpent*'s Don Ramón. Photograph by Ernest Gruening.

Plate 49. Dr. José E. Larumbe, the well-educated Mexican doctor who attended Lawrence in Oaxaca.

In her *South Dakota Review* memoir Brett wrote, "Marriage is something I have never liked or wanted." And since she was already forty-one when she was in Oaxaca, we can be sure she must have said it to Lawrence. The next part of his letter counseled her otherwise.

If ever you can marry a man feeling kindly towards him, and knowing he feels kindly to you, do it, and throw love after Murry. If you can marry in a spirit of kindliness, with the criticism and the ecstasy both sunk in abeyance, do it. As for Toronto, I don't think you have any warm feeling at all for him. I know your Captain Seeley: there is a kind of little warm flame that shakes with life in his blue eyes; and that is more worth having than all the highflown stuff. And he is quite right to leave his door open. Why do you jeer? You're not superior to sex, and you never will be. Only too often you are inferior to it. You like the excitation of sex in the eye, sex in the head. It is an evil and destructive thing. Know from your Captain that a bit of warm flame of life is worth all the spiritualness and delicacy and Christlikeness on this miserable globe.

No, Brett. I do *not* want your friendship, till you have a full relation somewhere, a *kindly* relation of both halves, not *in part,* as all your friendships have been. That which is in part is in itself a betrayal. Your "friendship" for me betrays the essential man and male that I am, and makes me ill. Yes, you make me ill, by dragging at one half at the expense of the other half. And I am so much better now you have gone. I refuse any more of this "delicate friendship" business, because it damages one's wholeness. . . .

So sit under your tree, or by your fire, and try, try, try to get a real kindliness and a wholeness. You were really horrid even with William: and no man forgives it you, even on another man's account. . . . Respect the bit of warm kindliness there is in people, even William and Rachel. And try to be *whole,* not the unreal half thing your brothers hated you for being, and that all men hate you for, even I. Try and recover your wholeness, that is all. *Then* friendship is possible, in the kindliness of one's heart. [P.S.] Remember I think Christ was profoundly, disastrously wrong.

This letter is not as unkind as it seems on first reading. Lawrence's criticism of Brett for "halfness" was not accusing her of insincerity. The wonderful "Parent Love" chapter in *Fantasia of the Unconscious* explains the reference, revealing Lawrence as a lay analyst trying to tell Brett the cause of her neurosis, and suggesting how it might be overcome. Since *Fantasia* was published two years earlier, he was lecturing her according to his own text, not so much fulminating against her personally as deploring all people blocked from certain aspects of their own nature in the way he felt she was.

In "Parent Love," Lawrence describes the upper and lower centers of human beings. The upper or "sympathetic" ones are located in the breast, the throat, and the mind, all organs above the diaphragm. They are, he says, the "centers of dynamic cognition." The "voluntary centers," those of "sensual comprehension," are in organs below the diaphragm, and these include the powerful centers of sex. If an individual's lower centers are not polarized with the lower centers of another, they will become strongly polarized to his/her own upper centers and the individual will begin to suffer from what Lawrence called "sex in the head." Because of the tendency for centers to polarize, Lawrence held that "the establishment of the upper love-and-cognition circuit inevitably provokes the lower sex-sensual centers into action, even though there is no correspondence on the sensual plane between the two individuals concerned." This, he held, was always disturbing, for an abiding relationship between individuals depended on a full dynamic communication at *both* the lower and the higher centers.

He was troubled by the distorting insistence that "for the first twelve years the parents and the whole [British] community forcibly insist on the child's living from the upper centers only, and particularly the upper sympathetic centers, without the balance of the warm, deep sensual self." Furthermore, this imbalance is increased in adulthood by idealism, particularly "the idealism of love and of the spirit: the idealism of yearning, outgoing love, of pure sympathetic communion and 'understanding.' It is time to drop the word love, and more than time to drop the ideal of love. Every frenzied individual is told to find fulfillment in love. So he tries. Whereas there is no fulfillment in love. Half of our fulfillment comes *through* love, through strong, sensual love. But the central fulfillment for a man is that he possess his own soul in strength within him, deep and alone."

As Lawrence was writing, another letter from Brett was on its way, enclosing another letter from Murry, and asking about her ear machine. Apparently she still had not received the bill and Rickards's intervention had been too late to circumvent the Vera Cruz repairers from sending the machine to Oaxaca. It arrived in a huge crate after Brett left and Lawrence had reshipped it to Mexico. He answered on Wednesday before she had time to reply to his long Monday letter.

> Dear Brett: Don't send me any more Murry letters. The smell of that London stink I want no more in my nostrils. I have written Murry also to that effect.
>
> I will write to the Drake man at Vera Cruz about that machine; though it does bore me. The box was sent to you at the Isabel Hotel. You should have it by now. Much best unpack the machine and put it in your trunk.

> I am tired to death of all the indecencies of intimacies. I want to
> be left alone. There must be a complete new attitude. And till then, si-
> lence about all this stuff.

Brett provided a footnote for this shorter letter when she wrote
me on 5 October 1962, that she received the hearing machine safely before she left Mexico City. And in *Lawrence and Brett* she showed that
she did not bear a grudge for the letter of analysis. When Frieda, Lawrence,
and Brett were together again that summer, new difficulties arose, even
though Brett stayed on the Hawk ranch, rather than on the Lawrences'.
"More and more trouble," she wrote. "One day brings fierce letters from
you; another awkward meetings with Frieda. But," she added, showing
she knew how to take such letters by now, "you are always gentle and
friendly after your angry letters."

THE EXPLOSION AGAINST MURRY

In Oaxaca Lawrence wrote three letters to Middleton Murry. Parts of the
first two have been quoted, and now chronology brings us to the third,
the outburst of 28 January 1925, detonated by the Murry letters Brett
forwarded. Because Lawrence's letter involves not only his relationship
with Murry, but also his friendship with Koteliansky, and the relations
between H. M. Tomlinson, Murry and Koteliansky, it requires considerable explication. When Harry T. Moore wrote Murry asking for help in
untangling his friendship-enmity with Lawrence, Murry answered in a
letter of 16 July 1953: "The truth about the Lawrence-Murry situation
in 1923-1924-1925 is very remote from anything that has appeared, or
is likely to appear in my lifetime." Then he added candidly, "though in
my considered judgment, I don't come out if it (i.e. the true story) any
better." Murry didn't think Lawrence would emerge very creditably either. This view comes in Murry's comment on Lawrence's four stories
featuring Murry as an unpalatable central character: "These, at the time
seemed to me just an outrage. And I still think they sprang from the worst
and most *dishonest* part of L. Considering what the real situation had been,
they strike me as a very shabby sort of revenge."

Murry died in 1957, and since then much of the truth has emerged.
Before turning to the central explosion, however, we need to understand
the role of H. M. Tomlinson.

Tomlinson and Murry became friends in 1917 when both were interested in peace, and working on the *Nation*. Later they shared part
of a house, and Tomlinson was one of the *Adelphi's* guiding spirits and
most frequent contributors. According to F. A. Lea, author of *The Life
of John Middleton Murry*, Tomlinson "remonstrated" with Murry against

the excerpts from Lawrence's *Fantasia of the Unconscious* which were published in the first three numbers of the new magazine. McDonald, the bibliographer-turned-friend, must have queried Lawrence about Tomlinson's opposition, for in Lawrence's reply, written from the ranch on 6 April 1925, he said: "Tomlinson—I saw him last year & he was most amiable—is mad, I suppose because I said the *Adelphi* magazine was slop: Murry's part anyhow. But then Tomlinson is a sort of a failure in himself."

Murry must have mentioned the Tomlinson attack in one of the letters Brett forwarded, for Lawrence wrote: "Please don't defend me to H. M. Tomlinson or to anybody else. As for your Tomlinson, I have seen him for about five minutes: can't imagine why you should have to defend me in his precious eyes."

That Tomlinson's attack still rankled shows in Lawrence's letter to Miss Pearn of the Curtis Brown office, telling her that he was "not so very keen" on letting Murry have "Mornings in Mexico" for the *Adelphi*. But Lawrence did not hold Tomlinson's words permanently against him and favorably reviewed Tomlinson's *Gift of Fortune* in the 1 January 1927 issue of *T. P. & Cassell's Weekly*. After summarizing Tomlinson's sketches of the Amazon, the Malay Straits, and Borneo, Lawrence concluded with words true also of his own writing: "Mr. Tomlinson gives us a new vision, what we might call the planetary instead of the mundane vision. The glimpses are of extreme beauty, so sensitive to the other life of things. And how grateful we ought to be to a man who sets new visions, new feelings sensitively quivering in us."

Lawrence thus proved himself more generous than Tomlinson, for the latter waited until Lawrence was dead before he disclosed what had made him angry the evening he seemed "most amiable." It was not because Lawrence had criticized the *Adelphi,* but because Lawrence had made fun of one of Tomlinson's idols, Norman Douglas. Tomlinson mounted his attack on the "personality-mongering" Lawrence in his little study *Norman Douglas,* published in 1931. There are digs at Lawrence throughout the book, including criticism of him for "maligning" Maurice Magnus, and a vivid account of the evening when Lawrence was unwittingly exasperating Tomlinson. The difficulty of interpreting such a man as Douglas in a fair and revealing way, wrote Tomlinson, was brought home to him on "the one occasion when I met D. H. Lawrence." The gathering was small, and he remembered the novelist as follows:

> [He] was very vivid and attractive, saying much, and saying it well; and it did not matter at all, so spontaneous were his images and pantomine, that he knew only the outside of what he was reporting, and not all of that, but only the superficies to which his creative predilections turned his attention. He had seen Douglas a few days before. And what, one of us asked, is the exile doing?

Lawrence surpassed himself. His comical caricature of Douglas, in mimicry of gestures and voice, in parodies of those occasions which make Douglas vocal and active, revealed something else, though that was not designed. It revealed the reason for the attraction D. H. Lawrence has for many readers; he was a delicate sensorium, quivering and vociferating to every physical fact. He did not resolve his sensations, but communicated them. He pictured Douglas as grotesquely as a cinema-camera in a "close-up." Yes, that was Douglas; his glance went like that sideways when he dropped a slow and artful comment, and that was the way he spoke when irritated, and those exaggerations mocked his ordinary movements. We laughed. But afterwards, not feeling satisfied with my easy diversion by this quizzical estimate, I saw that the excellent mimicry was no truer representation of Douglas than one of his old hats. All that was important was left out, because it was not important to Lawrence. What was important would not have heightened the illusion. You recognized the man again, recognized him instantly—an amusing and original fellow—but so might a bus-conductor who had seen him once or twice. That was as near as Lawrence got, and it pleased us mightily; a little fact though not unimportant, for Lawrence is widely advertised to be a great writer. Should we accept the report of a sensorium, however delicate, about the things of the mind?

The scene of mimicry that Tomlinson evokes is pertinent to Oaxaca, for it gives an indication of the sort of evening Carola and Hermann Kull enjoyed the day *Memoirs of the Foreign Legion* arrived, when Lawrence told them the story of Magnus.

Murry and Koteliansky were among those Lawrence invited to follow him to the New World at the Café Royal dinner. The interconnectedness between the three men was prepared in 1913 when Lawrence and Frieda first met Murry and Katherine Mansfield. Then in July 1914 on a walking tour through the Lake District, Lawrence met Koteliansky, who, having left his native Ukraine three years previously, had settled in London, where he was earning a meager living as secretary-translator for two lawyers. Koteliansky, a bachelor, was five years older than Lawrence, and the novelist introduced him to the Murrys a month after the walking tour. Murry began collaborating with Koteliansky as a translator of Russian classics before Lawrence did,[2] publishing a collection of I. A. Kuprin stories with him in 1915 and a volume of Chekhov ones in 1916. In 1916, the Lawrences and the Murrys had a period of near-communal living at St. Ives, Cornwall, with the two men oscillating between love and hate, until after two and a half months the Murrys moved thirty miles away. Early in 1920 Murry was completely estranged because he felt Lawrence had written him so unfeelingly about Katherine's consumption. But by spring 1923, when he was planning to start the *Adelphi*, Murry, carried away by his enthusiasm for *Kangaroo* and *Fantasia of the Unconscious*, had become reconciled to Lawrence. At the time of the Café Royal dinner the magazine had been in existence nine months; Murry was its editor and Koteliansky its business manager.

Because Koteliansky was planning a new publishing scheme, there was no question of his going to the New World, but at the dinner he was so effusive in his praise of the novelist—breaking a wine glass every time he affirmed that Lawrence was a great man—that the other guests were embarrassed. However, words passed between them before Lawrence sailed. According to Mrs. Carswell, Brett and Murry made the situation between Lawrence and Koteliansky difficult. Koteliansky withdrew "essentially" from the two intervening friends. Further, he disapproved of Lawrence's introduction of Magnus's *Memoirs of the Foreign Legion* and, according to Mrs. Carswell, "bluntly told Lawrence so. Lawrence was angry and hurt." No doubt he retorted roughly for he wrote from the *Aquitania* to their mutual friend Gertler: "I left Kot with a sore head." That Lawrence did not think it was anything serious is shown by what he added: "But that is better than a sore heart and spirit. It's no good, the old Jehovah does *not* rule the world any more. He's quit." After landing in New York, Lawrence consoled Koteliansky for the collapse of his publishing scheme, to which he had pledged 300 pounds: "My dear Kot, it's no good thinking of business unless you will go at it like a lion, a serpent, and a condor. You're well out of publishing. The world is a very vast machine, that grinds the bones of the good man gladly, if he's fool enough to let it."

Here, at least in publication, the Lawrence correspondence with Koteliansky suddenly breaks off. As Zytaruk shows in *The Quest for Rananim*, it does not resume until a year and nine months later. Since this is the only major break in the correspondence and since the resuming letter makes no reference to any length of time having passed between it and the previous one, Volume 10 of the Koteliansky papers in the British Museum probably contains letters filling the gap.[3] Letters to others show that the unavailable letters must touch on the novelist's later anger with Koteliansky and on a scandal involving Murry while Lawrence was in Oaxaca.

Part of the difficulty between Koteliansky and Lawrence arose because Koteliansky, according to Mrs. Carswell, "was definitely unable to accept or approve of Frieda." Mrs. Carswell's version of the difficulty between Koteliansky and Murry is that Koteliansky "withdrew himself also from the *Adelphi* into a special and respectable kind of solitude." Lea's biography claims that Koteliansky objected to Murry as editor for turning the *Adelphi* into a one-man show. Murry, he held, in imposing his own pattern on the magazine, was betraying the original idea of a review open to all shades of thought. Murry's response was to offer the magazine to Koteliansky. Kotelianksy accepted, only to find that others of the group, including Tomlinson and J. W. N. Sullivan, would not accept his leadership. Thereupon he "retired in a dudgeon." Murry's version, told in his *Reminiscences of D. H. Lawrence* published in 1933 largely to refute Mrs. Carswell's *Savage Pilgrimage,* said only: "Koteliansky and I had parted, very violently, over the *Adelphi,* on a fundamental issue, very soon after Lawrence left for America."

But to Lawrence in Oaxaca Murry must have complained bitterly about Koteliansky's actions, perhaps expecting sympathy, which was not forthcoming: "Remember," commented Lawrence, "you have betrayed everything and everybody up to now. It may have been your destiny. But in Kot you met a more ancient Judas than yourself. There are degrees of initiation into the Judas trick. You're not half way on yet. Even Kot is miles ahead of you. It's a case of *sauve-toi.* Judas was a Jew, and you're not quite that, yet."

Rancorous about Murry, Lawrence did not hold Koteliansky's quitting the *Adelphi* against him. Nor did his personal anger against Koteliansky—which made him avoid his old friend when he returned to London in October 1925—last very long. Before December 6 of that year—when the correspondence black-out was lifted—both men must have reached an accord and the reopening letter indicated previous recent communications. "Curtis Brown sent me the letters," are the starting words, and because Lawrence does not explain *what* letters, we know they must be letters Koteliansky had mentioned were coming. "We've got a villa here till the end of March," Lawrence continued chattily, referring to the Villa Bernarda that he had rented at Spotorno. "Send us news, if there is any. You are still Frieda's pet enemy, which is almost straining constancy, *stia bene,* D. H. L." This closing passage assumes an intimate understanding between the two men.

From then on the friendliness of the correspondence never wavered. In the last few months their mutual dislike of Murry comes out in their nickname, a private joke: Smerdyakov, taken from a Dostoyevsky character, meaning "the be-shitten." The last extended piece Lawrence wrote was a favor for Kot. Koteliansky had prepared a translation of "The Grand Inquisitor" scene from Dostoyevsky's *The Brothers Karamazov* that he wanted to publish in an expensive limited edition. Near death as he was, Lawrence wrote a preface of almost 4,000 words crediting Murry as the first to point out the key significance of the scene. In a reply preserved in the Lawrence satchel in Santa Fe, Koteliansky demurred at this favorable mention of "Smerdyakov." In his final letter to Koteliansky on 9 February 1930, when Lawrence weighed only ninety pounds, he said, "Yes, you can leave out Murry's name—put Katherine's instead, if you like." Koteliansky did, thus giving the credit to Katherine Mansfield.

The first of Lawrence's anti-Murry stories was "The Border Line" from which we have extracted the portrait of Frieda, barely disguised as Katherine. In it Frieda is pictured as married to Murry, here a journalist named Philip Farquhar, a "dark, insidious fellow," who had been a friend of her red-haired first husband Alan (a portrait of Lawrence). When the story opens Philip is on a journalistic assignment in Germany. Katherine, while journeying to join him, pauses in Strassburg, where she meets the ghost of Alan, who was killed in World War I. She realizes that in spirit she still belongs to her first husband. By this time, too, she has admitted Alan's merits and some of her own mistakes in not being more yielding in the marriage. Alan had been "a ceaseless born fighter, a sword not to be sheathed." When she arrives Philip is ill and strikes her as "a whimpering little beast." In contrast to Alan, he is "this cunning civilian, this subtle equivocator, this adjuster of the scales of truth." In Baden-Baden, Philip's illness becomes serious. Katherine feels indifferent. On one of her excursions from his hotel bedside, she meets Alan's ghost again in the Black Forest. This time he takes "complete possession of her." Later, as Philip is dying with his arms around Katherine's reluctant neck, the ghost enters and detaches Philip's clasping arms. Thereupon Philip dies. In the presence of the corpse, the ghost makes love to Katherine in the other bed.

Besides giving Lawrence a vent for his impulse to destroy Murry, it is a remarkably graphic assertion that Lawrence was the better man, not only as a man but as a love-mate. Though only a few insiders would know all its implications, its appearance before the British public in 1928 in *The Woman Who Rode Away and Other Stories,* must have given Lawrence considerable vindictive satisfaction.

In "The Last Laugh," he kills the Murry figure again. Marchbanks is introduced as the escort of Brett. "With his thick black brows sardonically arched, and his rather hooked nose . . . he seemed like a satanic young priest, ready to go to bed with a strange woman the moment she is willing." (Plate 47.) In "Jimmy and the Desperate Woman," the Murry figure is Jimmy, the "editor of a high-class, rather high-brow, rather successful magazine." Again he has "a pure Pan face, with thick black eyebrows cocked up and grey eyes with a sardonic goaty gleam, and nose and mouth curling with satire." This Murry figure is also a woman-chaser. The story tells how he uses his glamour as a lecturer-editor to persuade a poetry-writing miner's wife, whom he does not love, to leave her husband to come and live with him.

The three stories were written before Lawrence got to Oaxaca: "The Border Line" in Germany between his two London visits of the 1923-24 winter, and "Last Laugh" and "Jimmy" on the ranch before leaving for Oaxaca.

A significant fact that has emerged since the death of Murry and Frieda is that Murry was the man with whom Frieda had an affair during the 1923-24 winter. The story is told by both participants in letters published in 1964 in Tedlock's *Frieda Lawrence: The Memoirs and Correspondence*. Murry's letters also explain why he felt the real situation made Lawrence's stories "a very shabby sort of revenge." Murry, widowed just seven months before, refused when Frieda proffered her love out of respect for Lawrence, then traveling in Mexico with Gótzsche. "If I had known, then, truly, how things had been between Lorenzo and you, I believe I should have had the courage," he told Frieda in his later reminiscing. The "courage" came after Lawrence got back to England. In his 24 September 1953 letter to Frieda, Murry recalled: "The physical tenderness of love is just as much a spiritual thing as it is a physical. It is both at once—in a new, blessed reconciliation. Was it merely a physical attraction I felt for you? Nonsense. I wanted, needed, *all* of you. And the loveliness there was between us came out of the generosity of your soul as much as the generosity of your body."

Did Lawrence know about the affair at the time? Brett says he did. Mrs. Carswell says Murry confessed it publicly at the Café Royal dinner, and that Koteliansky, a strict moralist, could never "accept or approve of Frieda" for her infidelity to Lawrence and betrayal of the men's friendship. "The Border Line" shows that Lawrence knew, and further understood his wife with the sort of understanding he had urged on Sir Thomas Dunlap, whose marriage had taken an unhappy turn just as the novelist was about to marry Frieda. The story makes no bones about how hard it was for Katherine to live with the often "unyielding" and self-assertive Alan. "At first it was wonderfully pleasant and restful and voluptuous, especially for a woman of thirty-eight, to be married to Philip. Katherine felt he caressed her senses and soothed her, and gave her what she wanted." An added pleasure for forty-four-year-old Frieda may have come from the reassurance of attracting a man ten years her junior.

The year after Frieda's death, Aldous Huxley, a friend of Lawrence and Frieda, wrote to Nancy Kelly, an actress rehearsing the role of the Goddess, Huxley's portrait of Frieda, in the dramatization of his novel *The Genius and the Goddess*. Published in 1969 in *Letters of Aldous Huxley,* it said:

> Frieda and Lawrence had, undoubtedly, a profound and passionate love-life. But this did not prevent Frieda from having, every now and then, affairs with Prussian cavalry officers and Italian peasants, whom she loved for a season without in any way detracting from her love for Lawrence

or from her intense devotion to his genius. Lawrence, on his part, was aware of these erotic excursions, got angry about them sometimes, but never made the least effort to break away from her: for he realized his own organic dependence upon her.

Lawrence's own beliefs about marital fidelity are embodied in one of the new sections he wrote into *The Plumed Serpent* in Oaxaca. In the marriage ceremony Ramón performed for Kate and Cipriano, he says:

> Man shall betray a woman, and a woman shall betray a man, and it shall be forgiven them, each of them. But if they have met as earth and rain, between day and night, in the hour of the Star; if the man has met the woman with his body and the star of his hope, and the woman has met the man with her body and the star of her yearning, so that a meeting has come to pass, and an abiding place for the two where they are one star, then shall neither of them betray the abiding place where the meeting lives like an unsetting star. For if either betray the abiding place of the two, it shall not be forgiven, neither by day nor by night, nor in the twilight of the star.

Lawrence clearly felt that physical fidelity was less important in marriage than "the abiding place," something that comes into existence only when there has been a true meeting. It is this which must not be betrayed, for physical infidelity did not in itself constitute betrayal. Perhaps Frieda's affair with Murry helped motivate Lawrence to write this new chapter. Obviously, he felt that he and Frieda had met "as earth and rain, between day and night, in the hour of the Star." And the passage suggests he could always forgive her because, as Huxley suggests, her affairs never detracted from her essential love for him, thus, never betraying the abiding place where they were a single star.

A scene Brett recalled from that 1923-24 winter to John Manchester, her biographer, was "how white Murry's face was while Lawrence ranted at him about an affair with a simple good woman of the Midlands, saying Murry was only acting out one of Lawrence's books and was not sincere about the woman; that he would soon get bored with this affair and would hurt the woman in question." The situation of "Jimmy and the Desperate Woman," then, was based on fact.

Despite this and despite the affair with Frieda, Lawrence seemed friendly enough with Murry when they sailed and expected him to join them in America a little later, for he advised Murry to come straight to Galveston and avoid New York. Another letter written in New York was newsy and impersonal; and when Lawrence wrote in May about Murry's sudden and unexpected marriage to Violet le Maistre he was unaffectedly cordial about the change in plans: "Better, as you say, than wild-goose-chasing in other continents." This letter, however, may have disguised real disappointment, for about this time he reported bitterly to Mrs. Luhan: "Another letter from Murry—still putting up catty little defences—leaves me cold."

Lawrence's last letter to Murry before leaving for Oaxaca—3 October 1924—also refers to the broken promise: "We shall never 'drop in on one another,' again the ways go wide apart. Sometimes I regret that you didn't take me at what I am, last Christmas: and come here and take a different footing. But apparently you did what was in you: what is in me, I do it."

The tone of the letter was friendly. However, it showed that Koteliansky was troubling Murry; adultery may have been involved: "As for Kot there is nothing to say. It is absurd, but there it is. The ultimate son of Moses pining for heavy tablets. I believe the old Moses would not have valued the famous tablets if they hadn't been ponderous, and millstones round everybody's neck."

Lawrence wrote again from Oaxaca, a long description of their trip down, the visit to the governor, the market, and the beauty of the fawn-colored hills. Two days later, after having heard from Murry, Lawrence wrote an acerbic note calling Murry's letter a "little yellow cry" from his liver. Apparently the trouble with Koteliansky was worse. "You were bound to hate Kot," Lawrence commented, "and he you, after a while: though I don't suppose the hate is mortal, on either side." Murry must have complained, too, of how the *Adelphi* was going.

> The *Adelphi* was bound to dwindle: though why not fatten it up a bit. Why in the name of hell didn't you rouse up a bit, last January, and put a bit of gunpowder in your stuff, and fire a shot or two? But you preferred to be soft, and go on stirring your own finger in your own vitals. If it's any good, to you or to anybody, all right! But if it's no good, what the hell! It seems to me the telephone-book magazine, and the pale yellow *cri de l'âme* are equally out of date. Spunk is what one wants, not introspective sentiment. The last is your vice. You rot your own manhood at the roots, with it. But apparently it's what you want.

Murry had not after all, been forgiven. Furthermore, "Jimmy and the Desperate Woman," appeared in the October 1924 *Criterion*. Lawrence's own copy reached him in Oaxaca on December 1, and he wrote the same day to the editor, Richard Cobden-Sanderson that he was relieved the *Criterion* had intestinal fortitude (he used a blunter term) and wasn't another *Adelphi* or *London Mercury*.

One wonders if either the latest short story or the November 17 blast could have prepared Murry for the January 28 letter. "Dear Jack," it began: "Brett sent on your letters. That seems to be an absolutely prize sewer-mess, of your old 'group.'—Pray read my story in the *Criterion.* I doubt if Kot would be so kind to you, as to assert its 'truth.' Doesn't he know *all* the real truth?—much more suited to his purposes."

The "sewer-mess" in question, according to Brett, was a new instance of Murry's philandering. Despite his second marriage in April, he had launched an affair with the wife of a man who was a friend of Brett, Lawrence, and Katherine Mansfield. Brett gave the husband's name to Manchester, who passed it on to me. Subsequent circumstantial evidence makes the affair a possibility, but conclusive evidence is lacking.

The new anger reminded Lawrence of the dinner at the Café Royale, a memory so painful that six months later he had written Mrs. Carswell from New Mexico, "I never forget that fatal evening at the Café Royale. That is what coming home means to me. Never again, pray the Lord." Murry had recalled that at one point in the emotional evening Lawrence turned to him and pleaded, "Do not betray me!" Lawrence does not mention this in the letter, but he asked:

> You remember that charming dinner at the Café Royale that night? You remember saying: I love you Lorenzo, but I won't promise not to betray you? Well you can't betray me, and that's all there is to that. *Ergo,* just leave off loving me. Let's wipe off all that Judas-Jesus slime. . . .
>
> All I want to say is, don't think you can either love or betray me. Learn that I am not lovable: hence not betrayable.

This statement about betrayal represents Lawrence's belief that only betrayal of the "abiding place" constitutes true betrayal. He had recently written as part of Quetzalcoatl's wedding ceremony: "Whosoever betrays another man, betrays a man like himself, a fragment. For if there is no star between man and a man, or even a man and a wife, there is nothing." Lawrence was telling Murry that there had never been such a star between them.

The letter ends with Lawrence being deliberately vague about his future plans: "Frieda and I may come to England in the spring. But I shall not want to see anybody except just my sisters and my agent. Last time was once too many. One day, perhaps, you and I may meet as men. Up to now, it has been all slush. Best drop that Christ stuff: it's putrescence."

In his September 1953 letter to Frieda, Murry wrote, "I sometimes went on quivering inside for months after one of his letters." And one can easily imagine that this happened after this letter. In his *Reminiscences* Murry characterized it as "a letter of pure denunciation." "I had made

no reply,'' he added, ''and looked upon it as the end of our relation.''
Yet nine months later they were in touch again; and during the September 20 to October 29 visit to England, Lawrence invited Murry to come to see him. Murry agreed. Before Murry left, Lawrence went out to buy him ''some fresh figs and dates and Carlsbad plums'' to take back to Dorset. That was the last time the two friend-enemies saw each other. But the next January when Murry backed out of his promise to visit the Lawrences at Spotorno, Lawrence wrote his fourth and last Murry story, ''Smile,'' in which he depicts Murry feigning grief at the death of Katherine Mansfield and drawn sexually to one of the nuns who had helped lay the body out.

LETTERS TO THE HAWKS

On the last day of 1924, Lawrence having filled his purple scribbler, took up its mate and continued *The Plumed Serpent* from page 382 on. Now, although only a month had passed, the yellow-brown scribbler was filled too with another 376 pages of longhand. Lawrence needed only a few extra pages—thirty-eight, as it turned out—and did not want to start a new copybook. Turning the second scribbler containing the Chapala version upside down, he began writing from the last page. He was within a few pages of the end when he wrote his January 30 letter to Alfred Decker Hawk, owner of the Del Monte Ranch.

A. D. Hawk was a former banker from Purcell, Oklahoma, who in 1912, after he had contracted tuberculosis, had moved to New Mexico and bought the ranch seventeen miles north of Taos where he had built himself a large square, two-story adobe house with a high pitched green roof that Brett described as ''ugly yet comfortable looking.'' Born in Pennsylvania, Hawk was a dark-haired, very slight man, about five feet, nine inches tall, who turned sixty during the winter the Lawrences spent on his ranch. Lawrence, always addressing him as A. D., wrote him perhaps his most relaxed letters from Oaxaca.[4] They deal with A. D.'s brown-haired son, William, the four Lawrence horses, forwarding mail, and paying taxes. But always the basis was personal, and Lawrence sent the rancher news and descriptions, with greetings for everyone, including the pets. These letters show the affection with which Lawrence thought of the ranch area throughout his months in Oaxaca.

A. D. and his wife were, according to Brett, ''very kind and hospitable.'' Rachel, ''with bobbed, wavy golden hair,'' and William, with ''large, dark, blue-green eyes and a big, well-shaped curved nose,'' were a handsome couple. Five days after arrival in Oaxaca, Lawrence expressed concern about Azul, the big gray horse he had bought in the summer as a gift for his wife. According to Brett, it was so gaunt its bones stuck out painfully, but with good care it soon "grew fat and handsome and strong enough to carry Frieda." Lawrence called it old, but Rachel Hawk told me Azul was comparatively young. However, it developed mouth trouble shortly before the Lawrences left for Mexico and was taken to a veterinary in Taos. "I will write to Taos about the Azul," Lawrence wrote William in his November 14 letter, "—and get Tony to send him up if he has been attended to. . . . I would rather he were up at Del Monte with his pals." Bessie, Aaron, and Ambrose, the other Lawrence horses, would graze on the Lawrence ranch until the big snows in December. Then William agreed to bring them down to Del Monte to shelter and feed them until they could be let free to graze for themselves in the spring. On December 7 Lawrence was still worrying about the gray horse. " Have you seen the Azul?" he wrote William, underlining the question. "Poor old thing, I shant be happy till I know you've got him safe." When William reported that he had gathered up the horses, Lawrence wrote in his January 6 letter, "I'm glad you fetched down the horses. Frieda is always moaning about the Azul's jaw. Did he have his tooth out, poor devil?" This letter said that Lawrence was sending $25 for the horses, but he absentmindedly forgot to enclose the check.

The letters also tell the story of more pots. Despite the bad luck with the shipment of pottery from Tlaquepaque the year before and despite the first resolve not to try again, the Lawrences weakened. On December 7 he wrote they wanted to send some pots from Oaxaca. And a letter written a month later shows that the pots, packed since Christmas, were also intended for Rachel, and had still not been dispatched. But the parcel was finally sent by parcel post, and the February 7 letter, which asked if Rachel would let William wear his black and white blanket, also inquired about the pots and the horse. Feeling sympathy for the old horse, Lawrence asked William if he had seen Azul, for he himself would not be happy until he knew it was safe. Then in his January 6 letter, in response to William's report that he had gathered up the horses and brought them to Del Monte, Lawrence expressed relief. Had Azul's tooth been extracted, he asked, for Frieda was always worried about its jaw. The letters contain vignettes of life in Oaxaca:

> It's hot here, & I go about in sandals, barefoot:—there was a scorpion on the floor this morning. . . . There is the brilliant hot sun all day long & every day, & the mountains standing up dark and bluish from the yellow, blazing valley bed. . . . Yes, it will be good to smell the cows in the corral once more—though at this moment the patio is reeking with the scent of some sweet tropical flower. Damn tropical flowers anyhow.

The letters hop about, and the expletive about the tropical flowers was immediately followed by the question, "Ask your father if he got my letter & cheque, about those taxes." This referred to a letter Lawrence wrote the older Hawk on December 20, enclosing a $100 check to pay taxes due on Kiowa Ranch. News that those taxes were safely paid prompted the January 30 letter to the father; and it is extraordinary that it could have been written only four days after the "halfness" letter to Brett and two days after the "drop that Christ stuff" letter to Murry. It dramatizes the effect on Lawrence of finishing *The Plumed Serpent,* of reaching the end of the enormous task he had set for himself with the determination that it should be accomplished within ten weeks. The light-hearted relaxation suggests the inner tension which must have accounted for much of the fierceness with which he turned on his two old friends. In the Hawk letter he is almost boyish in his joy at knowing he will soon be on the move again. One sees him happily remembering friends he had known on Mount Lobo earlier: like Bobbie, the Hawks' younger daughter who was married to Ted Gillett, and concerning whom in December he had written Earl Brewster in Capri, saying "Thanks so much for promising to look after the Gilletts a bit. Probably by this time they are in Italy." Besides Bill and Rachel, another family member Lawrence was eager to see was A. D.'s wife Lucy Walton, formerly of Iowa. He was pleased that they would be on hand in the coming summer, for during the 1922-23 winter they had been in San Diego, making the novelist the oldest responsible male at Del Monte. Merrild and Gótzsche, the Danish artists, who had lived in an adjoining cabin that same winter, were others Lawrence remembered fondly. One also sees him eagerly anticipating resuming relations with old ranch neighbors, like Scott Murray, an obliging workman with a team of horses who lived in the village of San Cristobal. The summer before Murray had helped Lawrence with the irrigation ditch on Kiowa and, in the summer ahead, would increase Lawrence's indebtedness by helping him lay the pipes to bring Gallina Creek water to the house. Most cheering of all, one sees a resumption of Frieda sending "many greetings" along with his. This sign, which had revealed their happiness in the earlier letters, had, up to now, been conspicuously absent from the Oaxaca letters. So relations were better and Frieda was happier too.

The letter is another of those for which we are indebted to Moore, who published it first in *The Intelligent Heart.* It reveals how charming Lawrence could be when he was unreservedly friendly. The next day, he wrote another casual letter, a hitherto unpublished note to Consul Rickards on Saturday, January 31. It reported that Oaxaca was still quiet but he wanted to be on the move again. He and his wife would be arriving in Mexico City around February 5. Did the consul have information about freighters? He and Frieda would like to delay reaching England before spring by cruising first in the West Indies. For his part, Lawrence also wanted to smell the sea.

CHAPTER 11

HOW *THE PLUMED SERPENT* WAS CHANGED IN OAXACA

During my second reading of *The Plumed Serpent,* I indexed every trace of Oaxaca, hoping to analyze the city's influence on the novel. When L. D. Clark's study, *The Dark Night of the Body,* appeared at the end of 1964, I expected to learn of more Oaxaca influences. Clark's book, though only incidentally concerned with Oaxaca, mentioned a typescript of the Chapala version.[1] Clark, who summarized it, said it was in the Houghton Library at Harvard University. When I got to the Houghton myself in November 1970, I brought the Oaxaca version with me. Comparing the two versions chapter by chapter, I found little to extend my list of changes mainly *because* of Oaxaca, but supplementary changes I could not classify began piling up.

A few were based on Lawrence's intervening experiences in the American Southwest, such as the Hopi snake dance. More, like learning about Calles and meeting Quintanilla in Mexico City, were based on his experiences in the capital before leaving for Oaxaca. Still more were obviously the result of the novel's haunting presence at the back of his mind between the end of June 1923, when he finished the Chapala version, and 19 November 1924, when he began the Oaxaca one. "The first full sketch" was Lawrence's characterization of the Chapala draft for Baroness von Richthofen, and it worked on him as any well-started literary project influences a writer, making him alertly observant in particular directions and drawing new material to it as the fundamental vision developed and clarified.

The newly discovered changes, with the exception of the remodeling of Cipriano, proved more important than those obviously traceable to Oaxaca. They could not be ignored. Besides presenting Lawrence with a new environment, Oaxaca provided an isolated and circumscribed area in which his ideas could grow and interact. Throughout his Oaxaca sojourn, outward circumstances were never as important to him as his creative life. He needed seclusion from the other Anglos, not only for uninterrupted writing time, but for distraction-free time to integrate old and new ideas and to work them into the framework of his story.

Actually, *The Plumed Serpent* has two major stories: the story of upper-class Irish Kate Leslie, a strong-willed, introspective, articulate, and physically attractive widow of forty, who comes to Mexico when her life reaches a crucial watershed; and the story of a new religious movement set in motion by Ramón Carrasco, a Mexican intellectual, and his friend, Cipriano Viedma, an Oxford-educated Indian, general of Mexico's Army of the West. The stories intersect when Kate hears of the new movement and moves to the lakeside village where the two leaders have their headquarters. Kate, a mixture of Frieda and D. H. Lawrence, is an interesting, even if sometimes implausible and occasionally tiresome woman, but in many ways, including alienation from her background, she does not differ from other Lawrence heroines. It is the new religion, with its pageantry and dramatic implications, that sets the work apart as perhaps the most original and most controversial of Lawrence's novels. The religion of *The Plumed Serpent* is still so outrageous to many—especially to anthropologists, historians, orthodox Christians, progressives, and believers in liberal democracy—that Kate, too, has become an issue of controversy for succumbing to it to the extent that she did. It is seldom analyzed as a novel. Such is its power, it is usually denounced as misleading history, misrepresentation of Mexico, pernicious doctrine, or a combination of all three. That it should be weighed in historical terms and denounced in doctrinal ones is ironic. Both approaches show the extent to which Lawrence succeeded in achieving in Oaxaca in 1924-25 his two most ambitious aims. For the dimensions of history and religion were what he most wanted to add to the story that, in less than eight weeks, he had written neatly into the two dark blue copybooks he took to Chapala in 1923.

Lawrence's idea of what a novel should be kept changing. Witness how he withdrew form Garnett's tutelage once he had rejected the idea that a novel should present consistent characters within an accepted moral scheme. At that time—5 June 1914—his interest, he said, had passed from showing "the old-fashioned human element" in people to dealing with what was "non-human" in them. Later, as his conception of human nature clarified, he felt the need to depict men and women in fiction as "phenomena" of life rather than as "characters" tailored to established concepts. By 1922, when he was writing *Kangaroo,* he had reached the new position enunciated in the "Bits" chapter of that novel: "We insist that a novel is, or should be, also a thought-adventure, if it is to be anything at all complete." *The Plumed Serpent* certainly complies with that prescription, as do its predecessors, *Aaron's Rod* and *Kangaroo.* These three thought-adventure novels are most easily understood if read in the order in which they were written, especially if the Chapala version of *Serpent* is inserted as number three and the Oaxaca version is considered as number four. For Lawrence's personal thought-adventure was a continuing story, which went through new developments between Chapala and Oaxaca. And the different denouement of the second *Serpent* reflects a decisive stage in one of his chief explorations.

The thought-adventurers in the succession of novels begin with two in *Aaron's Rod:* Aaron himself, whose mental adventure barely begins as he walks out on his wife and his coal-mining background to venture into the larger world of London and sophisticated Florence; and Lilly, the Lawrence self-portrait, a writer who has advanced much further intellectually than Aaron, for whom he becomes a goad and only partially acknowledged stimulus. Lilly is married, and his wife, Tanny, distinctly resembles Frieda, but she is kept in the background. In *Kangaroo* there is no equivalent of Aaron (the adventurer just on the threshold of thought), but the Lawrence self-portrait (this time known as Richard Somers) steps forward to the center of the stage, and here his wife, Harriet (the Frieda portrait), becomes almost as important as her writer-husband, whose impulsiveness and idealism she continually mocks. In *Aaron's Rod* the two male thought-adventurers view a few incidents of rising fascism in Italy, but they are not involved as participants. In *Kangaroo* the single thought-adventurer is drawn closer to the vortex of action, for two leaders—"Kangaroo," the man animating a fascist-like group of World War I veterans, and Struthers, the Socialist leader—both ask him to serve their movements as an editor. In *The Plumed Serpent,* the alert male thought-adventurer of *Aaron's Rod* and *Kangaroo* is subsumed into the more complex figure of Kate. She too is asked to join a movement, this time a religious one. Unlike the central character in *Kangaroo,* who rejects and evades both movements by leaving the country (in this case Australia), Kate accepts the invitation, joins the movement and decides to remain in the country (in her case Mexico).

Lawrence's relations with Frieda were an essential factor in his consciousness as he began the Chapala version. Another was the conclusion that he felt all men must reach around the age of thirty-five, namely, that his chief goal as defined in *Fantasia of the Unconscious* should be "a passionate union in actively making a world." He had been disillusioned in democracy by World War I, in standard education by seven years as a school teacher, in industrialism by his experience as a coal-miner's son, and even more by commercialism and commercial prosperity. Thus he was disenchanted with economic roads to world betterment. But what about combined economic and political ones? "In the flush of youth," he wrote in *Assorted Articles,* "I believed in Socialism, because I thought it would be thrilling and delightful." Disillusionment came when he saw it ushering in a life even duller than life under capitalism. As a member of the working class, he knew its members too well to have faith in proletarian revolution as a means of redeeming the world. He did not like what he saw of early fascism in Italy. By the time he wrote *Kangaroo,* he had also given up on romantic love and wanted instead a deeper communion in "a vast, phallic, sacred darkness," where men and women could be enveloped in "the dark god at the lower threshold." Because Christianity denounced this god released into the life of the body through sex, he saw no hope for the world in Christianity. Seeing that average men and women showed no desire to regenerate themselves, he had lost faith, as his many expletives in Oaxaca show, in unaided, ordinary humanity. And the experiences first of Australia and then of the United States had brought him still greater distaste for the emptiness of the purely materialistic approach to life.

If democracy, education, industrialism, mechanization, commercialism, socialism, communism, fascism, love, Christianity and materialist humanism were all dead-ends, what purpose could he serve? For he could not accept despair. He believed in action. The question, to borrow a metaphor he put into Ramón's mouth, was how to "get inside the egg, right to the middle, to start it growing into a new bird," for he was no longer naive enough to have faith either in merely cleaning the nest or in "washing the outside of the egg to make it look clean."

"You want a new spirit in society, a new bond between men," is the way Struthers, the Socialist leader, enunciates the Lawrencean position in *Kangaroo.* And a few pages later, when Struthers presses for how these can be brought into being, Lawrence under the hero's name replies, "It *does* need some sort of religion."

Some sort of religion, then, was Lawrence's answer. It had to grow out of real belief and it also had to have the power to transform men by appealing to "the deeper man." Lawrence also wanted a new bond between men and felt Walt Whitman's "Love of Comrades" was the great factor likely to enkindle it. But his experience had convinced him that ordinary men were not capable of leading themselves or of revering the higher life. Leaders were necessary, both for the practical governance of life and to bring into the awareness of only half-awake human beings the concept of "mate-trust" and the potentialities of the vital unconscious. Besides wanting this new concept of brotherhood and a sense of the dark gods brought into consciousness, Lawrence wanted them held in highest honor. And since 1915 he had felt the low sights and the intransigence of ordinary men and women necessitated a hierarchy of leaders, with a disciple transmitting the chief's vision to others and providing the training and discipline necessary for the regeneration of society. In short, Lawrence believed in a theocratic form of government. "Our supreme judges and our master professors," he wrote in "Education of the People," "will be primarily *priests.* Let us not take fright at the word.

The true religious faculty is the most powerful and the highest faculty in man, once he exercises it."

In *Fantasia of the Unconscious* he added, "The secret is to commit into the hands of the sacred few the responsibility, which now lies like torture on the mass. . . . For the mass of people, knowledge *must* be symbolical, mythical, dynamic," with the interpretation of the symbols resting in "the higher, responsible, conscious classes." Since many of the world's longest-lasting and most civilized cultures have been theocracies, Lawrence's ideal was not unworthy. And *Kangaroo* is evidence of how strongly he had come to believe in it before he had left Australia, which was ten months before he began *Quetzalcoatl.*

"Can't a new great inspiration of belief in the love of mates be breathed into the white Peoples of the world, and a new day be built on this belief!" The hope implicit in this question, asked by *Kangaroo*'s hero, shows both Lawrence's own hope and suggests a further disillusion with his own culture. After crossing from Australia to the United States, Lawrence, as he confessed in *Studies in Classic American Literature,* encountered firsthand "this wild and noble America . . . the thing that I had pined for most ever since I read Fenimore Cooper, as a boy." And in New Mexico he met Indians related to those in the Leatherstocking books that he "loved so dearly." The North American Indians, he found, were governed by strong religious impulses and they seemed in touch with forces deep in their unconscious natures. White-skinned Americans, on the other hand, struck him as hard and tense. He began to feel that Anglo-Saxons were a lost cause and that only in the hearts of brown-skinned people could the spark he longed for be lit. On 16 November 1921, before he ever left Europe, Lawrence had written the Brewsters, "The Indian, the Aztec, old Mexico—all that fascinates me and has fascinated me for years." The Indians of the United States, then, had reanimated an old interest; and, being that much closer to Mexico meant its ancient cultures were now within train-riding distance. Heading south, therefore, was the logical next step in Lawrence's thought-adventure.

One of the most exciting discoveries in Mexican archaeology was made by Manuel Gamio late in 1919 at San Juan Teotihuacán, thirty miles north of Mexico City. (Plate 48.) There, by cutting into a crudely nondescript mound within the large patio known as the Ciudadela, Mexico's first Director of Anthropology exposed the remains of a much finer pyramid that had been deliberately covered. The hidden pyramid had six tiers, whose risers were adorned with some of the most dramatic sculpture that has been brought to light in Mesoamerica. Projecting from several risers were a series of large serpent heads with exposed fangs, each encircled by a feathered ruff that suggested representations of Quetzalcoatl. The undulating bodies of the plumed serpents ran in low relief between the heads. Alternating with the serpents were the heads of another Middle American god, Tlaloc, the god of rain, recognized by heavy "spectacles" and large teeth under a jutting upper lip. The newly discovered pyramid did much to increase the fame of Quetzalcoatl, one of the deities of the Classic Era between the birth of Christ and 900 A. D. This was a major development in Mesosamerican studies, for in Yucatan, where he was called Kukulcan, Quetzalcoatl had never seemed very important; but in the Valley of Mexico, where he had stood high, he had been reduced to a minor deity by the Aztecs in favor of their god-protector Huitzilopochtli. Gamio's discovery also shed light on the religious beliefs of the mysterious builders of Teotihuacán, who were still not known to be predecessors of the Toltecs who built Tula. This, then, was a major discovery of fact, as well as a major art discovery. Besides generating an interest that spread widely beyond archaeological circles, it created at the long-famous site a new focus for sightseeing that rivaled the previously supreme attraction of the Pyramid of the Sun.

When the Lawrences arrived in Mexico for the first time in March 1923, they went sightseeing. Bynner and Johnson went with them, and the latter took a photograph of his three friends on top of the Pyramid of the Sun, which Lawrence sent as a postcard to Mrs. Carswell on April 11. Lawrence's message on the reverse calls Teotihuacán "very impressive . . . far more than Pompeii or the Forum." Evidence that Gamio's discovery impressed him even more than the Pyramid of the Sun appears in a description of the site he would add to *The Plumed Serpent* in Oaxaca: "The ponderous pyramids of San Juan Teotihuacán, the House of Quetzalcoatl, wreathed with the snake of all snakes, the huge fangs white and pure today as in the lost centuries when his makers were alive. He has not died. He is not so dead as the Spanish churches, this all-enwreathing dragon of the horror of Mexico."

Lawrence's most extensive account of his response to Teotihuacán is in "Au Revoir, U.S.A." which Johnson published in his eighth number of *The Laughing Horse.* In developing his idea that North America was a fanged continent Lawrence wrote:

> And out at San Juan Teotihuacán where are the great pyramids of a vanished, pre-Aztec people, as we are told—and the so-called Temple of Quetzalcoatl—there, behold you, huge gnashing heads jut out jagged from the wall-face of the low pyramid, and a huge snake stretches along the base, and one grasps at a carved fish, that swims in old stone and for once seems harmless. Actually a harmless Fish! But look out! The great stone heads snarl at you from the wall trying to bite you: and one great dark,

green blob of an obsidian eye, you never saw anything so blindly malevolent: and then white fangs. Great white fangs, smooth today, the white fangs, with tiny cracks in them. Enamelled. These bygone pyramid-building Americans, who were a dead-and-gone mystery even to the Aztecs, when the Spaniards arrived, they applied their highest art to the enamelling of the great fangs of these venomous stone heads, and there is the enamel today, white and smooth. You can stroke the great fang with your finger and see. And the blob of an obsidian eye looks down at you.

Bynner's *Journey with Genius* describes how strongly Lawrence was affected by Gamio's discovery: "In the great quadrangle of Quetzalcoatl, we saw Lawrence looking and brooding. The colored stone heads of feathered snakes . . . were a match for him. The stone serpents and owls [meaning the Tlalocs] held something that he obviously feared. . . . Perhaps the germ of *The Plumed Serpent's* theme came to him then."

There are so many parallels between the life of Gamio and Lawrence's Ramón that the newly uncovered pyramid, besides giving Lawrence the idea of a novel about the religion of Quetzalcoatl, must also have sealed the basic story line in his mind: the story of a modern Mexican bringing the religion of Quetzalcoatl back into his people's lives. In a sense was that not what the excavator had done? Transforming the archaeologist into a religious leader was a simple step. The forty-two-year-old hero of the novel was Gamio's age, for Gamio was forty at the time Lawrence visited Teotihuacán. That Lawrence had Gamio in mind is more apparent in the Chapala draft than in the final novel, for the draft contains a subsequently eliminated flashback of Ramón's career that follows Gamio's almost to the letter, including a family wealthy in the days of Porfirio Díaz, study in the United States, and a return to Mexico in 1911, the very year that Gamio returned from New York. So Gamio, like Ramón, had been in a position, as a thoughtful adult with sympathies for both the old and the new, to observe the whole course of the Revolution. Gamio, like Ramón, was tall, dark, and handsome. Furthermore, Gamio was a close friend of Mrs. Nuttall's, making Casa Alvarado a logical place for one of his characters to meet a Gamio-equivalent. Whether it was before or after the visit to Teotihuacán that Lawrence learned the basic facts of Gamio's life, their inclusion in the Chapala flashback is proof that he learned them on his first visit to Mexico. Mrs. Nuttall, who was in a position to know, is the likely source. She had been affectionately disposed to Gamio since he was in his twenties, probably told Lawrence how handsome Gamio was, and had arranged Gamio's scholarship to Columbia University. Thus we can be sure she corrected Lawrence about Gamio going to Columbia, not to Harvard, as he had it in the Chapala version.

Ramón is even called an archaeologist in the newspaper story that tells Kate of the naked man who came of the the lake, saying he came from Quetzalcoatl. This does not mean that Ramón is a portrait of Gamio drawn from life. Lawrence never succeeded in meeting him. But Gamio undoubtedly provided the initial inspiration for the character. Lawrence may have borrowed some elements from John Dibrell, the American supporter of native costumes, who Bynner felt inspired Ramón; and even a trait or two from José Vasconcelos, whom several others, including Harry T. Moore, have suggested as the model. But neither Dibrell nor Vasconcelos had careers that matched Ramón's so well as Gamio.

Because Lawrence wanted to learn more about Quetzalcoatl and about Gamio himself, he wrote to the archaeologist in the spring of 1924 when he knew he was coming back to Mexico to redo the novel. By May 18 Gamio had replied, Lawrence reported the news to Seltzer and told his publisher that when he got to Mexico he would visit Gamio and discuss his novel with him. On June 9, he wrote Idella Purnell Stone, whose magazine *Palms* he had helped in Guadalajara, "I intend to come to Mexico in the autumn—I think in October—and I look forward very much to coming back. I have had a couple of letters from Manuel Gamio, the anthropologist in Mexico. He seems nice."

On June 14 he mentioned to Seltzer more letters from Gamio. Four months later, when Lawrence got to Mexico, he looked Gamio up, only to write bad-temperedly to Mrs. Luhan: "Gamio is reported to be in Yucatan: but I don't care where he is." To Johnson, he was half-rueful, half-humorous: "Garnio is in Yucatan with the Carnegie Institute excavators—at Chicken Ita—digging up the dead instead of looking after the living."[2]

When Lawrence first headed for Mexico it had been almost a year since he had worked on a novel. As he wrote on 26 May 1923 to Murry from Chapala, "I sort of wanted to do a novel here," but added, "I could never begin in Mexico [City]." But the sightseeing that had prevented him from making a start had given him an idea on how to begin. After he had rejected the idea of renting an apartment in Mrs. Nuttall's house and arrived at Lake Chapala, he found a congenial place in which to work and an environment, disguised under the name of the neighboring Lake Sayula, that would serve excellently as the setting for the story he had conceived. "I felt I had a novel simmering in me," he wrote Mrs. Carswell, "so I came here, to this big lake, to see if I could write it." On June 7, just a little more than a month after arriving in Chapala, he was able to tell Mrs. Carswell, "It goes fairly well, I shall be glad if I can finish the first draft by the end of this month." He could estimate the ending date because he was already more than half done. He met his hoped-for deadline. That he completed a draft of about 100,000 words in eight weeks is striking proof of how quickly he wrote. "The way things pour out of him, *he* seems only the pen," is how Frieda described it to Edward Garnett. He did most of his Chapala writing, as Johnson recalled, "towards a little peninsula where tall trees grew near the water." And Johnson's description, published in the 1930 summer issue of the *Southwest Review,* continues, "He sat there, back against a tree, often looking over the scene that was to be the background of his novel, and wrote in tiny, fast words in a thick, blue-boarded blank book."

Correlating Lawrence's references to *The Plumed Serpent* in his letters, one finds that his plans for it were formulated early. From the start he intended to write it twice, both times in Mexico with an intervening period. At first the interval between the two versions was to be only about ten months, and Secker was hoping to get the second version by October 1924 so he could bring it out the following January. The first delay was caused when Lawrence, deciding to join Frieda in England, cut short his second stay in Mexico, thereby abandoning his plan to rewrite the novel there that winter. Then from the ranch on April 10 Lawrence wrote Curtis Brown, "I shan't get my Mexican novel finished this year—shall stay the summer here, I think." In Lawrence's May 18 letter to Mrs. Carswell, the timetable had been extended even further: "I think we shall stay till October, then go down to Mexico, where I must work at my novel." Lawrence reaffirmed his plans when he wrote Earl Brewster on July 15: "I want to go down to Mexico City early in October. F. loves it here, but I hanker rather for old Mexico. And I have a novel half finished down there, which I want to get done this winter."

The Chapala version had the dual-stranded story already outlined. The heroine's name was Kate Burns; and, although two years younger than the final Kate Leslie, she was at a comparable crucial stage in her own life. She, too, went to the headquarters of the new Quetzalcoatl movement, and one of the climaxes of the now-intertwined story also appears in the final version: an attempt on the life of one of the leaders on the roof of his *hacienda*. Kate shoots a second assailant. The sequel to the raid is also the same: the ritual execution of the would-be murderers. Kate is asked to join them as a woman leader. In the Chapala version, Kate declines and packs to return to England. In the Chapala version, too, the Quetzalcoatl movement is still local, its successful sweep through the rest of Mexico was developed later in Oaxaca.

The essential content of the new religion—as distinct from its outward form—is also the same in the Chapala version. We have seen it earlier in *Kangaroo.* It was to be a religion to regenerate humankind, badly in need of new ideals. True manhood and the love of comrades were basic values. The dark gods of the unconscious were to be recognized and revered. The movement would derive from a spiritual leader and a second man, who would train and discipline other men so they could simultaneously fight for the new religion and serve as inspiring examples of the new manhood and brotherhood that would reanimate Mexico. In the Chapala version, too, a good deal of the leader's faith is based on the strong, deep connections of the brown-skinned Indians with their aboriginal natures.

The University of Texas acquired both manuscripts of *The Plumed Serpent* in the spring of 1964, an unexpected discovery on my first visit to Austin. My examination of the four copybooks disclosed that many pages of the two blue ones containing the first version had scratched-out passages with new material written above the lines but the Oaxaca copybooks contain hardly a crossed-out word, truly the "beautiful MS" Lawrence described to Brett during a bad period in September 1929 when it seemed to have been stolen. The unfaltering flow is evidence that Lawrence had worked out most of its problems in his mind. He knew how and where new material should be added, what old material should be cut, and what should be done with old material that needed elaboration, intensification, alteration, or shifting about. Because the revisions he made group themselves into recognizable types one can get a clear idea of what went on in his mind when he was thinking about the novel but not actually working on it. This is especially true, if one knows the details of his biography in the ruminative period. In a postscript to Garnett about the first draft of the novel that ultimately divided into *The Rainbow* and *Women in Love,* Lawrence admitted, "All along I knew what ailed that book." And the revisions of *Quetzalcoatl* show that this was also true in general terms for the Chapala draft of the Mexican novel. This knowledge made him alert to conversations, characters, scraps of knowledge, books, and telling experiences.

Lawrence's keen awareness of two of the Chapala draft's major ailments was illustrated by the four stories which let him try out solutions for Kate: "None of That," "The Woman Who Rode Away," *St. Mawr* and "The Princess." The Chapala handling of Kate—depicting her as just an observant tourist—made the novel a thinly disguised travel book. Her final departure made her a weak character who really participated only once, when she saved Ramón's life by firing on the man creeping up the stairs.

Novelist that he was, Lawrence knew he needed to make his setting still more vivid and real, even though its physical vividness was already the draft's greatest strength. Many incidents needed to be expanded and new elements of the plot developed. He also needed to improve his characterizations, all as part of his need to make his story more believable. Stronger characters would help, but the new religion of Ramón and Cipriano had to be convincing as a spiritual gospel. The essential holiness of its central vision needed clearer expression than in the Chapala version and its mythologically based ritual had to become compelling to Mexicans of Indian heritage.

Furthermore, the religion had to be a gospel that Lawrence himself wanted to preach. On the practical side, he wanted to create a colony whose members would be able to live by their best ideals because they had created an environment where such freedom was possible. On the theoretical side, he wanted his new religion to bring men and women into a nobler, more fulfilled existence. The colony idea had fallen through for the first time when nobody managed to get to Florida in 1915 and again by the time he got to Oaxaca because all but Brett backed out. Friends failing, almost certainly Lawrence placed compensating stress on creating a gospel that would inspire strangers.

As a final complication he had set his novel at a precise point in Mexico's history. Thus, the new religion must not only be Mexican in flavor and related to Mexico's cultural traditions but had to be one that might have arisen plausibly during his chosen period. Historic, political, and economic facts had to be accurate. Beyond facts, he had to capture the spirit and atmosphere of Mexico after fourteen years of revolution.

Lawrence also knew that every successful religion must have the equivalent of a Bible, with a cosmogony, creation myths, a Saviour, a cast of holy personages and ethical mandates, a hymnal, a Book of Common Prayer, and a collection of sermons, sacred images, a body of easily recognized visual symbols, and a repertoire of vestments, stances for praying at peak moments of worship, services for such occasions as marriage, burial, and ordination, each with its sacramental rituals, and regular services with established orders of procedures. Comparing the first and second versions of *The Plumed Serpent,* it is easy to deduce that Lawrence saw one of the chief deficiencies of the religion in the first draft: its liturgy was too thin. Present were the ethical ideas, the conviction of God, and intimations of God's various manifestations, but the first draft lacked nearly all the poems, hymns, and sermons that are one of the novel's distinguishing characteristics. It had only about 130 lines of verse, few visual symbols, and almost no religious ceremonies. So most of the panoply of Quetzalcoatl's religion, many of its services, and the bulk of its liturgy were invented by Lawrence between the two versions. The creative effort must have been enormous. He did not have to write a whole Bible, but he had to conceive one in his mind from which he could derive hymns, rituals, and services. He had to design banners, emblems, costumes, statues, ritual objects, blankets, etc., and even compose a primitive kind of music.

In the spring of 1911 when Lawrence's fiancée, Louie Burrows, had asked him about his new poetry, he said he would answer her questions when he saw her. "But remember," he cautioned, "I am not a very ready talker, about my own work especially." Eleven years later, when Lawrence was drafting *The Plumed Serpent* at Chapala, Bynner recalled how Lawrence "seldom talked about what he was writing." And Frieda has testified, "He really disliked talking about his writing." He seldom wrote his friends about his literary problems either. Thus, little in his own words reports the weaknesses he saw in the Chapala draft, although in Oaxaca he confided to Brett: "Chapala has not really the spirit of Mexico; it is too tamed, too touristy. This place is more untouched."

Repeatedly Lawrence strengthened both main male characters and integrated the essay-like sections on Mexico with the development of the protagonists. The revisions are striking evidence of Lawrence's powers to criticize his own work, emphasizing what trial-run stories revealed: how deliberately and self-consciously he worked to refine his art. A before-and-after will illustrate how he revised to bring his material into sharper focus and how he moved in more closely to everything in his story.

In the typescript (pp. 51-52) Lawrence speaks of "a churchful of dark-wrapped women kneeling like dark toadstools on the ground and silent in a devotion of fear." It is a vividly evocative sentence, but his revision eliminated the unfriendly toadstool image and added depth, not only to the description but to their devotion: "Many women kneeling in a dim church, all hooded in their dark-blue *rebozos,* the pallor of their skirts on the floor, their heads and shoulders wrapped dark and tight, as they swayed with devotion of fear and ecstasy! A churchful of dark-wrapped women sunk there in wild humble supplication of dread and bliss filled Kate with tenderness and revulsion. They crouched like people not quite created."

The second version thus does the double duty of explicating the heroine's feelings and becoming part of her story.

A more extended and more dramatic instance of Lawrence moving closer to his material is provided by the finale to "Auto da Fe," the chapter describing how the men of Quetzalcoatl took the images from the church of Sayula, loaded them on a large *canoa,* transported them to an island in the lake, and burned them. In both versions, the description of the images being carried from the church to the *canoa* are alike. The same figures are described: Christ in the glass coffin, the Virgin in her blue mantle, Saint Anthony with his child, Saint Francis looking at his cross, Saint Anne, and Saint Joaquin. But in the draft, the actual conflagration is only described as it appeared from the beach of Chapala—smoke threading up in the distance. In the novel the reader is taken to the island with the images and sees them set on the iron bars of a grill. Ramón kindles the fire below them with a magnifying glass, and then . . .

> There was a crackling, and a puffing of whitish smoke, the sweet scent of ocote, and orange-red tongues of half substantial flames were leaping

up in the hot white air. Hot breaths blew suddenly, sudden flames gushed up, and the ocote, full of sweet resin, began to roar. The glass of the great box emitted strange, painful yelps as it splintered and fell tinkling. Between the iron bars, brownish flames pushed up among the images, which at once went black. The little vestments of silk and satin withered in a moment to blackness, the caked wounds of paint bubbled black.

This is only part of what is described. Finally, the young priest who accompanied the images to the island flings his linen vestment, his stole, his chasuble and his black cassock, onto the fire and is revealed, surprisingly, as a convert to the new religion of Quetzalcoatl.

This revision, like that of the women in the church, is actually only an amplification of the original material. But there are many instances where the coming closer involves almost complete transformation. Between them, the amplifications and the transformations almost double the work, with the 469 pages of the Chapala draft developing into 796 in the Oaxaca one. A number of the Chapala chapters developed into separate chapters. The story of Kate's first visit to Ramón's *hacienda,* for instance, needs only a single chapter of twenty-one pages in the typescript, because she merely goes for tea. But in the novel she stays overnight, and the 100-page account is divided into four chapters. The novel has twenty-seven chapters against the draft's nineteen.

CHANGES BECAUSE OF OAXACA

Lawrence needed proper names that would disguise real places or personages yet seem convincingly Mexican. Montes, for example, masks President Calles. The most obvious proper name borrowed from the Valley of Oaxaca was that of Tlacolula, the town between Oaxaca and Mitla that has a famous Sunday market. In the Chapala version, Lawrence disguised Coyoacán, the suburb in which Mrs. Nuttall lived, as Tacubaya, but Tacubaya is really a suburb near Coyoacán: too close for comfort. Tlacolula was safer. Jamiltepec, in the Costa Chica where the Kulls were headed, provided a more convincing disguise than the draft's Las Yemas for El Manglar, the *hacienda* near Chapala that Lawrence borrowed as the model for Ramón's home.

Among the personal names suggested by Oaxaca contacts is José García, who went with the Lawrences to Mitla. The novelist used García for the young intellectual—partly Miguel Covarrubias and partly Genaro Estrada—who took Kate to see the Rivera and Orozco frescos. Another is that of Maruca, the daughter of Doña María Monros. In the novel he bestowed it on the traitorous sewing-girl implicated in the attempt on Ramón's life.

He borrowed the name of the Hotel Francia for the Orizaba Hotel where he introduced a new horror story of the arbitrary Laborites who spare one defiant hotel manager and shoot the next one before he can speak. Introducing grisly stories of banditry, like those of Winfield Scott (disguised as Bell), was part of Lawrence's campaign to reduce the tameness that he felt weakened his picture of Mexico in the Chapala version. He also borrowed from Oaxaca the reports of its foreign residents that marauding bandits made it unsafe to walk outside the city limits. Thus, in the new description of Chapala, "Kate was glad to be walking. The one depressing thing about life in the village was that one could not walk out into the country. There was always the liability to be held up or attacked. And she had walked already, as far as possible, in every direction, accompanied usually by Ezequiel. Now she was beginning to feel a prisoner."

Lawrence went outside geography altogether to rename his Oaxaca. Duke, the burglar-shooting Texan who tells the story of the dummy telephone, is described as "a man up from Mixcoatl . . . a capital way to the south." Mixcoatl is a Nahuatl name for a hunting god, later than Quetzalcoatl but earlier than the emergence of the Aztecs, and believed to be a ruler of the Place of the Dawn. Lawrence must have fished him from Spence's *The Gods of Mexico*. Although he used Mixcoatl as a pseudonym for Oaxaca, he did not work him into the pantheon of gods that Ramón was trying to bring back into the consciousness of his fellow-Mexicans. Lawrence used the dummy phone story, not only to provide a glimpse of Mexico outside the range of tourist vision, but to link his story more securely to history and the world of Mexican politics. It also contributed to his scornful picture of Mexican leaders, especially the labor leaders who had gained political power, and helped darken the background of cynicism and exploitation, illustrating that in a country like Mexico, democratic government was a grimly ineffective joke. Finally, the anecdote helped establish an atmosphere of hopelessness, lending plausibility to the people's receptiveness to a new religion.

The need to intensify Mexico's pre-Columbian past was part of Lawrence's multiple task in revising. Oaxaca's "hard . . . zig-zagging Mitla" provided him with another Mexican archaeological site, which he could add to those of Teotihuacán and Cholula. The Mitla description, besides evoking Mexico's ruined ancient past which inspires the new religion, also gives Kate another reason for wanting to leave Mexico.

Indian Mexico was another aspect of the country that Lawrence knew he had to intensify. For this need, too, he found help in Oaxaca; for, even though the middle class *mestizos* have notably increased, one of the charms of the city to this day is the preponderance of Indians among its inhabitants. Lawrence could observe Indians at close range, especially when he was at the Hotel Francia, and could add Zapotecs to the tribes he had met elsewhere. He provides a thumbnail catalogue of types of Indians: "the handsome men of Jalisco, with a scarlet blanket on one shoulder," "the too-often degenerate men of Mexico Valley, their heads through the middle of their ponchos" (types he had met on his first visit to Mexico), "the dark faces and the big black eyes on the coast of Sinaloa" (which he saw on his second trip down the west coast), and "the quick little Indians, quick as spiders, down in Oaxaca." "Most of Cipriano's men are Zapotecas from the hills," Ramón told Kate; and he added, "They love chasing men who aren't," which is a clear reflection of what Lawrence was told about Ibarra's *Serranos,* who frequently swept down from the Sierra de Juárez to drive out governors and install new ones. Shortly before the images are burned, a number of Cipriano's Zapotec soldiers appear in Sayula. "There must have been fifty or more, little men, not the tall soldiers in slouched hats. These were little, quick, compact men, like Cipriano, and they talked in a strange Indian language, very subdued." Lawrence borrowed heavily on his Zapotec neighbors for the outward appearance of the new Cipriano in the Oaxaca version of the novel: "His face was changeless and intensely serious, serious almost with a touch of childishness. But the curious blackness of his eyelashes lifted so strangely, with such intense unconscious maleness from his eyes, the movement of his hand was so odd, quick, light as he ate . . . and his dark-colored lips were so helplessly savage, as he ate or briefly spoke, that her heart stood still."

A major embellishment added to the new religion in the Oaxaca version was dancing. And the liveliest inspiration for the type introduced is worth circumstantiating.

Besides seeing the great dance of Taos Pueblo on the day of San Geronimo in 1922, Lawrence saw it again in September 1924, shortly before leaving for Oaxaca. Before each of these fiestas, Mrs. Luhan had Indians come to her studio to dance their round dance and to give her guests and other friends lessons so they could participate. "Last night," Lawrence wrote Mrs. Carswell on 29 September 1922, "the young Indians came down to dance in the studio, with two drums; and we all joined in. It is fun: and queer." The 1924 dancing in the studio is described in *Lawrence and Brett,* and after the Indian men had danced alone, Brett reports: " 'There is something new for you,' you [Lawrence]say to me; but I am too amazed, too overwhelmed by the strange beauty of it, to have anything to say. 'There are two dances we will be allowed to dance in,' you remark."

A little later the drum began for one of those other dances, and "suddenly a young Indian woman gets up and crosses over to you and says in a high tinny voice: 'Will you dance with me?' You are taken aback, but rising quickly, you reply nervously with a shy little giggle. 'Yes.' Then how shy, how embarrassed you are, as you and she alone in the middle of the room begin to dance."

The other dance Lawrence participated in was the Circle Dance. The chief step for both dances was a kind of treading, and one of the new sections describes how Kate learned the steps: "Her feet were feeling the way into the dance-step. She was beginning to learn softly to loosen her weight, to loosen the uplift of her life, and let it pour slowly, darkly, with an ebbing gush, rhythmically in soft, rhythmic gushes from her feet into the dark body of the earth." Presumably, Kate's learning describes Lawrence's own.

This treading step appears in a number of the regional dances of Oaxaca, especially those from La Cañada and the Isthmus of Tehuantepec. Although Lawrence wrote Mrs. Isaacs of *Theatre Arts Magazine* that "there's never a dance down here," he must have subsequently seen some dances or had his mistake pointed out to him. For one revision records how in some out-of-the-way plazas people were beginning to dance "the slow round dance" that Kate had joined, adding information that may be doubtful: "For the old dances of the Aztecs and the Zapotecs, of all the submerged Indian races, are based on the old, singing bird-step of the Red Indians of the north." As Carlota, Ramón's wife, lies dying, Kate sees men dancing "the old, barefooted, absorbed dancing of the Indians, the dance of downward sinking absorption. It was the dance of these people too, just the same: the Dance of the Aztecs and Zapotecs and the Huicholes, just the same in essence, indigenous to America."

Lawrence twice made use of Oaxaca's patroness, the Virgin of Solitude. In the first example the white-handed Virgin with "moon-like power and the intense potency of grief" is the object of Cipriano's devotion during boyhood. It also helped make it plausible why a man like Cipriano should fall in love with a woman like Kate. In addition, the sudden suggestion of the Virgin's hands as Kate wept into hers in remembering her dead husband creates a new incident for the developing relationship. The Virgin of Soledad reappears in the song, "Jesus' Farewell." Fairly early in the typescript, hints of hymns and lessons emerge, but no text is provided before the start of the ninth chapter. The first texts are all prose until the fourteenth chapter. In the revision, liturgical passages in poetic form appear almost as soon as Lawrence gets his heroine to Sayula.

"Jesus' Farewell," a rudimentary eighteen lines in the typescript, is the text that opens the ceremony of burning the images. Purportedly sung by the spirit of Jesus himself, it exhorts his saints to troop from their shrines and follow him away from Mexico "to the pool of peace and forgetting in heaven." Among the saints burned is Soledad.

Oaxaca, as we know, gave Lawrence a new character in the person of Eulogio Gillow, the city's first archbishop, a powerful influence on García Vigil and Padre Rickards. But the novel provides a further anecdote that sounds too probable to be apocryphal. In the Chapala account Cipriano saved his mistress's life after snakebite by sucking the venom from her ankle. The grateful woman has him educated in England. In *Kangaroo* Lawrence had likened stay-at-homes during World War I to jackals: "The bite of a jackal is blood-poisoning and mortification." Cipriano was feared because others believed that the venom would make his own bite poisonous. In the Oaxaca account, Lawrence omits the superstition that he was venomous; and it is his life that is saved by the bishop, a living figure the reader can like and admire, as well as one who could plausibly inspire the affection the new Cipriano always felt for him.

In the typescript, Kate learns the snake-bite story from her American cousin, Owen Rhys, with whom she goes to a bullfight. Owen, modeled on Bynner, had learned the story by hearsay. In the novel Lawrence exploits the new story much more cleverly by having Cipriano reveal aspects of himself as he tells it directly to Kate. After explaining that the bishop owned a large *hacienda* in Oaxaca, he continued:

"My father was one of the overseers of the *hacienda*. When I was a little boy I came running to my father, when the Bishop was there, with something in my hands—so!"—and he made a cup of his hand. "I was a small child—three or four years of age—somewhere there. What I had in my hands was a yellow scorpion, one of the small ones, very poisonous, no?" And he lifted the cup of his small, slender, dark hands, as if to show Kate the creature.

"Well, the Bishop was talking to my father, and he saw what I had got before my father did. So he told me at once, to put the scorpion in his hat—the Bishop's hat, no? Of course I did what he told me, and I put the scorpion in his hat, and it did not bite me. If it had stung me I should have died, of course. But I didn't know, so I supposed the *alacran* was not interested."

In other words, the alert bishop had extraordinary presence of mind, and because he provided his hat as a receptacle into which the scorpion could be dumped without being lifted, he saved the child's life. After this he became the boy's godfather.

Undoubtedly the most important alteration that Lawrence made in his novel because of Oaxaca was the new characterization of Cipriano. Lawrence's first description of Cipriano in the typescript is not of an Indian. He wears a pale-blue military cloak, "which made him seem Italian," is described as "a gentleman," and is the host at the dinner party Kate attends—not Ramón. Ramón actually began as more Indian in this manuscript. Lawrence had definitely decided by the thirteenth chapter of the draft that Cipriano was to be Indian, for Kate feels "the terrible distance between his blood and her own." He is never linked to a specific tribe and he is born and raised on a *hacienda* near Jalapa, in the state of Veracruz. But once Lawrence got to Oaxaca and encountered Zapotecs, Cipriano comes into focus, is given a new childhood and a seminary education, remains in England until his Oxford education is complete, then returns voluntarily at the age of twenty-two because he wishes to serve as a soldier in the Revolution. In the earlier draft, the death of his patroness brings him back due to lack of funds before the Revolution. He is then commissioned by the reactionary Díaz.

In the novel, Kate asks Cipriano how his feelings for Ramón compare with his feelings for his godfather. He likes the two men equally, he tells her, but the bishop, a sincere Roman Catholic, cannot see the real Mexico as clearly as Ramón. Furthermore, "How else should one believe, except by being compelled?" he asks Kate, showing how little he was an intellectual. "I like Ramón for that, that he can compel me. . . . When I grew up, and my godfather could not compel me to believe, I was very unhappy. . . . But Ramón compels me, and that is very good."

THE RELIGION LAWRENCE INVENTED

How much of the religion that Lawrence invented was conceived by the time the draft was completed? The principles of a hierarchy of leaders, its appeal to true manhood, the love of comrades, and the dark gods of the unconscious had been established as chief principles. Lawrence also knew that it was to be polytheistic; its gods were to be embodied in human beings; it was to interchange deities, with Christ and the Virgin Mary giving way to resuscitated pre-Columbian gods; the chief gods to be revived and embodied were Quetzalcoatl and Huitzilopochtli, the war god who guided the Aztecs on their pilgrimage to the Valley of Mexico, and it was to have a liturgy, extensive symbols, and dramatic rituals. But much of the theology is vague in the Chapala version, especially in the long lecture on the risen Adam redeemed by blood, which begins on page 331.

That Lawrence was thinking searchingly about the religion while he was in England between versions is evidenced by his January visit to Frederick Carter in Shropshire. Carter was a painter and illustrator who had become fascinated with the relationships between the symbols of the zodiac and those in the Revelation of John. He sent Lawrence a manuscript about his ideas in Chapala. It had an extraordinary effect. In the shorter of the introductions written in 1929 for a later installment of Carter's work, Lawrence said:

I have read books on astronomy which made me dizzy with the sense of illimitable space. But the heart melts and dies—it is the disembodied mind alone which follows on through this horrible void of space, where lonely stars hang in awful isolation. . . . Why then, this sense of release, of marvelous release, in reading the *Dragon?* I don't know. But anyhow, the *whole* imagination is released, not a part only. In astronomical space, one can only *move,* one cannot be. In the astrological heavens, that is to say, the ancient zodiacal heavens, the whole man is set free, once the imagination crosses the border. The whole man, bodily and spiritual, walks in the magnificent fields of the stars, and the stars have names, and the feet tread splendidly upon—we know not what, but the heavens, instead of untreadable space.[3]

This experience of the astrological heavens induced by Carter—and Lawrence says it was his first—greatly extended his idea of the cosmos. By showing him the heavenly bodies as they were known to the Chaldeans, Carter gave him back the sun and the moon, and gave him an extended sense of his own being as the macrocosm, "big and glittering and vast with a sumptuous vastness." Lawrence wanted to include this new feeling for the cosmos in his Mexican novel to reawaken a "responsive connection" with the cosmos, to borrow a phrase he used in developing the idea in his *Apocalypse.* Lawrence glimpsed how it could be done by apprehending relationships between the dragon of John's Revelation and the great plumed serpent of Mexico. But by mid-June, when the Carter manuscript reached him, the first version of the novel was nearly completed. Lawrence's changes would wait for the second.

Meanwhile, as he wrote on June 18, he hoped to see Carter when he came to England. Carter has vividly described the visit in his *D. H. Lawrence and the Body Mystical.* Beside a fire in the rectory, the two men discussed how to get Carter's work published. But Lawrence "came really to discuss the symbol of the dragon. He loved the dragon symbol—for its ubiquity I should think—it had met him everywhere in Old Mexico, staring out on him from old ruins, jaws gaping to hold doorways and gleaming here and there wherever he might be. It was a god there, a god he admired."

Ten months later Lawrence was back in Mexico City. Eduardo Rendón, who told me the scandal behind "None of That," was one of the Mexicans with whom Lawrence discussed his religious ideas. In 1971 in his home in Cuernavaca, Don Eduardo recalled how he had been sympathetic to a regeneration of Mexico's religious life and especially to new spiritual impulses that would help Mexico preserve its culture against the influences flooding in from the United States. "He could have made something really good," Don Eduardo told me, "if he had based it on the religion of the Franciscans of the sixteenth century and the sorcery of the Indians, with the two harmonized. The Franciscan beliefs could have made the Indians idyllic. Old Romance could have been revived here, and Mexico could have been the key to its revival. The thing needed was to do away with the Baroque: to revive the Romanesque world of Cortés and the friars who had fled Spain. And Lawrence could have done it for he had read Cortés's letters to the king of Spain. I urged him, too, to study the other Indians of Mexico, not the Aztecs. But Lawrence wouldn't listen. He was very dictatorial. He would lose his temper and we could never have a real discussion. And when I read *The Plumed Serpent* and saw that he had stuck to all his old ideas, I said 'This damn thing is nonsense.' ''

Lawrence himself did not want his religion to replicate the past. "We can never recover an old vision once it has been supplanted," he wrote in his introduction for Carter's manuscript. His ideal expressed in the introduction was "a new vision in harmony with the memories of old, far-off, far, far-off experience that lies within us." Undoubtedly, Rendón's ideas were unacceptable because of their Christian content. Lawrence's rejection of Christianity went back at least to 1916 as shown in a letter to Mrs. Carswell: "I count Christianity as one of the great historical facts, the has-been. That is why I am not a conscientious objector: I am not a Christian. Christianity is insufficient to me. I too believe a man must fight."

Although Lawrence rejected Rendón's suggestion, he explored ways to help him conjure up a vision that would harmonize with Mexican racial memories. He had written Gamio, then tried to see him in Mexico City. He had successfully located another archaeologist, the woman whose tea party was already in the first draft of his novel. Zelia Nuttall gave Lawrence one of her books, according to Frieda in rebutting William York Tindall's claim that Lawrence had access to Mrs. Nuttall's library. "He never stayed with Mrs. Nuttall," she wrote Tindall, "never had books out of her library, only the one of her own she gave him." It is not hard to deduce that Mrs. Nuttall's gift was her massive study, *The Fundamental Principles of Old and New World Civilizations,* because her only other book was *New Light on Drake* and there is no sign of Lawrence having read the Drake volume, whereas *Serpent* provides ample evidence that he read *Principles.* But when did Mrs. Nuttall give Lawrence her book? In the spring of 1923, when she had him to tea or in the fall of 1924 when the Lawrences lunched with her twice, the last time only two days before they left for Oaxaca?

Her *Fundamental Principles* influenced *The Plumed Serpent* in nine ways, striking and unmistakable,[4] but none of them appear in the first version. Clearly, then, it was during the 1924 meetings that Mrs. Nuttall gave Lawrence the book, probably because he discussed his ideas with her, as he had done with Rendón and wanted to do with Gamio. He read it in Oaxaca. It was even more of a godsend than Spence's *The Gods of Mexico* though that other major book he read in Oaxaca, as revealed in his Aztec fantasias, is not to be discounted. Mrs. Nuttall's book, with its emphasis on star worship, dualism, and the male and female principles, presented a reconstruction of pre-Columbian beliefs closer to Lawrence's own ideas, especially after he had embraced Carter's vision of the Chaldean cosmos. In consequence, *Principles* gave his imagination greatly welcomed stimulus for his liturgical labors.

To solve two of his problems—propagating a gospel that was convincing as religion and that was personally compatible—he transformed Ramón from a thought-adventurer into a fulfilled mystic. To achieve this end, he had to sacrifice one of the most interesting chapters, "Conversion," the flashback mentioned in the discussion of Gamio as the initial inspiration for Ramón. It traces Ramón's intellectual life through his research for a history of Mexico since independence, and his firsthand observation of the Revolution. Successive disillusionments convinced him that "you can do nothing in real achievement till you get down to the religious level." Yet he also came to the somewhat frustrating conclusion that he could not act until he had gained at least one disciple. In other words, this Ramón is a Western intellectual. In Lawrence's new concept, Ramón is a mystic who has fully learned how to open the doors of his soul to admit his Lord, thus feeling justified in assuming a god's role. From the start, the new Ramón is presented as an engimatic and mysterious figure, whose "eyes brooded and smouldered with an incomprehensible, unyielding fire"; he has compelling composure and speaks with effortless wisdom. That he is the genius behind the new religion of Quetzalcoatl appears only by degrees. His role is not confirmed until Kate's interest has been thoroughly aroused by repeated signs of the religion in action.

Once Kate has heard a man singing the first hymn of Quetzalcoatl and has joined in the dance of the two concentric circles, the reader, for the first time, learns that Ramón retires to pray naked in the darkness to achieve contact with the nameless god from whom he receives power, inspiration, and disengagement from ordinary concerns. Then she learns that he has a circle of initiates who gather to pray with him. In his sermon to them he stresses consciousness of the "Now and the I AM." The mysticism of the inner circle is nonspecific; the second hymn, spoken at this service, contains no reference to Quetzalcoatl but instead invokes the mystic place named as the Morning Star from which the power of the cosmos emanates. Ramón is recognized as the Lord of the Morning Star because of his contact with that place.

The novel really has two religions. Ramón's mysticism is something that he tries to share with a select few, including Cipriano, although his gifts are military rather than spiritual. The second religion, full of symbols, "manifestations," and ceremonies, Ramón has conceived so that the multitudes seeing "only the waving of wings" can still be brought to absorb some of the power, uplift, and idealism inherent in forces they do not understand. For himself, Ramón has to "keep his soul in touch with the heart of the world." His wife, Carlota, says, "He wants to make a new connection between the people and God." Kate, in a moment of agreement with his fundamental aims, says to herself: "We must go back to pick up old threads. We must take up the old, broken impulse that will connect us with the mystery of the cosmos again, now we are at the end of our tether."

That the underlying universal religion in *The Plumed Serpent* was Lawrence's own can be recognized by recalling the religious beliefs he had published in *Kangaroo,* and his description of how the cosmos was opened to his imagination as he read Carter's manuscript under the vast star-filled sky at Lake Chapala. The double concept of the Morning Star makes it more thoroughly Lawrencean. Ramón preaches that it is the sun behind the sun, the power source for the cosmos. It is a symbol for a concept of wholeness. Lawrence had used the crown in the British coat of arms as the symbol for reconciling and balancing, the lion symbolizing the powers of the body and the unicorn symbolizing the powers of the spirit. Later he saw the Holy Ghost in the same position between God the Father and God the Son. By the time he was ready to revise *The Plumed Serpent,* he had developed the idea of the Morning Star standing between the night and the day, as the new symbol bringing consummation through balancing two conflicting forces that must neither be denied nor confused. As the marriage service he added in Oaxaca indicates, because the innermost being could be fixed on the Star it could symbolize both an abiding place for the individual soul, and, for those loyal to the Star, the place of profoundest union.

Why, then, did Lawrence confuse this personal religion with a dubious Mexican one? Especially when, as we have seen, he was reaching forward to the soul as a new symbol for the surpassing element burning between the body and the spirit. An obvious answer is that he was writing a novel and not a bible. Another is given in the open letter that Ramón addresses to the clergy: "Different peoples must have different Saviours, as they have different speech and different colour. The final mystery is one mystery. But the manifestations are many. God must come to Mexico in a blanket and in *huaraches,* else He is no God of the Mexicans, they cannot know him."

Elsewhere Ramón defends his liturgy by saying: "One had to speak the language of one's own people." And in still another: "Quetzalcoatl is to me only the symbol of the best a man may be." Speaking of the "perfectly unfathomable life mystery at the center of the universe," he says, "If I call the mystery the Morning Star, surely it doesn't matter! A man's blood can't beat in the abstract."

My 1946 acquaintance with pre-Columbian deities when I first read *Serpent* was nil and I was mightily impressed that a visiting Englishman had found the time to learn about such obscure gods as Huitzilopochtli, Itzpapalotl, Tezcatlipoca, Tlaloc, and Malintzi and had such intimate knowledge of ancient religious ceremonies. I, like most readers unfamiliar with Mexico when they first read *Serpent,* thought it was all authentic. By the time of my second reading, however, I had been back to Mexico fourteen times, and began my 1961 reading of *Serpent* to sort out its pre-Columbian elements. I discovered that besides Quetzalcoatl, there were only five gods and three were window-dressing. Tezcatlipoca was mentioned once, Tlaloc twice, and Itzpapalotl four times. Malintzi was a Lawrence invention. There never was a Mesoamerican goddess of that name and Lawrence had borrowed her pseudonym from Malinche, the Indian gentlewoman who became Cortés's mistress and translator. Lawrence's knowledge of the ancient Mexican religions, then, was much skimpier than his imaginative powers had led me to think. As I read the draft of "Quetzalcoatl" at Harvard, I discovered that Lawrence had added Itzpapalotl and Tezcatlipoca in Oaxaca but had subtracted two Chapala deities, Coatlicue and Huichililobos (a variant of Huitzilopochtli).

In short, Quetzalcoatl and Huitzilopochtli are the only ancient Mexican gods who play substantial roles in either version of *The Plumed Serpent.* In the first, the two men merely set themselves up as living symbols by pretending to be manifestations of the gods. Occult symbolism is not introduced until the penultimate chapter and is largely borrowed from Theosophy and Rosicrucianism. Reading the Chapala draft, we see that in 1923 Lawrence understood that the serpent moved on the ground, yet had wings enabling it to fly. Thus, it symbolized a god with jurisdiction in two elements. But otherwise he perceived Quetzalcoatl in the disastrous role he played for the Aztecs in 1519: namely, that Quetzalcoatl was a white man who had brought their ancestors a high level of civilization, promised to return from the east, and then disappeared. Montezuma and many other Aztecs, identifying Cortés as this returning culture-hero-turned god, vacillated. Because Cortés obviously wasn't Quetzalcoatl, why not envision a modern man claiming that at last the ancient god really had returned?

In Oaxaca, however, Lawrence learned that Quetzalcoatl, among other things, was a wind god. The Kate of the novel, besides being two years older than the Kate of the draft, is also better informed about Quet-zalcoatl, which makes her more responsive to the new religious move-ment. The god's name thus evokes "the wind, the breath of life the eyes that see and are unseen, like the stars beyond the blue of day." The idea is developed again in the first of the prose sermons—another passage added in Oaxaca: "The man on the hill said: I am Quetzalcoatl, who breathed moisture on your dry mouths. I filled your breasts with breath from beyond the sun. I am the wind that whirls from the heart of the earth, the little winds that whirl like snakes around your feet and your legs and your thighs, lifting up the head of the snake of your body, in whom is your power."

Lawrence's imagination had obviously transformed the anthropo-logical facts into a beautiful and powerful concept of a wind god. More important, however, was Lawrence's discovery that Quetzalcoatl, accord-ing to legend, had been transformed into the planet we know as Venus.

Next to the sun and the moon, Venus is the largest and most bril-liant of the heavenly bodies seen from the earth. It is not surprising, there-fore, that a people who worshipped the sun and the moon also worshipped Venus. Sometimes it rises three hours before the sun; sometimes it sets the same length of time after the sun. Thus it is both the morning and the evening star. Because of its brilliance it outlasts the other stars in the morning and appears earliest in the twilight. In the latitude of Oaxaca, morning Venus is so large, white, and beautiful when the sky is still black three hours before dawn that one easily understands why the ancient people felt that it, as well as the sun and the moon, represented a god. Probably Lawrence was already familiar with Venus as the morning star, but the information that Quetzalcoatl was associated with Venus had provided the sanction to conceive the pre-Columbian deity as the Lord of the Morning Star. In Oaxaca, Lawrence composed the second hymn of Quetzalcoatl:

> The Lord of the Morning Star
> Stood between the day and the night:
> As a bird that lifts its wings, and stands
> With the bright wing on the right
> And the wing of the dark on the left
> The Dawn Star stood into night.

The Morning Star links the ancient religion of the historic Quetzal-coatl and Lawrence's personal religion. It also enabled him to make sin-cere use of the plumed serpent—another aspect of the multi-form Quetzalcoatl—as a symbol in both religions. Its dual characteristic, true of the ancient religion, symbolized for him the opposed forces of body and spirit that he felt had to be held in balance by the Holy Ghost in its new metaphorical guise as the Morning Star. The Quetzalcoatlism of *The Plumed Serpent,* then, may be dubious in its Mesoamericanism, but it is not dubiously Lawrencean. How far back into his life it reached can be gathered from his letter to Koteliansky of 3 January 1915, when he described the badge and flag he had in mind for their colony, Rananim. The bird for the badge was to be a phoenix, but the flag was to be like a Huitzilopochtli blanket: "the blazing, ten-pointed star, scarlet on a black background."

The novel's symbol for Quetzalcoatl—an eagle within a circle formed by a serpent with its tail in its mouth—is one of the picturesquely important elements Lawrence added to the work in Oaxaca. This symbol, sometimes referred to as the eye of Quetzalcoatl because, from a distance, it resembles a human eye, recurs repeatedly through the book— on leaflets, on *ponchos,* on *sombreros,* on the sail of the ship taking the images out to be burned, on the pendants given to Kate and Cipriano by Ramón as he married them, and on the tips of the steeples of the church as replacements for the Christian crosses. In doing so, it adds considerably to the reality of the new movement, corresponding to the star and the crescent, the hammer and sickle, and the cross. But like the goddess Malintzi, the symbol is a Lawrence invention with no exact counterpart in pre-Columbian religion. In fact, giving the serpent's feathers to the eagle runs counter to the significance of the plumed serpent. But alluding to the eagle of the coat of arms of modern Mexico contributes to Ramón's aim of appealing to Mexican national feeling. It was also in Oaxaca that Lawrence invented most of the other costume elements like the white *serapes* of Quetzalcoatl bordered with black and blue, the gorgeous scarlet and black *serapes* of the men of Huitzilopochtli, the different woven sashes, and the various types of *huaraches.* He also added Huitzilopochtli's black and red body paint, with the whitened jaw and the yellow band across the area of the eyes. As a result, Lawrence's living Huitzilopochtli in the person of Cipriano might be closer in appearance to the Aztec ceremonial figure than any of the others. But even he is far from an exact recreation. To bring the Huitzilopochtli of the novel a little closer to the Aztec war god, Lawrence had Cipriano stab the assailants of Ramón to the heart (in the Chapala version they were shot). But Cipriano did not pull out their hearts and the absence of human sacrifice as a religious ritual is the greatest divergence between Lawrence's religion and the ancient one. In matters of doctrine, Cipriano as Huitzilopochtli is chiefly an echo of Ramón as Quetzalcoatl, so we hardly know how Lawrence conceived the character of the true Huitzilopochtli. But where Cipriano speaks strongly and earnestly in his own voice—for example, his address to his soldiers in the greatly revised passage on his training methods—his chief message is "Try! Try for the second strength," meaning an inward strength that comes mysteriously to the brave and upright. This is hardly the message of a war god asking to be fed human hearts so he can be strong to aid his worshippers in battle.

In sum, though the Oaxaca version of the religion is more fully developed, Lawrence still transmits few authentic pre-Columbian elements. Readers should cease puzzling over which part is real, and anthropologists can stop wasting time on *The Plumed Serpent*'s "distorted" picture of ancient Mexico's religion, since Lawrence never tried to paint that religion accurately. As his own words show, he knew better than to try to recover a supplanted vision. Unlike the garbled and misrepresented Aztec creation myths in *Mornings in Mexico* which purported to set forth facts from a knowledgeable point of view, the novel is an imaginative work about a new religious movement, not an anthropological treatise. The novel's religion is meant to enhance life. Among other things, it brings new life to a white woman, the opposite effect of the primitive Mexican religion of "The Woman Who Rode Away," which ends in a white woman's sacrificial death. The religion Lawrence concocted for that short story and attributed to modern Indians living in Northern Mexico, is in the same category as the garbled essays, since its religion is presented as a genuine pre-Columbian survival. *The Plumed Serpent* never makes such a claim. Its aim is to create a new and awakening gospel, making use of some earlier elements with the hope that their echoes still have power.

A comparison of the two drafts shows how Lawrence labored in Oaxaca to make his new movement seem real, vivid, and dramatically appealing. Kate's first experience of a Quetzalcoatl service takes four paragraphs in the Chapala drafts and seventeen pages in the published novel. In the draft, she and Owen momentarily note in the plaza the intense singing of a man naked to the waist who appears to be blind and is perhaps a man of Quetzalcoatl. The words are not given. They only learn that such singing has been recurring in the village.

Owen, the character based on Bynner, goes ahead of her to El Fuerte (disguised as Orilla in both draft and final version), at the eastern extremity of the lake. There he greets her and Villiers (based on Spud Johnson), who had accompanied her from Mexico City. After the trio reach Chapala by boat, the two men remain close companions for more than a month. In the second draft, Lawrence makes Juana, Kate's Indian servant, her companion for the first Quetzalcoatl service because in Oaxaca he limits the Bynner figure to Mexico City. The Johnson figure disappears after he escorts Kate safely to Orilla. Thus, the setting is less touristy and Kate is the town's only foreign visitor. In the plaza scene in the novel, Kate and Juana hear a drum and a flute. (The Chapala draft guitars are nearly all replaced by drums, as more evocative of the "timeless, primeval passion of the prehistoric races.") They draw nearer and see the drummer and flutist wearing the Quetzalcoatl costume. Kate receives "a sort of ballad" printed with the Quetzalcoatl eagle within the encircling snake. The ballad tells of Jesus asking his brother Quetzalcoatl to help him get past the fierce heat of the sun on his way home. An old man comes forward holding a banner depicting the black sun behind the world's sun and a prose sermon, also given in full. Explicating the theme of the ballad— that Jesus and Mary want to leave Mexico to find rest in the sun behind the sun—he tells how the Father, the Nameless, is sending back Quetzalcoatl and exhorts the crowd to say "Welcome to Quetzalcoatl, Farewell to Jesus." Kate is unable to resist participating in the marvelous dance that follows when the women join with the men and the two circles rotate in opposite directions.

Kate's first visit to Ramón's *hacienda,* originally one chapter, develops into four in the second draft. In the Chapala version, Kate glimpses Ramón, naked to the waist, with blue and red cords securing his white pants at the ankles, teaching four men to sing to the accompaniment of guitars and violins. No text is given. In Oaxaca Lawrence has Kate arrive in the morning and stay till the next day. Carlota, Ramón's wife, gives Kate a lengthy and hostile version of her husband's religion. Kate sees a smithy making a symbol of the sun behind the sun; Ramón poses for a Quetzalcoatl statue to be used later in the church; there is a prayer meeting of the seven initiates with two more prose sermons and another Quetzalcoatl hymn; and an evening service for the *hacienda* peons, with a song for the man at the gates calling them in and another long prose sermon reversing Hopi ideas in which Ramón exhorts the peons to first gain the force of the "Snake that lies in the fire at the heart of the world." Then, exploiting the wind blowing up before the coming of the first rain, he invokes the great Bird of the Beyond and, in the pause before the "bird shakes water out of its wings," he tells them that "The Morning Star is sending you a messenger, a god who died in Mexico. But he slept his sleep, and the Invisible One washed his body with water of resurrection. . . . The Son of the Star is coming back to the Sons of Men."

Ramón's gifts as a showman make the reader feel the appeal of his movement, especially when coupled with his compelling presence and magnetic personality. Another factor, of course, is his extraordinary literary talent. Here, for instance, is how he tells his initiates to accept and endure suffering:

> And say to thy sorrow: Axe, thou art cutting me down!
> Yet did a spark fly from out of thy edge and my wound!
> Cut then, while I cover my face, father of the Star.

Endowing Ramón with true poetic gifts solved a number of Lawrence's problems. Besides making him a more interesting character, it helped make the appeal of his religion plausible, exploited his poetry and poetic prose to give the reader the sense of a genius whose religion had to be respected and to some degree absorbed, even if it was not always intelligible. Charming examples are Ramón's three songs for the watches of the day chanted by drummers to replace the village clock.

The Dawn Song is:

> The dark is dividing, the sun is coming past the wall.
> Day is at hand.
> Lift your hand, say Farewell! say Welcome!
> Then be silent.
> Let the darkness leave you, let the light come into you.

The Midday song also induces an exalted mood, and the Sunset Song is:

> Leave off! Leave off! Leave off!
> Lift your hand, say Farewell! say Welcome!
> Man in the twilight.
> The sun is in the outer porch, cry to him: Thanks! Oh, Thanks!
> Then be silent.
> You belong to the night.

A subsequent development in Lawrencean criticism lends additional interest to these beautiful songs, composed and added in Oaxaca. Because of his lessened concern with leadership after *The Plumed Serpent* and because of a frequently quoted letter that Lawrence wrote Bynner on 13 March 1928, a number of commentators contend that Lawrence repudiated the religion in his Mexican novel. He wrote Bynner: "On the whole, I think you are right. The hero is obsolete, and the leader of men is a back number. After all, at the back of the hero is the militant ideal: and the militant ideal, or the ideal militant, seems to be also a cold egg."

Refutation lies in "Apropos of *Lady Chatterley's Lover,*" an ultimate statement of belief written more than a year later:

> We *must* get back into relation, vivid and nourishing relation to the cosmos and the universe. The way is through daily ritual, and the re-awakening. We *must* once more practice the ritual of dawn and noon and sunset, the ritual of the kindling fire and pouring water, the ritual of the first breath, and the last. This is an affair of the individual and the household, a ritual of day. The ritual of the moon in her phases, or the morning star and the

evening star is for men and women separate. . . . To these rituals we must return: or we must evolve them to suit our needs. For the truth is, we are perishing for lack of fulfillment of our greater needs, we are cut off from the great sources of our inward nourishment and renewal, sources which flow eternally in the universe.

Obviously, Lawrence still held the same personal religion. In the posthumously printed *Apocalypse,* even though he rejected "the militant ideal," he did not repudiate his ideas about the value of leadership and of man's need for it:

> Power is there, and always will be [he wrote in that last book]. As soon as two or three men come together, especially to *do* something, then power comes into being, and one man is a leader, a master. It is inevitable.
>
> Accept it, recognize the natural power in the man, as men did in the past, and give it homage, then there is a great joy, an uplifting, and a potency passed from the powerful to the less powerful. There is a stream of power. And in this, men have their best collective being, now and forever, and a corresponding flame springs up in yourself. Give homage and allegiance to a hero, and you become yourself heroic. It is the law of man.

Such echoes from *The Plumed Serpent* in Lawrence's final works suggest that Lawrence felt *Serpent* outranked his other novels in importance because of its religious ideas. He repeats that estimate in a number of letters, in a context suggesting that its merits as a work of art were not primarily what Lawrence was weighing.

WAS LAWRENCE A FASCIST?

A number of writers have accused Lawrence of being a fascist. Others, like Moore and Mary Freeman, have defended him. The two versions of *Serpent* illuminate his views on fascism and theocracy.

The chapter called "Huitzilopochtli's Night" was extremely puzzling on first reading. Roughly five-sixths of the way through, the new religion sanctions the public murder of five people and presents Cipriano and Ramón as god-like heroes in the ritual slaughter. True, the victims were chosen with reason. The two strangled were the woman who enabled the would-be murderers to reach Ramón's roof and the man who fell in the attempt. The three stabbed were accomplices. The ceremony included a leaf-drawing lottery to insure that one accomplice would be spared. Nevertheless, the appeal of the new religion and its leaders suddenly disappeared.

The novel never lies, wrote Lawrence in his attack on Tolstoy, even though the novelist might try to. Perhaps *The Plumed Serpent* intended to make the reader turn from the new religion here. What had Lawrence himself intended? In a careful rereading, I discovered that the repugnance of the ritual execution was not its injustice—a crime *had* been attempted—but the two religious leaders' seizing of the law in a community where the legal system had not broken down. In taking over the administration of justice, the reader sees them acting like fascists. Yet clearly Lawrence labors to make the chapter seem like poetic tragedy. Part of it is in dramatic form, it has a higher percentage of poetry than any of the other chapters, and Ramón's beautiful threnody, added in Oaxaca, closes the scene. In short, Lawrence's own moral scheme put him on the side of his repellent protagonists. His nonlying novel had lifted the curtain on the "holy horror" that he envisaged in *Kangaroo* if man-and-man love ceased being guided by religion. But apparently he was too convinced that Ramón and Cipriano still had the "God-passion" to sense they presented "the rare gruesome sight" that the hero of the Australian novel knew would follow religious breakdown.

Contemporary history has dealt *The Plumed Serpent* a number of blows, most of them resulting from Lawrence's remarkable prescience about possibilities in the world of his time. In *Serpent*'s seventeenth chapter, for instance, Ramón expresses the wish that each nation might have a similar religious revival by reanimating its old gods. For he wishes "the Teutonic world would once more think in terms of Thor and Wotan, and the tree Igdrasil." That was written while Hitler was still in jail following the failure of his Munich beer hall putsch; and Lawrence had been dead for three years by the time Hitler became Chancellor of Germany. Yet even those aware of the sequence of events sometimes see in it evidence of Lawrence's incipient fascism, even if he did not live long enough to become one in fact. The fascist-like salutes that Lawrence invented for the guards of Quetzalcoatl and Huitzilopochtli, and the use of bonfires on tripodal supports for illumination at night meetings, give this retrospective credence. Lawrence was however, a theocrat, even though he was a naive one whose faith in "natural aristocrats" blinded him to the dangers of entrusting them with arbitrary power. One senses, too, that he saw little danger in the real possibility of theocratic intolerance and the excessive zeal of the reformer. But he was not a fascist. He denounced fascism in *St. Mawr,* written between the two *Serpents* . Having seen only early Italian fascism, he saw it as something that kept "the surface of life intact" but predicted that it would work up to a break, even if in the meantime it kept the "hemorrhage internal, invisible." In both *Serpents* , too, there is ample evidence that he was alert to the dangers of fascism and saw the risk that a religion such as Ramón's might be perverted to fascist ends. "We will be masters among men, and lords among men. But lords of men and masters of men we will *not* be," are the opening words of the second sermon to the seven initiates. The men Ramón saw as potential fascists were not his followers, but the Knights of Cortés, laymen willing to take up arms against his movement at the behest of the Catholic Church. Kate observes that her landlord is "a great Fascista. The reactionary Knights of Cortés held him in great esteem."

The Knights of Cortés represent a relatively late idea for they do not appear in the Chapala version until five chapters before the end, as Knights of Columbus named there for the American Roman Catholic fraternal society. In the Oaxaca version, they appear earlier to point up the struggle between fascist forces and Ramón's adherents. In a Chapala passage, Cipriano, who is a military power in Mexico, wants to use force to spread Ramón's religion. Ramón warns:

> Even if you do succeed in working the Church interest, and in getting together as Fascist reaction, you are only staving off the evil day. Fascism won't hold against the lust for anarchy which is at the bottom of the Fascisti themselves. The Fascisti only live because they think they can bully society. It is a great bully movement, just as communism is a bully movement. But communism is a more vital feeling, because of the big grudge that burns in a communist's belly. And in the end, that grudge will burn holes through all Fascism, and down you'll come again, and the Church with you in a big smash.

Perhaps, for the sake of his subsequent reputation, Lawrence should not have excised the passage in the Oaxaca version.

That Ramón has no fascist aims is supported further by his two refusals to enter the Mexican political arena when Cipriano, after pointing out Ramón's strong chances of achieving high office, urges him to do so. But if Ramón wanted to exert neither military nor political force, he was nevertheless realist enough to realize that his anti-Christian movement could not spread peacefully in a country where the Roman Catholic church was strong, without a military force ready to protect it. He knew Cipriano's role as his secular arm was necessary, requiring that Cipriano be admitted into the pantheon of embodied divinities. But Cipriano's desire to become a dictator made Ramón concerned to imbue Cipriano with his own spiritual ideals. Only after he is convinced that Cipriano has been suffused with the darkness of the Unknown—an experience with the divine—does Ramón invest him as the living Huitzilopochtli. The need for Cipriano's conversion is one of the strands that Lawrence strengthened in Oaxaca, and there is a vast difference between what James C. Cowan deftly calls the "Ordination" scene in the twenty-second chapter of the novel and its counterpart on page 278 of the typescript. In the earlier version Ramón merely hypnotizes Cipriano to bring him into consciousness of "his divine self," and Cipriano falls asleep. In Oaxaca Lawrence greatly extended the scene, elaborating the ritual with the five-fold binding of Cipriano—with belts of black fur around his eyes, his breast, his middle, his knees, and his ankles. The experience of passing into deep unconsciousness is such that Cipriano sleeps three times before awakening as his usual self.

Lawrence, then, did not preach fascism personally, and he saw his religion as anti-fascist in spirit. His Ramón, too, tries to insure that his religion will not become fascist. Yet such is the honesty of the novel that its religion takes the step of public murders as a fascist means to frighten the villagers from further attempts on their lives. Lawrence also inserts Ramón's discouraged question to himself, "Why have I started this Quetzalcoatl business?" And as the story follows the national success of the movement, Lawrence shows Ramón having more misgivings, having less control, wondering if he can hold out against the mounting pressures and crises. Perhaps if Lawrence had had the strength and will to write *The Plumed Serpent* a third time—as he was to do with *Lady Chatterley's Lover* he might have altered "Huitzilopochtli's Night" yet again. He might have added that the movement had taken a turn in the wrong direction and that Ramón's loving forgiveness of the accomplices in the final burial service did not sanctify an act of horror.

I still find "Huitzilopochtli's Night" a stumbling block but it no longer derails me completely. I also find the ending granting state-religion status to Quetzalcoatlism insufficiently thought out, but knowing Lawrence's mental and physical condition as he drove himself to his self-imposed deadline, I am disposed to be tolerant. And I applaud the way Lawrence allowed the novelist in him—as opposed to the religious theoretician—to end the story as a near-fiasco for Ramón instead of as a triumph of righteousness. George Pierce Baker, who taught drama at Harvard and Yale so outstandingly, formulated the critical dictum that a work of art should be judged by its abundance of power rather than by its absence of fault. By this criterion *The Plumed Serpent* emerges high among the novels of its period, high even among the novels of Lawrence. If it seems to veer toward fascism it remains a penetrating study of the course of a religious movement that grows powerful enough to develop a strong secular arm. It demonstrates, too, the thin line between theocracy and fascism, and how the God-centered idealism of the one imperils itself when it flirts with the brutal opportunism of the other. Ramón Carrasco is one of Lawrence's most important and successful male characters. "When people pose as gods," Lawrence said sagely in one of his later *Pansies,* "they are Crystal Palace statues, made into cement poured

into a mould, around iron sticks.'' Ramón's struggle with his own success, his inner strength and spiritual integrity threatened by the practical
demands of large-scale administration, is warmly human even while we
recognize him as a mystic genius. Because of ''a certain vulnerable kindliness about him,'' Ramón is also among the most appealing of Lawrence's
males.

THE NOVEL AND MEXICAN HISTORY

Because Lawrence sifted real history into his imaginary movement,
historians have dealt too seriously with *Serpent*'s historical parallels, even
though those parallels make Lawrence seem mysteriously clairvoyant.

Calles, whose position had been shaky when his regime began, knew
he needed to consolidate his power in the struggle between state and
church. Archbishop Mora, who defied Calles's enforcement of disregarded
anti-clerical provisions in the 1917 Constitution, was then a man of
seventy-two. He had been Archbishop of Mexico since the closing years
of Porfirio Díaz. Calles ordered a round-up—justified by the
Constitution—of foreign priests. Padre Rickards was among those bagged.
Calles asked for new legislation further restricting the church. On 14 June
1926, the Mexican Congress ratified the *Leyes Calles,* effective July 31.
One of the new restrictions, which obliged Padre Rickards to give up
his black suit and reversed collar, was that no priest could appear in public in a distinctive garb. Other provisions forbade priests to speak against
the Constitution or teach in a primary school. The number of priests allowed to serve in Mexico was limited, foreign priests were forbidden to
enter, and even Mexican priests were obliged to register as foreign agents.
Once the terms of the new legislation were known, Archbishop Mora
and his supporters decided on open but nonviolent resistance through
a clerical strike. The Episcopate decreed that all churches in Mexico should
be closed on August 1. When the priests obeyed, Calles immediately
retaliated. Calles arrested Mora and a number of other archbishops and
bishops, put them on a train without a change of clothing, and sent them
to the United States the same night.

After deporting the bishops, Calles took an interesting step. In February 1925, just after Lawrence completed *The Plumed Serpent,* a former
priest, José Joaquin Pérez, calling himself the Patriarch, had taken over
Soledad de Santa Cruz, a sixteenth-century church in Mexico City, as headquarters for his schismatic Mexican Catholic Apostolic Church. Roman
Catholics attacked him and drove him from the church, preventing Pérez
from holding services. Calles had not yet come out against the Catholic
Church, but he neither wanted to take sides with it nor repudiate the
patriarch. He took the noncommittal course of letting neither side use

the church and converted it into a library. After the priests had closed their own churches, however, Calles was willing to help Pérez openly, and he gave him the Church of Corpus Cristi in Mexico City as a "Cathedral" for the *Cismaticos.* That church, now the Museo Nacional de Arte Popular on Avenida Juárez, continued in existence until the patriarch's death in 1931.

Meanwhile, in January 1927, sporadic acts of violence intensified when Roman Catholic laymen, calling themselves *Cristeros,* began a long rebellion, driving federal troops from some places where priests were still active. On 23 November 1927, Padre Miguel Pro, one of the priests still ministering to Catholics behind closed doors, was arrested and executed without trial. He was accused of being involved in a plot to assassinate Obregón, who was slated to succeed Calles. Many other incidents followed. It was not until June 1929—three years after their closing—that the churches were reopened and peace was made between the Roman Catholic Church and the administration that succeeded Calles.

In repeating Lawrence's mocking joke that the Street Sweepers Band greeted Calles when he paused in New York, I mentioned one of Lawrence's plans for the revision in Oaxaca: to introduce Calles as an important character in his novel and thereby tie the novel more closely to the Mexican political and historical scene. A second purpose would be to expand the progress of the religious movement outside the confines of the village. In the revision the account of the movement's national progress is still sketchy, and certainly hurried too quickly to an improbable victory at the end, but introducing Calles in the second chapter and using him as a frequent offstage point of reference amplifies the outside Chapala aspect of the novel. But it must be emphasized that when Lawrence finished *The Plumed Serpent,* Calles had been in office only three months. Thus, because Lawrence wanted to carry the action of his novel forward by at least a year to allow the movement time to make its way and stir both enthusiasm and hostility, all the decisions pondered and the actions taken by Montes, the fictional Calles, had to be invented. All Lawrence knew was that Labor had been decisive in Calles's victory, that the insurrections expected from either the army or his political rival Angel Flores did not take place, that the first months of his regime were peaceful, and that Calles had hated the Roman Catholic Church. From then on, Lawrence had to imagine how the hard-bitten former schoolteacher with socialist leanings would react to an imaginary movement that aimed to supplant Catholicism with a new brand of Quetzalcoatlism.

Lawrence's Montes recognizes that the movement is aimed at men's souls, while he wants to concentrate on eliminating poverty and unenlightenment. But he is interested in it. He gives Cipriano the impression that he has "the cravings of a dictator," but pledges not to let the

Quetzalcoatl movement be interfered with. Feeling alone and disliking his colleagues, Montes is eager to win Ramón's support.

Later in the novel, after a minor rebellion against Montes has been suppressed and the Church has begun to oppose Ramón's movement, Ramón tells Cipriano, "Montes will stand for us, because he hates the Church and hates any hint of dictation from outside. He sees the possibility of a 'national' church." After Montes forbids religious processions and the public wearing of clerical habits, Montes is "meditating the expulsion of all foreign priests." Meanwhile the archbishop had issued orders against listening to anything concerning Quetzalcoatl. "But Montes had given orders to the police and the military to afford such protection to the Men of Quetzalcoatl as was accorded to any other law-abiding citizens."

Lawrence's anticipation of the expulsion of foreign priests and the ban on clerical garb seems uncanny. Neither had occurred when Lawrence imagined them, nor had the government shown any interest in a new "national" church.

In the novel, soldiers take copies of Ramón's hymns and sermons to converted proselytizers in all cities of the republic. These missionaries appear in villages too. As the clerical opposition to the new religion grows more menacing, Cipriano wants Montes to declare the religion of Quetzalcoatl the official religion of Mexico, and to back the declaration with the army. Ramón is opposed. Next we hear that the political opposition to Montes has broken his health, one of Lawrence's few wrong guesses. Later, comes an assassination attempt. (Guessed out of sequence and on a different man.) A recovered Montes acts decisively after the archbishop excommunicates Ramón, Cipriano, and their adherents by having him arrested while he is leading a procession against the House of Quetzalcoatl, the former church of San Juan Bautista.

> Then a kind of war began [the novel says]. The Knights of Cortés brought out their famous hidden stores of arms . . . and a clerical mob headed by a fanatical priest surged into the Zócalo. Montes had the guns turned on them. But it looked like the beginnings of a religious war. . . .

Lawrence, therefore, guessed right about the arrests, the *Cristeros* and their "holy war." When a general in Zacatecas "declared against Montes and for the Church," Cipriano and his well-trained soldiers defeat the rebellion. "Then Montes declared the old Church illegal in Mexico, and caused a law to be passed, making the religion of Quetzalcoatl the national Religion of the Republic." Three more Lawrence guesses turn out to be right: "All churches were closed. . . . The Archbishop was deported, no more priests were seen in the streets."

Of course, many details are wrong. Historically, the priests themselves closed the churches, the *Cristero* uprising came after the closing, rather than before, and the new religion Calles backed was a Christian schism rather than Quetzalcoatlism. But these partial errors seem slight, even though they attracted much criticism—ironically, because Lawrence was so right about the major happenings. Those with an accurate knowledge of Mexican history have jumped on the novel for not getting the facts straight, not realizing Lawrence was writing about the future.

Subsequent archaeological research has complicated the situation further. The great discovery in 1941 that Tula, not Teotihuacán, was the legendary Tollan of the Toltecs increased the importance of Quetzalcoatl, the priest-governor of that name who built and ruled Tula. It is not certain that his own people looked on him as a god and almost certainly he had only assumed the ancient wind god's name. But by the time of the Aztecs when the exact location of Tollan had been forgotten, legend had converted the builder into a white god who was expected to return to Mexico. The reader aware of Mexican archaeology since the 1940s would not find a Quetzalcoatl movement improbable. In the 1920s, however, Gamio pointed out in a 1956 letter to Edward Nehls: "There is no concrete memory whatever of Huitzilopochtli, Quetzalcoatl and other deities." There was, indeed, no continuous memory, but well before Gamio wrote—and partly because of his own efforts—Quetzalcoatl had come into the consciousness of hundreds of Mexicans. Since then, Mexico's enthusiasm for its pre-Columbian past has mounted steadily.

Events, then, have cooperated to make many people dismiss *The Plumed Serpent* as bogus in its pre-Columbianism, inaccurate in its Mexican history, and repulsive in its Hitlerian fascism. Lawrence's efforts to make his story seem so real as to be probable backfired, partly because of his artistic success and partly because history has made his story seem more realistic than it was, thereby engendering the criticism that it was not true enough. Some day, perhaps, when people can see the novel for what it is—not as anthropology, history, or political theory, but as a work of the creative imagination—it will come more fully into its own. Already it has won adherents in such critics as E. M. Forster, Katherine Anne Porter, Jascha Kessler, John B. Vickery, L. D. Clark, and the William York Tindall with whom Frieda disputed about Mrs. Nuttall's library. But Horace Gregory has called it "the worst of all Lawrence's novels," others have been almost as harsh, and few agree with Lawrence's own judgment as to its supremacy among his works of fiction.

WHAT TO DO WITH KATE?

The final artistic problem Lawrence had to solve for his novel in Oaxaca is that of Kate. His most important revision was to make her Cipriano's mistress. Because Cipriano was caught up in the Quetzalcoatl movement, Kate's new involvement linked her to the movement, paving the way for her ultimate, though hesitant joining.

Besides changing Kate's name and age, Lawrence also changed her nationality, gave her two children, and provided a second husband, from whose death she was still suffering. This man, a much more interesting and important character, in many ways resembled D. H. Lawrence. The only husband of the apparently childless Chapala Kate was Desmond Burns, a man who gave his life to Labor and socialism, and was, one gathers, rather a bore. The first husband of the Oaxaca Kate was a lawyer considerably her senior named Tylor. They were divorced and the children of that marriage at the time of the story are a boy of twenty-one and a girl of nineteen. Kate's second husband was Joachim Leslie, a tireless Irish patriot, who, like the socialist Burns, wore himself to death serving a cause—this one being politics and Irish nationalism. In contrast to the Chapala Kate's lukewarm feelings for the stolid Burns, the Oaxaca Kate had loved her husband passionately; and his death, after ten years of marriage, left her devastated. The Chapala Kate was the daughter of a Devonshire baronet; and in the flashback of her life in the penultimate chapter of the draft, Lawrence seems to have changed his mind and given her a son. In this flashback, cut entirely from the novel, one suspects that her vigorous old mother is drawn from Frieda's mother, the Baroness von Richthofen.

Undoubtedly Lawrence eliminated the flashback because it suddenly jerks the novel out of the Mexican setting. But its contrast with her life in Mexico makes many of Kate's snobbish reactions to dark-skinned people more understandable. Perhaps Lawrence could have worked more of her background into an earlier section of the novel. As it is, the only glimpse of Kate's childhood surviving in the novel is the four-year-old Kate telling her parents' guests at a large formal dinner that they are all monkeys, an estimate of people that, she tactlessly tells Ramón, has remained with her.

Making the Oaxaca Kate a woman of forty, as opposed to the thirty-eight-year-old Chapala Kate Burns, is a more significant change than might be apparent. By making her children older, it increases her freedom from them by lessening their need for her. Being adrift and older makes the new Kate's spiritual watershed more definite. Because she is unquestionably at the end of one period and the opening of another, the interest of her situation is heightened. More significantly, Lawrence intellectualized her character. As he changed Cipriano into a full-blooded Zapotec and Ramón into a fulfilled mystic, he assigned to Kate the role of the thought-adventurer. We assume that Lawrence made this change in the hope that her more significant personal story would balance the stronger and more original story of the religious movement. As a consequence, the Oaxaca Kate has the temperament and inclination to analyze her spiritual dilemmas more fully and to respond to new experience as an intellectual adventure. The new Kate, because she contains a stronger admixture of Lawrence himself, may be less plausible; but her powers of observation, her ability to line up elements in an argument, and her capacity to weigh her responses are all strengthened. Kate, like Somers, the thought-adventurer in *Kangaroo,* the Australian novel, is also a basically skeptical European faced with the difficulties of personal commitment. Lawrence carries the character a step further because Kate is confronted with the appeal of a religious movement, whereas Somers was faced with fascism and socialism.

The most striking example of Kate's ability to weigh her responses is the beautiful section describing her ride down the lake between her overnight stopping place at Orilla and her ultimate destination at Sayula. In the draft, this thirty-five-mile journey by launch is barely mentioned; but in Oaxaca, Lawrence not only devotes five evocative pages to it, he has Kate express her feelings about her chief concern—the state of her soul.

Her musings begin with the news paragraph about the man of Quetzalcoatl arising out of the lake, also expanded from the Chapala draft. "A different light than the common seemed to gleam out of the words," is Kate's reaction, but that light might be the reflected glow of her dawning maturity. She feels that, having gone beyond the stage of longing for the love of a man, the flower of her soul might be opening in a new era of peace. But even though she wanted to be "disentangled" from the past, she knew she wanted to be surrounded by "the silence of other unfolded souls." Later, she is aware of how the flow of her life was broken by her second husband's death and how she could not restart it in Europe. "Give me the mystery and let the world live again for me!" is her cry "as the motor-boat chugs peacefully through the fish-milk water gleaming and throwing off a dense light." Recalling how she had felt like a cogwheel in the United States, interlocked with workings that reversed her life-flow, she adds, "And deliver me from man's automatism." Once she moves into a pleasant house in Sayula she sums up her position: "Now I have only one thing to do: not to get caught up into the world's cogwheels any more, and not to lose my hold on the hidden greater thing."

Because Kate's former husband in the Oaxaca version had been involved in politics, Kate's shunning politics for religion is made more probable. And because Joachim's commitment to his cause was total, Kate's mistrust of a similar cause is also understandable. "When I was with Joachim absolutely alone in a cottage, doing all the work myself, and knowing nobody at all, just living, and feeling the greater thing all the time: then I was free, I was happy," Kate tells Ramón. Was Joachim happy in the same situation? She replies, with some of the self-centered lack of comprehension that repeatedly characterizes her: "He was *really*. But that's where the monkeyishness comes in. He wouldn't let himself be content. He insisted on having *people* and *cause,* just to torture himself with." In an earlier talk about her marriage Kate, ignoring how much she was setting her own will against Joachim's idealism, blamed him for his own death:

> He broke his own soul and spirit in those Irish politics [she told Carlota, Ramón's wife]. I knew it was wrong. What does Ireland matter, what does nationalism, and all the rubbish matter, really! And revolution! They are so, so stupid and *vieux jeu*. Ah! It would have been so much better if Joachim had been content to live his life in peace with me. It could be so jolly, so lovely. And I tried and tried and tried with him. But it was no good. He *wanted* to kill himself with that beastly Irish business, and I tried in vain to prevent him.

This passage echoes the struggles between Frieda and Lawrence, but the point Lawrence makes is that Kate-Frieda felt Ramón and Cipriano were wrong to subordinate their personal lives to a cause. Having been through one marriage with a man dedicated to a cause, she did not want to submit herself to another, particularly when there was an aspect of the new cause she could not believe in.

Ramón's interest in her, however, was more than simply as another convert. He wanted the Mexican love for the Virgin Mary, in the new religion, to be transferred to a female deity. He also felt the success of his movement depended on gods reappearing in the flesh. If the two chief male deities were to appear as men, there would have to be a real woman too. Being white, like the Virgin, gave Kate a major qualification for the third role. Her eyes were "a sort of hazel, changing grey-gold," and her statuesque beauty made her look "like an Ossianic goddess." So Ramón asked Kate to go before the people as a living manifestation of Malintzi, Lawrence's invented merciful, rain-giving goddess. The Chapala Kate was offended by the idea of impersonating a deity and certainly couldn't see herself in the role. In the end, she packs to leave Mexico.

This ending flaws the novel. The Oaxaca Kate, though still troubled by the idea of pretending godhood, finds sexual fulfillment and personal happiness living within the aura of the movement. Although she agreed to play Malintzi to Cipriano's Huitzilopochtli when they were alone after Cipriano's investiture in his god-role, she has not done so by the time the novel ends. We do not know if she makes that ultimate commitment. At the close of the novel, we see her as the wife of a rich Mexican general who, for her own reasons, has decided to remain in Mexico. Not only has she escaped the fate of a sex-starved middle-aged woman with nothing but her own luxurious, prowling life—the fate of many of her contemporaries in England—but she has come to love the color, beauty, and climate of Mexico; the pleasure of having courteous Indian servants, the tranquilizing effects of the slow-paced rural life of the villagers, and especially, the physical fulfillment provided by her new kind of husband who makes her blood "blossom" in her body.

Kate's willing "submission" with its surrender of much of her own ego is not a new solution in Lawrence. Lady Daphne, of "The Ladybird" and Alvina Houghton of *The Lost Girl* make similar choices for the sake of dark-eyed lovers. After trying out the four unsatisfactory solutions of "None of That," "The Woman Who Rode Away," *St. Mawr,* and "The Princess," Lawrence reverted to the solution of his heroines of Taormina days. In fact, the revised Cipriano resembles the small, dark Count Dionys, a follower of "the blessed god of destruction" for whom Daphne deserted her husband's bed.

Kate's decision to submit to Cipriano and remain in Mexico involved a whole series of other revisions. One was to make Cipriano a more worthy foil for Kate. Making him a proud Zapotec with an archbishop for a godfather were two steps Oaxaca suggested. Since Cipriano and Kate were to be more important to each other, their first meeting had to be strengthened. That meeting is outside the bleachers of the bullring as Kate leaves, disgusted after the goring of two horses. The new Cipriano is bravely indifferent to the possibility of being assassinated because of his military uniform, has an Imperial goatee, and is important enough to be recognized by the crowd—all touches lacking in the draft. When he helps Kate escape through the heavy rain, she responds:

> He was awfully nice. But he made her feel she wanted to get away from him too. There was that heavy, black Mexican fatality about him that put a burden on her. His quietness, and his peculiar assurance, almost aggressive; and at the same time, a nervousness, and uncertainty. His heavy sort of gloom, and yet his quick, native, childish smile. Those black eyes, like black jewels, that you couldn't look into, and which were so watchful; yet which, perhaps, were waiting for some sign of recognition and warmth.

When she goes to tea at Mrs. Nuttall's and meets Cipriano again and Ramón for the first time, Lawrence has the two invite her to dinner. Kate and Cipriano have a long scene alone on the verandah which is not in the draft. In this new scene, Kate weeps remembering Joachim, and Cipriano's heart goes out to her when her tears, falling through her wet fingers, remind him of the Virgin of Soledad. By the time of Kate's first visit to Ramón's *hacienda,* Cipriano asks her to marry him, whereas by this point in the draft, all we know is that Cipriano desires her. The first proposal is followed by a request for her to join the pantheon, then a second proposal. Ramón adds pressure by asking her if she might marry Cipriano, and afterwards asking her to marry Cipriano as a way of joining them. Finally, "the Pan-Male in Cipriano"—a totally new passage—overcomes Kate as she drives with him on another visit to the *hacienda*. At the *hacienda* Ramón tells her the name of the goddess he wants her to represent. (In the first draft, it is Itzpapalotl, a true Aztec goddess, rather than Malintzi.) Shortly after this, Kate takes a motorboat ride to Jaramay, where she and Cipriano have intercourse for the first time. This is not long after the two-thirds point of the book, whereas in the draft Kate never goes to bed with Cipriano, much less marries him. In the novel, she marries him twice: first in the private ceremony conducted by Ramón according to the rites of the new church of Quetzalcoatl, and later in a Mexican civil ceremony, after which she lives with him on a *hacienda* that Cipriano has rented on the lake front.

In Jaramay Kate discovered that when the strong, vigorous, athletic Cipriano makes love to her "she fused into a molten unconsciousness." In the last chapter but one, not only is Cipriano a lover of extraordinary physical appeal but he makes love with a special technique, *coitus reservatus,* developed in India, propounded in the sacred books known as *Tantras,* and used in both Hindu and Tibetan Buddhism from the sixth century on. Thus, Cipriano is heightened beyond other Lawrence male characters possessed of irresistible animal magnetism. Even knowledgeable critics have overlooked it, including Singhalese author Martin Wickramasinghe, who, in his *The Mysticism of D. H. Lawrence,* points out other Tantric influences in Lawrence. It involves literally hours of penetration and arousal but without rhythmic thrusting and ejaculation. This technique, Aldous Huxley points out in the "Appendix" to *Tomorrow, and Tomorrow, and Tomorrow* was favored by the Gnostics of the first Christian centuries, the Cathars of the early Middle Ages, and the Adamites, or American Brethren and Sisters of the Free Spirit of the nineteenth century. It was praised by the troubadour poets and the Petrarchians and was revived in the nineteenth century by members of Oneida, the longest-lasting of the Utopian settlements in the United States.

Lawrence may have learned about it during his visit to Ceylon in 1922, but it does not appear in any of the works written between Ceylon and *The Plumed Serpent,* pointing to Mexico as the place where he became familiar with it. Eduardo Rendón, besides giving Lawrence his ideas for a viable religious revival in Mexico, also told the novelist about *coitus reservatus,* which he had learned about in 1904 when he visited India. In Bombay, the English-educated eighteen-year-old scion of a wealthy Yucatecan family had found two dilapidated books in a second-hand store, technical treatises for Hatha Yoga, the branch of yoga dealing with psycho-physiological training. One was the *Hatha-Yoga Pradipikâ,* the other the *Shiva Samhitâ.* Because Lawrence showed such interest, Rendón gave him the dog-eared volumes.

> Curious as it may seem [the description of Cipriano's love-making opens], he made her aware of her old desire for frictional, irritant sensation. She realized all her old love had been frictional charged with the fire of irritation and the spasms of frictional voluptuousness.
>
> Cipriano, curiously, by refusing to share any of this with her, made it seem external to her. Her strange seething feminine will and desire subsided in her and swept away, leaving her soft and powerfully potent, like the hot springs of water that gushed up so noiseless, so soft, yet so powerful, with a sort of secret potency.

It must not be thought, however, that Lawrence cynically used sex as a *deus ex machina* to cement two parallel stories that were not integrated securely in the first version. He had deeper reasons than that, arising, largely, from another religion that was becoming more important to him than the one he tried to set forth symbolically in Quetzalcoatlism. Lawrence's rejection of romantic love and his related rejection of Christianity, led to a new religion where one is embraced by "the greater god" in the phallic darkness. This religion was already formulated by the time he wrote *Kangaroo.* Its hero, in reacting against the Christian Socialism of the leader who appeals to him for aid, muses on what he is rejecting, "It all seemed so far from the dark God he wished to serve, the God from whom the dark sensual passion emanates. He wanted men once more to refer the sensual passion of love sacredly to the great dark God, the ithyphallic, of the first dark religions." By the time Lawrence wrote *Lady Chatterley's Lover,* he made the novel his great "declaration of the phallic reality." His feeling for it is not so fully developed in *The Plumed Serpent,* but the elements are there. Kate realizes near the end that she was convinced "of one thing finally: that the clue to all living and to all moving-on into new living lay in the vivid blood-relation between man and woman."

In Lawrence's eyes, therefore, Kate was not settling for something trivial when she decided that staying was more important than her own individuality. His solution for her, besides giving him an ending, also enabled him to adumbrate one of his deepest conclusions and to sound a religious theme that in his remaining years was to seem more important than the regeneration of humankind through courage, the love of comrades, and communion with the forces of nature.

Despite the new happiness of her married life, the Oaxaca Kate remains hesitant about her commitment to the movement itself, sharing the Chapala Kate's vacillations because of recurring aversions to Mexico in general and Quetzalcoatlism in particular. Even after marrying Cipriano, she insists she must go home to England for a while, to slow the rapid changes. But after she has her ship reservation, she knows she does not want to leave, even for a short absence. In the final scene of the novel, she comes to tell Ramón and Cipriano. As she and Rosalino pause in the garden, her heart is further softened by hearing Ramón teaching one of the men of Quetzalcatl a new song—the only love poem among the book's twenty-four poems, and added in Oaxaca. Cipriano's apparent indifference to her decision confuses her; when she gets an admission that he cares very much, she exclaims happily and yet not quite certainly, "You won't let me go!"

Touchingly, those closing words of the novel echo a scene from the Lawrences' life that the young novelist reported to Edward Garnett on 3 July 1912, when they were in Italy, and Frieda, still not married to Lawrence, was tugged by home ties in England to leave him: "She lies on the floor in misery—and then is fearfully angry with me because I won't say 'Stay for my sake.' I say 'Decide what you want most, to live with me and share my rotten chances, or go back to security and your children—decide for yourself—choose for yourself.' And then she almost hates me, because I won't say 'I love you—stay with me whatever happens.' "

CHAPTER 12

THE RETURN TO THE FRANCIA

Monday, February 2, was when Lawrence planned to leave Oaxaca—at least when he wrote Curtis Brown on January 10 it was. But later he decided to allow himself a few days more. It would probably be February 5, he indicated to Consul Rickards, when he revealed his nostalgia for the sea on January 31. But the day after that letter, he "went down, as if shot in the intestines." And to Amy Lowell, to whom he gave this graphic description of his sudden sickness, he also gave the information that he was stricken "the very day" he finished *The Plumed Serpent.* Considering the tension and his final feverish activity in writing so many extra pieces, a breaking point is not surprising. Probably it was his desperate nearness to collapse from physical and emotional exhaustion that contributed to his lashing out at Brett and Murry. Obviously only his will had kept him going.

Aldous Huxley was frequently amazed by the extraordinary way Lawrence could bounce back from an illness that would lay an ordinary man low for months; and by February 4 Lawrence had rallied enough to scrawl a shaky note to Consul Rickards explaining the delay. The same day Frieda had written Brett, telling her that Lawrence would not be fit to travel for another ten days. The next day Lawrence wrote Brett himself, saying: "You have heard how my flu remains got tangled up with *malaria;* these houses have malaria mosquitoes from that little river, so I am still in bed—having quinine injections shoved into me. But hope to be up Sunday, and get away from Oaxaca next week. I hate the place—a let down. The doctor says the *race* is exhausted. But the novel is finished. I almost envy you the ranch . . . the feeling one's blood isn't being sullied—guess I've had malaria since December."

The day this letter was written, the Kulls left for the Costa Chica, so it was in the first day or two of this severe illness that the kindly Carola came up to the priest's house to sit by Lawrence's bedside so Frieda wouldn't lose her last opportunity for dental work. That he expected his "flu remains" to disappear shortly is evidenced by Carola's recollection of how, on the day she replaced Frieda, Lawrence pleaded with the

Kulls to delay their departure so the Lawrences could go with them. In their recollections of the "emaciated" Lawrence, they do not mention his novel, suggesting he had never revealed how it absorbed him. Naturally they saw no connection between its completion and his collapse. Two months later, in that same letter to Amy Lowell, Lawrence would write, "I daren't even look at the outside of the MS, it cost one so much, and I wish I could eat all the lotus that ever budded, and drink up Lethe to the source. Talk about dull opiates—one wants something that'll go to the very soul." The Kulls' silence about the novel was common to all Lawrence's contemporaries in Oaxaca I spoke to: not one knew how much of himself he was giving to the book.

Lawrence learned that many cases in the nearby military hospital were soldiers who had contracted malaria in the state's coastal low-lands. He believed he probably owed his malaria to them. But because Oaxaca City is too high for the mosquito that transmits the disease, the malarial element in his illness was likely a recurrence of his Ceylon infection. But typhoid fever was endemic to Oaxaca, as we have seen through the death of McEwen's five-year-old daughter and the near-death of Carola Kull. So it was not surprising that typhoid was part of Lawrence's trouble. Lawrence was probably correct in blaming it for the awful intestinal pain, for in his health report to Mollie Skinner he cited "typhoid condition inside" in addition to "chest going wrong with flu."

Probably the Kulls transmitted the news of Lawrence's illness to the foreign colony. One who heard promptly was Jean Akin, who was soon to help greatly in nursing him, and it was Mrs. Akin who first set me on the track of José E. Larumbe.[1] (Plate 49.)

The doctor who "shoved" quinine into Lawrence turned out to be a Carranzist colonel, the director of the Hospital Militar. He had come from the northern state of Nuevo León and had been in Oaxaca seven years. Two years older than Lawrence, he was well educated and cultured. After finishing his medical studies in Mexico, he had studied further in Galveston, Texas, and studied and worked in Berlin and Paris. Ophthalmology was his specialty, and his love of hunting had turned him into an amateur naturalist. Probably he also attended Lawrence for his stomach-ache at the Hotel Francia during the first days of his stay. Larumbe was accustomed to looking after the mine-owners in the hotel; and his explorations as a hunter-naturalist had put him into a position to do what Brett said the doctor did to Lawrence at the Francia: pour tales into his ears "of unspeakable horror in the mountain villages of nameless, incurable diseases."

In "The Flying Fish," Lawrence made double use of Dr. Larumbe. Besides introducing him directly as a character in the story, he took features of his career and combined them with discouraging things the Kulls told him about their projected trip to the Costa Chica to create a convincing occupational background for Gethin Day, the hero of the story. Larumbe was a wiry man of medium height with gray hair. Though tanned by the sun, he was not an Indian. Lawrence, however, made him one in the story, and the scene of his visit follows:

> The doctor came—an educated Indian: though he could do nothing but inject quinine and give a dose of calomel. But he was lost between the two days, the fatal greater day of the Indians, the fussy, busy lesser day of the white people.
>
> "How is it going to finish." he said to the sick man, seeking a word. "How is it going to finish with the Indians, with the Mexicans? Now the soldiers are all taking marijuana—hashish!"
>
> "They are all going to die. They are all going to kill themselves—all—all," said the Englishman, in the faint permanent delirium of his malaria. "After all, beautiful it is to be dead, and quite departed."
>
> The doctor looked at him in silence, understanding only too well. "Beautiful it is to be dead!" It is the refrain which hums at the center of every Indian heart, where the greater day is hemmed in by the lesser. The despair that comes when the lesser day hems in the greater. Yet the doctor looked at the gaunt white man in malice:—"What, would you have us quite gone, you Americans!"

In the story, the scene with the doctor occurs in a hotel bedroom and includes material from an earlier visit at the priest's house. The doctor's view that the race was exhausted indicated that Lawrence had passed it on to Brett while he was still at the Padre's. The exactitude of the detail about the soldiers smoking marijuana is startling. The further influence of the doctor and of the Kulls can be seen in the hero's background. In this case, the hero has just returned from the sort of trip to the coast that the Kulls were making.

> He lay in his bed in the hot October evening, still sick with malaria. In the flush of fever he saw yet the parched, stark mountains of the south, the villages of reed huts lurking among trees, the black-eyed natives with the lethargy, the ennui, the pathos, the beauty of an exhausted race; and above all he saw the weird, uncanny flowers, which he had hunted from the high plateaus, through the valleys, and down, to the steaming crocodile heat of the *tierra caliente,* towards the sandy, burning, intolerable shores. For he was fascinated by the mysterious green blood that runs in the veins of plants, and the purple and yellow and red blood that colours the face of flowers. Especially the unknown flora of South Mexico attracted him, and above all he wanted to trace to the living plant, the mysterious

essences and toxins known with such strange elaboration to the Mayas, the Zapotecas, and the Aztecs.

Lawrence gives a further picture of himself in his illness: "His head was humming like a mosquito, his legs were paralyzed for the moment by the heavy quinine injection the doctor had injected into them, and his soul was as good as dead with the malaria."

Lawrence's portrait of Dr. Larumbe contradicts Frieda's recollection of him in *"Not I, But the Wind . . . ."*: "I had a local native doctor who was scared at having anything to do with a foreigner and he didn't come." But Frieda was notoriously shy of doctors, sharing Lawrence's feeling that most of the time they were not necessary. She was so reluctant to seek and insist on good medical attention for her husband, in fact, that Aldous and Maria Huxley both subsequently lost their tempers with her. Writing to his brother, Julian, on 13 July 1929, Huxley says: "He is going to Germany now—or is just going: for he has been in Florence these last days—of all places in this weather! We have given up trying to persuade him to be reasonable. He doesn't want to be and no one can persuade him to be—except possibly Frieda. But Frieda is worse than he is. We've told her that she's a fool and a criminal; but it has no more effect than telling an elephant."

Jean Akin discovered in Oaxaca that Lawrence "did most of the cooking when he was strong" because Frieda "didn't care anything about housework" and "wasn't a very good housekeeper." Later she turns out not to be a good nurse. Mrs. Carswell, who had visited the Lawrences in England when he was sick, bluntly calls her a bad nurse "in the ordinary sense" although she "had a marvelous power of putting strength into Lawrence when he was ill." Two years after Lawrence's death, in a letter to Mrs. Strousse about the novelist's dependence on his wife, Huxley, in a more charitable mood wrote, "I have seen him on two occasions rise from what I thought was his death bed, when Frieda, who had been away, came back after a short absence." And twenty-five years later in a letter to Nancy Kelly, dealing with Frieda's infidelities, Huxley conceded, "Thanks to Frieda, Lawrence remained alive for at least five years after he ought, by all the rules of medicine, to have been in the grave."

In her own memoirs, Frieda "got him better by putting hot sandbags on him, that seemed to comfort his tortured inside," which was, as Mrs. Carswell noted, "his own treatment."

The rally that had enabled Lawrence to write Brett a short note on Thursday continued. On Saturday he wrote William Hawk the letter he had planned seven days sooner. It included the money for the horses that he had forgotten to enclose a month earlier, and a portion published in Moore's *The Intelligent Heart* relates to Lawrence's illness: "I have been steadily out of luck this trip down here: don't think I shall ever come to Mexico again while I live. I wondered why I wasn't well down here—thought it was the remains of the old flu—and so it was, with malaria. This place is full of malaria. I've had the doctor, and heavy quinine injections, and feel a rag: but much better." The letter continued: "We hope to get away some time next week, to Mexico City—and sail from Vera Cruz on the 20th (D. V.!)." And the letter told Hawk that Brett was leaving Mexico City for the ranch the next day. To make sure she got a good send-off, Lawrence telegraphed her the same day he wrote Hawk, reporting improved health and wishing her a good journey.

God was not willing. On February 8, the Sunday Brett left Mexico and the day Lawrence hoped to be up, he had a relapse so severe that Frieda felt she could no longer cope with his illness by herself and turned for help to the missionaries, who had the house up the street and around the corner on Liceaga.

Although Ethel Doctor has appeared frequently in this narrative, Norman Taylor and his wife Geraldine were not involved with the Lawrences until this point. They would naturally have been involved with the Protestants among the Mexicans. Furthermore, the semi-Bohemian Lawrence and the earnest Presbyterians would have found little in common. Taylor remembers three visits, and Frieda records in *"Not I, But the Wind . . ."* a preliminary call which suggests that the missionaries may have come to offer help.

"One day," she wrote, "we had met a missionary and his wife, who lived right in the hills with the most uncivilized tribe of Indians." The Taylors actually had come to Oaxaca to take over the hostel for Protestant children, relieving their predecessors, the Van Slykes. It was the Van Slykes who went to live in the hills. Frieda correctly noted that Taylor "didn't look like a missionary, he looked like a soldier. . . . He told me he had been an airman."

Born in Winnipeg, he had served in the Royal Canadian Air Force and was thirty-two when Frieda met him. Thanks to Miss Doctor, I corresponded with him and he reported serving five years in the Canadian Forces. "My squadron was No. 20," he said, "and we flew the Bristol fighter which, at that time, was one of the best planes in the air." During the war he decided to become a minister and began his theological studies as soon as he was discharged. McCormick in Chicago and Xenia in Pittsburgh were his seminaries. Geraldine Ely, the girl he married, was an American and also a missionary. He later became a U.S. citizen.

Frieda was enduring anxiety for a sick husband in a strange country far from her own people. An anecdote Taylor related touched her deeply: "There far away in Oaxaca he told me how he was there when Manfred Richthofen was brought down behind the trenches and in the evening at mess one of the officers rose and said 'Let's drink to our noble and generous enemy.' For me to be told of this noble gesture made in that awful war was a great thing," Frieda recalls.[2]

Like the Kulls, the Taylors never knew they had figured in a book. In 1962 when I sent Taylor Frieda's account, he replied:

> I suppose I must have known that Mrs. Lawrence was related to Richthofen or I would not have told her about the incident in our squadron mess. But I had forgotten it completely. What she quotes me as saying is not my language at all, and I cannot imagine myself saying anything like that. However, it is true that we drank to him and hoped that he had not been killed.
>
> In those days there was a great deal more chivalry than in the Second World War. If a German plane was shot down behind our lines, the following day we would drop a message on their side saying what had happened to the pilot. And they would do the same with us. But I am sure that none of us would have called him "Our noble and generous enemy." We admired his "guts" and his airmanship, but we had lost too many of our men, and some of us had been shot down by his circus, to call him noble and generous.

After the first visit of the missionaries, Lawrence grew worse and Taylor recalled, Frieda "came over to our home at the corner of the Llano and told us how sick he was. It was then that Mrs. Taylor made up some soup and took it to him." And Frieda recalled Mrs. Taylor appearing "with a very good bowl of soup when Lawrence was at his worst, and then prayed for him by his bedside in that big bare room. I was half afraid and wondered how Lawrence would feel. But he took it gently and I was half laughing, half crying over the soup and the prayer."

When I sent this account to Dr. Kull, the chuckling irreligious dentist commented, "Well, well, no doubt Norman Taylor, and especially his wife, Geraldine, tried to do a little missionary work among the Lawrences as well—as they did try it on us, again, especially she."

"At that time," wrote Mr. Taylor, "D. H. Lawrence was not as famous as he became later. To us he was just 'an author' who was very ill and needed sympathy and help."

When I asked the minister how Lawrence impressed him personally, he said: "He was a very sick man and our conversation on each occasion was very brief." Forty years later, no strong impression of Frieda remained in the missionary's mind either. "My remembrance of her is very vague," he wrote. And perhaps he never met Brett, for he said, "I only recall there was another lady with them, but remember nothing about her personally."

While Lawrence was too sick to talk and Frieda herself was feverish,

Oaxaca's earth shook as described in the account of the fate of the priest's house. In *"Not I, But the Wind . . ."* Frieda remembers crying out, "Let's get under the bed if the roof falls."

Brett, reconstructing the scene from Frieda's "scrappy accounts," wrote, "Of course there would be an earthquake, with you too sick to move and the old beams in the Padre's house moving in and out of their holes in the wall while you lie helpless, unable (as Frieda suggests from the next room) to get under the bed. You can't even turn over."

As 1925 had approached, Lawrence had written, "The next year will be momentous, one feels." Six weeks later, he was in danger of dying. Frieda recalls that "Lawrence himself thought he would die." As often as he had been ill in the past, there had never been a thought that he would not recover, but this illness was worse. Frieda's narrative continues:

> "You'll bury me in the cemetery here," he would say grimly.
>
> "No, no," I laughed, "it's such an ugly cemtery, don't you think of it."
>
> And that night he said to me: "But if I die, nothing has mattered but you, nothing at all." I was almost scared to hear him say it, that, with all his genius, I should have mattered so much. It seemed incredible.

Two months later, Lawrence wrote to Frieda's mother that he was "cross that I was so ill." And the nearest he came to confiding to a correspondent what really happened was early in 1926 when he wrote Murry, "Last year I nearly fell into the Styx." Despite his humor, his whole life was changed by the experience. From Oaxaca on he began to build his "ship of death" for the long voyage that he knew lay ahead. Even before he left Oaxaca, "The Flying Fish," the story he wrote in his last days there, records a man's feelings after experiencing death's presence. He would develop the theme more fully in 1929 in "The Escaped Cook," as he originally titled Part One of *The Man Who Died,* for this part evokes the speech and scenery of Oaxaca, and the yards, huts, and appearance of the villagers he saw on his walk to Huayapan. In 1927 he thought continuously of how death should be faced during his tour of the tombs and the lost cities of the Etruscans. Those reflections, which he hoped to augment by a second tour he was never strong enough to make, appeared in *Etruscan Places.* Awareness of peaceful oblivion brought a new note into his final poems, especially the several-times rewritten "The Ship of Death."

It must not be thought, though, that he grew increasingly morbid after the experience in Oaxaca. Finding that he could face and accept the prospect of his own death, in fact, seemed to liberate him. Perhaps no essays are so high-spirited and life-affirming as those written at Kiowa Ranch shortly after his return from Oaxaca published in *Reflections of the Death of a Porcupine.* Not only does a new joy come into his post-Oaxaca work, but an old urgency—mountingly present in the novels from *Aaron's Rod,* through *Kangaroo* to *The Plumed Serpent* —disappears completely. The duty of a man to help generate a new spirit in humankind is no longer a theme. Lawrence's new attitude, proclaimed in how he acted, as well as in what he wrote, is embodied in the words he put in the mind and on the lips of the man he depicted as having survived crucifixion:

> Let the earth remain earthy, and hold its own against the sky. I was wrong to seek to lift it up. I was wrong to try to interfere. . . . I have outlived my mission and know no more of it. . . . It had to be. But now I am glad it is over, and the day of my interference is done. The teacher and the saviour are dead in me; now I can go about my business, into my own single life. . . . Now I can live without striving to sway others any more.

Actually, in his remaining years Lawrence continued striving to sway others. But the mention of "the single life" is significant. From this point he would preach that individuals should seek salvation through what Philip Rieff calls "the intimate life." *Lady Chatterley's Lover* is Lawrence's fullest and most eloquent statement of this new gospel.

This encounter with death left Lawrence a partial invalid, with a restricted and slowly narrowing range of physical activities. The "vast reserves of energy" Frieda mentioned enabled him to still produce a great deal of work, and he traveled from place to place in search of salubrious climates, but after Oaxaca he was never the same again. On 27 May 1927, he admitted to Koteliansky: "I am sick of these bronchial colds, mixed with malaria. I've never been right since I was ill in Mexico two years ago—beastly bronchial trouble and the germs get in in an instant." A year later when he was trying Switzerland for his "bronchials," he wrote Harry Crosby:[3] "I only get depressed about my health—if only I am well I'm quite a happy soul. But I do get tired of not being well: it's three years now I'm shaky, since we came back from America last time."

The missionaries were not the only ones to offer help. In fact, every one was so kind that Frieda wrote:

> I can never say enough of the handful of English and Americans there: how good they were to us. Helping us in every way. I thought these mine-owners and engineers led plucky and terrible lives. Always fever, typhoid, malaria, danger from bandits, never feeling a bit safe with their lives. And so I was amazed at the 'Selbstverständichkeit' [matter-of-courseness] with which they helped us. It was so much more than Christian, just natural: a fellow-Englishman in distress: let's help him.

Padre Rickards was the nearest to an Englishman of those the Lawrences knew in the city, so he must have been especially helpful. Her mention of the mine-owners shows that Emma and William Thompson, who had loaned them furniture and lived across the Llano, must have pitched in too; and the reference to engineers indicates that Donald Miller, their across-the-street neighbor, who had sent in "cakes and jam" and driven them to Mitla, had probably sent in more than desserts in his neighborliness. Rosalino, Brett asserts, guarded Lawrence and served him with faithful devotion. Miss Doctor, reports that "the wild Wilson boys," whose father lived next door on Pino Suárez, were also helpful.

Jean Akin's involvement was extensive. She shared the nursing with Frieda, a skill acquired in caring for her sister Eva, who had become ill while Jean was in high school in Topeka. Eva was fifteen or sixteen years older than Jean and the younger sister loved her almost as if she were her mother. During Eva's long illness at St. Francis Hospital in Topeka, Jean visited her daily, did her homework beside her bed, and observed the ministrations of the nurses and doctors. As her sister's illness stretched out, she relieved the nurses and ended by giving her sister most of the care she needed. In following years, she went so far out of her way to help the sick that her family, including her elderly husband, joked about her "yen for taking care of all strays."

It must have been during this time that Frieda confided to Jean about her three children by a previous husband and that Jean saw what no one else saw in Oaxaca: Lawrence angry at Frieda. "We were very good friends," Jean recalled to me forty years later. "Poor Frieda, she had a life, I tell you. I felt so sorry for her. She always struck a tender spot in me, having been practically kicked out by her husband. I liked her better than I did him. After they left Oaxaca, we corresponded. But then we lost touch. I haven't any of her letters left."

Frieda's account of their Oaxaca days does not mention that Lawrence was moved from the priest's house. But Brett's hearsay account reports, "You were carried from the Padre's house to the [Francia] hotel, after the earthquake." The move came on February 14, for the following day, Lawrence had regained enough strength to write Curtis Brown: "Am still in Oaxaca—but was moved down to this hotel yesterday. Been having a devil of a time with malaria—think it's got under.—That comes of hot winter sun! I *hope* and pray we can get up to Mexico City in a week's time, out of the malarial areas.—With luck we should sail for England from Vera Cruz on March 10th—land in England about March 25th. I shall bring the MS. of *Quetzalcoatl* with me, and you can get it typed for me—then I can go over it. It is finished."

Perhaps he did not want to admit to Brown that he was so ill that he had to be taken on a stretcher. Old Bob Wilson, the Hamiltons' mine manager who lived next door, had an open touring car, a Moon, according to his son, Robert W. Wilson. He was not present at the time and was sixty-nine when I queried him. He had no recollection of the transfer. Clyde Wilson, the twenty-one-year-old son, was often Jean Akin's tennis partner on the Kulls' court, and probably Jean had enlisted his participation, for, she recalled, "Clyde Wilson was the one who helped drive him down to the Francia. He was on a stretcher then."

Perhaps on another trip Clyde and the Moon helped bring down the two trunks, the suitcases, and the hatbox, which Jean may have helped to pack. She does not recall what happened to the borrowed beds, rocking chairs, and the round table with the onyx top. Perhaps the Thompsons took some of their own things back; and I would like to think that the Lawrences left the Padre those pieces that had been bequeathed by the Kulls.

Jean persuaded Frieda to make the move because it would be easier for Jean to spell Frieda on the nursing at the Francia. Besides, the hotel, with its servants and dining room, was better equipped to be a substitute hospital than the bare house at the outskirts of the city. It was a correct decision. Lawrence's report to Brown was too optimistic, and he relapsed. His days spent in the hotel are vividly conveyed in his projection of himself as the hero of "The Flying Fish," including descriptions of the rooms and patio of the Francia:

> He lay in the nausea of the tropics, and let the days pass over him. The door of his room stood open on the patio where green banana trees and high strange-sapped flowering shrubs rose from the water-sprinkled earth towards that strange rage of blue which was the sky over the shadow-heavy, perfume-soggy air of the closed-in courtyard. Dark-blue shadows moved from the side of the patio, disappeared, then appeared on the other side. Evening had come, and the barefoot natives in white calico flitted with silent rapidity across, and across, forever going, yet mysteriously going nowhere, threading the timelessness with their transit, like swallows of darkness.
>
> The window of the room, opposite the door, opened on to the tropical parched street. It was a big window, came nearly down to the floor, and was heavily barred with upright and horizontal bars. Past the window went the natives, with the soft, light rustle of their sandals. Big straw hats balanced, dark cheeks, calico shoulders brushed with the silent swiftness of the Indian past the barred window-space. Sometimes children clutched the bars and gazed in, with great shining eyes and straight blue-black hair, to see the Americano lying in the majesty of a white bed. Sometimes a beggar stood there, sticking a skinny hand through the iron grille and whimpering the strange, endless, pullulating whimper of the beggar—

"por amor de dios" —on and on and on, as it seemed for an eternity. But the sick man on the bed endured it with the same endless endurance in resistance, endurance in resistance which he had learned in the Indian countries. Aztec or Mixtec, Zapotec or Maya, always the same power of serpent-like torpor or resistance.

What did Frieda do during these long days? Lawrence's use of her "pheasant" scribbler for his second start of the Quintanilla piece shows that at one time she took Spanish lessons. Brett recalls, "Frieda stitches away silently," and Mrs. Luhan remembers "that cigarette made her face look tough and formidable, while her hands held a bundle of knitting needles and yarn." Merrild also testifies how much Frieda knitted, and Lawrence frequently told Baroness von Richthofen of the clothes Frieda was making.

In a P.S. to one of Lawrence's letters during their first stay at the Francia, Frieda wrote to Clarence Thompson, Mrs. Luhan's blonde protégé: "It's such a lovely sun. The people gave us feasts in Mexico City— but a city goes a long way. There really is need for your rose-coloured trousers in the world. I do enjoy the exquisite bits you gave me—With all good luck to you! Love.—excuse pencil, I am writing in the patio—" (Three years later, Lawrence would write an article for the *London Evening News* called "Red Trousers," condemning socialism because it made for such a dull life, praising bright clothes, and advocating that more young men should wear them. "It takes," he wrote, "a lot of courage to sail gaily, in brave feathers, right in the teeth of a dreary convention.")

So probably Frieda spent long hours in the "lovely sun" of the hotel's patio, within earshot of the bedroom's open door. She wrote letters in this period too. One at the University of Texas to her "liebe Mère" reports that she struggled hard with Lawrence against his depression. Two owned by the University of Cincinnati were written to Brett in Mexico City.

Thanks to Tedlock's scrupulous description of the Lawrence manuscripts Frieda had in 1948, we know what happened next. After Lawrence had filled all but a few pages of "Record" and overflowed the two books he had bought in Mexico City for the second *Serpent,* he needed a new copybook. At a stationery store in Oaxaca run by Angel San-German, he bought one similar to the pair he had found at "El Bufete." Though it was a little narrower, it too was nine inches high, had lined pages, and had marbled boards. Considering how sick he was, it seems incredible that he should act on his own advice about Pisgah and precipitate a new adventure by starting another novel. He was too ill to write, so he dictated to Frieda. The first eight pages and all but the last of the ninth page are in her hand. He continued filling the pages from ten to forty, making occasional but extensive interlinear revisions as he did.

His first idea for a title was "The Weather Vane," though in small letters in his notes he also thought of "The Flying Fish." Because of those notes, included among the "Suggestions for Stories" in "Record," we know the novel was conceived before his illness. In fact, it dates from mid-January, for Lawrence summarized its plot before starting "Noah's Flood"; and internal evidence links it to both the Noah play and Kate's musing about Atlantis. "Fish" describes the Atlantic Ocean "like a cemetery, an endless infinite cemetery of greyness, where the bright lost world of Atlantis is buried." The natives of Oaxaca are described as "handsome, dangerous, wide-eyed men left over from the ages before the flood in Mexico." And "the sun behind the sun" is mentioned three times, twice described as a great bird—the image from "Noah's Flood" only with blue wings rather than white.

He also jotted down plots for three more stories that reflect the torments he felt over the Frieda-Brett conflicts. "The Wedding Ring," a title discarded from an earlier draft of *The Rainbow* and *Women in Love,* would deal with a wife who wants *"absolute* love" and throws her wedding ring at her husband before she leaves him. He then decides not to marry the rival, "the halfwoman." "The Dog" was to be about a wife who loves dogs and whose husband, a younger man, grows dog-like as her dog sickens. After the dog dies, the husband flies at her, and in his "maddened" eyes she sees her dead dog's eyes. The attack causes her to expire "in terror." "The Woman out of the Water" was to be about a woman with a motorcycle who rides into the sea and then, an "insidious separator" comes between the husband and wife who rescue her. "Wife fires her," continues the plot, "she has a vision of Christ. Husband follows her— loves her—finds she is really half a *fish. "*

"The Weather Vane" was the only one of the quartet that Lawrence started, and we know the general lines of its projected plot from his notes. The novel would take its title from the weather vane of Daybrook, the ancestral home of the Day family, said to be situated in Lathkill Dale. This vane is a curious affair—a fish surmounting a ring bearing the figures of the zodiac. The hero, forty-year-old Gethin is the last of the Days. The novel would tell of his return home, marrying a local girl, and his falling ill after she reverses the rotation of the zodiacal ring, making the fish swim belly up. They leave Daybrook at her request to live in town. Their child is born, she grows hostile towards Gethin, and is struck by lightning when she tries to turn the ring to its original rotation.

When Lawrence began dictating, he changed Lathkill Dale to Crichdale, showing that he had decided to set his novel in a Midlands valley he had visited on an Easter Monday when he was seventeen or eighteen and which he had already used in *Sons and Lovers.* The visit had been to see the ruins of the Earl of Shrewsbury's Wingfield Manor, where Mary

Queen of Scots was twice imprisoned. Largely destroyed by the Puritans in 1646, the manor no doubt suggested Daybrook to Lawrence, for his sister Ada, who was on the excursion, recalled how the manor was in the Derbyshire Hills "high up on a grassy slope," and Daybrook is described as "a sixteenth-century stone house, among the hills in the middle of England . . . standing upon a knoll." Gethin's sister is called a Derbyshire woman. Since Derbyshire adjoins Nottinghamshire to the west, and Wingfield Manor is only ten miles from Lawrence's native Eastwood, "The Flying Fish" was to be another novel laid among the scenes of his youth. Though he never completed it, he later used its projected setting for *The Virgin and the Gypsy.*

Before leaving Oaxaca Lawrence wrote only three sections: "Departure from Mexico," "The Gulf," and "The Atlantic." This last section breaks off with the subsiding of a storm three days out of Havana. Gethin, a naturalist who was formerly a soldier, never reaches Daybrook, to which he had been called by the death of his older sister. He is at last eager to get home and settle there as the last survivor of his ancient family. A family superstition is embodied in the couplet:

No Day in Daybrook:
For the Vale a bad outlook.

Sir Gilbert Day, an Elizabethan seaman, built the stone house and wrote the *Book of Days,* "a sort of secret family bible at Daybrook." Gethin knew it almost by heart because his sister had written out a copy for him, and its text haunts his meditations as he leaves Mexico.

Whether Lawrence wanted to abandon "The Weather Vane" for the "The Flying Fish" we do not know. Perhaps only the first section would be called "The Flying Fish," referring to the flying fish in the Gulf of Mexico rather than to the vane. But clearly there would be a symbolic connection between the metallic fish flying over Daybrook and the living fish that seemed like silver butterflies when Lawrence first saw them. The three sections written in Oaxaca were published in 1936 in McDonald's *Phoenix* as "The Flying Fish," the fifth of the Oaxaca pieces included without reference to the city, because its typescript, like those of the four others, gave McDonald no clue to its place of composition. Following "Resurrection" and "Noah's Flood," it was the third of the Oaxaca pieces written, in part, in Lawrence's biblical style.

The basic theme, the imagery, the manner of expression, the philosophy, and even the story line of "Flying Fish" go back far in Lawrence's earlier writings. He had the idea of going down into death and returning as a changed and better person as early as 1915. On 20 December 1915, he wrote Katherine Mansfield, trying to console her for the wartime death of her brother, Leslie Heron Beauchamp:

> Do not be sad. It is one life which is passing away from us, one "I" is dying; but there is another coming into being, which is the happy, creative you. I knew you would have to die with your brother; you also, go down into death and be extinguished. But for us there is a rising from the grave, there is a resurrection, and a clean life to begin from the start, new and happy. Don't be afraid. Don't doubt it, it is so.
>
> You have gone further into your death than Murry has. He runs away. But one day he too will submit, he will dare to go down, and be killed, to die in his self which he is. Then he will become a man: not till.

During the first year of the war Lawrence felt that he too had gone far into his own death. And by May 1916 when he had read Richard Henry Dana's *Two Years Before the Mast,* and later wrote about it in *Studies in Classic American Literature,* he had felt the pull of the basic story of a man returning home from a sea voyage "after passing into the black deeps" and having his consciousness almost swallowed up by the waters.

Three long sea voyages in 1922 and a fourth in 1923 also played shaping roles in "The Flying Fish." In 1922 he went from Naples to Ceylon via the Suez Canal. Coming into the Gulf of Aden, he first saw flying fish. As he wrote Baroness von Richthofen on March 7, "We see now the little flying fish. They are all silver and they fly like butterflies, so wee." On April 30, after the Ceylon visit, when he was four days short of his destination in Australia, he wrote Lady Cynthia Asquith of being "somewhere in a very big blue choppy sea" and seeing more flying fish "sprinting out of the waves like winged drops." The third voyage of 1922 was in May on the *Malwa* which took ten days to circumnavigate the underside of Australia from Fremantle in the west to Sydney in the east. In his *Moby Dick* chapter in *Studies in Classic American Literature,* he wrote:

> Well, I have seen an albatross, too, following us in waters hard upon the Antarctic, too, south of Australia. And in the Southern winter, And the ship a P. and O. Boat, nearly empty, and the lascar crew shivering.
>
> The bird with its long, long wings following, then leaving us. No one knows till they have tried, how lost, how lonely those Southern waters are. And glimpses of the Australian coast.
>
> It makes one feel that our day is only a day. That in the dark of the night ahead other days stir fecund, when we have lapsed from existence.

The 1923 voyage was on the freighter *Toledo,* on which he sailed with Gótzsche from Veracruz on November 22. Although he had already reconstructed this voyage (as if in the reverse direction) in the novella *St. Mawr,* it was this voyage that he exploited again in "The Flying Fish." Mrs. Carswell describes how Lawrence told her and other friends about it once he reached London. "While he talked, he left all the letters that had collected for him in London unopened—did not even glance at them. He had liked it in Mexico, he said, that there had been no mail for him and no English newspapers. He described with delight how on the voyage home he had hung over the bows, watching a school of porpoises playing about the steamer in the translucent water. Then later the rain on the surface of the black water . . . and the beauty of the flying fish. . . ."

In *Kangaroo,* the hero wishes "he could take to the sea and be a whale, a great surge of living blood: away from these all-too-white people." Lawrence is already anticipating the feelings of the later hero. Another anticipation appears when the *Kangaroo* hero watched birds diving for fish and reflects:

> Why be cloyed and clogged down like billions of fish in water, or billions of mice on land? It is a world of slaves. Then why not gannets in the upper air, having two worlds? Why only one element? If I am to have a meeting it will be down, down in the invisible, and the moment I re-emerge it shall be alone. In the visible world I am alone, an isolated instance. My meeting is in the underworld, the dark. Beneath every gannet that jumps from the water, ten thousand fish are swimming still. But they are swimming in a shudder of silver fear. That is the magic of the ocean. Let them shudder the huge ocean aglimmer.

Kangaroo records a scene based on a beach outing Frieda and Lawrence had taken. She laughs in recalling that Lawrence's hat had been blown from his head as he was wading, and how he had run deeper into the sea to rescue it.

"Like a flying-fish! Like a flying-fish dashing into the waves! Dashing into the waves after his hat—" is the way the heroine based on Frieda recalls the incident. "I shall call you the flying fish." The extent to which flying fish had influenced his meditations on the oceans' depths, the difference between life in them and life in the air, and how he had come to see the contrasting lives in symbolic terms is shown strikingly in the passage he added to *The Boy in the Bush* to describe how consciousness returned to Jack, after nearly dying while lost in the bush.

> The subconscious self woke first, roaring in the distant wave-beats, unintelligible, unmeaning, persistent, and growing in volume. It had something

to do with birth. And not having died. "I have not let my soul run like water out of my mouth."

And as the roaring and beating of the waves increased in volume, tiny little words emerged like flying-fish out of the black ocean of consciousness. "Ye must be born again," in little silvery, twinkling spurts like flying-fish which twinkle silver and spark into the utterly dark sea again. They were gone and forgotten before they were realised. They had merged deep in the sea again. And the roar of the dark consciousness was the roar of death. . . . You may be born again. But when you emerge, this time you emerge with the darkness of death between your eyes, as a lord of death.

Like "Climbing Down Pisgah," "The Flying Fish" exhibits a coming together of themes that had been developing in different compartments of Lawrence's mind. And the theme that coalesced with death and the ocean depths was the Day theme. His vision of a monkey whisking its tail in one day while he himself scratched his head in another showed how he was considering it as he wrote "Corasmín and the Parrots." By the time he had written "Resurrection," about three weeks later, he used a stronger image: "Man who can rise with the Son of Man, and ascend unto the Father will see the new day." In another, drawing his imagery from *Revelation* which he had already borrowed for *Aaron's Rod* —he wrote: "The tree shivers and sheds its leaves. Never was the tree so vast in stature and so full of leaves. But the new fire spurts up at its root, the boughs writhe, the twigs crackle from within, and the old leaves fall thick and red to the ground. That is how a new day enters the Tree of Life. [And later] If you cannot note the coming day, if you're blind to the morning star, it is because the shadow of the stone is upon you, rolling down from the mouth of the tomb."

The impressive invention of "The Flying Fish" is not the story, which, as far as it goes, is almost straight autobiography, nor the thinking behind it, most of which was done before Lawrence began, but the imaginary Elizabethan book, "beautifully written out on vellum and illuminated by Sir Gilbert's own hand." Besides conceiving the appearance of the *Book of Day,* Lawrence had invented it so fully that he quotes from it extensively in the story. It helps the hero understand not only the impact of Mexico itself but his experience of death in Mexico. Here, for instance, is one of Sir Gilbert's intuitions: "Beauteous is the day of the yellow sun which is the common day of men; but even as the winds roll unceasing above the trees of the world, so doth the Greater Day, which is the Uncommon Day, roll over the unclipt bushes of our little daytime. Even also as the morning sun shakes his yellow wings on the horizon and rises up, so the great bird beyond him spreads out his dark blue feathers, and beats his wings in the tremor of the Greater Day."

The hero is deeply affected by recalling this passage in Oaxaca:

> Gethin knew a great deal of his *Book of Days* by heart. In a dilettante fashion, he had always liked rather highflown poetry, but in the last years, something in the hard, fierce, finite sun of Mexico, in the dry terrible land, and in the black staring eyes of the suspicious natives, had made the ordinary day lose its reality to him. It had cracked like some great bubble, and to his uneasiness and terror, he had seemed to see through the fissures the deeper blue of that other Greater Day where moved the other sun shaking its dark blue wings. Perhaps it was the malaria; perhaps it was his own inevitable development. . . . which caused his old connexions and his accustomed world to break for him. He was ill, and he felt as if at the very middle of him, beneath his navel, some membrane were torn, some membrane which had connected him with the world and its day. The natives who attended him, quiet, soft, heavy, and rather helpless, seemed, he realized, to be gazing from their wide black eyes always into the greater day whence they had come and where they wished to return. Men of a dying race, to whom the busy sphere of the common day is a cracked and leaking shell.

A vivid idea of how Lawrence felt in his sickness, lying in bed in the Francia, follows:

> Now he was sick from the soul outwards, and the common day had cracked for him and the uncommon day was showing him its immensity, he felt that home was the place. It did not matter that England was small and tight and over-furnished, if the Greater Day were round about. He wanted to go home, away from these big wild countries where men were dying back into the Greater Day, home where he dared face the sun behind the sun, and come into his own in the Greater Day.

And the home that Lawrence was envisioning was part of the country near Eastwood that had seemed particularly lovely to him in late adolescence.

For Oaxaca's sake, it is unfortunate that Lawrence did not name the city in "The Flying Fish," for it was not until Joseph Foster's *D. H. Lawrence in Taos* that "the lost town of South Mexico" of the story was publicly indentified as Oaxaca. Highly praised as the Oaxaca sketches in *Mornings in Mexico* have been, they do not equal "The Flying Fish." His best portrait of the city is in the unfinished novel and the story itself is the finest new piece he produced there. One memorable feature is the account of the journey to Oaxaca in the days of the narrow-gauge railway.

Because the hero of the story was going from Oaxaca to Mexico City, the sequence of the stations is reversed. But they are easy to rearrange, and because of Brett's description of the journey down to Oaxaca, we can tell that Lawrence reconstructed it, rather than working with the nightmare journey, when he and Frieda left Oaxaca and he was still very ill. Furthermore, Lawrence dates the journey in November, the month when they went to Oaxaca. Thus, all we have of "The Flying Fish" was already completed before leaving Oaxaca.

The first leg of the trip was from Mexico City to Esperanza, a point on the line from the capital to Veracruz, via Córdoba. This line, which was opened in 1873, was the first important railroad in Mexico. It was financed, built, and, in Lawrence's day, still governed and owned by Englishmen. Lawrence must have known this and heard the nickname bestowed on it during Victoria's reign, for he calls it "The Queen's Own." Esperanza, which is on the capital side of the highest point of the line, provides a wonderful view of Mexico's loftiest volcano, the Pico de Orizaba, or Citlaltepetl ("Mountain of the Star"). This is Lawrence's description of the stopover, while waiting for the train to Tehuacán:

> Here in the big but forlorn railway restaurant the Englishman ordered the regular meal that came with American mechanical take-it-or-leave-it flatness. He ate what he could, and went out again. There the vast plains were level and bare, under the blue winter sky, so pure, and not too hot, and in the distance the white cone of Orizaba stood perfect in the middle air.
>
> He came at nightfall to a small square town [Tehuacán], more in touch with civilization, where the train ended its frightened run. He slept there. And the next day he took another scrap of a train. [One of the sights not far out of Tehuacán was] among mango trees, beyond the bright green stretches of sugar cane, white clusters of a village, with the coloured dome of a church all yellow and blue with shiny majolica tiles. Spain putting the bubbles of her little day among the blackish trees of the unconquerable.
>
> The little train, with two coaches, one full of natives, the other with four or five "white" Mexicans, ran fussily on, in the little day of toys and men's machines. On the roof sat tiny, earthy-looking soldiers, faces burnt black, with cartridge belts and rifles. They clung on tight, not to be shaken off. And away went this weird toy, this crazy little caravan over the great lost land of cacti and mountains standing back, on to the shut-in defile where the long descent began.

By the shut-in defile he meant what the Mexicans call "La Cañada," and he described the midday dinner stop at Tomellín, midway through the long gorge.

At a station . . . connected with old silver mines the train stood, and all descended to eat: the eternal turkey with black sauce, potatoes, salad, and apple pie—the American apple pie, which is a sandwich of cooked apple between two layers of pie-crust. And also beer, from Puebla. Two Chinamen administered the dinner, in all the decency, cleanness and well-cookedness of the little day of the white men, which they reproduce so well. There it was, the little day of our civilization. Outside the little train waited. The little black-faced soldiers sharpened their knives. The vast, varying declivity of the *barranca* stood in sun and shadow as on the day of doom, untouched.

When the hero embarks in "The Gulf" chapter, the evocative passages about the porpoises and the flying fish seen from the ship's bow show that the 1923 voyage away from Mexico was vividly in Lawrence's mind as he anticipated a similar one in 1925. However, those passages rightly belong to the story of Lawrence's second trip to Mexico, the one without Frieda. Here as elsewhere in the story of the journey the fictional experience of the hero and Lawrence's reconstructed memories combine to form a convincing work of fiction.

"The Flying Fish" was clearly going to be a thought-adventure novel, too, and two passages from the imaginary book reveal how the hero intended to face life once he got home. They also reveal the state of mind to which Lawrence's illness in Oaxaca had brought him. The first describes how he would henceforth see the world, continually aware of the Greater Day, and all the time hoping to be equal to its reality:

> For the little day is like a house with the family around the hearth, and the door shut. Yet outside whispers the Greater Day, wall-less and hearthless. And the time will come at last when the walls of the little day shall fall, and what is left of the family of men shall find themselves outdoors in the Greater Day, houseless and abroad, even here between the knees of the Vales, even in Crichdale. . . . The tall men will remain alone in the land, moving deeper in the Greater Day, and moving deeper. Even as the flying fish, when he leaves the air and recovereth his element in the depth, plunges and invisibly rejoices. So will tall men rejoice, after their flight of fear, through the thin air, pursued by death. For it is on wings of fear, sped from the mouth of death that the flying fish riseth twinkling in the air, and rustles in astonishment silvery through the thin small day. But he dives again into the great peace of the deeper day, and under the belly of death, and passes into his own.

The second passage shows the advice he had for himself in the interval before the ultimate plunge into death, the one from which there would be no returning, and it is interesting to see how the perpetually snow-capped Citlaltepetl, seen on the way to Oaxaca while waiting on the platform at Esperanza, influenced his imagery:

> Be still, then, be still. Wrap thyself in patience, shroud thyself in patience, shroud thyself in peace, as the tall volcano clothes itself in snow. Yet he looks down in him, and sees wet sun in him molten and of great force, stirring with the scald sperm of life. Be still, above the sperm of life, which spills alone in its hour. Be still, as an apple on its core, as a nightingale in winter, as a long-awaited mountain upon its fire. Be still, upon thine own sun.
>
> For thou hast a sun in thee. Thou has a sun in thee, and it is not timed. Therefore wait, Wait, and be at peace with thine own sun, which is thy sperm of life. Be at peace with thy sun in thee, as the volcano is, and the dark holly-bush before berry-time, and the long hours of night. Abide by the sun in thee, even the onion doth so, though you see it not. Yet peel her, and her sun in thine eyes maketh tears. Each thing hath its little sun, even in the wicked house-fly something twinkleth.

The fights with censors over *Lady Chatterley's Lover,* the police action against his paintings, and being bedeviled by miserable health would interfere with Lawrence's quest for inner stillness in his post-Mexican years. But he would remain ever aware of the sun in him, and of the sun latent in all living creatures. The joyful tone in the new essays for *Death of a Porcupine* continues in his portrait of the rooster in *The Man Who Died.* What happened to Lawrence after Oaxaca is revealed in the words about the revived man in the second part of the novella in terms Lawrence had already coined in Oaxaca: "He had come back to life, but not the same life that he had left, the life of little people and the little day. Reborn, he was in the other life, the greater day of human consciousness. And he was alone and apart from the little day, and out of the contact with the daily people."

When the risen man contemplates the life of the slaves around the temple of Isis where he has found refuge, he reflects: "It was the life of the little day, and life of little people. And the man who had died said to himself: 'Unless we encompass it in the greater day, and set the little life in the circle of the greater life, all is disaster.' " The similarity of the language to that used in "The Flying Fish" shows, in fact, as Gerald M. Lacy has pointed out in *The Escaped Cock* (his unexpurgated edition of *The Man Who Died*) that *Cock* was a second attempt to recreate in fiction Lawrence's recovery from near-death in Oaxaca, and the changes it wrought in him. Lawrence's changes in behavior and writing after leaving Oaxaca strikingly parallel the conduct of his crucified Man, liberated because he had outlived his mission.

"The Risen Lord," the already quoted article published in *Everyman* in 1929, suggests even more simply what Lawrence felt had happened to him in Oaxaca after he had taken the same last step as Whitman and "looked over into death": That he had "accomplished" his acceptance of death, and had died both to "self-importance and to self-conceit." The terminology tracing his progress can be extracted from *Fantasia of the Unconscious*. In having undertaken a "purposive action" by trying to establish a colony and then by outlining a new religion he had gone beyond the quest for love; in having now gone beyond his mission, he had crossed another great threshold.

If Lawrence had the time and strength to write *Lady Chatterley's Lover,* perhaps his most poignant paean to life, not once but three times, why did he never finish "The Flying Fish"? The Brewsters became interested in the work after he read it to them in Switzerland the summer of 1928. When they asked about its progress, he replied, "I've an intuition I shall never finish that novel. It was written so near the borderline of death, that I never have been able to carry it through in the cold light of day."

Because Doña María, the tall, majestic manager of the Francia Hotel, was so kind to Brett, we can assume that she was as diligent as her staff in seeing that Lawrence's wants were supplied. Taylor, the Canadian fighter-pilot-turned missionary, also visited him with his wife at the hotel. "I called upon him," said the seventy-year-old minister "and, if I remember correctly, read a passage or two from the New Testament. I remember distinctly leaving my leather-bound New Testament with him, because later someone told me that I had 'wasted' it upon a man who did not believe anything. But I felt that was all the more reason to have given it. I am not certain whether I led in prayer at the time, but think that it is very possible since that is the customary thing for a minister to do after reading the Scriptures. In regard to our attitude when we prayed, I think we probably just stood by the bedside."

Jean Akin must also have been in constant and efficient attendance. She was the only Oaxaca contemporary of his I talked to who referred to him as David, apparently not realizing his self-confessed "unreasonable dislike of the name." Jean's unself-consciousness in using the name suggests that he never winced at the appellation, an instance of something that friends have claimed and that he himself admitted in "Making Pictures," in *Assorted Articles:* "My kindliness makes me sometimes a bit false." Jean recalls during that convalescence: "David was almost cadaverous looking. He was just so thin. Later I used to tell him that he hid behind an alfalfa patch. That was what I called his beard. It was all in fun."

Because of his own recuperative power and the good care at the Francia, Lawrence, after about a week, was able to get out of bed. Writing about his alter ego in "The Flying Fish," he described the next stage. "At last, Gethin Day crawled out into the plaza." Through the enfeebled hero's eyes, Lawrence describes Oaxaca's state palace, where he visited the governor, and the municipal palace. The description is colored by his illness:

The square was like a great low fountain of green and of dark shade, now it was autumn and the rains were over. Scarlet craters rose: the canna flowers, licking great red tongues, and tropical yellow. Scarlet, yellow, green, blue-green, sunshine intense and invisible, deep indigo shade! And small, white-clad natives pass, passing across the square, through the green lawns, under the indigo shade, and across the hollow sunshine of the road into the arched arcades of the low Spanish buildings where the shops were. The low, baroque Spanish buildings stood back with a heavy, sick look, as if they too felt the endless malaria in their bowels, the greater day of the stony Indian crushing the more jaunty, lean European day which they represented. The yellow cathedral leaned its squat, earthquake shaken towers, the bells sounded hollow. Earth-coloured tiny soldiers lay and stood around the entrance to the municipal palace which was so baroque and Spanish, but which now belonged to the natives. Heavy as a strange bell of shadow-coloured glass, the shadow of the greater day hung over this colored plaza which the Europeans had created, like an oasis, in the lost depths of Mexico. Gethin Day sat half lying on one of the broken benches, while tropical birds flew and twittered in the green trees, and natives twittered or flittered in silence, and he knew that here, the European day was annulled again. His body was sick with the poison that lurks in all tropical air, his soul was sick with that other day, that rather awful greater day which permeates the little days of the old races. He wanted to get out, to get out of this ghastly tropical void into which he had fallen.

What a far cry from Lawrence's first day in Oaxaca when he, Frieda, and Brett had wandered round and round "the lovely, shady" *zócalo,* absorbing the town's peace and "remote beauty" and reveling in the perfect climate which permitted the women, even in winter, to wear cotton dresses!

Once Lawrence was no longer confined to bed, the interrupted plans to go to Mexico City could be resumed. Gerald Lacy's "Calendar" of the Lawrence letters marked February 24 as the new departure date. The Lawrences' personal belongings and some of their purchases in Oaxaca had been somewhat thinned when Brett had taken "a lot of bits of stuff" with her to New Mexico, including, perhaps, a beautiful green Oaxaca dish that Lawrence would smash with an ax in a fit of anger when it fell off a table. Still, there were those two trunks, those two suitcases, and Frieda's hatbox to be packed and transported to the station. But there was one procedure whereby the bulk and weight of things could be reduced—by giving them away. Two books that he gave away in Oaxaca provide clues to memories stirred before he left.

One was his first novel, *The White Peacock,* reissued by Duckworth from its third impression, dated April 1921. As we have seen, Lawrence associated *The White Peacock* with his mother's death and the bitter Christmas of 1910 when neither he nor his sister Ada could bear to stay home. In the introduction for McDonald's bibliography that Lawrence had written into "Record" shortly before coming to Oaxaca, he recalled the novel's arrival in the family home in Eastwood.

> The very first copy of *The White Peacock,* that was ever sent out, I put into my mother's hands when she was dying. She looked at the outside, and then at the title-page, and then at me, with darkening eyes. And though she loved me so much, I think she doubted whether it could be much of a book, since no one more important than I had written it. Somewhere in the helpless privacies of her being, she had a wistful respect for me. But for me in the face of the world, not much. This David would never get a stone across at Goliath. And why try? Let Goliath alone. Anyway, she was beyond reading my first immortal work. It was put aside, and I never wanted to see it again. She never saw it again.

The copy was an advance one that had been bound especially for him so he could present it to her "with love" while she still kept "the live consciousness." When one considers how thrilled an author generally is by the sight of his first book and how much of himself Lawrence had put into this particular novel, which had taken almost five years of effort, with most of it rewritten five or six times, one realizes the destroyed hopes and bitter grief behind his sentences.

In the same introduction, Lawrence said, "I have never read one of my own published works." Yet in Oaxaca he reread *The White Peacock* for he spoke about it a few months later when Kyle Crichton, an American journalist of twenty-nine who wrote for the *New York World,*[4] interviewed him at Kiowa Ranch: "It's awful to read stuff when it's once in book form [Crichton reported Lawrence as saying]. Last year in Mexico I reread *The White Peacock* for the first time in fifteen years. It seemed strange and far off and as if written by somebody else. I wondered how I could have thought of some of the things or how I could have written them. And then I'd come on something that showed I may have changed in style and form, but I haven't changed fundamentally."

Might *The White Peacock*'s evocation of the ruins of Felley Abbey, the valley, woods, streams, and pond that Lawrence loved as a boy have influenced him in conceiving "The Flying Fish"? It may well have intensified his homesickness while simultaneously inspiring him to return to a nearby setting for a later book.

The second book Lawrence gave away in his last days in Oaxaca was *Little Novels of Sicily* by Giovanni Verga. Of all the writers Lawrence helped, either as encourager, editor, translator, rewriter, reviewer, or drum-beater, Verga was unquestionably the most important. Not only was Verga a more significant artist than any of the others, but, by single-handedly translating three Verga books when he was already quite famous himself, Lawrence rendered the Sicilian novelist far greater assistance. In the introductions he wrote for those translations, Lawrence argued persuasively that Verga was a writer of the stature of Flaubert, Hardy, and Tolstoy.

An advance copy of *Little Novels of Sicily,* the second of Lawrence's three Verga translations, arrived from Basil Blackwood of Oxford, at the end of Lawrence's stay. (It was scheduled for publication in England in April.) He does not record his response to the arrival of the little yellow-bound book of 191 pages. It is unlikely that he reread it. Still, his translation of Verga's *Novelle Rusticane* must have brought him memories of Ceylon as well as Sicily.

Verga is best-known as the librettist of Mascagni's *Cavalleria Rusticana,* an opera which, as we know from Lawrence's letters to Louie Burrows, had thrilled him as early as 1911. Verga based his famous libretto on one of his own stories in *Vita del Campi,* the third Verga book Lawrence would translate under the title *Cavalleria Rusticana and Other Stories.* Though the octogenarian Verga had long given up writing,he was still living in Sicily when Lawrence moved there in 1920. The two novelists never met, but near the end of his second year at Taormina, Lawrence began reading the island's most famous chronicler. On 25 October 1921, he wrote Mrs. Carswell: "I have only been reading Giovanni Verga lately. He exercises quite a fascination on me, and makes me feel quite sick at the end. But perhaps that is only if one knows Sicily—do you know if he is translated into English?— *I Malavoglia* or *Maestro don Gesualdo* —or *Novelle Rusticane,* or the other short stories. It would be fun to do him—his language is so fascinating."

On November 10, just after his reconciliation with Edward Garnett, he wrote his old friend asking the same question about Verga translations in English. "He is *extra ordinarily* good—peasant—quite modern—Homeric—and it would need somebody who could absolutely handle English in the dialect, to translate him. He would be most awfully difficult to translate. That is what tempts me: though it is rather a waste of time, and probably I shall never do it. Though if I don't I doubt if anyone else will—adequately, at least."

Maestro-don Gesualdo, about a peasant who grew wealthy in the middle of the last century when Sicily was still part of the Bourbon kingdom of Naples, was Verga's last and finest novel and the first Lawrence tackled. In January he reported to Curtis Brown: "I am nearly half-way through the translation of a Sicilian novel, *Maestro-don Gesualdo* by Giovanni Verga. He just died—aged 82 in Catania. . . . I will send you the Ms.—all that is finished—before I leave."

In his wanderings after leaving England, Lawrence's two years at Taormina were an exceptionally stable period, but even the pleasures of Sicily finally palled, and in early 1922 he headed for Ceylon to visit the Brewsters as the first stage in his roundabout journey to the United States. On the voyage to Ceylon he finished translating *Gesualdo.* During his visit with the Brewsters at their large bungalow in Kandy, he began translating the twelve stories of *Novelle Rusticane.*

Because it was in Ceylon that Lawrence caught malaria, we can be sure the *Little Novels of Sicily,* coming to him in a place where the malaria had flared up again, reminded him of the connection. And thanks to the Brewsters' *Reminiscences,* we have a vivid glimpse of one of the scenes the pocket-sized volume must have brought back to him.

> Generally [recalled Achsah Brewster], we sat on the north verandah in the morning. There was early breakfast, then tiffin; then the child went to a little school and Earl studied Pali in a monastery across the lake. Frieda, stretched out on a rattan couch, sewed and embroidered with bright silks. Lawrence sat curled up with a schoolboy's copy-book in his hand, writing away. He was translating Giovanni Verga's short stories from the Sicilian. Across the pages of the copy-book his hand moved rhythmically, steadily, unhesitatingly, leaving a trail of exquisite, small writing as legible as print. No bolts, no scratchings marred its beauty. When the book was finished, he wrapped and tied it up, sending it off to the publisher. All of this went on in the family circle. Frieda would come for consultation as to whether the rabbit's legs should be embroidered in yellow or white. The pen would be lifted a moment and then go on across the page. Sometimes Lawrence would stop and consult us about the meaning of a word; considering seriously whatever comments were offered. He listened gravely and intently to everyone.

"I packed up to go to Mexico City," is all Frieda says of their departure from Oaxaca in *"Not I, But the Wind* . . . " But by this time Frieda was feeling feverish, too, so Jean Akin helped, arranging with young Clyde Wilson to come with the Moon on the morning of Tuesday, February 24,

LAWRENCE IN OAXACA

342

to drive the Lawrences and their luggage to the station. To show his appreciation to Jean for all she had done for them, Lawrence on his last night in Oaxaca gave her two gifts. One was the purple-covered Duckworth reissue of *The White Peacock,* the other was the new copy of *Little Novels of Sicily.* He inscribed both books on the flyleaf in his firm clear hand, using Jean's middle initial H. (which was also his own) showing he knew that the red-haired young woman with the blue eyes and the long lashes was the former Jean Harmon, born on a Kansas farm.[5]

Jean remembered that Lawrence was still very ill on the morning of his departure but could sit up. As we know from Brett's departure, five minutes past seven was the standard hour for leaving. The two trunks and Frieda's hatbox probably went into the baggage car, perhaps the two suitcases too, but it is likely that Lawrence, as he did on the way down, kept personal charge of the little brown satchel. Oaxaca weather being as consistent as it is, especially in the winter, one can assume that the morning resembled the one he imagined for the departure of his "Flying Fish" hero and which may have been based on the morning he and Frieda had seen Brett off six weeks earlier. Comments he made on Oaxaca later suggest that he felt the depression assigned to his hero, and further saw his own projected feelings as emanations of the place he was leaving. Gethin "felt an immense doom over everything, still the next morning, when, an hour after dawn, the little train ran out from the doomed little town, on to the plateau, where the cactus thrust up its fluted tubes, and where the mountains stood back, blue, cornflower blue, so dark and pure in form in the land of the Greater Day, the day of demons."

When Lawrence had been preparing to leave in the first week of February, he sent the news in a flurry of letters to his sister Ada, to Secker, to the older Hawk, and to Rickards, the Vice-Consul in Mexico City. In the rally after his first sudden sharp illness, he sent further letters saying the plans had been postponed, and the relapse and move to the Francia meant still more reports of delay. Perhaps learning not to write news that might have to be revoked, Lawrence refrained from letting anyone know they had left Oaxaca until they had actually done so. The next day in Tehuacán, where they broke their journey, Lawrence wrote his sister Emily that they would continue on to Mexico City that night. In *"Not I, But the Wind . . ."* Frieda wrote: "This was a crucifixion of a journey for me. We travelled through the tropics. Lawrence in the heat so weak and ill and then the night we stayed halfway to Mexico City in a hotel. There, after the great strain of the illness, something broke in me. He will never be quite well again, he is ill, he is doomed. All my love, all my strength will never make him whole again. I cried like a maniac the whole night. And he disliked me for it."

Lawrence said nothing to Emily about the weeping but revealed that Frieda was now sick too. After arriving in the capital, they remained incommunicado for five days in the comfortable Imperial Hotel. They booked passage for England on March 17, but Lawrence suffered another relapse and as he wrote Curtis Brown on March 11: "Still in bed here. Doctor made all sorts of examinations, blood tests, etc. says I must *not* risk a sea-voyage nor the English climate, for some months: must stay in the sun, either here, or go to the ranch. So as soon as I can travel we shall go to the ranch."

Two weeks later—March 24—they arrived at the ranch. He told Brett, "I looked so awful when I reached Mexico City from Oaxaca: just pale green. The people stared at me so in the streets that I could not bear it, so Frieda bought me some rouge. I rouged my cheeks and gave myself such a lovely, healthy complexion that no one ever turned to stare at me again. You should have seen me! I used the rouge all the time till I reached New Mexico—until I got past that terrible doctor at El Paso."

"This is rather a blow, indeed," Lawrence wrote as a P.S. to his news to Brown that he was not coming back to England as planned. Then he added, "It's been a series of blows lately." And that, perhaps, is a fitting epigraph for the last days of the Oaxaca story. Lawrence's life was full of new "beginnings" that ended in disillusion and sometimes downright misery. The episode in Cornwall during World War I, that ended with the impoverished Lawrences being driven from their beloved cottage on suspicion of being German spies, was perhaps the worst. But the Oaxaca experience might well qualify as the runner-up; and its end was all the sadder because of the bright hope with which it began. Lawrence's second enthusiastic visit to Mexico, as he told Mrs. Carswell, "spoiled" him for Europe and made him confident that Mexico was where the gods were. His health improved the moment he reached Oaxaca, but by the end of the stay he was at one of the lowest points in his life and his health was permanently broken.

Still, he had five more years, and Lawrence could hold out in spirit, even while his body weakened. He was one of those he praised in *Studies in Classic American Literature:* one who could "laugh and listen to the Holy Ghost," one, too, who furnished proof that "the brave soul of man refuses to have the life-quick pierced in him." The way his spirit could rally is vividly illustrated in summarizing letters from the ranch to two friends he made in Mexico. To Rendón, who had argued with him about his religious ideas, he wrote on May 21 about editors and *The Plumed Serpent:* "They urge me to go over the MS., but I still feel I can't look at it. It smells too much of Oaxaca, which I hated so much because I was ill." But twenty days later he wrote Conway, who had shown him many Spanish colonial documents: "I am about my normal self again—but shall never forgive Mexico, especially Oaxaca, for having done me in. . . . Quoth the raven: *Nevermore.* But this Nevermore is a thankful, cheerful chirrup, like a gay blackbird. Nevermore need I look on Mexico— but especially Oaxaca.—Yet my Quetzalcoatl novel lies nearer to my heart than any other work of mine. I shall send you a copy next year—D. V."

This time God was willing. Conway got his copy safely. But that story, and other events of the final years lie beyond the limits of this book.

THE LUCK OF THE DRAW

This book began with the discovery that there were several people alive in Oaxaca who remembered D. H. Lawrence. The task of research was a labor of affection. I did not, at that point, try to decide whether the Oaxaca chapter was a significant one in Lawrence's life. In fact, other writers had given me the impression it was minor, but it seemed worth recording because—despite Brett's beautiful memoir—it represented almost the least-known corner of his by now well-explored life.

Being able to reach a number of his Oaxaca contemporaries was only the first of many surprises. Another was discovering that Oaxaca was in such a significant state of its own development at the time of Lawrence's visit. Having seen the city so peaceful, friendly, and prosperous year after year, I had been lulled into feeling I had come to know its eternal aspect. Histories of the Mexican Revolution available in English had done nothing to dispel this illusion. Oaxaca's role was seldom typical and tends to be scamped by those wanting to tell a consistent story. Thus I did not know how much Oaxaca had suffered during the Revolution and that it was a city still scarred by a devastating rebellion when Lawrence came to it. Ignorant of so many specific events, I had not detected their influence on Lawrence nor realized how many of them he used in semi-fictional form for his Oaxaca writings. Lawrence, then—at least during his Mexican period—was much more of a political observer than I realized.

The next great surprise was discovering that he wrote so much more in Oaxaca than is commonly supposed. He was in the city only 106 days, but he rewrote the whole of one of his longest novels, he wrote nine essays of high quality, the beginning of an ambitious poetic drama, and the start of a novel so fine that it can stand independently as one of his most beautiful short stories. His numerous letters, more than sixty, were another surprise. When coordinated with the barely known Oaxaca writings and with the events of his life in the city, the letters provided insight into his inward life in Oaxaca.

Nor did I expect to find so much of his past flooding back on him: memories of his nature at twenty-six when he wrote *The White Peacock,* his mother's death, other Christmases, the help of Edward Garnett when he was still struggling for recognition; his memories of how *Sons and Lovers* was rejected and *The Rainbow* suppressed; the unhappy experience with Maurice Magnus; his hopes for a colony of kindred souls; the life in Sicily, and the journey to Ceylon; the sojourn in Australia and the rewriting of *The Boy in the Bush;* ranch life at Taos and the impact of Mabel Luhan; the temporary breach with Koteliansky; the anxiety of not being paid by his American publisher, and the relationship with Murry, so electric still with hate, love, and disappointment. Perhaps least of all did I expect to find Oaxaca so significant as a present experience in Lawrence's life; and one whose influence persisted so strongly into the future. As the whole rest of his output testifies, the visitation of death was one of the major experiences of his life. Oaxaca also marked one of the three or four greatest turning points of his career. Except for a recuperative six-months coda in New Mexico, it ended his adventuring not only in "the New World" of America, but, as Tedlock has pointed out, all New Worlds, for Australia must be included in this picture too. It brought the abandonment of his mission to try to regenerate his fellow men through political, social, and religious means. It closed his life as a man in reasonable health. It ended his attempts to write works of epic length, and it ushered in a new era of faith in the tenderness and releasing joy of sex as the great force in achieving individual peace and happiness, and of combating the anti-life effects of industrialism, commercialism, and over-intellectualized, urban living.

It was fortunate that the Lawrence chapter I wanted to write for love of Oaxaca had validity as a biographical unit. What might have been an arbitrary time division depending solely on geography proved to be a logical framework enclosing a build-up, a climax, and a significant resolution. The deeper the exploration of Lawrence's winter in Oaxaca took me into his life, the higher he rose in my estimation as a human being. Surely few men have walked the earth with such intense aspiration towards goodness, such extraordinary responsiveness to living, so much personal feeling, so original and searching a mind, so keen a desire to make life richer for others, an eye so alive to natural beauty, coupled with such remarkable gifts of expression to make us see and feel what he, as one of humanity's most gifted perceivers, saw and felt. He was a great and good man—a great writer and a sensitive and idealistic man who has helped interpret men and women to each other and extended the consciousness of us all. And because he left us his life, so courageously and quiveringly exposed, we have more than the legacy of a poet, novelist,and master story-teller for which to be grateful.

APPENDIX

AN ECHO OF
OAXACA IN
''THE LOVELY LADY''

Besides the echoes of Oaxaca in *The Man Who Died,* minor ones appear in *Reflections on the Death of a Porcupine* and in *Apocalypse.* Perhaps the most entertaining echo, however, is to be found in "The Lovely Lady," a short story that Lawrence wrote at the Villa Mirenda early in 1927. There one reads of the hobby of Robert, the titular lady's son:

> He had, unknown to everybody but his mother, a quite extraordinary collection of old Mexican legal documents, reports of processes and trials, pleas, accusations, the weird and awful mixture of ecclesiastical and common law in seventeenth-century Mexico. He had started a study in this direction through coming across a report of a trial of two English sailors, for murder, in Mexico in 1620, and he had gone on, when the next document was an accusation against a Don Miguel Estrada for seducing one of the nuns of the Sacred Heart Convent in Oaxaca in 1680.

George Conway, who gave Lawrence the little manuscript about the "beastly" Santo Domingo and to whom the recovered Lawrence chirruped like "a gay blackbird," was one of the Lawrence associates I had met. When I visited his home in Cuernavaca in 1948, he showed me through the library he had built in the lower part of his garden to house Spanish colonial documents he had either purchased or paid to have copies transcribed. So I recognized where Lawrence got the inspiration for his hero's unusual hobby, for I knew the Lawrences had visited the hospitable Conways in Cuernavaca. Because Conway loved showing his library, the story's description made plain that the library had been included in the Lawrences' tour of the Conway home, now the well-known restaurant "Las Mañanitas." George, Robert, and Graham were Conway's three given names; so Lawrence also borrowed his friend's middle name for his hero; though in other respects the wishy-washy lawyer of the story is not at all like the efficient English engineer who ran Mexico City's streetcar and electric power systems.

Although Oaxaca formerly had many convents, it did not have one of the Sacred Heart, which made me suspect that Lawrence contrived alternate names for the people and institutions involved in the cases described. But the docket itself sounded too circumstantial to have been wholly invented by Lawrence. Perhaps it was among the *legajos* he saw in Conway's library. Conway's papers were distributed among the Library of Congress, the University of Aberdeen, Cambridge University, and the Gilcrease Institute in Tulsa. Richard E. Greenleaf, director of the Center for Latin American Studies at Tulane University, made an initial search for me of the Library of Congress index of its Mexican Inquisition documents, which included the Conway papers. I made a second search myself in the Latin American Library of the University of Texas. Thinking it unlikely that Conway parted with an original colonial manuscript, even to Lawrence, I wondered if he had given the novelist one of the seven books that he issued in small, privately printed editions between 1921 and 1945. Most of these books, I knew, reprinted documents. *The Rare Travaile of Job Hartop* and *An Englishman and the Inquisition* dealt with difficulties of English sailors in Mexico, but their troubles were all considerably earlier than 1620. The other books were even further from the Lawrence mark. So I turned to the four issues of the *Hispanic American Historical Review* containing checklists of the Conway material. Again I found documents dealing with English sailors—mostly "Lutherans" tried for heresy between 1580 and 1601—but when title after title showed no evidence of two sailors tried for murder in 1620 or of the Miguel Estrada accused of seducing a Oaxaca nun in 1630, I accepted the idea that Lawrence had invented his criminals.

And I never found what manuscript Conway gave Lawrence dealing with Santo Domingo. But in the name the novelist gave the alleged nun-seducer, I think I discovered a hidden joke on the affable Genaro Estrada, the president of the Mexico P.E.N. Club. That relations with Estrada were resumed on a friendly basis after the return from Oaxaca is proved by a letter to Seltzer written from the Imperial Hotel after Lawrence had recovered enough to start seeing friends. Estrada must have called, for on March 5 the novelist asked his publisher to send Estrada a copy of Seligmann's little book, *D. H. Lawrence: An American Interpretation,* that he had brought out the previous fall. "Estrada," Lawrence explained, "is undersecretary for foreign affairs; and wants to write a critique of me." Apparently Estrada, who had been caught short on his Lawrence reading by the P.E.N. dinner, had found the time to bone up on the guest of honor in the meantime.

Prologue

1. This plaque was shaken loose by a minor earthquake sometime after October 1964 and it smashed on the sidewalk. By 20 December 1972, when the transferred museum was reopened in the monastic complex of Santo Domingo, the plaque had not been replaced. By the end of 1982, the plaque had still not been replaced, indicating a continuing lack of interest in the Vigil revival.

2. Jorge Fernando Iturribarria, *Oaxaca en la Historia* (Mexico City: Editorial Stylo, 1955), p. 309.

3. Miss Doctor continued as a missionary in Oaxaca until 1957 and outlived most of the other foreigners there during Lawrence's visit. She died 17 November 1978 at the age of eighty-six.

4. Iturribarria, *Oaxaca,* p. 421.

Chapter 1
Lawrence and the Governor

1. The letters, written between November 14 and 17, are to be found divided among the collections edited by Aldous Huxley (1932) and Harry T. Moore (1962).

2. This friendship dates from 1914. "Lawrence," said Mrs. Carswell in *The Savage Pilgrimage,* p. 19, "would always read anything that anybody tried to write." Their own friendship began when, after reading the manuscript of her first novel, *Open the Door,* Lawrence wrote "thousands of notes and opinions on the margin: suggesting improvements."

3. I am indebted to Villaseñor for a copy of the invitation to the dinner and the issue of the club's bulletin, *Volante,* no. 22, 24 January 1925, which published the addresses delivered by the Mexicans.

4. For a time I thought this "fresh and lively" Mr. Henry, who had stayed at the Hotel Francia in Orizaba, was a portrait of Frederick W. Leighton and when I showed the Henry passages to him, Leighton admitted he had been at the Nuttall tea and in Oaxaca shortly before. But after reading how Lawrence described Henry, he said, "It doesn't ring too much of a recognition bell in my mind. I think the character may have been Carlston Beals." Probably Lawrence drew on them both, for Beals was in the group waiting for Vasconcelos to take them to lunch. "When things went through the mill of Lawrence's mind," said Leighton, "they never came out as they were."

5. His son, B. C. Girdley, Jr., supplied this information. His father was later vindicated and reestablished, for he returned to Midland, entered the cattle business for himself, and in 1932 became a justice of the peace, a post he held for seventeen years.

6. Letter to author, 16 November 1962.

7. The clue is Gee's September 1924 message to the American Institute of Mining, Metallurgical and Petroleum Engineers: "hold magazines." Later he let the Institute know he had moved to Los Angeles, where he lived into his nineties.

8. Omitted from Moore's *The Collected Letters of D. H. Lawrence,* but included in Edward Nehls's earlier publication of the letter in *D. H. Lawrence: A Composite Biography,* vol. 2.

9. The original of this letter is in the Berg Collection of the New York Public Library. "Much" is the word Lawrence used, but both Huxley and Moore transcribed it as "mush" in their editions.

10. Although there is now doubt that the painting Ibarra pointed out was a genuine Cabrera, there was logic in his showing it, for Miguel Cabrera, often called "the Mexican Murillo," is one of Oaxaca's greatest native sons. There was also logic in the visit to Bazán's house, for he transformed the weaving of his village. Besides introducing pre-Columbian motifs into his designs, he introduced aniline dyes. The Indians of the American Southwest had been using aniline dyes for more than fifty years, but until Bazán's time the Teotitlán weavers had stuck to vegetable dyes.

Chapter 2
Lawrence's Landlord

1. His first appearance, unnamed, but in Lawrence's own words, was in 1932 in Huxley's edition of the letters. The next year in *Lawrence and Brett* the priest's kindly nature was brought into clear perspective through two or three vivid anecdotes, but Brett gave nothing of his antecedents and identified him only as "the Padre." In Frieda Lawrence's *"Not I, But the Wind . . ."* of 1934, the house, the parrots, the white dog and the *mozo* are mentioned, but there is no trace of the house's owner. In Richard Aldington's 1950 biography, *D. H. Lawrence: Portrait of a Genius, But . . .,* details of the house are borrowed from Lawrence's *Mornings,* but the priest's name is misspelled as Richards— the way Lawrence himself at first mispelled it—and Aldington contributed nothing new on the landlord. In *The Life and Works of D. H. Lawrence* of 1951, Harry T. Moore never mentioned the priest, and three years later when Moore brought out *The Intelligent Heart,* for all its wealth of new material, it had nothing new on the Padre. Instead, he followed Aldington's misspelling and Aldington's example of characterizing the house

by quoting a line or two from Lawrence's own description. It took the energetic and ingenious American researcher, the late Edward Nehls, while working on vol. 2 of his *Composite Biography* (1956), to find the connection between Padre Rickards and the father and son British Vice Consuls, Constantine G. and George E. Rickards. But because George wrote that his father had been a member of the Episcopal Church of England, Nehls made the mistake of calling Padre Rickards an Anglican. When L. D. Clark's *Dark Night of the Body* appeared in 1964, pictures of the exterior of the house, and the garden carved from the patio by tenants of the middle third of the house, were published for the first time, both taken by LaVerne Harrell Clark, who had accompanied her husband on a photographic tour of the Lawrence haunts in Mexico. Clark also interviewed people who remembered Padre Rickards, so he was able to correctly state that the priest was a Roman Catholic.

2. He also had a sixth notebook of the same kind, the first half reserved for diary jottings (mostly of financial transactions in connection with his work) and the second half for poems that were to be collected as *Birds, Beasts and Flowers.* The diary starts in Capri on 6 February 1920. Most of the entries date from his two years in Taormina, but there are also eleven entries from the 1922-23 winter at Del Monte Ranch. It is unfortunate that he only made two entries in it while in Oaxaca, the first recording the arrival at the Francia, the second saying he was moving the next day to the priest's house. E. W. Tedlock, Jr. published the complete diary, with a good description of the marbled black and green book, in *The Frieda Lawrence Collection of D. H. Lawrence Manuscripts: A Descriptive Bibliography* (Albuquerque: University of New Mexico Press, 1948).

Chapter 3
The Market

1. A *real,* an old term that has since almost died out, is twelve centavos; the equivalent of a "bit," as in the American slang "two bits." In United States terms, the vendor asked for "two and a half bucks."

2. Oaxaca now has a rival market, but the creation of the new market illustrates the tenacity of the vendors in the old market and their love for their venerable place of business in the center of the city. As Oaxaca's population increased, the old market grew larger and larger, expanding into the surrounding streets, with makeshift booths. Finally, it was estimated that the Saturday market was drawing 30,000 people to the area, with the vendors from the villages covering twelve city blocks. The shopkeepers in the side streets were unhappy about the stands in front of them. Vehicular traffic became impossible and even pedestrians

had to jostle each other to get through the crowds. In 1973 plans were drawn for a larger and more modern market on the outskirts of the city in the fields alongside the Atoyac River. When the new buildings were ready to accommodate the vendors, the market would be shifted there and the old "beehive" razed to make a park. By the fall of 1974 the new brick buildings were ready, as well as a new centralized bus station which would let the villagers load and unload their goods across the street from the largest of the new market buildings. But the people of the old market would not move to these new quarters. The new buildings stood vacant for four years. In August 1978 soldiers and police made the squatters on the street move to the new market, but the people in the covered sections were all rent-payers and could not be forced out. There was no resistance when the showdown came, but the old market has not been razed, and those who sell there, confident of their massed strength, are convinced it won't be. Oaxaca has grown large enough for two principal markets. The vendors at the new market are every bit as picturesque and charming as they were in the old. So now the city has two tourist attractions, and the market that Lawrence described so well has been saved.

Chapter 4
The Kulls and Their *Mozo*

1. Hermann wrote the story in detail in "Experiences of a Dentist in Tropical Mexico" in *The Dental Digest* (June 1926).

2. The Oaxaca Courts was an attractive motel run by Roy and Anita Jones from August 1947 to December 1970. It has since been enlarged, remodeled and renamed Misión de los Angeles. It stands in the map on p. 109. at the junction of the two roads just above the name Jalatlaco.

3. In searching for Zelia Nuttall letters there, I learned that the museum had the satchel. I am grateful to Michael F. Weber, the museum's curator of history, who allowed me to go through its contents, and to Nancy Gardett and Margaret Harrison, who helped sort the items that had been so long undisturbed.

4. Lawrence responded in an open letter published in *The New Statesman,* 20 February 1926. Because Douglas reprinted his attack in his book *Experiments,* Lawrence finally broke silence, urged to do so by Martin Secker, who had been his English publisher since 1918. Secker argued that Lawrence should not let the case go against him by default.

5. Lawrence did not need dental treatment in Oaxaca, Kull told me, but Rickards sometimes did. "He was a very nice man, but I only knew him as a patient," was the way Kull explained his lack of anecdotes about the priest.

Chapter 5
Rosalino

1. In later years he became well known as "Don Pancho" to visitors at the Pension Suiza.
2. A detail I owe to Dorothy Brett.
3. "The Market," originally to be called "Saturday Morning," was the second of the sketches to be written and was intended to be second in the sequence. Perhaps because of its strength it was shifted to the fourth and culminating place when the sketches were published in book form. The shift meant that the preparation for Christmas as the "fiesta" in "The Mozo" was weakened.

Chapter 7
Favors for Two Writers

1. Muray, a Hungarian-born photographer with a studio in Greenwich Village, was already well-known as a portraitist of celebrities. He tells the story of the sitting in *The Revealing Eye,* which before his death he coauthored with Paul Gallico. He mistakenly recalled 1923 as 1920. Lawrence first visited New York in 1923 and the portrait must have been taken then to be on hand before Lawrence's return to New York in March 1924. Muray's evidence also suggests that Lawrence and the editor met in 1923.
2. Besides three in 1924 and one in 1928, there were five in 1929; and in the fall of 1929 Crowninshield offered him a year-long contract for an article a month. Knowing his strength was failing, he refused to pin himself down; and his last appearance in the magazine consisted of three poems in March 1930, the month of his death.
3. A sequence in *Lawrence and Brett* gives a clue about how Lawrence chose Mirabal as the fictional pseudonym for Quintanilla. At the ranch in New Mexico before they set out for Oaxaca, Brett remembered a young man who rode over to the Lawrences' cabin and stayed for lunch, and in the afternoon Lawrence saw the visitor off by riding part of the way homeward with him. After they parted at the Hondo River, Lawrence rode fast until he reached the top of Kiowa Hill. From there he saw the guest in the distance "a tiny, clear, figure, riding along the ridge." The visitor saw his host and waved. Thereafter they kept turning back to wave at each other. Brett, not writing fiction, gave the guest's true name, Luis Mirabal, an English-speaking Indian from Taos Pueblo who often visited the Lawrences and demonstrated Indian dances for them. Frank Waters was the friend who confirmed the Indian's name for me.

4. The name José García solved one of my mysteries neverthe-less. In her book, Brett never identified Donald Miller's "engineer friend," who went with them to Mitla, but she included him in several of her photographs. Using the photos in hand, I asked many people who were in Oaxaca during the Lawrence period if they recognized him. Two did. Lawrence himself had written it on the back of a postcard. It is interesting to speculate whether this man, who helped in the guiding at Mitla, was the source of the pseudonym that Lawrence used for the guide in Mexico, partly based on Estrada.

5. This is the first publication for this item and the ensuing excerpts from "Mexico, Why Not." I am grateful to Quintanilla for entrusting the article to me in the first place and then for giving permission to publish parts of it.

6. Frieda's mention of *doctors* suggests that the "Uhlfelder" and the "analyst doctor" might not be the same. But one has to read carefully not to assume that "Uhlfelder" was the breaker of the bad news. Because it might have been another, and because Quintanilla's memory suggests that Frieda learned the diagnosis earlier than Lawrence did, I would like to identify "Uhlfelder" and suggest he was the kindly doctor of Quintanilla's memory, rather than the tactlessly cruel analyst.

Finding his identity was another stroke of luck. Martha Hitchens, whose mother, May Whittlesey, had been a friend of Zelia Nuttall, in racking her brains for the names of women of her mother's age still alive, came up with Mrs. Sydney Ulfelder. When she said Mrs. Ulfelder was the widow of a doctor, I felt sure I had finally identified Frieda's "Dr. Uhlfelder." But I called the widow to check. She was too old, deaf, and frail to come to the phone, but her daughter, Ruth Covo, agreed to query her mother for me. The old lady confirmed that Lawrence had been a patient of her husband, but she could recall no more than that she had met the Lawrences on the one occasion she and her husband had dined with them. Her memory of the dinner was no longer clear. Mrs. Covo had never known her father diagnosed Lawrence's illness. Willingly, she told me that her father was born in New York in 1875 and had been in Mexico since 1899. He was both a general practitioner and a surgeon, and had risen to be head of surgery at the American Hospital. Because he had enlisted the interest of the wealthy Lady Cowdray, he had also played a role in establishing the English Hospital. Lawrence, then, had one of the best doctors in Mexico.

7. After struggling to make ends meet as a literary man in Mexico, Maples Arce, in 1935, followed Quintanilla's example and entered Mexico's diplomatic service. He began as a secretary in the Mexican embassy in Belgium and rose to be an ambassador, serving successively in Panama, Chile, Japan, Canada, Norway, and Lebanon. He retired in 1967. When

I met him on 18 February 1974, he was a cordial and plump little man in a pinstripe suit, with failing eyes. He recalled very little from his meeting with Lawrence, but he remembered that the restaurant where they gathered was in the novelist's hotel, the Imperial, and that there was some kind of an argument. But Quintanilla, apparently, maintained silence on what had been said. Maples Arce said he had never understood what it was all about, and he chuckled when I told him it was about whether or not he was a genius. That he still cherished fond memories of his obstreperous days when he was the leader of the *Estridontistas* was proved by two books he gave me: *Soberana Juvenud,* the second volume of his autobiography, which recalled the movement from his own point of view, and *el Estridentismo,* an historical study of it by Luis Mario Schneider.

8. Original in the possession of the Library Board of Western Australia and paraphrased with the Board's permission.

9. "D. H. Lawrence and *The Boy in the Bush,*" in *Meanjin* 9 (University of Melbourne, Summer 1959), pp. 260-63.

10. *Letters from a Publisher: Martin Secker to D. H. Lawrence and Others, 1911-1929* (London: Enitharmon Press, 1970): p. 23.

11. Lawrence nearly always spelled her nickname with a "y," rather than an "ie." But he always addressed her directly: "Miss Skinner."

12. Original in the possession of the Library Board of Western Australia and paraphrased with the Board's permission.

13. Mollie Skinner's succeeding novel, "Eve in the Land of Nod," never found a publisher, but Lawrence kept his promise about helping her with it. After her death in 1955, when her executors found its manuscript among her papers, they found notes in Lawrence's handwriting on page after page. They must have been made before 3 December 1928, for Katharine Susannah Prichard, who saw a letter from Lawrence to Miss Skinner of that date, as well as the text, says Lawrence read the manuscript twice, and "put a great deal of work into it, cutting, pasting up and rewriting between pages." But finally he gave up, saying, "I can't do with it as I did with *Boy in the Bush.*" Lawrence was probably relieved that his preface was not published with *Black Swans.* In a letter to Middleton Murry of 12 December 1925 he mentions submitting to the *Adelphi* an article about a hospital that Mollie had written and that he had edited and partially rewritten. Lawrence confided to Murry that *Black Swans* had irritated him "by its foolish facility." Murry never used the hospital piece, despite Lawrence's emendations.

Chapter 8
Brett with Addenda

1. Miller, whose full name was Donald Gazley Miller, was born in Sandusky, Ohio, in 1888, graduated from the Irving School in New York in 1905, studied engineering at Columbia University and obtained

his E.M. degree there in 1909. His first job was in Mexico with the Montezuma Copper Company in Sonora. Later he was employed by Phelps Dodge at Bisbee, Arizona. During World War I his experience brought him an army commission and he served as a major in the fourth Engineer Training Regiment at Camp Humphreys, Virginia. After demobilization he worked in New Mexico and the Yukon before going to Oaxaca. Because he seemed younger than most, he was a Lawrence associate I hoped to reach personally. But a visit in January 1963 to the American Institute of Mining, Metallurgical and Petroleum Engineers, of which he was a member, brought the disheartening news that he had been dead for ten years.

2. Purchased in 1950 by Ervine R. Frissell, whose personal collection of antiquities became the nucleus for the museum. The University of the Americas bought the museum and the inn in 1959.

3. Its construction took six years and when it was opened with a performance of *Aïda* in 1909 it was called Teatro Luis Mier y Teran in honor of General Mier y Teran, a friend of Díaz, who had been the first magistrate of the state when the railway to Oaxaca was finished in 1892. It still had that name in Lawrence's day.

4. These were the traditional Christmas *buñuelos:* "a great wafer of a pancake with sweet stuff on it," as described by Lawrence in his account of their marketing on Christmas day.

5. Brett kept the painting in her personal collection for twenty-five years but finally sold it to Mae Reed Porter of Oklahoma, a collector who owned a number of Brett's works. The sale was before John Manchester became Brett's gallery manager, so he was not sure of the year, but he thought it was about 1950. He estimated the canvas at 24-by-16 inches. After Mae Porter's death, the painting became the property of her grandson, John Harvey of Sant Fe. It was reproduced in color on the cover of *The Sunstone Review,* 5, no. 3 (Santa Fe, New Mexico: 1976). Keith Sagar reproduced it again as one of the color plates in his *The Life of D. H. Lawrence* (New York: Pantheon books, 1980).

6. David Robb Farmer, who was then preparing his catalog of the University's Lawrence holdings, was the Lawrence scholar who described the books for me so meticulously. In return, I showed him how this letter proved that the copybooks he knew so well were a gift from Brett.

7. Two statistics substantiate facts given impressionistically by Brett. She was not exaggerating when she spoke of Lawrence being narrow-shouldered. Four years later, when he asked Maria Huxley to bring him a new blue coat, he explained "the measure is 15 1/2 inches across the back—between the sleeves." He mentioned his slightness in *Reflections on the Death of a Porcupine:* "Alas! my wife is about twenty pounds heavier than I am."

8. The calculation was made this way. Because Lawrence's letter, delivered in the morning, was dated "Friday evening," the next day scene had to be on a Saturday. Brett left on Monday, January 19, and there was more than one day between her decision to leave and her going. Thus, the Saturday in question could not have been January 17. It could not have been January 3, for references to her departure do not appear in letters until after January 10.

9. That Lawrence was not so indifferent to his headgear as Brett implied is shown in a letter to Secker from Baden-Baden in the fall of 1925. In London he had stayed at 73 Gower Street, and because Rina Secker, the publisher's wife, was about to come to the Continent, Lawrence wrote her husband, "I went and left my nice new felt hat at 73 Gower Street. If Rina is bringing a hat box, I wish she'd put it in it. It's been worn a few times. The woman at 73 is Mrs. Woodhouse—I'll write her. And if you would send your boy for it I'd be glad." Then in a P.S. he added, "If Rina's not bringing a hatbox, tell her not to bother at all."

Chapter 9
Correspondence and Other Writings

1. Chronologically, the communications are 1 December 1924, letter to Richard Cobden-Sanderson; December 7, postcard to William Hawk; December 20, letter to A. D. Hawk; December 23, letter to Lady Cynthia Asquith; 6 January 1925, letter to William Hawk; February 7, telegram to Dorothy Brett; and February 15, letter to Thomas Seltzer. For permission to draw on the first six I am obliged to Gerald Pollinger, agent for the Frieda Lawrence Ravagli Estate, and the University of Texas. I am also grateful for permission to paraphrase from the portions of the February 7 letter to William Hawk that Moore did not publish in *The Intelligent Heart.* The letter to Seltzer has since been published in *D. H. Lawrence: Letters to Thomas & Adele Seltzer,* ed. Gerald M. Lacy (Santa Barbara: Black Sparrow, 1976.)

Chapter 10
"Noah's Flood" and More Letters

1. Because Lawrence's ideas about Atlantis swept back on him in Oaxaca powerfully enough to prompt him to insert a new section into his novel and to start a play, a note should be added on when and where he got his Atlantean ideas. My first thought—that he probably picked them up from Ignatius Donnelly's *Atlantis* —vanished when I saw no internal evidence that Lawrence had used any of its ideas. Iverson Harris, former secretary to Katherine Tingley, who ran the Theosophical colony at Point

Loma, California, presented me with a copy of Helena P. Blavatsky's *Isis Unveiled*. Because William York Tindall, in *D. H. Lawrence and Susan his Cow,* has said Mme. Blavtsky had influenced *The Plumed Serpent,* I had investigated enough to know that Lawrence had definitely read the works of the controversial Theosophist. In the spring of 1919, he had written to Nancy Henry: "Try and get hold of Mme. Blavatsky's books—they are big and expensive—the friends I used to borrow them from are out of England now. But get from some library or other *Isis Unveiled,* and better still the 2 vol. work whose name I forget."

The larger work could only have been *The Secret Doctrine,* which besides giving Mme. Blavatsky's time-table for the destruction of the Atlantean continent, claims (Vol. II, p. 29) "There were four-armed human creatures in those early days of the male-female hermaphrodites," a sentence which echoes in Lawrence's "male-female" Japhet and his "female-male" Cosby. *Isis Unveiled* rounded out the evidence. Not only did it contain much about Atlantis—including what Lawrence lifted about easy round-the-world travel—in those times but it held that the Mexicans were among the descendants of the Atlantean people. This belief is common to many believers in Atlantis. Considerably more revealing is an extensive section about Noah and his sons. Most telling of all, Mme. Blavatsky, too, connected Noah's flood with the submersion of Atlantis, saying the Noah story was one of the "disfigured allegories" of the earlier cataclysm.

2. To use Lawrence's modest term, he "rubbed up into readable English" Koteliansky's draft translations. In the case of Leo Shostov's *All Things Are Possible,* Lawrence rewrote the whole translation in his own hand. What he did in 1919 to induce Secker to publish it, including bargaining to get his friend better terms, is revealed in *Letters from D. H. Lawrence to Martin Secker.* What he did two years later for the placement of another Koteliansky-Lawrence collaboration, the translation of Ivan Bunin's most famous story, "The Gentleman from San Francisco," is told in *D. H. Lawrence and the Dial* by Nicholas Joost and Alvin Sullivan. Almost the whole Koteliansky story is in *The Quest for Raranim: D. H. Lawrence's Letters to S. S. Koteliansky, 1914-1930,* edited by George J. Zytaruk.

3. Koteliansky died in 1955, and when he left his papers to the museum, his will stipulated that the contents of this volume should not be accessible to the public until fifty years after his death.

4. I have been able to round out the story presented by the published letters by drawing on the three unpublished ones and the unpublished part of a fourth listed in Ch. 9, note 1. I would also like to thank Mrs. Rachel Hawk for so willingly furnishing background facts.

Chapter 11
How *The Plumed Serpent* was Changed in Oaxaca

1. When Clark wrote, the manuscript of the Chapala version seemed to have been lost. In the spring of 1964 it appeared unexpectedly on the booksellers' market while his book was in press, too late for him to change what he had written.

2. "Garnio" is probably a deliberate misspelling on Lawrence's part, one of the two verbal jokes in the sentence, for Lawrence knew the sort "Spoodles" enjoyed. The other was making Chicken Ita sound like "Chicken Eater." Speaking of the Carnegie "Institute," when it should have "Institution" was an honest and often-made error.

3. This shorter introduction was published in July 1930 by the *London Mercury* and included by McDonald in the first *Phoenix* under the title "The Dragon of the Apocalypse" by Frederick Carter. The long introduction became Lawrence's own final book, *Apocalypse.* Both were written after the Carter-Lawrence friendship had been reactivated in 1929. According to Carter's *D. H. Lawrence and the Body Mystical,* Lawrence wrote the shorter introduction after he had decided not to offer Carter the long one after all. The fact that Carter never used it meant it was a second Lawrence preface that misfired. But it did not lie buried as long as the one for Mollie Skinner, and appeared five months after Lawrence's death.

The first part of Carter's manuscript that he sent to Lawrence in Chapala was published in 1926 as *The Dragon of the Alchemists.* More of Carter's work was published in 1931 as *The Dragon of Revelation.*

4. References to her pages are: a bright day sun and a black sun, p. 13; the worship of the morning star, p. 53; the dance with the concentric wheels, pp. 58-59; a female deity of great power associated with Huitzilopochtli, pp. 60-61; the Huitzilopochtli colors: red, black and yellow, p. 64; mating at the rainy season, pp. 101-02; the three watches of the night, p. 229; marriage with the star between, p. 319; and the Assyrian cult of the morning and evening stars, p. 338.

Chapter 12
The Return to the Francia

1. Mrs. Akin remembered only his last name, but Ethel Doctor, who knew the doctor was dead, steered me to his widow, Clara Reimers de Larumbe. Doña Clara knew Lawrence had been one of her husband's patients but had no personal recollection of the novelist. By giving me an excellent booklet on her husband by Dr. Luis Cervantes M. she enabled me to learn a good deal about Larumbe. He was born in Linares and became a military doctor during the Revolution when he was

commissioned as a lieutenant-colonel in a Coahuila cavalry division. He came to Oaxaca in 1918 at the age of 35. During Lawrence's stay, Dr. Larumbe was already on the track of his greatest discovery. Onofre Jiménez, while still a candidate for governor, had called the doctor's attention to the village of Tiltepec in the Sierra, where vampire bats had killed all the farm animals, and a large proportion of the 400 inhabitants were blind. The blindness, which afflicted many other villages in Oaxaca was *onchocercosos*. Several years after Lawrence left Mexico, Larumbe won national fame by being the first to discover the microscopic parasitic worm that caused this disease by getting into the ocular tissues of the victims. His widow lived until 13 March 1980.

2. "The Red Baron" was shot down 21 April 1918 by Captain Roy Brown of the Royal Canadian Air Force. But Taylor was not actually there when it happened. His squadron had fought across into Germany and was stationed in Kassel. Brown's squadron (the 209th) was in France and Richthofen was brought down near a ruined village on the French coast. Taylor later met Brown while they were both in the same hospital, but before that he had had no contact with Brown's squadron. Frieda's version of the story is understandable. Having suffered as a German in England during the war, she would have been hungry for any sign of reconciliation between enemies. She had never met her cousin Manfred personally, but, knowing he was thirteen years her junior, she would have recalled that he was only twenty-six when he was killed.

3. Crosby was a wealthy and generous young American who wrote poetry and published limited editions, including one of Lawrence's *Sun*. Lawrence aided his writing career by providing a preface for *Chariot of the Sun,* a collection of Crosby's poems.

4. The full interview, one of the best selections in Volume 2 of Nehls's *Composite Biography,* does not identify the place of the rereading, but two circumstances prove it was Oaxaca: the fact that Lawrence had the novel there and his acknowledgment that prior to Oaxaca he had never read one of his own books in print.

5. "Señora J. H. Akin from D. H. Lawrence, Oaxaca, 23 Feb., 1925," was the text of *The White Peacock* inscription. In the *Little Novels* he wrote "Mrs. Jean H. Akin from D. H. Lawrence." Jean and the Colonel never had any children, but Eva Winsor, Jean's older sister whom Jean had nursed so tenderly, had a son named Henry. Eva died in 1938, and four years later her husband died while Henry was in service during World War II. Henry lived with his aunt after the war, and she gave him her two inscribed Lawrence books sometime before she died in November 1969. Henry showed me the books a year later. His Aunt Jean, he said, had never spoken much to him about Lawrence until after she began receiving my letters. Because his Uncle Albert lived until 1956, dying at

the age of eighty-six, Henry knew his uncle well, but the Colonel never mentioned the novelist. Henry was grateful for what I could tell him about his aunt and uncle's days in Mexico. I was equally grateful to him for showing me his uncle's papers and his uncle's album of more than 300 carefully captioned photographs of those days. Through the carbon copies the Colonel kept of his own letters, I learned that the Akins stayed in Oaxaca until the fall of 1926. Henry added that then the Colonel spent three years in Fontana, California, as an orange-grower. The Depression took most of his remaining capital and an attempt to found a lumber mill in Jasper, Arkansas, failed. But the Akins remained in Jasper, the Colonel becoming a recluse while Jean abstracted deeds in real estate transactions. The Colonel's dated Oaxaca photos enabled me to pin down many of the events that Jean recalled. Unfortunately, the Colonel never took a picture of the Lawrences.

Lawrence gave away other books in Mexico as signs of his personal feeling for friends. When the English version of his edition of Magnus's *Memoirs of the Foreign Legion* reached him in Oaxaca, he presented it to Carola Kull. Later the Knopf edition of the *Memoirs* reached Lawrence and he gave this one to Consul Rickards, who assisted Brett with her hearing machine after she got back to Mexico City and continued to help the Lawrences in their trying final weeks in the capital. Lawrence wrote: "To Constantine G. Rickards from D. H. Lawrence with many thanks for the kindness received in Mexico City." Rickards later gave the inscription to Zelia Nuttall.

WORKS CONSULTED

Aldington, Richard. *D. H. Lawrence: Portrait of a Genius But. . . .* New York: Duell, Sloan and Pierce, 1950.

Amory, Cleveland, and Bradlee, Frederick. *Vanity Fair: A Cavalcade of the 1920s and 1930s.* New York: Viking Press, 1960.

Anonymous, "The Boy in the Bush." *Times Literary Supplement,* No. 1180 (28 August 1924).

_____, "A Look Inside a Mexican Indian's Head." *Literary Digest* 94, No. 13 (1921): 50, 52.

Asimov, Isaac. *The Kingdom of the Sun.* Rev. ed. New York: Abelard-Schuman, 1963.

Asquith, Cynthia. *Remember and Be Glad.* New York: Charles Scribner's Sons, 1952.

Blavatsky, Helena P. *Isis Unveiled: Volume 1, Science; Volume 2, Theology.* Centenary Anniversary Edition. Los Angeles, 1968.

Boulton, James T., ed. *Lawrence in Love: Letters to Louie Burrows.* Nottingham: University of Nottingham, 1968.

Bradomín, José María [Guillermo Villa Castañeda]. *Oaxaca en la tradición.* Mexico City: Privately printed, 1968.

Brett, Dorothy. "Autobiography: My Long and Beautiful Journey." *South Dakota Review* 5 (1967): 11-71.

_____. *Lawrence and Brett.* Philadelphia: J. B. Lippincott, 1933.

_____. *Lawrence and Brett.* Introduction, Prologue and Epilogue by John Manchester. Santa Fe, N.M.: Sunstone Press, 1974.

Brewster, Earl and Achsah. *D. H. Lawrence: Reminiscences and Correspondence.* London: Martin Secker, 1934.

Burwell, Rose Marie. "A Catalogue of D. H. Lawrence's Reading from Early Childhood." *D. H. Lawrence Review* 3 (1970): 3.

Bynner, Witter. *Journey with Genius: Recollections and Reflections Concerning the D. H. Lawrences.* New York: John Day, 1951.

Carrington, Dora. *Carrington: Letters & Extracts from Her Diaries.* Edited by David Garnett. New York: Holt, Rinehart & Winston, 1970.

Carswell, Catherine. *The Savage Pilgrimage: A Narrative of D. H. Lawrence.* With a memoir of Mrs. Carswell by John Carswell. London: Cambridge University Press, 1981.

Carter, Frederick. *D. H. Lawrence and the Body Mystical.* London: Denis Archer, 1932.

_____. *The Dragon of the Alchemists.* London: F. Mathews, 1926.

Cavitch, David. *D. H. Lawrence & The New World.* New York: Oxford University Press, 1969.

Cervantes, Luis M. *José E. Larumbe: Descubridor de la causa eficiente de la Ceguera onchocerosica.* Mexico City: Privately printed, 1960.

Chambers, Maria Cristina. "John of God, the Water Carrier." *New Criterion* 6 (October 1927): 312-331.

Clark, L. D. *Dark Night of the Body: D. H. Lawrence's The Plumed Serpent.* Austin: University of Texas Press, 1964.

Corke, Helen. *D. H. Lawrence: The Croydon Years.* Introduction by Warren F. Roberts. Austin: University of Texas Press, 1963.

Cowan, James C. *D. H. Lawrence's American Journey: A Study of Literature and Myth.* Cleveland: Press of Case Western Reserve University, 1970.

Delany, Paul, ed. "Twelve Letters." *D. H. Lawrence Review* 2 (1969): 195-209.

_____. *D. H. Lawrence's Nightmare: The Writer and His Circle in the Years of the Great War.* New York: Basic Books, 1978.

Díaz, Bernal. *The Bernal Díaz Chronicles: The True Story of the Conquest of Mexico.* Edited and translated by Albert Idell. Garden City, N.Y.: Dolphin Book Doubleday & Co., 1956.

Diccionario Porrua, Historía, Biografía y Geografía de Mexico. Suplemento. Mexico City: Editorial Porrua, 1966.

Donnelly, Ignatius. *Atlantis.* Rev. ed. Edited by Egerton Sykes. New York: Harper & Brothers, 1949.

Douglas, Norman. *D. H. Lawrence and Maurice Magnus: A Plea for Better Manners.* Syracuse, Sicily: Privately printed, 1924.

Dulles, John F. W. *Yesterday in Mexico: A Chronicle of the Revolution.* Austin: University of Texas Press, 1961.

Evans, Rosalie. *The Rosalie Evans Letters from Mexico.* Arranged with comments by Daisy Caden Pettus. Indianapolis: Bobbs-Merrill, 1926.

Farmer, David Robb. *Catalog of the D. H. Lawrence Holdings of the University of Texas* (Doctorate, University of Texas at Austin, 1970).

Firth, J. B. *Highways & Byways in Derbyshire.* London: Macmillian, 1905.

Foreign Office List & Diplomatic and Consular Year Book. London: Harrison, 1960.

Foster, Joseph. *D. H. Lawrence in Taos.* Albuquerque: University of New Mexico Press, 1972.

Freeman, Mary. *D. H. Lawrence: A Basic Study of His Ideas.* Gainesville, Fla.: University of Florida Press, 1955.

Gamio, Manuel. "Los Ultimos Descubrimentos Arqueologicos en Teotihuacán." *Ethnos* 1 (1920): 7-14.

Gaona, Rodolfo, as told to "Mono Sabio." *Mis 20 Años de Torero.* Mexico, City: Biblioteca Popular de "El Universal," 1924.

Gertler, Mark. *Mark Gertler: Selected Letters.* Edited by Noel Carrington. London: Rupert Hart-Davis, 1965.

Gregory, Horace. *D. H. Lawrence: Pilgrim of the Apocalypse.* New York: Viking Press, 1933.

Gruening, Ernest. *Mexico and its Heritage.* New York: Appleton-Century-Crofts, 1928.

Hammett, Brian R. *Politics & Trade in Southern Mexico, 1750-1821.* Cambridge, England: Cambridge University Press, 1971.

Howard, Michael S. *Jonathan Cape Publisher.* London: Jonathan Cape, 1971.

Huxley, Aldous. *Eyeless in Gaza.* New York: Harper, 1936.

————. *Letters of Aldous Huxley.* Edited by Grover Smith. New York: Harper & Row, 1969.

————. *Tomorrow and Tomorrow and Tomorrow.* New York: Harper, 1956.

————, ed. *The Letters of D. H. Lawrence.* New York: Viking Press, 1932.

Irvine, Peter L., and Kiley, Anne. "D. H. Lawrence and Frieda Lawrence: Letters to Dorothy Brett." *D. H. Lawrence Review* 9 (Spring 1976): 1-116.

Iturribarria, Jorge Fernando. *Oaxaca en la Historia.* Mexico City: Editorial Stylo, 1955.

Joost, Nicholas, and Sullivan, Alvin. *D. H. Lawrence and the Dial.* Carbondale, Il.: Southern Illinois University Press, 1970.

Keller, Hermann. *The Bible as History.* New York: William Morrow, 1956.

Krutch, Joseph Wood. *More Lives than One.* New York: William Sloane, 1962.

Kull, Hermann. "Experiences of a Dentist in Tropical Mexico." *The Dental Digest* (June 1926): 376-385.

Lacy, Gerald Morris. "An Analytical Calendar of the Letters of D. H. Lawrence"(Doctorate, University of Texas at Austin, 1971).

————. ed. *The Escaped Cock.* Los Angeles: Black Sparrow Press, 1973.

————. *D. H. Lawrence: Letters to Thomas & Adele Seltzer.* Santa Barbara: Black Sparrow Press, 1976.

Lawrence, Ada, and Gelder, G. Stuart. *Young Lorenzo: Early Life of D. H. Lawrence.* Florence: G. Orioli, 1931.

Lawrence, Frieda. *Frieda Lawrence: The Memoirs and the Correspondence.* Edited by E. W. Tedlock, Jr. New York: Alfred A. Knopf, 1964.

————. *"Not I, But the Wind. . . ."* New York: Viking Press, 1934.

Lea, F. A. *The Life of John Middleton Murry.* London: Methuen & Co., 1959.

Leavis, F. R. *D. H. Lawrence: Novelist.* London: Chatto & Windus, 1955.

Levy, Mervyn, ed. *Paintings of D. H. Lawrence.* New York: Viking Press, 1964.

Lucas, Robert. *Frieda Lawrence: The Story of Frieda von Richthofen and D. H. Lawrence.* New York: Viking Press, 1973.

Luhan, Mabel. *Lorenzo in Taos.* London: Martin Secker, 1933.

McDonald, Edward D. *A Bibliography of the Writings of D. H. Lawrence.* Philadelphia: Centaur Book Shop, 1925.

————. *The Writings of D. H. Lawrence, 1925-1930: A Bibliographical Supplement.* Philadelphia: Centaur Book Shop, 1931.

McDonald, Marguerite Bartelle. "An Evening with the Lawrences." *D. H. Lawrence Review* 5 (1972): 63-66.

Maples Arce, Manuel. *Soberana Juventud.* Madrid: Editorial Plenitud, 1967.

Mercurio, El. Marcelino Muciño, ed. Oaxaca daily newspaper. Issues from April 1924 to 6 March 1925.

Merrild, Knud. *A Poet and Two Painters: A Memoir of D. H. Lawrence.* London: George Routledge & Son, 1938.

Moore, Harry T. *The Intelligent Heart: The Story of D. H. Lawrence.* New York: Farrar, Straus and Young, 1954.

————. *The Life and Works of D. H. Lawrence.* New York: Twayne Publishers, 1951.

————. ed. *The Collected Letters of D. H. Lawrence.* New York: Viking Press, 1962.

————. ed. *D. H. Lawrence: A Critical Survey.* Toronto: Forum House, 1969.

Muray, Nicholas, and Gallico, Paul. *The Revealing Eye: Personalities of the 1920s.* New York: Atheneum, 1967.

Murry, John Middleton. *Reminiscences of D. H. Lawrence.* London: Jonanthan Cape, 1933.

————. *Son of Woman: The Story of D. H. Lawrence.* New York: Jonathan Cape and Harrison Smith, 1931.

Nahal, Chaman. *D. H. Lawrence: An Eastern View.* New York, A. S. Barnes, 1970.

Nehls, Edward. *D. H. Lawrence: A Composite Biography, Vol. 2, 1919-1926.* Madison: University of Wisconsin Press, 1958.

Nin, Anaïs. *D. H. Lawrence: An Unprofessional Study.* Chicago: Swallow Press, 1964.

Nottingham Festival Committee. *Young Bert: An Exhibition of the Early Years of D. H. Lawrence.* Nottingham: Nottingham Festival Committee, 1972.

Nuttall, Zelia. *The Fundamental Principles of Old and New World Civilizations.* Cambridge, Mass: Peabody Museum, 1901.

Parkes, Henry Bamford. *A History of Mexico.* Boston: Houghton Mifflin, 1938.

Parmenter, Ross. "Glimpses of a Friendship: Zelia Nuttall and Franz Boas." *Pioneers of American Anthropology.* Edited by June Helm. Seattle: University of Washington Press, 1966.

Prichard, Katharine Susanna. "Lawrence in Australia." *Meanjin* 9 (1950): 252-259.

Rieff, Philip. "Introduction," *Psychoanalysis and the Unconscious.* New York: Viking Press, 1960.

Roberts, Warren F. *A Bibliography of D. H. Lawrence.* London: The Soho Bibliographies, Rupert Hart-Davis, 1963.

Rojas, Basilio. *Un Gran Rebelde: Manuel García Vigil.* Mexico City: Editorial Luz, 1965.

Rosas Solaegui, Guillermo. *Anecdotario de Oaxaca.* Oaxaca: Rosas Solaegui, n.d.

————. *Multicosas de Oaxaca.* Oaxaca: Rosas Solaegui, n.d.

Sagar, Keith. *The Art of D. H. Lawrence.* Cambridge: Cambridge University Press, 1965.

————. *The Life of D. H. Lawrence.* New York: Pantheon Books, 1980.

————, ed. *D. H. Lawrence in New Mexico.* Salt Lake City: Gibbs M. Smith, Inc., 1982.

Santa Cruz, José, ed. *Reminiscences del Ilustrusimo y Reverendisimo Señor Doctor D. Eulogio Gillow y Zavalza, Arzobispo de Oaxaca.* Puebla: Escuela Linotipográfica en Salesiana, 1921.

Schneider, Luis Mario. *El Estridentismo: Una Literatura de la Estrategia.* Mexico City: Ediciones de Bellas Artes, 1970.

Secker, Martin. *Letters from a Publisher: Martin Secker to D. H. Lawrence & Others, 1911-1929.* London: Enitharmon Press, 1970.

————. ed. *Letters from D. H. Lawrence to Martin Secker: 1911-1930.* Bridgefoot Iver, England: Martin Secker, 1970.

Seligmann, Herbert J. *D. H. Lawrence: An American Interpretation.* New York: Thomas Seltzer, 1924.

Skinner, M. L. "D. H. Lawrence and *The Boy in the Bush.*" *Meanjin* 9 (1950): 260-263.

————. *Black Swans.* London: Jonathan Cape, 1925.

Spence, Lewis. *The Gods of Mexico.* New York: Frederick A. Stokes, 1923.

Taylor, William B. *Landlord and Peasant in Colonial Oaxaca.* Stanford, Ca.: Stanford University Press, 1972.

Tedlock, E. W., Jr. *D. H. Lawrence: Artist & Rebel.* Albuquerque: University of New Mexico Press, 1963.

————. *The Frieda Lawrence Collection of D. H. Lawrence Manuscripts: A Descriptive Bibliography.* Albuquerque: University of New Mexico Press, 1948.

Terry, T. Philip. *Terry's Guide in Mexico.* Hingham, Ma.: Rapid Service Press, 1909.

Tindall, William York. *D. H. Lawrence and Susan his Cow.* New York: Columbia University Press, 1939.

Tischendorf, Alfred. *Great Britain and Mexico in the Era of Porfirio Díaz.* Durham, N.C.: Duke University Press, 1961.

Tomlinson, H. M. *Norman Douglas.* New York: Harper, 1931.

Vasconcelos, José. *A Mexican Ulysses: An Autobiography.* Translated and abridged by W. Rex Crawford. Bloomington: University of Indiana Press, 1963.

Vivas, Eliseo. *D. H. Lawrence: The Failure and Triumph of Art.* Evanston, Il.: Northwestern University Press, 1960.

Volante. No. 22 (24 January 1925.) An occasional publication of the Mexico City P.E.N. Club.

Walker, Ronald G. *Infernal Paradise: Mexico and the Modern English Novel.* Berkeley: University of California Press, 1978.

West, Rebecca. "Elegy." *Ending in Earnest: A Literary Log.* Garden City, N.Y.: Doubleday, 1951.

Weston, Edward. *The Daybooks of Edward Weston: Vol. I, Mexico.* Rochester, N.Y.: George Eastman House, 1961.

Wickramasinghe, Martin. *The Mysticism of D. H. Lawrence.* Colombo, Ceylon: M.D. Gunasena, 1951.

Widmer, Kingsley. *The Art of Perversity: D. H. Lawrence's Shorter Fictions.* Seattle: University of Washington Press, 1962.

Womack, Jr., John. *Zapata and the Mexican Revolution.* New York: Alfred A. Knopf, 1969.

Zytaruk, George J., ed. *The Quest for Rananim: D. H. Lawrence's Letters to S. S. Koteliansky.* Montreal: McGill-Queen's University Press, 1970.

INDEX

LAWRENCE WORKS CITED

ABBREVIATIONS USED:

(AA) *Assorted Articles* (London, Secker, 1932), reprinted in *Phoenix II*
(P) *Phoenix* (New York, Viking, 1936)
(P II) *Phoenix II* (New York, Viking, 1968)

Aaron's Rod, xviii, 8, 93, 142, 196, 215, 235, 274-5, 324, 332
All Things Are Possible (Shostov translation), 358
"Altitude," 248-9
Apocalypse, 229, 232, 291, 301, 347, 359
Apropos of Lady Chatterley's Lover, 300
"Art and Morality" (P), 235
"Art and the Individual" (P II), 50
Assorted Articles (P II), 21, 191, 275, 337
"Au Revoir, U.S.A." (P), 278
"Autobiographical Sketch" (AA), 21

"Bibbles," 89
Birds, Beasts and Flowers, 33, 89-90, 245, 351
"Border Line, The," 159-60, 264-5
Boy in the Bush, The, with M. L. Skinner, ix, 6, 80, 87, 150-5, 190, 200, 215, 331, 345, 355

Cavalleria Rusticana and Other Stories (Verga translation), 340
Centaur Letters, The, 240
"Climbing Down Pisgah" (P), 249, 252, 254-5, 332
"Cocksure Women and Hensure Men" (AA), 96
Collected Letters of D. H. Lawrence, The, ed. Harry T. Moore, 107, 204, 213, 239, 349, 350
Colliers Saturday Night, A, 248
Complete Plays of D. H. Lawrence, The, 243
"Corasmín and the Parrots," 87, 88, 91-3, 332
"Craving for Spring," 253
"Crown, The" (P II), 233, 251
"Dance of the Sprouting Corn," 219
"Daughter-in-Law, The," 248

David, 248-9
D. H. Lawrence: Letters to Thomas & Adele Seltzer, x, 357
"Dog, The," 328
"Dragon of Apocalypse by Frederick Carter, The" (P), 91, 291, 359

"Education of the People" (P), 69, 157, 247, 251, 276
Escaped Cock, The, 323, 336
Etruscan Places, 221, 323

Fantasia of the Unconscious, 56, 90, 196, 215, 230, 237, 244, 249, 253-4, 257, 260, 262, 275, 277, 337
"Fight for Barbara, The," 249
"Flowery Tuscany" (P), 107
"Flying Fish, The" (P), 18, 73, 83, 165, 235, 318, 323, 326, 328-38, 340, 342, *plate 8*
"Fox, The," 198

"Gentleman from San Francisco, The" (Bunin translation), 358
"Grapes," 245

"Hopi Snake Dance, The," 32, 218, 221
"Humiliation," 203
"Hymns in a Man's Life" (AA), 232, 252

"Indians and an Englishman" (P), 33, 221
"Indians and Entertainment," 221
"Introduction, *Memoirs of the Foreign Legion*" (P II), 80, 262
"Introduction to Bibliography" (P), (McDonald's), 32
"Introduction to Pictures" (P), 190
"Introduction to These Paintings" (P), 92

"Jimmy and the Desperate Woman," 264-7
John Thomas and Lady Jane, 191

Kangaroo, ix, xviii, 50, 62, 78, 84, 127-8, 196, 215, 262, 274-5, 276-7, 281, 289, 294, 302, 310, 314, 324, 331

Lady Chatterley's Lover, 49, 81, 191, 218, 304, 314, 324, 336-7
Ladybird, The, 198, 224, 312
"Lady Wife," 196
"Last Laugh, The," 159-60, 264-5
Lemon Gardens, The, 251
Letters of D. H. Lawrence, ed. Aldous Huxley, 25, 213, 240, 349, 350
"Little Moonshine with Lemon, A," 221
Little Novels of Sicily (Verga translation), 217, 340-2, 360
Look! We Have Come Through, 84, 161, 203
Lost Girl, The, 80, 151, 215, 224, 312
"Lovely Lady, The," 347

Maestro-don Gesualdo (Verga translation), 340-1
"Making Pictures" (AA), 191, 337
"Man Is Essentially a Soul," 251-2
Man Who Died, The, ix, 229, 233, 323, 336, 347
"Market Day," 45, 47, 57, 85, 170
"Married Man, The," 248-9
"Merry-Go-Round, The," 248
"Moby Dick," 93, 330
"Morality and the Novel" (P), 235
Mornings in Mexico, ix, xi, xvi, 25-6, 30-1, 42, 45, 59, 65, 78, 83-4, 106-7, 110, 136, 142, 151, 185, 186, 199, 206, 218, 220-2, 228, 235, 260, 298, 333, 350, *plate 22*
"Mother and Daughter," 178
Movements in European History, 241
"Mozo, The," 65, 75, 107, 353

"New Mexico" (P), 218
"Noah's Flood" (P), 243, 245-7, 249, 252, 254, 328-9
"None of That," 223-4, 226-7, 282, 291, 312
"Novel, The" (P II), 154, 190, 229, 230, 235

"On Coming Home" (P II), 87
"On Human Destiny" (AA), 136

Pansies, 304
"Paul Morel," 156. See also *Sons and Lovers*
Phoenix, The Posthumous Papers of D. H. Lawrence, ix, xi, 136, 190, 228, 240, 249, 329, 359
Phoenix II, More Uncollected Writings by D. H. Lawrence, ix, xi, 158
Plumed Serpent, The, ix, xv, xvi, 4, 20, 21, 37, 87, 97, 128, 147, 224, 225, 227, 243-4, 271, 273, 274, 275, 279,

281, 273-315 passim, 317, 324, 343, 358, *plates 14, 48*
_____, first draft, xi, xxiii, 15, 32, 35, 36, 91, 140, 185, 224, 246, 269, 273, 274, 275, 279, 281-6, 289, 295, 298-9, 302-3, 306, 309-11, 315, 359
_____, second draft, xi, xviii, xx, xxiii, 6, 7, 11, 15, 27, 59, 83, 85, 87, 91, 95, 104, 106, 127, 136, 140, 175, 182, 193, 199, 216, 221, 232, 234, 235, 236, 266, 269, 273, 275, 278, 282-5, 289, 299, 302, 304-5, 309-13, 315, 327
"Preface to Black Swans" (P II), 151, 153, 155, 158, 199, 213, 241, 355
"Princess, The," 32, 87, 224, 225, 282, 312
"Proper Study of Mankind, The" (P), 135
Psychoanalysis and the Unconscious, 197, 215

Quest for Rananim, The: D. H. Lawrence's Letters to S. S. Koteliansky, 262, 358
"Quetzalcoatl," the working title for *The Plumed Serpent,* 32, 135, 176, 185, 214, 219, 246, 277, 282, 325

Rainbow, The, xv, xxviii-xxix, 8, 124, 139, 156-7, 215, 241, 246, 282, 328, 345
"Red Trousers" (AA), 327
Reflections on the Death of a Porcupine (P II), 230, 323-4, 336, 347, 356
"Resurrection" (P), 228-236, 244, 252, 329, 332
"Rex" (P), 89
"Risen Lord, The" (AA), 233, 337

St. Mawr, ix, 87, 92, 216, 223, 224, 282, 302, 312, 331
Sea and Sardinia, 215, 220, 221
"See Mexico After, by Luis Q." (P), 136, 145, 147, 158, 228, 246
"Ship of Death, The," 323
"Smile," 269
Sons and Lovers, xxviii-xxix, 6, 81, 156, 233, 239, 241, 255, 328, 345
Studies in Classic American Literature, ix, 33, 63, 145, 215, 230, 239, 251, 277, 330, 343
"Study of Thomas Hardy" (P), 229
"Suggestions for Stories," 236, 328
Sun, 360

"Taos" (P), 218
Tortoises, 241

Touch and Go, 215, 249
Trespasser, The, 93, 156, 198, 241
Twilight in Italy, 88, 165, 178, 221, 251

Virgin and the Gypsy, The, 329

"Walk to Huayapan," 109
"Weather Vane, The," first name of "The Flying Fish," 328-9

"Wedding Ring, The," 156, 228-9. See also *The Rainbow* and *Women in Love*
White Peacock, The, 155-6, 192, 198, 241, 252, 339-40, 342, 345, 360
"Why the Novel Matters" (P), 235
Widowing of Mrs. Holroyd, The, 248
"Woman out of the Water," 328
Woman Who Rode Away, The, 87, 224, 225, 227, 264, 282, 298, 312
Women in Love, xxix, 144, 156, 215, 242, 250, 282, 328

LAWRENCE IN OAXACA

Aaron, brother of Moses, 235, 253
Abraham, 153
Acevedo, Jesús, xx, xxii
Adamites, 313
Adelphi, 135-6, 219, 259-60, 262-3, 267
Agrarians, 7
Aguascalientes, xix, xxi, xxiii
Akin, Col. A. D., x, xxv, xxvii, 2, 3-4,
   15, 75, 164, 194, 360-1
Akin, Jean Harmon, x, xxv, 2, 3-4, 14,
   15, 22, 31, 33, 75, 79, 164, 170,
   171, 194, 318, 320, 325-6, 337,
   341-2, 359, 360-1
Alameda Hotel, later Monte Alban, 13,
   14, 36, 66
Alameda, Mexico City, 9, 138
Alameda, Oaxaca, 13, 110
alcalde, 102
Aldington, Richard, 141, 350
Alemania, Mexican town, 67
Alfareria Jiménez, *plate 38*
Allende, Calle, xvii
Allenta, Ramón, 185, *plate 43*
Almazán, Juan Andrew, xxv, xxvii, 77
Alonso, Francisco, 127
Alvarez Collado, José and Manuel, 39-40
Amazon River, 260
American Institute of Mining, Metallur-
   gical and Petroleum Engineers, 350,
   356
American Railway Express Company, 78
*Analytical Calendar of the Letters of
   D. H. Lawrence, An,* 213-4, 338
Anaximander, 233
"And the Fullness Thereof . . . ," 160,
   192, 201
Anna Karenina, 229, 231
Antarctic, 330
Apaches, 218, 221, 225
Apocalypse. See *Revelation of St. John
   the Divine*
Aqueduct of Oaxaca, 35, 173
Aquitania, 262
Aragón family, knifemakers, 179
Arbuckle, Roscoe, "Fatty," 223
Arce, Maples, 149, 354-5
Arizona, 219, 225, 356
Arkansas, 33
Arlen, Michael, 10
Asia, 244

Asquith, Lady Cynthia, 80, 125, 330,
   357
Assyria, 359
Atlantis, 244-6, 253, 328, 357-8
Atlantis, 357
Atoyac River, 4, 17, 28, 60, 352
Austin, Texas, 228, 236, 247, 282
Australia, 6, 21, 63, 78, 151, 157, 275-7,
   310, 330, 346
Austria, 16
"Autobiography: My Long and Beautiful
   Journey" (Brett), x
Avion, 138
Azompa, 64, 195
Azores, the, 244
Aztec Land Gallery, 9
Aztecs, 34, 56, 60, 90, 95, 175, 195,
   226, 278-9, 286, 288, 290, 292, 295,
   297-8, 308, 320, 327
Azul, Frieda's horse, 269-70

Baden-Baden, 186, 215, 264, 357
Baker, George Pierce, 304
Barmby, A. W., 135-6, 142, 206, 216-8
Bandol, 193
Barber Family, 192
Bazán, Eligio, 21, 350
Beals, Carlston, xxix, 349
Beals, Ralph L., 64
Beauchamp, Leslie Heron, 330
Bejarano, Manuel, 40
Belgium, 36, 354
Bennett, Arnold, 239
Berlin, 318
Bernabé, fruit collector, 118-20, 133
Bethlehem, 130, 189
Bethlehemite monks, xx, 111
Bible, The, 233, 246, 283
*Bibliography of the Writings of D. H.
   Lawrence,* 31, 32, 155, 230, 238-42,
   359
Birmingham, 26, 37
Black Swans, 6, 151-2, 157-8, 355
Blackwood, Basil, 340
Blavatsky, Helena P., 358
Bolaños Cacho, Miguel, xx, 34, 208
Bolivár, Simón, xvii
Bolshevism, 9
Bombay, 313
Boni, Albert, 217
Boni, Charles, 217

Book of Common Prayer, The, 283
Borneo, 260
Bournemouth, 21, 156
Bradford, Pa., 228
Bradlee, Frederic, 136
Bradomín, José María, 180
Brena, Enrique, 22
Brena, Guillermo, 22
Brenan, Gerald, 223
Brett, Dorothy, ix, x, xi, 3, 6, 7-8, 9,
    11, 12, 13, 15, 18, 28-9, 31, 33-4,
    45, 47-8, 52, 57, 62-3, 66, 68, 69-71,
    78, 79, 81, 84, 87, 91, 94, 97-8,
    100-1, 103-4, 105, 107, 131, 139,
    141, 145, 147, 150, 153-4, 159-214
    passim, 218, 223, 226, 239, 249-50,
    255-60, 262, 265-6, 268, 269, 271,
    282-4, 287, 317-321, 323, 325,
    327-8, 334, 337-8, 342-3, 345,
    353-4, 356-7, 361, *plates 36, 41*
Brewster, Achsah and Earl, x, 21, 161,
    213, 271, 281, 337, 341
Bribiesca, Dr. Macario, xxvii-xxviii
British Embassy and Consulate, 25, 28
Brothers Karamazov, The, 263
Brown, Curtis, 18, 28, 30, 135, 142,
    148, 214, 216-20, 240, 254, 260,
    263, 281, 317, 325-6, 341, 343
Brown, Roy, 360
Buddhism, 164, 313
"Bufete, El," 32, 327
Bunin, Ivan, 358
Buñuelos, 372
Burrows, Louie, 7, 14, 140, 283, 340
Bynner, Witter, xxiii, xxv, xxviii-xxix,
    4, 7, 17, 25, 86, 135, 186, 195, 215,
    223, 278-80, 284, 289, 298, 300

Caballero, Manuel, 167, *plate 39*
Cabrera, Miguel, 21, 350
Café Oriental, 7
Café Royal, 11, 261-2, 265, 268
Caldanza de la Republica, 28
Calendas, 40-2, 183-4, 194-5, 202
California, xxiv, 162, 180
Calles, Plutarco Elías, xviii, xx, xxi,
    xxiv, xxvi, xxviii-xxx, 11, 38, 127,
    140, 142, 273, 285, 305-6, 308
Cambridge University, 348
Campbell, Albert J., 53
Camp Humphreys, Va., 356
Canaan, 252-4
Cape, Jonathan, 151, 157
Capri, 161, 351
Cardenas, Lázaro, xxviii
Carden, Sir Lionel, 7, 28
Carmen Alto, Church of, 105
Carnegie Institution, 280

Carranza, Jesús, xix, xxvii-xxviii
Carranza, Venustiano, xviii-xxiv, 7
Carretera de la Patria, 23
Carrington, Dora, 223, 226, 255
Carswell, Catherine, x, 5, 10-11, 63,
    125, 168, 215-7, 229, 262-3, 265,
    268, 278, 280-1, 287, 292, 320, 340,
    343, 349
Carswell, Donald, 11
Carswell, John Patrick, x, 11
Carter, Frederick, xxiv, 91, 176, 216,
    290-4, 359
Casa Alvarado, 4, 279
Casa Aragón, 179
Casa Fuerte, 61
Caso, Alfonso, 3
Cathars, 313
Cathedral of Oaxaca, 13, 74, 338, *plates
    8, 27*
Cavalleria Rusticana, 14, 340
Cavitch, David, 50, 224
cazaquate, a plant, 116
Cazaquate River, 114, 115
Celaya, xviii, xix
Centaur Book Shop and Press, 230, 238
Century, 156
Cervantes M., Dr. Luis, 359
Ceylon, 21, 63, 94, 138, 313, 318, 330,
    340-1, 346
Chahuites, xxvii
Chaldeans, 244, 291
Chambers, Colin K., 108
Chambers, David, 37
Chambers family, 37, 229
Chambers, Henry Kellett, 107
Chambers, Jessie, 229
Chambers, María Cristina Mena, 107-8
Chapala, lake and town, xvi, xxiii, xxvi,
    4, 5, 10, 17, 21, 33, 94, 176, 186,
    246, 280-1, 284-5, 290, 294
Chapultepec, Lomas de, 68
Chapultepec Park, 10, 138
Chariot of the Sun, 360
Chase National Bank of N.Y., 6
Chekhov, Anton, 261
Chiapas, xxv, xxvii, xxviii
Chicago, 15, 321
Chicken Ita (Chichen Itza), 280
Chihuahua, 225
Chinese, 244
Chiricahuas, 225
chirimoyas, a fruit, 133
Cholula, 176, 286
Chopin, xvi
Christ, 61, 123-4, 228, 232-4, 251, 255,
    268, 271, 278, 284, 290, 294, 299,
    328
Christianity, 292, 314

Christmas, 103-4, 106, 192-3, 199, 215, 356
Citlalicuie, 95
Citlaltepetl, volcano, 334-5
Clarke, Ada Lawrence, 20, 84, 88, 161, 192, 213-4, 220, 242, 339, 342
Clark, LaVerne Harrell, 351
Clark, L. D., 27, 56, 72, 224, 273, 308, 351, 359
Coahuila, 360
Coatlicue, 295
Cobdnen-Sanderson, Richard, 267, 357
Codex Nuttall, xvi
Codex Rickards, 25, 28
coitus reservatus, 313
Coldwater, Oh., 239
Colegio Militar de Chapultepec, xxi
Colette, 89
Collings, Ernest H. R., 58, 155, 230, 236
Collins, Dorotha, 228
Colonia Reforma, 112
Columbia University, 279, 355
Compañia, La, Church of, 61, 165
Congregational, 252
Constitutionalistas, xix, xxiii, 3
Constitution of 1857, 137
Constitution of 1917, 38, 305
Contreras, Guillermo, 167, *plate 39*
Conway, George R. G., 164, 343-4, 347-8
Cooper, Fenimore, 277
Corasmín, Padre Rickards's dog, 30, 35, 42, 87, 89, 110, *plate 11*
Córdoba, 334
Cornish, Dr., 66
Cornwall, 32, 63, 84, 253, 343
Corpus Christi Church, 306
corredor, 29, 39-40, 253, 343, *plate 17*
Corriere de la Sera, 239
Cortés, Hernán, 55, 57, 292, 295
Cortés López, Genaro, 131-2
Cosiojeza, 60
Costa Chica, 79, 317, 319
Covarrubias, Miguel, 7
Covo, Ruth, 354
Cowan, James C., 303
Cowdray, Lady, 354
Coyoacán, 285
Coyotepec, 64
Crichton, Kyle S., 176, 339
Cristeros, 306-8
Criterion, 267-8
Crosby, Harry, 324, 360
Crowninshield, Frank, 135-6, 215, 353
Croydon, 21, 50, 88, 198, 229
Cruz, Inocente, 66-7, 75-9, 83, 105, 108
Cuernavaca, 65, 291, 347, *plate 46*
Cuicatlán, 94

Cuilapam, 22
Cummings, H. A. C., 7

Dana, Richard Henry, 330
Dark Night of the Body: D. H. Lawrence's The Plumed Serpent, 56, 273, 351
Darlington, 6, 151
Darwin, Charles, 91
Davidson Road Elementary School, 21
Davila, José Inés, xix-xx
Daybooks of Edward Weston, The, Vol. I, x, 10, 37, 141
Dead Sea, 252
de la Huerta, Adolfo, xviii-xxi, xxiv-xxvi, xxviii
de la Huerta Rebellion, xxv,xxix-xxx, 6, 11, 15, 16, 30-1, 68, 73, 77, 83, 183
Delany, Paul, 169
Del Monte Ranch, xxiv, xxv, xxx, 6, 46, 78, 90, 205, 210, 256, 259, 269-71, 351
democracy, 127-8, 275, 286
Dentists' Supply Co. of N.Y., 68
Derbyshire, 329
Devon, 309
D. H.Lawrence: A Composite Biography, Vol. II, 135, 136, 148, 213, 350-1, 360
D. H. Lawrence: An American Interpretation, 215, 218, 241, 348
D. H. Lawrence and Maurice Magnus: A Plea for Better Manners, 81
D. H. Lawrence and Susan his Cow, 358
D. H. Lawrence and the Body Mystical, 291, 359
D. H. Lawrence and the Dial, 358
D. H. Lawrence & the New World, 50
D. H. Lawrence: An Unprofessional Study, 50
D. H. Lawrence in Taos, 88, 358
D. H. Lawrence: Portrait of a Genius, Eut . . . , 350
D. H. Lawrence: Reminiscences and Correspondence, x, 214
D. H. Lawrence Review, 169
Dial, The, 221
Díaz, Bernal, 55-8
Díaz, Félix, nephew of Porfirio, xxi, xxiii
Díaz, Juan, 60
Díaz, Porfirio, xv, xviii, xix-xxi, 1, 3, 18, 27, 53, 72, 137, 148, 279, 290, 305, 372
Díaz Quintas, Heliodoro, 127
Dibbrell, John, 17, 280

Diéguez, Manuel M., xxvi, xxvii, xxviii, 77
Discovery and Conquest of Mexico, 56
Doctor, Ethel R., x, xxv, 1-2, 3, 6, 13, 16, 22, 25, 30, 31, 65, 73, 74, 81, 110, 127, 162, 321, 325, 349, 359
Dominicans, 60, 123, 165
Don Quixote, 128
Donaji, 109, 113
Donnelly, Ignatius, 357
Dorchester College, 36
Dorset, 269
Dostoievsky, Fyodor, 229, 263
Douglas, Norman, 81, 260-1, 352
Dover, N.J., 215
Dragon of the Apocalypse, The, 291, 359
"Dregs," 81
Drexel Institute, 239
Drinkwater, Rev. Harold, 26
druids, 244
Duckworth, Gerald, 156-7, 241, 339, 342
Duke, John. *See* Girdley, B. C.,
Duncan, Isadora, 80
Dunlap, Sir Thomas Dacre, 161, 265
Durán, Adela de Rickards, 27

earthquakes, 39-40, 323, 325
earwigs, 93
Easter, 219, 233
Easter Isles, 244
Eastwood, Lawrence's birthplace, 37, 192, 229, 252, 333, 339
Eder, David, 10
Einstein, Albert, 150
Ejutla, 17, 32, 67, 171, 179
"Elegy," (Rebecca West), 97
El Fuerte, 298
El Paso, 6, 147, 162-3, 343
England, xviii, xxiv, xxv, 36, 104, 147-9, 152, 161-2, 198, 199, 203, 223, 242, 265, 268-9, 281, 289-9, 312, 315, 320, 325, 333, 340, 343
Englishman and the Inquisition, An, 348
English Review, 156
Esher, Viscount, 6
Esperanza, xxvi, 4, 16, 78, 334, 336
Estrada, Enrique, xxvi
Estrada, Genaro, 7-9, 17, 137, 141, 285, 348, 354
Estridentistas, Los, 8, 149, 355
Etla, xxvi, 48, 63
Etruscans, 220-1, 244
Etztatlan, 5
Europe, 144, 233, 244, 277, 343
Evans, Rosalie, 6-7

"Eve in the Land of Nod," 355
Everyman, 233-4, 337
evolution, 91-2
"Experiences of a Dentist in Tropical Mexico," 352
Eyeless in Gaza, 77
Ezekiel, 233

Fairbanks, Douglas, 177
Farmer, David Robb, xi, 356
fascism, 275-6, 301-4, 308
Felley Abbey, 340
Fernández MacGregor, Genaro, 8
Ferrer, Mario, xxiii
Ferrocarril Mexicano del Sur, 4, 16, 36
Finney, Claude B., 1, 3-4
Flaubert, Gustave, 340
Florence, Italy, 81, 247
Flores, Angel, 11, 127, 306
Flores Magon, Nicolás, 127
Florida, 10, 283
Fontana, 361
Foreign Office List, 25
Forster, William, xi, xii, 206, 308
Fortín, El, xxvi, 20, 33-4, 74, 109, 172, 222, *plate 27*
Foster, Joseph, 6, 88, 124, 333
France, 9, 137, 150, 193, 218, 360
Francia, Hotel, 2-3, 12, 13, 15, 16, 30, 32, 37, 48, 52, 66, 78, 94, 165, 166, 168, 185, 189, 209-10, 213, 255, 286-7, 318, 326-7, 333, 337-8, 342, 349, 351, *plate 4*
Franciscans, 292
Freeman, Mary, 301
Fremantle, 152, 330
Frieda Lawrence Collection of D. H. Lawrence Manuscripts, The, 144, 228, 236, 351
Frieda Lawrence Ravagli Estate, x, xi, 236, 357
Frieda Lawrence: The Memoirs and Correspondence, ix, 265
Frissell, Ervine R., 356
Fundamental Principles of Old and New World Civilizations, xvi, 292

Galveston, 266, 318
Gamio, Manuel, 277-80, 292-3, 308, *plate 48*
Gaono, Rodolfo, 227
Garcés, Ubaldo, 85
García Cortés, Marciano, 122-5
García Díaz, Antonio, 166
García, José, 141, 173, 285, 354, *plates 29, 41*
Garcia, Lois, 247

García Vigil, Manuel, xv-xxx, 3, 22, 23, 26, 34, 36, 72-7, 83, 127, 171, 174, 289, 349, *plates 1, 27, 35*
Garda, Lake, 198
Gardiner, Rolf, 63, 251
Garita de Tepeaca, 48
Garnett, Edward, 87, 104, 122, 151, 155-8, 229, 233, 240-1, 274, 281, 282, 315, 340, 345
Garsington, 255, *plate 36*
gavilan, 117
Gee, J. Emerson, 14-5, 350
Genius and the Goddess, The, 265
Genoa, 161
George Washington, steamship, 11
Gerard, James Watson, 171
Germany, 88, 145, 171, 186, 216, 264, 302, 320, 360
Gertler, Mark, 199, 255, 262
Gesualdo, 341
Gettysburg Academy, 9, 137
Gift of Fortune, 260
Gilcrease Institute of Tulsa, 348
Gillett, Bobbie Hawk, 271
Gillett, Ted, 271
Gillow, Eulogio, xx, xxiii, 26-7, 35-6, 40, 60, 67, 71-2, 83, 289
Gillow, Thomas, 36
Girdley, B. C., x, 2, 4, 13, 14-5, 87, 127, 165-6, 286, 350
Girdley, B. C., Jr., x, 350
Gnostics, 313
Gods of Mexico, The, 91, 95, 178, 286, 293
God the Father, 232, 246, 251, 283, 294, 299
Goliath, 248
Good Friday, 233
Gómez, Felix, xxvii-xxviii
Gómez, José F., xxiii, xxvii, xxviii
González Mena, Josefina de Ruiz Bravo, 40
González, Pablo, xxi
Gopar, Eloy, 179
Gótzsche, Kai, xi, xxiv, 4-5, 8, 10, 46, 162, 203, 223, 265, 271
Great Britain, 7
grecas, frets at Mitla, 21-22, 141, 174, *plate 9*
Greenleaf, Richard E., 348
Greenwich Village, 353
Gregory, Horace, xxviii, 308
Grenzen der Seele, 157
Grether, Ernest, 42-3
Grummon, Stuart, 79
Guadalajara, xvi, 5, 46, 113, 153-4, 280
Guadalupe, Basilica of, 38
Guadalupe, Santuario of, Oaxaca, 111, 208
guaje, 86, 89

guayabas, or *guavas,* 119, 132
Guaymas, 10

Haggs, the, 37
Hamilton, Charles A., 1-2, 3, 23
Hamilton, Harloe, x, 2, 14-5, 23, 65
Handel, George Friedrich, 95
Hanley, T. E., 228
Hardy, Thomas, 340
Harris, Iverson, 357
Hartford, Conn., 239
Harvard University, xi, 246, 273, 279, 295, 303
Harvey, John, xii
Hatha Yoga, 314
Hatha-Yoga Pradipikâ, 314
Havana, 329
Hawk, Alfred Dekker, 169, 256-7, 269, 271, 342, 357
Hawk family, 46, 78
Hawk, Lucy Walton, 269, 271
Hawk, Rachel, 256-7, 269-71, 358
Hawk Ranch. *See* Del Monte
Hawk, William, xxx, 11, 18, 20, 28, 30, 46, 71, 80, 94, 168, 173, 205, 217, 236, 256, 269-271, 320-1, 357
Heinemann, William, 155-6, 240-1
Hellman, Geoffrey, 136
Henry, Nancy, 124, 358
Herald of Oaxaca, 22
Herrera, Jesús, 171
Hinduism, 164, 313
Hiroshige, 241
Hispanic American Historical Review, 348
Hitchens, Martha, 354
Hitler, Adolph, 302, 308
Ho Chi Minh, 150
Hohenzollern, 80
Holy Ghost, the, 251, 294, 297, 343
Holy Trinity Church, 1
Hospital Militar, 72, 318
Hospital Vasconcelos de Caridad, 40
Hotel Isabel, 255-6, 258
Houghton Library, xi, 246, 273
"House of Ellis, The," 6, 153
huaraches, 55-9, 99-100, 106, 174, 294, 297
Huayapan, 48, 50, 109-11, 113-5, 119-129, 133-4, 148, 165, 188, 323, *plates 30, 31, 32*
Hueffer, Ford Madox, 155-6
Huerta, Victoriano, xviii, xxi, 7
Hughes, Rosalind, x, xii, 2, 4, 12-14, 21, 31, 66, 69, 78, 162, 164, 166, 169-70, 171, 189, 193-4, 213, 255, *plate 6*
Huichilolobos, 295
Huicholes, 288

Huitzilopochtli, 21, 140, 224, 278, 290, 295, 297, 302-3, 308, 311, 359
Humboldt, Alexander von, 173
Huxley, Aldous, ix, 10, 25, 49, 77, 92, 203, 213, 240, 242, 265-6, 313, 317, 320, 349, 350
Huxley, Julian, 320
Huxley, Maria, 320, 356

Ibarra, Isaac M. x, xx, xxii-xxiii, xxvii, xxix-xxx, 1, 3-4, 14, 17-24, 26, 34, 42, 76-7, 83, 127, 165, 287, 250, plate 5
Ibsen, Hendrik, 239
Igdrasil, 302
I Malavoglia, 340
Imperial Hotel, 148-9, 343, 348, 355
India, 313
Indiana Oaxaca Mining Company of Indianapolis, 14
Indians, 5, 17, 20, 45, 52, 53, 85, 94, 96-7, 102-3, 106, 117, 120, 139, 168, 195, 224, 277, 282, 286-8, 292, 319
Instituto Nacional de Antropología e Historia, 172
Intelligent Heart, The, 164, 213, 229, 271, 320, 350, 357
Intimate Memories (Luhan), 226
Ireland, 311
Irvine, Peter, 204
Isaacs, Edith J. R., 219-20, 222, 288
Isis, 336, 358
Isis Unveiled, 374
Italy, 32, 58, 88, 100, 122, 150, 168, 221, 245, 247, 276, 315
Iturribarria, Jorge Fernando, 349
Itzpapalotl, 295, 313
Ixcotel, 48, 109
Ixtepec, xxvii, xxviii
Ixtlán del Rio, Nayarit, 5
Ixtlán, Oaxaca, 84

Jaffe, Else, Frieda's sister, 87, 193, 242
Jalapa, 290
Jalatlaco River, 17, 28, 30, 48, 109, 206
Jalisco, xxv, xxvi, xxvii, xxviii, 5, 77, 171, 187
James, Henry, 239
Jamiltepec, 285
Jardín Gonzatti, 15
Jarquin, Doña María de Monros, 1, 12, 47, 170, 185, 210, 285, 337, plate 43
Jasper, Ark., 361
Jericho, 252
Jester, David, 238-9
Jesuits, 61, 165

Jicarilla Reservation, 218
Jiménez family, potters, 166-7, plate 39
Jiménez Figueroa, Luis, xx
Jiménez, Onofre, xx, xxv, xxix-xxx, 19, 23, 126-7, 360
Jocotepec, 21
"John of God, the Water Carrier," 107
Johnson, Martyn, 8
Johnson, Willard ("Spud"), x, xxiii, xxiv, xxviii-xxix, 6, 8-9, 190, 219, 221, 278, 280-1, 298
Joost, Nicholas, 358
Jordan, 252
Journal del Société des Américanistes, 25
Journey with Genius, 4, 223, 279
Juárez, Benito, xix, xx, 34, 165
Juárez Maza, Benito, 52, 72
Juchitán, xxiii, xxvii, 56
Judas, 256, 263, 268

Kandy, 341
Kansas, 342
Kelly, Nancy, 265, 320
Kessler, Jascha, 308
King, Joan, 213
King, Margaret, 213
King, Norman, 7
King, Pamela ("Emily") Lawrence, 20, 84, 213, 220, 342-3
Kiowa Ranch, 6, 32, 46, 158, 162, 197-8, 204, 214, 215-6, 221, 223, 229, 239, 256, 260, 270-1, 281, 317, 321, 323, 339, 343, 353
Knights of Columbus, 303
Knopf, Alfred A., ix, 107, 216-7, 221, 361
Koteliansky, Samuel Solomonovich, 5, 10, 83, 180, 193, 255, 259, 261-3, 265, 267-8, 297, 324, 358
Krutch, Joseph Wood, 135
Kukulcan. See Quetzalcoatl
Kull, Carola, x, xxiii, 15, 21, 22, 30-1, 65-82 passim, 94, 127, 162, 174, 192, 202, 261, 285, 317-9, 322, 326, 352, 361, plate 26
Kull, Hermann, x, xii, xxiii, 3-4, 13-5, 21, 22, 30-1, 65-82 passim, 83, 127, 162, 171, 202, 261, 285, 317-9, 322, 326, 352, plate 26
Kull, Lydia, xxiii, 73, 74
Kuprin, I. A. 261

Labor in Mexico, 14, 286, 306, 309
Lachatao, 23
Lacy, Gerald Morris, x, 213, 336, 338, 357
Lagard, Ernest, 79

Lake District, 261
Lara, Eliseo, 167, *plate 39*
Lara, Guillermo, 167, *plate 39*
Larumbe, José E., Dr., 318, 320, 359-60,
    plate 49
Laughing Horse, 190, 219-221, 278
Lawrence and Brett, x, 7-8, 65, 70,
    141, 166, 168, 191, 213, 223, 228,
    259, 287, 350, 353
Lawrence, Arthur John, father of DHL,
    81, 161, 214
Lawrence, D. H., *plates 11, 12, 13, 17,
    19, 25, 29, 34, 35, 38, 40, 41, 43,
    44, 45*
_____, appearance, 13, 97, 199
_____, colony, 10, 196, 199, 207,
    281, 346. *See also* Rananim
_____, copybooks, 32-3
_____, Days with capital D, 92-3
_____, health, 21, 39, 71, 88, 148,
    150, 156, 198-9, 317-21, 323-7,
    334-7, 342-4
_____, house in Oaxaca, 27-31, 45,
    78, 85, 87, 140, 151, 163, 168, 193,
    229, 317, 323, 325, *plate 10*
_____, ideas of the novel, 229-32,
    274, 302
_____, memory, 54, 56
_____, phallic mystery, 224, 276,
    314
_____, rifts with Frieda, 161-2,
    184, 195, 199-211, 311
_____, whites, feelings against, 277
_____, writing style, 50-1, 139,
    232-3
Lawrence, Ernest, brother of DHL, 192
Lawrence, Frieda, ix, xxiii, xxiv-xxv, 5,
    6, 8, 9, 11, 13, 14, 18, 27, 29, 31,
    39, 47-8, 49, 54, 58, 63, 69-71, 78,
    79-80, 81-2, 104, 105, 110, 114,
    115, 116, 122, 125, 130, 138, 139,
    140, 144, 147, 148-9, 154, 155, 156,
    157, 158, 159-60, 161-2, 168-9, 170,
    173-5, 177, 178, 180, 186, 187-90,
    192-3, 196-8, 214-5, 217, 218, 223,
    226, 230, 240, 242, 246, 250, 255-6,
    259, 261-3, 165-6, 268-71, 275, 281,
    284, 292, 308, 315, 317, 320-8,
    334-5, 338-9, 341-3, 350, *plates 13,
    17, 19, 25, 29, 35, 37, 38, 40, 41,
    44*
Lawrence, Lydia Beardsall, mother of
    DHL, 81, 192, 339
Lea, F. A., 259, 262
Leake, R. E. *See* Skinner, M. L.
Leighton, Frederick W., x, xxviii-xxix,
    349
Le Maistre, Violet, 266

León, 227
Lerdo de Tejedo, Miguel, 137
*Letters from a Publisher: Martin Secker
    to D. H. Lawrence and Others,
    1911-1929,* 355
Letters of Aldous Huxley, x, 265
Levy, Mervyn, 191
Library Board of Western Australia, xi,
    xii, 355
Library of Congress, 348
Life and Works of D. H. Lawrence, 350
Life of D. H. Lawrence, 356
Life of John Middleton Murry, 259
Linares, 359
Linati, Carlo, 239
Literary Digest, 107-8
Llano, El, xxv, 3, 22, 27, 28, 30, 322,
    325
Lochaber, 140-1
London, 21, 104, 107, 135, 151-2, 216,
    219, 221, 240, 254, 261, 263-4,
    274-5, 357
London Evening News, 327
London Mercury, 267, 359
"Look Inside a Mexican Indian's Head,
    A," 108
López, Leonardo Santiago, 121-2
López Ortigoza family, 13
Lorenzo in Taos, 68, 220, 226, 248
Los Angeles, xxviii, 6, 143, 350
Lowell, Amy, 317-8
Lucka, Emil, 157
Luhan, Mable Dodge, xxv, 5, 6, 13, 68,
    88, 94, 141, 160, 169, 215, 218-21,
    226, 233, 248-9, 256, 267, 280, 287,
    322, 346
Luhan, Tony, 218-9
Lunes del Cerro, 222

McDonald, Edward D., 31, 32, 85, 117,
    136, 155, 230, 238-42, 243, 247,
    249, 260, 329, 339, 359
McEwen, Charles, 74, 171, 318
McLeod, A. W., 198
Madero, Francisco I., xviii, xxi, 3, 137
Magnus, Maurice, 80-1, 260-2, 346, 360
Malay Straits, 260
Malinche, 295
Malintzi, character in *The Plumed Ser-
    pent,* 295, 297, 311, 313
Manchester, John, x, 191, 209,223, 226,
    266, 268, 356
Mandrake Press, 92
Mansfield, Katherine, 62-3, 255, 261,
    264, 268-9, 329

Manzanillo, 5
Marconi, Guglielmo, 13, 159, 206
María de Jesús, 30, 40
María del Carmen, 30, 40
Market of Industry, 60
Mark Gertler: Selected Letters, 255, 262
Marquesas, 244
Marqués del Valle Hotel, 2, 180
Márquez, Vicente Fermín, 36
Martínez, Francisco, 85, 353
Mary, Queen of Scots, 329
Mascagni, Piero, 340
Maudslay, Alfred P., 1
Maximilian, Emperor, 3
Mayas, 320, 327
Maycotte, Fortunato, xxiii, xxv, xxvi,
    xxviii, 4
Mazatlán, 5
Meixueiro, Guillermo, xix-xxi, 19
Memoirs of the Foreign Legion, 80,
    262, 361
Mercado Benito Juárez Maza, 52, *plate
    19*
Mercado Veinte de Noviembre, 59
Mercedarian Order, 39, 41
Merced, La, Church of, 39, 40-1, 43,
    165, 222, *plates 15, 16*
Mercurio, El, xiii, xxix, 22, 33, 79, 94,
    177
Merrild, Knud, xi, xxv, 10, 203, 271,
    327
Mesoamerica, 277, 297
Methuen, Sir Algernon, 157, 241
Mexican Catholic Apostolic Church,
    305-6
Mexican Light and Power Company,
    164
Mexican Railway (Ferrocarril Mexi-
    cano), 4
Mexican Revolution, xvi, xxx, 1, 3, 6,
    9, 19, 27, 52, 67, 83, 97, 106, 117,
    125-6, 138, 148-9, 167, 171, 279,
    283, 290, 293, 345, 359
Mexican Ulysses, A, xi, xxix-xxx, 128
Mexico, Lawrence's first visit to, xxiii,
    4, 10, 90, 140, 227, 287
Mexico, Lawrence's second visit to,
    xxiv, 6, 10, 46, 140, 150, 162, 197,
    265, 281, 287, 343
Mexico, Lawrence's third visit to, 6, 16,
    140, 223
Mexico City, 4, 5, 6, 10, 11, 17, 25, 37,
    55, 67, 73, 77, 79, 91, 136, 142,
    148, 162-3, 180, 201-2, 206, 213,
    223, 227, 248, 255-6, 271, 273, 280,
    291, 292, 298, 321, 325, 334, 338,
    341, 342, 361

Mexico, the country, 5,7, 11, 58-9, 77,
    87, 88, 94, 106, 111, 113, 128,
    138-9, 143, 144, 147, 151, 226, 258,
    274, 278-80, 294, 307, 311, 333,
    335, 344
Miahuatlán, 63
Mictlan, 174
Midlands of England, 266
Midland, Texas, 14, 350
Mier y Teran, Luis, 372
Milan, 239
Miller, Donald Gazley, 4, 17, 32, 171-2,
    174, 177, 178-80, 325, 353, 355,
    plate 29
Miomandre, Francis de, 128
Mirabal, Luis, 353
Misión de los Angeles, 352
Mis 20 Años de Torero, 223
Mitla, 17, 21, 71, 79, 120, 140-141, 144,
    171-6, 209, 224, 285-6, 325, 354,
    plates 29, 35, 40
Mitla Road, 49, 51, 109, 169, 202
Mixcoatl, 286
Mixteca Alta, xix, 57
Mixtecs, xv, 52, 175, 222-3, 226, 327
Modotti, Tina, 8, 10, 142
Monros, Juan, 2
Monte Alban, xv, 3-4, 20, 34, 66, 71,
    116, 172
Monte Alban Hotel, 13, 110
Montecassino, 81, 196
Montes, Manuel, 7
Montezuma, 55, 295
Moore, Harry T., ix, 27, 107, 158, 164,
    204, 213, 226, 229, 239, 259, 271,
    280, 301, 320, 349, 350
Morales, Rubén, 127
Mora y Del Rio, José, Archbishop, 37-8,
    305
More Lives Than One, 135
Morning Star, the, 293-6, 299, 332, 359
Morrell, Lady Ottoline, 162, 255, *plate
    36*
Moses, 250, 252-3, 267
Mount Lobo, 271
Mountsier, Robert, 135
Muciño, Marcelino, 22, 33, 79
Munich, 302
Muray, Nicholas, 135
Murray, Scott, 271
Murry, John Middleton, 19-20, 21, 26,
    30, 31, 46, 49, 57-8, 62-3, 81, 135,
    159, 197, 215, 219, 220, 251,
    255-69 passim, 280, 317, 323, 330,
    346, 353, 355, *plate 47*
Museo Frissell de Arte Zapoteco, 173
Museo Regional de Arte Popular, 306
Museum of New Mexico, 78

Mysticism of D. H. Lawrence, The, 313

Nahuatl, 123, 286
Naples, 330, 341
Nast, Condé, 135
Nation, 135, 259
National Library, Mexico, 255
Natividad, Rickards's cook, 30, 40, 100
Navarro, Ramón, 143
Nehls, Edward, 136, 141, 148, 150, 213, 308, 350-1, 360
New Criterion, 107
New Light on Drake, 292
New Mexico, xxv, xxx, 6, 11, 52, 68, 87, 147, 149, 151, 154, 180, 205-6, 225, 248, 256, 268-9, 277, 338, 343, 346, 353, 356
New Orleans, xxiii
New Statesman, 352
New Testament, The, 244, 337
New World, the, 261-2, 346
New York, xxiv, 6, 11, 80, 107, 135, 146, 150, 162, 180, 206, 216-7, 219, 221, 240, 248, 254, 262, 266, 306, 353, 355
New Yorker, 136
New York Herald Tribune, 12
New York Public Library, 246
New York Sun, 218
New York Times, 11, 22, 221
New York World, 339
Nieves, Las, church of, 27
Nin, Anaïs, 50
Noah, 243-248, 358
Norman Douglas (Tomlinson), x
North America, 135, 244, 278
"Not I, But the Wind . . . ," ix, 9, 39, 48, 149, 162, 199, 320-1, 323, 341-2, 350
Nottingham, 21
Nottinghamshire, 329
Nottingham University College, 32, 37, 69
Novedades, 136
Novelle Rusticane, 217, 340-1
Nuttall, Zelia, xvi, 4, 6, 11, 14, 91, 140, 279-80, 285, 292-3, 308, 312, 349, 352, 354, 361

Oaxaca, City of, xv, xviii, xix, 4-6, 10, 12, 28, 60, 66, 75, 107-8, 109-10, 118, 128, 130, 147, 150, 154, 157, 163, 181-2, 194, 208, 213, 221-2, 239, 244, 248-9, 254, 267, 274, 276, 283, 329, 333, 336, 344, 346, *plate 2*

Oaxaca, State of, xv, xviii-xxiii, xxix-xxx, 19, 25, 47, 52-3, 73, 77, 128, 144, 178-9, 223, 240-1
Oaxaca, streets of:
—Abasola, 75
—Aldama, 52, 59
—Allende, xvii
—Armenta y López, 27
—Cinco de Mayo, 75
—Constitución, 105
—García Vigil, xvi-xvii, 52, 105
—Independencia, xxvii, 36, 67
—Jota P. García, 179
—Las Casas, 51
—Miguel, Cabrera, 52
—Pino Suárez, 26, 28, 39, 48, 85, 110, 325
—Reforma, 105
—Veinte de Noviembre, 3, 52, 67
Oaxaca Courts, 74, 352
Oaxaca en la Historia, 349
Oaxaca Lawn Tennis Club, 79
Oaxaca Museum, 349, 352
Oaxaca, Valley of, xv, xix, 285
Oaxaqueño, El, xxi
Obregón, Alvaro, xviii-xxx, 7, 11, 16, 19, 77
Ocotlán, xix, 48-9, 56, 57, 63, 112,
Old Testament, 248
Olmecs, xv
Olten, 65
Olviera, Urbano, 60
Omecihuatl, 95
Oneida, 313
Open the Door, 349
Oregon, 72
Orizaba, 12, 286, 349
Orozco, José Clemente, xxviii, 126, 137, 285
Oscott College, 26-7, 37
Ossian, 311
Oxford, 35, 255, 290, 340
Oxford University Press, 124

Pacific Isles, 244
Pagliacci, I, 14
Paintings of D. H. Lawrence, 191
Palacio del Gobierno, 18, 75
Palacio Municipal, xxix, 13, 39, 338
Palo Blanco. See *cazaguate*
Palo Verde, xxvi
Pan-American Highway, 34, 49, 109, 111, 180
Panteón, Oaxaca, 43
Paris, 216, 318
parrots, of Padre Rickards, 42, 89-90, 110
Partido Liberal Constitutionalista, xxi

Partido Liberal Independente, 127
Pascualita, 30, 40
Paseo de la Reforma, 148
Patmore, Brigit, 235
Patrocinio, Templo del, 30, 85, 111, 165, 208
Pearn, Nancy, 260
P.E.N. Club, English branch, 7-9
P.E.N. Club, Mexican branch, 7-9, 17, 137, 141, 142, 143, 146, 238
Pérez, José Joaquín, 305-6
Philadelphia, 85
Phoenix, ix, xi, 240
Phoenix II, ix, xi, 158
Pimentel, Emilio, xx-xxi, 27
Pisgah, 250, 252-3, 327
Pittsburgh, 254, 321
Plato, 245
Pleistocene Epoch, 244
Pochutla, xxvi, xxviii, 67
Poe, Edgar Allen, 251
Poet and Two Painters, A, xi, 203
Poetas Nuevas de Mexico, 7
Pollinger, Gerald, ix-x, xi, 236, 357
Pollinger, Laurence, ix
Pompeii, 278
Popocatépetl, 138, 146
Portales, 70
Porter, Katherine Anne, 308
Porter, Mae Reed, 356
Posadas, Las, 188-9
pre-Columbian times, 91-2, 106, 140, 176, 286, 290, 295-6, 298
Presbyterian Church of the U.S.A., Board of Foreign Missions, xxv
Prewett, Frank, 255
Prichard, Katharine Susannah, 355
Pro, Padre Miguel, 306
Puebla, xxiii, xxv, xxvi, 3, 36, 66, 335
Puerto Angel, 67
Purcell, Okla., 269
Puritans, 329

Quemada, La, 5
Querétaro, xxi, xxii
Quero, Ambrosio, 174-5, *plate 35*
Quero, Darío, 173-4
Quero, Fausto, 172
Quero, Felix, 172, 173
Quest for Rananim, The, 262, 358
Quetzalcoatl, in Lawrence's novel, 21, 60, 140, 176, 224, 232, 234-5, 237, 268, 281, 284-5, 293, 295-9, 302, 304, 306-7, 309-10, 313-5
Quetzalcoatl, the pre-Columbian deity, 96, 277-8, 280, 290, 308
Quintanilla, Jane, 9, 17, 138, 141, 145, 150

Quintanilla, José, 138, 149
Quintanilla, Luis, x, 8-9, 16-7, 19, 63, 136-150 passim, 162, 173, 186, 208, 218, 235-6, 246, 273, 327, 353-5, *plate 33*
Quintanilla, Luis Fortuño, 137
Quintanilla, Ruth Stallsmith, x, 9, 63, 138, 141, 145, 147, 148, 150

Radio, 138
Radishes, Feast of, 189-91
Rámirez de López, Soledad, 121-2
Ramos, Armando, 166, *plate 39*
Rananim, Lawrence's proposed colony, 10-11, 297
Rare Travaile of Job Hortop, The, 348
Read, H. Hudston, 53
"Record," the black copybook, xi, 32, 87, 145, 151, 218, 224, 228, 235, 241, 246-7, 249, 327-8, 339
Red Cross, 75
Reforma, Calle, Huayapan, 120, 127
Reform Laws, 120, 165
Reimers, Clara de Larumbe (doctor's wife), 359-60
Relaciones Exteriores (Dept. of Foreign Affairs), 7, 9, 17, 138-9, 140, 142
Reminiscences of D. H. Lawrence, 57-8, 263, 268, 341
Rendón, Eduardo, 223, 291-3, 313-4, 343, *plate 46*
Resurrection (Tolstoy), 230-2, 235, 246
Revealing Eye, The, 353
Revelation of St. John the Divine, 290, 332
Reyes, General Bernardo, xxi
Richthofen, Baroness Anna Marquier von, 5, 33, 69, 94, 145, 186, 197, 214, 273, 309, 323, 327, 330
Richthofen, Baron Manfred von, aviator, 31, 69, 321-2, 360
Rickards, Constantine G., xi, 1, 7, 25, 26, 27-8, 38-9, 42, 206, 271, 317, 342, 351, 361
Rickards, George E., x, 25-7, 30, 33, 38-9, 40, 42-3, 351
Rickards, Grace de Solano, 38-9
Rickards, Mabel, x, 26
Rickards, Padre Edward Arden, x, 25-43 passim, 72, 74-5, 83, 94, 103, 108, 109, 165, 170, 195, 206, 222, 229, 258, 289, 305, 325-6, 350-2, *plates 11, 13, 16*
Rieff, Philip, 324
Riga, 65
Rigoletto, 14
Rinconada, La, 84
Rivas, Alfonso, xii

Rivera, Diego, xxviii, 126, 137, 285
Riviera, Italian, 161
Road to Mitla, xii
Roberts, Warren F., xi, 158
Roman Catholic Church, 123, 303, 305-8
Romans, 220
Rome, 36
Roosevelt, Franklin D., 150
Rosalino, Lawrence's *mozo,* 32, 48, 83-5, 89-90, 93-4, 98-108 passim, 110, 113, 114, 116, 117, 119, 126, 129-33, 170, 178, 186, 190, 193, 204, 213, 325, *plate 25*
Rosalino's married sister, 84
Rosalino's mother, 102-3
Rosalino's younger brother, 84, 103, 157, 193
Rosicrucianism, 295
Royal Canadian Air Force, 321, 360
Royal Ontario Museum, 25
Ruins of Mexico, The, 1, 25, 27-8
Ruiz, Valentino, 122, 130
Russell, Bertrand, 150
Russell, Lt.-Col. George M., 79

Saint Andrew, 123
Saint Anne, 284
Saint Anthony, 284
Saint Catherine, 221
Saint Christopher, 123
Saint Dominic, 123
Saint Francis, 284
St. Ives, Cornwall, 261
Saint Joaquín, 284
Saint John the Baptist, 138
St. Louis, Mo., 179
St. Matthew, Gospel of, 232
Saint Sebastian, 181
Salina Cruz, xix
Salinas, Bethsabe, 40
Salinas, Maximiliano, 28, 35, 40, 110, *plate 13*
Salisbury, Conn., 240
San Andrés Huayapan. *See* Huayapan
San Angel, 139
San Antonio de Padua, 61
San Antonio, Texas, 246
Sanborn's restaurant, 9, 148
Sánchez, Guadalupe, xxiv-xxv, xxviii
San Diego, 271
Sandusky, Ohio, 355
San Felipe del Agua, 35, 40, 109, 113-4, 128, 170, 182, 187, 208, *plates 12, 13*
San Felipe Mountain, 109, 111-3
San Francisco, Calif., 1
San Francisco Caxones, 60

San Francisco de Paula, 61
San-German, Angel, 327
San Geronimo, 218, 287
San Gervasio, 245
San José, foster-father of Jesus, 61
San Juan Bosco, 61
San Juan Chilateca, xvii
San Juan de Dios, church of, 59-61, 165
San Juan de Dios Market, 84, *plate 23*
San Judas Tadeo, 61
San Luis Beltran, 109, 113
San Martín de Porres, 61
San Miguel Peras, 173
San Ramón, 40
Santa Catarina, convent, later a jail, 75, *plate 28*
Santa Fe, xxv, 78, 206, 263, 356
Santa Lucia del Camino, 109, 206
Santa Lucrecia, now Jesús Carranza, xxvii
Santa Rita, 61
Santa Vera Cruz, hermitage, 181
Sántibañez, José, 180
Santo Domingo, church of, xvii, 105, 110, 121-5, 164-5, 347-8
Santo Domingo Pueblo, 219, 349
Savage Pilgrimage, The, x, 215, 263, 349
Sayula, Lake, 280, 284, 287-8, 310
Scotland, 123
Scott, Winfield, 286
Secker, Martin, 80-1, 85, 151-2, 154, 158, 162, 168, 186, 213, 215, 220-1, 227, 281, 342, 352, 357-8
Secker, Rina, 357
Secret Doctrine, The, 358
Sedlacek, Dr. Francis, 79
Seeley, Capt., 256-7
Seligmann, Herbert J., 215, 218, 241, 348
Seltzer, Adele, xxiv, 5, 162, 215, 217
Seltzer, Thomas, xxiv, 5, 81, 87, 135-6, 154, 213, 214-8, 241, 280, 348, 357
Seminario Pontifico y Conciliar de la Santa Cruz de Antequera, xx, xxiii, 26, 40
Serranos, xix-xxiii, xxvi, xxix, 19, 22, 34, 74-5, 77, 78, 85, 287, *plate 27*
Shakespeare, William, 40
Shaw, George Bernard, 239
Sheffield, James Rockwell, 10
Shiva Samhità, 314
Shostov, Leo, 358
Shropshire, 290
Siberia, 229-31
Sicily, 69, 78, 81, 97, 340-1, 346
Sierra de Juárez, xix, 66, 84-5, 287
Sierra Madre, 67

Signature, The, 251
Sinaloa, 11, 287
Skinner, Maria Louisa, "Mollie," xii, 6,
    150-8 passim, 193, 213, 241, 318,
    355, 359
Smith, Hugh A., 75
Soberanistas, xix-xx, xxii
Socialism, 9, 19-20, 275, 276, 309
Solano, Manuel, 38
Soledad de Santa Cruz, church of, 165,
    305, *plate 44*
Sonora, xviii, 225, 356
Sorpresa, La, inn, 173-4, *plate 40*
South Dakota Review, x, 71, 249, 255,
    257
Southwest Review, 281
Soviet Union, 136
Spain, 227, 292
Spaniards, 60, 106
Spence, Lewis, 91, 95-6, 178, 286, 293
Spezia, 161
Sphere, The, 142
Spotorno, 161, 180, 193, 221, 263, 269
Stafford, Viscount, 153
Stalin, 150
Stone, Idella Purnell, x, 280
Stonyhurst College, 36
Strassburg, 264
Stridberg, August, 239
Strousse, Flora, 203, 320
"Structure of the Oaxaca Market, The,"
    64
Suez Canal, 330
Sullivan, Alvin, 358
Sullivan, J. W. N., 263
Sumner, John S., 215
Switzerland, 65, 81, 88, 324, 337
Sydney, Australia, 330

Tacubaya, 22, 25, 285
Tantras, 313
Taormina, 68, 78, 235, 340-1, 351
Taos, x, xxiv, 5, 13, 18, 131, 177, 191,
    218-9, 249, 269-70, 287, 346, 353
Tapanatepec, xxvii
Taviche, 1, 3, 15, 23, 75
Taylor, Geraldine Ely, xxv, 74, 171,
    321-2, 337
Taylor, Norman W., x, xxv, 74, 171,
    321-2, 337
Teatro Alcala, 1, 79, *plate 3*
Tecolote River, 114, 116
Tedlock, E. W., Jr., ix, 125, 144, 158,
    160, 224, 228, 235-6, 246, 247-8,
    265, 327, 346, 351
Tehuacán, Puebla, 4, 16, 17, 176, 334,
    342
Tehuantepec, 34

Tehuantepec, Isthmus of, xxvi, xxvii,
    49, 56, 288
Tehuantepec Railroad, 94
Teotihuacán, 176, 277, 278-9, 286, 308
Teotitlán del Valle, 21, 23, 46, 55, 64,
    222, 350
Tepache, 129
Tepic, 5
Terry's Guide to Mexico (1909), 172,
    177
Terry, T. Philip, 172, 174
Tezcatlipoca, 295
Theatre Arts Monthly, 218-21, 288
Theosophy, 295, 357-8
"Thief of Bagdad, The," 177-8
Thompson, Clarence, 13, 31, 168, 327
Thompson, Emma von Violand, 15-6,
    25, 30, 68, 193-4, 325-6
Thompson, G. William, 15, 193-4,
    325-6
Thor, 302
Tibet, 313
Tiltepec, 360
Times Literary Supplement, 152
Tindall, William York, 292, 308, 358
Tingley, Katherine, 357
Tlacolula, 49, 56, 63, 172, 206, 285
Tlalixtac, 48
Tlaloc, 140, 278-9, 295
Tlalteloco, 56
Tlaquepaque, 46, 270
Tlaxiaco, xix-xx
Tlazolteotl, 95
Toboada, Juan, 166-7, *plates 38, 39*
Tollan, 308
Tolstoy, Leo, 228-32, 234-5, 246, 302,
    340
Toltecs, 278, 308
Tomellín Canyon, 16, 17, 73, 334
Tomlinson, H. M., x, 259-61, 263
*Tomorrow and Tomorrow and Tomor-
    row,* 313
Tonacaciuatl, 95
Topeka, 75, 325
Toronto, 25, 28, 255, 257
T. P. & Cassell's Weekly, 260
Tulane University, 348
Tula. *See* Tule, Santa María del
Tule, Santa María del, 17, 109, 172,
    173, 278, 308
Turgenev, Ivan, 229
Turner, W. J., 255
Two Years Before the Mast, 330

Ukraine, 261
Ulfelder, Dr. Sydney, 149, 354
Ulfelder, Mrs. Sydney, 354
Ulise Criolla. See A Mexican Ulysses

United States Embassy in Mexico, 79
United States of America, 5, 6, 7, 33,
    63, 107, 146, 147, 225, 239, 276-7,
    279, 291, 305, 310, 313, 341
Universal, El, 223
University of Aberdeen, 348
University of Cincinnati, 94, 204, 327
University of Texas at Austin, xi, 32,
    35, 71, 87, 156, 166, 191, 209,
    213-4, 228, 236, 240, 282, 327, 357
University of the Americas, 356

Valentino, Rudolph, 143
Van Slyke, Mr. & Mrs., missionaries,
    321
Vanity Fair, 135-6, 141-2, 144, 147-8,
    186, 215
*Vanity Fair: A Cavalcade of the 1920's
    and 1930's,* 136
Vasconcelos, José, xi, xxviii-xxx, 4, 7,
    18, 23, 112, 126-8, 280, 349
Vatican Council, First, 36
Venus, the planet, 296
Veracruz, xxiv, xxvi, xxviii, xxx, 30,
    74, 138, 147, 169, 181, 206, 255,
    258, 321, 325, 334
Veracruz, state of, 76, 79, 149, 290
Verdi, Giuseppe, 14
Verga, Giovanni, 217, 340-1
Vickery, John B., 308
Victoria Hotel, 2
Victoria, Queen, 334
Vietnam, 150
Vigilista, 85
Viking Press, ix, xii, 243
Villa Alta District, xxv, 60
Villa Bernarda, 161, 263
Villa, Francisco, "Pancho," xviii, xix,
    xxiii-xxiv, xxvi, xxx, 75, 146
Villa Mirenda, 193, 220, 347
Villard, Oswald Garrison, 135
Villaseñor, Eduardo, 8, 349
Virgin Mary, 284, 290, 299, 311
Virgin of Carmen, 61
Virgin of Guadalupe, 61, 180
Virgin of Mercy, 41-2
Virgin of Soledad, 61, 123-4, 180-6,
    195, 210, 288, 312, *plate 42*
Virgin of the Light, 61
Virgin of the Rosary, 61
Vita del Campi, 340
Volante, 349

Wagner, Richard, 137
War and Peace, 229, 231

Warren, Dorothy, 10
Washington, D.C., 136
Weekley, Barbara, 161, 180, 186, 325
Weekley, C. Montague, x, 186, 242, 325
Weekley, Elsa, 161, 180, 186, 325
Weekley, Ernest, 31
Wells, H. G., 239
Welte, Cecil R., 109
West, Rebecca, 97
Weston, Cole, xii
Weston, Edward, xii, 8, 9-10, 37, 80,
    139, 141-6 passim, 186
Whitman, Walt, 250-1, 253-4, 276, 337
Whittlesey, May, 354
Wickramasinghe, Martin, 313
Wilson, Clyde, 2-3, 12-3, 325-6, 341
Wilson, Robert, 2-3, 29, 79, 325-6,
    plate 10
Wilson, Robert W., 2-3, 12-3, 325-6
Wingfield Manor, 328
Winnipeg, 321
Winsor, Eva, 360
Winsor, Henry, x, 360-1
Woodhouse, Mrs., 357
Wooton, Paul, 22
World War I, 14, 32, 69, 80, 84, 125,
    127, 171, 225, 229, 232, 234, 239,
    251, 264, 275, 289, 330, 343, 356
World War II, 114, 136, 322, 360
Wotan, 302
Written on Water, 128

Xolotl, 96

Yale University, 304
Young Lorenzo, 20, 192, 213
Yucatan, xxv, 143, 278, 280, 313
Yukon, 356

Zaachila, 60, 63
Zacatecas, 307
zaguan, 29, 33, 89, 99, 101
Zapata, Emiliano, xviii, xix, 41
Zapotecs, xv, xxv, 16, 18, 20, 28, 52,
    60, 72, 84, 98, 117, 122, 130, 175,
    222-3, 224, 287-8, 290, 309, 311,
    320, 327
Zavaleta, 1
Zimatlán, 63
Zócalo, xv, xvi-xvii, 1, 13, 18, 41, 45,
    52, 71, 121, 171, 180, 183-4, 194,
    202, 209, 307, 338
Zoogochí River, 114, 116, 119
Zoogochí, Santa María, 84-5
Zopilote, 131, 133
Zytaruk, George J., 262, 358

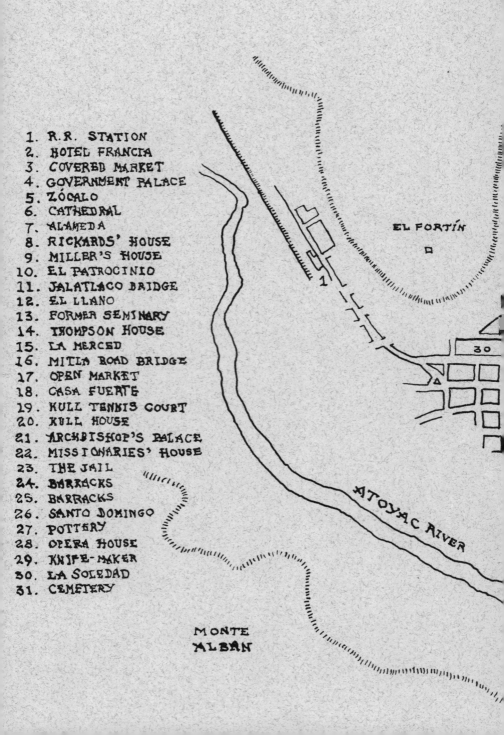

1. R.R. STATION
2. HOTEL FRANCIA
3. COVERED MARKET
4. GOVERNMENT PALACE
5. ZÓCALO
6. CATHEDRAL
7. ALAMEDA
8. RICKARDS' HOUSE
9. MILLER'S HOUSE
10. EL PATROCINIO
11. JALATLACO BRIDGE
12. EL LLANO
13. FORMER SEMINARY
14. THOMPSON HOUSE
15. LA MERCED
16. MITLA ROAD BRIDGE
17. OPEN MARKET
18. CASA FUERTE
19. KULL TENNIS COURT
20. KULL HOUSE
21. ARCHBISHOP'S PALACE
22. MISSIONARIES' HOUSE
23. THE JAIL
24. BARRACKS
25. BARRACKS
26. SANTO DOMINGO
27. POTTERY
28. OPERA HOUSE
29. KNIFE-MAKER
30. LA SOLEDAD
31. CEMETERY

EL FORTÍN

ATOYAC RIVER

MONTE ALBAN